BIRDS  1ST  11.50
198

# RARE BIRDS
## OF THE
# WEST COAST
### OF NORTH AMERICA

by Don Roberson

Color plates by:

    Donna Dittmann
    Dana Gardner
    Tim Manolis
    Marv Reif
    Ray Robinson

Line illustrations in the text by the author

First printing

Copyright © 1980 by Woodcock Publications, Pacific Grove, California. All rights reserved. No part of this work may be reproduced or transmitted in any form by any means, electronic or mechanical, including photo copying and recording, or by any information storage or retrieval system, without permission in writing from the publisher.

Library of Congress Catalog No.: 80-51054

ISBN 0-9605352-0-9

*It is only a matter of time theoretically until the list of California birds will be identical with that for North America as a whole.*
Joseph Grinnell (1922)

*This prediction is being rapidly fulfilled.*
Paul DeBenedictis (1971)

**Dedicated to Guy McCaskie and Rich Stallcup, who, more than any other observers, are most responsible for the rapid fulfillment of Grinnell's prophecy. They were the first to begin systematic searches for rare birds, they discovered many of the patterns described in this book, and they have been (and are still today) in the forefront of our developing knowledge of distribution and identification. Their influence has been felt not only in California, but along the entire West Coast.**

# TABLE OF CONTENTS

Preface and Acknowledgments .................................... v
Introduction .................................................... ix
   Records ..................................................... xi
      California ............................................... xi
      Oregon .................................................. xii
      Washington ............................................. xiii
      British Columbia ....................................... xiii
      Alaska ................................................. xiii
   Abbreviations and Citations ................................ xv
   Taxonomy and English Names ................................. xvi
   Graphs ..................................................... xvii
   Maps ....................................................... xviii
   Photographs ................................................ xviii
   Color Plates ............................................... xix
Standardized County Abbreviations ............................... xx
Maps with selected localities
   California ................................................. xxi
   Oregon ..................................................... xxii
   Washington ................................................. xxiii
   British Columbia ........................................... xxiv
   Alaska ..................................................... xxv
Patterns and Theories on Vagrancy .............................. xxvi

Species Accounts ................................................ 1
   Essays:
      Identification and Ageing of Stints ..................... 153
      Identification of *Empidonax* Flycatchers ............... 272
      Identification of *Catharus* Thrushes ................... 310
      Identification of Pipits ................................ 331
      Eastern Warblers in California .......................... 354
   Color Plates ..................................... between 224-225

Appendix A — Additional Alaska Rarities ........................ 479
Appendix B — Possible Vagrants from Eurasia .................... 480
Appendix C — Selected Reports Not Used ......................... 483
Appendix D — Selected Additional Records (1980) ................ 484
Literature Cited ............................................... 485
Index to Photographers ......................................... 491
Index to English Names ......................................... 492

# PREFACE AND ACKNOWLEDGEMENTS

At this very moment, somewhere near where the Pacific Ocean meets the west coast of North America, there is a rare bird. For several years I have been interested in these vagrants which have strayed outside the normal paths of their species. It has been twenty years since active field observers began to seriously pursue these stragglers and over the past decade we have trekked to obscure desert oases, fog-shrouded clumps of coastal cypress, lonely storm-battered Aleutian islands, and clutched the rails of wave-tossed fishing boats to the quiet amusement of their captians. As one of this cadre, I had often wished for some book which completely listed the records of rare birds, not only for the smugness that comes from knowing "I have just found the 17th record for California", but to note the patterns of past records which might reveal clues as to when the bird would next appear. Photographs of rare birds are another special interest, and I am not alone as one whose first impulse on receipt of a new issue of *American Birds* is to flip to the photos and attempt to identify them or whose response to the news of a very rare bird is "Was it photographed?". And how often had I heard birders wish for a publication which contained much of the recent advances in identification, which are not found in the standard field guides and, if published at all, are scattered among a complex variety of journals.

Sometime during the spring of 1978, I came upon Sharrocks' *Rare Birds in Britain and Ireland*. How fine it was to see maps, graphs, and an annotated text all about rare birds! The idea of putting together a similar book became too attractive and the result is in your hands. I have, like the Sharrocks, used maps and graphs extensively and have liberally annotated the text with references to further reading. I have also added features I have most wanted: numerous photos of the rarities, an expanded identification text, and color plates of those species not currently illustrated by the standard North American guides. The limitations of space have reduced some of the features which I might have preferred to have expanded. A fairly tight definition of "Rarity" reduced the number of species covered (occasionally "stretched" to meet special cases, especially warblers in California). Identification sections were limited to those birds which are not discussed in the standard guides or whose identification is difficult and not adequately discussed there. Much could be written about the identification of any bird and even when an identification section is included, it tends to be written in a telegraphic style. Information is packed together and can be difficult to read; I would have preferred longer and more thorough essays. The book

# PREFACE

does have a fairly representative collection of photographs of rare birds, but there are important photos I was not able to obtain and space prevented the publication of numerous others. The final result might be thought of as a hybrid field guide X reference book. The identification sections and the color plates should be useful in the field; the text, maps, and graphs do comprehensively compile all acceptable records of Rarities through 1979 (and sometimes into 1980).

The two years during which this project was undertaken were years of rapid advancements in birding expertise. I have attempted to keep abreast of these advances, but the reader will find some information outdated or expanded in the near future. The identification of stints (what we have called "peeps" in the past) is a good example. An early draft text was written after research in the literature, immediately revised upon examination of specimens, revised again after review by several authorities, revised yet again after the presence of several interesting West Coast birds which shed new light on the problem, and revised a final time just prior to going to press when Peter Grant and others suggested new features to separate very difficult birds (Little vs. Rufous-necked Stint is an especially rapidly-expanding case). Some of these final revisions occurred after the printing of the color plates and their facing pages and the careful reader will find a few discrepencies between the main text and the plates. The artists carefully followed my suggestions when painting the plates and the paintings were, when finished, as accurate as the information available to me at the time. But information continued to accumulate and a few of the paintings (juvenile stints, for example) would be further revised if it were practical to do so now. I believe they are more accurate in many respects than what is presently available and in print, but should the reader wish for the most up-to-date information available to me at this time (summer 1980), I suggest that the main text be given preference over the notes facing the color plates.

I also found that with each new rare bird one studied, interesting details (some minor, some more important) suggested a change in the identification text. A trip to Attu I. and St. Lawrence I., ALASKA, in May-Jun 1980 was most instructive in this respect. At this time much of the first half of the book was in final form and the printer was producing final proof sheets. I had this text and the finished color plates with me in Alaska'and was able to compare them first-hand with a number of rare birds. Some of the paintings and portions of the text were quite accurate, but I scrambled on my return to change the text of some birds (e.g. female Falcated Teal, Gray-tailed Tattler, Oriental Greenfinch) just prior to printing. There is no doubt that other portions are equally in need of further revision. Careful observers should consider this book as a base

# ACKNOWLEDGEMENTS

upon which to build. It is as accurate as possible at this time, but it should not be considered comprehensive. Whenever possible I have directed the reader to more thorough articles on identification. I have often summarized the high points of these articles and added new material, but the wise observer, faced with the identification of an interesting bird, will consult those articles which are in print and continue to search for additional material to be published later.

This book could not have been written without the assistance of many outstanding field observers, who took the time to review both the validity of records and the accuracy of the identification sections. Jon Dunn, Kimball Garrett, Paul Lehman, Joe Morlan, and Rich Stallcup were especially valuable reviewers of the entire text. Most of my experience has been in California. When I found (early in the project) that the patterns of occurrence became clearer when the scope was expanded to include the entire Pacific coast (and thus changing the book from one on California to one which includes all the West Coast states and provinces), it became necessary to depend heavily on local state and provincial authorities. The expertise of Daniel D. Gibson (Alaska), R. Wayne Campbell (British Columbia), Eugene Hunn (Washington), and Alan Contreras (Oregon) was invaluable. Members of the Oregon Records Committee were most cooperative — Clarice Watson, the current secretary, made the files available to me and kept me up to date, and useful advice was received from David Fix, Jeff Gilligan, Tom Lund, Harry Nehls, and Mark Egger. John Luther, secretary of the California Records Committee, was also very helpful in keeping me current with the workings of that committee. During the research for this book I was able to visit Seattle, Washington, and Victoria, B.C. Phil Mattocks kindly made the Washington rare bird files available and helpful comments were made by Dennis Paulson, Steve Speich, and Terry Wahl. The bird record and photoduplicate files at the British Columbia Provincial Museum were marvelously well organized and the days spent perusing them were among the most profitable of the entire project, producing numerous unpublished records, valuable descriptions, and photos.

I spent a fair amount of time working with museum specimens while looking into identification problems. Most of this time was spent at the Museum of Vertebrate Zoology, University of California, Berkeley, and I am grateful to Ned K. Johnson and Victoria M. Dziadosz for providing access to the collection (the Museum is funded, in part, by the National Science Foundation grant BMS 7200102). I was also able to visit collections at the California Academy of Sciences, courtesy of Laurence C. Binford; the San Bernardino Natural History Museum, courtesy of

# ACKNOWLEDGEMENTS

Eugene Cardiff; and the British Columbia Provincial Museum, courtesy of R. Wayne Campbell and Charles Guiget. Elizabeth Copper did some additional research for me at the San Diego Natural History Museum; Paul Lehman checked a point at the American Museum of Natural History in New York.

I was especially fortunate in having the identification sections of Eurasian species reviewed by Peter J. Grant, one of Britain's foremost field ornithologists and chairman of the British Rarities Committee. He was able to revise my drafts extensively and much of the credit for the accuracy in accounts of Eurasian birds are directly attributable to him.

Important new information based on recent research, and as yet unpublished, was generously provided by Lawrence Balch (Common v. Oriental Cuckoo), Joe Morlan (races of White Wagtail), and Claudia Wilds (Reed Buntings). Jon Dunn made available the draft of his text (with Thede Tobish) on the identification of pipits, to be published shortly in *Continental Birdlife*. Phil Unitt and H. Lee Jones commented on the identification of tropical seabirds.

The artists of the color plates — Donna Dittmann, Dana Gardner, Tim Manolis, Marv Reif, and Ray Robinson — have greatly added to the value of this book. Some of the plates were reviewed by Jon Dunn, Larry Balch, Rich Stallcup, and Phil Unitt, which allowed for corrections that made for greater accuracy.

Carol Deuel proofread portions of the text, for which I am appreciative.

I was only able to update the records of some species through 1979 by the willingness of *American Birds* regional editors to send me the unpublished drafts of their 1979 fall reports. My thanks to Guy McCaskie (Southern Pacific Coast) and Stephen Laymon and David Shuford (Middle Pacific Coast). Much of the information on eastern warblers in California was compiled in an unpublished manuscript by Dave DeSante and myself.

The response from photographers throughout the West Coast was enthusiastic and adds much to this effort. Point Reyes Bird Observatory made available a number of important photos from their files.

Though a tremendous amount of help was received from those listed above and others unmentioned, I made the final decision as to which records were published and which were not and on what to include in the identification sections. I am responsible for any errors contained therein.

Finally, without the support of B.B. Roberson, MD, this entire project would not have been possible. Many thanks to you all.

Don Roberson<br>
Pacific Grove, California<br>
October 1980

# INTRODUCTION

This book covers the status and distribution, and often the identification, of those birds considered to be Rarities on the West Coast of North America. The two capitalized terms have definitions specific to this book. The "West Coast" is the states of California, Oregon, Washington, and Alaska, and the province of British Columbia, in their entirety. It also includes offshore waters to a limit of 200 miles. When used in this book, the "West Coast" includes this entire area.

A "Rarity" is a species which has occurred, during the most recent five-year period, an average of four times or less in any West Coast state or province. When a bird has been averaging less than four birds a year in any of the states or provinces included, it is discussed in detail for the area (or areas) in which it is a Rarity. Each West Coast state and province is treated as a separate entity. If the bird meets the definition for Oregon (averaging four birds or less a year), its status and distribution in Oregon is discussed in detail. If it also meets the definition in Washington, it is discussed in detail for that state as well. But if it does not meet the definition in California (averaging over 4 birds a year there), its status in California is only briefly noted in the introductory paragraph and it is not covered in detail for that state (a few exceptions to this definition have been made, especially for California; these are described later).

The treatment of Alaska is somewhat different. The definition of Rarity has been stretched there to include all Eurasian species which have reached Alaska and are not covered by the standard North American field guides. These guides are considered to be Robbins' *Birds of North America* (1966) and the Peterson series: *A Field Guide to the Birds* (1947, 1980), *A Field Guide to Western Birds* (1961), and *A Field Guide to the Birds of Texas and Adjacent States* (1963). (Pough's *Audubon Western Bird Guide* (1957) included some additional species, but it is now out-of-print and not considered one of the standard guides). To make room for these species, those birds which meet the Rarity definition for Alaska, but are not Rarities in any other West Coast state or province, are relegated to Appendix A. This divergent handling of Alaska birds was chosen because it was felt that more readers of this book would prefer to learn about the status and identification of Long-toed Stint *Calidris subminuta* or Brambling *Fringilla montifringilla* (which do not meet the definition of Rarity in Alaska) than of the Alaska status of Wilson's Phalarope *Steganopus tricolor* or Bobolink *Dolichonyx oryzivorus* (which do).

In essence, this book might be thought of as one which deals with every Rarity in California, in Oregon, in Washington, and in British Columbia, and also as a book which covers all the Eurasian birds which have reached Alaska (even those which occur there with some regularity).

There are a few other exceptions to the general definition of Rarity. Birds which formerly occurred in a state or province but which are best considered extinct there are not covered (examples are Sharp-tailed Grouse *Pediocetes phasianellus* in California and Oregon, and California Condor *Gymnogyps californianus* in Oregon and Washington). Another exception is made for birds which do not meet the definition when a 5-year average is used, but whose occurrence within a state or province is erratic and irregular — numbers may be present some years, yet it may be absent the next year (examples include Blue-footed *Sula nebouxii* and Brown Booby *S. leucogaster* in California). A final exception is occasionally made in the case of some eastern species which average well over 4 birds a year in California but are still considered to be vagrants there. This exception has been made somewhat arbitrarily; I have included a discussion of the status of nearly every "eastern" warbler in California though only a few meet our "4 birds a year or less" definition.

288 species are covered by the main text. Each has an individual account which includes:

1) A brief synopsis of its regular breeding and wintering range. This information is very general and does not include areas of limited breeding or wintering. It is meant to give nothing more than a general impression of the regular range of the bird.

2) A general introductory paragraph which discusses the West Coast status of the bird and often highlights the information found in more detail in specific state and provincial accounts which follow. General trends of occurrence, some theories which might explain the trends, exceptional records, and taxonomic comments are often included in this introductory section.

3) Detailed state or provincial accounts for each area where the species meets our definition of a Rarity (or one of the exceptions to the definition). These accounts are grouped either from north to south or from south to north, depending on the general direction of the regular breeding area from the West Coast. Birds which primarily breed in northern North America or northern Eurasia have their area accounts listed from north to south; those which nest primarily in the Neotropics, the South Pacific, or eastern North America are listed from south to north. These accounts discuss all the records within the state or province (and to 200 miles offshore), discuss general trends, and often include graphs and maps.

4) An identification section is included if a) the species is not covered by the standard American field guides, or b) if the identification of the bird is difficult and is not adequately handled by the standard guides. If it seems probable that most observers could identify the bird, even if it turned up in an area where it was rare, by referring to the standard guides, an identification section is not included. When there is

information not included in the standard guides but which is important in the identification of a rare bird, an identification section is usually included. The limits of space have made the decision to include or not to include an identification section somewhat arbitrary, but for the most part an identification section should be considered as supplemental to the standard guides; it is not intended to repeat information available in those guides.

# RECORDS

This book contains a compilation of all acceptable records of West Coast Rarities through the end of 1979. A few additional records of importance from 1980 are also included.

The compilation of all acceptable records of Rarities is not without its difficulties. There is no central clearinghouse for records from the West Coast (as there is in Britain and Ireland) and for the most part I have relied on the opinions of regional authorities (published and unpublished), the workings of the California and Oregon Records Committees, the seasonal reports published in *American Birds,* reports published in the ornithological literature, and my own evaluation of suspect records. In some ways, it would have been preferable to cite the publication of each record used, but such a practice would have made the reading of this book more difficult and substantially increased its length. I have chosen to specifically cite only exceptional records or those not to be found in the discussion of records compilation to follow. The manner in which the records from each state or province were compiled and the authorities relied upon are these:

**CALIFORNIA** Records prior to 1940 were taken from Grinnell and Miller (1944). Any deviations from this authoratative work are discussed in the text. Records of extremely rare species since 1940 were taken from either McCaskie, DeBenedictis, Erickson, and Morlan (1979) — which covers northern California — or Dunn and Garrett (1981 — the authors kindly made their drafts available to me) — which covers southern California. The California Records Committee has an officially accepted state list; this was followed except for two species discussed in the text (Black Vulture *Coragyps atratus* and Anhinga *Anhinga anhinga,* both of which were unaccepted by the Committee on split votes) and there are a number of additional records of first reports for California which have not yet been reviewed by the Committee which are included in this book. I have followed the decisions of the California Records Committee, but the Committee has dealt with only a small number of the Rarity records from California. Most records since 1940 were taken from the pages of *American Birds;* fortunately the California birding community has rather good communication and one soon learns which records are considered acceptable by most and which to look upon with suspicion. Readers of the California section will find the individual records published in the authoratative works listed above or in *American Birds;* exceptions are usually cited directly.

A word about sight records and Records Committees is appropriate here. We have long since passed the day when it was necessary to collect a bird to substantiate its presence within a state. Careful sight records by knowledgeable observers are usually adequate to consider a record valid, and the rapidly increasing use of photography has usually made specimen evidence unnecessary. The Records Committee plays an important role in the substantiation of sight records and it is hoped that their coverage can be more complete in the future. The California Records Committee consists of ten voting members. Should a sight record receive unanimous approval or have only one member voting against the report, the record is considered accepted. But if two or more members vote to unaccept a report (either for identification reasons or for suspicions that the bird escaped from captivity), it is rejected. These extremely high standards of scrutiny do lend strong support to the claims of sight records, but they do, at times, account for the rejection of valid records and it can happen that two dissatisfied Committee members will vote down a report which is otherwise widely accepted within the knowledgeable birding community. Nevertheless, I have followed the decisions of the California Records Committee in nearly every case; exceptions are discussed in the text or the appendices. At the present time, very few records since 1977 have been reviewed by the Committee. The numerous important records in the late 1970s, which are included in this book, will probably be accepted by the Committee within the next few years.

Records from California which are substantiated by a specimen or are substantiated by the acceptance of the CAL Records Committee are indicated in the text in the following manner:

† = specimen record
\* = record accepted by the CAL Records Committee

**OREGON** Records prior to 1940 were taken from Gabrielson and Jewett (1940), except for a few cases when early records appear suspect (e.g.; Black Rail *Latterallus jamaicensis*). Records since 1940 were compiled from the appropriate regional summaries in *American Birds* and, to a lesser extent, from the *Auk, Condor, Western Birds, Murrelet,* and *Oregon Birds.* Records from the Oregon book and *American Birds* are not specifically cited in the text; records from other publications often are (especially when the citation includes a description of the bird). The recently formed Oregon Records Committee and its first secretary, Alan Contreras, were most helpful in evaluating records. The Committee has approved a tentative state list; this was followed for the most part. Unfortunately, the enthusiasm of the Oregon committee has sometimes out-stripped their expertise and there are a number of records accepted by the Committee which are not included in this book; I have reviewed the documentation of each case and found it unsatisfactory (these reports are listed in Appendix C). Nevertheless, I have followed the decisions of the Oregon Records Committee (which is patterned after the California model) in most cases and their decisions often provide necessary substantiation of sight records. The Oregon Committee has reviewed most important records through 1979. Records approved by them or

specimens in existence are indicated in the text in the following manner:
† = specimen record
* = record accepted by the ORE Records Committee

**WASHINGTON** Records prior to 1950 were found in Jewett, Taylor, Shaw, and Aldrich (1953) and records from 1950-1974 were taken from Mattocks, Hunn, and Wahl (1976). These two authoratative works provide a complete compilation of Rarity records through 1974 and are followed almost without deviation. Records published in these works are not specifically cited in the text, and the reader is referred to them by implication here. But on occasion an important record is cited directly to a journal when the authoratative works only cite the publication as well. Records since 1974 were taken mostly from the appropriate regional summaries in *American Birds;* Eugene Hunn provided some direction as to the validity of certain reports. Records from Washington which are substantiated by a specimen are indicated in the text in this manner:
† = specimen record

**BRITISH COLUMBIA** Records prior to 1945 were found in Munro and Cowan (1947); some important records since then were referred to in Godfrey (1966). Many records since 1945 were taken from the appropriate regional reports in *American Birds;* these records, and those from the works listed above, are not cited directly in the text. A number of records were found in the *Auk, Condor, Murrelet, Syesis, Western Birds,* and *Canadian Field Naturalist;* these are often cited directly in the text. Numerous additional records were found in the files of the British Columbia Provincial Museum, often with descriptions attached. Many were unpublished and appear first in print here. R. Wayne Campbell provided direction on the validity of a number of these records. Records which are substantiated by a specimen are indicated in this manner:
† = specimen record

**ALASKA** Records prior to the mid-1950s were found in Gabrielson and Lincoln (1959). Additional records through 1977 were taken from Kessel and Gibson (1978). These two works provide a comprehensive assessment of all Alaska Rarity records and are followed in all cases; records published in these works are not cited directly in the text, but the reader is referred to these publications in nearly every case by implication here. Records since 1977 were found in the regional reports in *American Birds* and also not cited. But in most cases where a very rare bird is involved, the original publication of the record in a journal is cited (even if it is repeated in the comprehensive works listed above). Journal articles which provide details on many Alaska Rarity records, not available in the two works listed above, include Kenyon (1961), Kenyon and Phillips (1965), Sladen (1966), Sealy, Bedard, Udvardy, and Fay (1971), Byrd, Gibson, and Johnson (1974), and Byrd, Trapp, and Gibson (1978). Daniel D. Gibson provided direction on the acceptance of a number of single observer reports. Records from Alaska which were substantiated by a specimen are indicated in the text in this manner:
† = specimen record

Despite the welcome help in evaluating records which is provided by Records Committees and regional authorities, over half of the records used in this book were first published in *American Birds* and have not received intensive review. *American Birds'* regional editors have varying standards of documentation which they require before publishing a record. In some cases (e.g., Guy McCaskie in the Southern Pacific Coast region) the records used are nearly always well documented and one can feel quite comfortable in using those published reports. But there have been times when some regional reports included numbers of undocumented and suspect sightings. My general approach to this problem has been this: if a record published in *American Birds* fits within a well-established pattern of occurrence for the species on the West Coast and there is nothing to suggest the report is suspect, I have used it without further review. In these cases, involving several thousand records, I have considered the review by *American Birds* regional editors to be adequate documentation. But when a published report fell outside the established patterns, I reviewed the record with more care, either directing questions to my state or provincial contact (listed in the acknowledgements) and relying on their opinion, or attempting to review details myself. Let me illustrate this process with the example of Buff-breasted Sandpiper *Tryngites subruficollis*. Well over 200 birds have been reported south of Alaska on the West Coast. Nearly all of the records published refer to birds present between mid-Aug and early Oct. Numerous photos, specimens, and Records Committee decisions document the fact that this early fall pattern is the established and expected one for this bird. But there are two published reports in May (one involving 200 birds!) and a couple from July. These records are considered outside the well established pattern and suspect on their face; they require further documentation. Subsequent inquiries did not produce any details of the sightings and regional contacts expressed doubts as to the validity of the reports. I have chosen not to use them in this book. This method of requiring documentation about records which I consider suspect on the face has led, no doubt, to the deletion of some valid reports. And it is possible that some suspect sightings which were within established patterns and not reviewed carefully are included. But given the immensity of the project — compiling over 10,000 records — this method was judged to be the best in screening unacceptable reports while at the same time completing as accurate a compilation as possible.

When there are less than 10 records for a state or province, each record is listed by date and locality (including the county in which the area is located in California, Oregon, and Washington; these counties are abbreviated and the key to the abbreviations is found next to the state maps on later pages of this introduction). Records are usually listed chronological, either for the area as a whole, or by season. In most cases when there are ten or more records for a state or province, the records are not listed individually but are illustrated by a graph. These graphs are explained in more detail a bit later.

The concept of a "record" can be troubling. I have handled the situation in this manner: each individual bird is considered a record except when 1) it is part of a flock and its movements appear to be strongly influenced by the movement of the flock as a whole, or 2) when it is a part of a pair of birds which appear to be interacting as a mated pair, or 3) when it seems reasonable to presume that an individual is the same bird which occurred at the same location in previous years. When a number of birds form a flock (e.g., 5 Emperor Geese *Philacte canagica* or 50 Common Redpoll *Carduelis flammea*), the entire flock is considered a single record, involving additional individuals. Many times a statement like "WASHINGTON 30 records, involving 36 individuals, graphed below" is found. This means that some records were of flocks (of 2 or more birds) and that each flock is graphed as only a single occurrence. When records are more detailed, the exact number of the flock is given: for example "6 Jun 1978 (3) at Los Angeles" would read "a flock (or group) of 3 birds at Los Angeles on 6 Jun 1978". In contrast to this "flock as one record" definition is the case when a single event can bring more than one bird to the same spot, but the birds should not be thought of as a flock. If, for example, a storm front brought 5 Siberian Rubythroat to the same patch of cover on Attu I., Alaska, on 30 May 1990, each bird would still be considered a single record, as it seems preferable not consider the event as a flock of Siberian Rubythroat.

## ABBREVIATIONS AND CITATIONS

A number of standard abbreviations are used throughout the text. Each month is abbreviated to a three-letter term and periods are omitted. Dates are written in scientific style (e.g., 13 Dec 1942). Each West Coast state and province, when referred to in the text in relation to specific rare birds, is capitalized (for ease of location) and usually abbreviated. These standard abbreviations are:

| CAL | = California | WASH | = Washington |
|---|---|---|---|
| ORE | = Oregon | B.C. | = British Columbia |
|  |  | ALASKA |  |

Points of the compass, when referring to an area designation, are abbreviated and capitalized. When points of the compass refer to direction, they are not capitalized. Thus "60 miles w of N CAL" reads "sixty miles west of Northern California".

Geographic features are often abbreviated. These standard abbreviations include:

| I. | = Island | Pen. | = Peninsula |
|---|---|---|---|
| Is. | = Islands | Pt. | = Point |
| Mt. | = Mountain | R. | = River |
| Mtns | = Mountains |  |  |

Standard abbreviations for citations used throughout the text are:

| A | = *The Auk* | CB | = *California Birds* (predecessor of WB) |
|---|---|---|---|
| AB | = *American Birds* |  |  |
| AFN | = *American Field Notes* (predecessor of AB) | CFN | = *Canadian Field Naturalist* |
|  |  | M | = *The Murrelet* |
| BB | = *British Birds* | OB | = *Oregon Birds* |
| C | = *The Condor* | WB | = *Western Birds* |

# TAXONOMY AND ENGLISH NAMES

In most cases, the taxonomy and English names used in this book follow the American Ornithologists' Union *Check-list of North American Birds* (Fifth Edition, 1957) and the more recent 32nd and 33rd supplements. In a few instances the sequence of species within an order has been altered to follow more recent information: herons follow the classification of Payne and Risley (1976); waterfowl follow the Johnsgard-Delacour-Mayr sequence (as in Johnsgard, 1968); shorebirds follow Jehl (1968); and pipits and wagtails follow Voous (1977). Following most waterfowl experts, "Bewick's Swan" *Olor "bewickii"* is considered conspecific with "Whisltling Swan" *O. columbianus* and I follow a number of recent works in referring to the complex as Tundra Swan. Since only species are discussed in the text, "Bewick's Swan" has been omitted, though it would have been a Rarity in ALASKA, ORE, and CAL. Its identification is discussed under Trumpeter Swan *O. buccinator*. It is possible that a number of other birds discussed in the text will be considered conspecific with more common West Coast birds in the future. This possibility is usually mentioned in the text.

In two cases a possible split of a species into two or more species has been anticipated, and complete text included for birds now considered subspecies by the AOU. "Black-vented" Manx Shearwater *Puffinus puffinus opisthomelas* and "White-vented" Manx Shearwater *P. p. puffinus* are both discussed in full; it would not be surprising to find them considered separate species in the future. The eastern race of Yellow-bellied Sapsucker *Sphyrapicus varius varius* may also be considered separate from the western races in the near future and a full text is included for it as well.

As birders and ornithologists begin to view avifuana in a world-wide scope rather than from a narrow regional one, English names have begun to undergo modifications. The American Birding Association's *Checklist* has adopted a number of English names different from those used in the AOU Checklist. Some of these are well received; others are poorly chosen and little used. The more modern trend is to adopt well-recognized and time-honored English names when available for North American species, but to defer to the English names in wide usage elsewhere when a species' primary origins are not North American. This book attempts to follow this course. As we deal with numerous rare birds which are not North American, the English names found here are those most commonly accepted where the bird is more common. Names of Eurasian species are generally those adopted by the British (as found in Voous, 1977, and other works); names of Neotropic species are generally those used by workers in Central and South America (following Eisenmann, 1955, in most cases). Alternate English names are often indicated parenthetically. In some cases one can only attempt to choose the most reasonable alternative. The ABA Checklist is followed in choosing "Band-rumped Storm-Petrel" for *Oceanodroma castro* (which has been known by several other English names), but I differ from the ABA Checklist in calling *O. tethys* the "Wedge-rumped Storm-Petrel" though the adoption of that name would seem to follow the same logic used for choosing the name of *O. castro*. It is hoped that some day we may all have a standardized set of reasonable English names; perhaps this book can be another small step in that direction.

# GRAPHS

In most cases when there are ten or more records of a Rarity from a state or province, the records are not listed individually but are illustrated by means of a bar graph. Every month has been divided into a four-week period in this manner:

Dates 1-8 = 1st week
Dates 9-15 = 2nd week
Dates 16-23 = 3rd week
Dates 24 to the end of the month = 4th week

If a bird was present during any portion of each weekly period, its presence has been graphed accordingly. Thus a bird present from 8-17 Oct will appear as a bar for the 1st through 3rd weeks of Oct. Note that the entire duration of the presence of each bird is graphed, not just arrival dates. The graphs illustrate during which weeks of the year most previous records have occurred. The reader may use them to anticipate the peak periods to search for the species. But since the entire stay is graphed, the reader should be aware that birds in winter tend to remain locally for long periods of time and that these records, when graphed, tend to pile up on each other, forming a misleading winter "peak" when compared to records during migration. Since records during migration are usually of birds which remain for a week or less, a solid bar through the entire month of Sep, for example, usually indicates four records, while a solid bar through the month of Feb usually indicates the presence of single bird which is wintering. Reference to the text will usually clear up any misunderstandings that might be engendered by the graphs. This style of graph has the advantage of indicating departure dates as well as arrival dates; a drop-off of records from Feb-Apr often indicates the departure of locally wintering birds.

Every available record has been graphed as accurately as possible. The same concepts of a "record" apply to the graphs as to the text. Flocks and pairs are graphed as single records, but multiple sightings of birds present at the same place at the same time but which are not part of a flock are graphed as multiple records. A bird which returns to winter for several years is only graphed once; in these situations the graph indicates the earliest ever arrival date and the latest ever departure date of the recurring individual.

The reader will note that the graph is usually started with the month of August. This procedure best suits the patterns of vagrants, for when there are numerous records of a vagrant the general trend is to find most records are of fall birds between Aug-Nov, a few from the spring between May-Jun, and a scattering of winter individuals present between Nov-Apr. The low point of the year for most vagrants is July; it seems best to break the year there, rather than at the end of December. A graph which begins with January and ends with December will show winter records — often of the same bird — far removed from each other and more difficult to read. For species which have a number of summer records lingering into August, the year is occasionally begun with September. On occasion the year is graphed from January, when winter records are not involved or when a single year (e.g. 1977) is illustrated rather than all the records of the Rarity. Single years are often used as "typical" examples to illustrate eastern warblers with numerous records in CAL. The reader should determine which pattern is being used before reading the graph.

## MAPS

In nearly every case when a Rarity has been recorded in a state or province, a map is included illustrating where the record occurred. Each record (keeping in mind the concept of a "record" discussed previously) is illustrated by the presence of a large or small dot at the location it was found. These dots are positioned on the maps as accurately as the scale allows. A small dot indicates that there are one or two records from the locality; a large dot indicates there are three or more records for that area:

- ● = 1 or 2 records
- ● = 3 or more records

Areas which have numerous records are usually discussed in the text and the exact number of records is often indicated there.

An additional feature included on maps of Eurasian vagrants in ALASKA is a smaller scale map of eastern Eurasia (with Alaska) which illustrates the breeding range of the species. The breeding range is shown as a shaded area in Eurasia and the reader can compare it with the records for ALASKA illustrated on the larger ALASKA map. Among the generalizations one can make from such a comparison is that Eurasian birds with northern ranges are most often encountered in ALASKA at Gambell, St. Lawrence I.; the Seward Pen.; or at Pt. Barrow. Birds which breed along the East Asian coast, in Japan, or on the Kamchatka Pen. are more often recorded on the western Aleutian Is. or on the Pribilof Is. The breeding ranges shown in Eurasia illustrate only the general range of the bird, and should not be used to exactly delineate the breeding range. Most of the ranges were drawn after Dement'ev, *et al* (6 volumes, 1951-1954) and modified after Cramp & Simmons (1977) and Flint, *et al* (1968). They are as accurate as these sources, but one might suspect them to be rather dated and lacking any recent information from Siberia.

## PHOTOGRAPHS

An attempt has been made to publish as many photographs of rare birds on the West Coast as could be obtained and which space permitted. Many are the only photos of the species within a particular state or province and several are the only photographs of the bird in North America. Some have been published previously elsewhere, but the majority are published here for the first time. The quality of the photos varies from poor to excellent and while I have chosen better photos when available, in a number of cases only a quick documentary snapshot was available. On the assumption that any photo is better than no photo, a number of these type of shots are included. The photographs are published as documentary photos of rare birds, but in many cases they also serve to illustrate field marks discussed in the identification sections. Each photo is labelled by date, locality (including standardized county abbreviations in CAL, ORE, and WASH), the number of the record which the photograph documents (if ten or less), and the photographer.

All but one of the photographs in this book are of vagrant birds on the West Coast. Photographs of the species under discussion were not included unless they documented a record of a rare bird on the West Coast, with the single exception of a photograph of a Wedge-rumped Storm-Petrel *Oceanodroma tethys* taken near the Galapagos Is., which illustrates the field characteristics of the bird well. In all other cases the reader can be assured that the photograph is of a rare bird taken on the West Coast.

# COLOR PLATES

The color plates illustrate nearly every species of bird which has occurred on the West Coast but which is not illustrated by the standard North American field guides. The few species which are not illustrated in either the standard guides or the color plates of this text are illustrated by line drawings in the text. The color plates also include paintings of more common West Coast species when a direct comparison between the rare bird and the common bird provides a clearer example of the identification problems than can be detailed in the text. Plate 10 illustrates Eurasian species which may, based on the nearness of their breeding range, occur on the West Coast in the future. Plate 11 contains five documentary photographs of rare shorebirds.

Each of the five artists commissioned to do the color plates has his or her unique style, but all paintings were done with reference to museum specimens, usually of the appropriate north-east Asian race. Whenever possible, the artists were supplied with photographs of the bird and with detailed identification articles from the literature (*British Birds* was particularly helpful). Some of the ducks were done from live captive birds.

The facing text to the color plates often highlights some of the more important identification features, but the reader is urged to turn to the main text for a more thorough account. In a few cases, the main text was revised after the printing of the color plates and their facing pages. Any inconsistencies between the facing page notes and the main text should be resolved in favor of the main text.

# Standardized county abbreviations

## CALIFORNIA

| | |
|---|---|
| Ala | Alameda |
| Alp | Alpine |
| Ama | Amador |
| But | Butte |
| Cal | Calaveras |
| Col | Colusa |
| C.C. | Contra Costa |
| D.N. | Del Norte |
| E.D. | El Dorado |
| Frs | Fresno |
| Gln | Glenn |
| Hmb | Humboldt |
| Imp | Imperial |
| Inyo | |
| Kern | |
| Kng | Kings |
| Lake | |
| Las | Lassen |
| L.A. | Los Angeles |
| Mad | Madera |
| Mrn | Marin |
| Mrp | Mariposa |
| Men | Mendocino |
| Mer | Merced |
| Mod | Modesto |
| Mono | |
| Mnt | Monterey |
| Napa | |
| Nev | Nevada |
| Orn | Orange |
| Pla | Placer |
| Plu | Plumas |
| Riv | Riverside |
| Sac | Sacramento |
| S.Bt. | San Benito |
| S.Bn. | San Bernardino |
| S.D. | San Diego |
| S.Bb. | Santa Barbara |
| S.F. | San Francisco |
| S.J. | San Joaquin |
| S.L.O. | San Luis Obispo |
| S.M. | San Mateo |
| S.Cl. | Santa Clara |
| S.Cz. | Santa Cruz |
| Sha | Shasta |
| Sie | Sierra |
| Sis | Siskiyou |
| Sol | Solano |
| Son | Sonoma |
| Stn | Stanislaus |
| Sut | Sutter |
| Teh | Tehama |
| Trn | Trinity |
| Tul | Tulare |
| Tuo | Tuolumne |
| Ven | Ventura |
| Yolo | |
| Yuba | |

## OREGON

| | |
|---|---|
| Bak | Baker |
| Ben | Benton |
| Clk | Clackamas |
| Clt | Clatsop |
| Col | Columbia |
| Coos | |
| Crk | Crook |
| Cur | Curry |
| Des | Deshutes |
| Dgl | Douglas |
| Gil | Gilliam |
| Grn | Grant |
| Har | Harney |
| H.R. | Hood River |
| Jck | Jackson |
| Jef | Jefferson |
| Jos | Josephine |
| Klm | Klammath |
| Lake | |
| Lane | |
| Lnc | Lincoln |
| Linn | |
| Mal | Malheur |
| Mar | Marion |
| Mor | Morrow |
| Mul | Multnomah |
| Polk | |
| Shr | Sherman |
| Til | Tillamook |
| Uma | Umatilla |
| Uni | Union |
| Wal | Wallowa |
| Wsc. | Wasco |
| Wsh | Washington |
| Whe | Wheeler |
| Yam | Yamhill |

## WASHINGTON

| | |
|---|---|
| Adm | Adams |
| Aso | Asotin |
| Ben | Benton |
| Che | Chelan |
| Clm | Clallam |
| Clk | Clark |
| Col | Columbia |
| Cow | Cowlitz |
| Dgl | Douglas |
| Fer | Ferry |
| Frk | Franklin |
| Gar | Garfield |
| Grn | Grant |
| G.H. | Gray's Harbor |
| Isl | Island |
| Jef | Jefferson |
| King | |
| Ksp | Kitsap |
| Ktt | Kittitas |
| Klk | Klickitat |
| Lew | Lewis |
| Lnc | Lincoln |
| Mas | Mason |
| Oka | Okanogan |
| Pac | Pacific |
| P.O. | Pend Oreille |
| Prc | Pierce |
| S.J. | San Juan |
| Skg | Skagit |
| Skm | Skamania |
| Sno | Snohomish |
| Spk | Spokane |
| Stv | Stevens |
| Thr | Thurston |
| Wak | Wahkiamkum |
| W.W. | Walla Walla |
| Wha | Whatcom |
| Whi | Whitman |
| Yak | Yakima |

In most cases when the county name is the same as the locality name, the county name is omitted (e.g. Gray's Harbor is in Gray's Harbor County). County names of offshore islands in California are omitted.

Some common abbreviations in locality names:
- NP = National Park
- NWR = National Wildlife Refuge
- NS = National Seashore
- NM = National Monument
- NF = National Forest
- SB = State Beach
- SP = State Park

**CALIFORNIA** Selected localities mentioned in the text and counties. Bold line separates northern and southern California (as defined by *American Birds*).

**OREGON** Selected localities mentioned in the text and counties (view sideways). Key to standardized county names is on page xx.

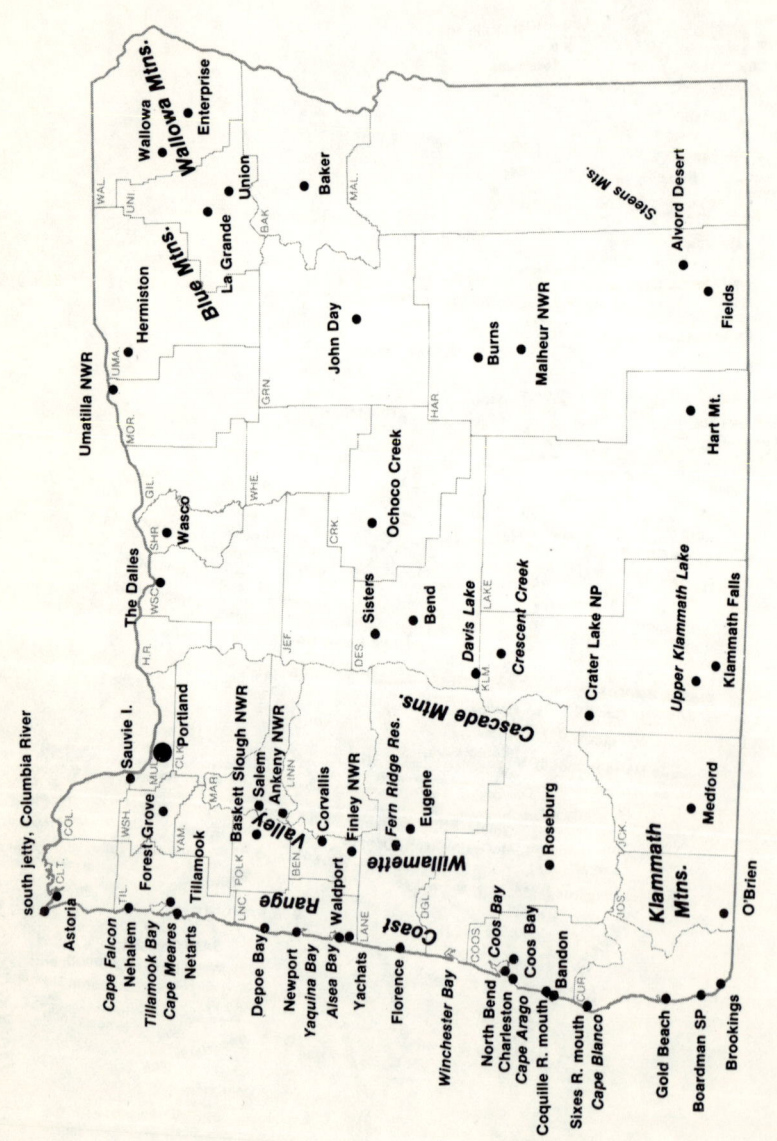

**WASHINGTON** Selected localities mentioned in the text and counties (view sideways). Key to standardized county names is on page xx.

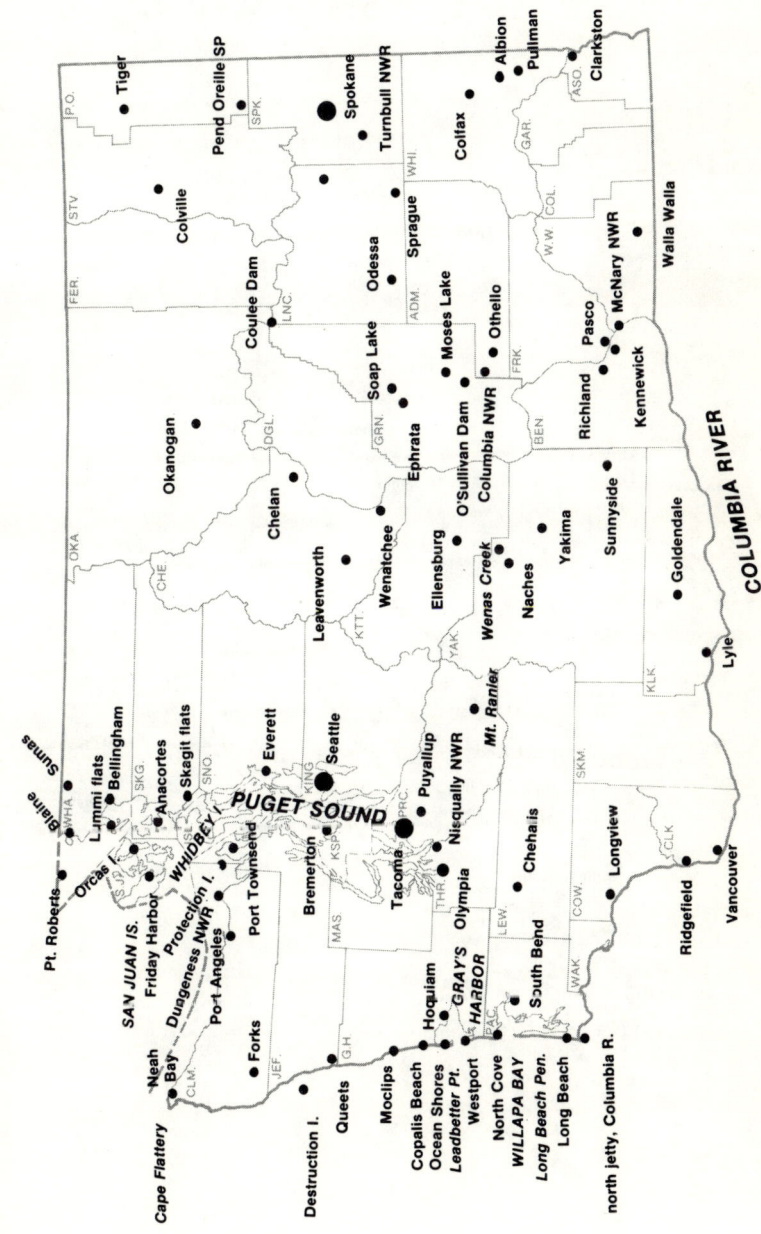

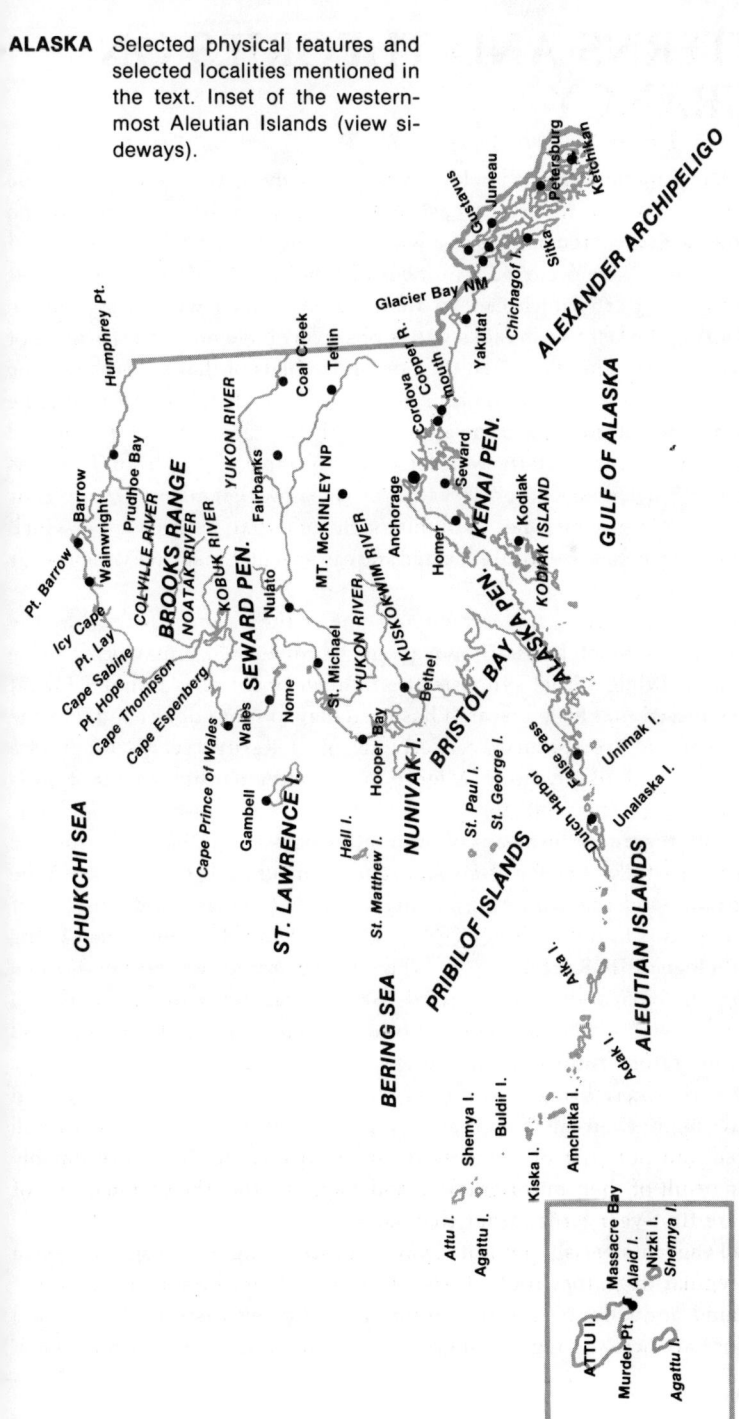

**ALASKA** Selected physical features and selected localities mentioned in the text. Inset of the westernmost Aleutian Islands (view sideways).

# PATTERNS AND THEORIES ON VAGRANCY

An important function of this book is to point out the patterns formed by the records of vagrants on the West Coast. Nearly every species covered here, no matter how rare, occurred as part of a wider pattern of records. The records of those birds which have occurred a number of times on the West Coast almost always form a pattern which can be analyzed and which we can attempt to explain. During the last two decades, active observers have noted the patterns of rarities and can often predict when the next individuals of that species are to be expected. Rare birds do not often occur because of a random "accident" and the term "accidental", often applied to vagrants by the literature, is misleading and inaccurate. Numerous eastern warblers, for example, have been listed as "accidental" or "casual" in California, yet today we know that many of them occur annually in the state, sometimes in numbers. Beyond that, we now know which periods of the year they are to be expected and can speculate as to why they occur then.

While we now may be understanding some of the patterns formed by the records of rarities, much less is known about the forces which may bring these vagrants to us. While a brief synopsis of a number of forces is found below, it should be stressed that little research has been done on the subject and that the theories suggested are speculative. Certainly most Rarity records occur as a result of the process of migration. Migration — the regular movement of birds between breeding areas and non-breeding areas — is a fascinating subject, especially with regard to the means of orientation of migrants. How do birds find their way successfully over the often thousands of miles of distance between the nesting ground and the wintering locality? A good popularized discussion of current theories is found in Fisher (1979); a more detailed review aimed at the field ornithologist is in Keeton (1979). When, for one reason or another, normal orientation or navigation fails, a bird may appear far from its expected destination. Here it is called a vagrant, a bird no longer a part of the regular and successful migratory routes of the species. Reoccurring misorientation errors and other forces may bring vagrants to the West Coast every year, in such numbers we might even call them regular vagrants, but these individuals are still misoriented and not part of a successful migratory route. Most presumably perish as a result of their misorientation and it appears that the vast majority of vagrants are first-year birds rather than adults.

Not all vagrants perish, nor is it always easy to distinguish a vagrant from a bird on a regular migratory route. It seems probable that a number of "eastern" species found annually in eastern California (and often eastern Oregon and Washington) are actually regular migrants in small numbers east of the Sierra.

Examples might be Black-and-white Warbler *Mniotilta varia*, Tennessee Warbler *Vermivora peregrina*, or Rose-breasted Grosbeak *Pheucticus ludovicianus*. These species are considered vagrants on the coast, but their status inland is more controversial and there is no good method of distinguishing a vagrant (a bird outside the normal and successful migratory routes) from a bird on a regular migratory route which is used by only a small portion of the population (a route which would be used successfully). We find the same blurring of the issue on the western Aleutian Islands, Alaska. A number of species are found there annually (examples include Wood Sandpiper *Tringa glareola* and Long-toed Stint *Calidris subminuta*) and we might call these species regular migrants there in spring and fall. On the other hand, more are found during "waves" of vagrants, often associated with storm fronts. Since we do not know the success of the movements which bring birds to the Aleutians, we cannot readily distinguish between regular migrants and misoriented vagrants. The success of an individual bird is not indicative of its status either. A tremendous array of vagrants have occasionally wintered or summered on the West Coast. Some have even found mates and nested in areas which superficially resembled the regular nesting area thousands of miles distant (Northern Parula *Parula americana* has nested twice in California). In this book, an attempt to distinguish between vagrants and regular migrants has been made, based on the evidence available, but the reader should understand that any label used is simply a "best guess". Others, looking at the same pattern of events, may use different terms.

Despite the difficulty in coming to terms with the distinction between a regular migrant and a vagrant, enough rare birds have occurred on the West Coast that a number of professional and amateur ornithologists have begun to speculate as to why they occur. The more important theories are discussed below. Throughout the book, these theories have been often applied to the patterns formed by the records of a rare bird and a possible reason for the appearance of the Rarity suggested. The major categories are 1) fall misorientation, especially mirror-image misorientation and reverse misorientation, 2) spring misorientation, 3) spring overshooting, 4) post-breeding dispersal, 5) winter invasions, 6) irregular nesting expansion, and, for pelagic species, 7) variable oceanic conditions. Weather can play an important role in several of these categories.

**Fall Misorientation.** Many Rarity records on the West Coast, especially in California, are of landbirds which nest in northern taiga forests or in the deciduous woodlands of eastern North America. The usual migration routes of these species take them east of the Rockies, and often to the coasts of northeastern North America, where it appears a large number orient SSW and follow the Atlantic coastline south to Florida, thence SE through the Caribbean Antilles to wintering grounds in the West Indies and South America (Richardson, 1976; Williams, Berkeley, & Harris, 1977). But a large percentage of migrants orient from the Atlantic coast to the SE and, following the passage of a cold front with its favorable winds, undertake long trans-oceanic flights (Richardson, 1972). These migrants need only continue their SE orientation, for strong NE trade winds over the Atlantic will curve them directly to South America (Williams, Williams, Ireland, & Teal, 1977). Should these migrants encounter very cloudy conditions, orientation may be lost. If, when disoriented, fast eastward-moving winds are encountered, a migrant may simply reorient downwind and these conditions may take the bird as a vagrant across the Atlantic to Britain or Europe (Elkins, 1979).

An understanding of the process of normal migration and orientation helps to explain the presence of eastern vagrants on the West Coast. DeBenedictis (1971) noted that eastern species with large populations account for many West Coast records. DeSante (1973) developed the mirror-image theory to explain how these birds arrive here. Working with eastern warblers, especially the Blackpoll Warbler *Dendroica striata*, he was able to show that these birds have become oriented to the SW, rather than to the SE as normal migrants are. Those species with a strong easterly, rather than southerly, component to their migration routes are the most numerous vagrants on the West Coast. Some portion of these populations are "mirror-image" misoriented — that is, unable to distinguish right from left in relating a migration direction to a compass reference point. Thus, rather than orienting SE over the Atlantic, they have become oriented SW and head towards the West Coast. Weather conditions over the center of the continent may play a part in determining how many of these misoriented vagrants reach the West Coast. A prolonged system of high pressure over Canada in August 1974 may have contributed to the greatest landfall of eastern warblers ever witnessed on the West Coast (Zimmerman, 1975).

While misorientation may occur to all points of the compass, and thus an individual may be simply randomly misoriented toward the West Coast, it does seem that a large population size, combining with the non-random misorientation suggested by DeSante's "mirror-image" theory, accounts for the presence of most immature fall vagrants from the East. DeSante and Ainley (1980) suggest an additional factor to account for differences in the numbers of vagrants between various species. They find it statistically significant that more nine-primaried passerines (wood warblers, icterids, and finches) occur on SE Farallon I., California, than do ten-primaried passerines (tyrant flycatchers, mimids, thrushes, and vireos). This fact is especially evident when comparing species of similar ranges, population size, and migratory patterns. They suggest that the nine-primaried species, which are theorized to be the most recently evolved group of passerines, have a higher degree of genetic variability and thus apt to more often produce individuals which are misoriented. Such vagrancy, they suggest, could eventually serve to enhance the species' position by the development of new breeding and wintering areas. The success of a few vagrants in summering and wintering on the West Coast may be steps in this direction.

The work of SE Farallon I. points out another aspect of the occurrence of vagrants in California, and perhaps the entire West Coast. The vast majority of records of eastern vagrants in California are from isolated groves of trees on coastal headlands or on offshore islands, or at desert oases in the interior. While the concentrating effects of these spots is apparent, it does seem that most misoriented birds continue to travel until the need for food or rest forces them down to the nearest available cover. This situation most often arises when crossing inhospitable desert or when finding themselves over open ocean. Observations of SE Farallon I., some 27 miles west of San Francisco, have shown that numerous vagrants appear there during a morning from the west, suggesting that the birds found themselves over ocean at dawn and back-tracked to the nearest land. Presumably most of these individuals continue their fatal misoriented oceanic route over the Pacific after "tanking up", but some do return to the mainland, as banded eastern warblers (presumably banded on the Farallones), have been seen on the central California coast as far south as Monterey. It would appear that some vagrants, having reoriented themselves to the mainland, might continue down the coast (similar to the situation with many birds in the East) and eventually winter successfully in California or western Mexico.

Mirror-image misorientation might also explain the presence of Eurasian vagrants on the Aleutians or elsewhere in Alaska, though nothing as yet been published on this subject. Numerous species which nest in NE Asia have migration routes which take them SW in the fall. If they were mirror-image misoriented — to the SE — their line of flight would take them to western Alaska and the Aleutian Is. A continuation of this hypothetical line of flight would bring some of these birds to the coasts of B.C., WASH, ORE, and CAL. Perhaps there is something to this theory, as a number of Eurasian vagrants have been recorded in the fall in these West Coast states and provinces.

Another phenomenon associated with fall migration might be called reverse misorientation. If a migrant should, for some reason, become disoriented, some birds will reorient themselves toward the direction they had just traveled. A bird moving south would, in this example, reorient itself towards the north. It is also possible that an individual would become oriented in the opposite direction at the beginning of its flight. By whichever method this reverse misorientation occurs, the net effect is to bring vagrants in the fall to areas north of the breeding range, when the species as a whole is travelling south. This phenomenon has been observed in eastern North America landbirds over the Atlantic (Williams, Williams, Ireland, & Teal, 1977) and may account for some records of Nearctic birds in Britain (Elkins, 1979). It may also account for the presence of numerous North American landbirds at Pt. Barrow, Alaska, in the fall, and records of

Mexican species in California in Oct-Dec. Some of the latter species, such as Tropical Kingbird *Tyrannus melancholicus*, occur annually in the fall on the West Coast and have occasionally remained to winter successfully. Others are much rarer, but records of Gray Kingbird *Tyrannus dominicensis*, Olivaceous Flycatcher *Myiarchus tuberculifer*, Coues' Flycatcher *Contopus pertinax*, Streak-backed Oriole *Icterus pustulatus*, and Varied Bunting *Passerina versicolor* may all fit into this pattern.

**Spring misorientation.** There does not appear to be a spring migration of eastern North American birds over the Atlantic (Richardson, 1974), migration taking place through the Caribbean and along the gulf coast of Central America and Texas. A large number of eastern vagrants have occurred on the West Coast in the spring, but the mechanics of misorientation have been little studied. Among the theories suggested is that migrants moving N or NE, which must reorient in mid-route to reach breeding grounds in central Canada or Alaska, occasionally reorient themselves to the NW too soon, thus reaching eastern California rather than NE British Columbia (for example). Another theory suggests that those birds whose departure from the wintering ground is delayed (for one reason or another), react to the stimulus for course changes at a lower latitude than the normally-departing migrants (star patterns, for example, have changed during the delay in departure) and thus arrive on the West Coast late and far south of their normal destination. These hypotheses have not been tested, but we can note that records of eastern vagrants are concentrated in late May-early Jun, considerably later than the migration of eastern species in similar lattitudes in eastern North America and that many records are from the desert oases of eastern California, while records of fall vagrants tend to occur most often on the coast.

**Spring overshooting.** Birds migrating north in the spring usually return to the area where they nested the year before or, if first year birds, to the area in which they were hatched. But numbers, often first year birds on their first northern flight, overshoot the area of their birth and appear far to the north (Pitelka, 1974). When the northward flight is accompanied by strong tailwinds, birds may overshoot spectacular distances, bringing southern species to New England or even American birds to Britain (Nisbet, 1963; Elkins, 1979). Similar forces must be at work in NE Asia, for every year numbers of Siberian birds occur to the north and west of their breeding grounds, especially on the outer Aleutian Is., the Pribilof Is., St. Lawrence I., the Seward Peninsula, and Pt. Barrow, Alaska. In some years these flights may be of so many birds that breeding activity is stimulated in some species. Wood Sandpiper *Tringa glareola* and the Ruff *Philomachus pugnax* have bred under these conditions; the Long-toed Stint *Calidris subminuta* and the Common Skylark *Alauda arvensis* are suspected of having nested. Local conditions for landfalls of Siberian overshoots on St. Lawrence I. or the Seward Pen. are clear and sunny days in mid-May to mid-Jun with S or SW winds, but storm fronts are associated with "waves" of vagrants reaching the western Aleutian Is. It may be that turbulent air moving in a predominately NE direction over the Sea of Japan may be responsible for bringing migrants to the western Aleutians, pushing them only slightly off-course from their intended destination on the Kamchatka Pen., NE Asia. It is as yet unknown whether these individuals are able to reorient themselves and eventually manage to nest in Asia.

Continual spring overshooting may result in the expansion of a breeding range. This seems to be the case with a number of primarily Mexican species in the southern California mountains (Johnson & Garrett, 1974). The Painted Redstart *Myioborus picta*, Zone-tailed Hawk *Buteo albonotatus*, and Pyrrhuloxia *Cardinalis sinuatus* have all nested in southern California in recent years, and the Grace's Warbler *Dendroica graciae* and Red-faced Warbler *Cardellina rubrifrons* have been found defending territory in what could be suitable breeding habitat.

**Post-breeding dispersal.** A number of birds, especially species breeding to the south of the West Coast, disperse widely after the completion of nesting. Immatures are often involved in these movements. Dispersal of west Mexican and Gulf of California birds occurs toward the west and north and is often concentrated at the Salton Sea, California. Some occur regularly — Wood Stork *Mycteria americana* and Laughing Gull *Larus atricilla* — and others irregularly — Blue-footed Booby *Sula nebouxii* — but the bulk of this dispersal is of pelicans, boobies, frigatebirds, herons, and gulls (see McCaskie, 1970). Similar dispersal occasionally occurs in species considered Rarities — White Ibis *Eudocimus albus* or Black-bellied Whistling Duck *Dendrocygna autumnalis*. Other post-breeding dispersals have taken California nesters to northern states or provinces where they are a Rarity; examples are the Fulvous Whistling Duck *Dendrocygna bicolor* and White-faced Ibis *Plegadis chihi*. Post-breeding dispersal at the Salton Sea is concentrated in Jul-Sep, but farther to the north records may extend through Oct-Nov.

**Winter Invasions.** A number of tundra or taiga nesting species stage periodic invasions to the south, often in response to a collapsing food supply. The Snowy Owl *Nyctea scandiaca* is famous for these cyclical movements, but Rarity records of Gyrfalcon *Falco rusticolus*, Hawk Owl *Surnia ulula*, and Boreal Owl *Aegolius funereus* may be related to similar phenomena. A variety of seed-eaters are affected by food and weather conditions in the north and have occurred in invasions; examples are redpolls *Carduelis sp.* and the Snow Bunting *Plectrophenax nivalis*.

**Irregular Nesting Expansion and Summer Invasions.** Some birds, particularly those nesting in desert or chapparal habitats, expand or contract their breeding range in response to environmental conditions. This is well documented in the case of the Cassin's Sparrow *Aimophila cassinii* (Hubbard, 1977), and a number of singing Cassin's Sparrows occurred in California in the summer of 1978 following draught-ending rains. Extremely favorable environmental conditions may cause temporary breeding expansion far from the normal nesting area (such as a nesting Lark Bunting *Calamospiza melanocorys* in SE California in summer 1978) or singing males beyond the breeding range (Black-chinned Sparrow *Spizella atrogularis* in Oregon).

Certain nomadic species, in response to food supplies, may wander to areas in which they are a Rarity during the summer. Following nesting in Oregon, the White-winged Crossbill *Loxia leucoptera* occurred in NE California in summer 1978.

**Pelagic Movements and Variable Oceanic Conditions.** A number of antarctic and sub-antarctic breeding seabirds are trans-equatorial migrants — Sooty Shearwater *Puffinus griseus* or South Polar Skua *Catharacta maccormickii* — and appear annually off the West Coast. Some, like the Mottled Petrel *Pterodroma inexpectata*, probably pass too far offshore to be detected annually along the southern West Coast. Northern nesting seabirds sometimes winter in great numbers in the central Pacific — the Horned Puffin *Fratercula corniculata* — but only stray to within the area covered here in response to still unknown environmental factors. Weather, currents, food availability, temperature, and salinity greatly affect seabird distribution (see Ainley, 1976 and Wahl, 1978). Pre-breeders do not always follow the general migratory patterns of the bulk of the species and some seabirds which do not breed until their fourth year or later — such as large albatross — may wander the seas for years. We know a number of tropical species — like the "Black-vented" Manx Shearwater *Puffinus puffinus opisthomelas* — follow the Davidson Current along the California coast north in the late fall and that temperature appears to affect the northern distributional limits of the Xantus' Murrelet *Endomychura hypoleuca* and Craveri's Murrelet *E. craveri*. Storm-petrels gather in huge flocks at the Monterey Bay upwellings in Sep-Oct, and Rarities like the Wilson's Storm-Petrel *Oceanites oceanicus* may be a regular part of this phenomenon. But as to what forces contribute to the presence of the Wandering Albatross *Diomedia exulans* or the Streaked Shearwater *Puffinus leucomelas* we can barely speculate. More thorough coverage, especially farther offshore, may provide more solid information. Indeed, the presence of Cook's Petrel *Pterodroma cooki* off California was not discovered until fall 1979. It is not yet known whether *Pterodromas* are regular off California, or simply occur irregularly when conditions are optimum.

# YELLOW-BILLED LOON

*OCT. 13, 1982*
*BODEGA BAY, CA*

*Gavia adamsii*

Breeds N North America, N Eurasia. Winters in northern coastal waters.

The Yellow-billed Loon in North America moves from its arctic and subarctic nesting grounds to wintering areas in cold coastal waters off S ALASKA and N B.C. Very small numbers winter south to Vancouver I., B.C. and Puget Sound, WASH, while fewer still migrate through these areas in <u>Sep-Oct towards</u> ORE and <u>CAL</u>, where it is a <u>Rarity</u>. The first loons to arrive off CAL (late Nov-Dec) seem to pass through quickly, perhaps to more southern destinations (though a single 24 Nov 1968 record from the Los Coronados Is., Mexico (C 72:376), just south of the international border, is the only evidence to date). Later arriving birds (peak in late Jan) tend to winter locally in N CAL and ORE, then move slowly back north in Feb-Apr, though a few stragglers have remained far south into the summer. A single sure record of a spring migrant in S CAL suggests a possible return migration of the southernmost wintering birds in Apr or early May. The Yellow-billed Loon prefers <u>shallow, sheltered waters</u> and most Rarity records are from suitable bays and river mouths. All acceptable records to date are <u>coastal</u>. For a more thorough discussion see Binford & Remsen (1975).

**OREGON**   12 records, graphed below. While there are 3 records of fall migrants and a local wintering record, most appear to be returning spring migrants from more southerly flights. 5 records are from Yaquina Bay, Lnc. A bird in summer dress on 15 Jul 1972 at Coos Bay must have been a very late straggler.

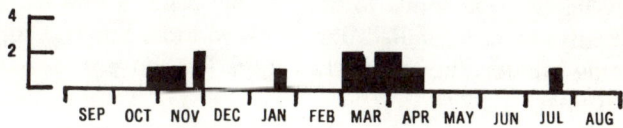

**CALIFORNIA**   33 records, graphed below. Now averaging about 3 birds a year, most are fall migrants (<u>Nov-Dec</u>) or local winterers (late Jan-Mar) in N CAL, with only two records south of Monterey Bay. One discovered 25 Jan 1976 at Berkeley, Ala., lingered until 2 Aug; another 17-25 Jun 1973* at Princeton, S.M., is the only other summer record. Spring migration is poorly documented. Most Apr-May birds have been in winter plumage and could be lingering winterers, but a breeding-plumaged bird passing Pt. Dume, L.A., on 20 Apr 1977 was clearly a spring migrant.

# YELLOW-BILLED LOON

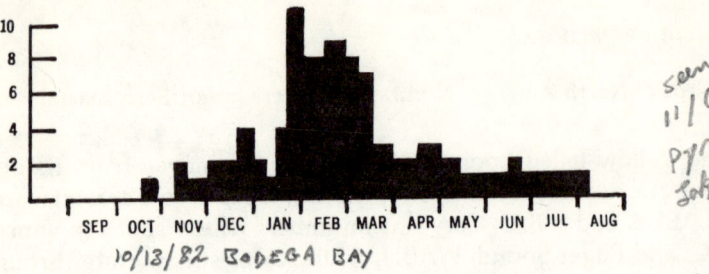

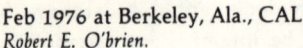

**I.D.** The Yellow-billed Loon in non-breeding plumage is often confused with the Common Loon *G. immer*. It differs in size and shape, being slightly larger, looking thicker-necked, flatter-crowned, and smaller-eyed, and has feathering at the base of the bill extending out from the chin towards the nostril. The plumage is generally browner and paler and often distinctly cross-barred on the back. An excellent mark is the paler face, usually showing a distinct auricular patch, which can be seen at great distances.

The standard guides emphasize unreliable bill shape differences and fail to portray the range of bill color in Common Loon. In winter, the bill of Yellow-billed Loon becomes a pale straw color, while that of Common Loon becomes pale grayish, and both may look quite light in the field. The color of the culmen is diagnostic. The culmen of Yellow-billed Loon, at least from the tip to the midpoint, is always pale, usually quite yellow. The culmen of Common Loon is always dark. While there are fine bill shape differences between the species (see Binford & Remsen, 1974), they are of little value in the field and the oft-mentioned greater gonydeal angle (upturn to the lower mandible) is not consistent. It is true that Yellow-billed Loon tends to hold its bill slightly upward and this posture accentuates a big-billed, long-headed look, but the "upturned bill" is of only minor value in identification. For more information see Binford & Remsen (1974).

Feb 1976 at Berkeley, Ala., CAL.
*Robert E. O'brien.*

# YELLOW-BILLED LOON

18 Feb 1980 at Richmond, Ala., CAL. *Steve Wilson.*

15 Jul 1972 at Coos Bay, ORE. 3rd record. *Paul Buckley.*

Jan 1969 at Monterey, CAL. 6th record. *Ronald L. Branson.*

# LEAST GREBE

*Podiceps dominicus*

Resident S Texas, W Mexico, S Baja to South America.

Individuals of the West Mexican race of the Least Grebe *P.d. bangsi* are thought to be scarce and local, but occasionally wander to the northwest. A single nesting record occurred in our area over 30 years ago, but two recent winter reports from S Arizona, including one from Oct 1976 to at least Mar 1978 at Quitobaquito, only about 120 miles distant, suggest the possibility of finding fall or winter vagrants in S Cal.

**CALIFORNIA**   One record: 18-23 Oct 1946† at West Pond, Imperial Dam, Imp. (C 49:125). A pair of adults were observed on the 18th, and 6 adults and 3 downy young were present of the 23rd, indicating local nesting. Other published reports are considered inadequately documented.

# WANDERING ALBATROSS   Plate 1

*Diomedea exulans*

Breeds subantarctic islands. Wanders widely in S temperate seas.

The Wandering Albatross is represented in our area by a single record, one of the very few for the Northern Hemisphere (see *Ibis* 109:141). This great albatross does not breed until its 8th or 9th year, and even then only every other year. Sub-adults disperse widely to 40° S with regularity. These extended sea flights, its great strength, and its known ship-following tendencies may all contribute to the presence of vagrants far to the north. While immature-plumaged birds might logically be most expected as vagrants, the single record is of an adult female.

# WANDERING ALBATROSS

**CALIFORNIA**  One record: 11-12 Jul 1967* at Sea Ranch, Son. (A 85:502). Found standing on the sea cliffs by local residents, it remained until the breeze came up, when it stretched its wings and departed seaward.

**I.D.**  The Wandering Albatross is a huge bird with wingspreads reported to 12 ft. Adults are almost all-white, with black tips to the flight feathers and tail, though younger adult females often show a neat dark cap. The Royal Albatross *D. epomophora*, another southern albatross, is most similar but has a distinct "cutting edge" to the bill, much reduced dark on the tail, and lacks any of the Wandering's many immature plumages. Very young Wanderings are all dark except for white underwings and a sharply contrasting white face and throat; older birds may show a blotchy "leopard" phase or a white-bodied plumage with dark upperwings and tail (see Harper & Kinsky, 1978). Some of these plumages might be confused with the Short-tailed Albatross *D. albatrus* and are covered under that account.

12 Jul 1967 at Sea Ranch, Son., CAL. 1st record. *Louis McLean.*

# SHORT-TAILED ALBATROSS       Plate 1

*Diomedea albatrus*

Breeds Torishima I., Japan. Wanders widely in N. Pacific.

The Short-tailed Albatross was formerly common along the entire West Coast, but hunters and volcanic eruptions on its Japanese breeding islands nearly extirpated this great bird by 1930. Reduced to only about 10 pairs in 1953, it has shown a gradual increase under protection and the 1978 population was estimated at 200 birds. For a recent account of its history and status see Harrison (1979).
   In the 19th century, it was said to be present year-round near the West Coast. Concentrations were found in the summer near the Aleutian Is., ALASKA. Young birds apparently predominated near the CAL coast. Only sightings from the 20th century are listed below. While ALASKA records are grouped in the summer, reports farther south show no apparent pattern.

**ALASKA**   Six records: 9 Jun 1940 in the Gulf of Alaska, 25 Nov 1947 about 50 miles se of Cape St. Elias, 14 May 1956 about 150 miles w of Sitka (M 45:47), 13 Aug 1962 some 42 miles sw of Attu I. (M 45:48), 16 Aug 1962 some 58 miles ne of Attu I. (M 45:48), and 27 Aug 1976 near Tanadak I., W. Aleutians. All but the 1947 and 1956 reports were adults. In addition, an immature outside the area on 24-26 Jun 1971 at 50° N, 145° W (CFN 86:285), in the southern Gulf of Alaska, completes the summer pattern of records in the NE Pacific.

**BRITISH COLUMBIA**   One record: an immature 11 Jun 1960 some 40 miles w of Vancouver I. (CFN 76:178).

**OREGON**   One record: an immature 11 Dec 1961 some 32 miles w of Yachats, Lcn. (C 65:163).

**CALIFORNIA**   Two records: an adult 17 Feb 1946 about 70 miles w of San Francisco, and an immature 28 Aug 1977* about 90 miles w of San Diego.

Note: A number of recently published reports of sub-adult Short-tailed Albatross appear to be misidentifications and actually refer to old or aberrant Black-footed Albatross or hybrid Laysan X Black-footed Albatross. This problem includes reports from WASH (CB 1:113), ORE (AB 33:206), and CAL (AB 32:1050), and is discussed briefly in the I.D. section.

# SHORT-TAILED ALBATROSS

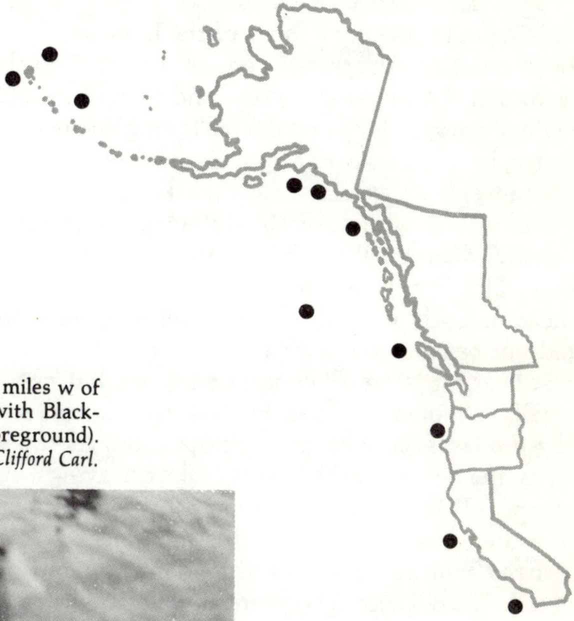

11 Jun 1960 about 40 miles w of Vancouver I., B.C. (with Black-footed Albatross, foreground). 1st recent record. *G. Clifford Carl.*

Captive Short-tailed Albatross. May 1971. *Mike Wihler.*

# SHORT-TAILED ALBATROSS

I.D. The Short-tailed Albatross is a very large, heavy albatross resembling in proportions those of the huge southern albatrosses, such as the Wandering Albatross *D. exulans*, rather than the smaller N Pacific Black-footed Albatross *D. nigripes* and Laysan Albatross *D. immutabilis*. The wings are very long and the bill is long and massive. In any plumage this huge, long bill, colored a light carmine-pink and looking nearly white at a distance, is an excellent field mark.

Adults, with white backs and a golden wash to the crown and nape, are easily distinguished from the dark-backed Laysan Albatross. Younger birds, with dark feathers in the back, will show much dark on the head and white areas on the upperwing near the body, and again should not be confused with the Laysan Albatross.

1st year birds are all chocolate-brown, but may be separated from young Black-footed Albatross by the huge, pink bill and light-colored feet and by the larger size in direct comparison. As the young Short-tailed matures, the face and belly become white, leaving a bird with a dark neck and throat. This plumage has been confused with very pale or very old Black-footed Albatross. These birds show an extensive white face, a dark breastband, whitish belly, and white flanks, rump, undertail coverts, and often tail. The bill becomes lighter as well, often a dull yellowish or dusky pink, and the feet are a light dusky-yellow. Some aberrant individuals, perhaps Black-footed X Laysan hybrids, may show whitish underwings. Whatever the state of these odd albatrosses, the Short-tailed Albatross differs by its large size, the long, clear pink bill, dark throat and neck (not breastband), dark flanks and undertail coverts, and dark tips to all tail feathers. As they become older, the dark throat, flanks, and undertail coverts are lost, but birds at this stage begin to show a white patch on the upperwings near the body, which becomes progressively larger with maturity. Aberrant Black-footed Albatross or hybrids will lack this patch.

In some of the young stages, Short-tailed Albatross may resemble immature Wandering Albatross. Wandering Albatross is larger, with longer wings, a discrete ear-patch, and shows all-white underwings as an immature (Short-tailed is mostly white-bodied before showing white underwings). The long bill and flat crown of the Wandering produce a long-headed appearance, accentuated by feathering extending out from the base of the bill to below the nostril. There is no lobe of feathers extending out at the base of a Short-tailed's bill.

# SHORT-TAILED ALBATROSS

General plumage sequence of Short-tailed Albatross from about 2nd to 5th year, dorsal views (left) and ventral views (right). Drawings after N. Yanagisawa in *Yacho* 38:44 (1973). The photos below illustrate aberrant or old Black-footed Albatross; compare them with the young Short-tailed Albatross.

Pale Black-footed Albatross. 12 Sep 1971 off Westport, WASH. *Dennis Paulson.*

# LAYSAN ALBATROSS

*Diomedea immutabilis*

Breeds Leeward Is., Hawaii. Wanders widely in N Pacific.

The Laysan Albatross is a highly pelagic species. It is considered a Rarity in a number of West Coast states and provinces, but is really quite common at times offshore the West Coast. Most birds appear to remain outside the 200 mile limit chosen for our area, but the movements of birds within our zone parallel the major movements in the annual cycle described by Sanger (1974).

Movements of birds away from the breeding grounds may be summarized as follows: In Jun-Jul, the bulk of the population is concentrated around the Aleutian Is., ALASKA. In Sep-Oct, birds begin moving from the Aleutian and w Gulf of Alaska waters to the south, appearing off B.C., WASH, and ORE and becoming common far offshore WASH-ORE in Oct. By late Nov, birds begin to arrive off CAL and by Jan are found commonly from N ORE to S CAL at distances greater than 500 miles offshore. By Mar, numbers begin to decline in these southern waters and a passage into the Gulf of Alaska begins, peaking in the Gulf in Apr-May, and shifting westward to the Aleutians in early summer.

The usual account by state or province does not lend inself well to discussing this bird. Instead, one might divide the West Coast south of ALASKA into two parts at Cape Mendocino, Men., CAL. In the northern half, birds are present year-round, as these waters fall within the southern part of the summering areas and the northern part of the wintering areas. A near-shore peak in Oct-Nov parallels abundance far offshore and may be influenced by high near-shore salinity. The Laysan Albatross prefers waters of high salinity (see Ainley, 1976).

In the southern half, near-shore occurrence also approximates abundance far offshore, with nearly all records occurring in Dec-May. Wintering Laysans seem to prefer areas of rich cold water upwellings (e.g., Monterey Bay; Cordelle Banks, off Bodega Bay, Son.) and annual temperature and salinity fluctuations probably affect local distribution. During the migration out of these wintering waters, in Apr-May, a few may be seen from shore (several recent records from sea-watches at Pigeon Pt., S.M.). Most unusual was a bird crossing the desert on 5 May 1976 near Desert Hot Springs, Riv., CAL. (WB 8:27). It is hypothesized that the bird may have become "trapped" in the Gulf of California while moving northward, and was continuing its flight via the Salton Sea, Coachella Valley, and San Gregorio Pass to the Pacific.

# LAYSAN ALBATROSS

26 Jan 1980 in Monterey Bay, CAL. *Don Roberson.*

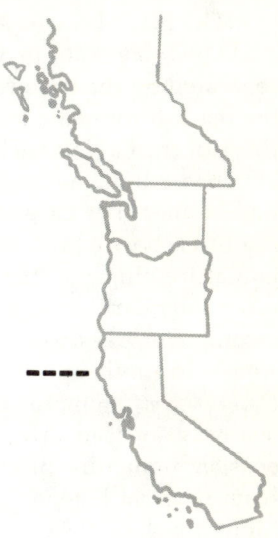

12 May 1975 west of Pt. Arguello, S.Bb., CAL. *John Butler.*

22 May 1976 about 18 miles w of Humboldt Bay, CAL. *Ron LeValley.*

I.D. In all flying stages, the Laysan Albatross is a white-bodied albatross with dark upperwings, back, and tail. Often there is some pale gray in the cheeks. Other white-bodied albatrosses are very rare along the West Coast. The endangered Short-tailed Albatross *D. albatrus* is white-backed as an adult and is a larger, heavier-billed bird; dark-backed sub-adults will show dark feathers on the head, neck, and underparts and white blotches on the upperwings.

# LAYSAN ALBATROSS

The Black-browed Albatross *D. melanophris*, a southern species which could possibly occur in our area, is very similar to the Laysan, but can be separated by the pattern of the underwings. The white underwings of the Black-browed are bordered with broad, straight-edged dark margins; those of the Laysan are bordered with irregular dark margins, with black blotches extending into and reducing the amount of white on the underwings. The Laysan also has diagnostic black axillaries ("arm-pits"); the Black-browed has white axillaries. While the Laysan lacks a distinct immature plumage, the Black-browed has an immature plumage with essentially dark underwings, variable amounts of gray on the nape, an incomplete breastband, and a dark-looking bill. In this plumage it is similar to another possible southern vagrant, the Gray-headed Albatross *D. chrysostoma*. Immature Gray-headed has even darker underwings and a distinct gray head, often with white cheeks. It is interesting to note that a possible immature Black-browed Albatross was seen on 24 Mar 1977 from shore at Pigeon Pt., S.M., CAL and that a bird on 28 Feb 1977 in Monterey Bay, CAL, was described as "similar to nearby Laysans, but smaller and with a distinctly dark head" and could have been a Gray-headed Albatross. For more on the identification of southern albatross, see Harper & Kinsky (1978) and Warham, Bourne, & Elliott (1974).

# WHITE-CAPPED ALBATROSS

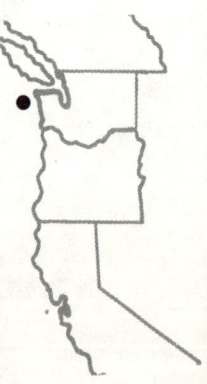

Plate 1

*Diomedea cauta*

Breeds islands in Australasia. Disperses widely into S subtropical seas.

The White-capped Albatross has occurred only once off the West Coast. The record, of an adult female, is the only one in the N Pacific and illustrates the potential for long-distance vagrancy in southern albatross.

**WASHINGTON** One record: 1 Sep 1951† about 40 miles west of the Quillayute R. mouth, G.H. (A 69:458).

# WHITE-CAPPED ALBATROSS

I.D. The White-capped Albatross is a huge albatross, surpassed in size only by the Wandering Albatross *D. exulans* and the Royal Albatross *D. epomophora*, and thus much larger than any regular West Coast albatross. The record is of the largest and most widespread race: *D.c. cauta*. It is a white-bodied, light-billed bird as an adult, with dark upperwings, back, and tail. The underwings are white, narrowly edged with black, and have a large black spot where the front margin meets the body. This underwing pattern, also present in immatures, and the large size should distinguish this bird from any other white-bodied albatross. Immatures have a grayish head and neck, a white throat, and a dark bill.

# CAPE PETREL

*Daption capense*

Plate 1

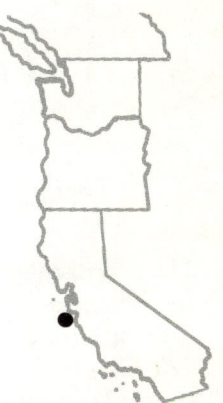

Breeds Antarctica, subantarctic and S Atlantic islands. Ranges widely in S hemispheric seas, north to the tropics.

The Cape Petrel, one of the commonest southern pelagics, has only rarely strayed north of the equator (see *Ibis* 109:141 and Cramp & Simmons, 1977). An old specimen attributed to Monterey Bay is best disregarded (CB 1:23), as should several sight records. The remaining sight record was very brief and has been questioned by some. It would be the only record for the N Pacific. The Cape Petrel follows cold currents into the tropics, and it is interesting to note that the year of the record (1962) was among th coldest in water temperature in Monterey Bay in a recent 20 year period (Ainley, 1976).

**CALIFORNIA** One record: 9 Sep 1962 in Monterey Bay (CB 1:39). Although the CAL Records Committee had previously accepted this report, it is recirculating the record and the status of this species on the CAL list is uncertain at this time (Jan 1980).

# CAPE PETREL

I.D.  The Cape Petrel is a sharply-patterned bird, with two large white patches on the black wings, a checkered back and rump, black head and tail, and white underparts (see Plate 1). The Northern Fulmar *Fulmarus glacialis*, which it resembles in size and shape, occasionally shows dark and light patches on the upperwings that may resemble the Cape Petrel's pattern. Partially albinistic Sooty Shearwater *Puffinus griseus* can vaguely resemble this bird. Observers should note the sharp contrast between a black head and white underparts and a white rump contrasting with a dark tail. The flight is said to be buoyant, with alternate gliding and wing-flapping (see Harper & Kinsky, 1978).

# MOTTLED (SCALED) PETREL

*Pterodroma inexpectata*

Breeds near New Zealand. Ranges S Pacific to N Pacific.

The Mottled Petrel is a transequatorial migrant, with at least a portion of the population moving north to spend the non-breeding season in the Gulf of Alaska, with a few straying as far north as the S Bering Sea. ALASKA records stretch from 4 May-25 Oct, but most are concentrated in Jun-Aug and are found well offshore. The high count was 40 birds on 20 Jun 1976 at 54° 20'N, 149° 50'W.

10 of the 13 West Coast records south of ALASKA are of dead or dying individuals, suggesting that migration occurs well offshore. All but two of the records fall between late Feb-early May, probably the timing of the northward movement. Beached birds in Jul-Aug may have been sick individuals south of the wintering area, since 7 birds collected 19 Nov 1906 about 600 miles w of Morro Bay, CAL, and another seen 26 Nov 1906 about 400 miles w of San Francisco (Loomis, 1918: 104) may indicate that the return migration occurs primarily in late fall. Near-shore occurrence of the Mottled Petrel may be correlated to major flights of the Northern Fulmar *Fulmar glacialis* (Ainley, WB, in press).

**BRITISH COLUMBIA**  One record: 24 Feb 1971 about 30 miles sw of Vancouver I. (CFN 87:179). In addition, another just outside our area on 17 Mar 1972†, some 300 miles sw of Queen Charlotte I., fits the migration pattern and two unidentified *Pterodromas*, thought to be this species, were about 100 miles nw of Vancouver I. in Jun & Aug 1969 (M 53:19) and may represent the southern limits of the wintering area.

# MOTTLED PETREL

**WASHINGTON** Four records: 23 Feb 1971 about 175 miles w of the Olympic Pen., 28 Feb 1976 at Ocean Shores jetty, G.H., and 2 beached birds on 6 Mar 1976† at Moclips and Twin Harbors S.P., G.H.

**OREGON** Three records: 25 Jul 1959† on a Lcn. Co. beach (C 63:417) and 18 Mar 1972 (2†) s of Newport, Lcn. All were beached specimens. Outside our area were two on 13 Dec 1978 about 350 miles w of S ORE.

# MOTTLED PETREL

**CALIFORNIA** Five records: 25 Feb 1976† at Pt. Reyes, Mrn.; 28 Feb 1976† at Cayucos, S.L.O.; 31 Mar 1976† at Cambria, S.L.O.; 11 Aug 1976† at the Mad R. mouth, Hmb.; and 1 May 1977† at Bolinas Lagoon, Mrn. The latter bird was picked up alive. All others were found dead on beaches, but CAL observers should be aware of the numbers taken far offshore in late fall, discussed in the general paragraph above.

1 May 1977 at Bolinas Lagoon, Mrn., CAL. 5th record. *Bruce Sorrie.*

24 Feb 1971 about 30 miles sw of Vancouver I., B.C. 1st record. *R. Wayne Campbell.*

# MOTTLED PETREL

I.D. The Mottled Petrel is illustrated in Robbins' guide, but the painting is misleading in some respects. *Pterodromas* are small, chunky, short-winged birds easily distinguished from West Coast shearwaters by their characteristic flight: a very rapid, constantly banking flight interspersed with high arcs. This character is as different from *Puffinus* shearwaters as the flight of a Common Snipe *Capella gallinago* is different from other shorebirds. The Mottled Petrel is larger than the tiny "Cookilaria" petrels—such as the Cook's Petrel *P. cooki*—and is about the size of the smallest West Coast shearwater: the Manx Shearwater *Puffinus puffinus*.

The Mottled Petrel, like smaller *Pterodromas*, has dark primaries and a dark bar across the upperwing coverts and uppertail coverts, forming a more or less distinct open 'M" across the upperparts. This pattern is less distinct in the Mottled Petrel than in the smaller, lighter-colored Cook's Petrel, but both birds have a pale gray back and head, with a dark eye-patch. The dark cap shown in Robbins' guide is misleading. The outermost tail feathers are mostly white and should be apparent in the field, though they are not as distinctive as those of the Cook's Petrel.

Perhaps the best marks of the Mottled Petrel are the broad black ulnar bar across the white underwings (see photo) and the extensively dark belly, contrasting with white throat and upper breast. This latter mark is variable and can be difficult to distinguish at a distance, when the most obvious mark will be the dark bar across white underwings. At a distance, then, it might be confused with a number of smaller *Pterodromas* with a black bar on white underwings. The Bonin Petrel *P. hypoleuca*, which nests in Hawaii and ranges to Japan, has a dark cap and nape and a distinctly dark tail, without white outer tail feathers. Gould's Petrel *P. leucoptera*, which nests in Australasia and ranges north to the Galapagos Is., is also distinctly dark-capped, merging into darker upperparts than those of the Mottled Petrel, and has an all-dark tail. The Black-winged Petrel *P. nigripennis*, which nests in Australasia and ranges north to Hawaii, resembles the Mottled Petrel with its pale head and dark eye-patch, but has much dark on the primaries of the underwings and a broad dark trailing border to the white underwings (see photo in Harper & Kinsky, 1978). The Mottled Petrel shows mostly white primaries from below and the dark trailing border is much reduced. All the small *Pterodromas* discussed are white-bellied. At close range, the Mottled Petrel's dark belly will identify it.

# COOK'S PETREL

*Pterodroma cooki*

Breeds New Zealand. Ranges S Pacific to N Pacific.

The Cook's Petrel was only recently discovered to occur off the West Coast in numbers. There are Jun and Aug records near the Aleutian Is., ALASKA and it may be that this species follows a migration route similar to Mottled Petrel *P. inexpectata*. But very little is known about the movements of Cook's Petrels away from the breeding islands. In 1967, one was taken on 1 Jun, ten on 29 Jul, and another on 3 Sep some 200-500 miles west of Baja, Mexico (G. McCaskie, pers. com.). Loomis (1918) considered it "common" off Baja. Thus while some Cook's Petrels may winter (during the northern summer) near ALASKA, others may winter far offshore south of the West Coast.

A pelagic survey in Oct 1979 found several off CAL and subsequent boat trips 40-60 miles west of Piedras Blancas Pt., S.L.O., over the Davidson Seamount, were successful in locating Cook's Petrels in Nov-Dec. It may be that future expeditions will find it regularly off CAL in Oct-early Dec, presumably during migration. It is also possible that water temperature (1979 was an abnormally warm water year) affects distribution and the species may remain irregular off the West Coast.

**CALIFORNIA** 8 records, all in fall 1979: 3 Oct 1979 about 50 miles w of Pt. Arena, Men., 7 Oct 1979 about 125 miles w of Pt. Sur, Mnt., 17 Nov 1979 (3) between 40-60 miles w of Piedras Blancas Pt., S.L.O., 24 Nov 1979 (2) about 50 miles w of Piedras Blancas Pt., and 1 Dec 1979 about 60 miles w of Piedras Blancas Pt. In addition, 13 unidentified *Pterodromas*, most of which were probably Cook's, were seen off CAL between 4 Oct-24 Nov 1979 and are indicated by open circles on the map. 8 of these were between 40-60 miles w of Piedras Blancas Pt., over the Davidson Seamount, in the same area as the identified Cook's. These records have not yet been reviewed by the CAL Records Committee.

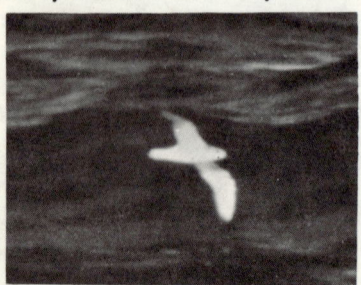

17 Nov 1979 about 60 miles w of Piedras Blancas Pt., S.L.O., CAL. 4th record. *Jeri Langham* (left); *Don Roberson* (right).

# COOK'S PETREL

**ALASKA** One record: lst week of Aug 1933† near Adak I. (A 57:77; it should be noted that some have questioned the origin of this record). In addition, one Cook's and a possible Cook's were seen over the N Pacific about 400 miles sw of Amchitka I. on 10 Jun 1975 at 45°57'N, 169°10'E (WB 9:45).

I.D. The Cook's Petrel is a very small *Pterodroma*, appearing smaller in the field than a Bonaparte's Gull *Larus philadelphia*. The flight is rapid and erratic, with nearly constant banking interrupted by high arcs. The entire underparts and underwings appear white in the field. The upperparts are a pale gray, with a dark open "M" across the mantle. The head is as pale as the back, with a dark eye-patch visible only at close range. The outer tail feathers are white and this mark can be very conspicuous, appearing as a white tail with a dark center.

# COOK'S PETREL

The only other small *Pterodroma* which appears to have all-white underwings in the field — the Stejneger's Petrel *P. longirostris* — is distinguished by its contrasting dark rear-crown and nape, a sharply defined white forehead, generally darker upperparts, and the lack of conspicuous white outer tail feathers. It should be noted that *Pterodromas* become darker with wear and very worn Cook's Petrels may be as dark-backed as fresh Stejneger's Petrels. The crown and nape of these worn birds remains concolor with the back; Stejneger's Petrels, in fresh plumage, show a contrasting dark cap and nape and white forehead. Other *Pterodromas* which might occur have a black bar on the underwings and are briefly discussed under Mottled Petrel.

Taxonomic note: The taxonomy of the small *Pterodromas* is unsettled due to the number of similar allopatric forms. Most previous literature has considered there to be two races of Cook's Petrel. However, Peters (1979) lists the apparently sedentary Chilean population as a separate species: *Pterodroma defilippiana*. It differs from nominate *cooki* in having a stouter bill.

Dorsal and ventral views of Cook's Petrel (left) and Stejneger's Petrel (right).

# STEJNEGER'S PETREL

*Pterodroma longirostris*

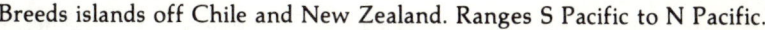

Breeds islands off Chile and New Zealand. Ranges S Pacific to N Pacific.

The Stejneger's Petrel is a little-known *Pterodroma*. It is a transequatorial migrant, spending the non-breeding season in the N Pacific near Japan. Several were collected well off CAL in Nov 1906, but it remained unrecorded in our area until sighted during a Nov 1979 pelagic trip which also turned up several Cook's Petrels *P. cooki*. Though the evidence to date is scanty, it may be that the Mottled Petrel *P. inexpectata*, the Cook's Petrel, and the Stejneger's Petrel all migrate regularly off the West Coast at distances beyond 50 miles offshore. The available information suggests a northward movement in late Feb-early May, "wintering" in the high latitudes of the N Pacific in Jun-Aug, and returning south in Oct-early Dec.

**CALIFORNIA** One record: 17 Nov 1979 about 55 miles W of Piedras Blancas Pt., S.L.O. In addition, 5 were taken between 17-19 Nov 1906 about 600 miles W of Morro Bay, S.L.O. The record has not yet been reviewed by the CAL Records Committee.

I.D. The Stejneger's Petrel is a very small *Pterodroma*, resembling in size, shape, and flight Cook's Petrel (see that account). The entire underparts and underwings appear white in the field. The upperparts are distinctly darker than those of Cook's in fresh plumage, with the open "M" across the mantle being less contrasting. The rear crown and nape are blackish and contrast with the grayer back. The back becomes darker with wear and the contrast between the nape and back can be obscured, taking on the upperpart pattern of Gould's Petrel *P. leucoptera*. But the white underwings of Stejneger's, without a black bar, will continue to identify it. In any state of wear, the forehead remains contrastingly white.

The only other small Pterodroma with all white underwings — the Cook's Petrel — is distinguished by a pale head with a small, dark eyepatch, paler coloration (in fresh plumage), and white outer tail feathers. Stejneger's typically has a uniformly dark tail.

Taxonomic note: The taxonomic relationships of small *Pterodromas* are unsettled. Peters (1979) lists the "Pycroft's" Petrel, often considered a separate species, as a race of Stejneger's Petrel: *P. l. pycrofti*. *Pycrofti*, which nests near New Zealand, may also be a transequatorial migrant. The nominate race, nesting off Chile, apparently accounts for all records off the West Coast. *Pycrofti* is similar to nominate *longirostris* but is a bit paler overall and shows some white on the outer tail feathers, though not as conspicuously as the Cook's Petrel.

# STREAKED SHEARWATER               Plate 1

*Calonectris leucomelas*

Breeds Japan, Korea, China. Winters W Pacific, Philippines to New Guinea.

The Streaked Shearwater has now been found on three occasions in Monterey Bay, all within a two-week period in early Oct. The close proximity of dates and place suggests that some factor, as yet unknown, may be contributing to their presence.

**CALIFORNIA**   Three records, all from Monterey Bay: 3 Oct 1975† (A 95:420), 9 Oct 1977* (AB 31:1097), and 14 Oct 1978.

I.D.   The Streaked Shearwater most resembles the Pink-footed Shearwater *P. creatopus*, being about the same size and generally gray-brown above, white below. It is somewhat differently shaped, being slimmer in the body and wings and with a more pronounced wrist angle. The most conspicuous field mark is a white face and crown; the dark eye stands out in contrast. The nape is heavily streaked and looks dark at a distance. The back is grayer than the upperwings and appears scaly. Individuals in molt - as some CAL birds have been - show white edgings to the rump, forming a long "U" visible at some distance. The entire underparts and underwings are white. The tail is dark and rather wedge-shaped. The feet are pink and the long bill is a dingy horn-color.

9 Oct 1977 in Monterey Bay, CAL. 2nd record. *Don Roberson.*

# STREAKED SHEARWATER

# GREATER SHEARWATER

*Puffinus gravis*

Breeds islands in S Atlantic. Winters in N Atlantic.

The Greater Shearwater has occurred only once on the West Coast, the record constituting the only report for the N Pacific. It has been suggested that a bird from the westernmost nesting islands, perhaps the small colony on the Falkland Is., wandered west of Cape Horn and became "trapped" in the Pacific, moving north on its annual trans-equatorial migration, and remained to summer (our winter) in the N Pacific in response to unfamiliar conditions. Whether or not this hypothesis approaches the truth, the record is of a bird far out of range and illustrates the potential for long-distance vagrancy in migratory seabirds.

CALIFORNIA   One record: 24 Feb 1979 in Monterey Bay. This report has not yet been reviewed by the CAL Records Committee.

I.D.   The dark cap and white rump shown in the field guides are important marks. The underwings are mostly white, without the large black "wrist" over-emphasized in some illustrations. A dark belly patch, often not pictured, is an excellent character, though difficult to see until the bird banks sharply towards the observer (see Finch, Russell & Thompson, 1978).

# MANX SHEARWATER

*Puffinus puffinus*

Since the two races of Manx Shearwater which have occurred off the West Coast show different distributional patterns and may prove to be separate species, the discussion of this bird is divided into two parts:

## "WHITE-VENTED" MANX SHEARWATER

*Puffinus puffinus puffinus*

Breeds islands in N Atlantic. Winters in S Atlantic.

The "White-vented" Manx Shearwater has not been collected or photographed in the N Pacific, but details of a number of West Coast sightings are sufficient to document its occurrence. Alaska summer records are best referred to this race and there are two fall records from CAL and another probable report from ORE. Specimens have been taken near Australia and New Zealand, documented the occurrence of this strongly migratory Atlantic race in the Pacific. Perhaps a few birds regularly wander west from their wintering areas in the S Atlantic, past Cape Horn, to the Pacific. Migration would send these birds to the Gulf of Alaska in summer and a return south along the West Coast in fall. This pattern is very different from the "Black-vented" Manx Shearwater, which wanders north to CAL in the late fall and reaches its northern limits in the winter, returning south in spring. Any Manx-type Shearwater on the West Coast in Jun-Sep should be carefully scrutinized. It may be that the "White-vented" Manx is more likely to occur during those months than the "Black-vented" Manx.

**CALIFORNIA** Two record: 27 Aug 1977 in Monterey Bay, and 28 Oct 1979 at Pt. Pinos, Mnt. These records have not yet been reviewed by the CAL Records Committee.

**ALASKA** Two records, both in the Gulf of Alaska: 4 Jun 1975 E of Barren I. (apparently this race, W. Russel, pers. com.), and 4 Jul 1976 at 57° 26' N, 145° 10' W (details suggest this race, J. Dunn, pers. com.). The details of an additional Alaska record - 5 Aug 1976 in Chiniak Bay, Kodiak I. - do not suggest racial affinity (D. Gibson, pers. com.), though the date suggests this race.

# "WHITE-VENTED" MANX SHEARWATER

In addition, a report from ORE - 10 Sep 1977 about 20 miles W of Coos Bay(OB 4(6):39) - may well have been this race. There are not, however, any acceptable records of either Manx Shearwater from ORE.

I.D. The "White-vented" Manx Shearwater is illustrated in Robbins' guide. It is a small shearwater, black above and white below. It is separated from the "Black-vented" Manx Shearwater by white sides, flanks, undertail coverts, axillaries (sometimes a bit of mottling) and more extensively white underwings. The wingbeats are fast and shallow.

Two other N Pacific races of Manx Shearwater have white sides, flanks and axillaries: "Newell's Shearwater" *P. p. newelli* in Hawaii and "Townsend's Shearwater" *P. p. auricularis* off W Mexico. Both are thought to be sedentary. They are distinctly smaller than the "White-vented" Manx, with shorter wings and a faster wingbeat, and tend to show white sides to the rump from above (expecially in Newell's). Newell's has white undertail coverts; those of Townsends' are black.

Ventral views of "White-vented" Manx Shearwater (left) and "Black-vented" Manx Shearwater (right).

# "BLACK-VENTED" MANX SHEARWATER

*Puffinus puffinus opisthomelas*

Breeds islands off Baja California, Mexico. Present year-round off Baja, late fall dispersal to S CAL.

The "Black-vented" Manx Shearwater is a winter breeding bird. It remains in warm Mexican waters until Davidson Current conditions in Nov-Jan bring it, along with warmer water temperatures, into S CAL. Abundance is correlated to maximum temperatures (Ainley, 1976), and in years of strong Davidson Current flow it occurs north to Monterey Bay with regularity, often as early as Sep-Oct. Most birds are found near shore, where temperatures are the highest. In very warm water years it has reached Men. Co., CAL recently. In the early 1900s it was found earlier and in greater numbers farther north than today and the specimen records far to the north (B.C.) were taken in the 19th century. It might be looked for from the coasts of ORE and WASH during warm water years in Nov-Jan, but there are no acceptable records from either state.

**BRITISH COLUMBIA**   Four records, all off Albert Head, V.I.: 24 Oct 1891 (2)†, Nov 1891†, and Feb 1895†.

**I.D.**   The "Black-vented" Manx Shearwater is illustrated in Peterson's Western guide. It resembles more a small Pink-footed Shearwater *P. creatopus* than the "White-vented" Manx, except for the rapid, shallow-stroking flight which is common to both Manx Shearwaters. An even brown above (which can look black in some lighting conditions), the white underparts are marked with dark sides, flanks, axillaries, undertail coverts and breast mottling. The latter is sometimes so extensive as to form a partial or complete breastband. It is distinguished from the Pink-footed Shearwater by its small size, slimmer build, rapid flight (rather than the Pink-footed's heavy, gliding flight), and more extensively white underwings.

# MANX SHEARWATER

Taxonomic note: The relationships of the Manx Shearwaters around the world are uncertain. Murphy (1952) considered the Manx to be a bird of world-wide distribution with numerous races, and most checklists have followed this treatment. Murphy's discussion acknowledges plumage differences but ignores those of breeding biology (e.g.: *opisthomelas* is a winter breeder, nearby *auricularis* is a spring breeder). Many workers use differing taxonomy (AOU, 1957; Slater, 1970; Jehl, 1974) and it may be that biological evidence will result in a revision of this complex in the future (*Birding* 9:115). It is very possible that the "White-vented" and "Black-vented" Manx Shearwaters will be considered separate species in the future.

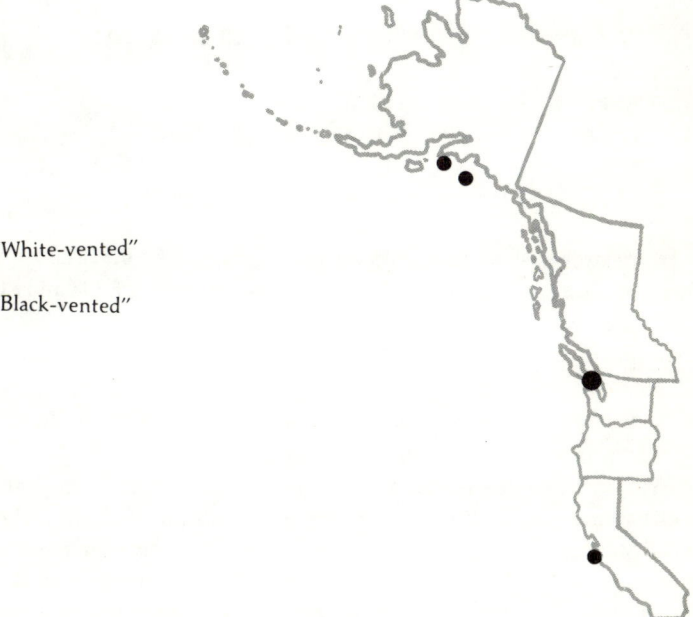

● "White-vented"

● "Black-vented"

# WILSON'S STORM-PETREL

*Oceanites oceanicus*

Breeds Galapagos Is., W South America, sub-Antartic is. Ranges to the C Pacific, N Atlantic.

# WILSON'S STORM-PETREL

The Wilson's Storm-Petrel is a Rarity anywhere off the West Coast, but in 11 of the past 13 years since 1967 it has been found in the great fall storm-petrel flock in Monterey Bay, CAL, where rafts of thousands of Ashy *Oceanodroma homochroa* and Black Storm-Petrel *O. melania* are found from late Aug-late Oct.

There are only two spring records from the West Coast. The northernmost of these (ORE) was recorded following several days of SW gales which produced numerous storm-petrel sightings from shore.

**CALIFORNIA** 17 records, involving up to 27 birds. The fall records from Monterey Bay are listed in the following table:

| Year | No. | Dates | Year | No. | Dates |
|---|---|---|---|---|---|
| 1910 | 1 | 24 Aug† | 1973 | 1 | 22 Sep-6 Oct* |
| 1967 | 1 | 7 Oct-1 Nov | 1974 | 1 | 5 Oct |
| 1968 | 1 | 7 Sep-16 Oct | 1975 | 2-3 | 4-5 Oct |
| 1969 | 1 | 12 Oct | 1976 | 1 | 9-17 Oct* |
| 1970 | 3 | 3 Oct | 1977 | 4-6 | 24 Sep-23 Oct |
| 1972 | 1 | 18 Aug-18 Oct | 1978 | 1-3 | 30 Sep-29 Oct |

Additional fall records are: 31 Aug 1935 off Pt. Loma, S.D. (C 62:141), 29 Aug 1959 near the Farallon Is. (C 62:141), 7 Sep 1969 off Morro Bay, S.L.O., and 6 Oct 1979 off Humboldt Bay.

The only spring record is 1 May 1978 in Monterey Bay.

**OREGON** One record: 31 May 1976* at the south jetty, Columbia R., Clt.

I.D. The Wilson's Storm-Petrel is a medium-sized, black storm-petrel with a bright white rump band. The rump band is wide and unmarked, often extending down onto the flanks, so the white is sometimes visible when the bird is sitting on the water. The tail is square-cut, looking slightly rounded in flight; this mark can be seen well at medium range. The leading edge of the wing is relatively straight and the wing-tips rounded, unlike the bent wrists and more pointed wings of the grayer Leach's Storm-Petrel *Oceandroma leucorhoa*. The white rump of the Leach's Storm-Petrel is variably divided by dark feathers in the center (visible at close range) and that species has a characteristic bounding flight. In direct flight, the Wilson's Storm-Petrel is rather swallow-like, but when feeding flutters over the surface, with long legs dangling and feet pattering over the surface. The yellow webbing of the feet is nearly impossible to see in the field. See also Band-rumped and Wedge-rumped Storm-Petrels.

# WILSON'S STORM-PETREL

# WEDGE-RUMPED (GALAPAGOS) STORM-PETREL

*Oceanodroma tethys*

Breeds Galapagos Is., Peruvian islands. Ranges at sea W Mexico to Peru.

The Wedge-rumped Storm-Petrel has occurred on the West Coast several times between Aug-Jan. Records include a bird picked up alive in a residential yard after Jan gales, another refound on several trips in the large storm-petrel flock in Monterey Bay, and solitary birds passing close to boats far offshore. The single specimen is of the small southern race *O. t. kelsalli*, nesting off Peru.

**CALIFORNIA** Four records: 21 Jan 1969† at Carmel, Mnt. (A 87:588), 18 Aug 1976 near Anacapa I., 24 Sep-9 Oct 1977 in Monterey Bay, and 1 Dec 1979 about 50 miles W of Piedras Blancas Pt., S.L.O.

# WEDGE-RUMPED STORM-PETREL

I.D.   The Wedge-rumped Storm-Petrel is the smallest white-rumped storm-petrel, being nearly as small as the tiny Least Storm-Petrel *Halocyptena microsoma*. In contrast to the Least's nearly tailless appearance in the field, the Wedge-rumped shows a long tail nearly covered by a wedge-shaped white patch extending down from the rump (see photo). At a distance the bird may look like a tiny, dark storm-petrel with an all-white tail. The tiny size and white rump wedge should separate this species from other white-rumped storm-petrels. The bird is grayer than the blackish Wilson's Storm-Petrel. The flight strokes are rather rapid and deep and the flight is most similar to that of the Least Storm-Petrel. Experience with the flight characteristics of the common West Coast storm-petreeels is necessary when attempting to distinguish a rare bird by flight.

Illustrative photo of Wedge-rumped Strom-Petrel near the Galapagos I., Dec 1970. *Tom Davis.*

# BAND-RUMPED (HARCOURT'S) STORM-PETREL

*Oceanodroma castro*

Breeds Galapagos Is., Hawaii, Japan, C Atlantic Islands. Ranges widely in C Pacific, C Atlantic.

# BAND-RUMPED STORM-PETREL

The Band-rumped Storm-Petrel has occurred only once on the West Coast, though it is regular in subtropical seas just to the south of our area (see King, 1974). In the Atlantic, storms have blown birds as far as Ontario and Indiana; storms might be expected to influence its presence off the West Coast. It is said to be solitary at sea and ship-following has been observed.

**CALIFORNIA**  One record: 12 Sep 1970 about 30 miles W of San Diego. This record is currently under review by the CAL Records Committee.

I.D.  The Band-rumped Storm-Petrel is a medium-sized, blackish storm-petrel with a continuous, unmarked white band over the rump and extending down to the sides of the undertail coverts. It may be confused with two other similarly-sized white-rumped storm-petrels: Leach's Storm-Petrel O. *leucorhoa* and Wilson's Storm-Petrel *Oceanites oceanicus*

The Leach's Storm-Petrel does not show an unmarked, continuous white band over the rump. The center is pinched together by dark indentations and often a gray center stripe divides the band in half. The irregular margins of the rump band are difficult to see at a distance, but the Leach's is further characterized by a distinctive erratic, bounding flight. The Leach's forked tail is difficult to see except at close range and the Band-rumped's less forked tail should not be considered a helpful field mark. Leach's is the common white-rumped storm-petrel off the West Coast and observers should be familiar with its flight characters before attempting to identify a Band-rumped Storm-Petrel out of range.

The Wilson's Storm-Petrel does show an unbroken white rump band extending far down to the sides of the undertail coverts. This band is wider than that of the Band-rumped, with the tail appearing to be about the width of the band. The tail of the Band-rumped appears to extend 1½ to 2 times the width of the white band beyond the rump patch. The Wilson's also has a distinctly square-cut end to the tail (slightly rounded when spread) and its feeding flight, fluttering low over the surface with long legs dangling, is distinctive. In direct flight, there is less fluttering and foot-dangling and observers should be aware that wind conditions affect the flight patterns of all storm-petrels.

The flight of the Band-rumped Storm-Petrel is more shearwater-like than other white-rumped storm-petrels, with fairly steady, high wing beats interspersed with glides on wings bowed below the horizontal. The combination of a clean, unmarked white rump and prolonged study of flight characters may identify this species to observers with pelagic experience.

# RED-BILLED TROPICBIRD

*Phaethon aethereus*

Breeds locally in tropics worldwide. Ranges widely in tropical oceans.

The Red-billed Tropicbird is regular on the West Coast only off S CAL, where an average of about 5 birds are found each year, particularly around the Channel Islands. A few birds may arrive as early as May, with numbers building through the summer, but most records are in Sep, when there is a sharp peak. A few may linger through Oct. Numbers have fluctuated annually, from 0 in 1972 to 9 in 1974 and 13 in 1968. There are 3 records from N CAL: 14 Jul 1970 in Monterey Bay, 5 Oct 1979 about 190 miles W of Bodega Bay, Son., and 6 Oct 1979 about 180 miles W of Pigeon Pt., S.M. A bird inland on 11 Sep 1976 at Morongo Valley, S.Bn., was deposited there by Hurricane Kathleen. There is one record north of CAL.

**WASHINGTON** One record: 18 Jun 1941† off Gray's Harbor, when a fisherman collected an unfamiliar bird (M 28:6).

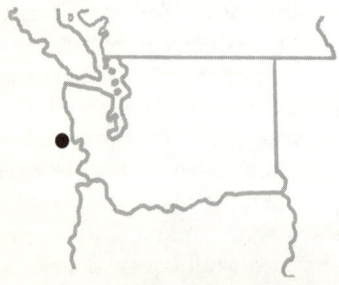

16 Sep 1979 near San Clemente I., CAL. *Herbert Clarke.*

## RED-BILLED TROPICBIRD

**I.D.** The adult Red-billed Tropicbird is covered by the standard guides. Immature or molting birds, lacking the long tail feathers, can be more difficult to identify. A rapid flight with deep wingbeats, rather pigeon-like, is characteristic of tropicbirds. Only the Red-billed Tropicbird shows a black nuchal crescent and black inner secondaries when viewed from below. Immatures are heavily barred above, and show the nuchal crescent and dark inner secondaries from below, lacking in other immature tropicbirds.

# RED-TAILED TROPICBIRD                Plate 1

*Phaethon rubricauda*

Breeds locally in tropical Pacific and Indian Oceans. Ranges widely in the tropics of these seas.

The Red-tailed Tropicbird is a bird of warm oceans and is recorded with some regularity off Baja California, Mexico, in winter; the nearest breeding areas are on Hawaii and the Galapagos Is. Five were recorded off the coast of CAL in 1979 between Jul-Oct. These dates correspond to higher than average ocean temperatures off CAL, which may have influenced the movement of these birds into our area. 3 of the 5 birds were found more than 100 miles offshore.

**CALIFORNIA**   Five records: 3 Jul 1979 on SE Farallon I., 30 Sep 1979 about 120 miles W of San Miguel I., 7 Oct 1979 about 200 miles W of Pt. Estero, S.L.O., 8 Oct 1979 about 95 miles SW of Pt. Buchon, S.L.O., and 8 Oct 1979 about 140 miles SW of San Miguel I. These records have not yet been reviewed by the CAL Records Committee.

**I.D.** The Red-tailed Tropicbird is mid-sized between the large Red-billed Tropicbird *P. aethereus* and the small White-tailed Tropicbird *P. lepturus*. The adult is easily recognized by the long red tail streamers and the white, virtually unmarked upperparts. Black edgings to the tertials are the only dark on the white back and upperwings. The underwings are also all-white, without the dark inner secondaries of the Red-billed Tropicbird.

# RED-TAILED TROPICBIRD

Immature Red-tailed Tropicbirds lack the tail streamers and are heavily barred above, rather like the Red-billed Tropicbird. They lack the Red-billed's nuchal crescent (showing only a dark eye patch, though the nape and crown may be barred) and lack dark inner secondaries on the underwings. Immature White-tailed Tropicbirds are very finely barred, have yellowish bills (flying stages of Red-tailed Tropicbirds usually have reddish bills), and at close range have yellowish (not bluish) feet.

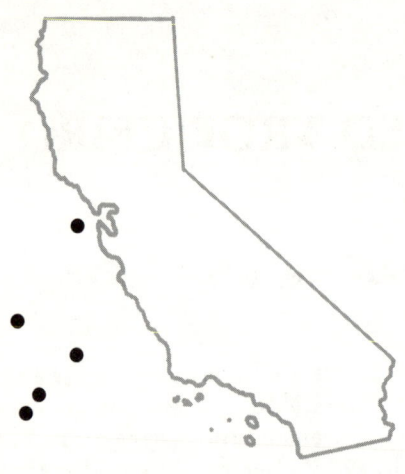

# WHITE-TAILED TROPICBIRD

*Phaethon lepturus*

Breeds locally in tropics worldwide. Ranges widely in tropical oceans.

The White-tailed Tropicbird has occurred only once on the West Coast. The nearest breeding birds are in Hawaii.

**CALIFORNIA** One record: 24 May-23 Jun 1964* at Newport, Orn. This adult was seen chasing remote-controlled model airplanes and even attempted to copulate with a grounded plane (C 67:186).

# WHITE-TAILED TROPICBIRD

23 Jun 1964 at Newport Bay, Orn., CAL. 1st record. *Wes Hetrick, courtesy Guy McCaskie.*

I.D.  The White-tailed Tropicbird is a small, graceful tropicbird easily recognized as an adult by the upperwing pattern illustrated in the standard guides, the dark eye-patches, and yellowish bill. Immature birds are rarely seen away from the breeding grounds. They are finely barred above and lack the tail streamers. The lack of a nuchal crescent and dark inner secondaries from below will separate them from the larger Red-billed Tropicbird *P. aethereus*. Small size, fine barring, yellowish bill, and yellowish feet will distinguish them from the Red-tailed Tropicbird *P. rubricauda*.

# BROWN PELICAN

*Pelicanus occidentalis*

Breeds locally coasts of S North America to N South America. Post-breeding dispersal to the N.

The Brown Pelican formerly nested on CAL coastal islands north to Pt. Lobos, Mnt., but a large-scale population collapse in the 1960s, linked to use of pesticides (see Schreiber & DeLong, 1969), dangerously reduced the CAL population. There has been a slow recovery in the 1970s and prospects appear good for the future.

During the 19th century, large flocks were found in the fall at the Columbia R. mouth and specimens were taken in B.C. Post-breeders continued to disperse to the north in Jul-Oct in this century, with a few stragglers wintering far north, but with the population collapse they became fewer. Numbers are no longer found north of C ORE in the fall, though a few continue to be recorded on the S WASH coast and a flock of 21 was counted on 16 Oct 1977 at LaPush, Jef., WASH. Yearly numbers in WASH fluctuate, but the average remains above the 4 per year definition of a Rarity. It is a Rarity in B.C., where there are only two records since 1940.

**BRITISH COLUMBIA**   9 records: Nov 1880† at the Fraser R. mouth, Jan 1898† at Race Rocks, V.I., 24 Nov 1904† at Esquinalt, V.I., 18 Jul 1913† in Queen Charlotte Straits, 19-23 Dec 1932 at Victoria, V.I., 7-16 Nov 1935 at Victoria, Aug 1939 at Race Rocks, 6 Aug 1972 at Folger I., Barkley Sound, and 12 Aug 1973 (2) at Victoria.

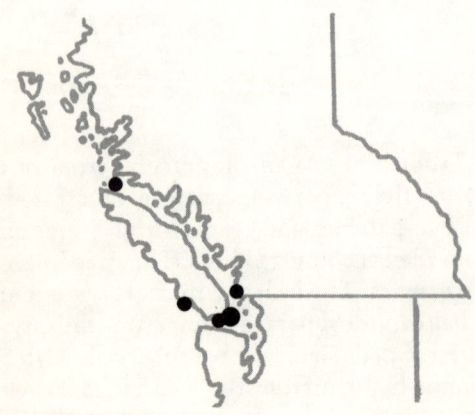

# MASKED (BLUE-FACED) BOOBY

*Sula dactylatra*

Breeds locally on tropical islands worldwide. Ranges in tropical seas adjacent to breeding sites.

The Masked Booby has occurred once off the West Coast. The nearest breeding islands are off Baja, Mexico within 600 miles of the U.S. border, but the single bird seen closely resembled the Hawaiian race. Boobies are known to "hitch-hike" aboard ships and their presence offshore the West Coast may be attributable to this passive assistance.

**CALIFORNIA**  One record: an adult 10 Jan 1977* about 20 miles SW of San Clemente I. (WB 9:175).

**I.D.**  The adult Masked Booby is pictured in the standard guides. It is the largest booby to occur on the West Coast and the large size is helpful in any plumage. The adult's bill may be orange-yellow or pink with a horn-colored tip; the legs may be grayish, greenish, or yellow; and the eye is yellow. Subadults have largely white underparts and underwings, but the head, throat, and neck are dark and sharply contrast with the white breast. Younger birds have dark upperparts, becoming white on the nape, back, and rump with age; older birds may show mostly white upperparts with a dark neck collar. The bill is slaty in young birds, becoming greenish or yellow with age (this bill color may remain until after acquiring adult plumage); the legs dark gray, greenish, or yellowish. Immatures are essentially all dark brown, with no noticeable contrast between breast and belly. The bill and legs are slaty. White feathers in the nape, back, and upperwing coverts occur at an early age. See also the discussion under Red-footed Booby *S. sula*.

# BLUE-FOOTED BOOBY

*Sula nebouxii*

Breeds on coastal islands Gulf of California, Mexico to Peru. Disperses after breeding to adjacent waters and irregularly north to CAL.

The Blue-footed Booby is an irregular post-breeding visitor to S CAL. In 8 of the most recent 10 years at least one booby appeared, but the vast majority of records occurred in irregular invasions. Invasion numbers occurred in 1969 (32), 1971 (80), 1972 (42), and 1977 (15). Most records are from the Salton Sea, with birds arriving as early as late Jul, numbers peaking from mid-Aug to late Sep, and dwindling in Oct. In invasion years, boobies have wandered up the Colorado R. as far as Lake Havasu; dispersed from the Salton Sea to the NW to desert reservoirs and north as far as New Hogan Res., Cal. (WB 7:155); and W by way of the Los Angeles basin to the coast. Coastal records date from 21 Aug-21 Nov and birds have been seen as far north as San Francisco. A very early (22 Jun 1976) and a late (8 Jan 1972) record come from near the Channel Is. Most birds probably perish, but where food is available, individuals have remained as long as 8 months. For more see McCaskie (1970).

There are 200 records for CAL. The single record to the north was during a peak time for booby dispersal but the distance involved suggests the possibility that the bird was ship-assisted.

24 Sep 1976 at New Hogan Res., Cal., CAL. *Don Roberson.*

# BLUE-FOOTED BOOBY

**WASHINGTON**  One record: 23 Sep 1935† near Everett, Sno. (M 26:45).

23 Aug 1977 at Salton City, Imp., CAL. *Jeri Langham.*

# BLUE-FOOTED BOOBY

I.D. The Blue-footed Booby is a mid-sized booby, with bright blue feet and bill as an adult. Adults are whitish with dark wings, back, and tail (which may fade to near whitish); the head is streaked with brown, often heavily. Immature birds are even more heavily streaked about the head and neck and look dark-headed at a distance; this dark color merges irregularly into the whitish breast. The upperparts may be dark as well, with only a few white feathers to nape or rump. The bill of young birds varies from grayish to bluish; the feet may be pinkish or bluish. Some immature Blue-footed Boobies have been misidentified as immature Brown Boobies *S. leucogaster*. The latter bird lacks any white feathering on the nape and rump and is a much richer chocolate-brown color than the grayish-brown cast of the Blue-footed Booby.

# BROWN BOOBY

*Sula leucogaster*

Breeds on tropical islands worldwide. Ranges in adjacent tropical seas.

The Brown Booby is an irregular post-breeding wanderer into S CAL from its breeding colonies in the Gulf of California, Mexico. Most records are of immatures.

**CALIFORNIA** 27 records, almost all falling between 15 Jul-30 Nov, with most occurring from Aug-Oct. 26 of the birds were found at the Salton Sea (or the adjacent Imperial Valley) and the Colorado River. The additional record was apparently the same adult at Prince Inlet, San Miguel I., in the summers of 1961, 1965 & 1968.

The histogram below illustrates the annual fluctuations in records since 1968. The highest numbers were recorded during invasion years for the Blue-footed Booby *S. nebouxii*.

Where food is available, the Brown Booby may survive for long periods. An adult was presumed to have over-wintered at the Salton Sea in 1969-70, and another was present at Martinez Lake, Imp. (on the Colorado R.), for over two years (1958-1960). For more details see McCaskie (1970).

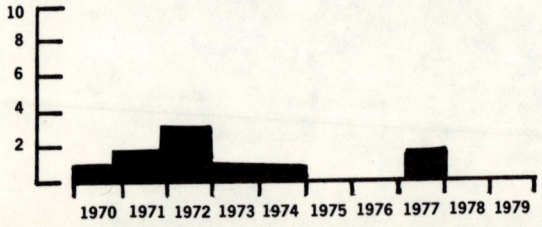

# BROWN BOOBY

4 Jul 1965 at Prince Inlet, San Miguel I., CAL. *Herbert Clarke.*

3 Sep 1977 at Lake Havasu, S.Bn., CAL. *Robert Witzeman.*

# BROWN BOOBY

I.D. The Brown Booby is a mid-sized booby, slightly smaller than the Blue-footed Booby in direct comparison. The adult is illustrated in the standard guides, though adults of the Baja race - *S. 1. brewsteri* - may show a pale patch on the back of the head.

Immatures are chocolate brown, much richer and darker in color than that of the grayish-brown immature Blue-footed Booby. The belly, though dark in young Brown Booby, is distinctly lighter than and sharply demarcated from the breast. The bill may be bluish or grayish, becoming yellowish with age. The feet are dirty yellow or greenish. Some plumages of the Red-footed Booby *S. sula* are all dark, but Red-footed Booby is smaller and lacks the white feathers in the underwing coverts, shown by immature Brown Booby.

# RED-FOOTED BOOBY  Plate 1

*Sula sula*

Breeds on tropical islands worldwide. Ranges widely in tropical seas.

The Red-footed Booby has occurred twice on the West Coast. The nearest breeding sites are on the Revilla Gigedo Is., off the W coast of Mexico (*S. s. websterii*) and the Hawaiian Is. (*S. s. rubripes*). Though perhaps the most pelagic and wide-ranging of all Pacific boobies, "hitch-hiking" aboard ships could have assisted the birds in reaching C CAL.

**CALIFORNIA** Two records, both from SE Farallon I: 26 Aug 1975* and 12 Oct 1975* (WB, in press). The first bird was banded and measured and proved to be *S. s. websterii*, the dark-tailed Mexican race. The second bird, an adult flying by the island, was white-tailed and could have been *S. s. rupripes*, the C Pacific race.

I.D. The Red-footed Booby is the smallest booby, with white-tailed and dark-tailed subspecies, both of which show dark and light color phases. The orange-yellow to deep red feet, which may occur in even all-dark young birds, are distinctive, as is the adult's bluish or green-tipped bill with a pink or orange base. The eye is dark; other adult boobies are light-eyed.

# RED-FOOTED BOOBY

Adult plumages may resemble those of the Masked Booby *S. dactylatra*, especially in dark-tailed races. These birds are all white except for a dark tail and dark flight feathers. However, the inner secondaries are white and thus the dark tailing edge of the wing does not reach the body, as it does in adult Masked Booby. The white tail in some races, the small size, soft part color, and the variable golden cast to the plumage will identify other adult plumages.

Dark morphs are a sleek tawny brown except for a white belly and rump (and tail in some races). Small size, white rump, and red feet will distinguish them from the adult Brown Booby *S. leucogaster*. Subadults may be dark above and whitish below, sometimes with an irregular dark breastband. Again, small size and soft part color is useful.

Immatures and some dark morphs may be all-dark and thus similar to immature Brown Booby. These birds can be identified by their small size, often by red or orange feet, by the lack of a sharply demarcated lighter belly, and by the lack of white feathers in the underwings.

26 Aug 1975 on SE Farallon I., CAL (with Western Gull, right). 1st record. *Jim Lewis, courtesy Point Reyes Bird Observatory.*

# NEOTROPIC (OLIVACEOUS) CORMORANT

*Phalacrocorax olivaceus*

Breeds E Texas, W Mexico to S South America. Mostly resident.

The Neotropic Cormorant has occurred only once on the West Coast, on the Colorado R. in extreme SE CAL. It has become a more regular visitor to Arizona, with records year-round. Some birds of the W Mexican race *P. o. chancho* wander north after the breeding season, in late summer, but the single West Coast record to date was a spring migrant.

**CALIFORNIA**  One record: an adult 13 Apr 1971* (CB 2:134), probably the same individual returning on 22-23 Apr 1972 & 7 Apr 1973, at West Pond, Imperial Dam, Imp.

**I.D.**  The Neotropic Cormorant must be carefully separated from the common Double-crested Cormorant *P. auritus*. The Neotropic is smaller and differently shaped, being about ¾ the length and ½ the bulk of the Double-crested, with a slimmer body, proportionately longer, wedge-shaped tail, and smaller head, neck, and bill. In breeding plumage the yellowish or pinkish throat pouch is bordered by white feathers. The Double-crested lacks this border and in any plumage shows a larger, conspicuous orange throat patch. Immatures of both species are grayish-brown, lighter on the throat and breast. The Neotropic immature looks darker in the field, especially on the head, with a dark brown cap extending below the eye. Double-crested immatures show pale cheeks.

In any plumage, the shape of the throat patch is distinctive. The Neotropic's pouch comes to a sharp point on the cheek and angles forward to the chin; the throat feathers forming an inverted "V" when viewed from below. The Double-crested's pouch is rounded against the cheek, continuing toward the throat without any sharp angle, thus looking rounded against the throat when viewed from below (see illustration).

# NEOTROPIC CORMORANT

Heads of Neotropic Cormorant (above) and Double-crested Cormorant (below).

# ANHINGA

*Anhinga anhinga*

Breeds W Mexico, E Texas to S South America. Post-breeders wander widely.

The Anhinga, a noted wanderer in the E United States, has occurred only once on the West Coast, in extreme SE CAL. This record and one from the Arizona side of the Colorado River date back to the early 1900s. More recent reports are best treated as escapees, as they pertain to birds near coastal urban centers that remained for long periods. The Colorado River and the Salton Sea would seem to be likely areas for true vagrants to visit.

**CALIFORNIA** One record: 9-12 Feb 1913 (2) at Potholes, Imperial Dam, Imp. This species has not yet been accepted by the CAL Records Committee as a member of the state's avifauna, but I find the descriptions by Allan Brooks (C 15: 182) and W.L. Dawson (C 18:24; Dawson, 1924, p. 1936) convincing. Birds at Lake Merced, San Francisco (2-29 Jun 1939) and Sweetwater Res., S.D. (4 Feb 1977-Dec 1978) have been judged probable escapees by the CAL Records Committee.

# MAGNIFICENT FRIGATEBIRD

*Fregata magnificens*

Breeds locally at coastal locations Baja, Mexico, N Caribbean to N South America. Post-breeding dispersal brings some north, regularly to CAL.

The Magnificent Frigatebird is a rare visitor to the West Coast, but is regular in small numbers at the Salton Sea and the coast of S CAL during the summer and fall (see McCaskie, 1970). Numbers vary from year to year, but a recent five-year average was about 18 birds a year. Most records are from Jun-Oct, but a few have been found into the winter. While most regular in S CAL, a few straggle north along the coast to N CAL and birds have reached Humboldt Bay. The largest invasion on record occurred in 1979 when at least 35-40 individuals reached the S CAL coast and up to 22 together were recorded at the Salton Sea. Six were found in N CAL during the summer 1979, including one inland over the Sacramento R. at Hamilton City, Gln. & But. This invasion brought one of the records north of CAL. Another in 1975 was during only a mild invasion in CAL.

The winter 1935 record in ORE is notable, but we have little information on invasions in CAL at that time.

Records north of WASH are less well documented. There are unconfirmed reports of several off Vancouver I., B.C. in the 1970s. The two Gulf of Alaska reports were by fishermen or government personnel, but the brief descriptions appear adequate and the dates (Jul-Sep) are during the height of frigatebird dispersal.

**OREGON**   Two records: 18-19 Feb 1935† at Tillamook Rock lighthouse, Clt., and 24 Jul 1979* at Gold Beach, Cur.

**WASHINGTON**   One record: 1 Jul 1975 at Umatilla NWR, Ben. (M 57:43).

**ALASKA**   Three records: Jul 1957 in Montague Strait, and 16 Sep 1969 (2) over Fairweather Bank. These areas are in the N Gulf of Alaska and the reports are discussed in Isleib & Kessel (1973), p. 138.

**MAGNIFICENT FRIGATEBIRD**

# GREAT EGRET

*Casmerodius albus*

Breeds S North America, South America, S Eurasia, Africa, Australia. Some northern populations winter to the south.

The Great Egret is a locally common nesting species in CAL and SE ORE. Though many move south in winter, a few winter regularly as far north as the ORE coast. The Great Egret was first recorded in WASH in 1949, but since that time it has become a rare, but regular, fall visitor and there are a number of records of spring overshoots and a few of wintering individuals. It is a Rarity in B.C., where nearly all records fall between Aug-Nov.

**BRITISH COLUMBIA**   13 records, graphed below. All are from the Vancouver and S Vancouver I. areas. The single spring record is 16 May 1975 at Victoria, V.I.

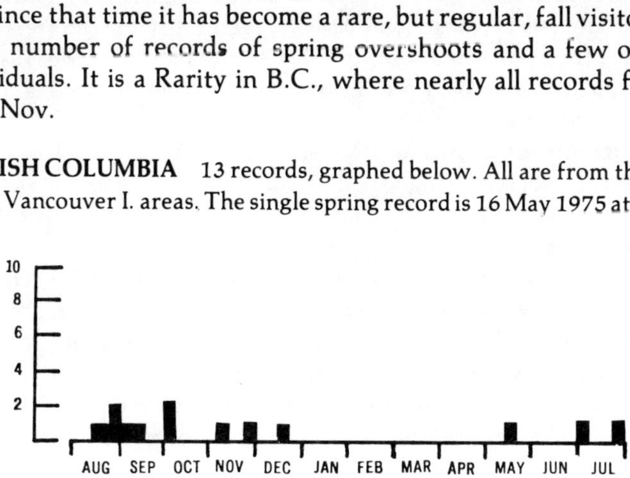

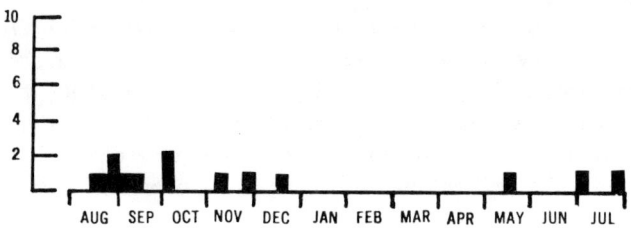

# GREAT EGRET

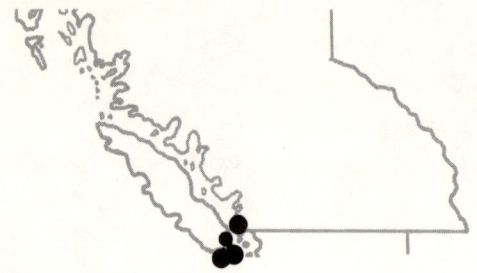

# REDDISH EGRET

*Dichromanassa rufescens*

Breeds W Mexico, Baja & SE U.S. to N South America. Non-breeding dispersal to N & W.

The Reddish Egret occurs in CAL irregularly. Most records are from the coasts of S CAL, especially around San Diego. A number of patterns emerge from the records, which have spanned all seasons. Numbers fluctuate annually; they may be absent for several years. High counts were 6 in 1969 and 1977.

**CALIFORNIA** 38 records, graphed below. In addition, 3 birds have been recorded on the Arizona side of the Colorado R. and are included in the general discussion below.

The pattern of CAL records is complex, but four general categories can be discussed:

1. Post-breeding dispersal: 14 records might be included here, most falling between early Jul-early Sep, with some birds lingering into Nov. Ten are from the coast, including the northernmost record - late Aug-8 Oct 1967 at Moss Landing, Mnt. The additional 4 records are divided between the Salton Sea and the Colorado River. Most are immatures.

2. Fall migrants: 10 records could be included here, of birds arriving in mid-Sep to mid-Oct but not remaining to winter. All are from the coast of S CAL and all but one (6-13 Oct 1963 at Bolsa Chica, Orn.) are from the San Diego area. Most are immatures.

3. Winter visitors: 10 records, often immatures, arriving mostly in Oct-Nov. Most were known to winter locally. 6 records are from coastal San Diego Co., another from Newport Bay, Orn., and 3 are from the Colorado R.

4. Spring migrants: 7 records, most probably overshoots, arriving in Apr-May, with a few lingering into late Jun. All are from the coast of S CAL. Another northern record - 9 Jul 1962 at Morro Bay, S.L.O. - might be best classified here.

# REDDISH EGRET

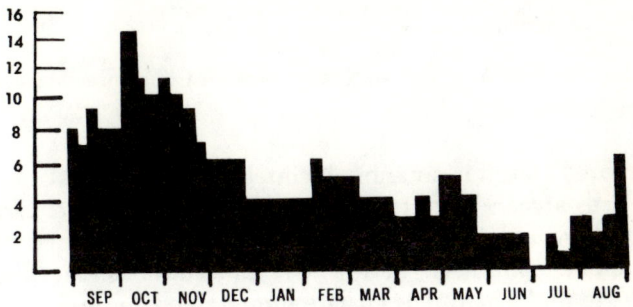

I.D.    Only dark-phase birds are present in W Mexican populations of Reddish Egret and they account for all West Coast records. The adults are illustrated in the standard guides, but the immatures are not. While retaining the characteristic shape and stance, these birds are essentially all gray, with dark legs and bill, and a distinctive white eye. Plumes are lacking, but the gray may be intermixed with various degrees of brownish, especially about the head and neck.

10 Oct 1977 at San Diego, S.D., CAL. *Linda Delaney.*

# TRICOLORED (LOUISIANA) HERON

*Hydranassa tricolor*

Breeds W Mexico, Baja & SE U.S. to N South America. Non-breeding dispersal to N & W.

The Tricolored Heron is an annual winter visitor to S CAL, averaging nearly 8 birds a year. Most records are clustered in S.D. & Orn. Cos., with up to five individuals at one locality. Two additional patterns, common among southern herons, are present. Post-breeding birds wander north to the Salton Sea in late summer and one was found far to the north at Honey Lake, Las. (24 Aug-26 Sep 1971; CB 3:19). Occasionally birds are found in late summer on the coast; the northernmost record was at Morro Bay, S.L.O. (14 Jul 1976). Spring migrant overshoots have occurred at the Salton Sea and on the S CAL coast in Apr-Jun. The records north of CAL would seem attributable to spring overshooting (May) and post-breeding dispersal (Oct).

**OREGON** Two records: 31 Oct 1943 at Malheur NWR, Har.† (C 46:124) and 12-30 May 1976* at Finley NWR, Ben.

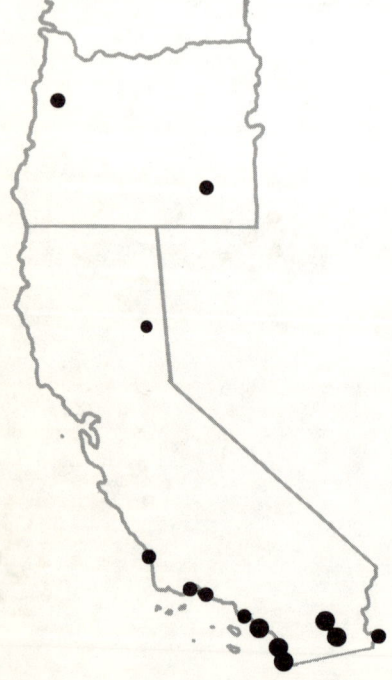

14 May 1976 at Finley NWR, Ben., ORE. 2nd record. *Larry B. McQueen.*

# CATTLE EGRET

*Bubulcus ibis*

Breeds S North America & South America, Africa, Asia. Rapid range extension through New World in this century.

The Cattle Egret first appeared on the West Coast in the Tijuana R. Valley, S.D., CAL (7 Mar 1964). Since then, it has become established in S CAL (5000 pairs nesting at the Salton Sea in 1977) and become increasingly regular farther north, with breeding confirmed in Hmb. Co. in 1978. The first ORE records occurred in the late 1960s and it has since become regular there. Still a Rarity north of ORE, it has been found with increasing frequency as a late fall straggler. It seems likely that it could be established to S B.C. by the end of this century.

**WASHINGTON** 13 records, involving 22 individuals, graphed below. Since the first record on 16 Oct 1967 at McNary NWR, W.W., all birds have arrived in late fall or early winter. The Cattle Egret recently nested in SW Idaho and might be expected to move into E WASH as a breeding species in the future.

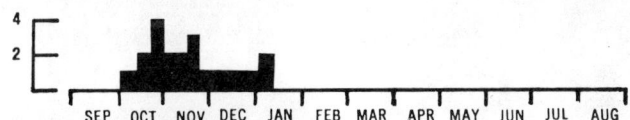

14 Nov 1977 at Errington, B.C.
Neil K. Dawe.

# CATTLE EGRET

**BRITISH COLUMBIA**   16 records, graphed below. All fit the late fall - early winter pattern shown by records in WASH. The first record was on 12-21 Dec 1970 at Iona I., Vancouver and most records since have been from Vancouver and Vancouver I. areas.

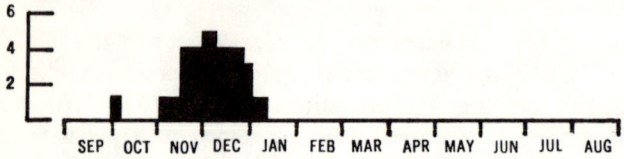

4 Jan 1975 near Ferndale, Wha., WASH. 5th record. *Terence R. Wahl.*

# LITTLE BLUE HERON

*Florida caerula*

Breeds W Mexico, SE U.S. to S South America. Post-breeders and some winterers move N and W.

The Little Blue Heron was first recorded on the West Coast in CAL in 1964, but since that time has become increasingly common there. There are now at least 61 records for the state and its status was summarized by Unitt (1977). Hybridization with Snowy Egret *Egretta thula* has been suspected in the San Francisco Bay area several times in the last 15 years.

# LITTLE BLUE HERON

In the late 1970s, adults began frequenting a Cattle Egret *Bubulcus ibis* colony in the Imperial Valley, Imp., and in the summer of 1979 a pair successfully nested there. There is only one record north of CAL, during a time of fall dispersal northward.

**WASHINGTON and BRITISH COLUMBIA**  One record: an immature 15 Oct 1974-5 Jan 1975 at Judson Lake, near Abbotsford, B.C., frequented both sides of the international border (WB 9:33).

**I.D.**  Immature Little Blue Heron may be confused with immature Snowy Egret, both of which have yellowish-green legs and feet and bluish-looking bills. Little Blue Heron may be distinguished by its bluish (not yellow) lores, a two-tone bill with distinct black tip, duller white plumage, and a slimmer build.

Jan 1973 at Bolsa Chica, Orn., CAL. *John Butler.*

# SNOWY EGRET

*Egretta thula*

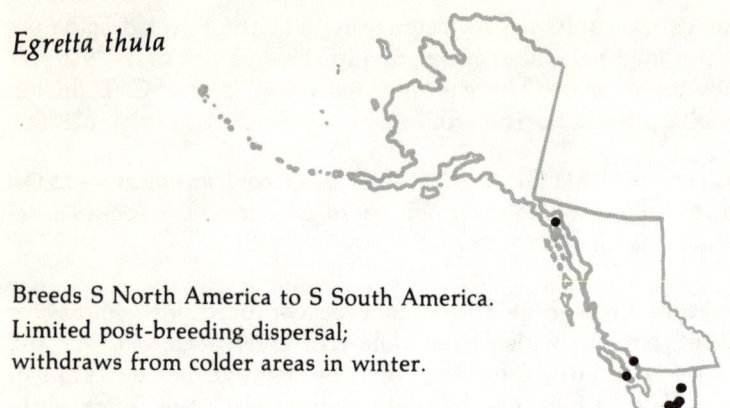

Breeds S North America to S South America.
Limited post-breeding dispersal;
withdraws from colder areas in winter.

The Snowy Egret is a common species in much of CAL and nests in SE ORE. Further north it is a Rarity, where spring overshooting and post-breeding dispersal seem to account for the records.

**WASHINGTON** Five records: 4 May 1975 at the Tucannon R. mouth, Col.; 11-12 May 1975 at the Yakima R. mouth, Ben.; 23 Jun 1976 at McNary NWR, W.W.; 14 Aug 1976 at Wallula, W.W.; and 20-27 May 1977 at Badger Lake, Spk.

**BRITISH COLUMBIA** Two records: 23-26 May 1972 at Pitt meadows, E of Vancouver, and 22-27 Aug 1972 at Victoria, V.I.

**ALASKA** One record: 18-24 May 1957 at Juneau.

I.D. The Snowy Egret is covered by the standard guides in comparison to other North American herons. The Little Egret *E. garzetta*, a Eurasian species which has occurred in NE North America and is a remote possibility in Alaska, is very similar. Western populations of Little Egret (which are responsible for vagrants to E North America) can be distinguished from Snowy Egret by gray or gray-green lores (not yellow), and a heavier-billed look. In addition, the base of the bill may be gray (Snowy's bill is usually all black) and Little Egret lacks the yellow stripe up the back of the leg present in immature (but not adult) Snowy Egret (see BB 72:128 and BB 73:39). Eastern populations, however, tend to have yellower lores, only slightly duller and greener than those of Snowy. Thus a vagrant to Alaska may be more difficult to identify. Complicating the situation is the fact that lore color becomes more intense during a brief period during courtship (yellow to yellow-green in Little; pinkish to red in Snowy), but it is unlikely a vagrant would show these colors. SE Asian races of Little Egret lack yellow feet; they are not expected to occur as vagrants on the West Coast.

# SNOWY EGRET

27 Aug 1972 at Victoria, V.I., B.C. 2nd record. *Enid Lemon.*

# CHINESE EGRET  Plate 1

*Egretta eulophotes*

Breeds NE Asia. Winters E Asia to Indonesia.

The Chinese Egret has occurred only once on the West Coast, as an apparent spring overshoot in the westernmost Aleutians, ALASKA. The world population of the Chinese Egret is small and it is listed as rare and local in the International Red Data Book.

**ALASKA** One record: an adult 16 Jun 1974† on Agattu I. (C 80:309).

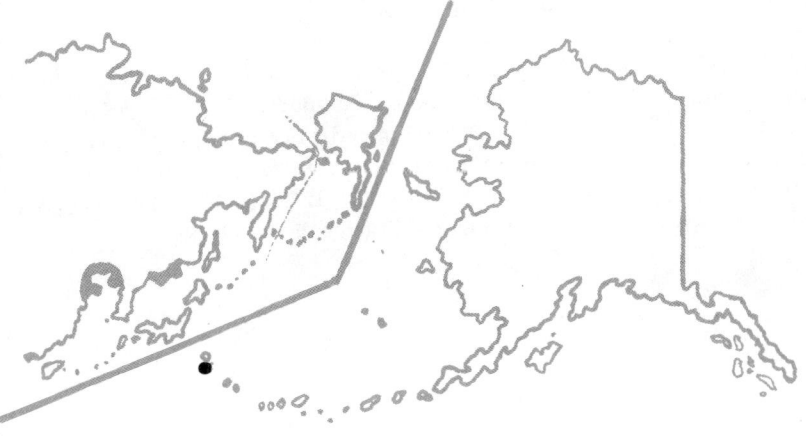

# CHINESE EGRET

I.D. The Chinese Egret is slightly larger than a Snowy Egret *E. thula*, which it generally resembles, including black legs and yellow feet in breeding plumage. It differs in this plumage by its short, shaggy crest, all yellow bill, and dark blue lores. In non-breeding plumage the Chinese Egret loses its short crest, the legs become yellowish or bluish-green, and the bill becomes dark with the yellow being restricted to the base of the lower mandible. Though restricted, the extent of the yellow on the lower mandible is greater than that shown by the Snowy Egret or Little Egret *E. garzetta* (difficult to see any yellow on the bill of either species in the field), and should serve to distinguish mostly dark-billed Chinese Egrets, even those with black legs and yellow feet during transitional plumages.

# YELLOW-CROWNED NIGHT HERON

*Nyctanassa violacea*

Breeds W Mexico, Baja & E U.S. to C South America. Limited post-breeding dispersal; some northern populations winter to the south.

The Yellow-crowned Night-Heron is a very scarce visitor to the West Coast. Most records seem attributable to spring overshooting, but post-breeding dispersal and fall vagrancy may account for the summer and fall records, respectively. One individual returned to the same San Francisco Bay locale for six consecutive summers.

**CALIFORNIA** Nine records: late Jun 1951 at Venice, L.A.; 3 Nov 1962 at Imperial Beach, S.D.; 27 Mar-6 Apr 1963 at Claremont, L.A.; 30 May-2 Jun 1963 at Harbor Park, L.A.; 22-25 Oct 1963† at Imperial Beach; 12 Jul-25 Aug 1968 at San Rafael, Mrn., and returning the next five summers with extreme dates of 3 May-20 Nov; 11 May 1977 at Irving, Orn. (WB 9:177); 5 Jul 1977 at Tomales Bay, Mrn; and 3 Apr-2 May 1979 at Imperial Beach and San Diego.

# YELLOW-CROWNED NIGHT HERON

I.D. The adult Yellow-crowned Night-Heron is well illustrated in the standard guides, but the immature is less adequately discussed. Compared to the young Black-crowned Night Heron *Nycticorax nycticorax*, it is a darker chocolate-brown bird with fine white streaks to the crown and neck becoming heavy on the breast. Immature Black-crowned Night-Herons are a lighter warm brown with broader, buffy streaks to head and neck, with the breast looking off-white heavily streaked with brown. The Yellow-crown's less-tapered, more dagger-like bill and chin feathering extending well beyond the level of the forehead gives the head a different profile. The legs are longer in Yellow-crowned, and in flight extend beyond the tail to nearly the knee; only the feet and lower tarsi extend beyond the tail in flight in Black-crowned.

11 May 1977 at Irving, Orn., CAL. 7th record. *Don Hoechlin*.

# LEAST BITTERN

*Ixobrychus exilis*

Breeds locally S North America to C South America. Northern populations winter to the south.

The Least Bittern is a secretive species which nests very locally in CAL and apparently in the Klammath and Malheur marshes of S ORE. ORE and NE CAL birds withdraw to the south in winter. There are only two records north of ORE.

## LEAST BITTERN

**BRITISH COLUMBIA** Two records: 30 Jul 1955 at Vernon (M 36:44) and 16 Jun 1974 at Vancouver.

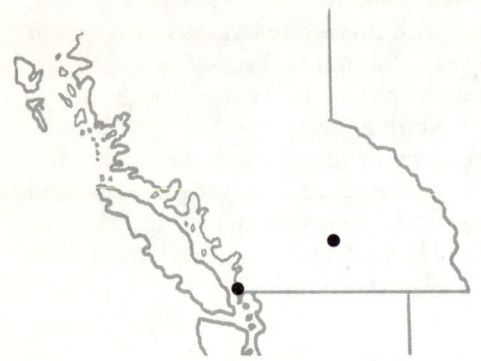

16 Jun 1974 at Vancouver, B.C. 2nd record. *Michael Oldfield.*

## WOOD STORK

*Mycteria americana*

Breeds W Mexico, SE U.S. to S South America. Post-breeding dispersal to the N & W.

The Wood Stork is a noted post-breeding wanderer and is regular in summer and early fall at the Salton Sea in S CAL. In some years, birds are more widespread in CAL, moving up the Central Valley, while others have reached the coast. Most extralimital records occur between Jul-Nov, the northernmost in CAL occurred in Mod. Co. There is only one record north of CAL.

**BRITISH COLUMBIA** One record: 15 Sep 1970† at Telegraph Creek.

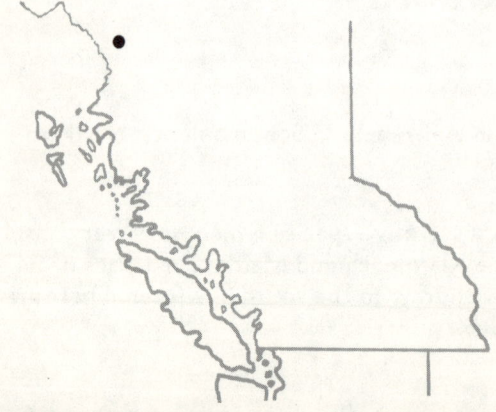

# WHITE-FACED IBIS

*Plegadis chihi*

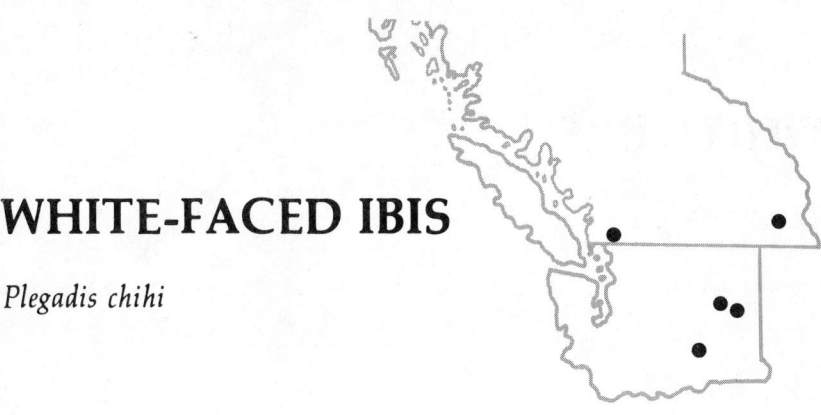

Breeds locally W U.S. to S South America. Post-breeding dispersal to N & W.

West Coast populations of the White-faced Ibis have been much reduced in recent years. It formerly bred in the Great Basin areas of NE CAL and SE ORE and the Central Valley and S coast of CAL. Oregon's only breeding colony is at Malheur NWR, Har. Only sporadic breeding has been reported recently in CAL, at Tule Lake, Mod., in 1967, at Honey Lake, Las., in the 1970s, and at Carlsbad, S.D., in 1979. When it was common, vagrants strayed north and west to the coast as part of late summer dispersal and spring & fall migrations. These movements account for records north to WASH and B.C.

**WASHINGTON** Three records: 30 Oct 1909† at Clear Lake, SW of Spokane (C 27:211), 26 May-2 Jun 1951 at O'Sullivan Dam, Grn. (M 32:43), and mid-May 1974 at Reardon, Lcn.

**BRITISH COLUMBIA** Two records: Nov 1907† at Sardis on the Luckakuck R., and 9-12 May 1967 at Wasa Slough, NW of Cranbrook.

I.D. The White-faced Ibis is likely to be confused only with the Glossy Ibis *P. falcinellus*, a possible (though unlikely) vagrant from the East. Though the standard guides emphasize the white feathers bordering the bare face in breeding plumaged White-faced Ibis, perhaps easier to see at a distance is the reddish face, often pinkish bill, and red legs of the White-faced Ibis in breeding plumage, present from about Feb-Aug. Similarly plumaged Glossy Ibis have dark blue facial skin, an olive-gray bill, and dark legs with reddish only about the knee. Both species show dark gray bare parts in fall and winter and may be inseparable in the field at these times, except for the White-faced Ibis' reddish iris (not dark brown), a most difficult field character to distinguish at a distance. For more information and color illustrations see Pratt (1976).

# WHITE IBIS

*Eudocimus albus*

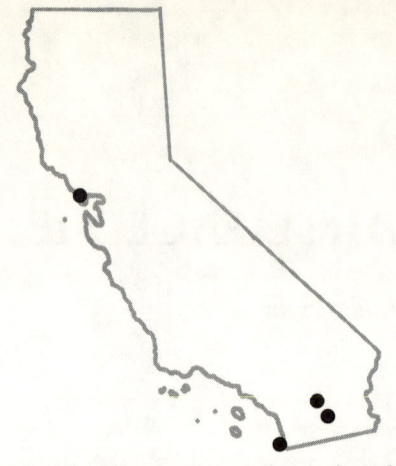

Breeds W Mexico, Baja & SE U.S. to N South America. Limited post-breeding dispersal to N & W.

The White Ibis has occurred on the West Coast as a post-breeding visitor to the Salton Sea, with additional records in spring and fall on the coast of CAL. It is kept in captivity in several metropolitan areas and young birds were known to escape in the Los Angeles area in 1978.

**CALIFORNIA**   Four records: 20 Nov 1935† at Pt. Loma, S.D.; 14-19 May 1971 at Bolinas Lagoon, Mrn., probably the same bird present 27 Jun-9 Sep 1971 at San Rafael, Mrm.; 10-24 Jul 1976* at the north end, Salton Sea, Riv., possibly the same bird 5 Aug 1976 at the south end, Salton Sea, Imp.; and 25 Jun-14 Jul 1977 at the south end, Salton Sea. Immatures in Mar-Apr 1978 at Malibu, L.A. and Jun 1978 at Pt. Mugu, Ven. are best treated as escapees. Many birders prefer to treat the Mrn. Co. bird similarly, but possible captive origin could not be hypothesized (as with the L.A. known escapees) and the record was accepted by the authoritative work on N CAL (McCaskie, DeBenedictis, Erickson, & Morlan, 1979).

# ROSEATE SPOONBILL

*Ajaia ajaja*

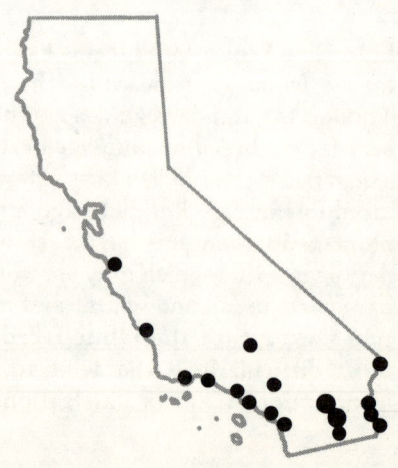

Breeds W Mexico, SE U.S. to S South America. Irregular post-breeding dispersal N & W.

# ROSEATE SPOONBILL

The Roseate Spoonbill occurs on the West Coast during irregular invasions involving post-breeding birds. It is not currently listed as a species reviewed by the CAL Records Committee. but its occurrence is irregular and birds are not present in the state every year. Per year averaging does serve to describe the status of this bird and I have chosen to include it though not technically a Rarity.

**CALIFORNIA** The irregular nature and invasion characteristics of the Roseate Spoonbill in CAL are clear in the chart below, which graphs individuals from 1970-1979. Many appeared as part of small flocks and the graph indicates individuals present, not "records" in the strict sense.

Roseate Spoonbills have been reported since 1903. The pattern in each invasion has been similar: birds first appear around the Salton Sea in late Jun-Jul (earliest arrival was 5 May) and numbers there build to peaks in Aug-Oct (highest count was 35 on 13 Oct 1973). Paralleling this movement, much smaller numbers may appear along the Colorado River. During major invasions, birds may strike west from the Salton Sea to the coast, arriving as early as 20 Jun, while others may move up to the S Central Valley. Small groups that reach the coast seem to disperse and wander individually, mostly to the north; in 1973 & 1977 birds reached Goleta, S. Bb. from late Jul-Oct. A very few have wintered locally; another continued north and reached Castroville, Mnt. (1 Jan-13 Feb 1978) for the northernmost record.

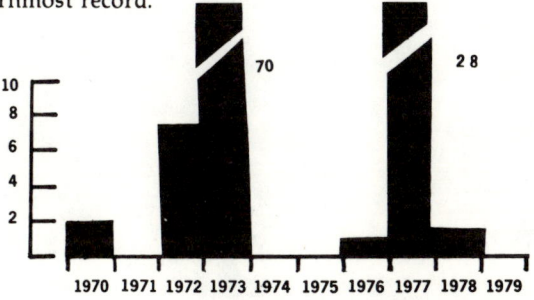

12 Jun 1977 at the Salton Sea, south end, Imp., CAL. *Robert Copper.*

# FULVOUS WHISTLING DUCK

*Dendrocygna bicolor*

Breeds locally S U.S., Mexico to S South America; E Africa; India. Wanders N as a post-breeder; some populations winter to the S.

The Fulvous Whistling Duck is much reduced as a breeding bird on the West Coast. Formerly it nested in S San Francisco Bay, the San Joaquin Valley, and the S coast of CAL. Nesting is now restricted to the S end of the Salton Sea, Imp., and is irregular at best (Remsen, 1977). When it was common, vagrants strayed north to Honey Lake, Las., in the interior and along the coast to N CAL. It is now very rare anywhere in N CAL. In the fall of 1905 flocks were seen N to WASH and B.C.

**WASHINGTON**   One record: 3 Oct 1905† (1 shot out of a flock of 10) at Gray's Harbor.

**BRITISH COLUMBIA**   One record: 29 Sep 1905† (5 shot from a flock of 11) at Alberni, V.I.

# BLACK-BELLIED WHISTLING DUCK

*Dendrocygna autumnalis*

Mostly resident W Mexico, S Texas to S South America. Post-breeding dispersal to N & W.

The Black-bellied Whistling Duck has occurred on the West Coast as a post-breeding wanderer, presumably from the W Mexican populations. All the records are from summer and fall and all but one were recorded at or near the south end of the Salton Sea, CAL. A number of coastal and northern reports have been dismissed as escapes from captivity, but some of these may pertain to true vagrants: a 27 Sep 1969 report from Oroville, But., CAL is an example of a report in this category. Only widely accepted records are listed below.

Black-bellied Whistling Ducks have nested in SE Arizona recently and it is possible that post-breeders or even wintering birds may be found along the Colorado R. in the future.

**CALIFORNIA** Six records: "fall" 1912† in the Imperial Valley, Imp.; 12 Jun 1951 at Calipatria, Imp.; 2 Jun-5 Aug 1972 (4 - not all together) at the south end, Salton Sea, Imp.; 15 Oct-4 Nov 1973 (3)* at the south end, Salton Sea; 19 Nov 1973 (3 - possibly the same individuals as the Salton Sea 1973 record) at Bakersfield, Kern; and 4-14 Aug 1977 at Brawley, Imp.

7 Aug 1977 at Brawley, Imp., CAL (with Fulvous Whistling Ducks, right). 6th record. *Linda Delaney.*

# WHOOPER SWAN

*Cygnus cygnus*

Breeds N Eurasia. Winters W Europe, S Russia, Japan, E China.

The Whooper Swan winters with some regularity in the outer Aleutians but is rare elsewhere on the West Coast. In Eurasia it winters south to 35° N (latitude of C CAL) and a fall migrant record from S ALASKA suggests that it has already wandered towards the S West Coast.

**ALASKA**   Regular winterer in small numbers in the W & C Aleutians from Nov-Apr (extreme dates: 26 Oct-8 May). Often occurs in family groups or small flocks, the high count was 31 (10 Apr 1970 - Amchitka I.). Winterering Whoopers have appeared as far east as St. Paul I., Pribilofs.

Records in W Alaska and the Bering Sea appear to be spring overshoots (14 May-3 Jul). The single fall migrant record was of two birds with 26 Trumpeter Swans *C. buccinator* on 23 Oct 1977 at Cordova in S ALASKA. Presumably this flock wintered somewhere to the south.

**I.D.**   The Whooper Swan is a large swan, similar in size and shape to the Trumpeter Swan *C. buccinator* and thus larger than the Tundra (Whistling) Swan *C. columbianus*. The flat profile of bill and forehead, large size, "kinked-neck" at ease posture (see Trumpeter Swan), lower-pitched bugled call, and shape of the yellow patch on bill will distinguish the Whooper from the Eurasian race of the Tundra Swan("Bewick's" Swan), which is a vagrant to ALASKA, ORE, and CAL. From a variable yellow base, the yellow on the bill of Whooper Swan extends as a wedge angling to a point below the nostril or beyond. This distinct wedge shape is lacking in "Bewick's" Swan, the yellow being confined to an irregularly-shaped patch on the basal third of the bill, only extending to the level of the nostril occasionally along the culmen. The yellow patch on the "Whistling" Swan is even more restricted and the "Whistling" lacks a yellow stripe on the underside of the lower mandible, present in "Bewick's."

The head and neck of the adult Whoopers may be stained with rusty. Immatures show grayish-brown heads and necks, with the bill patch dirty pink or white. The feet are dark gray, becoming black with age.

# WHOOPER SWAN

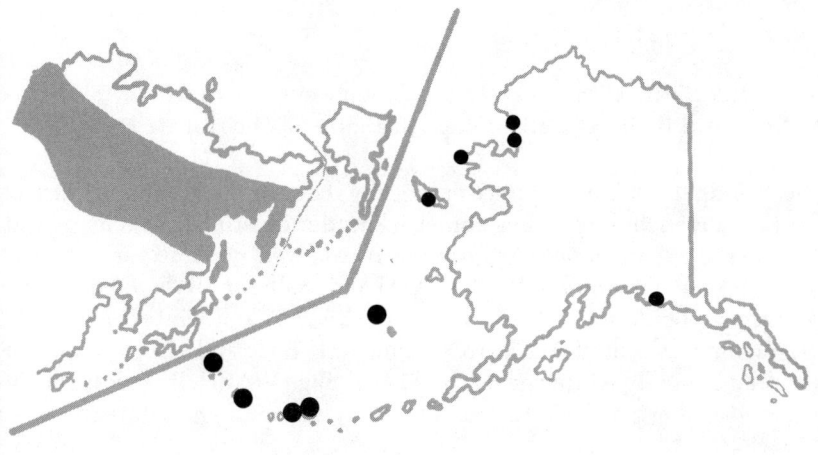

Heads of Trumpeter (left) and Tundra (Whistling) Swans (right), above; and at ease postures of Whopper Swan (left) and Tundra (Bewick's) Swan (right), below.

# TRUMPETER SWAN

*Cygnus buccinator*

Breeds NW North America. Alaska population winters coastal S ALASKA to N WASH; Great Basin populations (including introduced birds) are resident.

The Trumpeter Swan was once drastically reduced throughout its range, but has staged an impressive comeback under careful management and widespread re-introductions. Among introduced populations are resident flocks at Turnbull NWR, E WASH and Malheur NWR, E ORE. The migratory population nests in interior ALASKA and winters along the coast from the Gulf of Alaska to Vancouver I., B.C., and a flock of about a hundred annually winter near Clear Lake, Skg., WASH. It is occasionally found elsewhere in WASH and is a Rarity south of that state.

**OREGON** Considered common during winter in the 1880s along the Columbia R., with reports scattered throughout the Willamette Valley and southeast to Malheur, the Trumpeter Swan was virtually extirpated from ORE by 1900. Today, an introduced population is established and resident at Malheur NWR. Records of non-introduced birds are very rare. Recently it has been noted annually during the winter in flocks of Tundra (Whistling) Swan at Sauvie's I., Col., where it was recorded between Nov-Feb during every winter since 1975-76. The high count there was 6 birds on 21-22 Jan 1978. The only other ORE records since 1900 are: 7 Sep 1929 at Davis Lake, Des., and 26 Dec 1976 (3) near Eugene, Lane.

**CALIFORNIA** Reported with some regularity in winter before 1900, though unsubstantiated by specimen. Only 15 records, involving about 25 birds, since 1900, graphed below. Family groups (2-5 birds) account for about a third of the reports. Occasionally a bird or group will return for successive winters: one on Pt. Reyes, Mrn., from 25 Dec 1961-9 Mar 1962 returned in Dec 1962 & Dec 1963, and 5 at Santa Rosa, Son., from 31 Dec 1967-14 Jan 1968 returned from 8 Feb-14 Mar 1969. Most records are of birds not associating with other swans.

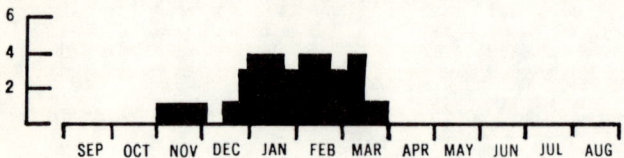

# TRUMPETER SWAN

22 Jan 1973 on Carrizo Plain, S.L.O., CAL (alert posture, with Tundra "Whistling" Swan, left). *Brad Schram.*

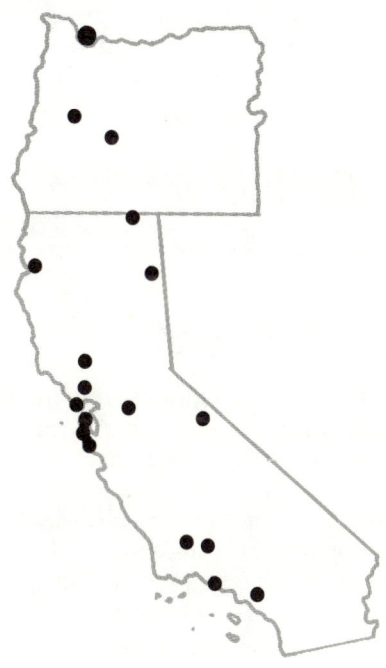

# TRUMPETER SWAN

I.D. The Trumpeter Swan must be carefully distinguished from the Tundra (Whistling) Swan *C. columbianus*. The Trumpeter is a larger bird, though without direct comparison this is difficult to judge. Better marks are the flat bill and forehead profile (Tundra Swans show more rounded foreheads), a straight or slightly convex upper edge to the bill (Tundra Swans show a slightly concave upper edge), a wide angle to the area of the bill before the eye (Tundra Swans show a narrower angle - see illustration), and a proportionately longer neck which, during at-ease posture, is held in a "kinked-neck" position, being curved back from the breast and arising vertically out of the upper back (see illustration). This mark must be used with caution, since alert or disturbed birds will hold the neck erect. The head and neck are often stained with rusty.

Most Trumpeter Swans lack any yellow on the bill, but a few show a yellow spot before the eye. Some Tundra Swans lack any yellow on the bill. The red "lips" discussed in the standard guides are present, but Tundra Swan has a pinkish stripe along the edge of the bill and this "field mark" is of little value. Immatures have a grayish cast to the head and neck, and often show a pinkish blotch on the bill. The grayish plumage is retained into spring; immature Tundra Swan becomes white by spring.

The deep, sonorous call of the Trumpeter Swan is distinct from the high-pitched soft calls of the Tundra Swan. Observers unfamiliar with either call might compare a Trumpeter call to that of Sandhill Crane *Grus canadensis*, while those of the Tundra Swan are more reminiscent of Snow Goose *Chen caerulescens*.

# BEAN GOOSE                                     Plate 2

*Anser fabalis*

Breeds N Asia. Winters W Europe, China, Japan.

The Bean Goose is a rare but regular spring migrant on the outermost Aleutian Is. It is very scarce elsewhere in ALASKA. Spring overshooting may account for the easternmost records.

**ALASKA**   30 records, involving 49 birds, graphed below. It is now considered a rare, but regular, spring migrant in the western Aleutians. Multiple records are from Buldir I. (6), Amchitka I. (5), Attu I. (5 - including flock of 9 on 11 May 1979), Alaid I. (3), Adak I. (3), and Shemya I. (2). Away from the Aleutians, the only records are from Gambell, St. Lawrence I. (3), St. Paul I., Pribilofs (2), and Safety Sound on the Seward Pen. (9 Jun 1974).

# BEAN GOOSE

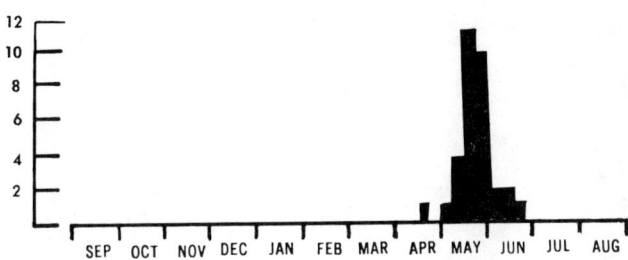

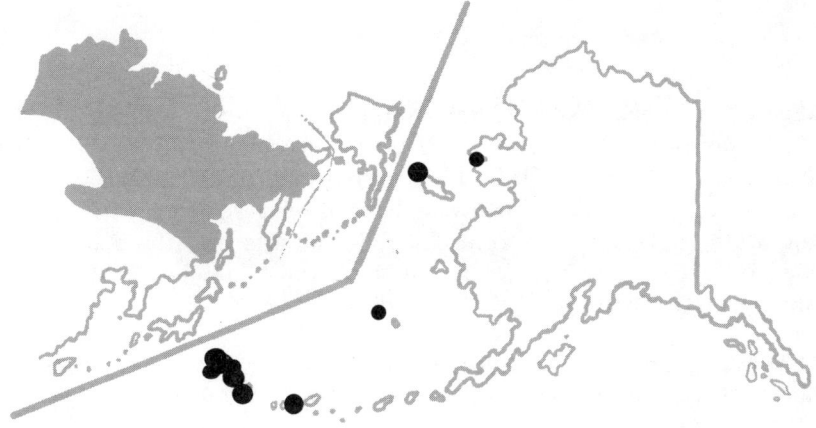

I.D.   Two races of the Bean Goose have been collected in Alaska : *A. f. serrirostris*, the most common, is a tundra bird, while *A. f. middendorfi* is an interior forest breeder. Both races lack the strong dark head-light body contrast of the European subspecies. They most closely resemble the Greater White-fronted Goose *A. albifrons* but are larger and heavier. They also lack white feathering on the face and black belly bars. Immature Greater White-fronted Goose, lacking the white on the face, can be distinguished from Bean Goose by the shape and color of the bill. The White-fronted's bill is short and compact, pinkish in color, smudged with dusky in immatures. The Bean Goose has a heavier, longer bill and it is distinctly two-toned: black with an orange band around the middle. The bill of *middendorfi* is even longer than that of *serrirostris*, giving the entire head a rather Canvasback-like profile.

# ROSS' GOOSE

*Chen rossii*

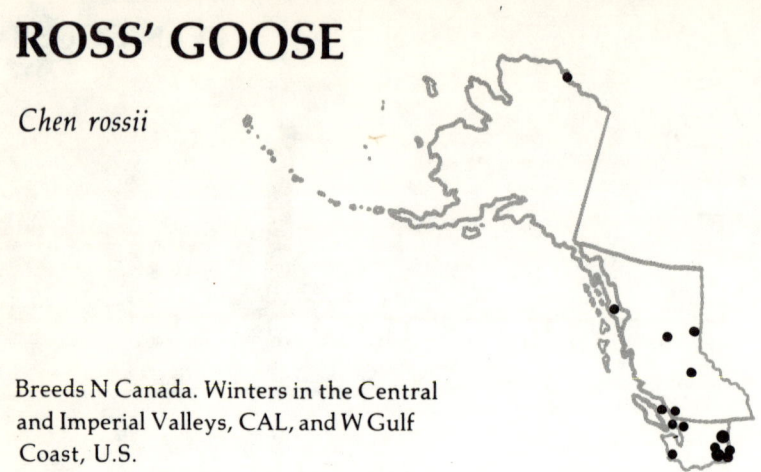

Breeds N Canada. Winters in the Central and Imperial Valleys, CAL, and W Gulf Coast, U.S.

Most of the world's Ross' Geese winter in the interior valleys of CAL. Migration routes take them over SE ORE and occasionally one will stray to the coasts of CAL or ORE. It is a Rarity north of ORE. Nearly all the coastal records in the Northwest have been associated with spring migration. E WASH has recorded fall vagrants and twice has held wintering birds. Summer records in N ALASKA may be non-breeders summering to the west of their breeding range.

**ALASKA**   Three records: 15 Apr 1907† in the Stikine R. delta; 15 Jul 1976 and 18 Aug 1977 (4), both northeast of Teshekpuk Lake, N ALASKA.

**BRITISH COLUMBIA**   8 records, two coastal: 4 May 1974 (4) at Iona I. jetty, and 30 Jan 1979 at Sea I. jetty, both near Vancouver. Older interior records are 1889† at Stuart Lake, 1895† at Kuper I., Dec 1892† at Comox, spring 1921† at Rawlings' Lake, 15 May 1942† at 149 mile, Caribou, and 8 Nov 1962† at Leo Lake.

**WASHINGTON**   11 records, involving 16 individuals, graphed below. Both coastal records are in spring: 8 May 1971 at Leadbetter Pt., Pac., and 13 Apr 1976 at Anacortes, Skg.

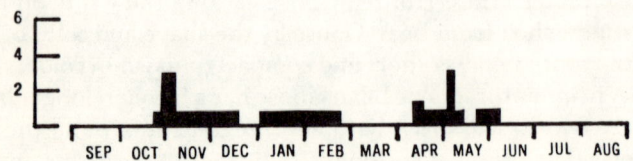

# EMPEROR GOOSE

*Philacte canagica*

Breeds W Alaska, NE Siberia. Winters in Aleutians and Gulf of Alaska; NE Asia.

The Emperor Goose is found during most winters along the West Coast south of ALASKA, but numbers are irregular and it remains a Rarity in every state and province. A distinctive species, the Emperor Goose was first taken in CAL in 1884, in B.C. in 1894, in ORE in 1920, and in WASH in 1922. Since then, hunters and casual observers account for numerous records prior to the rise of modern birding and these reports have become difficult to trace in the mists of the past. The graphs below represent as complete a compilation as possible.

While most records are from the coast, some Emperor Geese (including small flocks) have joined flocks of other geese and subsequently wintered in the Klammath Basin of SE ORE - NE CAL and even the Central Valley of CAL.

**BRITISH COLUMBIA** 24 records, involving 29 birds, graphed below. While there have been a number of wintering individuals, most records appear to be migrants in Nov and late Feb-Apr. An individual at White Rock (just N of the international border) returned for 4 consecutive winters from 1968-69 to 1971-72. There are 4 records from Victoria, V.I. and 5 from Masset, Q.C.I.

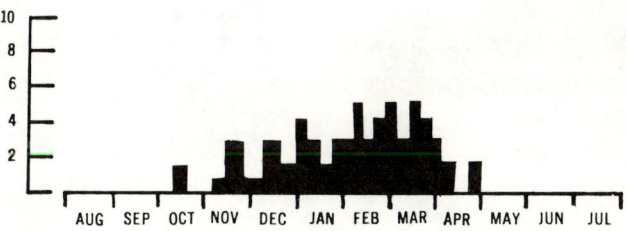

**WASHINGTON** 13 records, involving 16 birds, graphed below. All are from the Puget Sound area or the coast. Records are about evenly divided between local winterers and apparent migrants. There are 5 records, of 8 birds, from Willapa Bay, Pac.

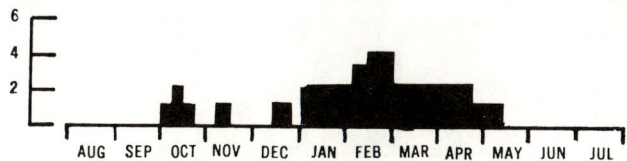

# EMPEROR GOOSE

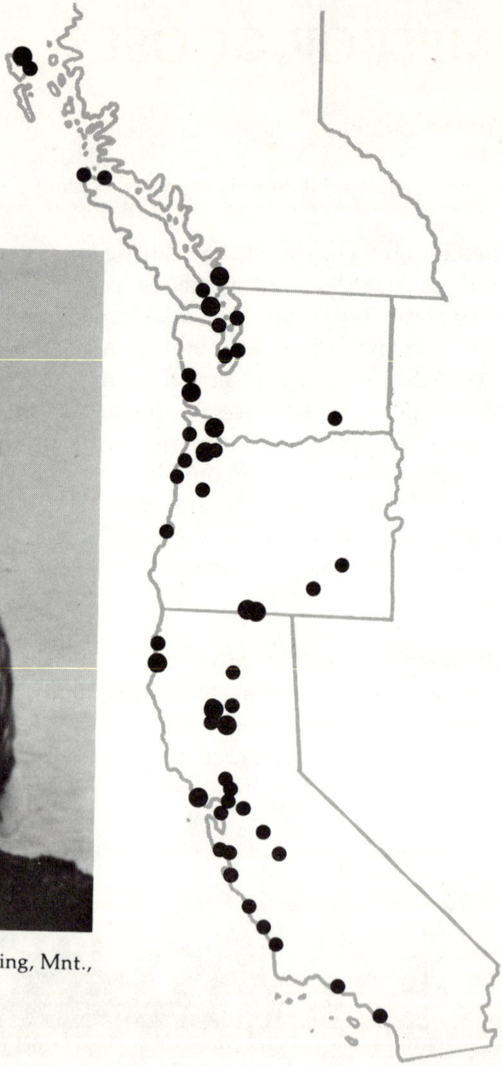

Jan 1978 at Moss Landing, Mnt., CAL. *Jeri Langham.*

**OREGON** 16 records, involving 36 birds, graphed below. Most are from the coast, including a flock of 17 at Gold Beach, Cur. from 1 Apr-8 May 1943 (M 24:29). There are 4 records from Sauvie I., Col. Records in the Klammath Basin date from the 1930s, mostly from hunters' bags. Precise information on these records has been elusive and since it appears the majority were taken in CAL, they are briefly discussed there.

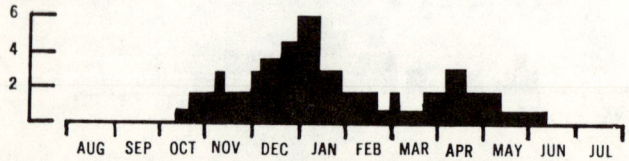

## EMPEROR GOOSE

**CALIFORNIA** 69 records, involving at least 132 birds. Those for which accurate dates exist are graphed below. 33 records, involving 51 birds, are from the coast; there are numerous records from the Humboldt Bay area, the Tomales Bay-Pt. Reyes, Mrn., area, and the Monterey Peninsula. The southernmost record was at Seal Beach, Orn., where a flock of 5 on 15 Dec 1968 was reduced to a lone bird by 8 Mar 1969.

36 records, involving at least 81 birds, are from the interior, especially the Klammath Basin, Sis., in the extreme NE. Most birds were taken from hunters' bags and a number may have been taken in ORE. A "flock of 25" was reported in 1964 and an additional 9 in 1965 (M 52:16). Unlike the coast, where wintering birds predominate, most interior records are from Oct-Nov. The southernmost interior record was at Ingomar, Mer. (12 Dec, early 1900s).

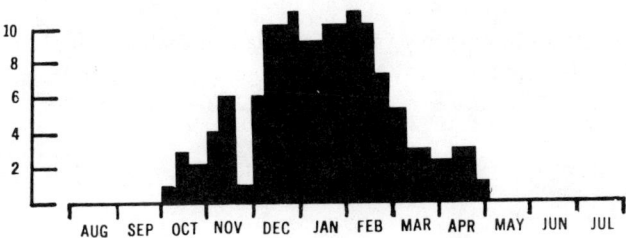

# FALCATED TEAL  Plate 2

*Anas falcata*

Breeds N Asia. Winters Japan to S China.

The Falcated Teal has occurred on the West Coast primarily as a spring vagrant to the Aleutian and Pribilof Is. of ALASKA, presumably as a result of spring overshooting. A handful of fall and winter records in the Aleutians seem to indicate the occasional tendency to wander toward the continental West Coast, where reports present problems of acceptability as wild birds. The spring 1932 record listed below for B.C. is a classic example: the bird probably wintered far south of B.C. and was discovered during the northward movement in the spring. But 1932 was during the height of live market activity in waterfowl in CAL (see C 34:259), where the Falcated Teal was the 3rd most common duck held for sale. Could the

# FALCATED TEAL

B.C. bird have escaped in CAL and joined a flock moving north? Or was it a genuine Asiatic stray that wintered on the West Coast? In many cases (such as two CAL reports: 5 Apr-21May 1953 near San Francisco and Jan-Feb 1961 at Newport Bay, Orn.) the weight of the evidence argues against the acceptance of the reported wildfowl. In other cases (Garganey, Tufted Duck) there is no doubt that genuine vagrants occur. But the Falcated Teal, S of ALASKA, remains problematical. The records listed may or may not be valid records, but are best enumerated in the hope that time will furnish a discernable pattern.

**ALASKA**  12 records, involving 20 birds, graphed below. Half of the 8 spring records are of pairs on the westernmost Aleutians. 3 records are from Adak I. (4 birds) and 2 from Attu I. (2 pairs). Males were recorded twice on St. Paul I., Pribilofs (8 Apr 1917†, 3 Jun 1962).

The four fall and winter records are from Adak I: female captured on 15 Oct 1970, 5 female-plumaged birds on 7 Nov 1970, and one remaining from 29 Nov 1970-9 Feb 1971 (C 76:288).

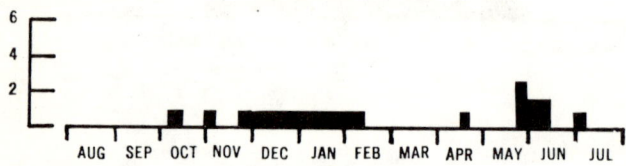

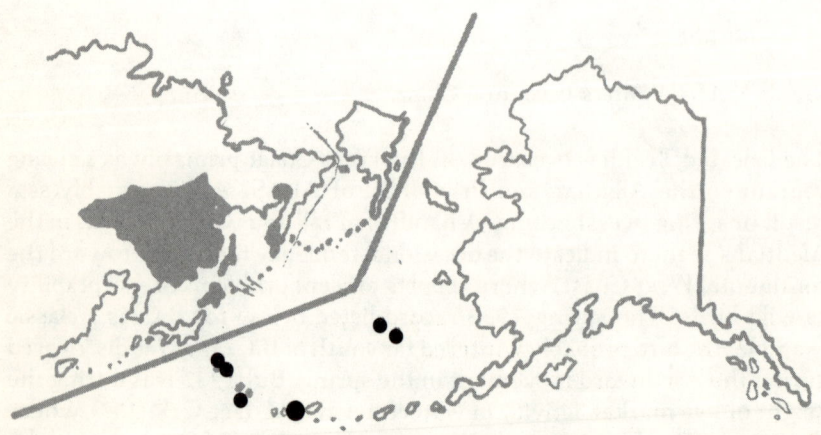

# FALCATED TEAL

**BRITISH COLUMBIA** One record: 5 Apr 1932 at Swan Lake, Vernon (C 44:33). The validity of this record as a wild bird is discussed above.

**WASHINGTON** One record: 3 Jan 1979† at Willapa Bay, Pac. The Falcated Teal is currently rare in captivity (see Ryan, 1972) and the date appears reasonable; this record may be of a wild bird.

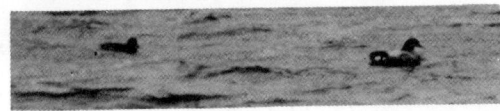

31 May 1980 on Attu I., ALASKA. *Don Roberson.*

**I.D.** The Falcated Teal is about the size of a Gadwall *A. strepera*; the male is distinctive (see plate). The female generally resembles female Gadwall, but is darker, possesses an all gray bill (not orange-sided), and is dark-bellied. A short mane on the nape can cause a big-headed look, but this is difficult to see at a distance. The plain gray-speckled head and unmarked body produce a field impression similar to female Eurasian Wigeon *A. penelope*, especially on the water. Note the lack of pinkish sides, gray (not bluish) bill, and whitish outer tail feathers; in flight, Falcated Teal is more easily identified by dark (not whitish) belly and a blackish speculum bordered fore and aft by prominent white bars. The underwings and axillaries are white.

# BAIKAL TEAL                                            Plate 2

*Anas formosa*

Breeds N Asia. Winters Japan to China.

The Baikal Teal has occurred on the West Coast most often as a spring overshoot in W ALASKA. Fall migrants have been recorded on the Seward Pen. and the Pribilof Is. and may represent individuals wandering towards the SE, where there are 6 records of wintering birds on the West Coast, all in Dec-Jan. All the winter records are of males taken by hunters. The question of possible escape from captivity arises in the case of the Baikal Teal. During the live market days of waterfowl, the Baikal Teal was the 2nd commonest duck imported at San Francisco and at least one published record is best disregarded in consideration of this fact (13 Dec 1931 at Brentwood, C.C., CAL.; see C 34:259). Today the Baikal Teal is expensive and rare in captivity (see Ryan, 1972 and *Birding* 11:74). The closeness of the dates, the distance from centers of captive holdings of the birds shot, and the presence of immature markings on several specimens (young birds are most likely to become fall vagrants) provide evidence that the Baikal Teal does occur as a genuine Asiatic stray in winter on the West Coast.

# BAIKAL TEAL

**ALASKA**   11 records, involving 18 birds, graphed below. There are no records from the Aleutians. The six spring records are from coast of W ALASKA and nearby King I., the summer record (23 Jul 1937 - pair) is from St. Lawrence I., and the 4 fall records are from St. Paul I., Pribilofs and Wainwright, far to the north. Two of the spring records were of pairs and up to 4 were found together in the fall (9 Sep 1971).

Despite an increase in Alaska birding activity, the Baikal Teal has not been found with increasing regularity. There is a record from the '20s, three from the '30s, two from the '40s, one from the '50s, and three from the early '60s; but only one from the '70s (1 May 1976 at Nanvak Bay). Whether this indicates a decrease in the breeding population on the Chuckchi Pen. across the Bering Strait or a shift in birding activity away from the Bering Sea coast, to the Aleutians, is an open question.

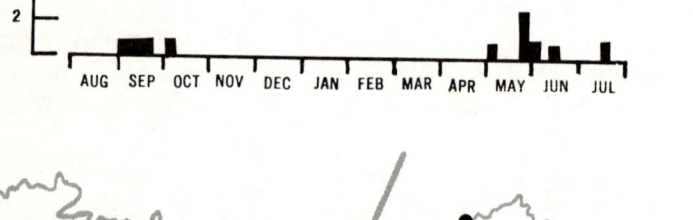

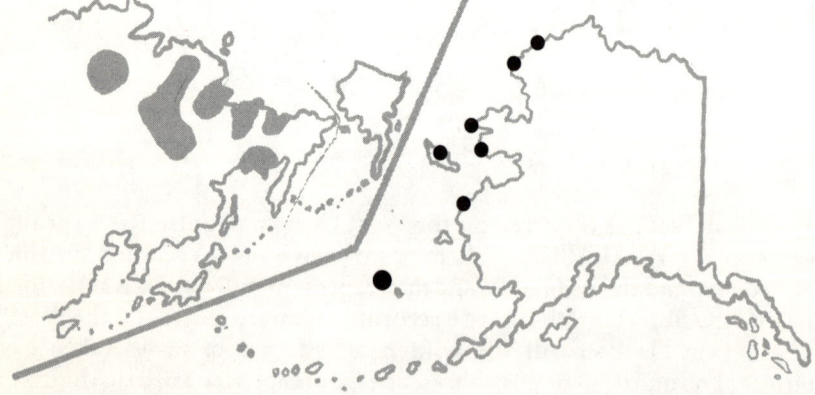

**BRITISH COLUMBIA**   One record: 20 Dec 1957† at Ladner (C 62:480).

**WASHINGTON**   One record: Jan 1920† at Dungeness, Clm. (M 6:41). In addition, a bird on 4 Jun 1979 S of Anacortes, Skg., is listed as a "probable escapee".

**OREGON**   One record: 12 Jan 1974† near Finley NWR, Lane.

# BAIKAL TEAL

**CALIFORNIA** Four records: 29 Dec 1946† at Niland, Imp.; 12 Jan 1974† at Riverside; 1 Dec 1974† at Honey Lake, Las.; and 4 Jan 1975† at Gray Lodge refuge, But.

I.D.   The Baikal Teal is a small duck, slightly larger than Green-winged Teal *A. crecca*. The male is easily recognized (see plate). The female is simitar to female Green-winged Teal, from which it differs by the noticeable white spot on the face at the base of the bill, a darker-capped appearance, pale lores (rather than the Green-wing's dark line from bill through the eye), more uniform back (less checkered), and warm rufous wash to breast. The female Garganey *A. querquedula* shares the white spot at the base of the bill (though typically smaller and less distinct), but has an uninterrupted dark eyeline, light gray upperwing coverts, a blackish speculum glossed with green, and lacks any rufous tone to the breast.

# AMERICAN BLACK DUCK

*Anas rubripes*

Breeds NE North America. Winters SE North America.

The valid occurrence of the American Black Duck on the West Coast remains a complex question. Two spring records in E ALASKA appear to be genuine spring overshoots, and the Alaska winter record is probably a wild bird as well. But the presence of several introduced breeding populations in the Northwest, its popularity in captivity, and its tendency to hybridze with the Mallard *A. platyrhychus* (some authorities consider them conspecific) has clouded its status as a species and as a genuine vagrant.

A brief synopsis of its movements in the East may shed some light on the question. The Black Duck is a common breeder in forested country and is somewhat less migratory than other ducks, moving south typically only with freezing water and diminishing food supplies. Northern interior birds move first, passing beyond more sedentary southern populations. Migration is underway in the far North in early Sep, reaches the N U.S. by early Oct, and extends to its southern limits by early Dec. Movement north coincides with the first break in winter weather, typically about mid-to-late Feb, and is completed by mid-Apr (Palmer, 1976).

The published records of Black Ducks and known Black Duck X Mallard hybrids are graphed below, excluding the acceptable Alaska records and known escapees from the Seattle area. Migration periods in the East are also shown. One would expect that records of a genuine vagrant would form an explainable pattern, probably of winter records with perhaps a few during migration. The graph illustrates this pattern is lacking.

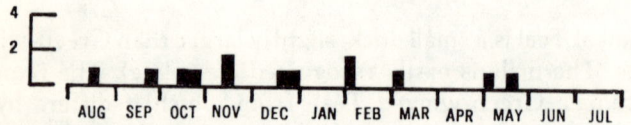

Introduced populations, some partially stocked by local fish & game departments, are present at Marysville and Everett, Sno., WASH and near Vancouver, B.C. The existence of these populations, for at least the last ten years, make any sighting of a Black Duck in the Northwest suspect and perhaps taints any recent record on the West Coast.

# AMERICAN BLACK DUCK

The tendency to hybridize with the Mallard further complicates the situation. Reported from such widely separated areas as the Copper R. delta, ALASKA, Seattle, WASH, and the Salton Sea, CAL., hybrids may account for a number of reports from hunters. In captivity, Black Ducks are listed as "regular but not abundant" (Ryan, 1972) and hybrids are raised. The distribution shown in the graph appears to be more closely approximate random escapes from captivity than the movements of wild birds. For this reason, coupled with the presence of introduced populations and the problem of hybrids, the American Black Duck is best considered less than a valid addition to the list of any state or province south of ALASKA, a position recently taken by the CAL Records Committee.

**ALASKA**  Three records: 5 May 1972 at Fairbanks and 17 May 1975 at Cordova, both probably spring overshoots. One returned for 4 consecutive winters at Gustavas from Dec 1969 to Jan 1973.

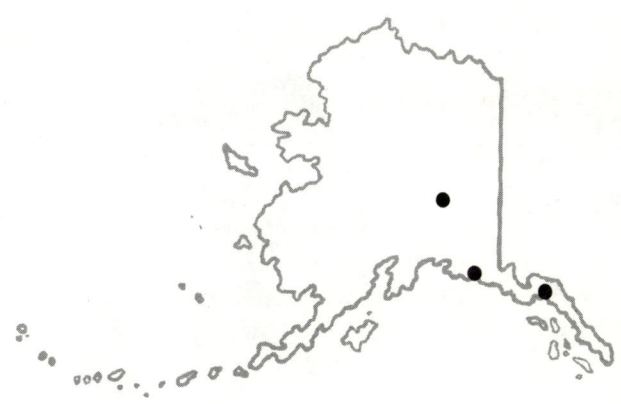

I.D.  Identification of "pure" Black Duck is covered by the standard guides. Hybrid characteristics in males include greenish feathers about the head (esp. the eyestripe), greenish sheen to back or rump, speculum tending more to blue than violet, presence of a distinct white bar in front of the speculum, reddish feathers in the breast, and an upturning of the tail feathers. At least the first two of these characters are latent in pure Black Duck stock and may not indicate hybridizism, although it often does indicate mixed ancestry. Hybrid females may be indistinguishable in the field.

# SPOTBILL DUCK

Plate 2

*Anas poeciloryncha*

Breeds NE Asia, India. Siberian races winter S to S China.

The Spotbill Duck has occurred twice in ALASKA. The first individual was seen locally for over a year. The second bird, far to the east on Kodiak I., may have been deposited there by tropical storm *Harriet*.

**ALASKA**   Two records: 10 Apr 1970-18 Apr 1971 on Adak I., and 30 Oct-1 Nov 1977† at Kalsin Bay, Kodiak I. (WB 9:127).

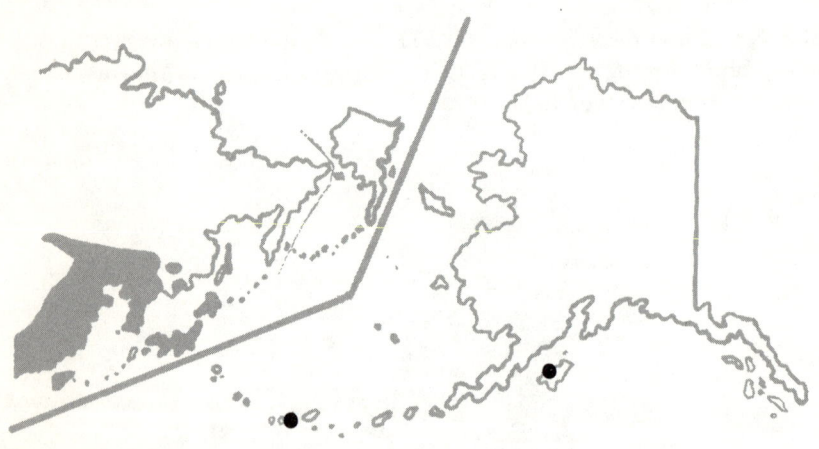

I.D.   The Spotbill Duck generally resembles the American Black Duck *A. rubripes*, with a dark body and pale head. It is slightly larger and differently proportioned, appearing longer-necked in the field. The speculum is violet-blue and bordered fore and aft with white. The underwings are whitish, like those of the Mallard *A. platyrhynchos*. The yellow tip to the dark bill is distinctive, as is the dark cap, dark eyeline, and conspicuously pale supercilium. The race collected in ALASKA - *A. p. zonorhyncha* - has a faint moustachial stripe.

# GARGANEY

Plate 2

*Anas querquedula*

Breeds N Eurasia. Winters W Africa, S Eurasia, SE Asia, New Guinea.

The Garganey has one of the longest migration routes among waterfowl and vagrants have occurred from the mid-Pacific Ocean to the West Coast. It is a rare, but regular, spring overshoot in the outer Aleutians and there are a number of fall records there as well. In Eurasia, fall migration at the latitudes of S B.C. to CAL is undertaken from Sep-Nov and spring migration from Mar-May. No fall migrants have been fround on the West Coast (hardly surprising as fall migration coincides with the autumn molt and female or eclipse male Garganeys are unlikely to be identified in the field). Every Garganey record south of ALASKA fits neatly into the timing of spring migration and there is little doubt that these records are of wild birds that wintered somewhere in the New World, especially since Garganeys are very rare in captivity (Ryan, 1972; *Birding* 11:74). All records S of ALASKA are of adult males; one returned with migrant teal in 3 of 4 consecutive years.

**ALASKA** A rare, but regular, spring migrant (10 May-21 Jun) on the outer Aleutians, where there are at least 25 records. Most occur singly or in pairs; the high count is 5 on Shemya I. (25-26 May 1976). There is a single summer record:11 Jul 1976 on Buldir I.

In the fall, it is a rare migrant from mid-Aug-early Oct on the outer Aleutians. About 40 individuals were recorded in the falls of 1976-77-78-79, and it was seen almost daily during fall visits to Shemya I. and Attu I. There is a lone record from the Pribilofs: 28 Aug 1975 on St. Paul I.

# GARGANEY

**BRITISH COLUMBIA** Two records: 14-28 May 1977 at Sea & Iona Is., Vancouver, and 8-12 Jun 1979 at Iona I.

**CALIFORNIA** Two records: 15 Mar 1972 at Long Beach, L.A., presumably the same individual returning on 4 Apr 1974 and 19 Mar 1975*, and 21 Mar-4 Apr 1979 at Lake Elsinore, Riv.

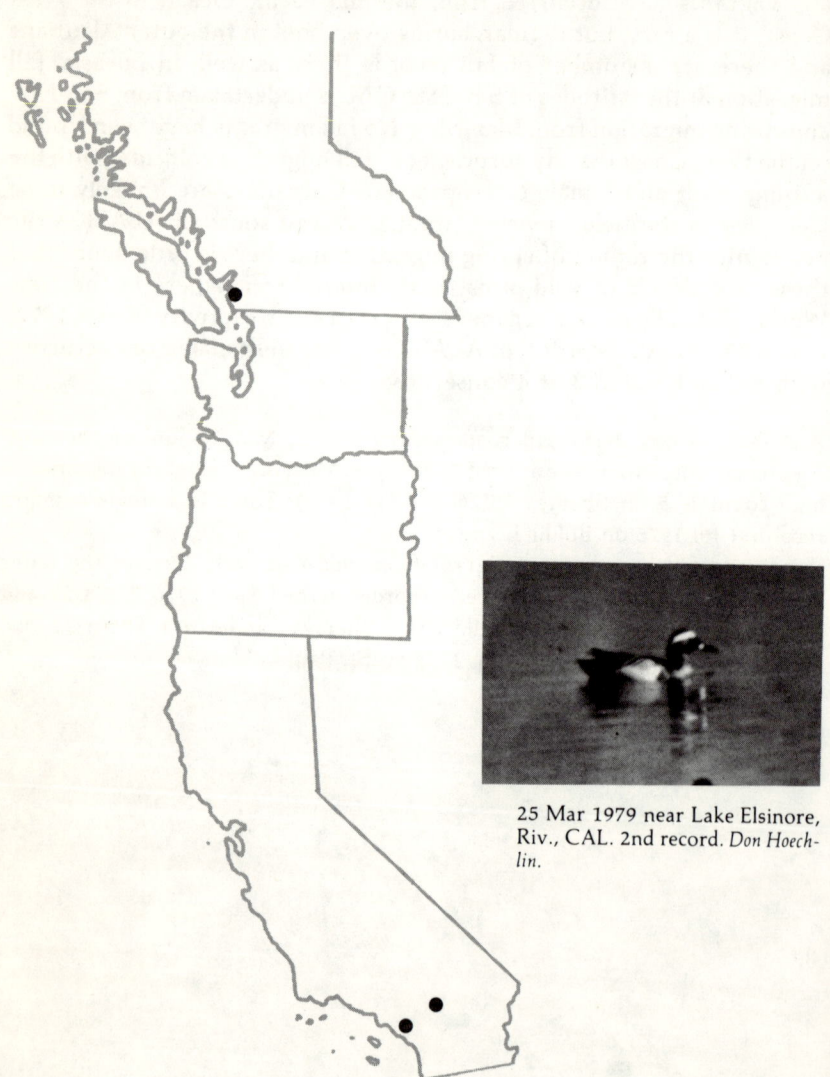

25 Mar 1979 near Lake Elsinore, Riv., CAL. 2nd record. *Don Hoechlin.*

# GARGANEY

Jun 1977 on Amchitka I., ALASKA (with "Eurasian" Green-winged Teal, foreground). *Robert P. Schulmeister.*

14 May 1977 at Iona I., Vancouver, B.C. 1st record. *Bruce A. Macdonald.*

I.D. The Garganey is about the size of Green-winged Teal *A. crecca;* the male in breeding plumage is easily recognized (see plate). Females and "eclipse" males are much more difficult to identify. They are often compared to female Blue-winged *A. discors* and Cinnamon Teal *A. cyanoptera,* but contrary to some of the literature the Garganey does not show a pale forewing in flight (the forewing of Blue-winged and Cinnamon Teal is bluish; see Wallace & Ogilvie (1977) for a good discussion of this difficult identification problem). Female Garganey is very similar to female Green-winged Teal: both have greenish speculums and a bold face pattern with dark cap, pale supercilium, and dark eyeline. Garganey tends to be a paler, grayer bird and shows a more conspicuous pale spot on the face at the base of the bill. The uninterrupted eyeline should separate it from female Baikal Teal *A. formosa.*

# COMMON POCHARD

Plate 2

*Aythya ferina*

Breeds N Eurasia. Winters N Africa, S Eurasia, Japan.

The Common Pochard occurs on the West Coast most often as a spring migrant in the outer Aleutians, where it is found nearly annually. The breeding areas are rather distant from ALASKA and spring overshoots may account for many records.

**ALASKA** Rare, but regular, spring migrant (28 Apr-19 Jun) in the outer Aleutians. Within the 1970s, at least 26 birds were on Adak I., 15 on Shemya I., 10 on Amchitka I., 7 on Attu I., and 1 on Buldir I. The first Aleutian record was from Amukta I. (16 Jun 1936). Farther east, there are 4 records from St. Paul I., Pribilofs, including two old records (1846† and 4 May 1912†).

The single fall record is 16 Oct 1973 (2) on Adak I.

May 1974 on Palisades Lake, Adak I., ALASKA. *Dewayne Ash, courtesy Daniel D. Gibson.*

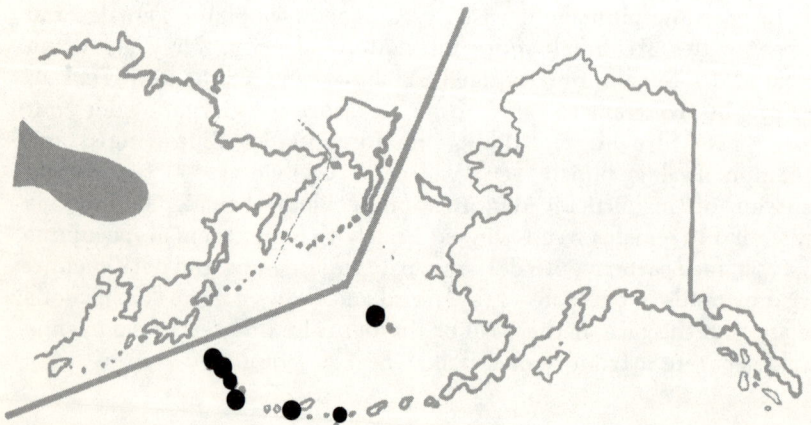

# COMMON POCHARD

I.D. The Common Pochard resembles the Redhead *A. americana* in size and pattern, but the coloring of the male is more like that of the Canvasback *A. valisineria*, with a whitish back and sides rather than the Redhead's darker gray back. The head shape is also reminiscent of the Canvasback, with a sloping forehead rather than the Redhead's rounded head, but not as extreme as the Canvasback's profile (see plate). This head shape, and the bill pattern, will separate adult Pochards of either sex from similarly-plumaged Redheads. The Pochard's bill is dark basally, has a distinct light midsection (reduced to a narrow band in females), and a dark tip with a small nail; the Redhead's bill is mostly light, with a dark tip and heavy nail. Female Common Pochard is further separated by a gray wash to the back. Young birds resemble females but lack the distinct bill pattern and the gray wash on the back and may be difficult to distinguish in the field. Head shape and nail size may be useful guides at close range.

# TUFTED DUCK

*Aythya fuligula*

Breeds N Eurasia. Winters N Africa, S Eurasia, Philippines, Japan.

The Tufted Duck is now recorded annually on the West Coast. Most records are of spring and fall migrants in the outer Aleutians, ALASKA, but in most years a few birds will migrate south along the West Coast to winter locally between S B.C. and CAL. Some individuals return to the same wintering area year after year (a male returned for 5 successive winters in S CAL). Tufted Ducks are often found in the company of scaup *A. marila, A. affinis* or Ring-necked Duck *A. collaris*. Apparent Tufted Duck X Ring-necked Duck and Tufted Duck X Greater Scaup hybrids have been encountered and may suggest that the Tufted Duck has attempted to breed somewhere in North America. There are summer records of Tufted Duck in ALASKA, but most have been thought to be non-breeders.

**ALASKA** Regular spring and fall migrant in the outer Aleutians, often occurring with flocks of Greater Scaup, but single-species flocks of up to 43 have been found (17 May 1975 on Shemya I.). Migrants have been recorded on the Bering Sea islands, the Seward Pen., and N to Pt. Barrow. A few have been recorded in winter on the outer Aleutians, and there are winter records from the E Aleutians, Kodiak I., and Cordova in S ALASKA (1 fall and 2 winter records). There are at least 14 summer records from the outer Aleutians and Pribilof Is., presumably non-breeders.

# TUFTED DUCK

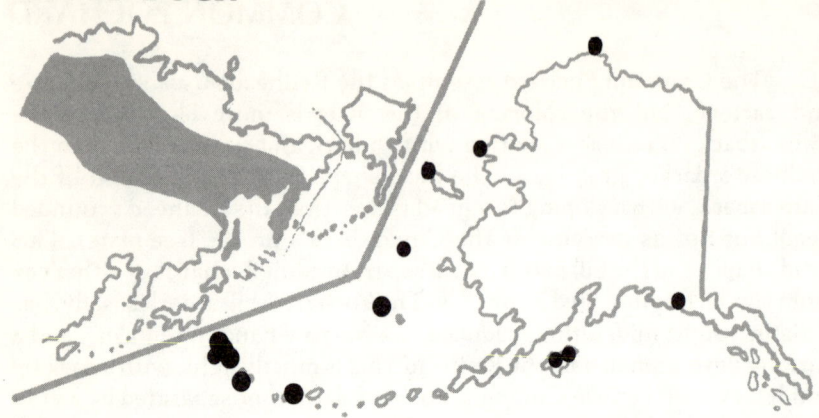

**BRITISH COLUMBIA** 35 records, graphed below. All are from the Greater Vancouver area or S Vancouver I. Despite a number of mid-winter records, only 4 birds have remained locally for over a week and it would seem that most B.C. records are of migrants that winter somewhere to the south. The graph shows a sharp peak during fall migration (Oct-Nov) but a more protracted spring migration (Feb-May) with a few birds, perhaps non-breeders, lingering as late as Jul. For more information see Campbell & Weber (1976).

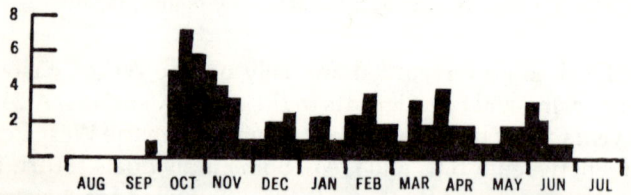

14 Oct 1967 at Lost Lagoon, Vancouver, B.C. 3rd record. *Lothar Kirchner.*

9 Mar 1972 at Ganges, Salt Springs I., B.C. *Ian Robertson.*

# TUFTED DUCK

**WASHINGTON**   Five records: 31 Dec 1967 (2 males) at Seattle, King, with one remaining to late Feb 1968 - a male (perhaps the latter individual) returned to this location each successive winter through 30 Dec 1970, 18-27 Feb 1979 at Everett, Sno., 20-27 Oct 1979 at Ocean Shores, G.H., and 26 Oct-Dec 1979 at Hoquiam, G.H.

**OREGON**   One record: 14 Feb-26 Mar 1960* at Portland, Mul. (A 78:638).

21 Feb 1972 at Golden Gate Park, San Francisco, CAL. 3rd record. *Van Remsen.*

**CALIFORNIA**   15 records, graphed below. At least 5 of the records refer to individuals that returned for successive winters, including males returning for 3 winters at Lake Merritt, Oakland, Ala. ('76-'77 to '78-'79), and 5 winters at Lake Sherwood, Ven. ('73-'74 to '77-'78). Most records are of birds that wintered locally, though fall (Nov) and spring (Apr) migrants have occurred. The validity of the record of a male that appeared at Arcata, Hum., on 10 Apr 1968 and was seen in the vicinity until 17 Jul 1970 is problematical. Though removed from centers of captive waterfowl, the bird was present during dates outside the known pattern for CAL and the length of its stay renders the record suspect. Tufted Ducks are kept commonly in collections (Ryan, 1972), but records within the known pattern of occurrence are best considered wild birds; for a full discussion see McCaskie (1973).

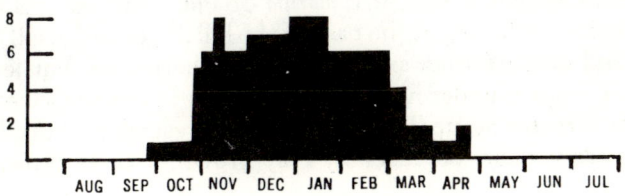

# TUFTED DUCK

Feb 1960 at Portland, Mul., ORE. 1st record. *David R. Marshall*.

Nov 1976 at Lake Merritt, Oakland, Ala., CAL (male & female). 5th & 6th records. *Al Ghiorso*.

I.D. Most Tufted Ducks can be identified by the unique tuft on the nape. Males are patterned somewhat like the Ring-necked Duck *A. collaris*, but differ in having a rounded head, white sides, and bills lacking the white band around the base. Females and first-year males (until midwinter) resemble female scaup *A. marilla* or *affinis*, but possess a short tuft. Any white feathering at the base of the bill (if present at all) is more restricted and obscure than similar white feathering on female scaup. Tufted Duck has a rounder head than the Lesser Scaup and a less heavy bill than the Greater Scaup. First-winter males resemble adults, but the while sides are variably obscured by gray-brown or rusty brown.

# COMMON EIDER

*Somateria mollissima*

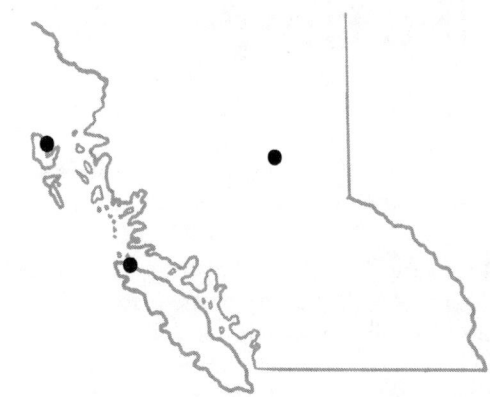

Breeds N North America, N Eurasia. Winters circompolar in N coastal waters.

The Common Eider on the West Coast is confined to ALASKA, wintering south of the sea-ice near the Aleutian Is. and Gulf of Alaska, but numbers dwindle rapidly in the Alexander Archipeligo. There are 3 B.C. records in Oct-Dec - including one in the interior - but none have been recorded south of ALASKA since 1949.

**BRITISH COLUMBIA** Three records: 26-27 Oct 1934† at Hardy Bay, V.I. (C 44:33), 4 Dec 1945† at Masset, Q.C.I., and 31 Oct 1949† near Prince George, far inland in NE B.C.

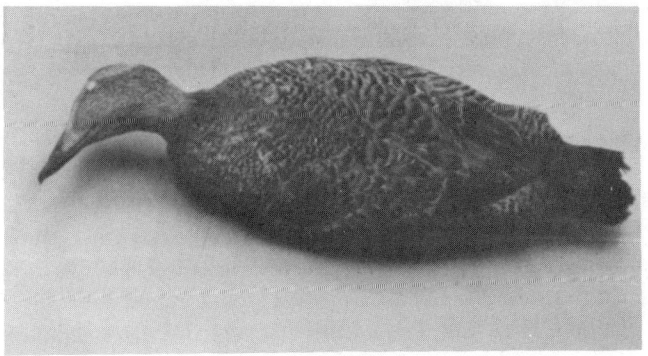

27 Oct 1934 at Hardy Bay, V.I., B.C. 1st record. Museum of Vertebrate Zoology, U.C. Berkeley #99537. *Don Roberson.*

# KING EIDER

*Somateria spectabilis*

Breeds N Holarctic. Winters coastal waters off Scandinavia, NE Asia, NE North America, W & S Alaska.

Most King Eiders on the West Coast concentrate in winter on coastal waters off the E Aleutians, the Alaska Pen., and Kodiak I., but occassionally an individual will wander south to the coasts of B.C. to CAL. Winter records dominate in these areas, but fall migrants have been recorded and there are a handful of spring records.

**BRITISH COLUMBIA**  Six records: 18 Oct 1938† at Hardy Bay, V.I. (C 44:33), 11 Jan 1942† at Sooke Harbor, V.I. (M 23:62), 15 Dec 1971-16 Jan 1972 at Queen Charlotte City, Q.C.I., 17 Nov 1973-20 May 1974 at Pt. Grey, Vancouver, 22 Feb 1975 at Port Edward, and 14 May 1977 at Sandspit, Q.C.I.

**WASHINGTON**  9 records: 23-30 Oct 1948† at Lincoln Beach, Seattle, King, 28 Oct 1965 at Blaine, Wha., 22 Feb 1967 (2) at Orcas I., S.J. (M 48:7), 29 Dec 1973-19 Jan 1974 (2) at Bellingham, Wha., 6 Apr 1977 at Port Angeles, Clm., 23 Oct-4 Nov 1977 at Pt. Roberts, Wha., and 1-15 Jan 1979 at Pt. Roberts.

The B.C. and WASH records are graphed below. They appear to be of fall migrants (Oct-Nov), local winterers (Dec-Jan), and two records of spring migrants.

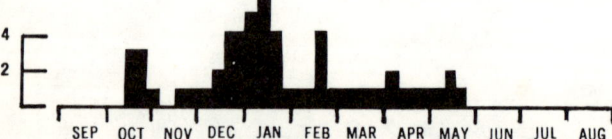

**OREGON**  One record: 10-20 Mar 1976 at Tillamook Bay.

**CALIFORNIA**  18 records, graphed below. The first was of a bird taken in the winter of 1879-80 and winter records constitute the bulk of sightings since then. One female returned to Monterey for three successive winters ('69-'70 to '71-'72) and once lingered to 1 Aug; another discovered at Moss Landing, Mnt., on 25 Mar 1961 remained as late as 26 Aug. The southernmost record was 22 Nov 1973-28 Jan 1974* at Malibu, L.A.

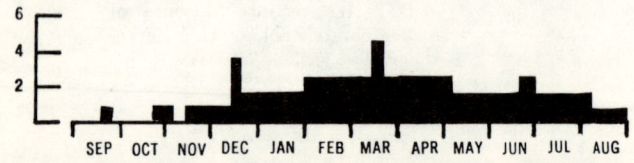

# KING EIDER

5 Jan 1974 at Monterey, CAL. *Van Remsen.*

Dec 1969 at Monterey, CAL. 11th record. *Ronald L. Branson.*

18 Nov 1973 at Vancouver, B.C. 4th record. *G. Allen Poynter.*

# STELLER'S EIDER

*Polysticta stelleri*

Breeds NE Asia, W & N Alaska. Winters off the Kamchatka Pen., NE Asia and Alaska Pen., Alaska.

The Steller's Eider has occurred on the West Coast south of ALASKA only in B.C. Most of the American population concentrate near the Alaska Pen. in late Oct-Nov and remain until Mar-Apr. Pre-breeders wander farther and linger later during this winter movement, and two of the B.C. records occurred during this time. But what can be said of an adult male in B.C. in mid-Jun?

**BRITISH COLUMBIA** Three records: 15 Oct 1948† at Masset, Q.C.I. (M 64:51), 14 Jun 1970 at Mitlenatch I., SE of Cambell River, V.I. (CFN 85:330), and 13 Feb-27 Mar 1976 at Sidney, V.I.

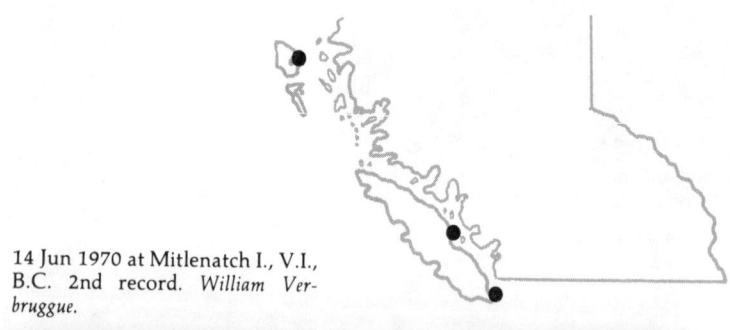

14 Jun 1970 at Mitlenatch I., V.I., B.C. 2nd record. *William Verbruggue.*

## STELLER'S EIDER

13 Feb 1976 at Sidney, V.I., B.C.
3rd record. J. E. Williams.

# SMEW   Plate 2

*Mergus albellus*

Breeds N Eurasia. Winters W Europe, Middle East, China, Japan.

The Smew is a scarce migrant and winter visitor on the outer Aleutian Is., ALASKA. It is very rare away from the Aleutian and Pribilof Is., and the few records south of ALASKA fall between Nov-Mar. Smews are extremely scarce in captivity (Ryan, 1976) and all West Coast birds are best considered genuine vagrants. For a more thorough discussion of Smews in North America see Weber & Campbell (1976).

**ALASKA**   Rare, but regular, spring migrant, fall migrant, and winter visitor in the W Aleutians. At least 55 birds have occurred in ALASKA, graphed below. Multiple records have been recorded on Adak I. (20), Shemya I. (10), Attu I. (9), Amchitka I. (8), and on St. Paul I., Pribilofs (7). Though most records are of single individuals, small flocks of up to 6 birds have been encountered. Far from the Aleutians was a bird from 7 Mar-25 Apr 1976 at Chiniak Bay, Kodiak I.

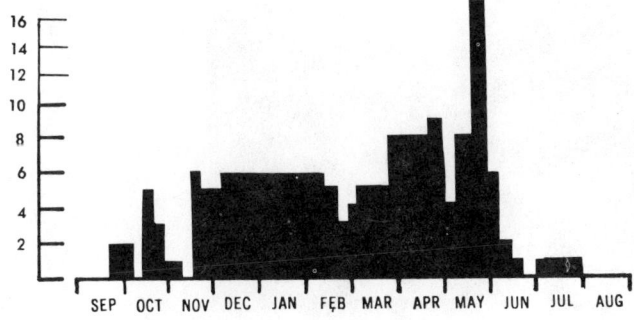

# SMEW

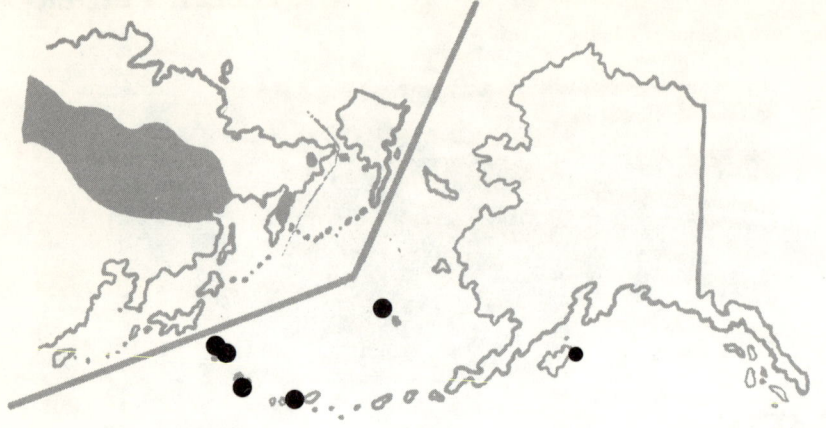

**BRITISH COLUMBIA** Three records: 14-23 Nov 1970 at Lost Lagoon, Vancouver, 28 Feb-21 Mar 1974 at Reifel refuge, Vancouver, and 14 Jan-30 Mar 1975 at Reifel refuge. The first and third records are of adult males. The second record was female-plumaged, but some observers felt it may have been a 1st-winter male and could have been the same individual that returned in adult plumage the following winter (see Weber & Campbell, 1976).

20 Jan 1975 at Reifel refuge, Vancouver, B.C. 3rd record. *Ervio Sian.*

# SMEW

19 Mar 1974 at Reifel refuge, Vancouver, B.C. 2nd record. *Ervio Sian.*

**I.D.** The Smew is any plumage is easily recognized (see plate). First-year males resemble adult females (though they lack the black lores in autumn), but begin showing characteristics of adult males by mid-winter. Eclipse males also resemble females, but are blacker-backed and retain a large white patch on the upperwing coverts.

# AMERICAN BLACK VULTURE

*Coragyps atratus*

Breeds W Mexico, SE U.S. to S South America. Local winter movements.

The Black Vulture has been reliably reported on the West Coast, but as yet it has not been accepted on any official state list. Its status in captivity is unclear and a minority of Rarity Committee members have felt the possibility of the reports referring to escaped birds is too great for acceptance. However, the Black Vulture is locally common in S Arizona and might be expected to appear in CAL, where single records of spring and fall migrants may be of genuine vagrants.

**CALIFORNIA** Two records: 13 Apr 1972 near Chico, But., and 5 Sep 1977 at Parker Dam, S.Bn. Although a majority of CAL Records Committee members voted to accept these records, both were unaccepted by narrow margins. I consider both to be valid records.

# WHITE-TAILED KITE

*Elanus leucurus*

Resident W U.S. to S South America.

The White-tailed Kite is locally resident in much of CAL. Formerly thought to be endangered, it has adapted to the spread of agriculture in the western U.S. and has expanded its range dramatically. It has been resident in the Rogue R. Valley of S ORE for a decade and has occasionally bred as far north as Finley NWR, Ben. (WB 9:131). Though only recently recorded in WASH, pairs have been noted and it may be that the White-tailed Kite will become part of the breeding avifauna of S WASH within the next decade.

**WASHINGTON** 5 records: 10 Jul 1975 at Nisqually NWR, Thr.; 27 Nov 1977 at Raymond, Pac., with presumably the same bird present irregularly through 1979 and joined by another in winter 1978; fall 1978 at Ridgefield NWR, Clk., with a pair present (perhaps the same bird joined by another) on 8 Mar 1979 at Vancouver, Clk. (these birds could be those that have frequented Sauvie I., Col., ORE for several years); 17 Aug 1979 at Ocean Shores, G.H., and 14 Nov-Dec 1979 at Snohomish, Sno.

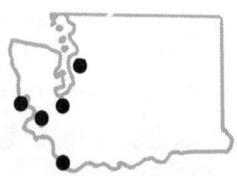

# MISSISSIPPI KITE

*Ictinia mississippiensis*

Breeds SE U.S. Winters S U.S. to S South America.

The Mississippi Kite has recently been extending its range westward and small numbers have been detected nesting in SE Arizona. On the West Coast all the records are from CAL. Over half of these occurred during a 4-week period in late May-early Jun on the Furnace Creek golf course in Death Valley.

# MISSISSIPPI KITE

**CALIFORNIA** Nine records: 18 Jun 1933† at Goleta, S. Bb., 2-5 Jun 1968 at Furnace Creek, Inyo, 3 Jun 1970 at Santa Barbara, 21-22 May 1973* at Furnace Creek, 21 May-3 Jun 1973* at Furnace Creek, 14 Jun 1973 at Furnace Creek, 6 Sep 1975* at Cape Mendocino, Men, 25-26 May 1976* at Furnace Creek, and 13 Sep 1976* at Pt. Diablo, Mrn. All refer to adult birds, except the Cape Mendocino record.

26 May 1976 at Furnace Creek, Death Valley NM, Inyo, CAL. 8th record. *Van Remsen.*

# WHITE-TAILED EAGLE

Plate 2

*Haliaeetus albicilla*

Breeds N & C Eurasia. Mostly resident.

The White-tailed Eagle is a widespread, mostly resident, Eurasian species that has occurred recently on the West Coast only on the Aleutian Is. of ALASKA. Bones have been found in kitchen middens on Kodiak I., suggesting it was resident there sometime in the past. Recent observations on Attu I., the westernmost of the Aleutians, suggest a few are resident there.

**ALASKA** Two records: 5 Oct 1895† at Unalaska, and a few (at least 2 adults and an immature) on Attu I. during the springs of 1977, 1978, 1979, & 1980. Dates of observations on Attu I. stretch from 13 May-16 Jul and have included a pair engaged in apparent courtship activity. Since observations on Attu I. are limited to a small coastal strip at the SE corner of the island, it seems highly probable that this species is also resident elsewhere on the 40 mile long island.

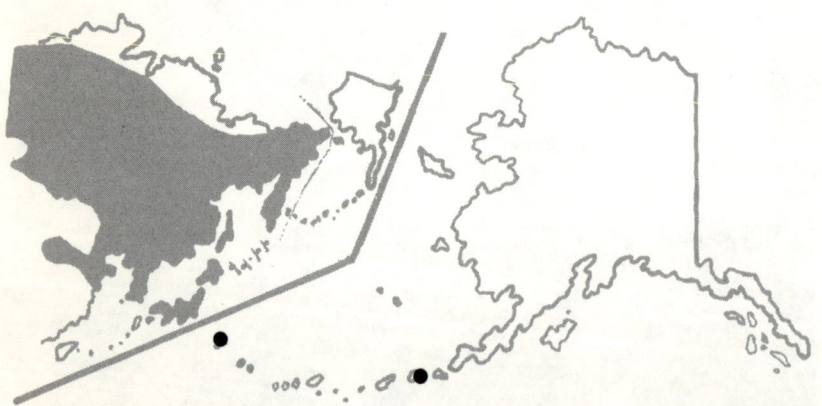

**I.D.** The White-tailed Eagle is a large, heavy eagle with very broad wings and a short, wedge-shaped tail. Its plumages are similar to those of the smaller Bald Eagle *H. leucocephalus*. Adults of both species have white tails, but the head and neck of the White-tailed Eagle are buffy brown (creamy white on very old birds), not the sharply contrasting white head of the Bald Eagle. Immatures are more similar. Juvenile White-tailed Eagles are dark with a few rusty-yellow streaks on the breast, a pale axillary patch and diffuse pale bar on the median underwings coverts, and whitish centers to the tail feathers. Older birds become rather mottled, especially on the upperparts, and the tail gradually whitens with age. Young Bald Eagles have similar patterns.

# WHITE-TAILED EAGLE

In flight, the broad wings of White-tailed Eagle are held straight, so that the wing-tips are nearly parallel, resembling a giant flying door. When gliding, the wings may be bent at the wrist, somewhat like a giant Osprey *Pandion haliaetus*. The head and long neck of the adult protrude as much in front of the wings as the short, wedged tail does from behind. Immatures have longer tails that are less wedge-shaped, but body proportions, large size, and flight silhouette continue to provide means of separating them from immature Bald Eagle. For more information see Porter, *et al* (1976).

# STELLER'S SEA EAGLE                        Plate 2

*Haliaeetus pelagicus*

Breeds NE Asia. Winters NE Asia, Korea, Japan.

The Steller's Sea Eagle is extremely rare on the West Coast; the only record in the past 50 years comes from the westernmost Aleutian Is., ALASKA. It may once have been more regular in ALASKA, as bones have been found in kitchen middens on Kodiak I., but there are only 4 records from the 1900s. The total world population of this impressive eagle is small and may be declining.

**ALASKA**  Four records: 26 May 1906 at Unalaska, 15 Dec 1917† on St. Paul I., 10 Aug 1921† on Kodiak I., and 13 May 1980 on Attu I.

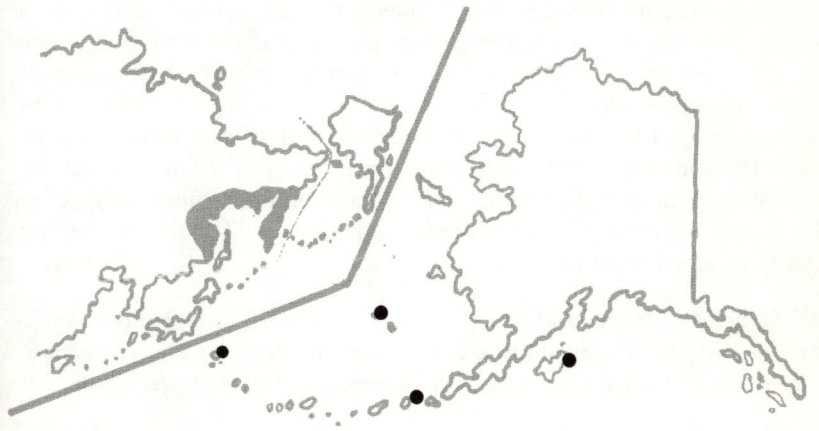

# STELLER'S SEA EAGLE

**I.D.** The Steller's Sea Eagle is the largest eagle to have reached the West Coast and the adult is unmistakable, being all dark except for a white rump and tail, shoulders, thighs, and forehead (sometimes an entire white crown). The tail is strongly wedge-shaped, even more so than the White-tailed Eagle *H. albicilla*. The yellow bill is very large and high, dwarfing the bills of smaller eagles. The immature is essentially all dark with a dirty white tail, and is distinguished from other immature eagles by its dark coloration, its large size, its heavy bill, and the strongly wedge-shaped tail.

# HARRIS' HAWK

*Parabuteo unicinctus*

Breeds SW U.S. to S South America. Mostly resident.

The Harris' Hawk was formerly resident along the Colorado R. and in the Imperial Valley of S CAL. Its decline in the state, attributable to habitat destruction and falconry (Remsen, 1977), began by the late 1950s and perhaps the last nesting birds disappeared by the mid-1960s. It formerly occassionally wandered north from Baja California, Mexico to the coast of San Diego Co. in late fall, by all recent records from that area are best treated as escapees from falconers. Indeed, the popularity of this species in falconry (especially to the inexperienced) has made every report in the last 15 years difficult to evaluate. Numerous reports have been of obvious escapees, with bands, jesses, or extreme wing and tail wear. In the summer of 1976 the CAL Fish & Game Dept. released a confiscated pair at the south end of the Salton Sea, Imp., where they unsuccessfully attempted to nest. Additional releases have occurred, including some near Yuma, Arizona on the Colorado R., making it difficult to judge the validity of any recent reports.

**CALIFORNIA** Now extinct as a breeding species in the state, but occassional stragglers from small populations in S Arizona might occur along the Colorado R. 1 recent record, perhaps of a wild bird: an immature Sep 1978 near Bythe, Riv.

# RED-SHOULDERED HAWK

*Buteo lineatus*

Breeds CAL, NW Baja and E North America, E Mexico. Some northern populations are migratory.

The Red-shouldered Hawk is mainly resident along the coast and in the Central Valley of CAL (see Wilbur, 1973). Vagrants occasionally wander to the deserts and Great Basin of CAL. It is a Rarity to the north of CAL, but a number of recent records from extreme SW ORE suggest it is regular there, especially in winter, and it has been suspected of nesting in the Rogue R. Valley. Several rehabilitated Red-shouldered Hawks were released near Grant's Pass, ORE, in the fall of 1978 and more releases are expected, complicating the acceptance of reports as valid.

**OREGON** Formerly nested in SE ORE, as eggs were taken and adults described along Archies Creek, Har., in Apr & May 1878 (see M 54:34). At least 14 recent records, those with known dates are graphed below. 6 of the records are from near the CAL-ORE border in Curry Co. One returned to territory along the Rogue R. in the springs of 1976-77-78 and a pair was suspected of nesting at Gold Ray Dam, Jck., in summer 1978; exact dates are not available and these occurrences are not shown on the graph. There are 4 records from the Willamette Valley: 3 Jan 1973 on Sauvie I., Col., 11-15 Jan 1977 at Fern Ridge Res., Lane, 1-22 Jan 1979 at the Eugene Airport, Lane, and 26 Dec 1979-Jan 1980 (2) at Fern Ridge Res. For more details see Rogers (1979).

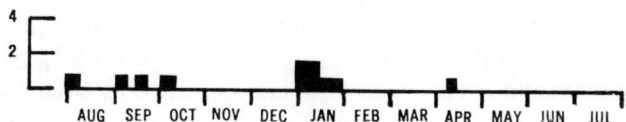

**WASHINGTON** One record: 21 Dec 1979-Jan 1980 at Nisqually NWR, Thr. This record fits the pattern shown by the northernmost records in ORE.

# RED-SHOULDERED HAWK

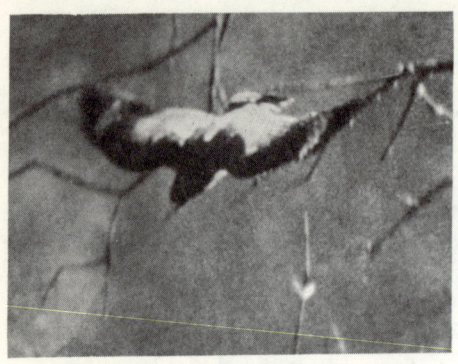
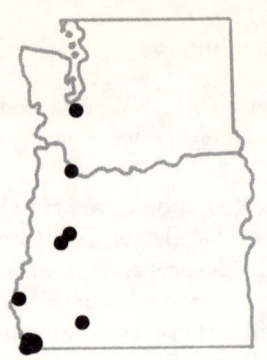

11 Jan 1977 at Fern Ridge Res., Lane, ORE. *Larry B. McQueen.*

# BROAD-WINGED HAWK

*Buteo platypterus*

Breeds E North America. Winters SE U.S., Central America to NW South America.

The Broad-winged Hawk was not recorded on the West Coast until Dec 1966 (Imperial Beach, S.D., CAL; C 70:93), but since that time it has been found as a regular fall migrant in small numbers in CAL, with a few wintering there, and a very scarce spring migrant. The Broad-winged Hawk nests west to C Alberta, and the CAL migration is suspected of originating from the NW portion of the breeding population, since 3 dark-phase birds, which appear to be limited to that portion of the population, have been recorded at Pt. Diablo, Mrn., CAL.

At least 222 Broad-winged Hawks have been recorded in CAL; about 60% of those (at least 131 birds) were seen from the hawk lookout at Pt. Diablo since its discovery in fall 1972 (see Binford, 1979). Since that time, CAL has averaged about 25 Broad-winged Hawks a year. The route that brings these numbers to CAL is still undiscovered; there are no records from ORE or WASH, and only two (both fall migrants) from B.C.

**BRITISH COLUMBIA** Two records: 28 Aug 1974† at Mile 54 near Fort St. John, and 5 Oct 1978 at Vancouver.

# BROAD-WINGED HAWK

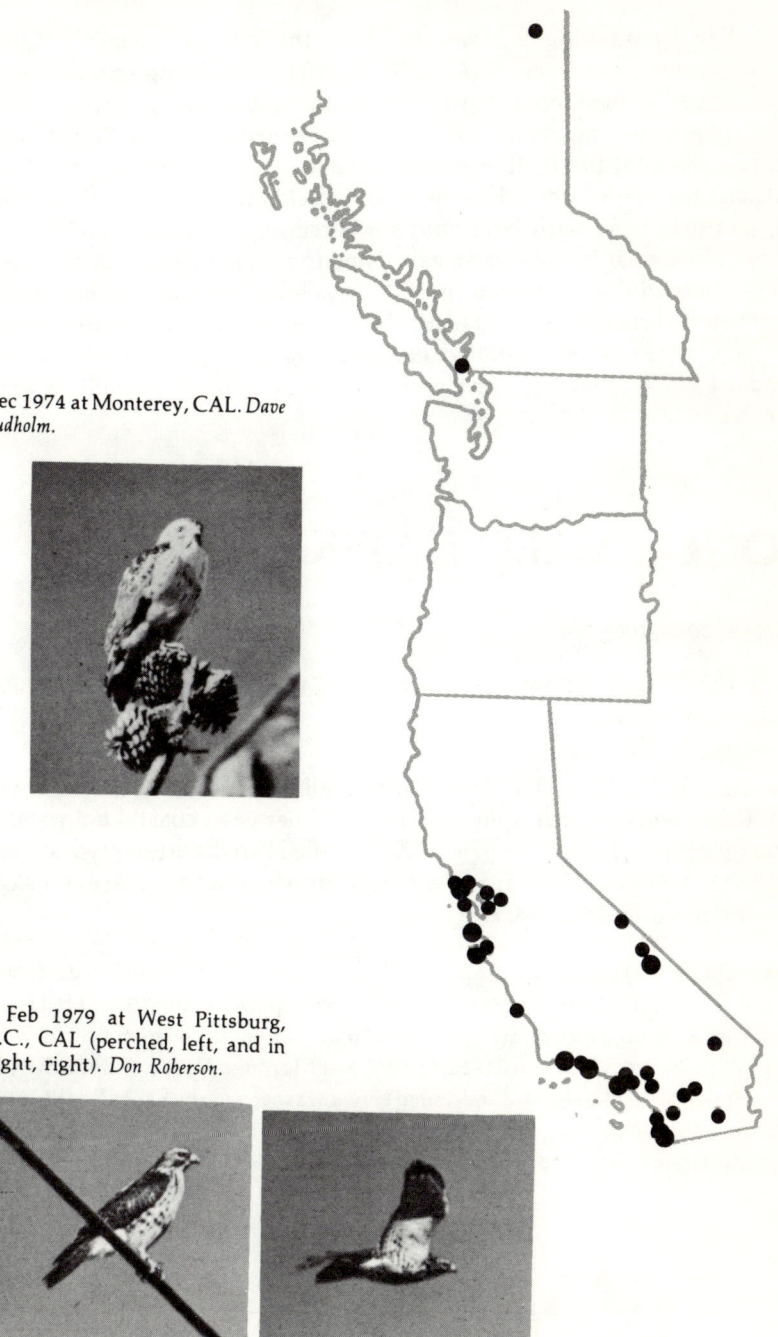

Dec 1974 at Monterey, CAL. *Dave Rudholm.*

3 Feb 1979 at West Pittsburg, C.C., CAL (perched, left, and in flight, right). *Don Roberson.*

# BROAD-WINGED HAWK

**I.D.** The Broad-winged Hawk is about the size of Cooper's Hawk *Accipiter cooperii*, but very differently proportioned, being chunky with short, broad wings and a short, broad tail. Adults are pictured in the standard guides. Immatures, which comprise the bulk of the West Coast records, are identified by their size and shape, the very white underwings (without the black "wrist" shown in some field guides), narrowly barred tail, and pale head with bold white supercilum and broad, dark malar stripe. The breast is variable streaked and the back may be mottled with white. Sub-adults, recorded in fall, resemble immatures but have acquired the broadly banded tail of adults. The rare dark phase resembles the dark phase of Short-tailed Hawk *B. brachyurus*, illustrated in the standard guides, but lacks the white forehead usually present in that species.

# ZONE-TAILED HAWK

*Buteo albonotatus*

Breeds Baja, Mexico & SW U.S. to N South America. Northern populations winter to the south.

The Zone-tailed Hawk has occurred as a fall, winter, and spring vagrant in S CAL, with records split about evenly between coastal points and desert localities. In 1979, a pair of Zone-tailed Hawks attempted to nest in S CAL. It is possible that this attempt foreshadows a range extension into the mountains of S CAL.

**CALIFORNIA** 14 records, graphed below. 8 of 9 fall and winter records are from S.D. and Orn. Counties; the additional record is 27-28 Aug 1972 at Big Pine, Inyo. The 3 spring records are: 9 May 1970 at Morongo Valley, S.Bn., 22 May 1976* at Ft. Piute, S.Bn., and 21-22 Apr 1978 at Morongo Valley, S.Bn. & Riv. In the summer of 1978 a single Zone-tailed Hawk was seen in the Santa Rosa Mnts., Riv., and during Jul-Aug 1979 a pair attempted to nest at this location. This breeding attempt was thought to be unsuccessful.

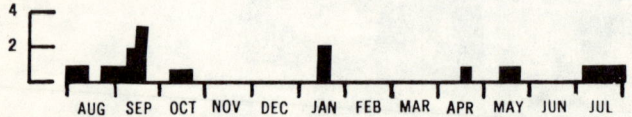

## ZONE-TAILED HAWK

11 Jul 1979 in the Santa Rosa Mtns., Riv., CAL. *Lawrence Sansone*.

# EURASIAN KESTREL           Plate 10

*Falco tinnunculus*

Breeds Eurasia, Africa. Northern populations winter to the south.

The Eurasian Kestrel has occurred only in the outer Aleutian Is., ALASKA. Both Sep 1978 records were suspected of being blown there by a storm originating over the Sea of Japan.

**ALASKA** Two records: 5-9 Sep 1978 on Shemya I., and another there in Sep 1978, details of which have yet to be published.

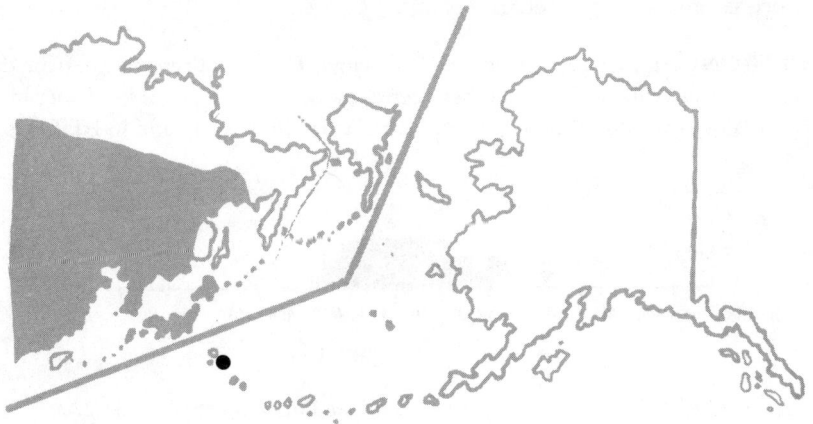

# EURASIAN KESTREL

**I.D.** The Eurasian Kestrel vaguely resembles the American Kestrel *F. sparverius*, but is distinctly larger and proportionately longer-tailed. The male Eurasian Kestrel differs considerably from the American Kestrel, as the former shows a gray head and tail, and chestnut upperwing coverts (gray in American Kestrels). The underparts of the male Eurasian Kestrel are a richer chestnut (less orange) and more heavily spotted than the American bird. Females are more similar, sharing chestnut backs and tails that are heavily barred, but Eurasian Kestrel has only a single vertical bar on the face (below the eye) while American Kestrel has a second vertical bar below the ear and shows a dark spot in the center of a pale area behind the ear. Female and immature Eurasian Kestrels are heavily streaked with dark on the underparts (American Kestrels are less streaked below and in a warmer brown tone) and show a broad dark subterminal bar on the tail. Both sexes of American Kestrel show a chestnut spot on a gray crown; Eurasian Kestrel lacks this feature.

# GYRFALCON

*Flaco rusticolus*

Breeds N North America, N Eurasia. Winters south to N U.S., C Europe, Japan. Occurrence in the southern parts of its winter range is irregular.

The Gyrfalcon on the West Coast is a breeding species in ALASKA, but occurs south of there during the winter (mostly Oct-Mar) with some regularity to south coastal B.C. and NW WASH. It is a Rarity in ORE and there is only a single record from CAL.

**OREGON** At least 10 records, graphed below. The recent reports are from the coast or the Willamette Valley between Nov-Mar, but there are old specimen records of birds along the Columbia R. near Sauvie I., Col., and in NE ORE.

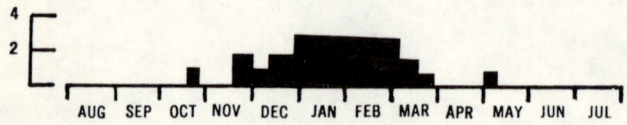

**CALIFORNIA** One record: 23 Oct 1948† at Tule Lake, Sis. (C 51:233).

# GYRFALCON

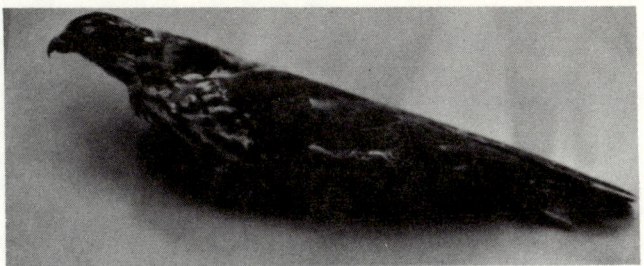

23 Oct 1948 at Tule Lake, Sis., CAL. 1st record. Museum of Vertebrate Zoology, U.C. Berkeley. *Don Roberson.*

I.D.   The Gyrfalcon is found in the field guides' "gray phase" plumage on the West Coast. The largest falcon, it has rather chunky proportions, with relatively short broad wings and resembles more in shape the Prairie Falcon *F. mexicanus* than the Peregrine Falcon *F. peregrinus*. Lacking the Prairie Falcon's black axillaries and pale brown tones, it is more likely to be confused with the Peregrine Falcon. The Gyrfalcon is larger and heavier, with broader, more rounded wings, and lacks the Peregrine's very dark upperparts and pronounced face pattern. Immatures may show a clear malar stripe merging into dark ear coverts, but not the Peregrine's strong pattern. Unlike the broadly spaced, thin pale bands on the tail of the Peregrine Falcon, the Gyrfalcon has numerous pale bands (10-12) and the backs of some immatures are also banded. At rest, the wingtips of the Gyrfalcon do not reach the end of the tail.

# COMMON CRANE

Plate 1

*Grus grus*

Breeds N Eurasia. Winters N India, China.

The Common Crane has been recorded only once on the West Coast, in interior ALASKA, but there are several records from central North America, presumably of individuals that joined flocks of Sandhill Cranes *G. canadensis* in NE Asia and passed through Alaska on their journey south to the Great Plains. The record for ALASKA is during the spring, following a winter that brought two reports of the Common Crane in Alberta (Dec 1957 & Mar 1958). Another Common Crane (perhaps the same individual returning) was found in Alberta in Sep 1958 and yet another occurred in Nebraska in Mar 1974. These records suggest that the Common Crane may occassionally follow flocks of Sandhill Cranes wintering in North America and might be looked for in ALASKA in spring and fall and farther south on the West Coast in winter.

**ALASKA** One record: 24 Apr-10 May 1958 near Fairbanks (A 75:465).

I.D. The Common Crane is about the size and shape of the Sandhill Crane, but adults show a different head pattern: black neck, broad white stripe from eye to hindneck, and a red bare crown limited to a small area on the back of the crown. Immatures lack the head markings, but all Common Cranes have black primaries and secondaries; all Sandhill Cranes have back restricted to the tips of the primaries and show gray secondaries.

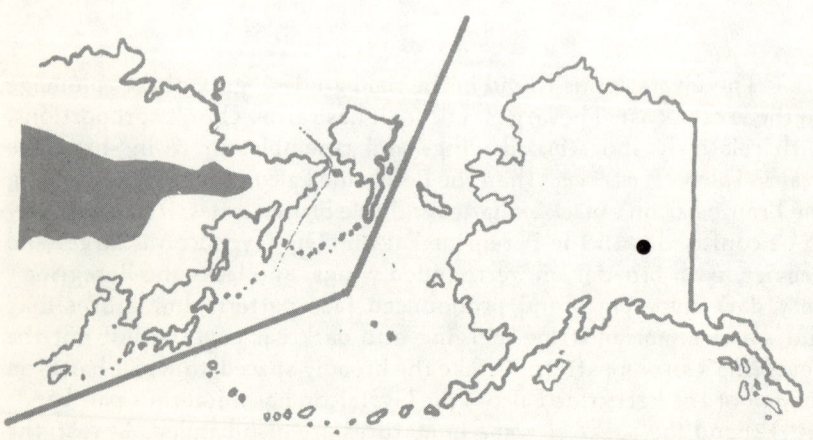

# YELLOW RAIL

*Coturniceps noveboracensis*

Breeds N-C North America. Winters SE U.S.

The Yellow Rail formerly was a breeding species along the eastern edge of the Sierras in CAL and a substantial population wintered along the coast and in the Central Valley of CAL, and perhaps north along the coasts or inland valleys of ORE and WASH. Today it is a Rarity in all areas, the breeding population having been extirpated by 1940 and the wintering population suffering similar declines. Land-clearing and cattle grazing are most responsible for its demise as a breeder (Remsen, 1977) and the disappearance of extensive coastal marshes and interior wet short-grass meadows have limited its potential wintering habitat. Recent reports are from remnants of appropriate habitat from Oct-Apr.

**WASHINGTON** Two records: 16 Nov 1935† (M 19:16) at the Skagit R. mouth, Skg. (perhaps an indication of a formerly more substantial wintering population in the Puget Sound area) and 30 Apr 1969 at Herman Slough, near Othello, Adm. (M 55:25).

**OREGON** One record: 1 Feb 1900† at Scio, Linn.

**CALIFORNIA** Formerly bred east of the Sierras at Bridgeport and Long Valley, Mono and probably Quincy, Plu., these records probably representing only a portion of the breeding population. At least 35 records from 16 localities before 1920 represent a sizeable wintering population on the coast from Humboldt Bay to Newport Bay, Orn., with concentrations around San Francisco Bay, and in the Central Valley. Specimens were taken in these areas from 1884-1914 and fall between Oct-Jan.

Three recent records: 13 Feb 1961 at Tomales Bay, Mrn., 2 Oct-1 Nov 1970 at Pacific Grove, Mnt., and 15-19 Apr 1978 at San Jacinto Lake, Riv.

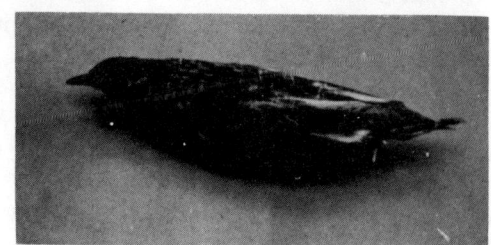

27 Dec 1903 at Locks Swamp, Santa Cruz, CAL. Museum of Vertebrate Zoology, U.C. Berkeley #91349. *Don Roberson.*

# YELLOW RAIL

I.D. The Yellow Rail is a small, chunky rail with a yellow chicken-like bill. It appears much darker in the field than the standard guides indicate, especially on the back, where each feather is a dark brown broadly edged in buff and tipped with a white crossband. Though the head and neck are a rich buffy-yellow, the wings and back look quite dark and when flushed the appearance is of a dark bird. Under these circumstances the best mark is the white tips to the secondaries, creating a long white patch on the inner trailing edge of the wing in flight.

Immature Sora *Porzana carolina*, which can be quite buffy, have been misidentified as Yellow Rail. The Sora is a larger bird, lacks the white crossbanding to the back feathers, lacks the rich golden-buff feather edgings, has greenish (not flesh-colored) legs, shows no white in the wing (though light-colored coverts, but not secondaries, may be seen in flight), is less secretive, and occurs in reedy marshes as well as short-grass marshes (Yellow Rail prefers the latter).

# AMERICAN PURPLE GALLINULE

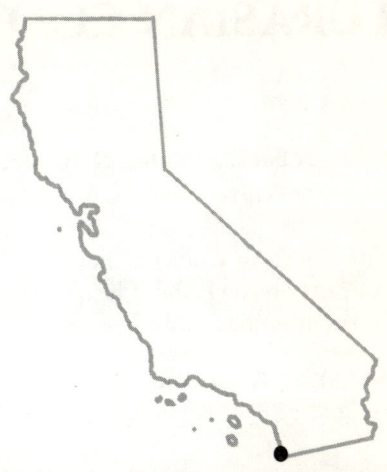

*Porphyrula martica*

Breeds SE U.S., Mexico to N South America. Northern populations winter to the south.

The American Purple Gallinule is represented on the West Coast by a single specimen of an immature picked up injured in coastal S CAL. The nearest breeding areas are in W Mexico, but there are a number of fall and winter records from Arizona and two records, one spring and one fall, near Las Vegas, Nevada. Additional CAL records might be expected from the Colorado River or the SE CAL deserts.

**CALIFORNIA** One record: 1 Oct 1961† on Pt. Loma, S.D. (A 79:483).

# COMMON GALLINULE

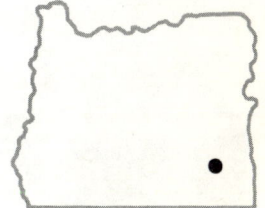

*Gallinula chloropus*

Breeds warmer areas nearly worldwide. Some populations winter to the south.

The Common Gallinule on the West Coast is a local resident from C CAL south, especially in the Central & Imperial Valleys. There is some winter movement and strays occasionally occur. One, presumably a spring overshoot, wandered to SE ORE.

**OREGON** One record: 20 May 1972 at Malheur NWR, Har. This record has not been reviewed by the ORE Records Committee.

# EURASIAN COOT

Plate 5

*Fulica atra*

Breeds N Eurasia. Winters N Africa, S Eurasia, Philippines. Resident populations in Indonesia, New Guinea, Australia.

The Eurasian Coot has been recorded on the West Coast only as a fall vagrant on the Pribilof Is., ALASKA. The specimen taken was identified as the nominate race *F. a. atra*.

**ALASKA** One record: 31 Oct-5 Nov 1962† on St. Paul I. (A 83:131). In addition, an unidentified coot on 24 Oct 1962 on St. George I. was probably this species.

I.D. The Eurasian Coot resembles the American Coot *F. americana* but may be identified by its all-white bill, including the shield on the forecrown (American Coots have a red shield), bill shape (see Plate 5) and black undertail coverts (feathers may be lightly fringed with white). American Coot has white undertail coverts divided by a black central stripe.

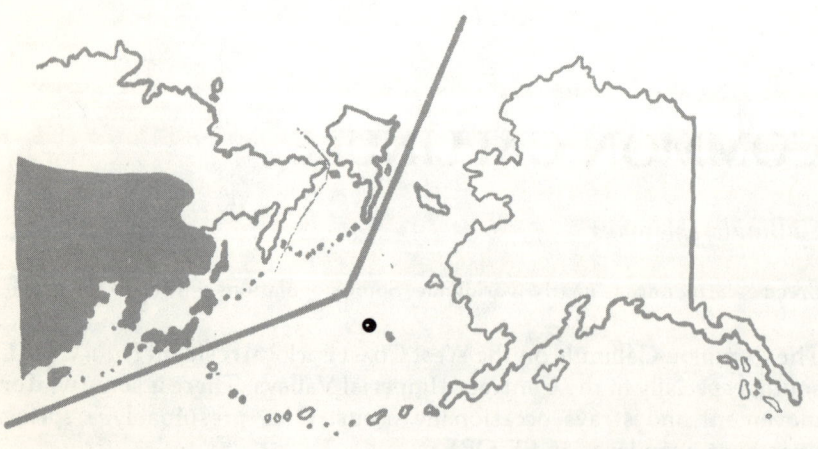

# AMERICAN OYSTERCATCHER

*Haematopus palliatus*

Breeds Baja, Mexico & E U.S. to S South America. Mostly resident.

The American Oystercatcher has occurred along the coast of CAL north to Monterey Bay, on the Channel Is., and at the Salton Sea. Coastal records span dates from Oct-Apr, with spring records perhaps involving migrant overshoots from Baja. Records from the Salton Sea are in Aug and may refer to birds wandering north from the Gulf of California as part of post-breeding dispersal. Records from the Channel Is. involve individuals that have established permanent residency. The species was suspected of breeding on Santa Barbara I. in 1863, 1 or 2 birds have been resident on Santa Cruz I. since at least 1966, and one has been found year-round on Anacapa I. from 24 May 1964 through at least May 1979*. This latter record would seem to involve a single long-lived individual coexisting with resident Black Oystercatchers *H. bachmani*. At times this bird has seemed to be paired with a Black Oystercatcher, but no evidence of interbreeding has been obtained. A probable American X Black Oystercatcher has been seen on Santa Cruz I.

**CALIFORNIA** 9 records. Resident or probably resident records from the Channel Is. are discussed above. Additional records are: 16 May 1862† at Pt. Loma. S.D., 12 Feb 1910 at White's Landing, Santa Catalina I., 3 Apr 1964 at Pt. Lobos, Mnt., 25 Oct 1964-20 Feb 1965 at Avila Beach, S.L.O., 14-19 Aug 1977 (3*) at Salton City, Imp. and rediscovered 20-30 Aug 1977 at Salt Creek, Riv., 20-21 Apr 1978 at Pt. Loma, and 23 Dec 1978-14 Jan 1979 at Pt. Fermin, L.A.

Apr 1975 on Anacapa I., CAL. 5th record. *Dave Rudholm.*

# AMERICAN OYSTERCATCHER

24 Aug 1977 at Corvina Beach, Salton Sea, Riv., CAL. 7th record. *Jeri Langham.*

# BLACK-NECKED STILT

*Himantopus mexicanus*

Breeds W U.S. to N South America. Some northern populations winter to the south.

The Black-necked Stilt is a common species throughout much of CAL and is a summer resident in S ORE. It was formerly very rare north of S ORE, but during an invasion in spring 1977, apparently in response to draught conditions, numbers were recorded into E-C WASH. Successful nesting was recorded at two sites and several other breeding attempts were made. Birds have now returned to these nesting sites, in Grant & Adams Cos., for 3 consecutive years and appear to be established. There are only 3 records for B.C., all spring overshoots, but surprisingly all were prior to 1977.

**BRITISH COLUMBIA** Three records: 13-14 May 1971 at Sea I., Vancouver (CFN 86:296), 4-7 May 1974 at Sea I., and 17 May 1974 at Hansen's Lagoon, V.I.

# BLACK-NECKED STILT

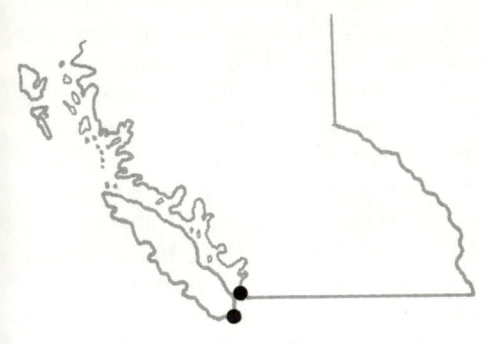

5 May 1974 at Sea I., Vancouver, B.C. 2nd record. *G. Allen Poynter*.

# LITTLE RINGED PLOVER    Plate 3

*Charadrius dubius*

Breeds N Eurasia. Winters S Eurasia, Africa, New Guinea.

The Little Ringed Plover is represented on the West Coast by a single record of a probable spring overshoot on the outer Aleutians Is.

**ALASKA**   One record: 15-16 Jun 1974† on Buldir I. (C 80:310).

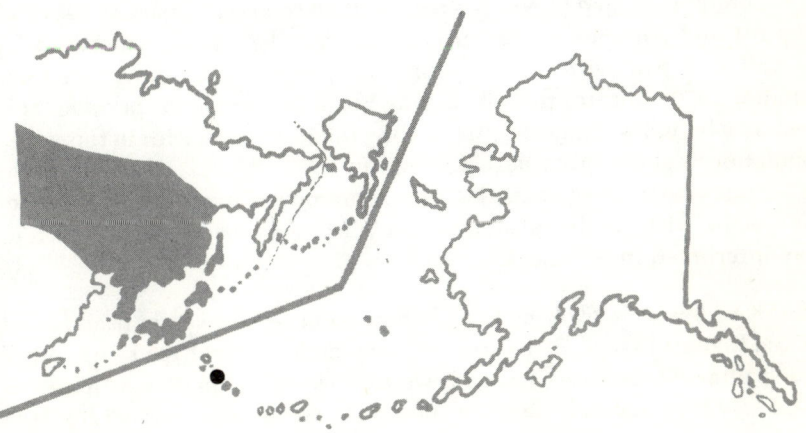

# LITTLE RINGED PLOVER

I.D.   The Little Ringed Plover most resembles the Semipalmated Plover *C. semipalmatus* and the Common Ringed Plover *C. hiaticula*, though it is smaller with proportionately longer legs and thus looks daintier than the more chunky birds of the Semipalmated-Ringed Plover complex. In breeding plumage, the Little Ringed Plover differs from this complex by 1) showing no wingstripe, 2) showing less of a tail pattern in flight, 3) having dull-colored legs (flesh-colored, yellowish, or greenish) rather than bright orange legs, 4) having an essentially all-dark bill with only some yellow at the base, rather than a black-tipped, orange bill, 5) usually showing a white band above the black patch on the forecrown, and 6) having a distinctly yellow eye-ring. These marks are of less value on winter-plumaged birds, when soft part colors are faded, and in juveniles, which have black areas on the head and breast replaced with brown and do not show a white band over the forecrown. In these plumages, the lack of wingstripe, the shape of the bill, and the call are useful.

In any plumage, the bill of the Little Ringed Plover is thinner and more pointed than the stubbier, almost bulbous-tipped bills of Semipalmated and Ringed Plover. The call—a short, descending "piu"—is unlike the upward whistled "tu-weep" call of the Semipalmated Plover.

# COMMON RINGED PLOVER

*Charadrius hiaticula*

Breeds NE Canada, N Eurasia. Winters S Eurasia, Africa, Australia.

The Common Ringed Plover has occurred on the West Coast as a spring migrant and summer visitor on the Aleutian Is. and St. Lawrence I., ALASKA. A pair with downy young discovered on St. Lawrence I. in summer 1970 indicates that the Bering Strait may be on the periphery of the bird's breeding range. Future nesting might be looked for in this area; copulation was observed here during Jun 1979.

Some authorities consider the Common Ringed Plover to be conspecific with the Semipalmated Plover *C. semipalmatus*, with which it may interbreed in NE Canada.

**ALASKA**   8 records involving 15 birds. Successful nesting was confirmed 16 Jul 1970 at Koozata Lagoon, St. Lawrence I., with the discovery of a pair with downy young. Other St. Lawrence I. records were at Gambell: 8 Jun 1976, 10 Jun 1976, 28-29 May 1978, and early Jun 1979. Aleutian Is. records are: 15 May 1973 (3) on Amchitka I. and 22 Aug 1975 (2†) on Adak I.

# COMMON RINGED PLOVER

I.D. The Common Ringed Plover is very similar to the Semipalmated Plover, especially the small, dark Ringed Plover that reach North America. While the Semipalmated Plover possesses webbing between both the outer and middle toe and the inner and middle toe, the Ringed Plover lacks webbing between inner and middle toe and has only reduced webbing between the outer and middle toe. This mark is of little value except at close range, but some Ringed Plovers may be identified by the combination of a wider breastband and more extensive white to the collar, forehead, and post-ocular patch.

In breeding plumage, the breastband of the Ringed Plover tends to be wider than those of the Semipalmated Plover and sometimes extends up toward the throat like an inverted "V", a feature lacking in Semipalmated Plover. The breastband is also wider and tends to narrow less in the center in winter-plumaged and juvenile Ringed Plovers when compared to similarly plumaged Semipalmated Plovers, but there is overlap and probably only extreme individuals can be identified on this basis. Ringed Plovers usually show a broad white collar and large white patch above and behind the eye, features that are reduced in many Semipalmated Plovers. Ringed Plovers also tend to have more white on the forehead and a slightly longer, wider white wingbar. While there is overlap in any single character, a bird combining a wide breastband, wide white collar, and large white post-ocular and forehead patches should be a Ringed Plover. A careful check of the toes may confirm this.

The call of the Ringed Plover is a flat, mellow "poo-eep", recognizably different from the more whistled "tu-wep" call of the Semipalmated Plover with experience.

Typical Semipalmated Plover (left) and Common Ringed Plover (right) in breeding plumage.

# COMMON RINGED PLOVER

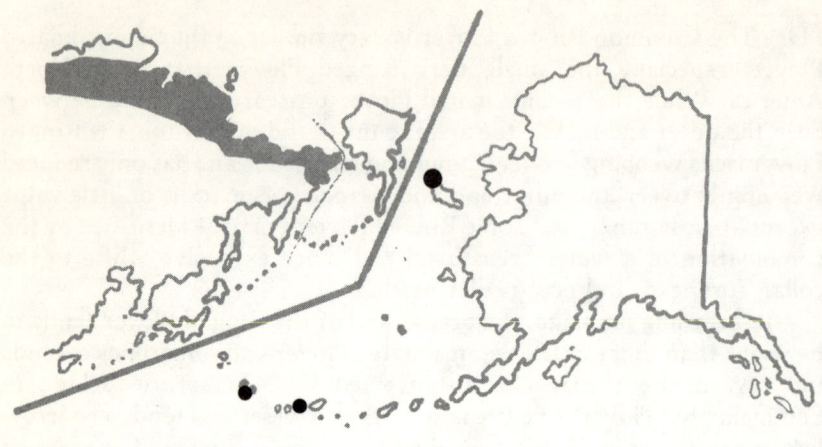

# WILSON'S PLOVER

*Charadrius wilsonia*

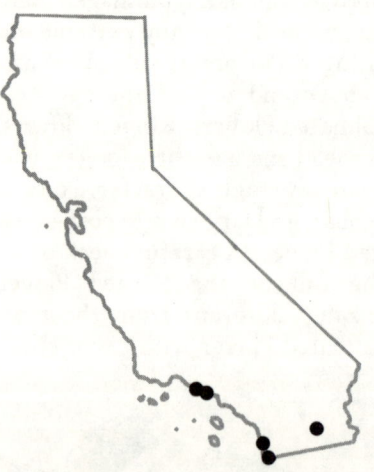

Breeds coastal shores Baja, Mexico & E U.S. to N South America. Some northern populations winter to the south.

The Wilson's Plover has occurred on the West Coast as a spring and summer vagrant on the beaches of S CAL and once nested at the Salton Sea.

**CALIFORNIA**  Five records, 4 from the coast: 29 Jun 1894† at Pacific Beach, S.D., 11 May 1918† at Imperial Beach, S.D., 27-29 Jun 1977* at the Santa Clara R. mouth, Ven., and 21 Apr-24 Jun 1979 at Pt. Mugu, Ven. The nesting record is of a pair with eggs 20 May 1948 near Mullet I., south end of Salton Sea, Imp.

# WILSON'S PLOVER

28 Jun 1977 at Santa Clara R. mouth, Ven., CAL (note how different positions may affect whether a breastband is apparent). 4th record. *Brad Schram*.

I.D. The race of Wilson's Plover illustrated in the standard guides is not the W Mexican race *C. w. beldingi* which is apparently responsible for all West Coast records. *C. w. beldingi* does not typically have a breastband as wide as those pictured in the standard guides nor show the broad continuous white band from forehead through supercilium. Some breeding-plumaged males may have a rufous tone to the nape, while some breeding-plumaged females may show a rather rufous breastband. The best marks remain a disproportionately long and heavy bill and long pale legs, giving the bird a distinctive shape, somewhat like putting the bill and legs of a Killdeer *C. vociferus* on the much smaller Semipalmated Plover *C. semipalmatus*, though the Wilson's bill is distinctly heavier (but not longer) than that of a Killdeer.

# PIPING PLOVER

*Charadrius melodus*

Breeds N-C & E North America. Winters SE U.S.

The Piping Plover has occurred twice on the West Coast. Both records are of birds that wintered on S CAL beaches; one returned for four successive winters.

**CALIFORNIA** Two records: 14-18 Apr 1971 at Goleta, S.Bb., and returning 16 Dec 1971-22 Apr 1972, 16 Dec 1972-21 Jan 1973, and 16 Dec 1973-3 Mar 1974\*; and 18 Nov 1973-16 Apr 1974\* at Malibu, L.A.

# PIPING PLOVER

18 Dec 1971 at Goleta, S.Bb., CAL. 1st record. *Herbert Clarke.*

Apr 1972 at Goleta, S.Bb., CAL (same bird as above, now in breeding plumage). *Brad Schram.*

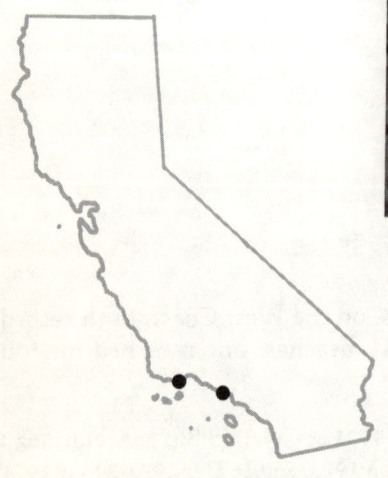

# PIPING PLOVER

**I.D.** The Piping Plover is easily recognized in breeding plumage by its very pale back and crown, its single black breastband (not always complete), a black bar over the crown from eye to eye, whitish uppertail coverts (not divided by a dark center), orange legs, and short, black-tipped yellow bill. In winter or juvenile plumage, the Piping Plover more closely resembles the Snowy Plover *C. alexandrinus*. The Piping Plover has paler upperparts, paler ear coverts, orange legs, paler center to uppertail coverts (not a dark center) and a distinctly shorter, blunter bill (see photo). The call—a plaintive descending "peep-lo"—is distinguishable from the drawn-out upslurred "chew-weep" of the Snowy Plover.

# SNOWY PLOVER

*Charadrius alexandrinus*

Breeds locally worldwide. Some northern and inland populations winter to the south.

The Snowy Plover is a local breeder along the West Coast north to SW WASH and in appropriate Great Basin and desert habitat in SE ORE and CAL. Coastal populations in CAL and ORE are resident, but WASH breeders and Great Basin birds are migratory. Records north of WASH would seem to be spring overshoots moving north along the coast.

**BRITISH COLUMBIA** Two records: 29 Apr-13 May 1972 at Tofino, V.I., and 14 Jun 1976 at Iona I., Vancouver.

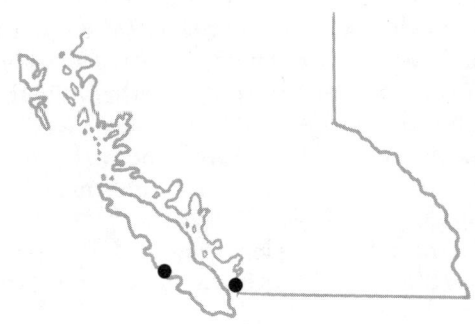

# MONGOLIAN PLOVER

Plate 3
Plate 11

*Charadrius mongolus*

Breeds E Asia. Winters E Africa, S Asia, Australia.

The Mongolian Plover is a rare but regular spring migrant on the outer Aleutians and the Bering Sea islands and coast and has nested or suspected to have nested on at least four occasions in W ALASKA. It is much rarer as a fall migrant in these areas, but the records south of ALASKA on the West Coast are during fall migration. Most interesting is a spring record from Louisiana (AB 31:140), which suggests that the Mongolian Plover has successfully wintered somewhere in the New World.

**ALASKA** Rare but regular spring migrant (11 May-9 Jun) on the outer Aleutian Is. and St. Lawrence I. and there are a number of spring records from the Pribilof Is. and the coast of W Alaska. Nesting has been confirmed only once (10 Jun 1933 at Goodnews Bay; C 36:89), but has been suspected (pairs in summer) on at least 3 other occasions on the Seward Pen. or in the Brooks Range. There are only about 10 fall records for Alaska, including one from Barrow [16 Aug 1971 (2)]. The south-easternmost record was in spring: 10 Jun 1959† at Augustine I., Cook Inlet.

**OREGON** Two records: 11-17 Sep 1977* at Bayocean spit, Tillamook Bay, and 6-21 Oct 1979* at the south jetty, Columbia R., Clt.

I.D.   The Mongolian Plover is a small plover, but distinctly larger and longer-billed than Semipalmated Plover *C. semipalmatus*. Breeding-plumaged adults are easily recognized by the broad chestnut breastband, the contrasting white throat (usually narrowly bordered below by a black line), and a chestnut nape and crown. A blackish "mask" and white forehead (in NE Asia races) complete the face pattern. Adults in winter lose the chestnut and black. They are grayish-brown above, and have broad grayish patches on the sides of the breast (often joined in the center). This breastband continues to contrast with a sharply defined white throat and remains an excellent mark. Above the white throat, the head is brown, with a thin white supercilium and a small white patch on the forehead. Juveniles are similar, but show some rusty edges to the coverts and tertials and may have some rusty intermixed with the breastband.

   The bill is black year-round and the legs grayish. The call is said to be a short "pip'ip" or a short, dry "drrit" (King & Dickenson, 1975).

# MONGOLIAN PLOVER

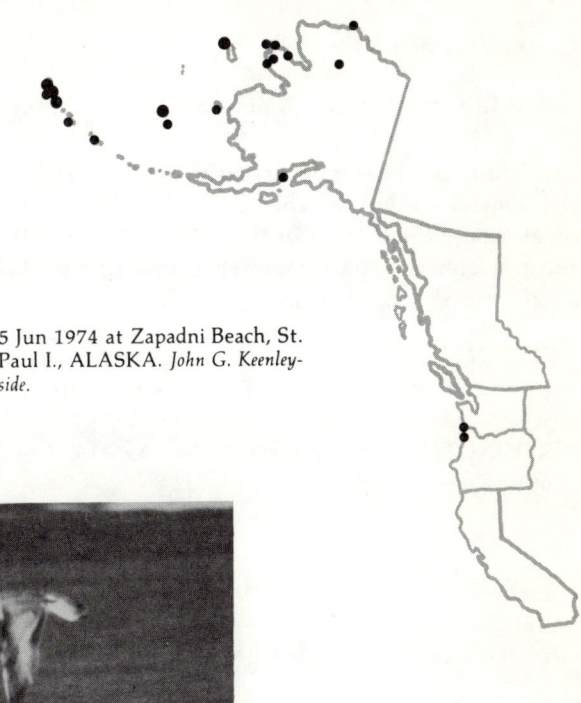

5 Jun 1974 at Zapadni Beach, St. Paul I., ALASKA. *John G. Keenleyside.*

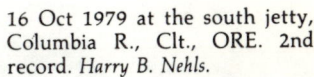

11 Sep 1977 at Tillamook Bay, Til., ORE (see also Plate 11). 1st record. *Jeff Gilligan.*

16 Oct 1979 at the south jetty, Columbia R., Clt., ORE. 2nd record. *Harry B. Nehls.*

# MOUNTAIN PLOVER

*Charadrius montanus*

Breeds C North America. Winters SW U.S. to C Mexico.

The Mountain Plover occurs on the West Coast as a local winterer along the western edge of the Central Valley, the Imperial Valley, and occasionally the S coast of CAL. North of CAL there are two fall (Nov) records from the coast, a winter record from the Willamette Valley, and a single spring record from the interior.

**OREGON** Two records: 2 Jan-10 Mar 1967 (2 - 1† taken 3 Jan) at Corvallis, Ben., and 19-26 Nov 1977* at Tillamook Bay jetty.

**WASHINGTON** Two records: 28 Nov 1964† at North Cove, Pac., and 6 May 1968 at Turnbull NWR, Spk.

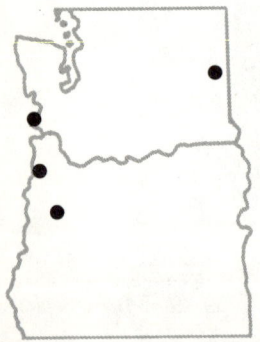

19 Nov 1977 at Tillamook Bay, Til., ORE. 2nd record. *Jeff Gilligan.*

# DOTTEREL

Plate 3

*Eudromias morinellus*

Breeds N Eurasia, W Alaska. Winters N Africa, SW Asia.

The Dotterel is apparently a local breeder on St. Lawrence I., the Seward Pen., and the NW coast of ALASKA, though no nest has been found to date (breeding evidence includes eggs and developed ova in collected females and distraction behavior). All spring and summer records are from the Bering Strait area and NW ALASKA, as far N as Pt. Barrow. There is a single fall record from the outer Aleutians and two fall records for the West Coast south of ALASKA.

**WASHINGTON** Two records: 3 Sep 1934† at Westport, G.H. (C 37:82), and 8 Sep 1979 at Ocean Shores, G.H.

**CALIFORNIA** One record: 12-20 Sep 1974* on SE Farallon I. (WB 10:92).

I.D. The Dotterel is a medium-sized plover possessing in all plumages a bold white supercilium and a white crescent across the lower breast. Adults in breeding and winter plumage are portrayed in Robbins (1966), though they often show more white or cinnamon edges to the back and wing covert feathers than is illustrated there. Juvenile Dotterels (Plate 3) have even more broadly-edged back and wing covert feathers, giving the upperparts a spangled appearance; a buffy-orange lower breast crossed by the white crescent; a pale gray upper breast that is fainted streaked; and lack a strong facial pattern except for the bold supercillium.

The flight call is a soft "pip-pip" or "pip-pip-pip", or a more rapid "pipipip".

8 Sep 1979 at Ocean Shores, G.H., WASH. 2nd record. *Dennis Paulson.*

# DOTTEREL

16 Sep 1974 on SE Farrallon I., CAL. 1st record. *Dave DeSante.*

# BLACK-TAILED GODWIT    Plate 5

*Limosa limosa*

Breeds N Eurasia. Winters S Eurasia, C Africa, Australia.

The Black-tailed Godwit has occurred on the West Coast only during spring migration on the westernmost islands of ALASKA. It may be considered regular on the outermost Aleutians in very small numbers in late May.

**ALASKA**   At least 24 records, graphed below. Nearly all are from the W Aleutians, including multiple records from Shemya I. (7), Attu I. (6), and Buldir I. (3). 15 of these records occurred during spring 1976; there had been only 2 previous ALASKA records. Away from the Aleutians, there are records on St. Paul I. [21 Jun 1976 & 19 May 1978 (2)], Gambell, St. Lawrence I. (25 May 1976†), and Little Diomede I. (22 May 1907†).

# BLACK-TAILED GODWIT

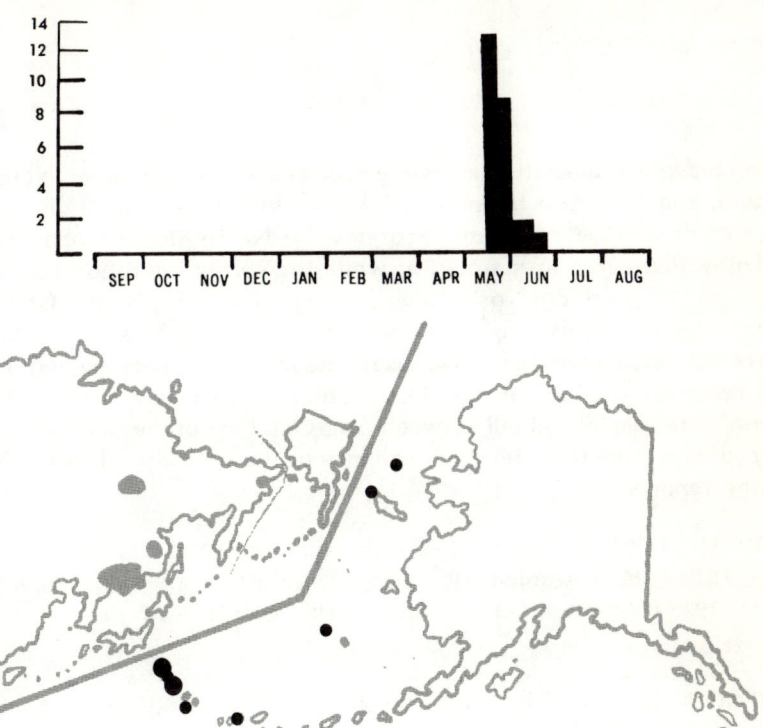

I.D. The Black-tailed Godwit is a godwit with a comparatively heavy, straight bill. It most resembles the Hudsonian Godwit *L. haemastica*, from which it can be distinguished in flight, in any plumage, by the Black-tailed's white underwings (black in Hudsonian) and broader, but shorter, white wingbar. In breeding plumage, the Black-tailed has ruddy-orange underparts with a white belly and undertail coverts; the breeding-plumaged Hudsonian is a darker, richer, rusty color, with this color extends onto the belly and undertail coverts and the Hudsonian has a distinctly streaked neck and throat, lacking in the Black-tailed. Juvenile and winter-plumaged Hudsonian Godwits tend to be washed with tawny on the underparts and the edges of the tertials; comparably-plumaged Black-taileds look whiter below, with tawny wash restricted to the breast, and tend to have whitish tertial edges. Hudsonian Godwit has a slightly more upturned bill and in winter plumage is darker-capped than Black-tailed Godwit, but any Black-tailed/Hudsonian Godwit out of breeding-plumage on the West Coast should have its underwing covert color carefully noted.

# HUDSONIAN GODWIT

*Limosa haemastica*

Breeds in disjointed areas of W Alaska, N Canada. Winters S South America.

The Hudsonian Godwit is a nesting species around Cook Inlet, Norton Sound, and Kotzebue Sound in ALASKA. In fall, the migration route appears to take these birds to the coasts of NE North America for a trans-Atlantic flight to South America, while the spring migration route is through the interior of North America. In spring, the Hudsonian Godwit is considered a regular migrant in extreme NE B.C. (Peace R. district) and there is a nesting record from Chilkat Pass in N B.C. There are about 10 fall records from coastal SW B.C. Farther south it is a Rarity. Most records are coastal and fall between Aug-Oct. One of the two mid-May records was from the interior, which may be the area to produce further spring reports.

**WASHINGTON**  Five records, four in the fall: 12 Sep 1959† at O'Sullivan Dam, Grn., 15 Sep 1961 at Reardon, Lnc., 24 Sep 1966 (3) at Ocean Shores, G.H., and 6-24 Sep 1975 at Aberdeen, G.H. The single spring record is 14 May 1977 at Ocean Shores.

**OREGON**  One record: 10-19 Sep 1978* at the Coquille R. mouth, Bandon, Coos.

**CALIFORNIA**  Three records: 9-10 Aug 1973* at Arcata, Hmb., 9 May 1975 at Daggett, S.Bn., and 9-11 May 1980 at Edwards marsh, Antelope Valley, L.A.

4 Aug 1970 at Iona I., Vancouver, B.C. *R. Wayne Campbell.*

# HUDSONIAN GODWIT

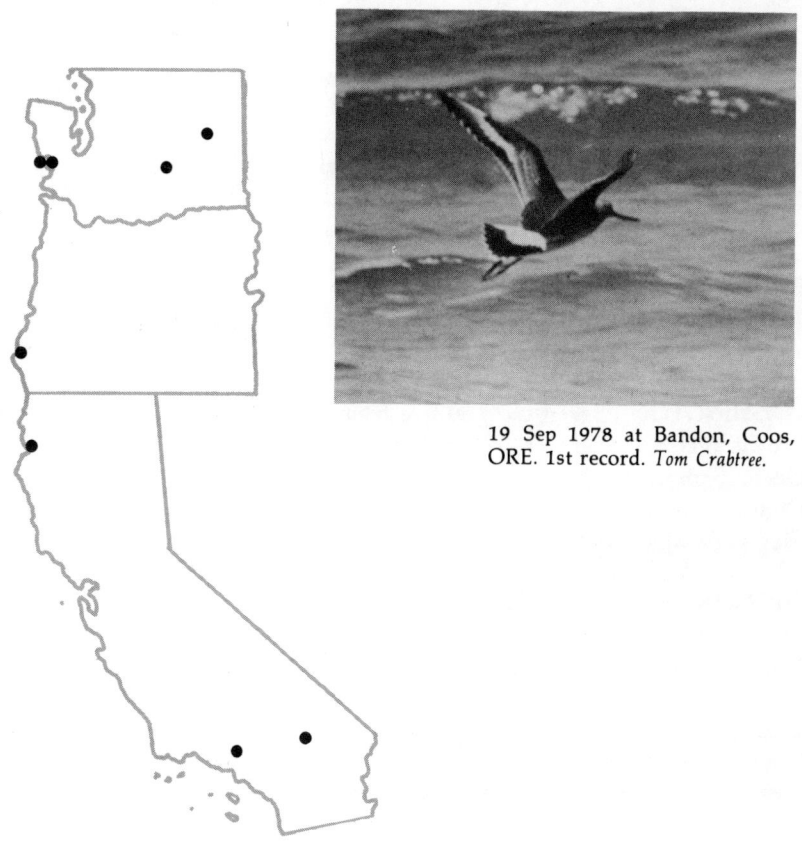

19 Sep 1978 at Bandon, Coos, ORE. 1st record. *Tom Crabtree.*

I.D. The standard guides discuss the identification of the Hudsonian Godwit in comparison to other American godwits. It is similar to the Black-tailed Godwit *L. limosa*, but can be separated in any plumage by the Hudsonian's black axillaries and underwings (whitish in Black-tailed). See the discussion under Black-tailed Godwit for other details.

# BAR-TAILED GODWIT

*Limosa lapponica*

Breeds N Eurasia, W & N Alaska. Winters S Eurasia, W Africa, Australia, S Pacific.

The Bar-tailed Godwit nests in ALASKA, but winters in the Old World, so it is a Rarity on the West Coast south of ALASKA. Most records are from the fall and stretch from mid-Jul to late Nov. There are three spring records, including a flock of six, and a single bird wintered in Los Angeles in 1976. All acceptable records to date have been coastal.

**BRITISH COLUMBIA**   Four records: 31 Oct 1931† at Colebrook (C 39:176), 9-10 Sep 1972 at Saanich Inlet, V.I., 16-30 Sep 1972 at Reifel refuge, Vancouver, and 29-30 Aug 1973 at Masset, Q.C.I.

**WASHINGTON**   Seven records, five from fall migration: 4 Sep 1973 at Pt. Brown, G.H., 25 Sep-1 Oct 1977 at Ocean Shores, G.H., another on 1 Oct 1977 at Ocean Shores, 22-28 Oct 1978 at Dungeness, Clm., and 1-12 Aug 1979 at Dungeness. The spring records are: 8 Jun 1974 (6) at Leadbetter Pt., Pac., and 13 May 1979 (2) at Tokeland, Pac.

**OREGON**   Five records, four from the fall: 23-26 Sep 1976 at Bandon, Coos, 11-15 Sep 1977* at Bandon, 6-8 Aug 1978 at Alsea Bay, Lnc., and 14-22 Sep 1979 at Yaquina Bay, Lnc. The single spring record is 28 May 1978 at Nehalem, Til.

**CALIFORNIA**   Four records, three from the fall: 11-17 Jul 1968* at Arcata, Hmb., 26 Oct-30 Nov 1973* at Bolinas, Mrn., and 17 Jul-4 Sep 1974* at Arcata. One winter record: 11 Feb-2 Mar 1976* at Playa del Rey, L.A.

4 Sep 1973 at Pt. Brown, G.H., WASH. 1st record. *Terence R. Wahl.*

# BAR-TAILED GODWIT

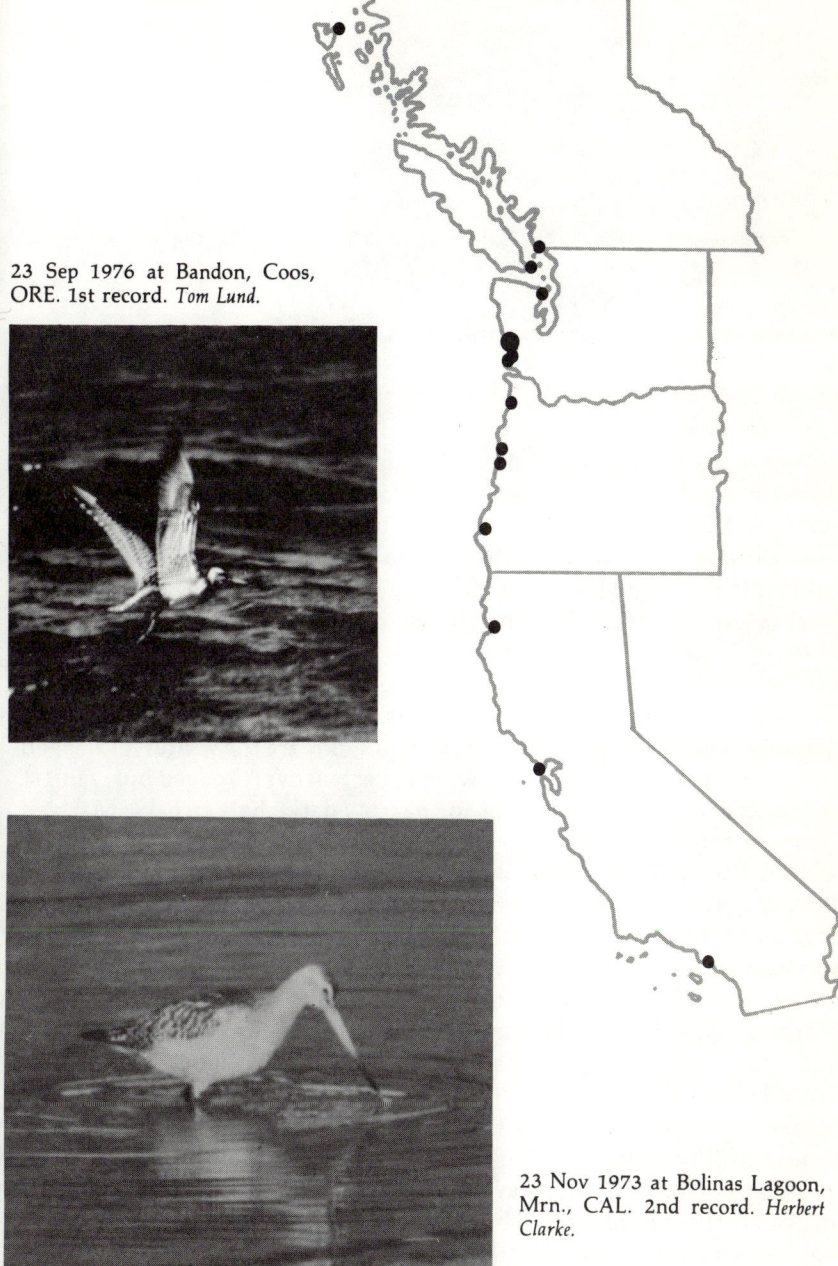

23 Sep 1976 at Bandon, Coos, ORE. 1st record. *Tom Lund.*

23 Nov 1973 at Bolinas Lagoon, Mrn., CAL. 2nd record. *Herbert Clarke.*

# BAR-TAILED GODWIT

8 Jun 1974 at Leadbetter Pt., Pac., WASH. 2nd record. *Harry B. Nehls.*

I.D. The Bar-tailed Godwit discussed in the standard guides is the European race; all West Coast records have apparently been of the Siberian-Alaska race, *L. l. baueri*, which does not show an unmarked white rump, and is much more likely to be confused with the Marbled Godwit *L. fedoa*. Both species show a barred rump and tail, though the Bar-tailed Godwit has a somewhat whiter background color to these areas, and this mark is less important than the guides suggest. The bill of the Bar-tailed Godwit, especially that of the female, is as long as the Marbled and similarly-shaped, making for a bird not too disimilar to the Marbled Godwit, especially on the ground. Birds in breeding plumage (Mar-Jun), with orangish underparts, are not difficult, nor are the winter-plumaged birds, with pale gray backs and wing coverts (coverts edged buffy in 1st winter birds), unmarked except for narrow dark shaft streaks. Marbled Godwits retain a speckled pattern to the upperparts throughout the winter. But juveniles (Jul-Nov), which account for most West Coast records, are more similar to the Marbled Godwit. Both have buffy edgings and tips to back and wing covert feathers and show similarly speckled upperparts. But while the Marbled Godwit is cinnamon-colored below, the Bar-tailed is whitish, looking quite pale from afar. Worn Marbled Godwits, especially in spring, can become quite whitish on the underparts, but retain cinnamon underwings (white in Bar-tailed). Juvenile Bar-tailed Godwits should be in winter plumage (without any speckling to the back) by the time a Marbled Godwit is worn enough to appear whitish below.

The Bar-tailed Godwit averages smaller than the Marbled Godwit and can further be identified by its bolder white supercillium and shorter legs, which extend only slightly beyond the tail in flight (the entire feet and lower tarsi extend beyond the tail in flight in Marbled Godwit).

# FAR EASTERN CURLEW  Plate 5

*Numenius madagascariensis*

Breeds NE Asia. Winters Philippines to Australia.

The Far Eastern Curlew has been recorded on the West Coast only during a spring migration in W ALASKA.

**ALASKA**  11 records, involving 14 individuals, graphed below. All records are during spring migration and probably refer to overshoots. There are 4 records for both Adak I. and Amchitka I.; singles were on St. Paul I., St. George I., and at Wales. Additionally, a curlew at St. Michael, Norton Sound on 19 Jun 1874, identified as a Long-billed Curlew *N. americanus*, was probably this species. Except for this probable report, all other records have been since 1961.

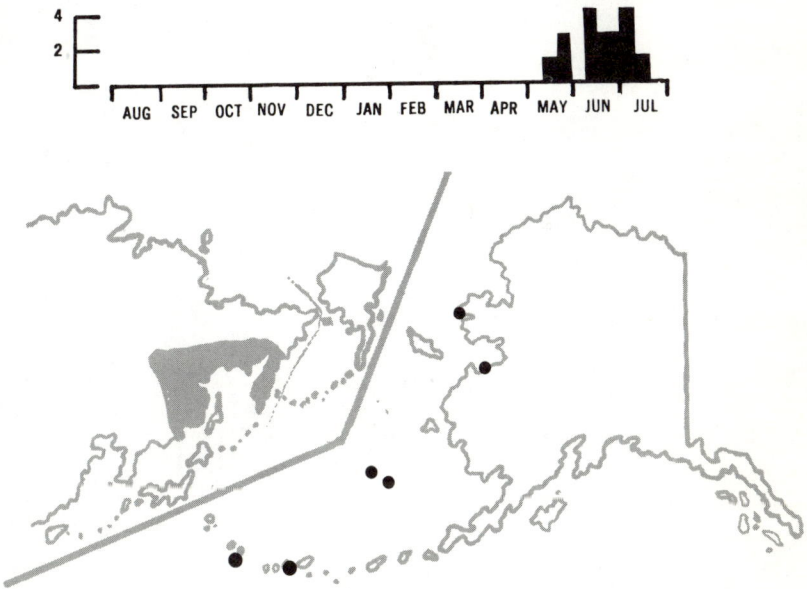

**I.D.**  The Far Eastern Curlew is the world's largest curlew and generally resembles the Long-billed Curlew, though it lacks the very cinnamon tones and possesses a comparatively shorter bill. Diagnostic are the heavily barred white underwings, rather than the Long-billed's cinnamon underwings. The underparts are also more heavily marked than those of the Long-billed Curlew. The Far Eastern Curlew may be separated from the possible vagrant Eurasian Curlew *N. arquata* by the lack of a white rump and lower back and the heavily barred underwings. The Eurasian Curlew has largely unmarked, white underwings.

# BRISTLE-THIGHED CURLEW

*Numenius tahitiensis*

Breeds W Alaska. Winters C & S Pacific.

The Bristle-thighed Curlew is a species with a small population, nesting only in W ALASKA, especially about the mouth of the Yukon R. The trans-Pacific migration route takes it due south from ALASKA, and it has strayed to elsewhere on the West Coast only once.

**BRITISH COLUMBIA** One record: 31 May 1969† at Grant Bay, V.I. (A 87:815).

# UPLAND SANDPIPER

*Bartramia longicauda*

Breeds locally N North America. Winters S South America.

The Upland Sandpiper is a local nester in E ALASKA and NE B.C., and there are small colonies in the Spokane Valley, WASH and in NE ORE. It is a Rarity in CAL, with records split about evenly between spring and fall.

**CALIFORNIA** Ten records, five fall and five spring. The fall records: 8 Aug 1896† at Tule Lake, Sis., 11 Sep 1952† at Needles Landing, Lake Havasu, S.Bn., 22-24 Aug 1968† on SE Farallon I., 10 Sep 1973† at Colton, S.Bn., and 9 Sep 1979 at Pt. Mugu, Ven. The spring records: 13 May 1959 at Furnace Creek, Inyo, 23 May 1969 on SE Farallon I., 23 May 1975 on Santa Barbara I., 15 May 1976* at Furnace Creek, and 28 May 1979 at Deep Springs, Inyo.

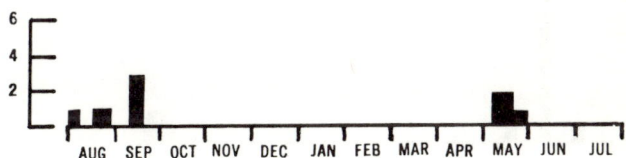

28 May 1979 at Deep Springs, Inyo, CAL (flying away; only photo from the state). 9th record.
*Jeri Langham.*

# SPOTTED REDSHANK

Plate 5

*Tringa erythropus*

Breeds N Eurasia. Winters S Eurasia, N Africa, Indonesia.

The Spotted Redshank has occurred on the West Coast most often as a fall migrant in the Aleutians and Pribilof Is., ALASKA (Aug-Oct) and there is a single fall record farther south in B.C. There are four spring records, all on the outer Aleutians, presumably of overshoots.

**ALASKA** 16 records, graphed below. 6 of the fall records were from 19-22 Sep 1961 on St. Paul I., Pribilofs; all other records are from the W Aleutians. The spring records are: 30 May 1971 on Adak I., 22-23 May 1976 on Alaid I., 21 May 1979 on Attu I., and 22-24 May 1979 on Attu I.

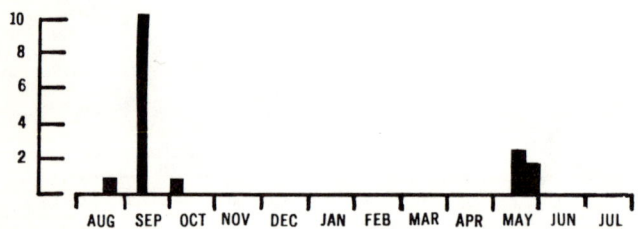

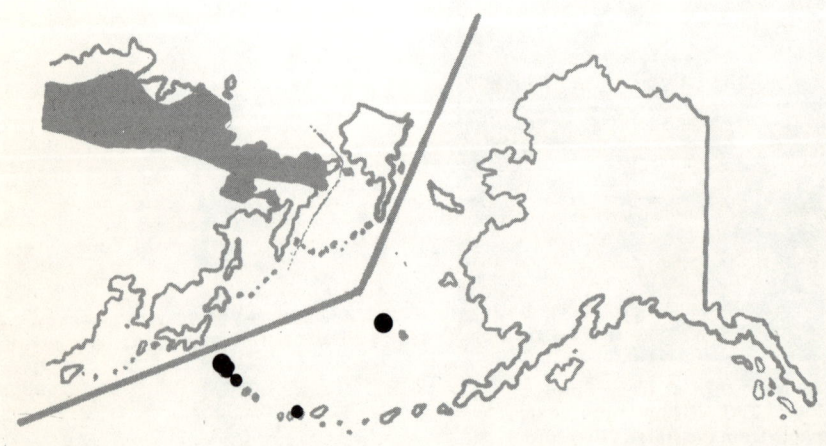

136

# SPOTTED REDSHANK

**BRITISH COLUMBIA** One record: 24 Sep-11 Nov 1970 at Reifel refuge, Vancouver.

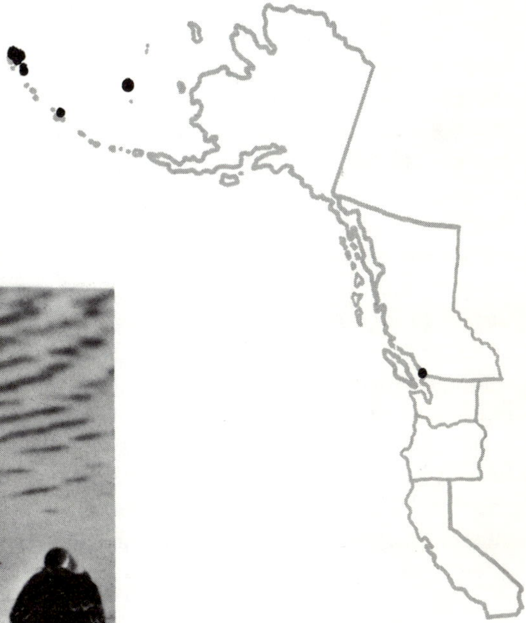

17 Oct 1970 at Reifel refuge, Vancouver, B.C. (both photos; with dowitchers). 1st record. *Rudolf H. Drent.*

# SPOTTED REDSHANK

I.D. The Spotted Redshank is mid-sized between the Greater Yellowlegs *T. melanoleuca* and the Lesser Yellowlegs *T. flavipes*. Breeding-plumaged adults are easily recognized by their black head and underparts, white spotting on the dark back, white eyering, and dark red legs (often look dark in the field). Winter plumage, acquired by adults in Jul-Sep and by juveniles in Oct-Nov, is also unlike any yellowlegs plumage, being an even gray above and whitish below, with a grayish wash to the sides of the breast. Juveniles (Jul-Oct) have extensive white spotting on dark wings and back. The whitish underparts are heavily streaked and washed with gray and the flanks are barred.

Bill shape, leg color (usually), and shape of white rump patch will separate the Spotted Redshank from any yellowlegs. The Spotted Redhsank has a rather long, thin, straight bill, with a slight droop at the tip, which is dark with a reddish base (dull red in juveniles). The long legs are a dark red color (may be dull orange-red in juveniles). The tail and uppertail coverts are heavily barred, but an unmarked white wedge extends from the rump to the lower back, producing a flight pattern not unlike dowitchers *Limnodromus sp*. The Greater Yellowlegs is larger and bulkier, with a thicker-based, slightly-upturned bill, and the white patch is restricted to a square area on the rump, not extending up the back. The Lesser Yellowlegs is smaller, with a more delicate build; has a much shorter bill; has less heavily streaked face, neck, and breast; shows a supercillium; and the white rump patch does not extend up the back like a dowitcher. Both yellowlegs show bright yellow legs, but occassionally they may be reddish and oiled yellowlegs with reddish legs have been mistaken for Spotted Redshank. The long bill and white wedge up the back may give the Spotted Redshank a somewhat dowitcher look, but the long legs, upright stance and lack of any really similar plumage to dowitchers should help avoid this confusion. However both Spotted Redshank and dowitchers often feed by wading belly-deep in water and plunging their bills into the mud.

The call - an upslurred "chuit" - recalls the Semipalmated Plover *Charadrius semipalmatus*, but is sharper and more emphatic.

# MARSH SANDPIPER  Plate 5

*Tringa stagnatilis*

Breeds locally E Europe, C Asia, N China. Winters Africa to Australia.

The Marsh Sandpiper is a long-distance migrant and, despite the distance of its breeding range from the West Coast, some migrational error was sufficient to send a single individual far to the north and east of its normal route, where it appeared in the outer Aleutians, ALASKA, in the fall.

# MARSH SANDPIPER

**ALASKA**  One record: 2 Sep 1974† on Buldir I. (C 80:310).

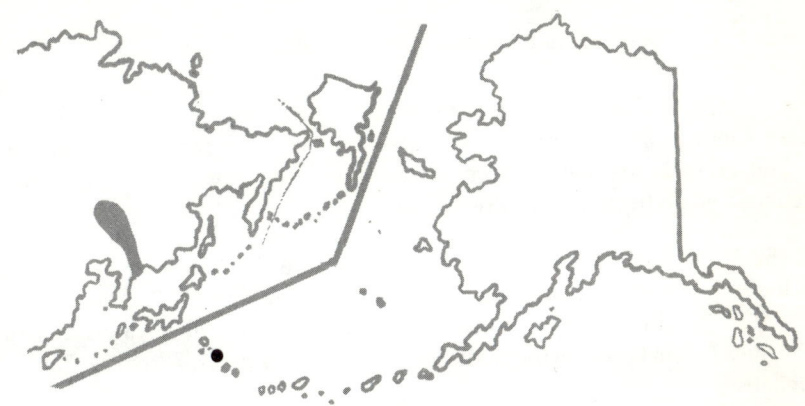

I.D.  The Marsh Sandpiper is a small, graceful *Tringa*, a bit smaller than a Lesser Yellowlegs *T. flavipes*, with a long, slim, sharp-pointed bill and disproportionately long, spindly olive-green legs. The whitish tail is heavily barred and a white rump patch extends up the back in a wedge similar to that of a dowitcher *Limnodromus sp*. In breeding plumage the black-centered back and wing feathers are edged buffy, giving a boldly spotted appearance. The plumage of Common Greenshank *T. nebularia* may be similar, but the Greenshank is a larger, heavier bird and lacks a long, needle-thin bill and long legs extending well beyond the tail in flight. Other similarly-sized shorebirds that combine a white rump with unmarked wings - Wood Sandpiper *T. glareola*, Green Sandpiper *T. ochropus*, Lesser Yellowlegs, or even Stilt Sandpiper *Micropalama himantopus* - all differ in lacking the long, straight, needle-thin bill; all have white rump patches restricted to the rump not extending up the back like a dowitcher; and are shorter-legged (Wood and Green) or show bright yellow legs (Lesser Yellowlegs) or have a dark tail and slight droop to bill (Stilt Sandpiper).

Juvenile and winter plumages of the Marsh Sandpiper recall the Wilson's Phalarope *Steganopus tricolor* in similar plumages, with pale unmarked upperparts, whitish underparts, barred tail, white rump, straight needle-like bill, and greenish legs. The Marsh Sandpiper can be distinguished by its different shape - longer bill and distinctly longer legs, more delicate build, and larger size - and by the white rump patch extending as a wedge up the lower back. The face and forehead are paler than a Wilson's Phalarope (apparent at some distance) and the Marsh Sandpiper is a bird of different habits, feeding by wading along the edges of marshy pools (like a Lesser Yellowlegs) and not dashing after prey on mudflats or swimming and spinning like the phalarope.

# COMMON GREENSHANK    Plate 5

*Tringa nebularis*

Breeds N Eurasia. Winters S Eurasia, Africa, Australia.

The Common Greenshank is a rare but regular spring migrant on the outer Aleutian Is. and spring migrants have occurred east to the Pribilof Is. Fall records are very scarce; all are from the Aleutians. It has not occurred elsewhere on the West Coast.

**ALASKA**   At least 41 birds have been recorded, mostly in ones and twos, but a flock of 9 has been encountered. The records (considering the flock as a single record) are graphed below. Multiple records include birds on Shemya I. (17), Attu I. (7), and Buldir I. (5). Farther east, there are 5 spring records from St. Paul I., Pribilofs.

There are four fall records: 14 Jul-6 Aug 1976 and 4 Sep 1975 (2), both from Buldir I.; 6 Sep 1978 on Agattu I.; and 6 Sep 1978 on Shemya I.

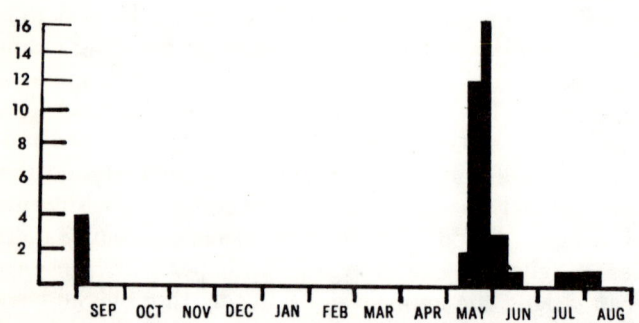

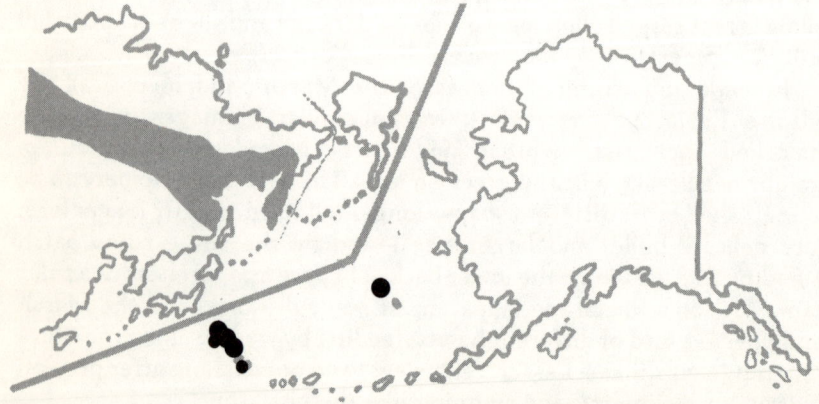

# COMMON GREENSHANK

21 May 1980 on Attu I., ALASKA. *Don Roberson.*

I.D. The Common Greenshank is a large, stout *Tringa*, about the size and shape of a Greater Yellowlegs *T. melanoleuca*, with a stout, slightly upturned bill. It is separated from the Greater Yellowlegs by the Greenshank's white rump patch extending up the lower back as a wedge recalling a dowitcher *Limnodromus sp.* The legs are grayish or olive-green, only rarely yellowish, and not the bright yellow of the yellowlegs. Plumages tend to parallel those of the Greater Yellowlegs, but the Greenshank averages paler, especially about the head and neck, and contrast with darker upperparts at any age. The call - a strident single to quadruple "tew" - recalls the Greater Yellowlegs.

The large size and stout bill should serve to eliminate smaller Eurasian *Tringas* with white wedges on the rump and lower back. The Nordmann's Greenshank *T. guttifer*, a NE Asian species which has occurred once on the Commander Is. west of Attu (22 May 1883†, see A 78:44), is similar but has yellower legs and a yellowish base to the bill, has distinctly shorter legs, has pure white underwing coverts (the Common Greenshank has lightly barred underwings), and at close range shows webbing between all toes (the Common Greenshank has webbing only between the outer pair). The call - a loud piercing scream "keyew" (sometimes repeated) - is said to be sharper and less musical than that of the Common Greenshank (King & Dickinson, 1975).

# GREEN SANDPIPER  Plate 5

*Tringa ochropus*

Breeds N Eurasia. Winters S Eurasia, Africa, Indonesia.

The Green Sandpiper has occurred only on Attu I., the westernmost of the Aleutian Is., during spring migration.

**ALASKA**  Two records, both on Attu I.: 13 Jun 1978 (T. Savaloja, pers. com.) and 22 May 1979. The first report was by a single observer and could not be accepted as the first North American record until further documentation (the 1979 record) was obtained.

# GREEN SANDPIPER

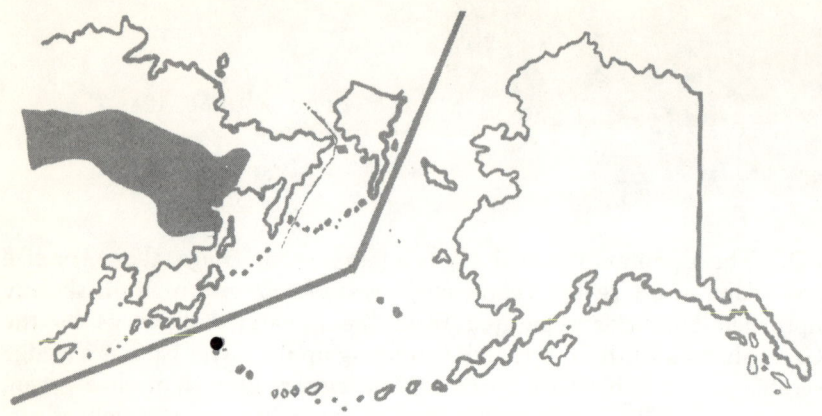

I.D. The Green Sandpiper closely resembles the Solitary Sandpiper T. *solitaria* in any plumage, including the habit of teetering, flying with deep, jerky wingbeats, and a sharp, shrill, rapid "pwi-pwi-pwi" call. The Green Sandpiper differs in possessing a white, triangularly-shaped rump patch, a white tail barred with black cross-bars (may be incomplete across uppertail coverts), and black underwings, producing a very dark-winged effect in flight. See also the identification section of Wood Sandpiper *T. glareola*.

# WOOD SANDPIPER

*Tringa glareola*

Plate 5
Plate 11

Breeds N Eurasia. Winters S Eurasia, Africa, Australia.

The Wood Sandpiper is a regular migrant in the Aleutian and Pribilof Is. of ALASKA, and breeding has been confirmed on the outer Aleutians. Spring and summer records of overshoots are scattered about W & N ALASKA. It has been reported south of ALASKA in North America only once - a probable fall record from Louisiana (AB 31:139) - but seems to be a likely candidate to occur in fall on the West Coast south of ALASKA.

**ALASKA** Regular migrant and rare breeder on the outer Aleutians and occurring with some regularity farther east in the Aleutians and on the Pribilof Is., where up to five have been found in midsummer and breeding has been suspected. Spring birds arrive mid-May to mid-Jun, usually singly or in small groups, but in some years - especially 1976 - larger flocks were encountered. On 16 May 1976 on Shemya I. at least 142 birds were counted, in flocks up to 45.

# WOOD SANDPIPER

Farther away, spring and summer birds have occurred on St. Lawrence I., the Seward Pen., and Pt. Barrow.

Confirmed breeding has occurred on Amchitka I. (3 downy young in Jul 1969 and 3 pairs bred in 1973) and Attu I. (downy young in Jun 1973). Displays and song on the Pribilof Is., in 1954 and 1961, suggest nesting there as well (see discussion in A 91:175).

Fall migrants, in small numbers, are found on the outer Aleutians from early Aug-mid Sep.

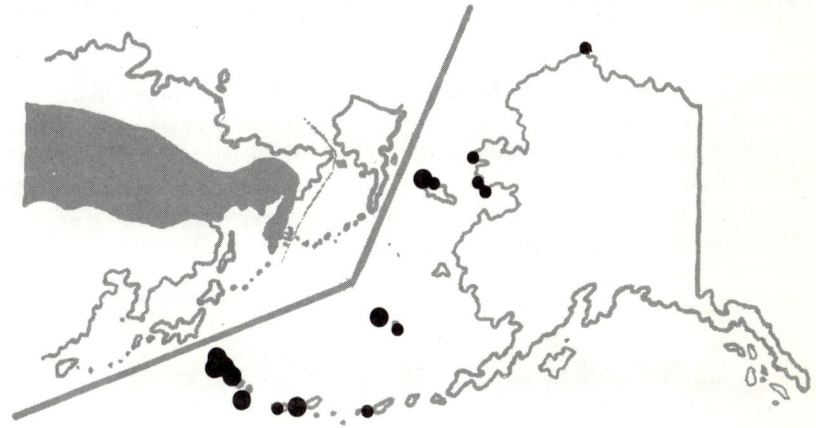

I.D. The Wood Sandpiper is about the size of a Solitary Sandpiper *T. solitaria*, but possesses a white tail barred with dark and a white rump patch and is generally paler than the Solitary Sandpiper. Its plumages more resemble those of the Lesser Yellowlegs *T. flavipes*, which is larger and longer-legged, shows bright yellow legs (not the Wood's greenish or yellowish-brown legs), and which looks more elongated in the field, with longer legs, longer neck, smaller head, and finer, longer bill. Confusion is most likely with juvenile Lesser Yellowlegs, which is decidedly browner than the adult. The Wood Sandpiper has darker wing-coverts, thus contrasting more with the white spotting, a shorter, stouter bill, and decidedly shorter legs (see BB 72:550). The call - a musical, high, shrill "chew-chew-chew" - or its liquid, trilling notes are different from the Lesser Yellowlegs softer, lower-pitched "tu" calls. The Wood Sandpiper also has the habit of flying high when flushed.

The Green Sandpiper *T. ochropus* is similar to the Wood Sandpiper, but the Green is a darker bird with a longer bill and less delicate build and shows blackish underwings in flight, unlike the whitish, faintly barred underwings of the Wood Sandpiper.

# WILLET

*Catoptrophorus semipalmatus*

Breeds Great Basin, N-C & E North America. Winters S U.S. to N South America.

The Willet, which nests in the Great Basin of NE CAL & SE ORE, is a common winterer on the CAL coast and winters locally north along the coast to Willapa Bay, Pac., WASH. Most records north of WASH were during the fall, but winter, spring, and summer birds have been recorded.

**BRITISH COLUMBIA** 14 records, graphed below. First taken in 1898† at Victoria, V.I., all records since have been from the Vancouver area or Vancouver I. Most are from the fall. The two winter records are: 26 Jan 1950† at Comox, V.I. and 22-30 Jan 1972 at Iona I., Vancouver. The single spring record was on 22 May 1977 at Willow Pt. Bay, V.I. A summering bird remained from 22 Jun-8 Sep 1974 at Crescent Beach, south of Vancouver.

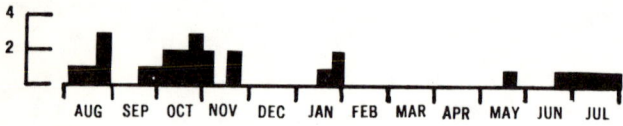

**ALASKA** One record: 8-9 Aug 1961 (2) at Minto Lakes, 50 miles W of Fairbanks (C 65:167).

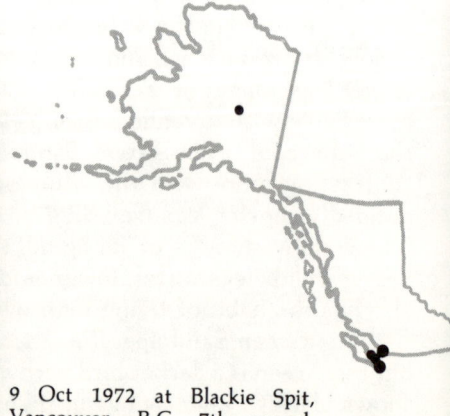

9 Oct 1972 at Blackie Spit, Vancouver, B.C. 7th record. *Richard Knapton.*

# TEREK SANDPIPER                                           Plate 3

*Xenus cinereus*

Breeds N Eurasia. Winters S Eurasia, Africa, Australia.

The Terek Sandpiper has been recorded on the West Coast only in ALASKA, where a number of spring overshoots have occurred, two as far east as Anchorage. A number of fall records suggest a tendency for a few birds to wander toward the West Coast in fall. There are unconfirmed reports from WASH (27 Oct 1972 at Dungeness, Clm.) and Alberta and this species might be expected to occur on the West Coast south of ALASKA in the future.

**ALASKA** 12 records, graphed below. 7 of the 8 spring records fall between 24 May-8 Jun on the outer Aleutians, St. Lawrence I., and the Seward Pen. Most unusual was one on 18 Jun 1977 at Anchorage. The 3 fall records occurred between 26 Aug-8 Sep on Buldir I., Agattu I., and St. Lawrence I.

Occurring too late to be included on the graph was an incredible record of at least 22 Terek Sandpipers on Attu I. from 25-27 May 1980, including a flock of 20 on 25 May.

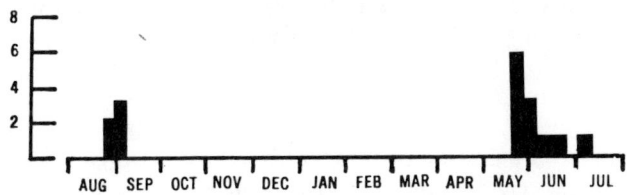

145

# TEREK SANDPIPER

**I.D.** The Terek Sandpiper is larger than Spotted Sandpiper *Actitis macularia*. The upturned bill is unique in small shorebirds. The bill may often have an orange-yellow base, but many look all black in the field. The bright orange-yellow legs are disproportionately short, adding to a distinctive profile. Breeding-plumaged birds are grayish above with a pair of prominent black scapular lines. Winter-plumaged adults are an even gray above. Juveniles are grayish-brown above with dark "V-shaped" marks on the scapulars. The underparts are whitish year-round. The white tips to the secondaries produce a prominent white trailing edge to the inner wing in flight.

The Terek Sandpiper often feeds by dashing about, but when standing often bobs like Spotted Sandpiper. The flight call is a rapid, fluted "tu-du-du" or a rolled "trrrut".

# COMMON SANDPIPER  Plate 3

*Actitis hypoleucos*

Breeds N Eurasia. Winters S Eurasia, Africa, Australia.

The Common Sandpiper is a rare, but regular, spring migrant on the westernmost Aleutian Is., ALASKA. There are a few spring records elsewhere in ALASKA. It is very scarce during the fall; all records have been on the Aleutians.

**ALASKA** Well over 50 records, nearly all from the W Aleutians, where it is a rare, but regular, spring migrant. About 35 of the records occurred during the spring of 1976; it has averaged only about 4 birds a spring during other recent years (but most islands are not covered daily). Occurs singly or in pairs, but 7 were counted on Buldir I. on 7 Jun 1976. Nearly all the records are from Buldir I., Shemya I., and Attu I.; in addition there are about 7 from Gambell, St. Lawrence I. Elsewhere it is very rare: only a single record on Adak I. and two from St. George I., Pribilofs.

4 of the 5 fall records occurred between 26 Aug-16 Sep; the other was 26-28 Jul 1976. All were on the outermost Aleutians.

26 May 1980 on Attu I., ALASKA. *Don Roberson.*

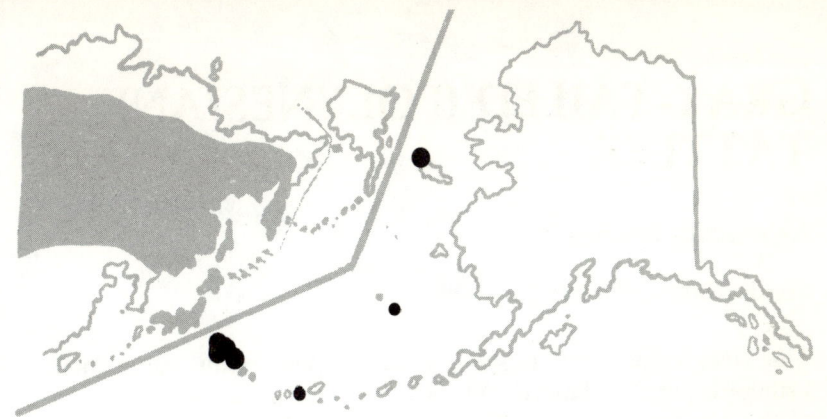

I.D. The Common Sandpiper is very similar to the slightly smaller Spotted Sandpiper *A. macularia*, although breeding-plumaged Spotted Sandpiper is easily identified by the spotting on the underparts. Juvenile and winter-plumaged birds may be identified by a combination of marks including: 1) the Common is differently shaped, having a proportionately longer tail, so that the wings reach only to the base of the tail (when viewed at rest); the wings of Spotted reach to mid-tail, 2) the Common shows a flight pattern with a long tail outlined in white and a bolder, longer wingbar; Spotted has the outlining of the tail obscured with dark marks and shows a white wingbar not extending to inner secondaries, and 3) the Common has more crisply marked underpart pattern, with sullied chin and throat; Spotted tends to have a pure white chin and throat, with dark patches reduced to the sides of the breast. In addition, juveniles can be separated by the pattern of wing coverts and back. On Common, both the wing coverts and back are obscurely barred, showing little contrast between wing and back; on Spotted, the wing coverts are more boldly barred with black, contrasting with an unmarked back.

The color of the legs and bill is less useful than the literature suggests. While the Common tends to have an all-dark bill and dull straw-colored or grayish legs and the Spotted tends to have a pale base to the bill and brighter yellow legs, there is much overlap. Some fall Spotteds have grayish-olive legs (see BB 73:185) and many spring Commons have bright yellowish legs and two-toned bills.

The call of Common Sandpiper is a muted "teep-teep", "weet-lo-eet", and "tloo-it", distinguishable with practice from the typical call of Spotted Sandpiper — a more ringing, whistled "tsee-wee" or "tsee-wee-wee". Spotted Sandpiper, however, can give softer calls much more similar to the calls of Common Sandpiper.

Both species share the habit of constant bobbing, though the Common Sandpiper's bob looks more exaggerated and forceful. It should be noted that some first-summer Spotted Sandpipers do not attain breeding dress and that a spring date, though suggestive, does not absolutely identify an unspotted bird of this group. For more information see Wallace (1970) and Prater *et al* (1977, p. 152).

# GRAY-TAILED (POLYNESIAN) TATTLER

Plate 3

*Heteroscelus brevipes*

Breeds NE Asia. Winters E Asia, Philippines, Australia.

The Gray-tailed Tattler is a regular migrant in the outer Aleutians, Pribilof Is., and St. Lawrence I., ALASKA and probably breeds just west of the Aleutians on the Commander Is., USSR. Spring overshoots have reached as far north as Pt. Barrow. The regular fall migration in ALASKA, a record in the E Aleutians, and the long migration route are indications that the Gray-tailed Tattler might occur on the West Coast south of ALASKA.

**ALASKA** About 60 records, about 20 during spring migration (18 May-17 Jun - peak in early Jun) and about 40 during fall migration (27 Jul-4 Oct - peak in late Aug-early Sep). While most birds were on the westernmost Aleutians, there are a number of spring records from Gambell, St. Lawrence I. and several fall records from the Pribilof Is. (including the only two Oct reports). Spring overshoots have twice reached Barrow: 10 Jun 1972† and 19-20 Jun 1977†. Three birds were identified far east in the Aleutians on 24 Sep 1974† on Unalaska I.

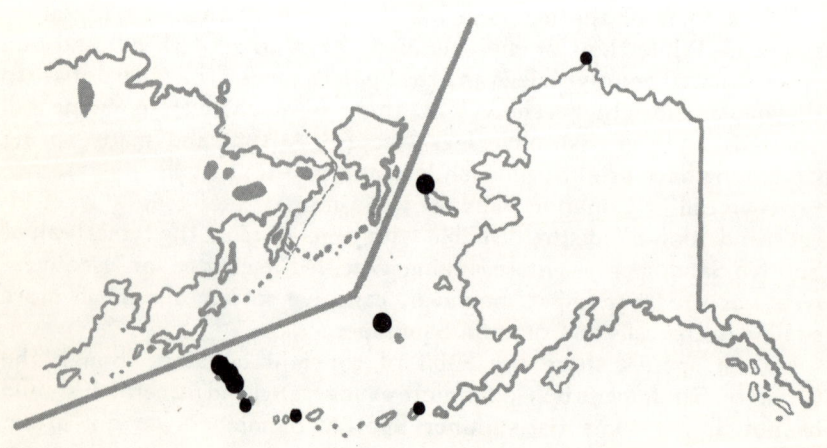

# GRAY-TAILED TATTLER

I.D. The Gray-tailed Tattler is similar in any plumage to Wandering Tattler *H. incanus*. In breeding plumage, Gray-tailed is identified by its more finely barred underparts with white belly and undertail coverts (fine barring restricted to the sides of the undertail coverts), fine white edgings to the uppertail coverts (looking like a pale patch on the rump in flight), and slightly paler gray upperparts; the Wandering has more heavily barred underparts including much of the belly, barred undertail coverts, unmarked uppertail coverts, and a slightly darker, more slaty cast to the upperparts. Many late summer and early fall Wandering Tattlers, molting into winter plumage (and even some full breeding-plumaged birds) show white bellies in the field. It is the width of the barring and the undertail coverts pattern that should be carefully noted.

Juvenile and winter-plumaged birds are much more difficult to separate. Gray-tailed tends to be a warmer brown-gray color and often show a pale area on the face at the base of the bill (lacking in Wandering); birds in very fresh plumage may show pale edgings to the uppertail coverts, but this mark is soon lost. The call — a sharp, whistled "too-weet", accented on the second syllable — is distinguishable from the Wandering's plaintive, repetitious, whistled, ringing "pew-tu-tu-tu". This call will identify Gray-tailed Tattler, but it is noted that Gray-tailed can give a call similar to Wandering (D. Gibson, *pers. com.*).

Of value in the hand, but absolutely no value in the field, is the length of the nasal groove on the bill: that of Gray-tailed is short, reaching to the half-way point on the bill or less; that of Wandering is longer, reaching beyond the mid-point and often to two-thirds the bill length. Grooves of both species become quite shallow at the distal end, thus the end is invisible in the field, so that a tattler with a groove apparently stopping at the mid-point of the bill in the field is usually a Wandering Tattler. For more information see Gibson (1978).

Comparison of Gray-tailed Tattler (left) and Wandering Tattler (right). Both photos taken 25 May 1980 on Attu I., ALASKA. *Don Roberson.*

# EURASIAN JACKSNIPE      Plate 3

*Lymnocryptes minimus*

Breeds N Eurasia. Winters S Eurasia, C Africa, Philippines.

The Eurasian Jacksnipe has occurred only twice on the West Coast: a spring record, probably an overshoot, in ALASKA, and a late fall record from CAL. Both specimens were taken before 1940 and there have been no recent sightings.

**ALASKA**   One record: "spring (probably Apr)" 1919† on St. Paul I., Pribilofs (C 22:173).

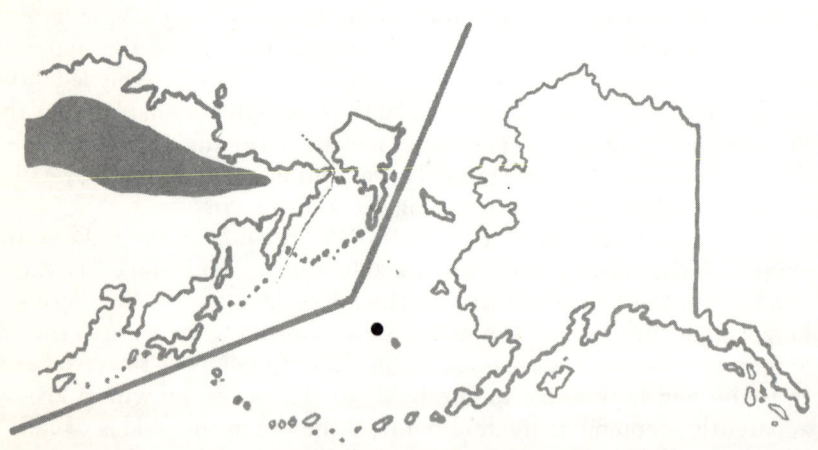

**CALIFORNIA**   One record: 20 Nov 1938† near Gridley, But. (C 41:164).

# EURASIAN JACKSNIPE

20 Nov 1938 near Gridley, But., CAL. 1st record. Museum of Vertebrate Zoology, U.C. Berkeley. *Don Roberson.*

I.D.   The Eurasian Jacksnipe is much smaller than the Common Snipe *Capella gallinago*, being about the size of a Dunlin *Calidris alpina*. It differs further from the Common Snipe in having a proportionately much shorter bill with a pale base, dark crown without a central stripe, more prominent creamy stripes on the back, streaked (rather than barred) flanks, and a wedge-shaped, brown tail. It usually flushes only at close approach and flies off silently, dropping back fairly quickly to cover, without the Common Snipe's distinctive call or wild, zig-zag flight. In flight the short bill is obvious, and the wings are more rounded and "fluttery" than Common Snipe.

   The Broad-billed Sandpiper *Limicola falcinellus* is vaguely similar, but is smaller (stint-sized), has a distinctive drooped tip to the bill, has a dark-centered, rounded tail, and behaves like a stint, not a snipe.

# GREAT KNOT

Plate 3

*Calidris tenuirostris*

Breeds NE Asia. Winters SE Asia, Philippines, Australia.

The Great Knot has occurred on the West Coast only during spring migration in western ALASKA. Most records are of single birds in late May-early Jun, but a pair in mid-Jun could suggest nesting attempts, which might be watched for in the future.

**ALASKA**   Eight records: 22 May 1922† on Cape Mt., Seward Pen., 4 Jun 1971† on Adak I., 16 Jun 1973 on Sevuokuk Mt., St. Lawrence I. (pair), 8 Jun 1973 at the Nome R. mouth, 24-27 May 1976 on Shemya I., 26 May 1976† on St. Paul I., 8 Jun 1977 at Gambell, St. Lawrence I., and 3-4 Jun 1979 at Gambell.

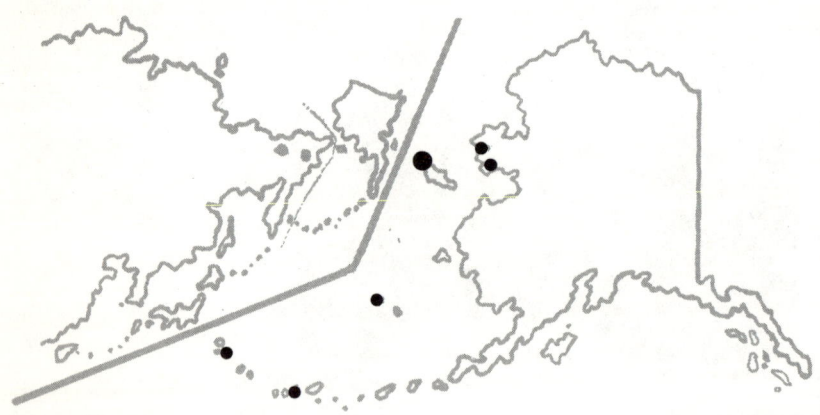

I.D.   The Great Knot is the largest *Calidris*, noticeably larger than a turnstone *Arenaria sp.* It shares the basic structure and tail pattern (white rump, gray tail) of the Red Knot *C. canutus*, but is much larger, with a longer, slimmer bill (slightly drooped at the tip) and lacks a clear wingstripe. In breeding plumage, the Great Knot is finely streaked on the face, heavily streaked on the neck and back, and has large spots on the breast and sides, becoming heart-shaped spots on the flanks. It shows striking chestnut scapulars in this black, gray, and white plumage and is easily distinguished (see plate). Juvenile and winter-plumaged Great Knots remain much more heavily streaked on the crown, breast, and neck than the very fine facial and breast streaking of the smaller Red Knot, and the Great Knot is darker above, showing a contrasting dark back and tail with the white rump. Red Knot is a paler gray on the back and tail, making the white rump less conspicuous. The call is a high, rolling "waaa, waaa, waaa" or a harsher "char, char, char, char".

# IDENTIFICATION AND AGEING OF STINTS

Before an observer attempts to identify the rarer species of stints (small species of the genus *Calidris*) on the West Coast, an ability to age stints and identify the common species is necessary. The field guides depict breeding (summer) and non-breeding (winter) plumages, but fail to discuss juvenile (first-autumn) plumages. Most rare shorebirds found in the fall are in juvenile plumage, as are the bulk of the scarce regular migrants (Baird's Sandpiper, Pectoral Sandpiper, etc.). Juvenile plumage is acquired on the nesting grounds and is worn through fall migration, until it is molted for a winter plumage resembiling that of adults in winter in Oct-Nov. Adults acquire breeding plumage in Apr-May during spring migration and wear it through the nesting season and during fall migration, usually until the wintering grounds are reached. However, adult stints migrate much earlier, on the average, than juvenile birds, thus passing in greatest numbers down the West Coast in Jul-Aug, while juveniles migrate in Aug-Oct. Adults reach their wintering grounds earlier and thus molt into winter plumage in late Jul-late Aug, while juveniles do not typically attain this dress until late Sep-Oct or even as late as Nov.

When adults molt into breeding plumage in the spring, the feathers are new and often characterized by broad, unworn brightly-colored edges, often whitish, chestnut, or yellow. By fall migration in Jul-Aug these feathers are worn and have lost their crisp edgings, appearing mottled, frayed, and without a crisp pattern to the upperparts and wing coverts. In contrast, juveniles during Jul-Sep are in new juvenile plumage and have broad, unworn, brightly-colored (white, reddish, yellow) edges to the feathers of the back and wing coverts. Wear begins around the neck, and typical juveniles in late Aug-Sep have grayish collars of worn feathers across the nape, but show distinct edgings to the back and wing covert feathers. Winter plumage is characterized by grayish, evenly-colored feathers on the back and wings, with either dark shaft streaks (Western, Semipalmated, Rufous-necked, Little) or dark centers (Least, Long-toed), without bright edges, giving the bird a very plain appearance on the upperparts. Adults begin showing these feathers by Jul-Aug, but juveniles do not molt into them until several months later. These feathers are fresh and unworn in early fall, but become quite worn by early spring.

# IDENTIFICATION AND AGEING OF STINTS

Once an observer can age a stint, care must be taken to carefully eliminate the two common species: the Western Sandpiper *C. mauri* and the Least Sandpiper *C. minutilla*. Both are illustrated on Plate 4. The Western Sandpiper is the larger of the two, with the longest bill of any stint (females have a longer bill than males and show a more distinct droop to the tip), and have black legs with webbing between the toes. The breeding plumage is characterized by bright chestnut edgings to the feathers of the crown, ear coverts, scapulars, and back and by a broad band of distinct streaks across the breast, extending down the sides and flanks as "V"-shaped chevrons. Winter plumage is characterized by the even gray back and wings, a paler forehead and face, a broad, square-ended supercilium, and very pale underparts with breast streaking, if any, reduced to fine streaks on the sides of the breast. Some first-winter birds retain rusty scapular edges. Juveniles are characterized by the extensive chestnut edgings to the feathers of the back, wings, and crown. All the feathers in the center of the back, between the pair of indistinct whitish lines, are edged chestnut. The scapular and tertial edgings are often very bright. There is often a few light streaks across the breast. The common call is a high "jeet". A solid background in the plumages of the Western Sandpiper is a must for observers searching for rarer species. Male Westerns, with shorter bills than the field guide pictures, can be mistaken for other species.

The Least Sandpiper is the smaller species, with a short, finely tapered bill, and greenish-yellow or brownish-yellow legs, without webbing. All plumages are much browner than those of the Western, and all have considerable streaking or smudging across the breast, which is quite distinct from the Western's pale breast in juvenile and winter plumage. Least Sandpipers in breeding plumage are characterized by blackish upperparts narrowly edged with white and rusty and broad, dark gray streaking across the breast. Winter-plumaged birds are very brownish appearing, with darker brown centers to each feather and a smudgy band of streaks across the breast. Juveniles also look very brown, with pale edgings to back and wing coverts feathers. The common call is a high, thin "preet".

The presence of these birds in numbers on the West Coast provide ample opportunity to study the plumage sequences of two basic types of stints and to practice distinguishing webbed toes (Western) from unwebbed toes (Least). For more information on stint plumages, see Prater *et al*(1977), Wallace (1974), and Dunn (1979 a). Stint identification is difficult at best and full of pitfalls. Identification must be based on a combination of characters, not a single "field mark". Some of the problems are discussed in Wallace (1979) and a note in *British Birds* 70:165.

# SEMIPALMATED SANDPIPER    Plate 4

*Calidris pusilla*

Breeds N North America. Winters C America, West Indies to C South America.

The Semipalmated Sandpiper is a nesting species across much of arctic ALASKA, but its major migration routes take it through E North America and it is scarce on the West Coast south of ALASKA. There is a regular migration of small numbers along the Pacific shoreline and interior of the West Coast, as it is recorded annually in all states and provinces and small concentrations are found, especially in the fall, around the Vancouver area, B.C. and Puget Sound, WASH. Fall migration occurs between mid-Jul and mid-Sep (adults early in the period, juveniles later). Spring migration occurs between late Apr-late May. It is very difficult to determine the magnitude of these migrations. During the research for this book, numerous descriptions and photos of "Semipalmated Sandpipers" were examined. A large percentage of these reports (including about half of the Vancouver I. reports) were found to be in error, referring instead to adult male Western Sandpipers in winter plumage. On the other hand, there is no doubt that small numbers occur annually. Semipalmated Sandpiper becomes decidedly scarcer in ORE & CAL. The records suggest that from the concentrating areas around Vancouver (such as Iona I.) and Puget Sound, only a portion of the birds continue south towards CAL. Another portion appears to move east, through the interior of WASH, and bypasses ORE & CAL.

**OREGON**  At least 4 records: 21 Aug 1972 at Fern Ridge Res., Lane, 19 Aug 1977* at Agate Res., Jck., 20 Aug 1977* at Tillamook Bay, and another 28 Jul 1979 on Tillamook Bay. The first 3 records are juveniles; the latter is an adult. In addition, there are a number of published reports during Apr-May and Jul-Aug. Some may be correct, but in light of the study of B.C.-WASH discussed above and a number of proven incorrect reports in ORE, I have chosen to include only those records accepted by the ORE Records Committee or photos I have examined.

28 Jul 1979 at Tillamook Bay, Til., ORE (adult in worn breeding plumage). *Harry B. Nehls.*

# SEMIPALMATED SANDPIPER

**CALIFORNIA** 63 records, graphed below. 36 of these are from the fall; 27 are during the spring. Most of the fall records are coastal, though there are a scattering from the Antelope Valley, L.A., the Salton Sea, Imp., and Baker, S.Bn. Extreme fall dates are 27 Jul-15 Sep. Nearly all have been juveniles; the single known adult was on 8 Aug 1979 at Moss Landing, Mnt.

19 of the spring records are from the Salton Sea, Imp & Riv., and 4 additional spring records are from the interior. This suggests that the spring movement of Semipalmated Sandpiper through CAL is primarily inland.

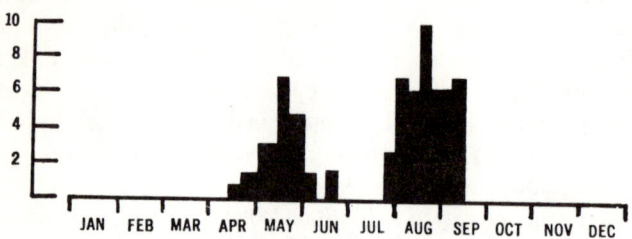

10 Sep 1978 at Imperial Beach, S.D., CAL (juvenile; with juvenile Western Sandpiper, right) *Linda Delaney.*

# SEMIPALMATED SANDPIPER

3 Aug 1975 at Pescadero SB, S.M., CAL (juvenile). *Dave Rudholm.*

10 Sep 1978 at Imperial Beach, S.D., CAL (juvenile). *Linda Delaney.*

I.D.  The Semipalmated Sandpiper is best compared to the common Western Sandpiper *C. mauri*. See p. 153 for a discussion of that species and of ageing stints. The Semipalmated is a bit smaller than the Western and looks stockier and more round-headed in the field. The bill is quite short (but there is overlap between female Semipalmated and male Western). In profile, the bill looks thick and blunt and from above it is typically bulbous-tipped (although there is variation in the extent of this "blob-tipped" look) and is thick throughout its length, without much tapering. Female Westerns have much longer bills, which taper down to a distinct droop at the tip, recalling the Dunlin *Calidris alpina*, though shorter. Males have shorter bills, without much of a droop to the tip, but are tapered to a slim tip, lacking the bluntness and thickness of the Semipalmated. The legs of a Semipalmated are black and partially webbed between all the forward toes.

# SEMIPALMATED SANDPIPER

In breeding plumage, the Semipalmated is distinct from the Western, as it lacks the latter's extensive rusty edges, showing only a bit of rusty on the crown, back, and ear-coverts. The upperparts are a darker gray or brownish than the paler gray of the Western, most edgings are yellowish or orange rather than bright chestnut, and the breast streaking is confined to a band of fine streaks across the breast, without the Western's broad gorget of streaks and lacking the Western's pattern of striking chevrons on the sides and flanks. Winter plumage is much like the Western, but tends to be browner. The breast is smudged with gray, often with distinct fine streaks across the breast (but much less than Least Sandpiper *C. minutilla*).

Juveniles are much less rusty than juvenile Western (or Rufous-necked Stint), typically a light brown on the upperparts with a regular pattern of buffy edges, producing in most birds a scaly appearance recalling that of a juvenile Baird's Sandpiper *C. bairdii*. The scapulars and tertials may be edged red, but the back (between the pair of indistinct whitish lines) is not edged with red on all feathers (a mixture of red and white or white and yellow is typical) nor are the wing coverts all edged red.

The calls of the Semipalmated Sandpiper are lower-pitched and rougher in quality than the high-pitched calls of the Western, and are typically transcribed as "cherrup" or "treep". Observers experienced Western calls can easily distinguish them.

While breeding-plumaged Semipalmated is fairly easy to distinguish and winter-plumaged birds are unlikely to occur on the West Coast, the identification of juvenile birds is complicated by the possibility of Rufous-necked Stint *C. ruficollis* and Little Stint *C. minuta*. These two species have more tapered bills, lack webbing between the toes, have extensive rusty edges to the upperparts (without the Semipalmated's buffy, scaly look), and have higher-pitched calls, lacking the rough quality of the Semipalmated. For more, see the discussion under those species.

# RUFOUS-NECKED STINT  Plate 4

*Calidris ruficollis*

Breeds NE Asia, W & N Alaska. Winters E Asia, Philippines, Australia.

The Rufous-necked Stint breeds, or is suspected of breeding, on St. Lawrence I., the Seward Pen., and at Barrow, ALASKA and summer birds have been found along much of the northern coast, while spring migrants have reached as far east as the Coleville R. delta. It is a rare but regular migrant through the Pribilof Is. and the outer Aleutian Is. While the bulk of the population migrates down the Asian coast, fall records from SE ALASKA (18 Aug 1976 at Valdez Narrows and 23 Jul 1965 (4) at Glacier Bay) and farther south on the West Coast suggest that a small number may migrate down the western coast of North America and winter somewhere in the New World. Perhaps due to the small number involved and the difficulty in identification, few are detected.

13 Jun 1972 at Barrow, ALASKA (adult in breeding plumage). *Van Remsen.*

**BRITISH COLUMBIA** Four records, all at Iona I., Vancouver: 24-25 Jun 1978, 13-15 Jul 1978, 25-26 Aug 1978, and 6 Aug 1979. All have shown traces of breeding plumage. The species has an early departure from the breeding grounds and may retain breeding plumage through Jul-Aug, so all records should be considered fall migrants.

**CALIFORNIA** Four records: 5 May 1969* at Arcata, Hmb., 18 Jun 1974 at Crescent City, D.N., 17 Aug 1974† at the Salton Sea, south end, Imp., and 1-6 Sep 1978 at the Santa Clara R. mouth, Ven. The first record is clearly a spring migrant, but all others probably refer to birds in fall migration. The Crescent City bird showed traces of breeding dress, the Salton Sea specimen was a winter-plumaged adult, and the final record is of a juvenile.

# RUFOUS-NECKED STINT

17 Aug 1974 at the Salton Sea, south end, Imp. (adult in winter plumage). 3rd record. *John Butler.*

3 Sep 1978 at Santa Clara R. mouth, Ven., CAL (juvenile). 4th record. *James M. Greaves.*

# RUFOUS-NECKED STINT

I.D. The Rufous-necked Stint is often compared to Semipalmated Sandpiper *C. pusilla*, which it resembles in size and bill length, but its plumages are more similar to those of Western Sandpiper *C. mauri*. See p. 153 for a discussion of ageing stints and the common species. The bill of Rufous-necked is short, like Semipalmated, but more tapered and less bulbous-tipped, though it still may show some swelling of the tip from above. The legs are black and the toes unwebbed, a mark that can be clearly seen at close range (beware of muddy conditions which may make the distinguishing of webbing difficult).

In breeding plumage the Rufous-necked Stint is quite distinctive, with bright chestnut face, throat, and upper breast (supercilium not strongly marked, incorrectly shown on Plate 4). The upperparts are mostly pale gray, with rufous edgings to the back and scapulars, but not the wing coverts (similar to Western; note the different pattern of Little Stint *C. minuta*, p. 164). Winter plumage is very similar to Western and Semipalmated Sandpipers, with grayish upperparts and whitish underparts. Bill shape, lack of webbing, call, and typically a whiter forehead than the other species may be useful in this plumage. Both Western and Semipalmated show webbing between the toes. The breast is mostly unmarked, with gray patches reduced to the sides of the breast with little streaking, similar to many Westerns (most Semipalmateds show fine streaks on the sides of the breast).

Juvenile Rufous-necked is similar to juvenile Western, but have shorter bills and unwebbed toes. The edges of the feathers on the crown, back, and scapulars are crisply edged in red and usually all the feathers on the center of the back, between the pair of sometimes conspicuous white lines, are edged red. The brightness of the upperparts recalls Western Sandpiper and is unlike the buffy, scaly upperparts of the Semipalmated, which has reddish edgings reduced to a few scattered feathers on the tertials and back. The Rufous-necked may show a few feathers with red edgings on the wing coverts, but the coverts are not usually all edged in red (contrary to the pattern shown on Plate 4). This lack of much red on the coverts may be a useful mark in separation from juvenile Little Stint, which typically shows all reddish edgings to the wing coverts. Again the reader is cautioned that the identification of stints is difficult and requires close study, with identification based on a combination of marks well seen. Our knowledge of stint identification is still in infancy.

The calls of Rufous-necked Stint are short and "clipped", distinct from the high-pitched "jeet" of Western and the low, rough "cherrup" or "treep" of Semipalmated. A number of twittering notes are shared by most stints, but the Rufous-necked gives a sharp "jit", recalling the flight call of Sanderling *C. alba*, which is apparently not given by other stints.

# LTTTLE STINT

Plate 4
Plate 11

*Calidris minuta*

Breeds N Eurasia. Winters S Eurasia, Africa.

The Little Stint has occurred three times in ALASKA: twice as a spring overshoot in W & N ALASKA and once as a fall vagrant on the outer Aleutians. While birds in breeding plumage are readily identified in the field, its similarity to Rufous-necked Stint *C. ruficollis* in juvenile and winter plumage make it very difficult to identify should it occur in the fall.

**ALASKA** Three records: 28 Jun 1976 at Pt. Barrow (C 80:451; photo on Plate 11), 17 Sep 1979† on Attu I., and 8 Jun 1980† at Gambell, St. Lawrence I.

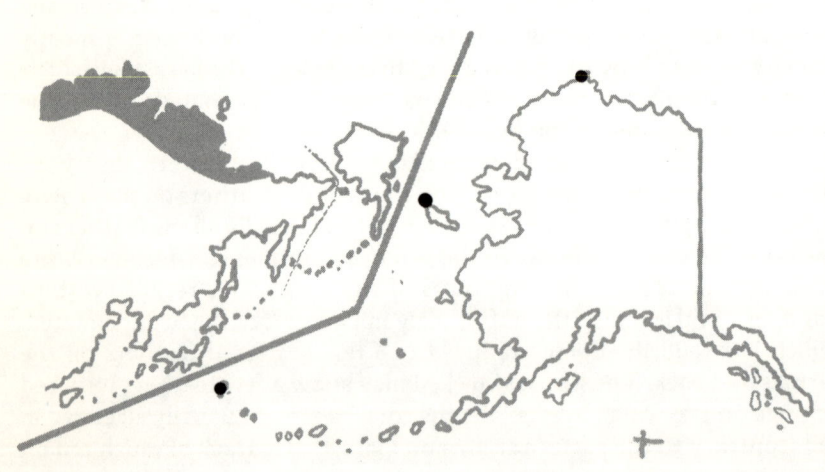

**I.D.** The Little Stint most closely resembles the Rufous-necked Stint *C. ruficollis*, and is very difficult to distinguish from that species except in fresh breeding plumage. The bill is short and tapers to a fine point, similar in proportions to that of the smaller Least Sandpiper *C. minutilla*.

# LITTLE STINT

The legs are black and the toes unwebbed. In breeding and juvenile plumages, the Little Stint shows a conspicuous white "V" on the back and less prominent white lines on the scapulars. Other similar stints (Western, Semipalmated) show less obvious white lines, but the most similar stint - the Rufous-necked - may also show a distinct "V" on the back, especially in juvenile plumage.

In breeding plumage, the Little Stint is distinctive. The head and breast are pale rufous or orange (rather than the rich chestnut of Rufous-necked), the throat is whitish (Rufous-necked usually has chestnut throat and white chin), the breast has an admixture of dark streaks across the center (this area is typically uniform chestnut on Rufous-necked), and the feathers of the wing coverts and tertials are brightly edged orange (wing coverts are typically edged grayish in Rufous-necked). The supercilium is very poorly marked (unlike illustration on Plate 4; see photo on Plate 11). In late summer the effects of wear and molt may reduce the obviousness of these differences from Rufous-necked Stint. In winter plumage the Little Stint is generally gray above, white below, like most other stints. Bill shape and call may be the only clues in this plumage (an unlikely plumage to be found on any Little Stint on the West Coast).

Juvenile Little Stint is brightly marked, with reddish feather edgings to the upperparts similar to those of Western Sandpiper C. *mauri* or Rufous-necked Stint. A recently discussed feature that may be of value in separating Little Stint from Rufous-necked Stint (both of which have unwebbed toes) is the color of the edgings of the wing coverts: typically all reddish-edged on Little Stint, mostly whitish or buffy-edged on Rufous-necked (other than this possibly useful character, identification can be very difficult; see Wallace, 1969). The supercilium tends to be less defined than on other stints and is generally forked above the eye. In the hand, note the pattern of the central tail feathers, illustrated below.

The call of Little Stint is a high-pitched, short, sharp "tit", more like a Western in pitch than the lower-pitched Rufous-necked and the rough call of Semipalmated Sandpiper C. *pusilla*. For more information on stints and especially this species, see Wallace (1974 — some of this information proved not to be useful and has been updated in these discussions).

Central tail feathers of juvenile Little Stint (left) and juvenile Rufous-necked Stint (right).

# TEMMINCK'S STINT  Plate 4

*Calidris temminckii*

Breeds N Eurasia. Winters S Eurasia, Africa, Indonesia.

The Temminck's Stint has occurred during both spring and fall migrations in W ALASKA. It remains very rare, but birds have appeared in numerous locations.

**ALASKA** 16 records, graphed below. Most spring records are from the westernmost Aleutians (3 from Buldir I.) and Gambell, St. Lawrence I. (4), but there is a mainland record on 13 Jun 1975 at Cape Prince of Wales. Summer reports are from Buldir I. (14-18 Jul 1976) and St. Matthew I. in the Bering Sea (28 Jul 1977); both may have been fall migrants. The four fall records are from Buldir I. (20-25 Aug 1976), Shemya I. (4 Sep 1977†), and St. George I., Pribilofs (24 Aug 1965 & 23 Aug 1968†).

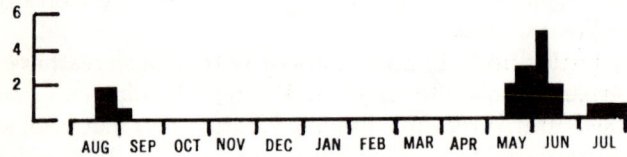

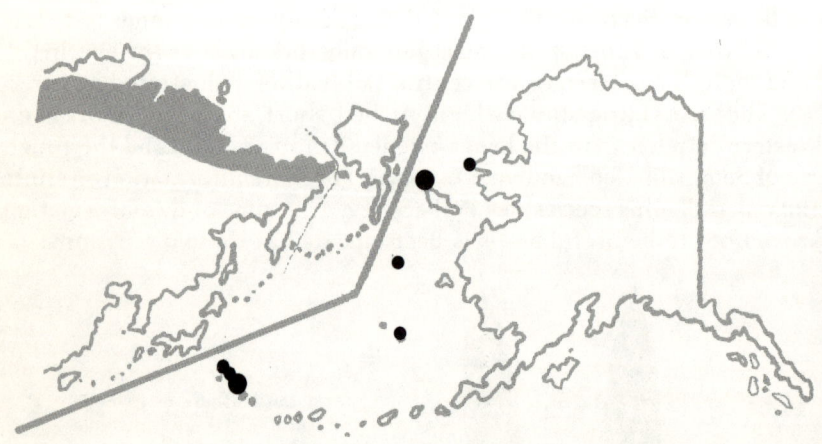

## TEMMINCK'S STINT

I.D. The Temminck's Stint resembles no other stint in its plumages, which are comparatively plain and without the bright feather edgings found on similarly-sized stints in breeding and juvenile plumages (nor is the supercilium well-marked, incorrectly portrayed on Plate 4). The bill is short, thin, and straight. The legs are greenish-yellow or brownish and the toes unwebbed. The bright white outer tail feathers, best viewed in flight, are unique (but beware that any stint may show pale grayish outer tail feathers). The posture of Temminck's is often hunched. Its typical habitat is marshy edges rather than mudflats.

In breeding plumage, Temminck's Stint is buffy-brown above with dark feather centers, with rusty edges restricted to the tertials. The sides of the breast are densely streaked and sharply cut-off from the white belly. Adults in winter plumage are a uniform grayish or olive-brown above with a broad gray wash in a clear-cut band across the breast. Juveniles are similar to winter plumage, with only a few fine pale buff edges to the back and wings, very unlike the boldly-patterned juvenile plumages of other stints. At a distance, the uniform upperparts and patches on the sides of the breast give the impression of a diminutive Spotted Sandpiper *Actitis macularia* in non-breeding plumage.

The flight call - a rapidly repeated series of short, dry trills, almost like a muted rattle - is very different from the calls of other stints.

# LONG-TOED STINT     Plate 4

*Calidris subminuta*

Breeds NE Asia. Winters SE Asia, Philippines, Australia.

The Long-toed Stint is a regular migrant in the outer Aleutians, ALASKA, and breeding may occur some years, though documentation is lacking. Despite it regularity in W ALASKA, observers there should not immediately identify any yellow-legged stint as a Long-toed: the Least Sandpiper *C. minutilla* has been recorded on St. Lawrence I. (4-6 Jun 1978).

**ALASKA** Rare, but regular, migrant during spring (mid-May to early Jun) and fall (late Jul to mid-Sep) migration on the westernmost Aleutian Is. Most occur singly or in small groups, but a high count of 40 on Shemya I. on 16 May 1976 included flocks up to ten. The species breeds on the Commander Is., U.S.S.R., and apparent courtship flights have been observed on Attu I. Like the Wood Sandpiper *Tringa glareola*, Long-toed Stints may nest in years when enough are present to stimulate breeding activity (see C 80:312). Additional spring records, perhaps overshoots, have occurred east to Amchitka I. and north to St. Lawrence I., the Pribilof Is., and Wales, Seward Pen.

# LONG-TOED STINT

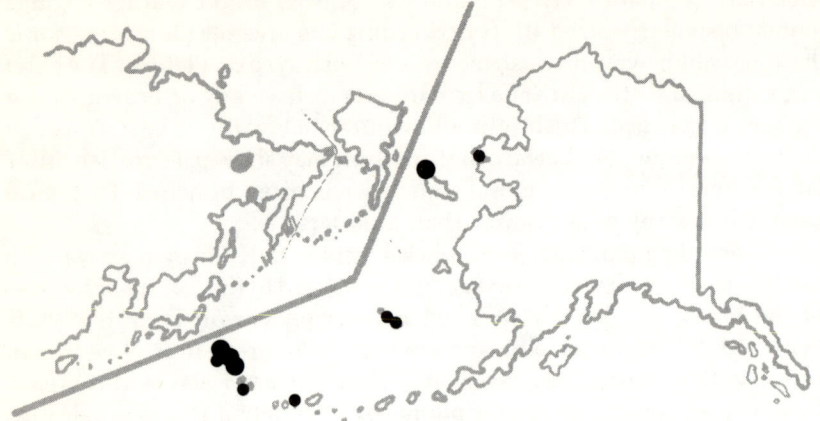

I.D. The Long-toed Stint is very similar to Least Sandpiper: both have short, fine bills, similar plumage sequences, and yellowish legs with unwebbed toes. See p. 153 for a discussion of ageing stints and the plumages of Least Sandpiper.

In breeding plumage, many Long-toed Stints are easily separated from Least Sandpiper by their brighter coloration, with feathers of the crown and back boldly black-centered and brightly edged in rufous. The breast is washed with orange and has a gorget of well-defined streaks. Except for the extent of the breast streaks, the entire effect is not unlike that of a minature juvenile Sharp-tailed Sandpiper *C. acuminata*.

Juvenile and winter plumage is much more similar to Least Sandpiper and out-of-range birds would be extremely difficult to identify. Useful points would include longer legs and toes (looking like it is wearing flippers as it walks), a more upright stance, and often a pale base to the bill, sometimes looking two-tone (but many Long-toed Stints have all-dark bills, as does Least). In hand, the central toe measures 22-26 mm long; that of Least measures 18-21 mm.

19 May 1980 on Attu I., ALASKA. *Don Roberson.*

### LONG-TOED STINT

The call is described as a dry, purring "prrp", rather than Least's high, thin "preet". For more information see Wallace (1974), Kitson (1978), and Prater *et al* (1977).

# WHITE-RUMPED SANDPIPER

*Calidris fuscicollis*

Breeds N North America. Winters C & S South America.

The White-rumped Sandpiper breeds across arctic ALASKA, but its long migration route takes it east to NE North America in the fall, for a transoceanic flight to South America, while spring migration is undertaken through the interior of North America, east of the Rockies. All records of the White-rumped Sandpiper on the West Coast south of ALASKA have been of spring migrants straying west, between the dates of 16 May-16 Jun, and most are from the interior of the West Coast states and provinces.

**BRITISH COLUMBIA** Two records, both from the interior in spring: 24 May 1931† at Atlin, and 29 May 1938† at Tupper Creek.

**WASHINGTON** Two records, both at Reardon, Lnc.: 20 May 1962 and 23 May 1964.

**CALIFORNIA** Four records: 7 Jun 1969† at the Salton Sea, north end, Riv., 16 Jun 1976* at the Salton Sea, south end, Imp., 2-7 Jun 1978 at the Carmel R. mouth, Mnt., and 11 Jun 1978 at Keyhoe Beach, Pt. Reyes, Mrn.

23 May 1964 at Reardon, Lnc., WASH. 2nd record. *Jim Acton.*

# WHITE-RUMPED SANDPIPER

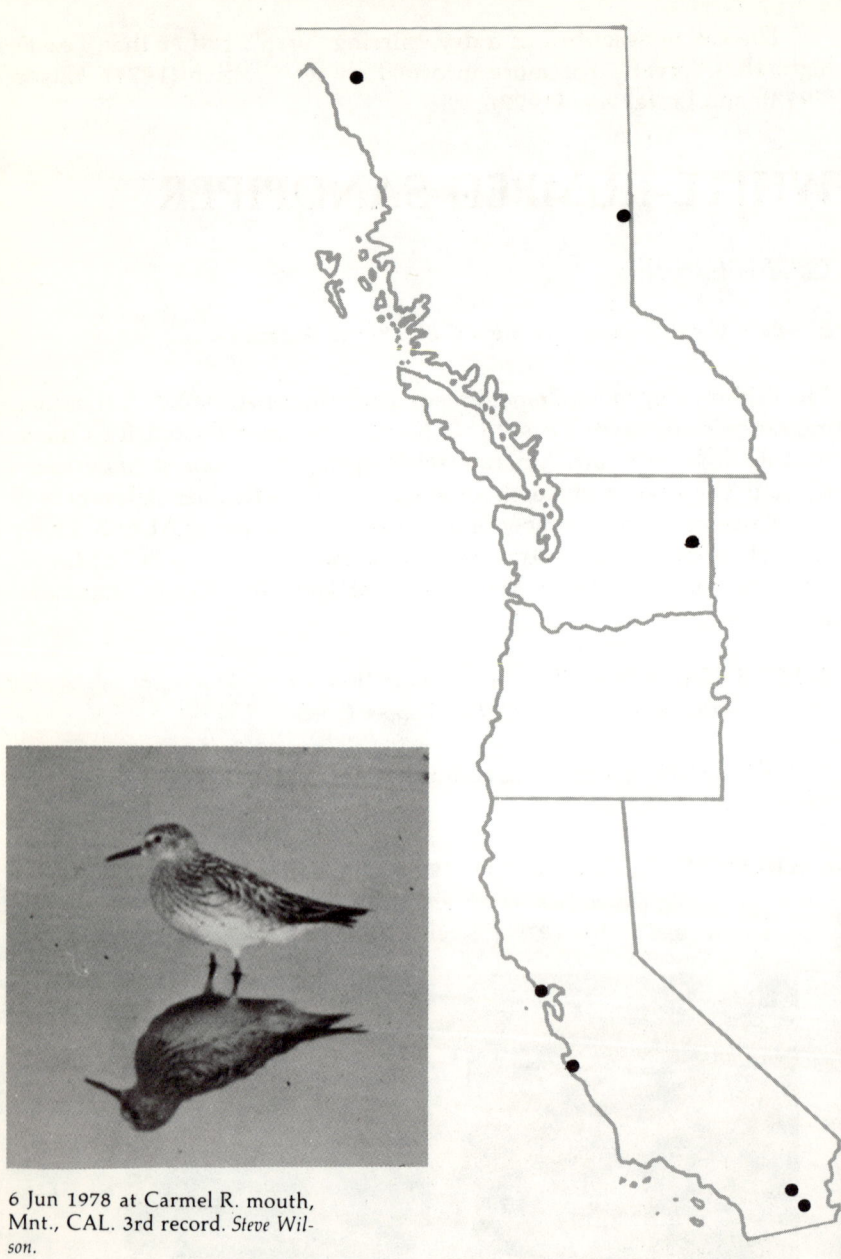

6 Jun 1978 at Carmel R. mouth, Mnt., CAL. 3rd record. *Steve Wilson.*

## WHITE-RUMPED SANDPIPER

I.D. The white rump of the White-rumped Sandpiper is emphasized by the standard guides, but note also the distinctive shape of the bird, being short-legged and long-winged, with the wings extending beyond the tail at rest, resembling in silhouette the Baird's Sandpiper *C. bairdii*. In breeding plumage, the breast streaking forms a gorget and continues down onto the flanks. This pattern, combined with a slight droop to the tip of the bill, resembles breeding-plumaged Western Sandpiper *C. mauri*, but the elongated shape, lack of rusty crown or ear coverts, and larger size will identify the White-rumped Sandpiper even if the rump is not seen. Adults in winter plumage are gray above and white below and this plumage is pictured in the standard guides, though it is not likely to be found on any White-rumped Sandpiper on the West Coast. Juvenile plumage is very different, with the dark-centered feathers of the upperparts being boldly edged in red, buff, and white. The breast and flanks are washed buffy or buff-gray and are finely streaked.

The call - a high, thin, almost insect-like "jeet" - is distinctive.

## SHARP-TAILED SANDPIPER        Plate 3

*Calidris acuminata*

Breeds NE Asia. Winters New Guinea to Australia, New Zealand.

The Sharp-tailed Sandpiper occurs on the West Coast most often as a fall migrant, when it is regular in small numbers throughout much of W ALASKA and has recently been regular (averaging about 10 each fall) at shorebird concentration areas near Vancouver, B.C., with others scattered along the B.C. coast and on Queen Charlotte I. and Vancouver I. It is still considered a Rarity south of B.C., but recent records suggest that there is a regular migration of Sharp-tailed Sandpipers, in small numbers, along the entire West Coast in fall. CAL has recently averaged about 6 birds a year. Fall migration south of ALASKA occurs between Sep-Nov and is composed almost entirely of juveniles. There is one winter record from S CAL.

# SHARP-TAILED SANDPIPER

The Sharp-tailed Sandpiper is very rare during spring migration in ALASKA and is unrecorded in the spring south of that state. Yet there are 4 spring records from Juneau (12 May 1969, 17 May 1970 (2), and 23 May 1973), suggesting returning birds from wintering grounds either in the New World or from islands in the E Pacific. More expected are 4 spring records from Gambell, St. Lawrence I., another at Nome, Seward Pen. (9 Jun 1977), and two far north at Barrow (11 Jun 1972 & 1 Jun 1973). Summer records, suggesting possible breeding, come from Kivalina in NW ALASKA, including 4 breeding-plumaged birds together (28 Jun 1967).

**WASHINGTON**   About 50 records, most graphed below. It is now considered annual in Sep-Oct, especially at Whidbey I., Isl., Leadbetter Pt., Pac., and Ocean Shores, G.H. All records are of juveniles, except for an adult reported 1 Oct 1977 at Ocean Shores. All records are coastal, except for 3 inland: 15 Sep 1972 at Soap Lake, Grn. (M 54:21), 13 Oct 1973 at Sunnyside, Yak., and 28 Sep-5 Oct 1975 at Richland, Ben.

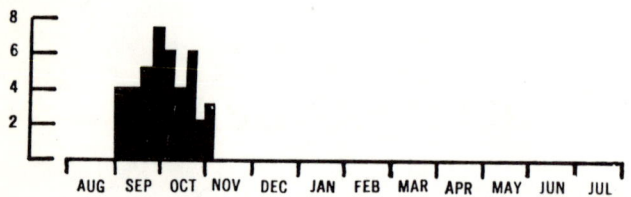

**OREGON**   9 records, all juveniles: 16 Oct 1965 at Tillamook Bay, 24 Sep 1967 at the south jetty, Columbia R., Clt., 1 Sep 1968 at the south jetty, Columbia R., 26-29 Oct 1969 at Fern Ridge Res., Lane, 22-23 Aug 1973 (2) at Eugene, Lane, 27-30 Sep 1974 at Sauvie I., Col., "fall" 1975 at Yaquina Bay, Lnc., 23 Oct 1977* at Tillamook Bay, 13 Aug-20 Sep 1978 (2-3)* at the south jetty, Columbia R., and 7-28 Oct 1978 (2-3) at the south jetty, Columbia R.

**CALIFORNIA**   50 records, involving 69 individuals, graphed below. All have been juveniles during fall migration. All have been coastal, except for these four records from the Central Valley: 6-7 Sep 1971 at Woodland, Yolo, 4-16 Oct 1973* at Woodland, 11 Oct 1976 at Visalia, Tul., and 1 Oct 1978 (3) at Dinuba, Tul. Favored coastal areas include Lake Talawa, D.N. (3 records, 7 birds), coastal Marin Co. (9 records), Santa Maria R. mouth, S.L.O. (3 records), Goleta, S.Bb. (5 records), and Santa Clara R. mouth, Ven. (3 records). Extreme dates of fall migrants are from 3 Sep to 13 Dec. The only winter record was on 19 Jan 1980 at Pt. Mugu, Ven.

# SHARP-TAILED SANDPIPER

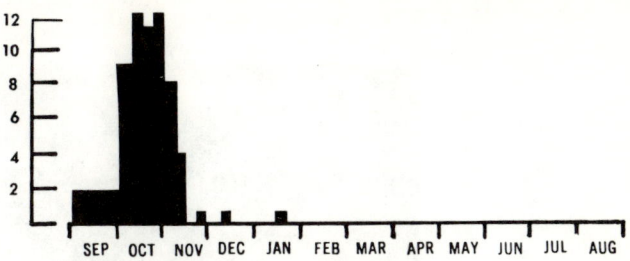

13 Oct 1978 at the south jetty, Columbia R., Clt., ORE (two with Sanderling, right). 8th record. *Harry B. Nehls.*

Oct 1978 at Carmel R. mouth, Mnt., CAL. *Ronald L. Branson.*

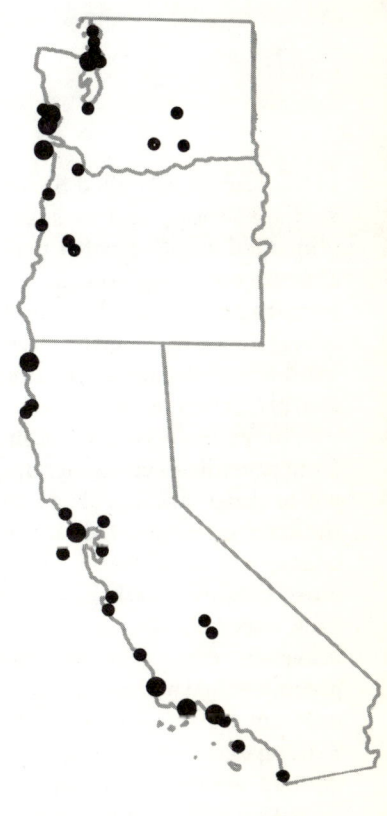

# SHARP-TAILED SANDPIPER

9 Sep 1979 at Goleta, S.Bb., CAL.
*James M. Greaves.*

I.D. The Sharp-tailed Sandpiper most resembles the Pectoral Sandpiper *C. melanotos*, and is basically similar in size and shape. Breeding-plumaged adults are distinctive (see plate). Winter-plumaged adults are almost unknown on the West Coast, but are basically like dull immatures, lacking the bright feather edgings to the cap, back, and wing coverts, and lacking the juveniles orange breast, but retaining the thin band of streaks across the upper breast, distinct from the Pectoral's wide, sharply demarcated gorget.

Juveniles account for nearly all West Coast records. These differ from juvenile Pectoral Sandpiper by the bright rusty cap and contrasting white supercilium; a broad wash of orange across the breast, with a thin necklace of streaks below the throat, very different from the Pectoral's heavily streaked breast, sharply cut-off from the white belly; and often more brightly marked upperparts, with rusty edges to the wings and back, especially about the scapulars and tertials (some juvenile Pectorals, however, may have brighter edgings to the upperparts than some juvenile Sharp-taileds). Juvenile Ruff *Philomachus pugnax* is typically uniform buffy-orange on the face and breast (recalling Buff-breasted Sandpiper *Tryngites subruficollis*), but lacks the necklace of streaks, a well-defined white supercilium, and the pair of white lines on the back of Sharp-tailed Sandpiper. Ruffs, even females, are larger (about the size of a Lesser Yellowlegs *T. flavipes*) and bulkier, and show more extensive white sides to the rump in flight. For more information see Webb & Conry (1979).

# CURLEW SANDPIPER

*Calidris ferruginea*

Breeds N Asia. Winters Europe, S Asia, Africa, Australia.

The Curlew Sandpiper has twice nested in N ALASKA and has been suspected of attempting to nest several other times. It has also occurred in ALASKA as a spring overshoot in the extreme NE and a fall migrant in W ALASKA. Farther south, spring (late Apr-early May) and fall (late Jul-mid-Sep) vagrants have appeared in every state and province on the West Coast.

**ALASKA** Most Alaska records are from Pt. Barrow, where it was taken on 6 Jun 1883† and nesting has been proved or suspected in the summers of 1962 (10 birds, 2 nests found; A 81:362), 1972 (7 nests found), 1973 (calling male), and 1974 (pair on territory). Fall records are: 8-9 Aug 1972 (3)† at Oliktok Pt. in N Alaska, 4-5 Aug 1975 at Pt. Barrow, 14-15 Aug 1975 at Old Chevak, W Alaska, and 11 Sep 1977† on Shemya I., Aleutian Is. The North Slope records could be of juveniles hatched in Alaska.

Spring records are: 8 Jun 1975 at Gambell, St. Lawrence I., 22 Jun 1976 at Cape Espenberg, and 3 May 1978 at Egg I., Copper R. delta, S Alaska. While the first two records may be of spring overshoots or migrants moving to Alaska nesting grounds, the latter record would seem to be of an individual returning north after wintering somewhere in the New World.

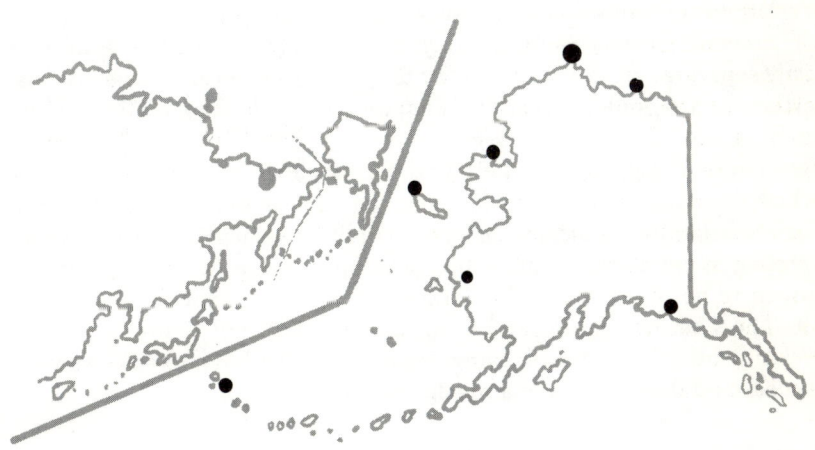

# CURLEW SANDPIPER

**BRITISH COLUMBIA**   Two records: 31 Jul 1936† at Masset, Q.C.I. (C 39:176) and 30-31 Jul 1977 at Iona I., Vancouver (*Discovery*, New Series, 6:89).

**WASHINGTON**   One record: 10 May 1972 at Potholes Res., Grn. (M 54:21).

**OREGON**   Two records: 21 Jul 1976* at Yaquina Bay, Lnc., and 16 Aug 1976* at Seven Devils wayside, Coos.

**CALIFORNIA**   Five records: 7 Sep 1966* at Rodeo Lagoon, Mrn., 16-17 Sep 1972* at Pescadero, S.M., 27-28 Apr 1974* at Salton City, Imp., 7-14 Sep 1974* at Bolinas Lagoon, Mrn., and 27-28 Sep 1979 at the Santa Clara R. mouth, Ven.

I.D.   The Curlew Sandpiper is slightly larger than a Dunlin *C. alpina*, with obviously longer neck and legs and a more upright stance, giving it a sleeker appearance. It would seem to be unmistakeable in breeding plumage, but the Red Knot *C. canutus* has been misidentified as a Curlew Sandpiper: note the Curlew Sandpiper's shape, longer bill, much deeper red color, and extensive red on back. Winter-plumaged Curlew Sandpipers are unrecorded on the West Coast, though this is the plumage generally pictured in the field guides. The shape, white rump patch, and bill evenly decurved along its entire length should distinguish it from the Dunlin; smaller size, shorter black legs (not pale), evenly decurved and finely-tipped bill, and wingstripe will separate it from the Stilt Sandpiper *Micropalama himantopus*, which is also gray-backed and white-rumped in winter plumage. Bill shape, not bill length (which may overlap with Dunlin), is an important character.

Juvenile Curlew Sandpiper, which account for most fall records, is easily separated from the Dunlin by the scaly back, recalling the juvenile pattern of the smaller Baird's Sandpiper *C. bairdii*, the similarly-sized Buff-breasted Sandpiper *Tryngites subruficollis* (which does not have black legs, white rump, or long bill), and the larger Ruff *Philomachus pugnax* (which is much bulkier and has pale legs and a shorter bill). Juvenile Curlew Sandpiper typically has a peach or buff-washed breast and shows a strong supercilium. A published account of a Curlew Sandpiper has proven to be of a Wilson's Phalarope *Steganopus tricolor* with a deformed bill. The Curlew Sandpiper has an all-dark tail (not white with dark flecking), black legs, shows a wingstripe, is less slender-necked and small-headed, and does not have a needle-like bill.

# CURLEW SANDPIPER

10 May 1972 at Potholes Res., Grn., WASH. 1st record. *Darlene Meyer.*

8 Sep 1974 at Bolinas Lagoon, Mrn., CAL. 4th record. *John Luther.*

31 Jul 1972 at Barrow, ALASKA (male of breeding pair). *Van Remsen.*

# SPOONBILL SANDPIPER

Plate 4

*Eurynorhynchus pygmeum*

Breeds NE Asia. Winters SE Asia.

The Spoonbill Sandpiper has occurred three times on the West Coast: as an apparent spring overshoot and fall vagrant in ALASKA and as a fall vagrant in coastal B.C.

**ALASKA**  Two records: 15 Aug 1914† (2 collected from a "flock of possibly ten"; A 35:387) at Wainwright, and 2 Jun 1977† on Buldir I., Aleutian Is. (A 96:189).

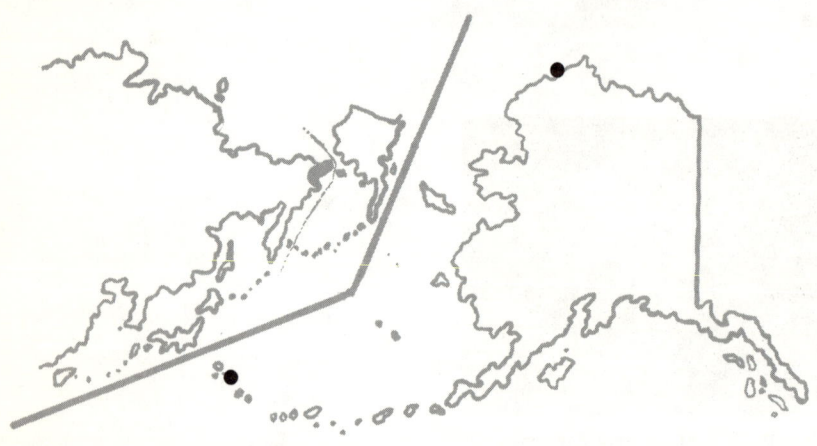

**BRITISH COLUMBIA**  One record: 30 Jul-3 Aug 1978 at Iona I., Vancouver (AB 32:1062).

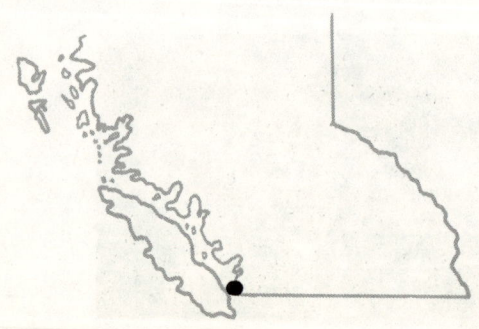

# SPOONBILL SANDPIPER

2–3 Aug 1978 at Iona I., Vancouver, B.C. (two views). *Ervio Sian.*

I.D.   The Spoonbill Sandpiper is about the size of a Western Sandpiper *Calidris mauri* and possesses a unique, spatulate-tipped bill. Though diagnostic when seen, this remarkable shape can be hard to see in profile. The plumages generally resemble those of the Rufous-necked Stint *C. ruficollis*. In breeding plumage the face, throat, and upper breast are washed with rufous and the blackish upperparts are edged with rusty (color photo in Prater *et al*, 1977). Juveniles show rusty and white-edged upperpart feathers and white underparts, washed with buff across the breast. Winter-plumaged birds are grayish above, white below. The general shape is chunky (more so than a Western Sandpiper) and the bird is said to have a tendency to stand with the head held high. For more information see Sauppe, Macdonald, & Mark (1978).

# BROAD-BILLED SANDPIPER

Plate 3

*Limicola falcinellus*

Plate 1?

Breeds N Europe, N Asia. Winters S Eurasia, Africa, Australia.

The Broad-billed Sandpiper has two disjunct breeding areas in Eurasia: in Scandinavia and in N Siberia. Vagrants from the Siberian population (presumably) have reached the West Coast on the outer Aleutian Is., ALASKA during the fall. 5 of the 6 records occurred on a single island during the fall of 1978.

**ALASKA**   6 records: 19 Aug 1977† on Adak I. (A 96:189) and 5 were found 30 Aug-6 Sep 1978 on Shemya I.

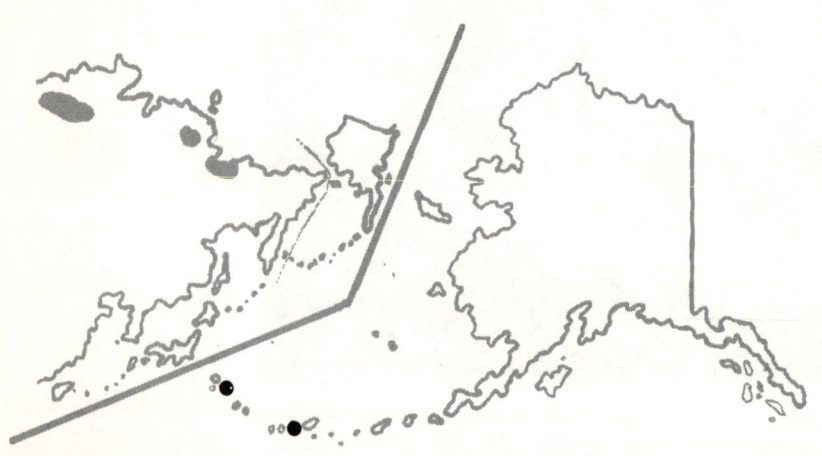

**I.D.**   The Broad-billed Sandpiper is about the size of a Dunlin *Calidris alpina*, but has shorter legs and is distinctively plumaged with a double supercilium. The bill is thick, with a marked droop or kink at the tip. The back shows a strong white "V" in breeding and juvenile plumages against richly-fringed, blackish back feathers, giving the upperparts a snipe-like appearance. The breast is crossed by a broad band of streaking, extending onto the flanks. In winter plumage, the "V" becomes less distinct, and the breastband is reduced to a narrow necklace of fine streaks. Bill shape, short legs, and double supercilium continue to give it a look of no other small shorebird. Juveniles have chestnut edgings to the feathers of the upperparts and show a gorget of breast streaks.

## BROAD-BILLED SANDPIPER

In flight, the inner half of the leading edge of the grayish wing is black, sometimes showing as a black shoulder patch at rest. The legs are blackish, greenish, or yellowish. The call is described as a "dry trill 'chrrreep'" (King & Dickinson, 1975).

# STILT SANDPIPER

*Micropalama himantopus*

Breeds N North America. Winters S South America; small numbers winter in S CAL.

The Stilt Sandpiper is considered a Rarity only in ORE. This anomolous situation arises as the species nests in N ALASKA, small numbers regularly winter in CAL, and it averages over 4 a year during small passages through SW B.C. and NW WASH in spring and fall. The major migration routes of the species are east of the Rockies, but small numbers migrate through the Great Basin, especially in fall. A percentage of these birds pass through the shorebird concentration areas near Vancouver and on S Vancouver I., B.C., each fall, and continue to the Great Basin via Puget Sound and E WASH. In CAL, fall migrants are quite rare but have occurred from late Jul-Oct, mostly on the coast. Small numbers winter annually at the Salton Sea, Imp., and occasionally elsewhere in S CAL. Except at the Salton Sea, spring records are very few and there is only one for N CAL. Likewise, it is very rare during spring migration in WASH & B.C., and is as apt to occur in the interior as on the coast. Since the regular movement of a small number of fall migrants bypasses ORE, it remains a Rarity there. All acceptable records to date are from fall migration.

**OREGON**   15 records, graphed below. All are from the coast or the Willamette Valley, except for a bird on 24 Aug 1974 at Baker, Bak. The late Aug-early Sep peak is similar to the pattern shown by migrants in coastal WASH-B.C. For more information see Fix (1979).

# STILT SANDPIPER

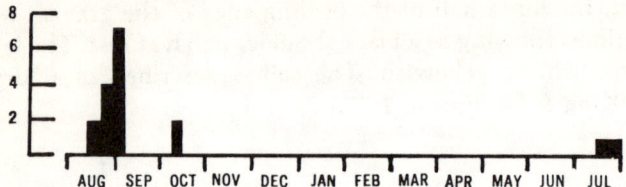

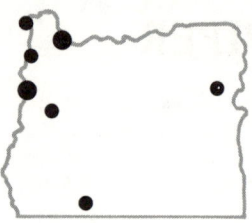

30 Aug 1974 at the south jetty, Columbia R., Clt., ORE. 5th record. *Harry B. Nehls.*

# BUFF-BREASTED SANDPIPER

*Tryngites subruficollis*

Breeds N North America. Winters S South America.

The Buff-breasted Sandpiper nests in arctic ALASKA, but its migration route is east of the Rockies and only rarely do individuals or small flocks wander to the West Coast south of ALASKA. All Rarity records fall between Aug-Oct, most are coastal, and apparently only juveniles have been involved. Exceptionally large numbers were recorded the falls of 1978 (46 birds) and 1979 (58 birds).

**BRITISH COLUMBIA**   Taken as early as 1889, small numbers have been found in most recent falls. 33 records, involving 48 birds, are graphed below. Favored localities include Oak Bay, Saanich Pen., and Comox airport, all on Vancouver I., and Iona & Sea Is., near Vancouver. For more information see Campbell & Gregory (1976).

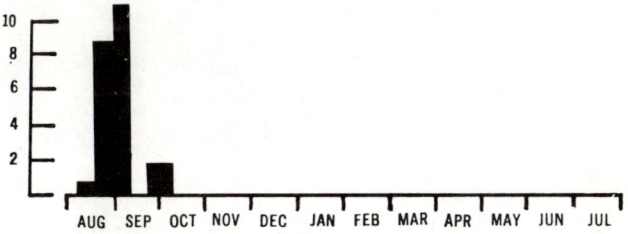

**WASHINGTON**   At least 30 records, involving up to 82 birds, graphed below. At least 21 were recorded in fall 1978 and at least 32 birds, including a flock of 20 at Ocean Shores, G.H., were found in fall 1979. About half of the records are from Ocean Shores; another location with multiple records is Leadbetter Pt., Pac. Although nearly all records are coastal; E WASH recorded birds in "fall" 1962 and 7 Sep 1968 at Reardon, Lnc.

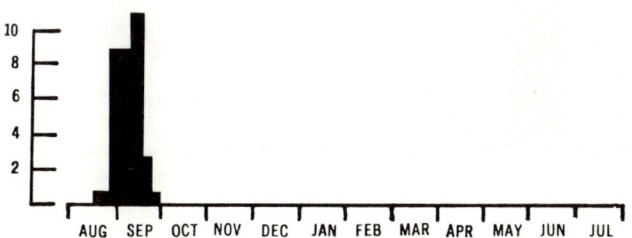

# BUFF-BREASTED SANDPIPER

**OREGON** 17 records, involving 23 birds, graphed below. The flight years brought 6 birds in 1978, including 3 at the south jetty, Columbia R., Clt., and another 6 in 1979.

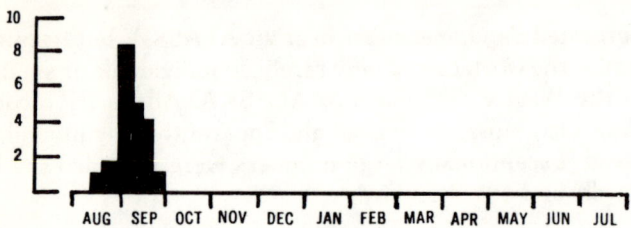

6 Sep 1975 at Sixes R. mouth, Cur., ORE. 8th record. *Tom Lund.*

**CALIFORNIA** 32 records, involving 55 individuals, graphed below. All have been found singly or in twos, except for a flock of up to 11 birds on Tomales Pt., Mrn., from 26 Aug-10 Sep 1978, 4 at the Santa Clara R. mouth, Ven., on 6 Sep 1979, and up to 7 at Pt. Mugu, Ven., between 16-18 Sep 1979. The invasion year of 1978 brough 18 birds to 7 localities in CAL; 1979 added an additional 18 birds. The only acceptable interior record is 27 Aug-1 Sep 1978 at Lakeside, Riv.

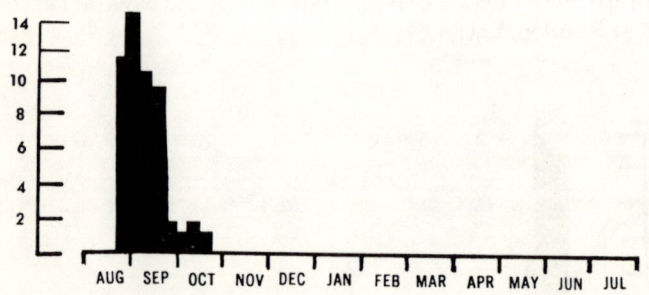

# BUFF-BREASTED SANDPIPER

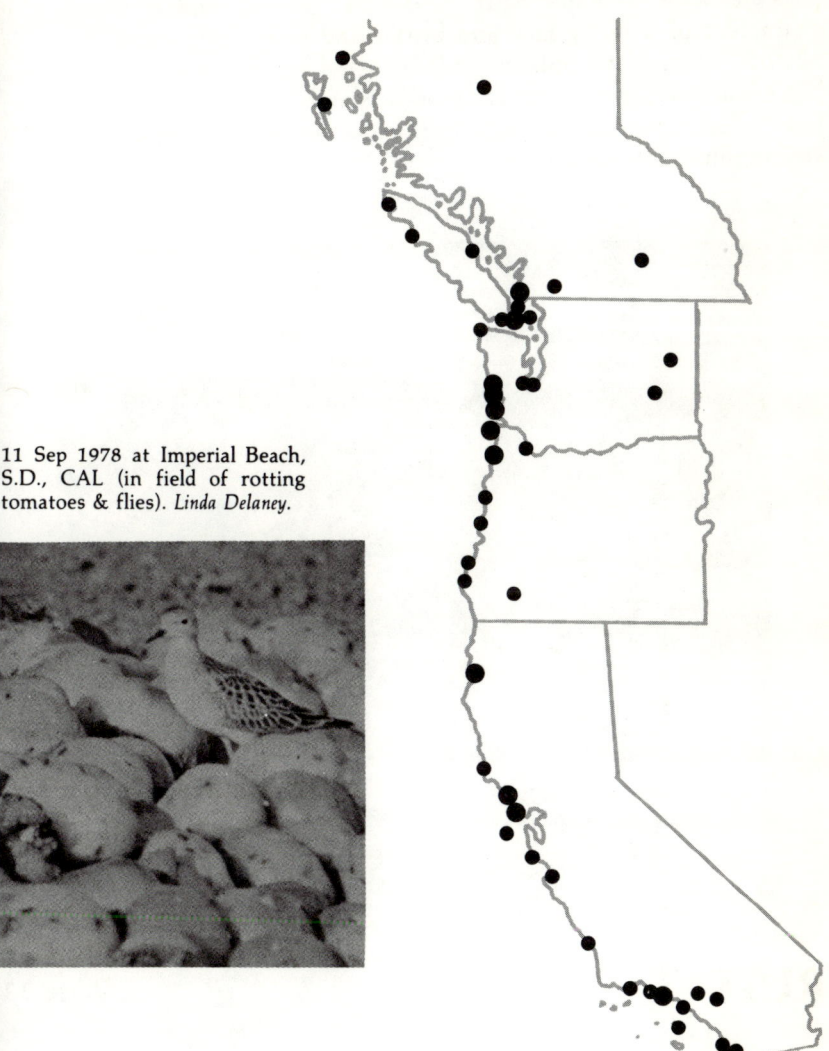

11 Sep 1978 at Imperial Beach, S.D., CAL (in field of rotting tomatoes & flies). *Linda Delaney.*

I.D. The standard guides do not picture the juvenile plumage of the Buff-breasted Sandpiper, though juveniles account for all West Coast Rarity records. In this plumage the belly is white (not buffy) and the back is very scaly, recalling a juvenile Baird's Sandpiper *Calidris bairdii*, though the Baird's has black, not yellowish, legs and is distinctly smaller. The flight of the Buff-breasted is quite graceful, on long wings, and the underwings are a gleaming white with a black "wrist" mark. Confusion is

## BUFF-BREASTED SANDPIPER

possible with juvenile Ruff *Philomachus pugnax*, which shares the characters of a buffy face and breast and scaly upperparts, but it is obviously larger and bulkier. Buff-breasted Sandpiper has a short, fine bill; small head, long-necked appearance; and show a bold buffy eyering, but confusing individuals might be flushed to note the plain rump and the striking underwing pattern.

3 Sep 1978 at Pt. Reyes NS, Mrn., CAL. *Truman Holtzclaw.*

# RUFF                                                    Plate 11

*Philmachus pugnax*

Breeds N Eurasia. Winters S Eurasia, Africa, Indonesia.

The Ruff has occurred on the West Coast as a rare breeder in N ALASKA, a spring and fall migrant throughout the area, and as a winterer in CAL. This complex pattern is more fully explained by state or province below.

# RUFF

**ALASKA** Rare, but regular, spring (mid-May - mid-Jun) and fall (mid-Aug - mid-Sep) migrant in the outer Aleutians and the Bering Sea islands and coastline. Fall birds have twice reached Pt. Barrow and the Coleville R. delta on the North Slope, while another was recorded at Cordova in S ALASKA.

Breeding has been proved once on the North Slope: a female with 4 eggs discovered 21 Jun-6 Jul 1976 at Pt. Lay (WB 8:25). Breeding activity noted elsewhere include a male courting 2 females on 12 Jun 1976 at the Arctic R. mouth on the Seward Pen., and over 40 birds, with flocks up to dozen, in early Jun 1979 at Gambell, St. Lawrence I. Observers noted courting males and copulation.

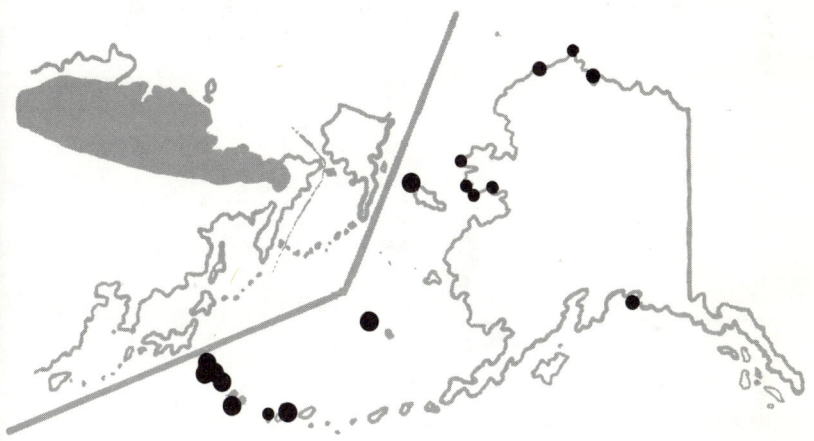

3 Jun 1977 on Buldir I., ALASKA (male in breeding plumage). *Robert H. Day.*

# RUFF

**BRITISH COLUMBIA**  9 records, graphed below. 8 are during fall migration and most occurred around Vancouver, especially Iona I. and Reifel refuge. The late Jun to early Aug pattern here is in contrast to the Sep-Oct showings of fall migrants further south and may consist of adults, rather than the juveniles which dominate fall records from WASH to CAL. The lone spring record is 27-29 May 1976 at Iona I.

# RUFF

**WASHINGTON** 12 records, graphed below. Nearly all are coastal and most occurred at Ocean Shores, including up to 4 from 31 Aug-15 Sep 1979. The only inland record was the first for the state: 22 Sep 1972 at Reardon, Lnc.

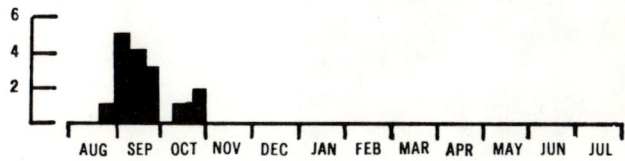

**OREGON** One record: 8-15 Sep 1979 at the south jetty, Columbia R., Clt.

**CALIFORNIA** 52 records, graphed below. All have been from the coast or coastally-influenced areas, except for birds 19 Dec 1962 at Lower Klammath NWR, Sis., 9 Oct 1974 at Hanford, Kng., 23-29 Mar 1975 at Los Banos, Mer., and 3 Oct 1979 at Lancaster, L.A. The graph would appear to show two patterns: 1) fall migrants (perhaps all juveniles) passing through CAL in Sep-early Oct, and 2) wintering birds arriving between late Oct-mid-Dec and leaving between late Feb-early Apr. To date, no birds in breeding plumage nor any that could be termed spring migrants have been found.

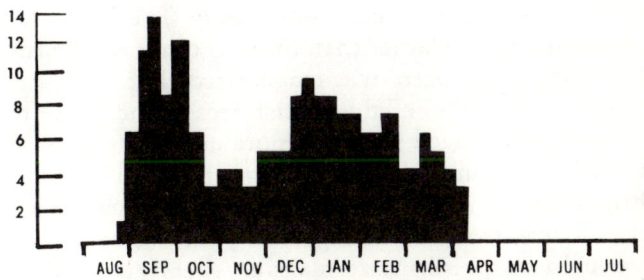

3 Sep 1978 at Limantour, Pt. Reyes NS, Mrn., CAL. *Jeri Langham.*

# RUFF

Feb 1977 at Pacific Grove, Mnt., CAL. *Robert E. O'brien.*

8 Sep 1979 at the south jetty, Columbia R., Clt., ORE. 1st record. *Owen Schmidt.*

I.D. The Ruff is a distinctly-shaped shorebird, being small-headed and thick-necked, with long legs and a bulky body. The white ovals at the sides of the rump can be larger than those of other shorebirds, but the value of this mark has been over-emphasized. The very scaly-backed appearance of the juvenile and the whitish area on the face at the base of the bill in winter-plumaged birds are more immediate clues. Breeding-plumaged males are unmistakable. The fairly thick bill is medium-length and slightly decurved, with a pale base to the lower mandible. Leg color is extremely variable, from red, orange-red, yellow, greenish, or grayish. There is sexual dimorphism in size: males are slightly larger than a Lesser Yellowlegs *Tringa flavipes* and a good deal heavier, females are about the same size and bulk as a Lesser Yellowlegs. The male also has a larger bill and longer legs. Juveniles are typically buffy-orange on the face and breast, and have each back and wing covert feather broadly edged with buff, recalling the scaly pattern of the juvenile Baird's Sandpiper *Calidris bairdii*. See the discussions under Sharp-tailed Sandpiper *C. acuminata*, Curlew Sandpiper *C. ferruginea*, and Buff-breasted Sandpiper *Tryngites subruficollis* to avoid possible confusion with those species.

# GREAT BLACK-BACKED GULL

*Larus marinus*

Breeds NE North America, N Europe. Winters coasts of E North America, Europe.

The Great Black-backed Gull has occurred only once on the West Coast. This species has been expanding its range in eastern North America in recent years and vagrants have occurred farther and farther west. Recent reports have come from Texas and Colorado. Though the Aug date of the CAL record was surprising, the occurrence of this species on the West Coast was not totally unexpected.

**CALIFORNIA**  One record: 11 Aug 1977 at Newport Bay, Orn. This record did not come to the attention of West Coast observers until early 1980, when a photograph taken by a foreign visitor was forwarded to the *American Birds* regional editor. This record has not yet been reviewed by the CAL Records Committee.

# SLATY-BACKED GULL

*Larus schistisagus*

Breeds NE Asia. Winters coasts of NE Asia south to China.

The Slaty-backed Gull is a very rare visitor to W & N ALASKA; it has recently been averaging about 7 sightings a year. Most have been recorded during the spring and summer months, which may reflect the concentration of birding efforts as much as the distributional pattern of this species. There is a single record on the West Coast south of ALASKA.

**ALASKA**  At least 95 records, those with known dates graphed below. Numbers of immatures and adults (perhaps non-breeders) have occurred during the summer months around the Bering Sea and in N ALASKA. 5 have been found far north at Pt. Barrow; the westernmost records on the Arctic coast come from Prudhoe Bay (31 Jul 1977) and the Colville R. mouth (Aug 1977). Records from the Aleutians have been mostly during spring migration (high count were at least 12 on Shemya I. from 30 Apr-3 Jun 1977). There are 5 winter records from the central and eastern Aleutians; two others occurred in S ALASKA: 23-25 Feb & 11-13 Apr 1978 at the Buskin R. mouth, Kodiak I. (same bird?) and 28 Oct-13 Nov 1979 at Anchorage.

# SLATY-BACKED GULL

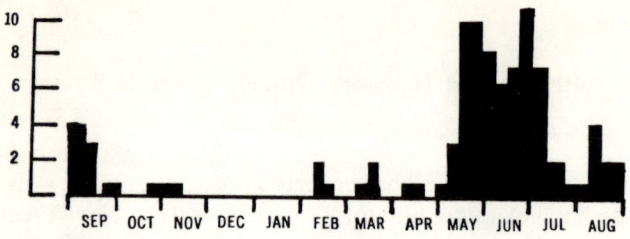

**BRITISH COLUMBIA**   One record: 1 Mar 1974 at Clover Pt., Victoria, V.I.

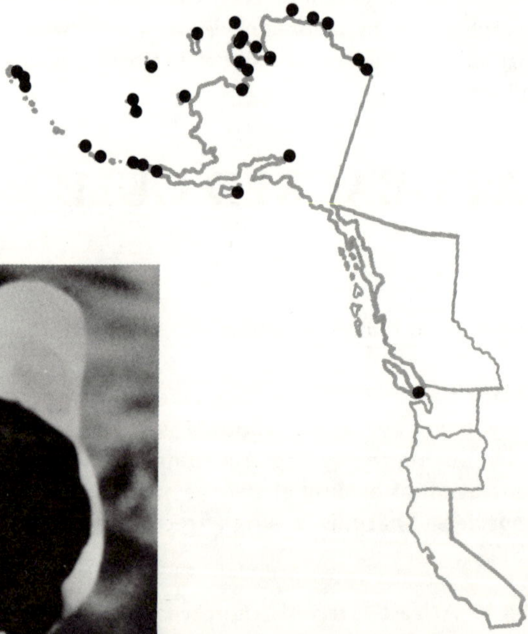

1 Mar 1974 at Clover Pt., Victoria, V.I., B.C. 1st record. *J. E. V. Goodwill.*

# SLATY-BACKED GULL

I.D. The Slaty-backed Gull is about the size of Western Gull *L. occidentalis* and closely resembles that species. Coastal Western Gulls are divided into two races which are often identifiable in the field: *L. o. wymani*, common in S CAL, is distinctly darker-mantled (2nd winter birds to adults) than *L. o. occidentalis*, the common race from C CAL to WASH. The mantle of Slaty-backed Gull is slightly darker than that of *L. o. wymani* (which is unrecorded north of CAL), so that this darker shade is distinguishable from the lighter-mantled northern race of Western Gull anywhere north of CAL. In addition, compared to Western Gull, the Slaty-backed Gull appears heavier, with a more massive head and bill, and often shows a pale gray "tongue" across the bases of the black tips of the inner primaries, thus separating the dark gray mantle from the black wingtips (vaguely reminescent of the wingtip pattern of adult Franklin's Gull *L. pipixcan*). Western Gull lacks these "tongues", as the dark gray mantle merges into the black wingtips. The illustration on Plate 5 compares adults in flight and portrays these differences. The observer should be aware that the effects of wear alter the wingtip patterns to some degree.

Soft part color becomes apparent after second-winter plumage; discussion of these characters for adults will also apply to appropriate sub-adult plumages. The legs of adult Western and Slaty-backed Gulls are pink, but those of Slaty-backed tend to be brighter and a deeper pink-red. While the iris color of Western Gull is quite variable, from dark to pale yellow, the iris of Slaty-backed Gull tends to be a clear yellow. The eyelid color (which becomes much brighter as breeding season approaches) of Western Gull tends to be orange-yellow; that of Slaty-backed Gull ranges from pink to red-purple.

Other large dark-mantled gulls may pose identification problems. The "Yellow-footed Gull" *L. o. livens*, perhaps a separate species, is a regular summer visitor to the Salton Sea, CAL, but is unrecorded north of S CAL. It is similar in size to Slaty-backed Gull and is nearly as dark-mantled, but has yellowish legs and a clear yellow eyelid. The Lesser Black-backed Gull *L. fuscus* has been recorded in C CAL and Colorado, but is distinctly smaller than Slaty-backed Gull, does not have pink legs, and is much slimmer-billed. The Great Black-backed Gull *L. marinus*, now recorded in S CAL and Colorado, is distinctly larger than Slaty-backed Gull, has a blackish mantle which is not noticeably lighter than the wingtips, and is long-legged and shows a longer, more massive bill. For a fuller discussion see Binford (1978).

# SLATY-BACKED GULL

The identification of first-year birds is even more difficult and little has been published. The brief data to date suggests that the immature plumages of Slaty-backed Gull resemble those of the larger Great Black-backed Gull, with whitish-appearing feathers on the wing coverts and back in first-winter birds and with very pale wing coverts of 2nd-winter birds contrasting sharply with dark gray back feathers. In Alaska, the situation is confused by the presence of the Siberian race of Herring Gull *L. argentatus vegae,* which averages larger than the usual North American Herring Gull *L. a. smithsonianus* and is somewhat darker-mantled as an adult than the North American Herring Gull (though still much lighter-mantled than Slaty-backed Gull). First-year Siberian Herring Gulls resemble first-year Slaty-backed Gull, but are distinctly slimmer-billed and lack the very pale look of some young Slaty-backeds.

Identification of any unusual gull (and, for that matter, many common species) is greatly facilitated by an understanding of their molt timing (in most species there is a molt of head and body feathers in late winter to spring, and a complete molt in late summer to fall), and knowledge of the progression of plumages from juvenile to adult, which takes one or two years in most small species and three or four years in the largest. A chart showing typical molt timings and immature plumage progression of gulls is given in part 1 of "Identification of West Palearctic Gulls" (Grant 1978): three parts of this five-part series have already been published (Grant 1978, 1979, and 1980), and the entire series (which will eventually be published in book form) is highly recommended.

# LESSER BLACK-BACKED GULL

*Larus fuscus*

Breeds N Europe to C Russia. Winters Europe, Middle East to C Africa.

The Lesser Black-backed Gull has occurred only once on the West Coast. During the 1970s, this species was encountered in eastern North America with increasing frequency (perhaps due to the continent-wide expansion in coverage and increases in birding expertise). An interior record occurred in Colorado in Dec 1976 (WB 9:171). The CAL and Colorado birds were judged to be the British race of Lesser Black-backed Gull *L. f. graellsii,* and it has been hypthesized (WB 9:173) that a small number of this race may regularly wander SW to NE North America,

# LESSER BLACK-BACKED GULL

with a few continuing onward to wintering areas in S North America, Central America, or the Caribbean (yet to be substantiated). Thus an occasional bird might be expected to wander toward our area, especially in Dec-Jan.

**CALIFORNIA**  One record: 14 Jan 1978* at Robert's Lake, Seaside, Mnt. (WB 9:141).

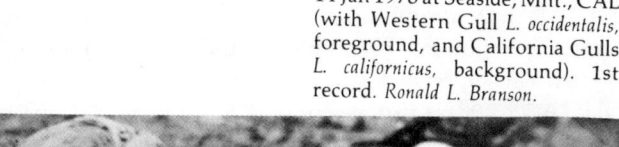

14 Jan 1978 at Seaside, Mnt., CAL (with Western Gull *L. occidentalis*, foreground, and California Gulls *L. californicus*, background). 1st record. *Ronald L. Branson.*

I.D. The Lesser Black-backed Gull is slightly larger than California Gull *L. californicus* and about the size of a small Herring Gull *L. argentatus*. The mantle of adult birds (attained by 2nd-winter) is a dark gray, distinctly darker than every regular West Coast gull (except Slaty-backed Gull in Alaska, which see). It is a full shade darker than the northern race of Western Gull *L. o. occidentalis*, with which it is likely to be compared as a vagrant on the West Coast, and the color is most similar to the back of an American Coot *Fulica americana*. The bill is long and very slim for a medium-sized gull; adults typically show an oblong red spot on the bill, an atypical pattern for common West Coast gulls. The legs of the British race of Lesser Black-backed Gull *L. f. graellsi*, which accounts for the West Coast record, are described as buffy-yellow. The iris is pale and the eyelid bright red. The heads of adults in winter are finely streaked on the face, crown, and nape. For a more through discussion of the adult and a comparison with other dark-mantled gulls, see Binford (1978).

The identification of immature plumages is more complex and not dealt with here. A detailed discussion of all plumages is contained in Grant (1980). For a discussion of possible problems presented by hybrid Great Black-backed *L. marinus* X Herring Gull, see Foxall (1979).

# BLACK-TAILED GULL

*Larus crassirostris*

Breeds NE Asia to E China. Winters Japan to S China.

The Black-tailed Gull has occurred only once in North America: an adult which reached Attu I., the westernmost Aleutian Is., ALASKA, during the spring. This species is regular as far north as the Kurile Is. in NE Asia and it is not totally surprising that one should reach the Aleutians, especially following favorable winds or storm fronts.

An earlier record of a bird collected on 28 Nov 1954 at San Diego, CAL (A 72:208) is not acceptable. San Diego is home port to numerous U.S. Navy ships which regularly enter the range of this species. The bird could have easily been captured and later released on the Naval Center at which it was collected. The possibility that this coastal gull crossed the Pacific Ocean on its own is extremely remote and the CAL Records Committee considers the specimen to be of an escapee (see CB 1:24).

**ALASKA**  One record: an adult 29 May 1980 on Attu I. The bird was flying by Murder Pt. ahead of a rain squall and observed by three experienced birders who happened to be seawatching at the time (D. D. Gibson, T. Moore, A. Driscoll, *pers. com.*).

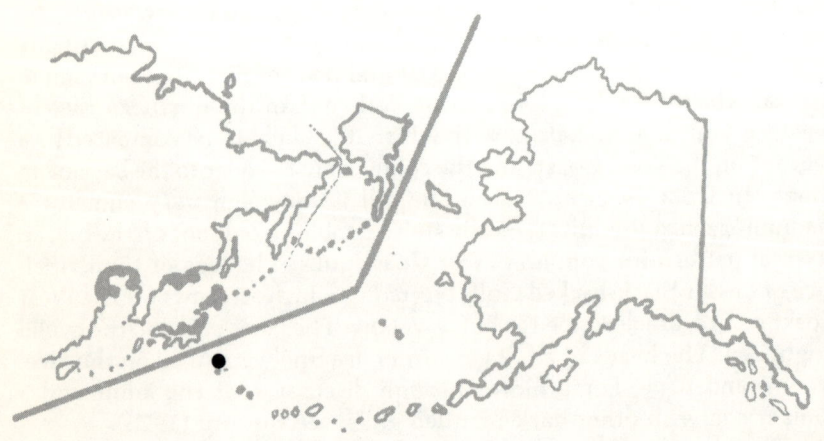

# BLACK-TAILED GULL

I.D. The Black-tailed Gull is about the size of California Gull *L. californicus*, but differently shaped with disproportionately long narrow wings producing a shape in flight unlike other similarly-sized gulls. Adults have a very dark blackish mantle with little contrast between the primaries and the rest of the wing and usually lack any white spots at the tips of the primaries (present in all other large adult West Coast gulls). A sharply demarcated black subterminal band on the white tail is unique. The bill is long and has a black ring behind a red tip. The legs are greenish-yellow. The eye is yellow; the eyering red. Some third year gulls with dark mantles, such as Slaty-backed Gull *L. schistisagus,* may lack white spots on the primaries, show a dark ring on the bill, and have a tail band. Black-tailed Gull is distinguished from these birds by the evenly dark mantle (Slaty-backed shows some contrast between primaries and upperwing), the very sharply demarcated tail band (third-year gulls have irregular bands), the red tip to the bill, a different shape, and greenish (not pink) legs.

Little has been published on the identification of subadult plumages since Dwight (1925, pp. 162-165). Black-tailed Gull is a medium-sized gull with a three year plumage sequence. First-year birds are mostly rich brown with blackish wings and tail and a flesh-colored bill with a sharply demarcated dark tip. The back becomes grayer and the underparts whitish during the first winter, but the wings and tail remain all dark. 2nd winter birds are very like the adult (having, like the adult, streaking on the head in winter) but differ in having the tail band extending to the outer tail feathers (outer tail feathers all white in adult), some mixture of brownish on the wing coverts, and a less well-defined bill pattern.

# BLACK-HEADED GULL

*Larus ridibundus*

Breeds N Eurasia, recently a few have bred NE North America. Winters S Eurasia, N Africa, Philippines.

The Black-headed Gull is regular on the West Coast only during spring migration on the Aleutian and Pribilof Is. of ALASKA (high count was 25 on 21 May 1979 on Attu I.). There are a scattering of spring and summer records along the Bering Sea coast, but very few fall records anywhere in ALASKA. A fall record from SE ALASKA (12 Sep 1977 at Cordova) would seem to be of a bird wandering toward the West Coast south of ALASKA, where it is a Rarity.

Rarity records of Black-headed Gulls have spanned the seasons. Most have been observed with flocks of Bonaparte's Gulls *L. philadelphia*. Interestingly, at least 4 times these same flocks have also included a Little Gull *L. minutus*. This coincidence(?) has raised an interesting question of possible origin of the Black-headed Gulls. The initial reaction to the presence of a Black-headed Gull on the West Coast would be that it was probably Siberian in origin. Alaska specimens have proven to be from NE Asia and it would seem likely that some other West Coast records would have originated there. But West Coast records of Little Gull, Lesser Black-backed Gull *L. fuscus,* and Great Black-backed Gull *L. marinus* presumably originated in NE North America or N Europe. The recent range expansion of Black-headed Gull to NE North America suggests the possibility that some West Coast birds could have occurred as a result of a cross-continental migration. Especially interesting is a bird that returned to winter for a second year (presumably the same individual) with a flock of Bonaparte's Gulls in the Central Valley of CAL; this flock also contained a Little Gull returning to winter for a second year.

15 Aug 1975 at Clover Pt., Victoria, V.I., B.C. 2nd record. *John B. Steeves.*

# BLACK-HEADED GULL

**BRITISH COLUMBIA**   Six records, five from Victoria, V.I.: 27 Oct-13 Nov 1974 (*Syesis* 9:361), 15 Aug-8 Nov 1975, 19 Oct-8 Nov 1975, 28 Jul-6 Aug 1976, 22 Sep 1979, and one from Tsawwassen: 26 Aug 1977.

**WASHINGTON**   One record: 4 Nov 1972 at Ocean Shores, G.H. This record is listed as hypothetical on the WASH checklist because, though well described, it was seen only by a single observer.

**OREGON**   One record: 27 Jun 1977* at Sunset Beach, Coos.

**CALIFORNIA**   Seven records: 23-24 Jan 1954 at Richmond, Ala., 4 Jan 1956 at Oakland, Ala., 16-23 Jul 1972 at Arcata, Hmb., 5-8 Apr 1976* in Tomales Bay, Mrn., 19 Feb-5 Mar 1978* at Arcata, Hmb., 30 Dec 1978 several miles offshore Santa Barbara, and 20 Mar-8 Apr 1979* at Stockton, S.J., presumably the same individual returning 4 Feb-late Mar 1980.

27 Oct 1974 at Clover Pt., Victoria, V.I., B.C. 1st record. *R. Wayne Campbell.*

27 Jun 1977 at Sunset Beach, Clt., ORE. 1st record. *Joe Gnagey.*

# BLACK-HEADED GULL

Early Apr 1979 at Stockton, S.J., CAL (with Bonaparte's Gull *L. philadelphia*, foreground). 7th record. Jeri Langham.

I.D. The Black-headed Gull in any plumage resembles Bonaparte's Gull *L. philadelphia*, though it is distinctly larger and has a heavier, longer bill and longer legs. Like Bonaparte's Gull, it reaches adult plumage by the 2nd winter.

Adults may be identified by the all dark red bill, dark brown hood in summer ( not extending as far down the nape as on Bonaparte's), and underwing showing a prominent blackish area on the inner primaries, contrasting with the white outer primaries and underwing coverts. Adults in winter also have a slightly lighter tone to the mantle than Bonaparte's, a whitish (not gray) nape, and dull red bill and legs (may look dark at a distance), rather than the black bill and red-orange legs of winter-plumaged Bonaparte's.

First-winter Black-headed is identified by shape and structural differences; pale, dark-tipped bill; lighter brown carpal bar; blackish-streaked inner primary coverts (see BB 72:33); slightly lighter gray mantle (this color not extending forward onto the nape); and the lack of neat white spots on the inner primary tips (but these may be worn off in some Bonaparte's).

The Black-headed Gull has a slower wingbeat and is less agile in flight than the more tern-like Bonaparte's Gull. A thorough discussion of this species is in Grant (1978).

# LAUGHING GULL

*Larus atricilla*

Breeds E North America, W Mexico to N South America. Winters SE U.S. to C South America.

The Laughing Gull formerly bred at the Salton Sea, CAL; today it occurs there annually as a part of post-breeding dispersal and numbers are found during the summer and early fall. Elsewhere in CAL it is very rare, with only about 10 records from the S CAL coast and fewer still along the N CAL coast (the northernmost was at Arcata, Hmb., on 4-18 Sep 1973). There is only one acceptable record north of CAL.

**WASHINGTON**   1 Sep 1975 at the north jetty, Columbia R., Pac.

I.D. The Laughing Gull can be confused with Franklin's Gull *L. pipixcan*, though adult plumages are distinctive and are pictured by the standard field guides. In any plumage, the Laughing Gull is a larger bird, with a noticeably longer bill (bills of both species are rather stout) which droops at the tip, and proportionately longer legs. First-winter birds of both species have dusky mantles, dark subterminal tail bands, and dark half-hoods. As well as size and structural differences, first-winter Laughing is identified by its extensive gray breastband, a dark half-hood merging into the dark nape and breast (Franklin's has a clear cut dark half-hood separated cleanly from white nape and breast), and the tail band extending onto the outer tail feathers (Franklin's has all-white outer tail feathers).

Franklin's Gull appears to have a complete molt in both spring and fall, unlike any other gull (except perhaps Sabine's Gull *Xema sabini*). First-summer plumage is characterized by a partial or complete black hood, a mostly white tail, and extensive black on the primaries with no white bar separating this black from the gray of the mantle. This plumage is similar to the field guide pictures of adult Laughing Gull and it is suspected that many summer records of vagrant Laughing Gulls actually refer to first-summer Franklin's Gull. The adult Laughing Gull is distinguished by the

# LAUGHING GULL

size and structural differences described above, an all-white tail (Franklin's has grayish on the central tail feathers and often an incomplete tail band), and gray primary coverts (Franklin's has its primary coverts washed with black during the first-summer).

The second-winter Franklin's Gull is white-tailed (except for some pale gray on the central tail feathers) and still does not have the white bar separating the black primaries from gray mantle as do adults; this plumage can be mistaken for adult winter Laughing Gull. Laughing Gull has a less clear-cut dark hood and has mostly black-tipped primaries (Franklin's has white-tipped primaries). See Grant (1979) for a complete discussion of both species.


# LITTLE GULL

*Larus minutus*

Breeds NW to C Eurasia, has recently bred around the Great Lakes, North America. Winters Europe, N Africa, Middle East.

The Little Gull is a Rarity anywhere on the West Coast. Records are scattered nearly year-round, but most birds have been found with migrant or wintering flocks of Bonaparte's Gulls *L. philadelphia*. All West Coast records of Little Gull are suspected of refering to birds which originated in NE North America (perhaps from the Great Lakes breeding area) or even N Europe and arriving after cross-continental flights. Most interesting is a bird (presumably the same individual) which returned to winter for a second year with a flock of Bonaparte's Gulls in the Central Valley, CAL.

**CALIFORNIA**  Ten records: 16-21 Nov 1968 at Mecca, Riv.; 22-25 Dec 1969 at Redondo Beach, L.A.; 3 Dec 1972 at the Salton Sea, south end, Imp.; 19 Jan-1 Mar 1975* at Zmudowski SB, Mnt.; 13 Apr 1977 at Pajaro R. mouth, S.Cz, presumably the same bird 16 Apr 1977* at Pigeon Pt., S.M.; 14-22 Apr 1977* at Goleta, S.Bb.; 21 Feb-5 Mar 1978* at Arcata, Hmb.; 7 Oct 1978 at Manilla, Hmb.; 20 Mar-17 Apr 1979 at Stockton, S.J., presumably the same individual returning 4 Feb-late Mar 1980; and 19 Apr 1979 at Pigeon Pt.

**OREGON**  Two records: 20 Oct-4 Nov 1975 at Tillamook Bay, and 11 Aug-20 Sep 1979* at Yaquina Bay, Lnc.

# LITTLE GULL

17 Apr 1977 at Goleta, S.Bb., CAL. 6th record. *Robert Copper.*

23 Jan 1975 at Zmudowski SB, Mnt., CAL. 4th record. *Gary Zamzow.*

20 Mar 1979 at Stockton, S.J., CAL. 8th record. *Don Roberson.*

# LITTLE GULL

**WASHINGTON** Ten records: 2 Sep 1974 at Penn Cove, Widbey I., Isl., 5 Oct & 7-9 Nov 1974 at Everett, Sno., with a second bird present 8 Nov 1974, 21 Sep 1975 at Ocean Shores, G.H., 15 Nov 1975 at Seattle, King, 30 Nov 1976 at Seattle, 2-30 Oct 1977 at Everett, 1 Apr 1978 in the Pt. Wilson stream, off Port Townsend, Jef., 8 Oct 1978 at Everett, and early Sep 1979 in the San Juan Is., S.J., possibly the same bird in Oct 1979 at Pt. Roberts, Wha.

7 Nov 1974 at Everett, Sno., WASH. 2nd record. *Dennis Paulson.*

Sep 1979 at Yaquina Bay, Lnc., ORE. 2nd record. *Robert Lucas.*

# LITTLE GULL

**BRITISH COLUMBIA**  Eight records: 24 Oct-19 Nov 1972 at Victoria, V.I., 17 Dec 1972 at Pt. Grey, Vancouver, 18-19 May 1974 (2) at Sea I., Vancouver, 31 Oct-7 Nov 1974 at Victoria, 27 Feb 1976 at Victoria, 30 Aug 1979 at Victoria, and 24 Oct 1979 at Iona I., Vancouver (perhaps the same bird as in N WASH in fall 1979).

**ALASKA**  One record: 4 Sep 1975 at Cordova. This record is considered hypothetical on the Alaska checklist because, though there are good details, it is based on a sighting by a single observer.

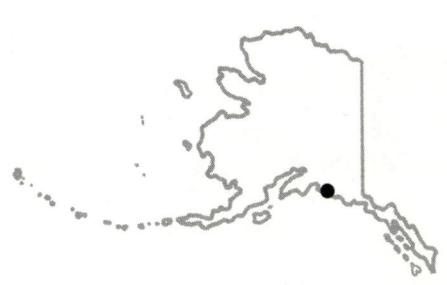

I.D. The Little Gull is portrayed in some of the standard guides, but the pictures are misleading to some extent. The world's smallest gull, it is distinctly smaller than Bonaparte's Gull *L. philadelphia*, with more rounded wing-tips, tiny bill, and short legs. Adults in breeding plumage have a black hood, pale gray back and upperwings (the latter with a thin white border around the tip and along the trailing edge), and wholly blackish underwings. Adults in winter show a small round ear-spot, neat dark cap, and wing pattern as in breeding plumage. Second-year birds resemble adults, but have whitish inner underwing coverts contrasting with the blackish remainder of the underwing (though the entire underwing still appears dark at a distance), and, usually, small black spots or lines near the tips of the outer primaries.

First-winter birds are identified by their small size and proportions, blackish-brown carpal bar and blackish outer wing (forming a "W" pattern across the wings in flight), faint dark bar on the secondaries (the remainder of the upperwing is pale gray, like the back), white underwing, neat round ear-spot and dark cap, and black tail band.

For a complete discussion see Grant (Part 4, to be published in BB, Feb 1981).

# IVORY GULL

*Pagophila eburnea*

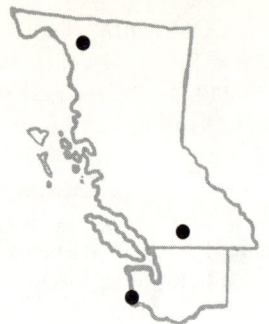

Breeds northernmost arctic islands and coast. Winters on holarctic arctic coasts and over pack ice.

The Ivory Gull is a fairly common pelagic migrant in the Chukchi and Bering seas off ALASKA, and is a less common winter and summer visitant to arctic seas around ALASKA. It is a rare vagrant to S & SE ALASKA, where there are five records: 13-14 Apr 1963 at Homer, 1 May 1963† at Anchorage, 7 Nov 1975 at Skagway, 7 Nov 1975 at Little Port Walter, Baranof I., and 13 Jul 1976 at Glacier Bay. There are two records from the interior of B.C., both from the fall and both taken before 1900, and a recent winter record from the WASH coast.

**BRITISH COLUMBIA** Two records: Sep 1889† at Dease Lake, and Nov 1897† at Penticton.

**WASHINGTON** One record: 20 Dec 1975 at Gray's Harbor.

# RED-LEGGED KITTIWAKE

*Rissa brevirostris*

Breeds locally on Pribilof and Aleutian Is., Alaska, and Commander Is., U.S.S.R. Post-breeders wander N to Bering Sea and E in the N Pacific.

The Red-legged Kittiwake is a Rarity anywhere south of ALASKA. The three Rarity records (all found dead on Oregon beaches) fall between Jan-Mar, but records in the N Pacific (most around Kodiak I., ALASKA) stretch from Oct-May and a recent bird found dead far inland at Corn Creek, near Las Vegas, Nevada (3 Jul 1977) illustrates the potential for long-range vagrancy in this species at nearly any time of year.

# RED-LEGGED KITTIWAKE

**OREGON** Three records: 28 Jan 1933† at Delake, Lcn., 25 Mar 1951† at Waldport, Lnc. (M 34:48), and 12 Mar 1955† at Nehalem, Til. (M 36:29).

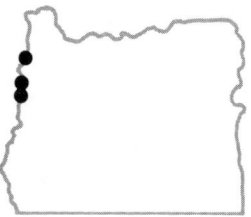

I.D. The adult is discussed in the standard guides (red legs, dark underwings, short bill). First-year birds are also distinctive, lacking the dark on the tail, nape, or carpal bar. At a distance, the immature appears to be a small white gull with a pale gray back and upperwing coverts, a white square tail, and black outer primaries. This pattern recalls a winter-plumaged adult Sabine's Gull *Xema sabini* and it is possible that some winter reports of Sabine's Gull (which is very rare off the West Coast from Dec-Mar) could refer instead to immature Red-legged Kittiwake. Sabine's Gull is separated by its more extensively black primaries and darker gray upperwing coverts — forming a more striking pattern — and a forked tail. At close range, young Red-legged Kittiwake shows a dark, smudgy eye-patch and dusky underwings.

# ROSS' GULL

*Rhodostethia rosea*

Breeds locally in NE Siberia (esp. Kolyma R. delta). Post-breeders move nearly circumpolar in arctic seas.

The Ross' Gull is regular on the West Coast only in coastal arctic ALASKA, where it is a fairly common fall migrant (most notably at Pt. Barrow) and a scarce spring migrant and summer visitant. It is very rare south of the Bering Strait and the southernmost ALASKA records come from the Pribilof Is. Nevertheless, fall and winter vagrants have appeared as far south in North America as Massachusetts, Illinois, and Victoria, B.C.

# ROSS' GULL

**BRITISH COLUMBIA**  One record: 9 Nov 1966 at Clover Pt., Victoria, V.I.

9 Nov 1966 at Clover Pt., Victoria, V.I., B.C. 1st record. *Ralph Fryer.*

## ROSS' GULL

I.D. The Ross' Gull is pictured in the standard guides, but recently additional identification material has been published (Miliotis & Buckley, 1975). In any plumage the small size (only slightly larger than Little Gull *Larus minutus*), tiny bill, long wedge-shaped tail, and long pointed wings are useful. In winter, the adult is essentially white with a very pale gray mantle (lighter than on other similar small gulls). The upperwings are pale gray with a broad white trailing edge, and a black outer web on the leading primary. A dusky eye-patch accentuates the black eye and there is a dark ear-spot or a hint of a dusky collar on the sides of the short neck. There is often a pale gray cap. The underwing coverts and the underside of the outer primary may look quite dark from a distance, recalling the dark underwing of Little Gull, but there is a broad white trailing wedge formed by white secondaries and inner primaries.

First-winter birds have a flight pattern similar to that of Black-legged Kittiwake *Rissa tridactyla*, with blackish outer primaries and carpal bar (forming a "W" pattern across the upperwings) and a dark terminal band on the tail. There may be dark barring on the rump. Ross' Gull lacks the Kittiwake's dark nape bar, but the best distinction is its small size and wedge-shaped tail. First-summer birds retain the first-winter wings and tail, but may have pinkish underparts and a full, thin black neck ring, like the summer adult.

# LEAST TERN

*Sterna albifrons*

Breeds C CAL to Baja, Mexico and E U.S. to N South America. Winters South America.

The Least Tern on the West Coast is regular only in CAL, where it is a local summer visitor along the coast north to San Francisco Bay. The CAL breeding race *S. a. browni* is now considered endangered: less than 1000 pairs are thought to exist (Wilbur 1974). The few records north of CAL appear to be spring overshoots and an early fall vagrant.

**OREGON** 2 records: 21 May 1964 (2†) at Ft. Stevens, Columbia R. mouth, Clt. (M 53:52), and 31 May 1976* at the south jetty, Columbia R., Clt.

**WASHINGTON** One record: 26-31 Aug 1978 at Ocean Shores, G.H.

# LEAST TERN

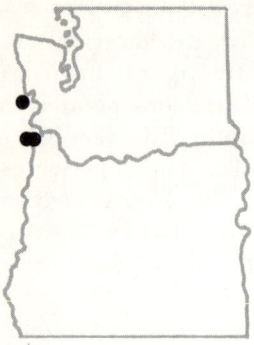

31 May 1976 at the south jetty, Columbia R., Clt., ORE (with Forster's Terns *S. forsteri*, left). 3rd record. *Harry B. Nehls.*

# SANDWICH TERN

*Sterna sandvicensis*

Breeds E U.S. to Caribbean; Europe to NW Africa. Winters SE U.S., S Mexico to C South America; S Europe to Middle East.

The Sandwich Tern does not nest in the Pacific (nearest colonies are along the American Gulf Coast and on islands off the Yucatan Pen., Mexico), but birds regularly winter on the Pacific coast of S Mexico and in the Gulf of Panama. It has occurred only once on the West Coast, when a spring vagrant reached S CAL.

**CALIFORNIA**  One record: 11-14 May 1980 in S San Diego Bay, S.D. The bird was discovered in an Elegant Tern *S. elegans* colony and during its brief stay attempted (unsuccessfully) to present fish to nesting Elegant Terns. This record had not yet been reviewed by the CAL Records Committee.

# WHITE-WINGED BLACK TERN

*Chlidonias leucopterus*   Plate 5

Breeds E Europe to SE Siberia. Winters Africa to Australia.

Though a long distance migrant with a tendency to wander (Sharrock, 1976), the White-winged Black Tern breeds far from the West Coast. The lone record could have been a spring overshoot far to the northeast.

**ALASKA** One record: 12 Jul 1976† at Nizki I., Aleutians. The adult was observed flying about an Arctic *Sterna paradisaea* and Aleutian *S. aleutica* tern nesting colony and was constantly harassed by the former species (C 80:312).

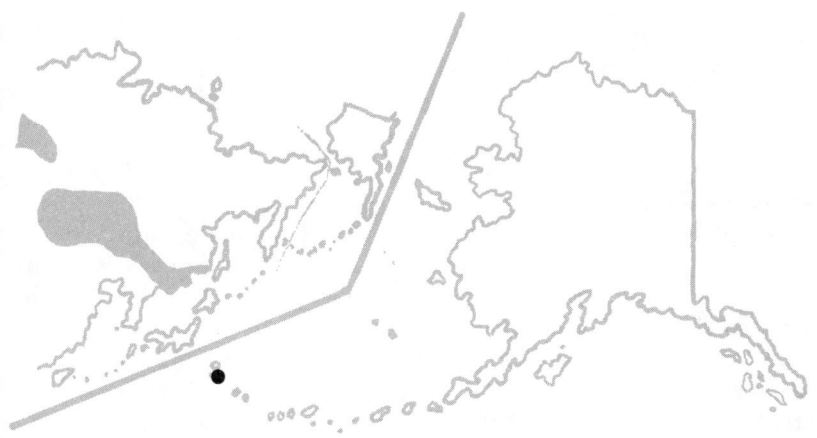

I.D. The White-winged Black Tern most resembles Common Black Tern *C. niger*. Subtle differences in structure and flight, such as its slightly heavier build, shorter bill, squarer tail, broader-based wings, and slower and shallower wingbeats, are difficult to discern even when the two species are together. Adults in breeding plumage are easily recognized by the white rump, tail, and leading upperwing coverts; black underwing coverts; and red bill and legs. Adults in winter are similar to Black Terns, but lack dark patches on the sides of the breast, show a discrete ear-patch clearly separated from a black-flecked crown, have a pale gray or white rump, and sometimes retain reddish legs. Black Terns in winter have obvious dark patches on the sides of the breast, a dark cap joined to the black ear-coverts, and a brownish-gray rump.

## WHITE-WINGED BLACK TERN

Juvenile and first-winter White-winged Black Terns have a "saddle-backed" look with a dark brown back contrasting with the pale gray upperwing coverts, white collar and rump; an ear-patch usually separated from the cap; and no black marks on the sides of the breast. Black Terns of the same age have a white collar but are otherwise dingy brown-gray above, including the rump, and the dark cap is joined to the ear-coverts. For a more thorough discussion see Williamson (1960).

## THICK-BILLED MURRE

*Uria lomvia*

Breeds circumpolar in N latitudes, S to Aleutians, Alaska, and the Gulf of St. Lawrence. Winters coastal waters south to N B.C., E U.S., NW Europe, and NE Asia.

The Thick-billed Murre winters on the West Coast from S ALASKA to N B.C.; it is a Rarity anywhere south of that province. All Rarity records have occurred in fall and winter and the majority were recorded around the edges of Monterey Bay, CAL. There it was found nearly annually from 1964-1974, but only one has been found there since then. It could be suggested that the warming temperatures in Monterey Bay during the late 1970s may have limited winter distribution at this southern locality. The general dearth of records between the more normal wintering areas and Monterey Bay is probably due to few observers, difficulty in identification, and the pelagic habits of this species.

2 Oct 1966 at Monterey, CAL (with Common Murre *U. aalge*, background). 3rd record. *Herbert Clarke*.

# THICK-BILLED MURRE

**WASHINGTON**  Five records: 19 Feb 1933† at Westport, G.H., 22 Sep 1976 about 25 miles w of Copalis Beach, G.H., 6 Dec 1979 at Friday Harbor, San Juan I., S.J., and 15 Dec 1979 (2) at Ocean Shores, G.H.

**OREGON**  Two records: 30 Jan 1933† near Mercer, Lane, and 15 Sep 1972† at the south jetty, Columbia R., Clt. (WB 5:137).

**CALIFORNIA**  17 records, graphed below. All but two were found in Monterey Bay, most along the shorelines of Monterey and Pacific Grove. Extreme dates are 27 Aug 1964 (CB 1:107) to 9 Apr 1965; birds occurred in 1964 (1), 1965 (1), 1966 (1), 1968 (1), 1972 (3), 1973 (3), 1974 (3), 1975 (1), and 1978 (1). The additional CAL records are: 7 Sep 1974* in Humboldt Bay and 3 Jan 1977 at the Eel R. mouth, Hmb.

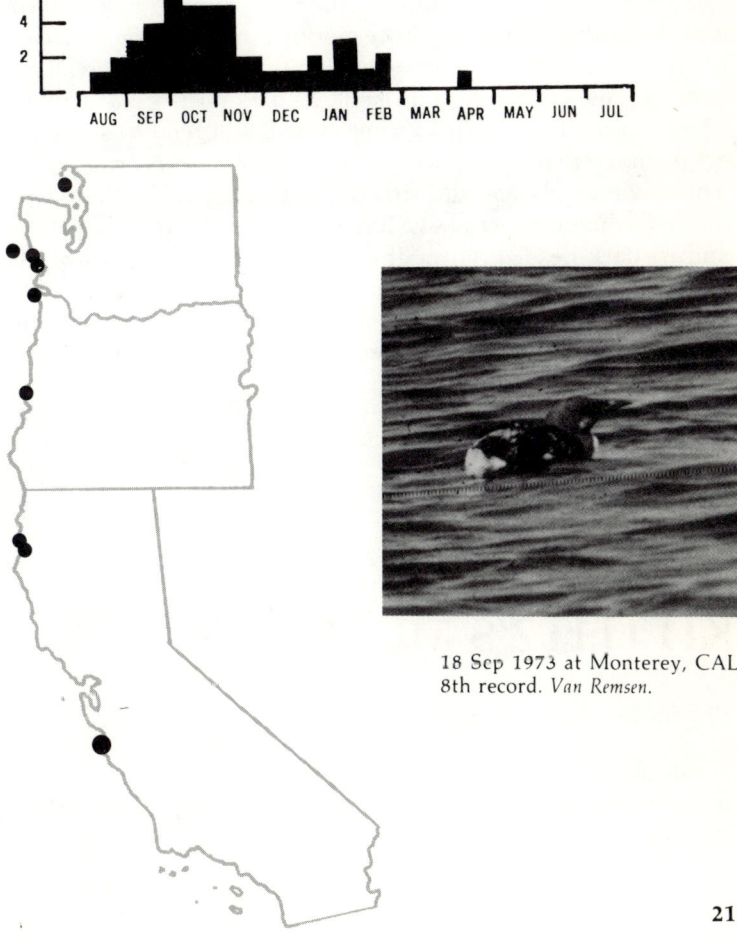

18 Sep 1973 at Monterey, CAL. 8th record. *Van Remsen.*

# THICK-BILLED MURRE

I.D. In the Pacific, the Thick-billed Murre is likely to be confused only with Common Murre *U. aalage,* which it resembles in any plumage. The best means of separation is bill shape: that of Common Murre is rather long and narrow and usually looks slightly upturned in the field; that of Thick-billed is decidedly stouter, with a decurving culmen throughout its length (see photos). Breeding-plumaged Thick-billed Murre shows a white stripe along the lower edge of the upper mandible and this mark is sometimes retained in winter plumage; a few Common Murre, however, show a similar pale line on the bill.

Plumage differences are also useful. The Thick-billed Murre in breeding plumage is decidedly black, rather than the dark brown of Common Murre (beware of lighting conditions which may make dark brown appear as black). The white chest of Thick-billed Murre extends up into the throat as a sharp inverted "V" in breeding plumage, a pattern not usually shown by Common Murre. In winter, Thick-billed Murre is dark-headed, with the dark face merging into a whitish throat. Common Murre in winter has white extending up the sides of the face to the ear-coverts, this white area is broken by a dark post-ocular stripe. Common Murre in molt, with dusky cheeks, will still tend to show some white areas above this line as soon as white begins appearing on the throat. These winter-plumaged distinctions are of value in the fall, but by Jan many Common Murre have already begun to attain breeding plumage and are dark-headed. Throughout the year the black back of Thick-billed Murre is a useful mark. In winter, the head of Thick-billed Murre may become brown, but the back remains black and at this time the contrast between brown head and black back (seen in good light) is a field character. Common Murre has a grayish cast to the back in winter-plumage; it will not look black in good light.

# KITTLITZ'S MURRELET

*Brachyramphus brevirostre*

Breeds SE, W, and N Alaska and NE Asia. Northern populations apparently winter off NE Asia, south to the Kurile Is.; other populations winter in adjacent open waters.

# KITTLITZ'S MURRELET

The Kittlitz's Murrelet is a Rarity on the West Coast anywhere south of ALASKA, where there is a single winter record from the Puget Sound area. More controversial is a record of a juvenile found beached 16 Aug 1969 at La Jolla, S.D., CAL (CB 3:33), far to the south. The date seems very early for a juvenile to be that far south of the breeding ground; capture and assisted passage aboard a ship could have accounted for its presence. The CAL Records Committee, in a split vote, has chosen not to include it on the CAL state list.

**WASHINGTON**   One record: 2 Jan 1974 at Friday Harbor, San Juan I., S.J.

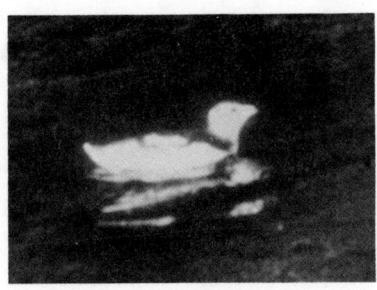 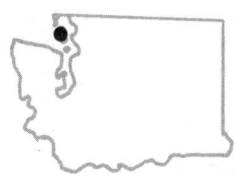

2 Jan 1974 at Friday Harbor, San Juan I., WASH. 1st record. *Dennis Heinemann.*

I.D. The Kittlitz's Murrelet is similar to Marbled Murrelet *B. marmoratus*, which also has white scapulars in winter plumage, but can easily be separated by plumage differences and the very short bill, distinctly more stubby than that of Marbled Murrelet. In breeding plumage, the overall effect of Kittlitz's Murrelet is of gray and fulvous speckles, including a very gray, white, and fulvous speckled back. Breeding-plumaged Marbled Murrelet looks uniformly dark brown above (rich red-brown barring visible only at close range) and heavily barred below. At a distance, Marbled Murrelet looks dark-capped; the head color of Kittlitz's is uniform.

In winter plumage, Kittlitz's is grayer than Marbled, and is identified by a white face and complete collar, white tail (hard to see); white edges to secondaries, and often a black crescent before the eye. Immatures resemble winter adults, but have fine barring on the face, nape, underparts, and tail. See Devillers (1972) for a more thorough discussion.

# XANTUS' MURRELET

*Endomychura hypoleuca*

Breeds Channel Is., CAL, and San Benito & Guadalupe Is., Mexico. Post-breeding dispersal generally north, regularly to Monterey Bay, CAL.

The Xantus' Murrelet breeds on the Channel Is. off S CAL and disperses north during the fall, regularly to Monterey Bay, especially during Aug-Oct. A few birds have been found off N CAL in every month; most have been of the CAL breeding race *E. h. scrippsi*, but there are fall records of the southern race *E. h. hypoleuca* in Monterey Bay and a winter record well offshore S.L.O. Co. The Xantus' Murrelet is a Rarity north of CAL, but a fair number have reached WASH during the fall (Aug-early Dec); most were identified as *scrippsi*, but *hypoleuca* has been collected. The northernmost record — off B.C. — was during the fall. Most interesting is a nominate *hypoleuca* photographed off ORE in Jun. Most Rarity records have been of pairs (each pair is considered a single record).

**OREGON** Four records: 28 Jul 1969 about 115 miles w of Cape Falcon, Til. (C 73:254), 19 Nov 1969* (pair) about 65 miles w of Newport, Lnc., 1 Sep 1970 (pair) some 132 miles w of Cape Falcon, and Jun 1973* about 165 miles w of Newport (*E. h. hypoleuca*).

**WASHINGTON** At least 22 records, graphed below. Most have been of pairs sighted during the fall on pelagic trips out of Westport, G.H., including a high count of 9 pairs on 8 Oct 1978. Most have been *scrippsi*, but *hypoleuca* has been collected (7 Aug 1947) and sighted (11 Sep 1978). The late 1970s featured a warming trend in mean ocean temperatures off the West Coast and this trend probably influenced the spattering of Xantus' records far to the north. The late record (6 Dec 1941†) was of a bird washed up on Copalis Beach, G.H.

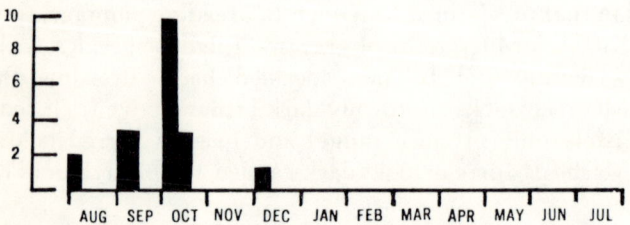

**BRITISH COLUMBIA** One record: 25 Oct 1971 some 57 miles se of Moresby I., Queen Charlotte Sound (C 75:253).

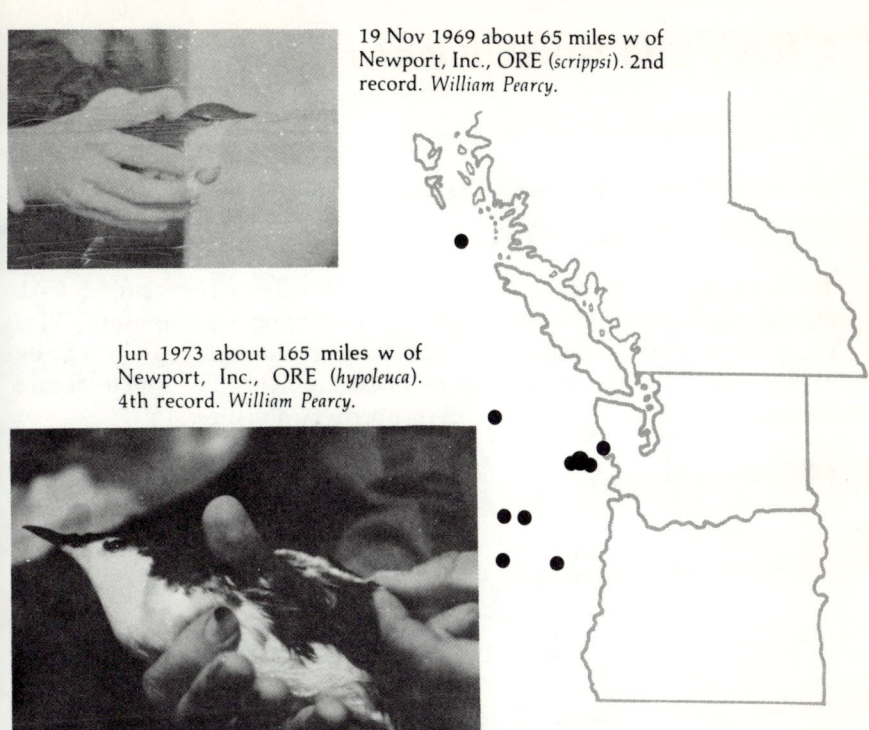

19 Nov 1969 about 65 miles w of Newport, Inc., ORE (*scrippsi*). 2nd record. *William Pearcy.*

Jun 1973 about 165 miles w of Newport, Inc., ORE (*hypoleuca*). 4th record. *William Pearcy.*

I.D. *Endomychura* murrelets are small, thin-billed alcids with only a passing resemblance as "tiny murres"; they sit low in the water and the white sides illustrated in the standard guides are not visible in the field. The two West Coast species — Xantus' and Craveri's Murrelets — are quite similar but can be separated by a variety of characters under good conditions. The southern race of Xantus' *E. h. hypoleuca* is easily identified by a broad white broken eyering, conspicous at a distance (other *Endomychura* have hard-to-see white eyelids only). The northern race of Xantus' Murrelet *E. h. scrippsi* is the race usually illustrated. It is separated from Craveri's Murrelet by 1) almost pure white underwing — Craveri's are blotched with dusky and sometimes appear quite dark (underwings of flying murrelets are often hard to see; other marks are equally good), 2) a shorter, stouter bill (compare photos of both species), 3) the dark cap extending down the face only to the middle of the bill — Craveri's extends down to the lower edge of the bill, and 4) a slight grayish cast to the dark upperparts — Craveri's has slightly darker upperparts with a brownish cast. Furthermore, most Craveri's Murrelets show a more or less sharply pointed dark mark extending down from the shoulder, sometimes visible on the water, but more apparent as a dark half-collar in flight. For more information see Dunn (1978b) and Jehl & Bond (1975).

# CRAVERI'S MURRELET

*Endomychura craveri*

Breeds on islands off Baja and in the Gulf of California, Mexico. Post-breeding dispersal generally north, regularly to S CAL.

The Craveri's Murrelet is found nearly annually in waters off S CAL during Aug-Oct, sometimes dispersing as far north as Monterey Bay, especially in years of strong Davidson Current conditions (which bring higher than average temperatures farther north). The single record north of CAL fell into this period of northward dispersal.

**OREGON**   One record: a week-old specimen found 15 Aug 1975 on Siltcoos SB, Lane (WB 6:109).

I.D. See the discussion under Xantus' Murrelet *E. hypoleuca*.

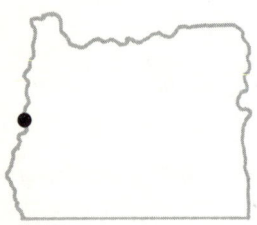

7 Oct 1978 at Moss Landing, Mnt., CAL. *Don Roberson.*

# PARAKEET AUKLET

*Cyclorrhynchus psittacula*

Breeds islands in Bering Sea and Aleutian Is., Alaska; Commander Is. and NE Asia. Winters in adjacent waters south to S Alaska and N Japan.

The Parakeet Auklet is now a Rarity anywhere on the West Coast south of ALASKA, but numbers were taken in Monterey Bay, CAL, in the early 1900s and the species may have previously been a regular winterer that far south. Most recent records are of birds found dead on beaches. It may be that a yet undiscovered wintering area exists well offshore (similar to the situation of Horned Puffin *Fratercula corniculata*). Jul-Aug records could be records of non-breeders attempting to summer far to the south of the breeding range.

# PARAKEET AUKLET

**BRITISH COLUMBIA** One record: 24 Feb 1971 (3) about 15 miles sw of Estevan Pt., V.I. (CFN 87:179).

**WASHINGTON** 7 records: 1863† on the WASH coast, 18 Dec 1934† at Westport, G.H., 11 Apr 1944† at Copalis, G.H., 17 Apr 1944 at Long Beach, Pac., 31 Jan 1950 (2†) at Westport (M 31:46), and 18 Jul 1976† at Westport. All were found dead on beaches. In addition, several live birds were reported between Port Townsend, Ksp., and Cape Flattery, Clm., on 15 Jan 1907.

**OREGON** One record: 3 Dec 1977† found dead at Bayocean spit, Tillamook Bay.

**CALIFORNIA** At least 29 were taken or found dead prior to 1945 along the entire CAL coast from Humboldt Bay to La Jolla, S.D. Dates range from 17 Dec-9 Apr. 14 were collected in Monterey Bay from 13-30 Jan 1908, where it must have been present in numbers. Only one recent record: one found dead in late Jun 1974† at Moss Landing, Mnt.

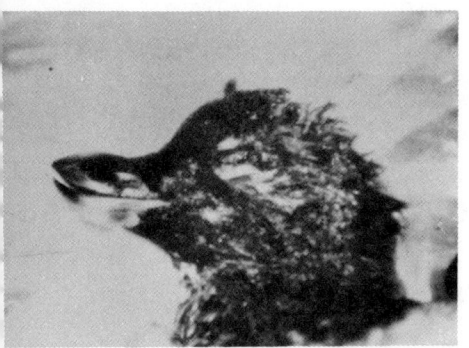

3 Dec 1977 at Bayocean Beach, Til., ORE (head of bird found dead on beach). 1st record. *Harry Nehls*.

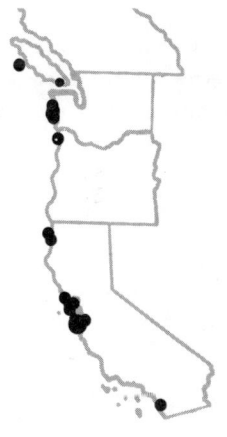

**I.D.** The stubby, upturned bill of Parakeet Auklet is unique, but the standard guides do not indicate that the bill of Rhinoceros Auklet *Cerorhinca monocerata* is often orange and can look quite reddish in the field; a number of recent reports of Parakeet Auklet have proven to be Rhinoceros Auklets with bright-colored bills. Like the Rhinoceros Auklet, the Parakeet Auklet acquires breeding plumage in mid-winter (all the Jan specimens from CAL which were examined proved to be in breeding plumage). Besides the unique bill, observers should note the Parakeet's smaller size, single facial plume, and white breast (Rhinoceros has only a white belly).

# CRESTED AUKLET

*Aethia cristatella*

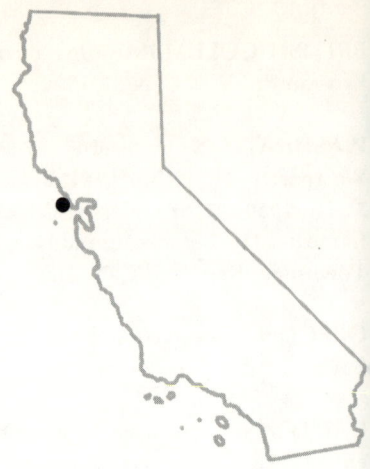

Breeds islands in Bering Sea and Aleutian Is., Alaska; NE Asia. Winters Bering Sea to Japan.

The Crested Auklet has been found along the West Coast south of ALASKA only once, when a bird was beached in C CAL in mid-summer and subsequently expired. The Jul date seems very odd for a bird to be this far south of the breeding areas, but another, apparently healthy, Crested Auklet was found even farther south in summer 1980: near Cedros I. off Baja California, Mexico (G. Friedrichsen, *per. com.*).

**CALIFORNIA** One record: a beached bird was observed 16 Jul 1979† at Pt. Reyes NS, near Bolinas, Mrn. It was found dead the next day.

# HORNED PUFFIN

*Fratercula corniculata*

Breeds NE Asia, Alaska to N B.C. Winters in adjacent open water and perhaps the mid North Pacific.

The Horned Puffin along the West Coast has shown interesting changes in distribution during this century. It breeds on islands in the Bering Sea and the Aleutian Is. and eastward along the southern coast of ALASKA to the Alexander Archipeligo. Recently a small breeding colony was discovered near Queen Charlotte I., B.C., stretching the breeding range

# HORNED PUFFIN

south from Forrester I., ALASKA to N B.C. (for a discussion of the B.C. status of Horned Puffin prior to this discovery, see *Syesis* 6:51). A few adults have been found during the last few summers around Triangle I., at the NW tip of Vancouver I., suggesting breeding even farther south.

The Horned Puffin is a Rarity south of B.C. In the early 1900s, numbers were found dead on beaches, nearly all during the winter. "Dozens" were washed up dead on ORE beaches from late Dec 1932 through mid-Feb 1933 and 70 were found dead on a Westport, WASH beach on 1 Apr 1959. But since 1953 birds have occurred mainly during the summer months; in the mid-1970s numbers of live birds were found offshore S CAL, while other healthy individuals summered near alcid colonies from WASH to C CAL. While there seems adequate evidence that Horned Puffins regularly winter well offshore in the North Pacific in lattitudes as far south as S CAL, it has been hypothesized (Hoffman, Elliott & Scott, 1975) that large-scale changes in the atmosphere-ocean system of the North Pacific during this century have contributed to the reduction of near-shore occurrences during the winter and the near-shore dispersal of birds, probably non-breeders, during the spring and summer.

**WASHINGTON** Over 75 records, but about 70 of these were found dead on beaches near Westport, G.H., on a single day: 1 Apr 1959 (M 40:21 — large numbers of Tufted Puffins *Lunda cirrhata* were also found in this wreck). The other records are: 27 Jan 1919† at Tatoosh I., Clm., 29 Jan 1933† at Westport (corresponding to a large scale die-off in ORE), 2 Jul 1977 at Cape Flattery, Clm., 15 Dec 1978 about 75 miles w of Gray's Harbor, 28 Jan 1979† at Dungeness, Clm., 22 Jul 1979 off Westport, and 5-26 Aug 1979 at Protection I. Most unusual was a live bird picked up well over 100 miles inland from salt water in Jun 1967 at Coulee City, Grn. (Larrison & Sonnenberg, 1968).

**OREGON** Probably well over a hundred records, but most were found on ORE beaches during a major wreck from 27 Dec 1932-15 Feb 1933. There are five other records of beached birds prior to 1967 (Nov-1, Feb-2, Mar-2). All but three records (5 Aug 1969 at Florence, Coos, 28 May 1978 at Yaquina Bay, Lnc., and 30 Mar 1979 at Tillamook Bay) since 1967 have been of live birds: 21 Jul 1968 at Cape Lookout, Til., 21-22 Jun 1973 at Yaquina Head, Lnc., 13 Jul 1973 (2) between 10-35 miles w of Newport, Lnc., 27 Jul 1975 (2)\* at Boardman SB, Cur., 25 Jun 1976\* at Cape Lookout, a bird (same individual?) returning here from Jun-Aug 1977, and 3 Jul 1979 at Island Rock, s of Port Orford, Coos.

# HORNED PUFFIN

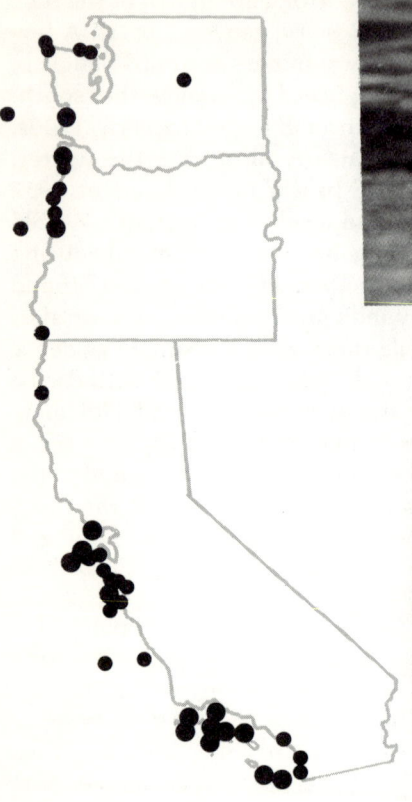

16 Aug 1979 at Protection I., Clm., WASH. *Jan Smith*.

29 May 1975 between Oxnard, Ven., and Santa Barbara I., CAL. *John Luther*.

**CALIFORNIA** About 340 records: 19 dead birds on beaches prior to 1967 (Aug-4, Jan-2, Feb-7, Mar-1, May-4, Jun-1), 9 dead on beaches since 1967 (Aug-4, Feb-1, Mar-1, Jun-1, Jul-2), and over 300 live birds, all found since 1967. Beached birds have been found along the entire coast: Samoa, Hmb. to La Jolla, S.D. Most live birds have been off S CAL during May-Jun, especially around the vicinity of the Channel Is. Numbers of live birds off CAL during May-Aug since 1967 are listed in the table below:

| | | | |
|---|---|---|---|
| 1967 | 1 | 1974 | 1 |
| 1968 | 0 | 1975 | 210 (total includes a few off |
| 1969 | 0 | | N Baja, Mexico) |
| 1970 | 0 | 1976 | 71 |
| 1971 | 1 | 1977 | 4 |
| 1972 | 0 | 1978 | 0 |
| 1973 | 6 | 1979 | 2 |

## HORNED PUFFIN

The reasons behind the "invasion" years of 1975 & 1976 have yet to be explained. High single day counts during those years included 25 from a boat between Oxnard, Ven., and Santa Barbara I. on 29 May 1975 and 39 to the south of San Miguel I. on 8 Jun 1976.

Fall and winter records of live birds are very scarce: 26 Sep-23 Oct 1974* at SE Farallon I., 2-8 Oct 1975 at SE Farallon I., 18-19 Mar 1977 at SE Farallon I., 26 Feb 1978 at San Nicolas I., and 8 Mar 1980 about 50 miles w of Pt. Piedras Blancas, S.L.O.

# WHITE-WINGED DOVE

*Zenaida asiatica*

Breeds SW U.S., Caribbean to C South America. Some northern populations are migratory.

The White-winged Dove is a summer visitor in the deserts of SE CAL. Vagrants have occurred in N CAL, primarily along the coast, from late Jul-early Feb. It is a Rarity anywhere north of CAL on the West Coast, where all the records fall within the same dispersal period as shown by vagrants in N CAL.

**OREGON** Two records: 28 Aug 1976* at the south jetty, Columbia R., Clt., and 28-29 Oct 1979* at Newport, Lnc.

**WASHINGTON** One record: 7 Nov 1907 in the Puyallup R. valley, Prc.

**BRITISH COLUMBIA** One record: Jul 1918† at Renfrew, V.I. The specimen has been identified as the SW U.S. race *Z. a. mearnsi*.

# ORIENTAL CUCKOO                                   Plate 6

*Cuculus saturatus*

Breeds E Asia. Winters Philippines to Australia.

The Oriental Cuckoo has occurred on the West Coast as a Jun-Jul vagrant to western outposts in ALASKA; most were probably spring overshoots. There are a number of specimens prior to 1946 but only two acceptable recent sight records due to the difficulty in separating this species from Common Cuckoo *C. canorus* (see the discussion under that species). A number of unidentified cuckoos, listed under Common Cuckoo, seen in recent years could have included additional records of this bird. All specimens have proved to be the northern race *C. s. horsfeldi*.

**ALASKA**   Seven records: 4 Jul 1890† on St. Paul I., Pribilofs, 1 Jul 1930† at Gambell, St. Lawrence I., 14 or 15 Jul 1935† on St. Lawrence I., 24 Jun 1937† on Rat I., Aleutians, 28 Jun 1946† at Cape Prince of Wales, Seward Pen., and 18 Jun 1979 (2) on St. Paul I. (B. King, *per. com.*).

I.D. See the discussion under Common Cuckoo.

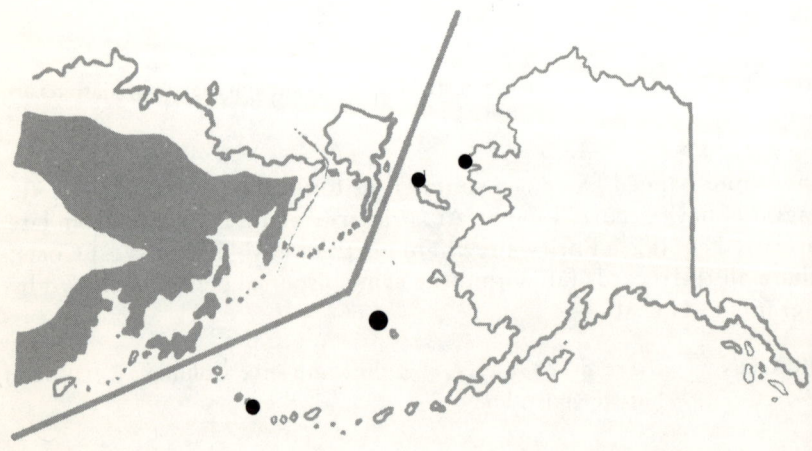

# COMMON CUCKOO                                    Plate 6

*Cuculus canorus*

Breeds Eurasia. Winters Africa to Indonesia.

The Common Cuckoo has occurred on the West Coast only as a spring overshoot in the Aleutian Is. and W ALASKA. In addition, a number of unidentified *Cuculus* cuckoos have occurred during the spring and summer on the Aleutians and Pribilofs; most are suspected of referring to this species, though some could have been the very similar Oriental Cuckoo *C. saturatus*.

**ALASKA**  Twelve records (through spring 1980), graphed below. Note that the peak of records falls in mid-Jun; it appears this species arrives later than most other Alaska vagrants. There are nine records from the western Aleutian Is. (Buldir-2, Kiska-3, Amchitka-3, Adak-1), two from St. Paul I., Pribilofs, and one in mid-Jun 1979 in the Yukon-Kuskowim R. delta.

In addition, unidentified cuckoos were seen on 8-10 Jun 1970 on Attu I., 7 Jul 1971 on Amchitka I., 14-28 Jun 1972 on Amchitka I., and 22 Jun 1972 on Attu I. (see C 80:312).

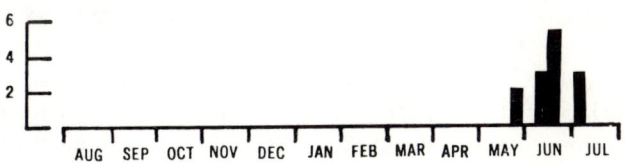

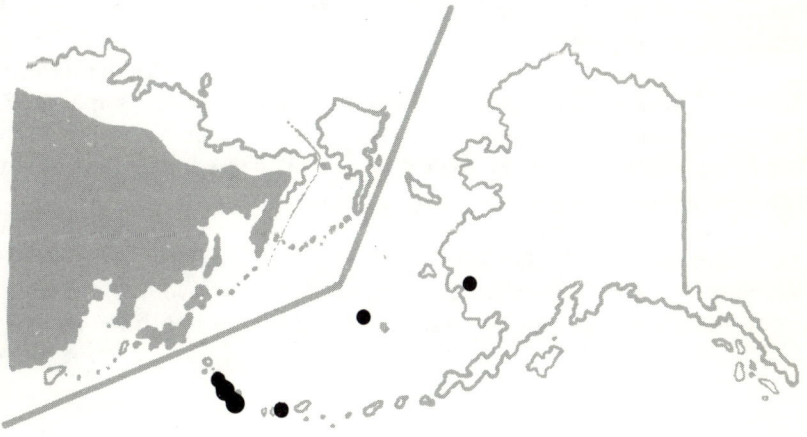

# COMMON CUCKOO
# ORIENTAL CUCKOO

I.D. The Common Cuckoo and Oriental Cuckoo are unlike American cuckoos *Coccyzus sp.*, being larger and showing conspicuous barring on the underparts (adults) or over most of the body (immatures). The shape is also different, with slim pointed wings and long tail in flight, recalling a small falcon. The adult of both species has a gray head, breast, upperparts and uppertail (except for the hepatic-phase female, which has these areas rufous barred with black). Immatures are gray-brown above with dark bars and fine white feather fringes on the head and upperparts, and white with close blackish barring on all the underparts.

Under good conditions, adults may be separated by Common Cuckoo's slightly longer, thinner bill; lighter gray breast; gray back contrasting with the darker gray uppertail; and finer barring across the belly. The Oriental Cuckoo is generally darker, with little contrast between the dark gray back and uppertail, the bars across the belly are distinctly wider and fewer than those on Common Cuckoo, and the bill is shorter and stouter.

Hepatic-phase females may be difficult to identify, but some percentage can apparently be separated by the pattern of barring on the upperparts. If the entire upperparts, including the rump and tail, are heavily barred, with the dark color predominating over the rufous, the bird is an Oriental Cuckoo. If the barring is narrow on the back and there is a complete lack of barring on the rump and only fine barring to portions of the uppertail coverts, the bird is a Common Cuckoo. Birds with average barring, which includes a barred rump, might be either species. Careful notes on the bill size and shape, barring pattern and color, and tail pattern might prove useful when later compared with an adequate collection of specimens.

Little is presently known about the identification of immatures. Juvenile Common Cuckoo shows a whitish patch on the nape, which juvenile Oriental Cuckoo lacks, but this is lost as the bird matures. In the hand, the white area under the carpal joint is barred gray in Common Cuckoo, but is mostly white in Oriental Cuckoo.

The call of the male Common Cuckoo is a far-carrying, mellow "cuc-coo", with the second syllable lower in pitch; females give a wierd "water-bubbling chuckle". The call of male Oriental Cuckoo is very different — a monotone booming call of four notes: "hoo-hoo-hoo-hoo" (King & Dickinson, 1975).

# COLOR PLATES

Donna Dittmann (Plates 3, 4, 5)
Dana Gardner (Plates 6, 9)
Tim Manolis (Plate 8)
Marv Reif (Plates 7, 10)
Ray Robinson (Plates 1, 2)

**PLATE ONE**  Not to scale; see text for size comparisons.

1A. **Wandering Albatross** *Diomedea exulans,* adult. Huge size, massive bill, plumage all white except for tips of flight feathers and tip of tail. P. 4.
1B. **Wandering Albatross,** immature (one of several sub-adult plumages). Huge size, massive pink bill, plumage mostly dark with white face and throat, dark auricular patch.

2A. **Short-tailed Albatross** *Diomedea albatrus,* adult. Large size, massive pink bill, white back and upperwing coverts, golden wash to head. P. 6.
2B. **Short-tailed Albatross,** immature. Large size, all dark plumage, massive pink bill.
2C. **Short-tailed Albatross,** subadult (possibly 3rd year). Large size, massive pink bill, white face and belly, dark lower throat, flanks & undertail coverts, white patch on upperwings (not shown, see text).

3A. **White-capped Albatross** *Diomedea cauta,* adult, ventral. Large size, heavy yellow bill, underwings narrowly outlined in black with black spot at juncture of forewing and body. P. 12.
3B. **White-capped Albatross,** adult, dorsal. Dark back and upperwings (this figure to much smaller scale).

4. **Cape Petrel** *Daption capense.* Black head, white underparts, checkered back and rump, striking upperwing pattern. P. 13.

5. **Streaked Shearwater** *Puffinus leucomelas.* White face and underparts, heavily streaked nape, gray scaly back, white edges to rump during molt (shown here). P. 22.

6A. **Red-tailed Tropicbird** *Phaethon rubricauda,* adult. Red bill and tail streamers, upperwings essentially all white. P. 34.
6B. **Red-tailed Tropicbird,** immature. Back and upperwing coverts heavily barred, lack of nuchal crescent, white inner secondaries on underwings (not shown).

7A. **Red-footed Booby** *Sula sula,* immature. Small size, plumage tawny brown, lack of white in underwings (not shown, see text). P. 42.
7B. **Red-footed Booby,** sub-adult, dark-tailed race (one of numerous sub-adult plumages). Small size, tawny wash to head (not always present), reddish feet.
7C. **Red-footed Booby,** adult, white-tailed race. Small size, red feet, black trailing edge to wing does not reach body.

8. **Chinese Egret** *Egretta eulophotes,* adult, breeding plumage. Yellow bill, bluish lores, shaggy crest, black legs, yellow feet. P. 54.

9A. **Common Crane** *Grus grus,* adult. Striking head pattern, red bare rear-crown. P. 108.
9B. **Common Crane,** adult in flight. Black primaries and secondaries.

**PLATE TWO**  Ducks to approximate scale, eagles and goose not to scale; see text for size comparisons.

1A. **White-tailed Eagle** *Haliaeetus albicilla,* adult. Large size, short wedge-shaped white tail, buffy-brown head. P. *98.*
1B. **White-tailed Eagle,** immature in flight. Large size, broad wings with wingtips held nearly parallel, light axillaries and median underwing coverts, whitish centers to tail feathers.
2A. **Steller's Sea Eagle** *Haliaeetus pelagicus,* immature in flight. Huge size, strongly wedge-shaped tail, dark plumage, huge bill. P. *99.*
2B. **Steller's Sea Eagle,** adult. Huge size, huge bill, white wedge-shaped tail, white shoulders and forehead.
3. **Redhead** *Aythya americana,* adult male. Compare to Common Pochard: round head, gray back, light bill, heavy nail. *See p. 84.*
4A. **Common Pochard** *Aythya ferina,* adult male. Compare to Redhead: sloping forehead, whitish back, dark bill with light midsection, small nail. P. *84.*
4B. **Common Pochard,** adult female. Sloping forehead, dark bill with light ring, small nail, grayish wash to back.
5A. **Baikal Teal** *Anas formosa,* adult male. Striking head pattern, angular head shape, ruddy breast. P. *75.*
5B. **Baikal Teal,** adult female. Whitish spot at base of bill, pale lores, dark postocular stripe, ruddy wash to breast.
6A. **Falcated Teal** *Anas falcata,* adult male. Striking head pattern and head shape. P. *73.*
6B. **Falcated Teal**, adult female. Short mane, plain face, dark bill.
7A. **Garganey** *Anas querquedula,* adult male. Striking head pattern, bluish forewing and long scapulars. P. *81.*
7B. **Garganey,** adult female. Strongly contrasting face pattern with dark cap and light supercilium, pale gray forewing in flight (not shown).
8. **Spotbill Duck** *Anas poecilorhyncha,* adult. Yellow tip to dark bill, pale head and dark body, strong facial pattern, white edges to tertials, broad white rear border to speculum. P. *80.*
9A. **Smew** *Mergus albellus,* adult female. Striking head and neck pattern. P. *93.*
9B. **Smew,** adult male. Mostly white plumage with striking black patterns.
10. **Bean Goose** *Anser fabalis,* adult. Large, heavy goose; dark bill with orange mid-section, sloping forehead. P. *68.*

**PLATE THREE**  Figures to approximate scale.

1. **Eurasian Jacksnipe** *Lymnocryptes minimus*, adult, winter plumage. Small size, comparatively short bill, broad creamy back stripes, dark wedge-shaped tail. P. 150.

2 **Broad-billed Sandpiper** *Limicola falcinellus*, juvenile. Double supercilium, thick bill with drooped tip, conspicuous "V" on back. P. 178.

3A. **Sharp-tailed Sandpiper** *Calidris acuminata*, juvenile. Orange wash to breast with fine gorget of streaks confined to lower throat, rusty cap, white supercilium. P. 169.
3B. **Sharp-tailed Sandpiper**, adult, breeding plumage. Bold spotting on orange breast, very rusty upperparts, rusty cap.

4. **Little Ringed Plover** *Charadrius dubius*, adult, breeding plumage. Small size, head pattern, yellow eye-ring, black bill, dull-colored legs. P. 115.

5. **Dotterel** *Eudromias morinellus*, juvenile. Bold supercilium, buffy-orange lower breast with white crescent, spangled upperparts. P. 125.

6A. **Gray-tailed Tattler** *Heteroscelus brevipes*, adult, breeding plumage. Fine barring to underparts, white belly and undertail coverts, white edgings to rump. P. 148.
6B. **Gray-tailed Tattler**, adult, winter plumage. Brownish-gray plumage, whitish edgings to rump, pale area on face at base of bill.

7A. **Mongolian Plover** *Charadrius mongolus*, juvenile. White throat, rusty wash to breastband, scaly edgings to upperparts (mostly lost by Sep). P. 122.
7B. **Mongolian Plover**, adult male, breeding plumage. Rusty crown, nape, and breast, sharply defined white throat.

8. **Common Sandpiper** *Actitis hypoleucos*, juvenile. Long tail, dark bill, dull legs, little contrast between barring of wing coverts and back. P. 146.

9. **Spotted Sandpiper** *Actitis macularia*, juvenile. Short tail, two-toned bill, yellowish legs, crisply barred coverts contrast with relatively unmarked back. See p. 146.

10A. **Great Knot** *Calidris tenuirostris*, adult, breeding plumage. Large size, boldly patterned breast and upperparts. P. 152.
10B. **Great Knot**, juvenile. Large size, comparatively heavy streaking on crown, neck, and breast, darker upperparts than Red Knot *C. canutus*.

11A. **Terek Sandpiper** *Xenus cinereus*, adult, breeding plumage. Unique upturned bill, short orange legs, black lines on back. P. 145.
11B. **Terek Sandpiper**, adult, winter plumage. Unique upturned bill, short orange legs, pale gray upperparts.

**PLATE FOUR**  Figures to approximate scale.

**1A.** **Rufous-necked Stint** *Calidris ruficollis,* adult, winter plumage. Black legs, unwebbed toes, short bill (see text). P. 159.
**1B.** **Rufous-necked Stint,** adult, breeding plumage. Rufous face and throat.
**1C.** **Rufous-necked Stint,** juvenile. Extensive rusty feather edgings to back and coverts, short bill, unwebbed toes (see text).
**2A.** **Semipalmated Sandpiper** *Calidris pusilla,* juvenile. Buffy feather edgings produce scaly effect to back and coverts, short blunt bill, webbed toes (see text). P. 155.
**2B.** **Semipalmated Sandpiper,** adult, breeding plumage. Brownish upperparts, narrow gorget of breast streaks, short bill (see text).
**2C.** **Semipalmated Sandpiper,** adult, winter plumage. Black legs, webbed toes, short blunt bill (see text).
**3A.** **Western Sandpiper** *Calidris mauri,* adult, breeding plumage. Extensive rusty feather edgings to crown and back, broad gorget of breast streaks and markings on sides and flanks, longer bill, webbed toes. See p. 153.
**3B.** **Western Sandpiper,** juvenile. Extensive rusty feather edgings to back and coverts, longer bill, webbed toes (see text).
**3C.** **Western Sandpiper,** adult, winter plumage. Whitish underparts, black legs, webbed toes, longer bill (see text).
**4A.** **Little Stint** *Calidris minuta,* adult, breeding plumage. Rusty face, white throat, bold orange feather edgings to back and coverts. P. 162.
**4B.** **Little Stint,** adult, winter plumage. Black legs, unwebbed toes, very fine bill, forked supercilium (see text).
**4C.** **Little Stint,** juvenile. Extensive rusty feather edgings to back and coverts, very fine bill, unwebbed toes, "V" on back (see text).
**5A.** **Temminck's Stint** *Calidris temminckii,* juvenile. Nearly unmarked upperparts, gray patches on sides of breast, white outer tail feathers, short thin bill. P. 164.
**5B.** **Temminck's Stint,** adult, breeding plumage. Buffy-brown upperparts with dark feather centers, densely streaked breast, white outer tail feathers.
**6A.** **Least Sandpiper** *Calidris minutilla,* adult, breeding plumage. Short pale legs, fine black bill, less boldly patterned upperparts (see text). See p. 153.
**6B.** **Least Sandpiper,** juvenile. Short legs, brownish breast streaking, brownish upperparts, fine black bill (see text).
**7A.** **Spoonbill Sandpiper** *Eurynorhynchus pygmeus,* adult, breeding plumage. Unique bill, rusty face and throat, boldly patterned upperparts. P. 176.
**7B.** **Spoonbill Sandpiper,** juvenile. Unique bill, extensive rusty feather edgings to back and coverts.
**8A.** **Long-toed Stint** *Calidris subminuta,* juvenile. Long pale legs, brownish breast streaking, brownish upperparts, long central toe, fine bill with pale base to lower mandible (see text). P. 165.
**8B.** **Long-toed Stint,** adult, breeding plumage. Long pale legs, fine bill with pale base to lower mandible, boldly patterned upperparts, long central toe (see text).

Note: Before attempting to identify any unusual stint, the observer should know how to age stints, be familiar with the common species, and understand the timing of migration See essay on p. 153.

**PLATE FIVE**   Shorebirds to approximate scale, other figures not to scale; see text for size comparisons.

1. **Slaty-backed Gull** *Larus schistisagus,* adult, in flight. Large size, massive head and bill, dark gray mantle, pale gray tongue between mantle and black wingtips. P. 189.
2. **Western Gull** *Larus o. occidentalis,* adult, northern race, in flight. Large size, heavy bill but less massive than Slaty-backed Gull, medium gray mantle merging into black wingtips. See p. 190.
3A. **White-winged Black Tern** *Chlidonias leucopterus,* adult, breeding plumage. White upperwing coverts, rump, and tail. P. 207.
3B. **White-winged Black Tern,** adult, winter plumage. Pale gray upperparts, black ear-coverts isolated from black-flecked crown, no shoulder mark (see text).
3C. **White-winged Black Tern,** juvenile. Saddle-backed appearance, white collar and rump, ear-coverts isolated from crown.
4. **Eurasian Coot** *Fulica atra,* head of adult. Bulbous white shield above bill, black undertail coverts (not shown). P. 112.
5. **American Coot** *Fulica americana,* head of adult. Reduced red shield above bill, white undertail coverts (not shown). See p. 112.
6. **Lesser Black-backed Gull** *Larus fuscus graellsii,* adult. Medium size, dark gray mantle, comparatively slender bill with oblong red spot, buffy-yellow legs (see text). P. 191.
7. **Far Eastern Curlew** *Numenius madagascariensis,* adult. Large size, buffy-tan plumage, coarsely marked underparts, heavily barred white underwings (not shown). P. 133.
8A. **Common Greenshank** *Tringa nebularia,* adult, breeding plumage. Stout, slightly upturned bill, olive-green legs, white wedge on rump and lower back. P. 140.
8B. **Common Greenshank,** juvenile. Stout, slightly upturned bill, olive-green legs, white wedge on rump and lower back, paler head and neck than back.
9A. **Black-tailed Godwit** *Limosa limosa,* adult, breeding plumage. Ruddy-orange breast, white belly and undertail coverts, in flight note white rump and white underwings (not shown). P.126.
9B. **Black-tailed Godwit,** juvenile. Mostly white underparts with tawny wash restricted to breast, comparatively heavy straight bill, in flight note white rump and white underwings (not shown).
10A. **Marsh Sandpiper** *Tringa stagnatilis,* adult, breeding plumage. Long slim bill, long greenish legs, delicate shape, boldly spotted upperparts. P. 138.
10B. **Marsh Sandpiper,** juvenile. Long slim bill, long greenish legs, delicate shape, very pale face.
11A. **Spotted Redshank** *Tringa erythropus,* adult, breeding plumage. Mostly blackish plumage, white spotting on back, long straight bill with droop at tip, dark reddish legs. P. 136.
11B. **Spotted Redshank,** juvenile in Oct, has acquired mostly winter plumage but retains juvenile coverts and traces of flank bars. Long bill with slight droop to tip, long reddish legs.
12. **Green Sandpiper** *Tringa ochropus,* adult, breeding plumage. Dark plumage, white rump, dark underwings (not shown). P. 141.
13A. **Wood Sandpiper** *Tringa glareola,* adult, breeding plumage. Paler plumage, much white spotting to upperparts, white rump, whitish underwings (not shown). P. 142.
13B. **Wood Sandpiper,** juvenile. Brownish plumage, white rump, whitish underwings (not shown).

**PLATE SIX**  Not to scale; see text for size comparisons.

1A.  **White-throated Needle-tailed Swift** *Hirundapus caudacutus,* ventral. Large size, sharply-defined white throat, white "U" formed by white flanks and undertail coverts. P. 236.

1B.  **White-throated Needle-tailed Swift,** dorsal. Pale wedge-shaped patch on lower back, white tertials, glossy green sheen to upperwings.

2.  **Common Swift** *Apus apus.* Size of Black Swift *Cypseloides niger;* narrow-winged and short-tailed, moderate fork to tail, mostly sooty plumage with ill-defined pale throat. P. 238.

3.  **Fork-tailed Swift** *Apus pacificus.* Larger than Black Swift; white rump, long deeply-forked tail, dark plumage with ill-defined whitish throat. P. 237.

4.  **Common House Martin** *Delichon urbica,* adult. White uppertail coverts, short forked tail. P. 291.

5A.  **Common Cuckoo** *Cuculus canorus,* hepatic female in flight. Falcon-like flight pattern, rufous upperparts with narrow dark barring (see text). P. 223.

5B.  **Common Cuckoo,** adult male. Grayish upperparts, narrow bars on belly, gray rump contrasts with black tail, long slim bill.

6.  **Oriental Cuckoo** *Cuculus saturatus,* adult male. Very dark gray upperparts, wide bars on belly, little contrast between rump and tail, short thick bill. P. 222.

7.  **Common Scops Owl** *Otus scops.* Small size, short ear tufts, much rufous to facial disc and on underparts. P. 229.

8.  **Streak-backed Oriole** *Icterus pustulatus,* adult male. Scarlet head, black rows of spots on yellow back. P. 411.

9.  **Hoopoe** *Upupa epops.* Striking plumage, long crest, long thin bill. P. 249.

10.  **Jungle Nightjar** *Caprimulgus indicus,* adult male. Gray throat, white patches in wings and on corners of tail, rounded wings, fluttery flight. P. 234.

**PLATE SEVEN**  Larger thrushes to approximate scale, other figures not to scale; see text for size comparisons.

1. **Fieldfare** *Turdus pilaris,* adult. Large size, gray head and rump, rusty back, buffy throat. P. 303.

2. **Dusky Thrush** *Turdus eunomus,* adult. Prominent supercilium, mottled breast (variable), rusty wings. P. 305.

3. **Rufous-backed Robin** *Turdus rufopalliatus,* adult. Similar to American Robin *T. migratorius,* but rufous back, paler breast, no eyering. P. 304.

4A. **Eye-browed Thrush** *Turdus obscurus,* adult male. Gray head, breast, and throat, white supercilium, rufous sides. P. 307.
4B. **Eye-browed Thrush,** adult female, head only. Gray head, white supercilium, white throat, rufous breast and sides.

5A. **Brown Shrike** *Lanius cristatus,* adult. Small shrike, rusty-brown upperparts. P. 348.
5B. **Brown Shrike,** immature. Small size, rusty-brown upperparts, fine barring on breast and sides.

6A. **Siberian Rubythroat** *Luscinia calliope,* adult female. Small size, often cocked-tail stance, white supercilium, whitish throat and grayish-brown breastband, buffy undertail coverts. P. 318.
6B. **Siberian Rubythroat,** adult male. Striking red throat and white malar stripe, white supercilium.

7. **Sooty Flycatcher** *Muscicapa sibirica,* adult. Upright stance, whitish throat, dark sides to breast and dark sides, whitish center of breast and belly, whitish eyering, dark gray-brown upperparts. P. 327.

8. **Gray-spotted Flycatcher** *Muscicapa griseisticta,* adult. Upright stance, distinctly spotted breast, gray upperparts, whitish eyering. P. 328.

9A. **Red-breasted Flycatcher** *Ficedula parva,* adult male. Black tail with white base to outer feathers, often flicked upward; gray upperparts, reddish throat, grayish breastband (in NE Asia races). P. 326.
9B. **Red-breasted Flycatcher,** adult female. Black tail with white base to outer feathers, often flicked upward; brownish upperparts and breastband, contrasting white throat.

**PLATE EIGHT**  Figures approximately to scale.

1. **Dusky Warbler** *Phylloscopus fuscatus*. Dark dusky-brown upperparts, whitish underparts, buffy undertail coverts, no wingbar, thin bill, rounded tail, active skulking habits. P. *321*.

2. **Willow Warbler** *Phylloscopus trochilus*. No record for West Coast (see Appendix B). NE Asia race pictured: grayish above, whitish below without noticeable yellow, no wingbar, fine supercilium.

3. **Wood Warbler** *Phylloscopus sibilatrix*. Yellow throat and upper breast contrasting with white belly, well-marked yellow supercilium, greenish-yellow upperparts. P. *320*.

4. **Middendorff's Grasshopper Warbler** *Locustella ochotensis,* fall immature. Large size, white-tipped tail, dark upperparts with indistinct streaks, buffy-yellow throat and breast indistinctly streaked. P. *323*.

5. **Siberian Accentor** *Prunella montanella,* adult male. Striking face pattern, buffy underparts. P. *330*.

6. **Olive-backed Pipit** *Anthus hodgsoni,* spring adult. Olive-green back, well-marked supercilium buffy before eye, pale post-auricular spot, buffy throat and breast, thrush-like spots on breast. P. *332*.

7A. **Red-throated Pipit** *Anthus cervinus,* adult female in spring. Reddish face and throat, white underparts, streaked back. P. *337*.
7B. **Red-throated Pipit,** fall immature. Heavily streaked back, whitish-buff underparts without contrast between background of breast and belly, heavily streaked breast, nape streaks obscured, "U" shape edge to lower throat.
7C. **Red-throated Pipit,** adult male in spring, head only. More extensive reddish on face and throat.

8. **Tree Pipit** *Anthus trivialis,* fall immature. General buffy coloration, nape and back streaks obscured, thrush-like breast spots. P. *334*.

9. **Sprague's Pipit** *Anthus spragueii,* fall immature. Large size, plain buffy face, scaly-looking back, breast streaks fine and restricted, more white on outer tail. P. *340*.

10. **Pechora Pipit** *Anthus gustavi,* spring adult. Heavily streaked back and nape, rusty fringes to upperparts, contrast between yellowish-buff background to breast and white belly, square-cut edge to lower throat, very skulking habits. P. *335*.

11A. **Gray Wagtail,** *Motacilla cinerea,* fall immature. Long slim shape, white throat, yellow undertail coverts. P. *343*.
11B. **Gray Wagtail,** adult male in spring. Gray back, black throat, yellow rump.

**PLATE NINE**   Figures to approximate scale.

- **1A.** **Hawfinch** *Coccothraustes coccothraustes,* adult male. Huge bill, tawny plumage, white band on wing, short white-tipped tail. P. 438.
- **1B.** **Hawfinch,** adult female. Huge bill, grayish plumage, black throat, white band on wing, short white-tipped tail.
- **2.** **Eurasian Wryneck** *Jynx torquilla,* adult. Unique shape, mottled plumage, small bill, long banded tail. P. 250.
- **3A.** **Eurasian Bullfinch** *Pyrrhula pyrrhula,* adult male. Chunky shape, rose-red underparts, black face and cap, stubby bill. P. 440.
- **3B.** **Eurasian Bullfinch,** adult female. Chunky shape, grayish plumage, white rump, black tail, stubby bill.
- **4A.** **Brambling** *Fringilla montifringilla,* adult male in spring. Black head, rusty chest and shoulders, white rump. P. 435.
- **4B.** **Brambling,** fall female. Brownish crown, grayish face, rusty shoulders, white wingbars, white rump.
- **5A.** **Oriental Greenfinch** *Carduelis sinica,* adult male. Dark greenish plumage, gray head, yellow patches in wings and tail. P. 444.
- **5B.** **Oriental Greenfinch,** adult female. Sandy-brown plumage, yellow patches in wings and tail.
- **6A.** **Common Rose Finch** *Carpodacus erythrinus,* adult male. Red crown and throat, unstreaked belly and undertail coverts. P. 441.
- **6B.** **Common Rose Finch,** adult female. Plain face, distinct white throat bordered below by gorget of streaks, unstreaked belly, wingbars.
- **7A.** **Little Bunting** *Emberiza pusilla,* adult male in spring. Small size, rusty cheeks, brownish lesser wing coverts. P. 475.
- **7B.** **Little Bunting,** fall immature. Small size, fine bill, eye ring, brownish lesser wing coverts, crisp streaking to underparts, pale medium stripe on crown reaches bill (see text).
- **8A.** **Gray Bunting** *Emberiza variabilis,* adult male. Large size, slaty-gray plumage, heavy dark bill with pale base to lower mandible. P. 478.
- **8B.** **Gray Bunting,** adult female. Large size, smudgy streaking to dingy underparts, plain face with whitish malar stripe, heavy dark bill with pale base to lower mandible.
- **9A.** **Rustic Bunting** *Emberiza rustica,* adult female. Rusty breastband (variable), rusty wings, tawny ear-coverts with pale spot in rear-center, bold malar stripe, much white in outer tail. P. 476.
- **9B.** **Rustic Bunting,** adult male in spring. Black head, white post-ocular stripe, rusty breastband.
- **10A.** **Pallas' Reed Bunting** *Emberiza pallasi,* fall immature. Buffy plumage, distinct pale rump, malar stripe distinct from breast streaks (see text). P. 479.
- **10B.** **Pallas' Reed Bunting** adult male in spring. Black and pearly-gray back and wings, distinct whitish rump, white collar washed with yellow.
- **11A.** **Common Reed Bunting** *Emberiza schoeniclus,* fall immature. Large size, stubby bill, heavy malar stripe merges into breast streaking, rusty lesser wing coverts, broad smudgy breast streaking, no eyering, pale median stripe on crown does not reach bill (see text). P. 481.
- **11B.** **Common Reed Bunting,** adult male in spring. Rusty wings, black and buffy back, white collar, rump concolor with back.

**PLATE TEN**  Figures to approximate scale.

The birds on this plate were chosen in fall 1978 as among those most likely to occur on the West Coast, but for which there were no acceptable records. Since that time there have been acceptable records of Eurasian Kestrel and to date (Mar 1980) there are good single observer reports for Hobby, Stonechat, and Yellow-breasted Bunting, pictured here, and Eurasian Siskin, not pictured here. While the remaining species seem potential candidates to occur in the future (based on geographic range and migratory patterns), others not pictured here would seem equally likely. See Appendix B for a discussion of these possible vagrants.

- **1A.** **Eurasian Kestrel** *Falco tinnunculus*, adult male. Large size, gray head, rufous back and wing coverts. P. 105.
- **1B.** **Eurasian Kestrel**, adult female. Large size, long tail, face pattern.
- **2.** **Hobby** *Falco subbuteo*, adult. Slaty upperparts, strong face pattern, heavily streaked underparts, rufous thighs.
- **3.** **Redwing** *Turdus iliacus*, adult. Brownish upperparts, prominent supercilium, streaked underparts, rufous flanks and underwing coverts.
- **4A.** **Stonechat** *Saxicola torquata*, adult male in spring. Black head, rufous breast, white shoulder stripe. NE Asia race has supercilium, unmarked orange-white rump, and pale breast.
- **4B.** **Stonechat**, fall immature. Brownish head and streaked back. NE Asia race has whitish throat, pale underparts, pale unmarked rump, supercilium, and conspicuous pale edges to tertials and secondaries.
- **5A.** **Siberian Thrush** *Turdus sibirica*, adult female. Barred underparts, buffy supercilium, white bands on dark underwings (not shown).
- **5B.** **Siberian Thrush**, adult male. Slaty plumage, white supercilium, white bands on black underwings (not shown).
- **6.** **Lanceolated Warbler** *Locustella lanceolata*, adult. Densely streaked upperparts, finely streaked underparts, unmarked tail, skulking habits.
- **7.** **Yellow-browed Warbler** *Phylloscopus inornatus*, adult. Prominent wingbars, yellowish supercilium, pale base to lower mandible, no white in tail (see text).
- **8A.** **Siberian Blue Robin** *Erithacus cyane*, adult female. Buffy throat and scaly breast, unmarked upperparts without rufous, white undertail coverts.
- **8B.** **Siberian Blue Robin**, adult male in spring. Dark blue upperparts, black stripe from bill to sides of breast, white underparts.
- **9A.** **Pine Bunting** *Emberiza leucocephala*, adult female. Heavily streaked breastband, streaked crown, face pattern.
- **9B.** **Pine Bunting**, adult male in spring. White crown, white and chestnut face pattern.
- **10A.** **Red-flanked Bluetail** *Tarsiger cyanurus*, adult female. Olive-brown upperparts, bluish rump and tail, whitish throat, dingy breast, pale rufous flanks.
- **10B.** **Red-flanked Bluetail**, adult male. Bright blue supercilium, forehead, shoulder, and rump; rufous-orange flanks.
- **11A.** **Yellow-breasted Bunting** *Emberiza aureola*, fall immature. Broad yellow supercilium, pale yellow throat and breast, two pale wing bars, narrow buff crown stripe.
- **11B.** **Yellow-breasted Bunting**, adult male in spring. Black face and throat, yellow underparts, rufous nape and narrow breastband, white shoulder patch.
- **12.** **Pintail Snipe** *Gallinago stenura*, adult. Conspicuous buff mottling on upperwing coverts; in flight shows barred underwings and lacks prominent white trailing edge to secondaries on upperwings.

# PLATE ELEVEN

Color photographs

Top: **Ruff** *Philomachus pugnax,* juvenile acquiring winter plumage. 8 Oct 1978 at Santa Clara R. mouth, Ven., CAL. *Lawrence Sansone.*

Middle, left: **Broad-billed Sandpiper** *Limicola falcinellus,* juvenile. 2 Sep 1978 on Shemya I., ALASKA. 3rd record. *Robert H. Day.*

Middle, right: **Mongolian Plover** *Charadrius mongolus,* adult, winter plumage. 11 Sep 1977 at Tillamook Bay, Til., ORE. 1st record. *Jeff Gilligan.*

Bottom, left: **Wood Sandpiper** *Tringa glareola,* adult, breeding plumage. 28 Jun 1973 on Attu I., ALASKA. *Gerald Maisel.*

Bottom, right: **Little Stint** *Calidris minuta,* adult, breeding plumage. 28 Jun 1976 at Pt. Barrow, ALASKA. 1st record. *J. P. Myers.*

# YELLOW-BILLED CUCKOO

*Coccyzus americanus*

Breeds very locally in CAL; much of S & E North America. Winters in South America.

The Yellow-billed Cuckoo has suffered catastrophic range reductions on the West Coast. Formerly breeding north to S B.C. (shaded area on map), nesting is now confined to local areas in the upper Sacramento, Owens, Amargosa, Kern, Santa Ana, and Colorado R. valleys of CAL (black areas on CAL map). Today it is a Rarity north of CAL, where most recent records are well to the east of the former range and probably represent spring overshoots or misdirected fall vagrants from populations to the southeast, rather than the CAL breeding race *C. a. occidentalis*, which is now on the Federal Endangered list. Calling birds during the summer suggest a possible colonization in E WASH or E ORE in the future.

**OREGON** Formerly bred in the Willamette and Rogue R. valleys and along the Columbia R., but disappeared from these areas by 1945. Seven recent records: 20 May 1970 at Malheur NWR, Har., 2-6 Jun 1972† at Malheur NWR, 1-8 Jul 1975 (2 — possible pair?) at Baker, Bak., 4 Jul 1976† near Sandy, Clk., 7 Jun 1977* at Hart Mt., Lake, 19 Jun 1977† at Echo, Uma., and 2-28 Sep 1977 at Sauvie I., Col.

**WASHINGTON** Formerly a rare summer visitor (extreme dates: 3 May-27 Sep) in W WASH, especially around the Puget Sound area, but disappeared from its breeding range by 1934. The reasons for this collapse are somewhat mysterious. Certainly habitat destruction was instrumental (perhaps the most substantial factor in CAL), but much apparently suitable habitat remains. Four records since 1934: 21 Jun 1956 north of Coulee Dam, Oka., 10 Jul 1974† at Beaux Arts, King, 21 Jun 1978† at George, Grn., and 26 Jul-1 Aug 1979 along the Skykomish R., near Sultan, Sno. The latter bird was calling and may have been defending territory: pairs could potentially breed in E WASH in the future.

**BRITISH COLUMBIA** Formerly bred on S Vancouver I. and SE B.C., as at least 12 specimens were taken during the summer between 1884-1927. Old records come from Victoria, V.I., Vancouver, Pitt Meadow, Huntingdon (and just across the international border at Sumas, WASH), and Chilliwack. There are no recent records.

# YELLOW-BILLED CUCKOO

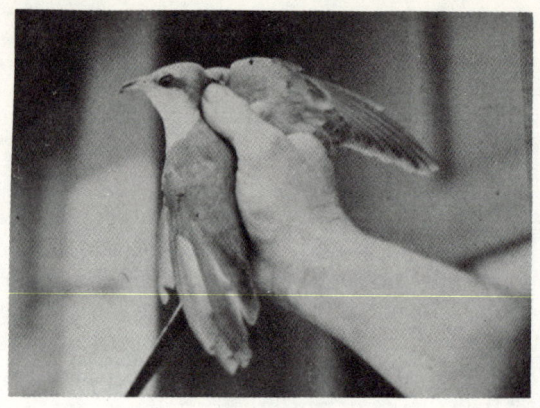

7 Jun 1977 at Hart Mt., Lake, ORE. 5th recent record. *Chris Kornet, courtesy L. Richard Mewaldt.*

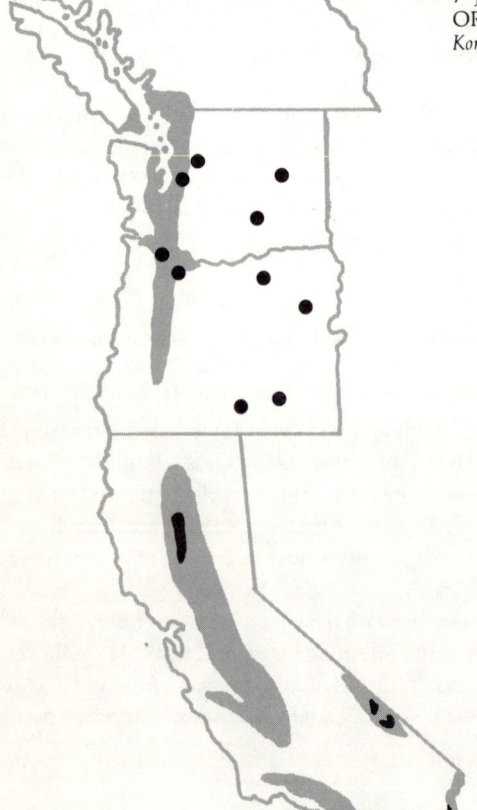

# BLACK-BILLED CUCKOO

*Coccyzus erythropthalmus*

Breeds E North America. Winters NW South America.

The Black-billed Cuckoo is a Rarity anywhere on the West Coast. Birds from the interior of B.C. and WASH would seem to be overshoots beyond the north-central Great Plains woodland breeding areas; some have been heard calling during Jun-Jul in woodland habitat and could have been attempting to set up territories. Coastal birds have been late spring and fall vagrants, probably misoriented. The retiring habits of this bird make it one of the more prized eastern vagrants to discover.

**BRITISH COLUMBIA**   Three records: a calling bird 8 Jun-6 Jul 1958 at Brisco (M 40:12), another tape recorded during the summer 1958 near Quesnal, and 8 Jun 1973† at Windemere.

**WASHINGTON**   Three records: 1 Jul 1952† at Kamiak Butte, near Albion, Whi. (M 33:44), 22 Jun 1958 and several days thereafter near Albion (M 40:12), and 26 Jun 1978† at Bremerton, Ksp.

**CALIFORNIA**   Three records: 22 Sep 1965 at Pt. Reyes, Mrn. (C 69:318), 8 Sep 1976* at the Carmel R. mouth, Mnt., and 3 Oct 1979† on the north spit, Humboldt Bay, Hmb.

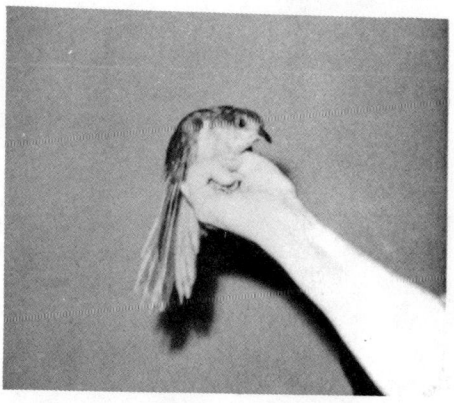

22 Sep 1965 at Pt. Reyes NS, Mrn., CAL. 1st record. *Lillian Henningsen, courtesy Point Reyes Bird Observatory.*

# BLACK-BILLED CUCKOO

# GROOVE-BILLED ANI

*Crotophaga sulcirostris*

Breeds S Texas, W Mexico to C South America. Post-breeding dispersal to W, N, and E.

The Groove-billed Ani has straggled to the West Coast twice during the fall, probably as part of the species' post-breeding dispersal.

**CALIFORNIA**   Two records: 4-16 Nov 1974* at Lakeview, Riv., and 13-17 Sep 1978 at Oak Canyon nature center, Anaheim Hills, Orn.

# GROOVE-BILLED ANI

Nov 1974 at Lakeview, Riv., CAL.
1st record. *Robert Copper.*

# COMMON SCOPS-OWL    Plate 6

*Otus scops*

Breeds S & C Eurasia, Japan, S & C Africa. Northernmost populations are migratory.

The Common Scops-Owl has occurred on the West Coast as a spring and summer overshoot on the outer Aleutians, ALASKA. Only the NE Asia races of Common Scops-Owl are migratory and vagrants would be expected to be of these birds. Some authorities consider Scops-Owl from E Asia (including the migratory races) to be a separate species: the Oriental Scops-Owl *O. sunia.*

# COMMON SCOPS-OWL

**ALASKA** Two records: a dried wing was found 5 Jun 1977† on Buldir I. (A 96:189), and late June 1979† on Amchitka I.

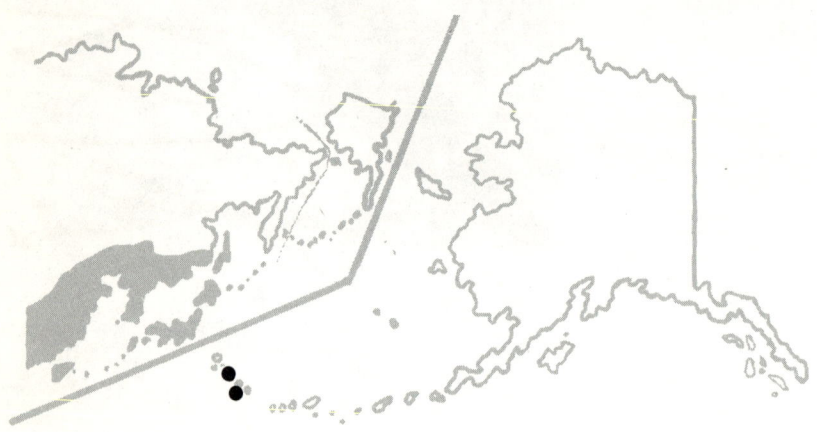

I.D. The Common Scops-Owl might be compared to Common Screech-Owl *Otus asio*, though it is decidedly smaller and more compact, resembling more the proportions of Flammulated Owl *Otus flammeolus*. Both Scops-Owl and Screech-Owl have yellow eyes and a wide variation of plumages on numerous subspecies. The migratory races of Scops-Owl in NE Asia tend to be less well-marked than Screech-Owl, lacking the bold underpart streaks and crossbars, and show buffy patches about the face and neck. The facial disc is washed with rufescent and many of the fine streaks on the underparts are edged with rufous. The upperparts are a mottled gray, without a buffy collar. The ear-tufts are quite short.

The call of NE Asia birds is said to be a measured, throaty "yu-kyu-hu".

# SNOWY OWL

*Nyctea scandiaca*

Breeds circumploar on arctic tundra. Winters irregularly south to N U.S., C Eurasia.

The Snowy Owl appears south of its tundra summer home during winter flights, sometimes occurring in major invasions which send stragglers (usually young birds) far to the south. These invasions are irregular, perhaps tied to population cycles of prey, and large flights have varied between 8 and 50 years apart. The Snowy Owl reaches S B.C. and N WASH with some regularity; it is a Rarity south of WASH on the West Coast. Impressive flights of Snowy Owls occurred in the winters of 1896-97, 1916-17, and 1973-74. Occasionally an "echo" flight year follows the winter of a major influx.

**OREGON** Occurs during irregular invasion; large numbers (exact total unknown) occurred in the flight years listed above. Birds moved down the northern coast, into the Willamette Valley, and into the NE corner of the state. Besides the large numbers during invasions, small numbers were found in the winter of 1966-67, and echo flights occurred in 1917-18 and 1974-75. Additionally, single birds were found in Nov 1929 (Seaside, Clt.), Dec 1971-Feb 1972 (Eugene, Lane, and Happner, Mor.), Mar 1977 (Beaverton, Wsh.), and winter 1978-79 (south jetty, Columbia R., Clt.). Dates in flight years stretch from mid-Nov to 5 May.

**CALIFORNIA** Has been recorded during 6 winters; when present birds have always frequented the coastal dunes of the northwest coast (D.N. and Hmb). "Flocks" in 1896-97 sent birds as far south as Alameda and Santa Cruz. One bird was found in Dec 1908 at Eureka, Hmb. About 19 birds were found in the northwest in the winter of 1916-17, with one inland at Gridley, But. Four were observed from Dec 1966-Mar 1967 in Hmb. Co., while one bird straggled south and inland to Sacramento. A total of 43 birds were found in the winter of 1973-74: 15 in D.N. Co., 20 in Hmb. Co., 1 at Bodega Bay, Son., 2 at Pt. Reyes, Mrn., and singles at San Francisco; Berkeley, Ala.; Alameda; Ano Nuevo SB, S.M.; and the Salinas R. mouth, Mnt. Two birds were in the Arcata, Hmb., area from Nov 1977-late Feb 1978. Dates in flight years stretch from 26 Oct-27 Mar.

# SNOWY OWL

Dec 1977 at Arcata, Hmb., CAL.
*Dave Rudholm.*

# SNOWY OWL

6 Jan 1974 at Pt. Reyes NS, Mrn., CAL. *Van Remsen.*

# HAWK OWL

*Surnia ulula*

Breeds N North America, N Eurasia. Winters irregularly south of its breeding range.

The Hawk Owl nests in much of interior ALASKA and across N B.C., occasionally moving south in winter to S B.C., probably when pressured by lack of prey or severe winter conditions. On the West Coast this winter movement rarely reaches WASH, where most records are from the NE reaches of the state and all records fall between Sep-Jan.

**WASHINGTON**  9 records: 15 Sep 1897† at Marlin, Grn., 24 Sep 1914† at Kachess, Ktt., 21 Dec 1914† at Pullman, Whi., winter 1919-20 (2†) along Skagit R. near B.C. border, Wha., 12 Nov 1922† at Camano I., Isl., 5 Dec 1926† at Yakima, Yak., 1 Dec 1959† on Grassy Top Mt., P.O., and 30 Oct 1966 near Tiger, P.O.

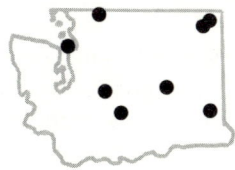

# BOREAL OWL

*Aegolius funereus*

Breeds in boreal forests of N North America and N Eurasia. Winters irregularly south to N U.S. and C Eurasia.

The Boreal Owl nests throughout much of the interior of ALASKA and across N B.C.; it is a Rarity south of B.C. Early explorers listed it as occurring in the "Oregon Territory" in the 1800s, but the only undisputed records are based on two specimens taken in winter: an old record from ORE and a recent specimen from WASH.

**WASHINGTON** One undisputed record: 10 Jan 1974† at Pullman, Whi. (A 93:195).

**OREGON** One record: 21 Mar 1902† at Ft. Klammath, Klm.

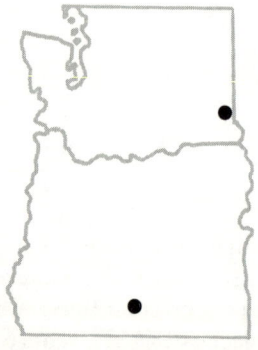

# JUNGLE NIGHTJAR  Plate 6

*Caprimulgus indicus*

Breeds E Asia, India. Winters S Asia, Indonesia, New Guinea.

The Jungle Nightjar has occurred only once on the West Coast, as a probable spring overshoot on the outer Aleutians, ALASKA. This species breeds farther northeast in Asia than other caprimulgids and would seem to be the only one of its family likely to occur in W ALASKA.

# JUNGLE NIGHTJAR

**ALASKA** One record: the dried remains of a female were found on 31 May 1977† on Buldir I. (A 96:189).

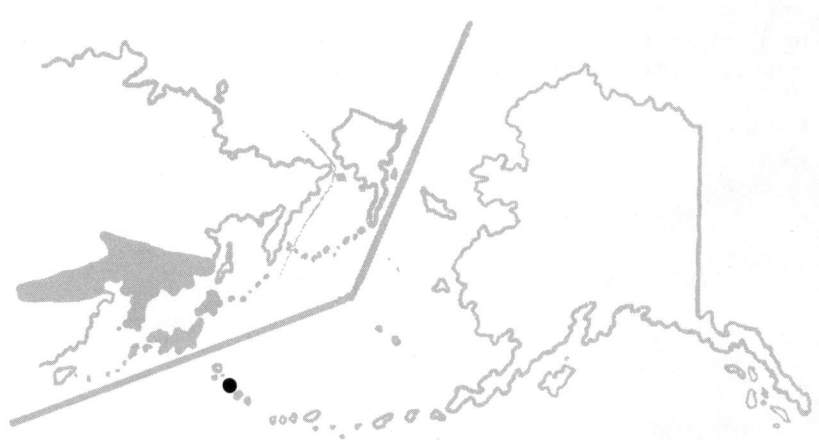

I.D. The Jungle Nightjar is a large, mottled gray caprimulgid, with rounded wings and a fluttery flight, about the size and general shape of a Whip-poor-will *C. vociferus*. Males have a white bar across the primaries, reminescent of Lesser Nighthawk *Chordeiles acutipennis*, and a large white subterminal patch on the outer tail corners. Females have a reduced buffy wing patch and much smaller tail patches. The rounded wings, long rounded tail, and fluttery flight will separate Jungle Nightjar from nighthawks; a white throat, the large size, mottled gray plumage, and wing patches will distinguish it from other North American caprimulgids. The wing patches often show at rest.

The call is described as a hard, sharp "tchuck" repeated rapidly (King & Dickinson, 1975).

# WHITE-THROATED NEEDLE-TAILED SWIFT

Plate 6

*Hirundapus caudacutus*

Breeds NE Asia, Japan. Winters Indonesia to Australia.

The White-throated Needle-tailed Swift has a long migration route; spring vagrants have twice reached the outer Aleutian Is., ALASKA.

**ALASKA** Two records: 21 May 1974† on Shemya I. (A 94:389) and 24 May 1978 on Attu I.

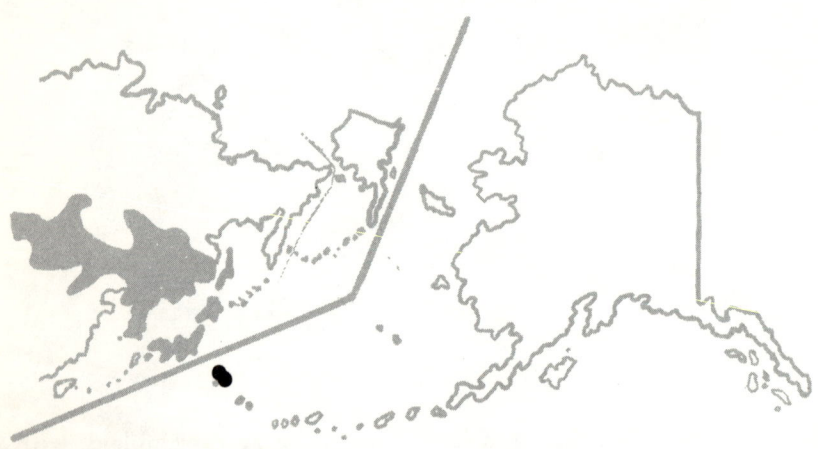

**I.D.** The White-throated Needle-tailed Swift is a chunky, dark swift, much larger than any North American swift. Conspicuous marks include a white forehead and throat; a white "U-shaped" patch on the underparts formed by white flanks and undertail coverts; and a triangular-shaped pale patch on the upperparts, cut squarely across the mid-back and extending as a wedge down to the rump. The tail is short and square, with needle-like projections seen only at very close range. Small white patches on the tertials are also difficult to see. At close range the wings and tail are glossed with an oily blue-green sheen.

The flight is powerful and at a distance it appears as a very large, heavy-bodied, broad-winged, short-tailed swift.

# FORK-TAILED SWIFT

Plate 6

*Apus pacificus*

Breeds E Asia. Northern populations winter south to Australia.

The Fork-tailed Swift has occurred on the West Coast as an apparent spring overshoot, summer wanderer, and fall vagrant on the Aleutian and Pribilof Is., ALASKA. Specimens have proved to be the nominate race *A. p. pacificus*.

**ALASKA** Five records: 1 Aug 1920† on St. George I., Pribilofs (C 23:93), 13 Jun 1949† on St. Paul I., Pribilofs (several other swifts, probably this species, were also seen on St. Paul I. during Jun-Jul 1949; A 82:633), 24 Jun 1976 on Agattu I., Aleutians, and 22-24 Sep 1977 (2-1†) on Shemya I., Aleutians.

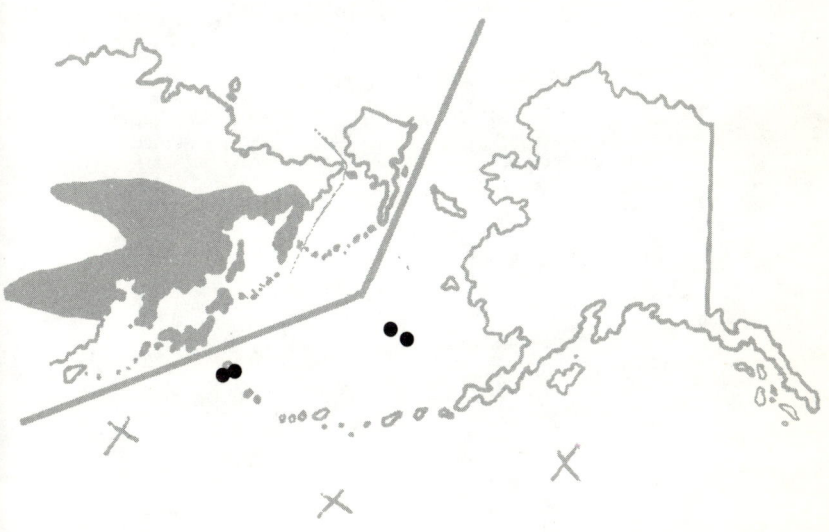

I.D. The Fork-tailed Swift is a large, white-rumped swift with slender, tapered wings and a leisurely flight, somewhat larger than Black Swift *Cypseloides niger*. The tail is long and deeply forked, the fork visible even when the tail is fanned. Except for the distinct white rump, the overall appearance is of a blackish bird, with a poorly-defined whitish throat. Narrow white scaling on the underparts is visible only at very close range.

# COMMON SWIFT

Plate 6

*Apus apus*

Breeds N & C Eurasia, India, N Africa. Winters Africa.

The Common Swift has occurred only once on the West Coast, as an apparent spring overshoot on the Pribilof Is., ALASKA. The specimen proved to be the NE Asia breeding race *A. a. pekinensis*.

**ALASKA**  One record: 28 Jun 1950† on St. Paul I., Pribilofs (A 82:633).

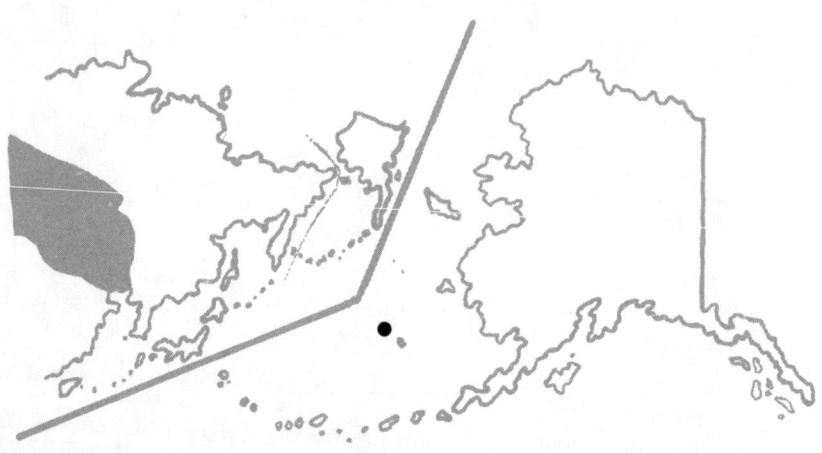

I.D. The Common Swift is a large, dark swift with narrow, long wings and a rapid, graceful flight, about the size of Black Swift *Cypseloides niger*. The tail is relatively short and only moderately forked. An ill-defined whitish throat is visible only at close range, so the general impression is of a large, slender-winged, brownish-black swift, slightly paler below, but otherwise unmarked.

# RUBY-THROATED HUMMINGBIRD

*Archilochus colubris*

Breeds E North America. Winters C Mexico, SE U.S. to Costa Rica.

The Ruby-throated Hummingbird breeds west to C Alberta, but there is only one acceptable record from the West Coast: a specimen of a fall vagrant totally lost in W ALASKA. The species might be expected as a spring or fall vagrant from WASH to CAL, but the difficulty in identifying females and immatures (and perhaps even males) might prevent detection even if birds did stray our way.

**ALASKA** One record: "late fall" 1925† at St. Michael.

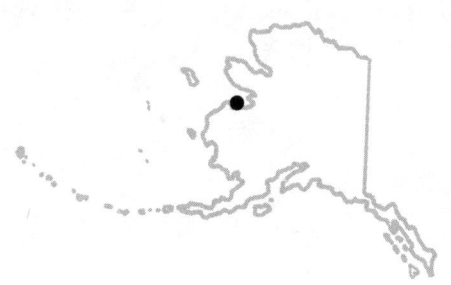

I.D. The Ruby-throated Hummingbird is a small hummingbird the size of Black-chinned *A. alexandri* and Costa's Hummingbird *Calypte costae*. Full-gorgetted males are separated from Broad-tailed Hummingbird *Selasphorus platycercus*, which also has a red throat and green crown as an adult male, by its small size, ruby-red (not rose-red) gorget, forked tail, and lack of a loud buzzing sound caused by the wings in flight; Broad-tailed nests in E CAL and SE ORE but has not been recorded as a vagrant on the West Coast. Females and immatures may be indistinguishable from similar plumages of Black-chinned Hummingbird (for separation from Costa's Hummingbird, see discussion under that species). A key may lie in vocalizations but they have yet to be worked out; some observers believe Ruby-throated and Black-chinned are separable by voice, others can hear no differences. In hand or under the most ideal of field conditions, note the rounded tips to the outer tail feathers; those of Black-chinned are blunt-pointed (compare sketch of Black-chinned in Stiles (1971) with photo of Ruby-throated in Reilly (1968), p. 261).

# COSTA'S HUMMINGBIRD

*Calypte costae*

Breeds SW U.S., NW Mexico. Northernmost populations winter south of the breeding range.

The Costa's Hummingbird is a resident in coastal southern CAL and is a common breeder in the CAL deserts, while a few are summer visitors in the Coast Range north to C CAL. Records of vagrants have reached north to Hmb. Co. and six have reached ORE, where it is a Rarity. Records there include probable spring overshoots, summer and fall vagrants, and a local winterer.

**OREGON**  6 records: 5-20 Apr 1972* at Astoria, Clt., 12-16 Apr 1974 at Eugene, Lane, mid-summer to 17 Nov 1977* at Portland, Mul., 15 Nov 1977* at Roseburg, Dgl., 26 Jun-20 Jul 1979* at Molalla, Clk., and Dec 1979-4 Feb 1980* at Florence, Lane. All have been males at feeders.

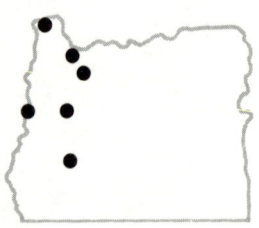

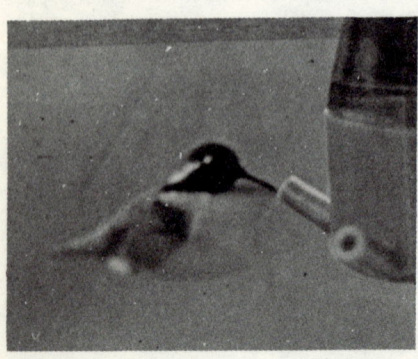

5 Apr 1972 at Astoria, Clt., ORE.
1st record. *Charles Linehan.*

## COSTA'S HUMMINGBIRD

I.D. The identification of males is adequately discussed in the standard guides, but the identification of females and immatures is extremely difficult. These are very similar to comparable plumages of Black-chinned Hummingbird *Archilochus alexandri*. The most important difference is in voice. The chip note of Costa's is a very high, light and sharp "tik" or "tip", sometimes rapidly run together and resembling the call of Bushtit *Psaltriparus minimus*. The chip note of Black-chinned is a low-pitched, softer, slurred "tew" or "tchew", almost never run together.

Plumage differences are more subtle. In general, Costa's is whiter below (especially as an immature; juvenile plumage is recognized by broader, paler edgings to the feathers of the upperparts), has a shorter bill (Black-chinned looks slightly decurved in the field, as well as slightly longer), generally lacks buffy flank spots (present in most Black-chinneds), and on the West Coast a white stripe behind the post-ocular white spot separates the dark ear-coverts from the crown (usually lacking on the CAL, but not Arizona, Black-chinned), and in hand by rounded tips to the outer tail feathers (Black-chinned are blunt-pointed; but see discussion under Ruby-throated Hummingbird *A colubris*). Distinguishing both vocal and plumage differences requires previous experience with these species; observers should not attempt to identify vagrant females or immatures without ample previous experience with these birds. For a more detailed discussion see Stiles (1971).

# ALLEN'S HUMMINGBIRD

*Selasphorus sasin*

Breeds SW ORE to SW CAL. Winters SW CAL to NW Mexico.

The Allen's Hummingbird is a breeding bird of the coast ranges of CAL and SW ORE. Birds have occasionally been reported farther north, where it is a Rarity, but the difficulty of identifying this species, even as an adult male, limit acceptable records (for the present) to specimens.

**WASHINGTON**   One record: 27 May 1894† at Seattle, King.

# ALLEN'S HUMMINGBIRD

I.D. The Allen's Hummingbird is very similar to Rufous Hummingbird *S. rufus*. Males with complete and full red gorgets can usually be identified by their green back, but observers should be aware that male Rufous Hummingbird show green backs and upper wing-coverts while acquiring the red gorget and one must first determine if the male has acquired full breeding plumage. Even then the identification may be tentative, since it has been reported that even full-gorgetted male Rufous may have a green back (see Phillips, 1975), though apparently this occurrence is rare. Females and immatures usually cannot be identified in the field, though in the hand or under ideal conditions, known age birds might be separated by Allen's narrower outer tail feathers (see Stiles, 1971 and Stiles, 1972). It seems that, at present, little is known about ways to separate these two difficult species and it would seem very difficult to identify vagrants with any degree of certainty.

# BLUE-THROATED HUMMINGBIRD

*Lampornis clemenciae*

Breeds S Arizona, SW Texas to S-C Mexico. Winters in Mexico.

The Blue-throated Hummingbird has occurred only once on the West Coast. The strange saga of this individual is set out below.

**CALIFORNIA** One record: a female appeared 27 Dec 1977\* at a feeder in Three Rivers, Tul, and remained to 27 May 1978. In early spring she consorted with a male Anna's Hummingbird *Calypte anna*, built a nest, laid eggs, and fledged three young. When examined shortly before fledging, the young appeared to best match Anna's X Blue-throated Hummingbird hybrids. Following this success, she rebuilt the nest, laid eggs, and hatched more young, which did not survive. The only male known to be present during this second attempt was a Black-chinned Hummingbird *Archilochus alexandri*.

# BLUE-THROATED HUMMINGBIRD

Jan 1978 at Three Rivers, Tul., CAL. 1st record. *Frank Baldridge.*

# VIOLET-CROWNED HUMMINGBIRD

*Amazilia verticalis*

Mostly resident NW Mexico to S Mexico. Has bred in SE Arizona, where it appears more regularly during post-breeding dispersal.

The Violet-crowned Hummingbird has occurred only once on the West Coast: a bird appeared for two consecutive summers at a feeder in coastal S CAL, perhaps as part of post-breeding dispersal.

**CALIFORNIA** One record: 6 Jul-late Dec 1976 at Santa Paula, Ven., presumably the same individual returning from 29 Jun-5 Jul 1977 (WB 9:91 contains a full discussion of this occurrence, including research which indicates that the possibility of this bird being an escape from captivity is minimal).

# VIOLET-CROWNED HUMMINGBIRD

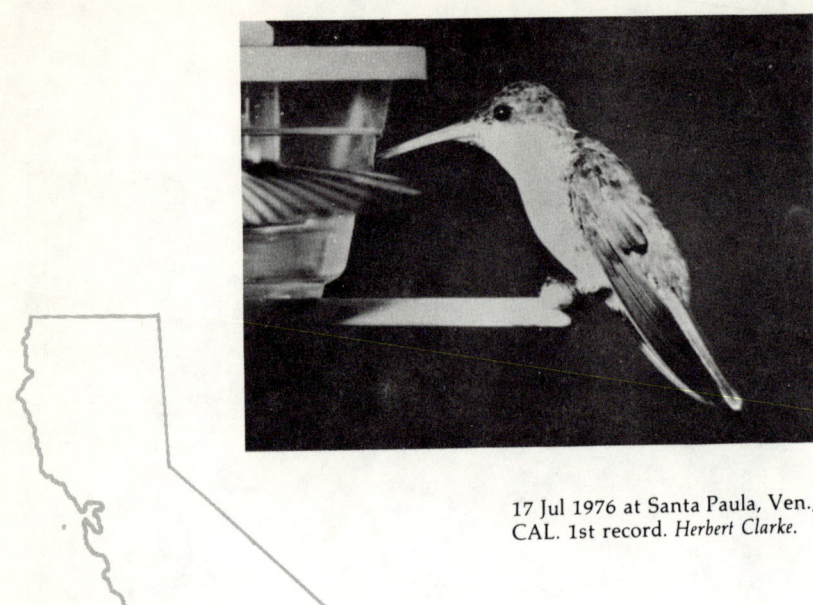

17 Jul 1976 at Santa Paula, Ven., CAL. 1st record. *Herbert Clarke.*

# BROAD-BILLED HUMMINGBIRD

*Cynanthus latirostris*

Breeds SE Arizona, SW New Mexico to S-C Mexico. Northern birds withdraw south to winter in Mexico.

The Broad-billed Hummingbird has occurred on the West Coast most often as a winter visitor to S CAL and there are records of spring and fall vagrants. 13 of the 19 records occurred during the last three years covered in this book (1977-1979); this increase seems to correspond to an increase in birding activity and reports from casual observers with feeders. Half of the West Coast records are of birds that visited hummingbird feeders, often for weeks.

# BROAD-BILLED HUMMINGBIRD

**CALIFORNIA** 19 records, graphed below. The first five records are discussed in CB 1:111. Birds known to winter locally have appeared as early as 30 Sep and lingered through late Mar. 6 records (including 3 fall vagrants) are from the Imperial Beach-San Diego, S.D., area, and 3 each are from western Riv.-S.Bn. Cos. area, Los Angeles area, and coastal S.Bb. Co. The single spring record was 21 Apr 1969 at Pacific Grove, Mnt., which also provides the northernmost report.

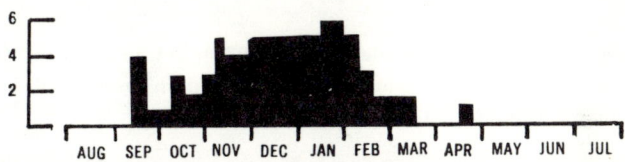

Jan 1977 at Agua Caliente, S.D., CAL. 7th record. *Robert Copper.*

17 Oct 1979 at Gaviota, S.Bb., CAL. *Kimball Garrett.*

# HOOPOE

Plate 6

*Upupa epops*

Breeds C Eurasia, India, Africa. C Eurasian and European populations winter to the south.

The Hoopoe has occurred only once on the West Coast, as a fall vagrant in W ALASKA.

**ALASKA** One record: an adult male 2-3 Sep 1975† at Old Chevak, Yukon-Kuskokwin R. delta (A 94:601). A local resident noted an unusual bird on his woodpile and shot it the next day.

I.D. The Hoopoe is unmistakeable: the head and underparts are pale dull pink, the wings and tail are boldly barred black and white, and it has a long black-tipped erectile crest and a long curved bill. It is about the size of Common Flicker *Colaptes auratus* and its undulating flight and habit of feeding on the ground recalls that species. In flight the tail appears quite long and the wings are broad and rounded.

The call is a carrying, low, soft "hoop-hoop-hoop".

# EURASIAN WRYNECK  Plate 9

*Jnyx torquilla*

Breeds N Eurasia, NW Africa. Winters S Asia, C Africa.

The Eurasian Wryneck has occurred only once on the West Coast, as a fall vagrant in W ALASKA. The specimen, found dead, proved to be the NE Asia race *J. t. chinensis*.

**ALASKA**  One record: a bird found dead on 8 Sep 1945† near Wales, Seward Pen.

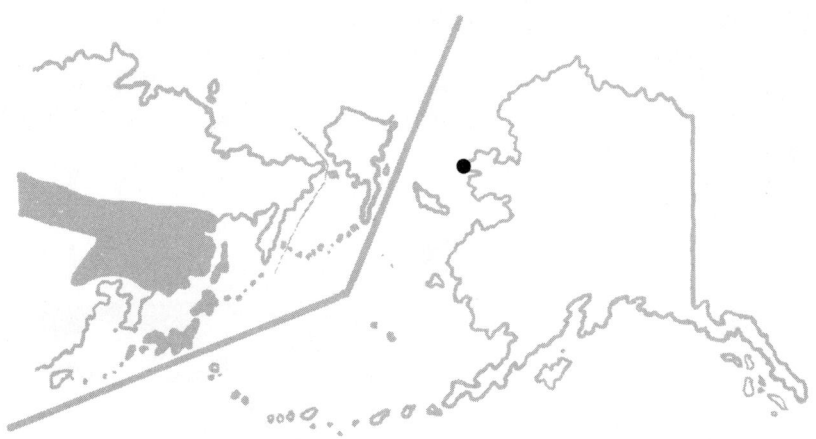

I.D. The Eurasian Wryneck is a uniquely-patterned member of the woodpecker family, about the size of Hairy Woodpecker *Picoides villosus*. Although it may perch on tree trunks and limbs, it often feeds on the ground with its tail raised, looking more like a passerine than a woodpecker. In its mottled gray, brown, and buff plumage, with dark mask, short bill, and long banded tail, it resembles no other bird. It is usually shy and retiring. The flight is undulating.

The call, usually only given on the breeding ground, is a loud shrill "quee-quee-quee-quee", constantly repeated. The alarm note is a series of short "tuck"s.

# RED-HEADED WOODPECKER

*Melanerpes erythrocephalus*

Breeds E North America. Northern populations move south in winter.

The Red-headed Woodpecker is a Rarity anywhere on the West Coast. The species breeds west to S Saskatchewan and E New Mexico; West Coast records to date have occurred during the summer and fall in interior B.C. and at the Salton Sea, CAL.

**BRITISH COLUMBIA** Two records: 11-13 Jul 1965 at Lavington, near Vernon (M 47:45), and 13 Sep 1978 south of Tatla Lake.

**CALIFORNIA** One undisputed record: 17 Jul-22 Aug 1971* at the Wister Unit, Salton Sea NWR, near Niland, Imp. (CB 3:23). Another was found dead on 20 May 1962 at La Puente, L.A. (C 65:332), but the origin of this specimen has been questioned, suggesting it arrived lodged in the front of a vehicle (CB 1:25). Opinion about the acceptability of this latter record is split among CAL observers.

7 Aug 1971 at Niland, Imp., CAL. 1st record. *Steve Cardiff.*

# ACORN WOODPECKER

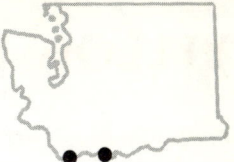

*Melanerpes formicivorus*

Mostly resident W U.S. to Colombia, South America. Occasionally stages irregular movements away from the breeding area, perhaps in response to diminishing food supplies.

The Acorn Woodpecker on the West Coast breeds north to the north end of the Willamette Valley and at The Dalles, on the Columbia R., ORE. It is a Rarity north of ORE; both Rarity records are of birds just across the Columbia R. from the resident populations.

**WASHINGTON**   Two records: 29 Sep 1978 at Washougal, Clk., and 3 May 1979 at Lyle, Klk.

# NUTTALL'S WOODPECKER

*Picoides nuttallii*

Resident Sierra foothills and coast ranges of CAL to NW Baja, Mexico.

The Nuttall's Woodpecker is locally common in CAL west of the Sierra and deserts. There is a local breeding population in Sis. Co. at the north end of the Central Valley; the old ORE records were taken not too far north of this population, suggesting the range was more widespread before 1900.

**OREGON**   Two records, both at Ashland, Jck.: 3 Feb 1881† and 4 Feb 1881†. Specimens were also said to be taken in this area in Aug 1851 but cannot be located. Considering that the species is very resident and not prone to wander, it seems likely that a small resident population existed in extreme S ORE during the 1800s, not far north of the present CAL residents.

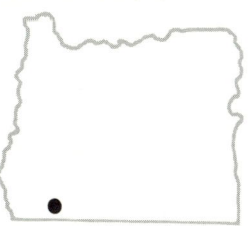

# YELLOW-BELLIED SAPSUCKER

*Sphyrapicus varius varius*

Breeds E North America. Winters SE U.S., Central America.

The Yellow-bellied Sapsucker is presently considered by the AOU Checklist (1957) to be a subspecies of a more widely nesting species which also includes Red-breasted Sapsucker *S. v. ruber & daggetti* and Red-naped Sapsucker *S. v. nuchalis,* both of which breed widely on the West Coast (Red-breasted mostly west of the Sierra Nevada and Cascades, Red-naped mostly east of these mountains). I prefer to follow Short (1969) in treating Yellow-bellied Sapsucker as a separate species (another possible treatment would be to combine Yellow-bellied and Red-naped Sapsuckers and separate out Red-breasted Sapsucker). Whatever the taxonomic treatment, Yellow-bellied Sapsucker is a Rarity south of B.C. on the West Coast. Its breeding range includes NE B.C. and wintering birds have been found irregularly west to Arizona. On the West Coast, most records are of fall migrants in desert oases in E CAL and nearly all have been juveniles. There are a few wintering records (including a bird returning for two consecutive winters in coastal S CAL) and one of a spring migrant. There are two records of summer birds in NW ORE. In addition, a few hybrids have been recorded, all as winter birds in S CAL.

**OREGON** Two records, both at Henry Hagg Lake, Forest Grove, Wsh.: a male on 9 Jul 1976 and a female on 20 Jul 1976. No evidence that these birds constituted a pair was obtained.

**CALIFORNIA** 24 records, graphed below. 8 records (7 from Oct-Nov) are from the Death Valley NM area, Inyo. About 5 birds could be considered winter records, including a male which wintered at Refugio SB, S.Bb. in 1978-79 and returned (presumably the same individual) for winter 1979-80, and a juvenile female from 31 Dec 1977-11 Mar 1978 at Tiburon, Mrn., which also provides the only N CAL record. The single spring record was 13 Jun 1976 on San Nicolas I. A dead bird was found 19 Jul 1950† at Pasadena, L.A. (some have questioned the origin of this bird, see CB 1:25).

In addition, two hybrid Yellow-bellied X Red-naped Sapsuckers have been collected in winter along the Colorado R. and two additional sightings of possible hybrids come from S CAL in winter.

# YELLOW-BELLIED SAPSUCKER

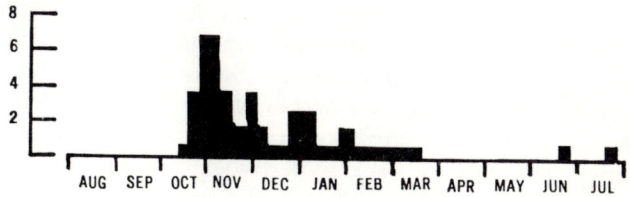

20 Feb 1978 at Tiburon, Mrn., CAL (immature female). *Al Ghiorso.*

# YELLOW-BELLIED SAPSUCKER

I.D. The Yellow-bellied Sapsucker closely resembles Red-naped Sapsucker. The adult, with clear black, white and red facial patterns, black back, and black breastband, may be identified by noting the throat and nape color and the back pattern. Yellow-bellied Sapsucker has a white (or buffy-tinged) nape and a black back barred with white, usually washed with golden-buff. Red-naped Sapsucker has a red nape (can be worn off in late summer) and a black back with two lines of white droplets (sometimes washed with buffy-gray), though females have more barred backs, more similar to the Yellow-bellied pattern. Adults with all red throats are males. In Yellow-bellied Sapsucker, the black border around the throat entirely encloses it and separates the red from the white malar stripe; in Red-naped Sapsucker the red color of the throat breaks through the surrounding black border to touch the white malar stripe. Throats of females are entirely enclosed by black, but the throat of female Yellow-bellied Sapsucker is all white; that of Red-naped Sapsucker is red with a white chin. Some female Red-napeds have only a few white feathers on the chin, thus looking mostly red-throated in the field and difficult to separate from male Yellow-bellied. Note the nape color and back pattern on these confusing individuals.

Juveniles are striking different from adults, with brownish feathers replacing the black on the face, back, and breastband and showing less distinct patterns. The crown of juvenile Yellow-bellied Sapsucker is spotted red and white; that of juvenile Red-naped Sapsucker is evenly red. Furthermore, juvenile Red-naped Sapsucker usually acquires adult plumage by early fall, before migration, while Yellow-bellied Sapsucker retains juvenile plumage until late winter. Thus a bird of this type in juvenile plumage in late fall or winter is most likely a Yellow-bellied Sapsucker.

Hybrids are rare and show a combination of characters. One CAL specimen was a female with a brown breastband (in Feb) and the white throat showed red corners while the whitish nape had a few red feathers.

For more information see Devillers (1970) and Dunn (1978f).

# NORTHERN THREE-TOED WOODPECKER

*Picoides tridactylus*

Mostly resident N Eurasia, N North America and south along Rockies to C New Mexico.

The Northern Three-toed Woodpecker on the West Coast is a resident species from ALASKA south through the southern Cascade Mtns. of ORE. It has seemed to be extending its range south in recent years. The single CAL record comes from the Klammath Mtns. not far south of the Cascades. It is possible that an undetected population now exists there, or if it does not, it is possible that it might become established in the future.

**CALIFORNIA**  One record: 29 Apr 1979 at Castle Lake, Sis. This record has not yet been reviewed by the CAL Records Committee.

# GRAY KINGBIRD

*Tyrannus dominicensis*

Breeds SE U.S., Caribbean. Winters Caribbean to N South America.

The Gray Kingbird has occurred only once on the West Coast. Although the record is extraordinary, several other species of southern *Tyrannids* are known to indulge in occasional "wrong-way" flights far to the north in the fall (Tropical Kingbird *T. melancholicus* does it with some regularity) and this species might be looked for again on the West Coast from Sep-Dec.

**BRITISH COLUMBIA**   One record: 29 Sep 1889† at Cape Beale, V.I.

# TROPICAL KINGBIRD

*Tyrannus melancholicus*

Breeds SE Arizona, W Mexico to S South America. Northern populations are migratory.

The Tropical Kingbird appears along the coast of CAL with some regularity every fall (mostly late Sep-early Dec) and has recently averaged 21 records a year (1975-1979). It has been recorded as early as early Aug and a few birds have remained locally to winter (lingering as late as May). There are only a handful of records of apparent spring overshoots. Nearly all records are from the immediate coast or offshore islands and numbers decrease along the N CAL coast. Interestingly, this species is the most likely kingbird to be encountered on the West Coast north of Santa Barbara from mid-Oct through Mar. It is a Rarity north of CAL, where all records were during Sep-Feb and were along the immediate coast.

# TROPICAL KINGBIRD

Until very recently, this species and the Couch's Kingbird *T. couchii* (which nests from S Texas to the Yucatan Pen., Mexico) were considered conspecific. Traylor (1979) published the definitive account which split the two sibling species. Specimens taken along the West Coast have proved to be *T. melancholicus,* but it should be noted that to date no sight record of a West Coast Tropical Kingbird has dealt with the issue of separating these two species, which are best distinguished by voice. Field identification of the two has yet to be worked out (but see I.D. section).

**OREGON** Five records: 14 Nov 1965 at Cape Meares, Til., 30 Sep 1973 at Devil's Elbow SP, Lane, 13 Oct 1973 at Taft, Lnc., 9-10 Oct 1976* at Harris Beach SP, Cur., and 27 Oct 1979* at Bandon, Coos.

**WASHINGTON** Four records: 18 Nov 1916† on Destruction I., Jef., 26 Nov 1927† at Westport, G.H., 17 Nov 1953† at Hoquiam, G.H. (M 35:49), and 6-16 Nov 1976 at Ocean Shores, G.H.

**BRITISH COLUMBIA** Six records: Feb 1923† at French's Beach, V.I. (C 30:251), 16-22 Oct 1972 at Victoria, V.I., 11 Oct 1976 at Tofino, V.I., 20-23 Oct 1976 at Sea I., Vancouver, 26-30 Oct 1977 at Colwood, V.I., and 22-23 Oct 1978 at Metchosin, V.I.

22 Oct 1972 at Cadboro Bay, Victoria, V.I., B.C. 2nd record. *Stuart Johnston.*

# TROPICAL KINGBIRD

**ALASKA**  One record: 23-24 Oct 1976 at Ketchikan. This species is considered hypothetical on the state list because, though well described and undoubtedly correct, it was seen by only a single observer.

I.D. The Tropical Kingbird most often appears along the West Coast as an immature during the fall. These birds most resemble Western Kingbird *T. verticalis* with pale gray head and white throat. They are identified by 1) a slaty ear-patch which contrasts with the rest of the head, 2) brighter and more extensive yellow underparts, 3) greenish (rather than gray) back, 4) olive sides to the breast, 5) whitish-buff edgings to the wing coverts, and 6) a brownish, forked tail. Another excellent character is the long, heavy bill (distinctly heavier than Western or Cassin's Kingbird *T. vociferans*, but not as heavy as Thick-billed *T. crassirostris* or Gray Kingbird *T. dominicensis*). For more information see Dunn (1979f).

Vocal differences during breeding season are the best means of separating Tropical from Couch's Kingbird (see Traylor, 1979). Visual methods noted in that discussion are comparative: Tropical has 1) a longer bill, 2) a smaller size and bulk, 3) less yellowish underparts, 4) darker brown wings and tail, and 5) a more deeply forked tail. In hand, note that the 5th primary is longer than the 10th (outer) primary.

# CASSIN'S KINGBIRD

*Tyrannus vociferans*

Breeds SW U.S. to S Mexico. Winters NW Mexico to Central America.

The Cassin's Kingbird on the West Coast is a locally common nesting bird along the coast of S CAL and north in the Coast Range to about the San Francisco Bay area. It also locally nests in desert oases and the pinyon-juniper belt of SE CAL and is a rare, but regular, winterer along the S CAL coast. It has been found north of CAL only once on the West Coast, though spring vagrants have reached Ontario in the East.

**OREGON** One record: 4 Aug 1935† at Mercer, Lane (M 57:44).

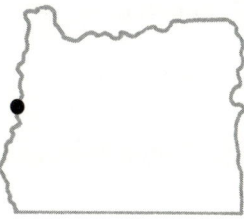

I.D. The Cassin's Kingbird is discussed in the standard guides, which tend to emphasize the differences in tail pattern from Western Kingbird *T. verticalis*. More apparent characters (especially in late summer when kingbirds are worn and when Western may lose its white outer tail feathers during molt) are the darker gray-olive cap, back, and breast of Cassin's, which contrast sharply with a whitish throat. The call — a loud 'chi-bur" — is distinctive and is given in migration and in winter. For more information see Dunn (1979f).

# THICK-BILLED KINGBIRD

*Tyrannus crassirostris*

Breeds SE Arizona, SW New Mexico to W Guatamala. Northern populations are migratory.

The Thick-billed Kingbird has occurred on the West Coast only as a fall vagrant. Except for an Aug record along the Colorado R., which may have occurred as part of post-breeding dispersal, all records would seem to be of birds which migrated "wrong-way", similar to the pattern shown by some other southern *Tyrannids*. All these records are suspected of referring to immature birds.

**CALIFORNIA**   Seven records: 19 Oct 1965 at Imperial Beach, S.D. (C 69:85), 3 Dec 1966 at Pt. Loma, S.D., 26-27 Dec 1966 at Bonita, S.D., 18-23 Oct 1967 at Pt. Loma, 27 Oct-19 Dec 1974* at McLaren Park, San Francisco, 5 Aug-15 Sep 1978 near Blythe, Imp., and 20 Dec 1979 at Lost Lake, near Blythe, Imp.

**BRITISH COLUMBIA**   One record: 20 Oct-11 Nov 1974† at Qualicum Beach, V.I.

Dec 1974 at McLaren Park, San Francisco, CAL. 5th record. *Dave Rudholm.*

# THICK-BILLED KINGBIRD

I.D. The Thick-billed Kingbird pictured in Robbins *et al* (1966) is an adult in breeding plumage; West Coast records have been of immatures. These birds differ from adults by having the yellow of the underparts much more extensive (except for a whitish throat and pale gray breastband, all the underparts are yellow) and by showing rufous edgings to the wings and tail. The most similar species is Tropical Kingbird *T. melancholicus*; Thick-billed is distinguished by 1) the much heavier bill (see photo), 2) the much darker head and back (Thick-billed has a dark gray cap, a slaty ear-patch, and olive-brown back; Tropical has a grayish head with less distinct ear-patch and a greenish back), 3) rufous (not whitish-buff) feather edgings on wing coverts, and 4) by the lack of olive sides to the breast.

# SCISSOR-TAILED FLYCATCHER

*Muscivora (=Tyrannus) forficata*

Breeds S-C U.S. Winters S Mexico to Panama.

The Scissor-tailed Flycatcher wanders as much as any member of the *Tyrannidae*. On the West Coast, where it is a Rarity, spring and fall vagrants comprise the bulk of the records, but wintering birds and mid-summer stragglers occur as well. Coastal vagrant "traps" and desert oases in CAL have been most productive, but a smattering of records north of CAL include a number of birds from the interior of B.C. and one north to ALASKA. Most interesting was a female apparently paired with a Western Kingbird *Tyrannus verticalis* along the Colorado R., CAL, which laid eggs, but later abandoned the nest.

**CALIFORNIA**  48 records, graphed below. The peak in late May-early Jun corresponds with peaks of other "eastern" vagrants in CAL; fall and winter records are more dispersed. A female discovered 26 May 1979 at Needles, S.Bn., was apparently paired with a Western Kingbird. She built a nest, laid 5 eggs, but then abandoned them in early Jun, though she remained present in the area through the end of the month.

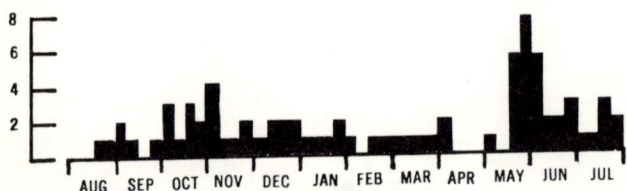

**OREGON**  At least one documented record: 13-14 Jun 1978* at Davis Lake, Klm.

**BRITISH COLUMBIA**  Eight records: 24 May 1964 at Enderby, 31 Aug 1966 ne of Quesnel, 2 Jun 1967 on Salt Spring I., V.I., 7-10 Oct 1967 at Patricia Bay, V.I. (M 49:14), 23 Sep 1968 at Grand Forks (CFN 83:62), 20 May 1972 nw of Trail, 13 May 1973 in Revelstoke NP, and 7 Jun 1974 at Port Neville.

**ALASKA**  One record: 22 Jul 1972 at Gustavus. This species is considered hypothetical on the state list because, though well described, the record is by a single observer.

# SCISSOR-TAILED FLYCATCHER

Nov 1974 at San Elijo Lagoon, S.D., CAL. *John Butler.*

13 May 1973 at Revelstoke NP, B.C. 7th record. *Bob Greyell.*

261

# SULPHER-BELLIED FLYCATCHER

*Myiodynastes luteiventris*

Breeds SE Arizona, N Mexico to Costa Rica. Winters W & C South America.

The Sulphur-bellied Flycatcher has occurred three times in coastal S CAL. All records to date fall within the 2½ week span between 22 Sep-9 Oct.

**CALIFORNIA**   Three records: 22 Sep-5 Oct 1974* at Pt. Mugu, Ven., 6-9 Oct 1978 at Goleta, S.Bb., and 7 Oct 1979 at Pt. Loma, S.D.

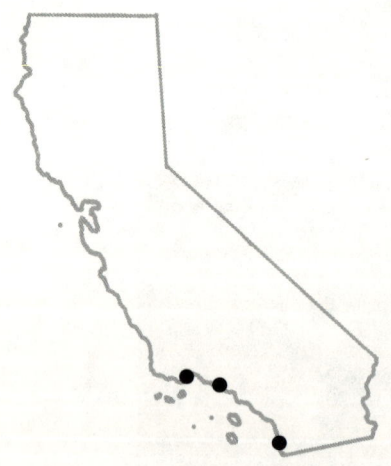

# SULPHUR-BELLIED FLYCATCHER

8 Oct 1978 at Goleta, S.Bb., CAL.
2nd record. *Brad Schram.*

I.D. The distinctive Suphur-bellied Flycatcher is pictured in the standard guides: a kingbird-sized flycatcher possessing heavily streaked yellowish underparts, streaked upperparts, and a bright rusty tail. There are two southern flycatchers that are similar and do migrate; they could occur and the observer should be able to eliminate them from consideration. Streaked Flycatcher *M. maculatus* is similarly-sized and is streaked above and below, but has a yellowish supercilium and whitish underparts (Sulphur-bellied has a whitish supercilium and yellowish underparts). Sulphur-bellied also has a dusky (not whitish) chin. Variegated Flycatcher *Empiconomus varius* has a similar facial pattern, but is distinctly smaller (size of a phoebe *Sayornis sp.*); has a much shorter, smaller bill; is only lightly streaked below without strong yellow tones; has a generally unmarked back; and has only the uppertail coverts and feather edgings of the tail rusty, not the entire tail. For a discussion of the latter bird, which has occurred in Maine, see Abbott & Finch (1978).

# GREAT CRESTED FLYCATCHER

*Myiarchus crinitus*

Breeds E North America. Winters E Mexico to N South America.

The Great Crested Flycatcher has occurred on the West Coast only as a fall vagrant along the coast of CAL. All records have occurred within a narrow time span in late Sep-mid Oct and are suspected of refering to misoriented migrants, probably immatures.

**CALIFORNIA** 16 records, graphed below. Seven were recorded on SE Farallon I. The nine mainland records come from Pt. Loma, S.D. (20 Oct 1974, 19 Sep 1975*, 6 Oct 1978); Pt. Fermin, L.A. (26 Sep 1970); Santa Barbara (13-14 Oct 1979); Goleta, S.Bb. (27 Sep 1974); Bolinas, Mrn. (19 Oct 1974, 3 Oct 1976*); and Arcata, Hmb. (13 Oct 1978).

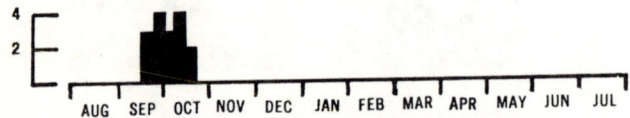

19 Oct 1974 near Bolinas, Mrn., CAL. 9th record. *Ian Tait, courtesy Point Reyes Bird Observatory.*

# GREAT CRESTED FLYCATCHER

I.D. The Great Crested Flycatcher must be carefully distinguished from Ash-throated Flycatcher *M. cinerascens* (see also the discussion under that species), which is a common summer resident and migrant in CAL. Great Crested is only slightly larger and is best identified by a combination of 1) darker mouse-gray breast, 2) brighter yellow belly (but beware that immature Ash-throated is more yellow-bellied than the adult), 3) an olive-green wash to the back and sides of the breast, and 4) a pale base to the lower mandible (sometimes hard to see). Experience with Ash-throated is necessary to note these clear, but subtle, differences. Pale edgings to the tertials and wing coverts are usually more pronounced in Great Crested, contrasting with darker brown wings. In hand or under excellent conditions, the tail pattern is useful. Each tail feather, except the central pair, are rufous on the inner web in both species. On Ash-throated this rufous reaches to the central shaft, but not to the tip, which is brown. On Great Crested the rufous reaches nearly to the shaft and continues to the tip. Juveniles, however, have almost all-rufous tail feathers and this mark cannot be used until after mid-Sep.

The call of Great Crested Flycatcher is a loud, whistled "wheep" with a rising inflection, quite different from the rolling "ku-brick" (accented on the second syllable) of Ash-throated Flycatcher. Both species may give a rolling "prrrt" call, though Great Crested tends to give it louder and more accented. For more information see Dunn (1978c).

# ASH-THROATED FLYCATCHER

*Myiarchus cinerascens*

Breeds W U.S. to SW Mexico. Winters N Mexico to Central America.

The Ash-throated Flycatcher nests in the Coast Ranges of CAL and SW ORE and locally in the desert and Great Basin regions of CAL, ORE, and SE WASH. It is a Rarity north of WASH, where records appear to be of spring overshoots and early fall vagrants.

**BRITISH COLUMBIA** 11 records, graphed below. All 3 spring records are from the interior. 7 of the 8 fall records are from the Vancouver area; the other is from Kleena Kleene in the interior (15 Aug 1964).

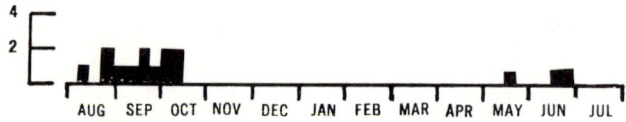

11 Sep 1971 at West Vancouver, B.C. 8th record. *G. Allen Poynter.*

# ASH-THROATED FLYCATCHER

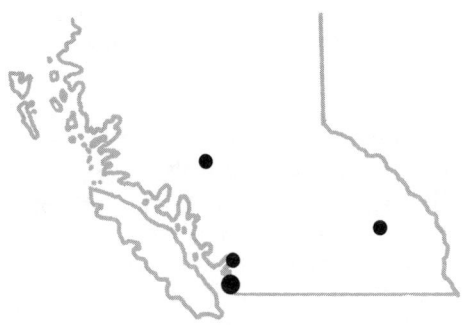

I.D. The Ash-throated Flycatcher is the expected *Myiarchus* in CAL, ORE, and WASH. It is illustrated in the standard guides. Great Crested Flycatcher *M. crinitus* is similar (see the discussion under that species) but is a very rare vagrant on the West Coast. Wied's Crested Flycatcher *M. tyrannulus* is also similar; it nests locally in SE CAL and vagrant Ash-throated Flycatchers have occasionally been misidentified as Wied's Crested (for example, a 22 Sep-12 Oct 1976 bird at Reifel refuge, Vancouver, B.C.).

Wied's Crested Flycatcher is very similar to Ash-throated Flycatcher, but is substantially larger and has a longer, heavier bill (but experience with Ash-throated is necessary to detect these differences; an Ash-throated will look large-billed to the novice with *Myiarchus*). The yellow of the belly of Wied's Crested is brighter than Ash-throated, but it must be remembered that a fall Ash-throated is in fresh plumage and appears brighter and more yellow-bellied than it has looked all summer. Under ideal conditions, the tail pattern (except in juveniles from Aug-mid Sep) is useful. The Ash-throated has a complete brown tip to each tail feather, preventing the rufous on the inner web from reaching the tip. On each Wied's Crested tail feather, the rufous on the inner web extends to the tip. The large size, paler breast, brown back, and all-black bill separate Wied's Crested from Great Crested Flycatcher.

The call of Ash-throated Flycatcher is a rolling, non-musical "ku-brick", accented on the second syllable, and a rolling, burry "prrrt". Wied's Crested common call is a musical, three part, whistled "pre-le-lip", often rolled out into a longer series of calls, or an upslurred, whistled "whip", rather like that of Great Crested Flycatcher, though shorter. For a more detailed discussion see Dunn (1978a).

# OLIVACEOUS FLYCATCHER

*Myiarchus tuberculifer*

Breeds SW U.S. to S South America. Northern populations winter from N Mexico south.

The Olivaceous Flycatcher has occurred on the West Coast only in S CAL during the late fall and winter. The records to date follow a pattern similar to that of another *Tyrannid* with a similar breeding range: Coue's Flycatcher *Contopus pertinax*. Birds arrive in late fall, having (presumably) migrated the "wrong-way". Some have successfully wintered.

**CALIFORNIA** Five records: 23 Nov 1968† at Furnace Creek, Inyo (CB 1:79), 29 Nov 1975-4 Jan 1976* at Furnace Creek, 7 Dec 1975-11 Apr 1976* at the Carmel R. mouth, Mnt., 9-14 Nov 1977† at Walter's Camp, Colorado R., Riv., and 30 Dec 1979-3 Feb 1980 at Irving, Orn.

Dec 1975 at the Carmel R. mouth, Mnt., CAL. 3rd record. *Ronald L. Branson.*

# OLIVACEOUS FLYCATCHER

I.D. The Olivaceous Flycatcher is distinctly the smallest *Myiarchus* in North America, but its shape, stance, and rufous edgings to the wings will identify it to genus. Unlike other American *Myiarchus*, the tail looks brown in the field, having only thin rufous edges (except for Jul-Aug juveniles, which have mostly rufous tails). Though smaller than Ash-throated Flycatcher *M. cinerascens*, it has almost as long a bill, thus looking big-billed (long and thin) in the field. Other characters include a dark brown cap and, in the fall, a grayish breast and a rather bright yellow belly. For more information see Dunn (1978c).

The call of Olivaceous Flycatcher is a mournful, whistled "pee-ur", first ascending and then descending. This call is very unlike any other American *Myiarchus*; it is more similar to the call of Say's Phoebe *Sayornis saya*.

# EASTERN PHOEBE

*Sayornis phoebe*

Breeds C & E North America. Winters SE U.S., N Mexico to S Mexico.

The Eastern Phoebe nests in NE B.C. Until recently, it was considered a Rarity on the West Coast south of B.C. In 1979 it was deleted from the CAL Records Committee list of birds to be reviewed, having averaged 4½ records a year during the 1970s. Nearly all these records are of wintering birds. It has yet to be convincingly recorded from ORE or WASH, suggesting that wintering birds in CAL originate not from the Phoebe's western outposts but from farther east.

**CALIFORNIA**  81 records, graphed below. It was first recorded in 1901, but over half the records (42) come from the last five years (1975-79). This increase probably reflects the recent increase in birders, areas covered, and expertise rather than an increasing number of Eastern Phoebes. As the graph indicates, most records are of birds during the winter and numerous individuals have been known to winter successfully, including one (presumably the same bird) which returned for a second winter at Santee Lake, S.D. (1976, 1977). The graph also illustrates a migrant peak in late Oct-early Nov of birds which do not winter locally; most of the few desert oases records occurred during this period. The vast majority of winter records are along the coast and in the L.A. basin; these birds seem to arrive in late Nov-early Dec (earliest arrival date for a known winterer is 26 Oct) and leave in early Mar. The higher peaks in late Dec-early Jan may reflect more an increase in coverage (associated with the annual Christmas Counts) rather than true arrival dates of wintering birds. Four records fall outside the normal dates of occurrence. Two are early fall birds: 18 Sep 1970 at Goleta, S.Bb., and 30 Sep 1968 at San Luis Waterfowl Management Area, Mrc. The other three are spring vagrants at traditional vagrant "traps" during the peak of spring vagrant season: 18 May 1968 on SE Farallon I., 21 May 1973 at Furnace Creek, Inyo, and 6-8 Jun 1975 on SE Farallon I.

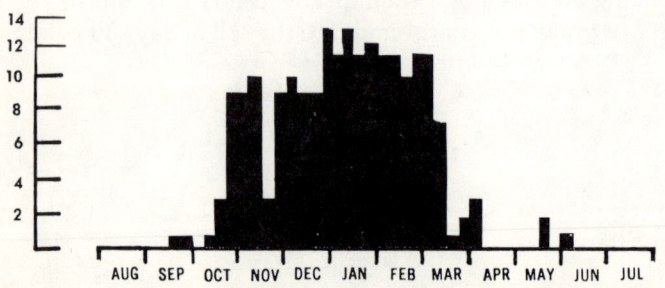

# EASTERN PHOEBE

# BLACK·PHOEBE

*Sayornis nigricans*

Breeds SW U.S. to S South America. Mostly resident but some local post-breeding and winter movements.

The Black Phoebe is a locally common resident throughout much of CAL and is a rare breeder in extreme SW ORE. It is a Rarity north of ORE, where the substatiated records are during the fall and winter.

**WASHINGTON**   One record: 27 Feb 1980 at Moclips Beach, G.H.

**BRITISH COLUMBIA**   One record: 11 Nov 1936† at Vancouver (C 41:123).

# IDENTIFICATION OF *EMPIDONAX* FLYCATCHERS

The identification of *Empidonax* flycatchers is a notoriously difficult problem and one of the standard guides (Peterson, 1961) goes so far as to state that "it is a standing joke among western ornithologists that no one seems to have an infallible way of telling Hammond's and Dusky Flycatchers apart in the field". The status of this problem today is much different. Active and experienced field observers, especially in CAL, routinely identify correctly most Hammond's and Dusky Flycatchers they encounter, even in migration, and have recently begun to find Rarities, such as Least Flycatcher, annually in CAL. Among the hardcore, today's discussions have moved from Hammond's vs. Dusky to the more difficult problems of Western vs. Yellow-bellied or Willow vs. Alder. In the mid-1960s Guy McCaskie, Pierre Devillers and Dave DeSante trapped and banded numbers of *Empidonax*, identified them in hand with proper keys, and then watched their field behavior and characters after release. They were able to pass on the expertise gained to a new generation of birders. Today the better field observers will usually agree on the identification of a migrant *Empid*. Selective collecting in the 1970s (Van Remsen, Steve Cardiff *et al*) proved the reliability of those identifications. The discussion below summarizes this knowledge and that published by Jon Dunn (1977c, e, g, h); it is one way to approach the problem (others might do it differently).

A caution is appropriate here. Despite increasing expertise, the identification of *Empidonax* is a subtle and complex problem and requires much field experience. The novice should not attempt to identify out-of-range birds. A beguiling trap for the unwary has arisen concurrent with increases in our knowledge of *Empidonax* identification. Much too often I have seen the less active or experienced birder use a recently discussed field character (for example, "Hammond's flicks its wings, Dusky doesn't") and attempt to identify flycatchers on that single character alone. More often than not, this leads to numerous misidentifications, as in the identification of *Empidonax* it is essential to note a combination of characters. The example listed above is typical; it is a generalization about migrants but there are plenty of exceptions. All *Empidonax* may flick their wings just after landing, and both Hammond's and Dusky are vigorous wing-flickers while singing on the breeding ground. Even experienced observers cannot identify *every Empidonax* they see; a small percentage of birds remain "Dusky/Hammond's" types or just *Empidonax sp?*.

# IDENTIFICATION OF *EMPIDONAX* FLYCATCHERS

All that having been said, most *Empidonax* can be identified in the field by a combination of characters and by progressively eliminating from consideration the common or distinctive species. The discussion below centers on the identification of migrant *Empidonax;* song and habitat are useful on the breeding grounds in summer. An excellent discussion of these characters for western *Empidonax* is in McCaskie, DeBenedictis, Erickson, & Morlan (1979). Knowledge of migrant timing and distribution is also very valuable; the Dunn series is especially good in this regard for S CAL.

Western Flycatcher *E. difficilis* is a common local nesting bird from SE ALASKA through CAL and is a common migrant. It is the *Empidonax* most often encountered in migration along the coast and is not uncommon as a migrant in the deserts of CAL. It may be the easiest western *Empid* to identify (except for worn birds in early fall), showing a combination of yellow underparts, including the throat; an olive-green back; a long, wide bill with an orange or yellow lower mandible; and an almond-shaped eyering tapering out to a point behind the eye. No other western *Empid* has a yellow throat, as green a back, or this eyering shape (but see the discussions under Yellow-bellied *E. flaviventris* and Acadian Flycatchers *E. virescens*). Worn or washed-out birds in the summer or fall may have very little yellow on the throat and can look browner above; note the bill size and color, eyering shape, actions, and call. Western Flycatcher often actively flicks its wings and tail in migration. The common call is a soft, thin "peet", recalling the note of White-crowned Sparrow *Zonotrichia leucophrys*. Another call given in migration, and commonly on the breeding ground, is a whistled, upslurred, snappy "su-wheet!". Both calls are unlike any other western *Empid*.

Willow *E. traillii* and Alder Flycatchers *E. alnorum* have in the past been lumped under the name "Traill's Flycatcher". Willow Flycatcher is the nesting species of this complex from Vancouver I. and extreme SE B.C. through CAL. It is a fairly common migrant in the interior of CAL, ORE, and WASH, but the timing of migration is later than other western *Empids*, usually not appearing in numbers in the spring until mid-May; it also departs earlier in the fall (Aug-early Sep). Alder Flycatcher is the nesting species in C & S ALASKA and N & C B.C. There is only one record on the West Coast south of B.C.

# IDENTIFICATION OF *EMPIDONAX* FLYCATCHERS

Willow Flycatcher is easily separated from other *Empids* (except Alder) by a combination of the lack of an apparent eyering in the field (shows a faint, thin eyering at close range; this very useful field character is not shown by any of the standard guides); a white throat; generally brownish upperparts; and a long, wide bill with a yellow or orange lower mandible. It is large for an *Empid* and looks small-headed and long-tailed in the field. The brownish coloration, white throat, and lack of an apparent eyering are like no other *Empid* in CAL, ORE, or WASH; indeed, Willow Flycatcher is much more often mistaken for Western Wood Pewee *Contopus sordidulus* or even Eastern Phoebe *Sayornis phoebe* than another *Empid*. Willow Flycatcher often flicks its tail up during migration. Its call is a loud "whit". Western Wood Pewee is a darker olive-gray color, has a peaked shape to the head, does not flick its tail, and does not have a "whit" call. Eastern Phoebe is larger and darker, especially darker-capped, has an all dark bill, lacks distinct wingbars (though Willow's are dull for an *Empid*), dips its tail downward, and does not give a "whit" call.

Alder Flycatcher is very similar to Willow Flycatcher and the only easy way to separate the two is by song on the nesting ground: Alder sings a buzzy "vee-bee-o" and gives a buzzy "veer" and rising "vee"; Willow gives an emphatic "fitz-bew", sometimes uttered during migration as well. Plumages are nearly alike, though Alder tends to be a bit greener on the back (Willow shows only a tinge of green on the lower back and rump) and sometimes a bit yellower on the belly. Alder Flycatcher shows a more apparent eyering than Willow; especially noticeable in western populations is a pale spot on the lores. Experienced observers might separate the two by call: Alder gives a buzzy "bic" or a sharp "pic", somewhat like the call of Hammond's Flycatcher. Willow gives a loud, mellow "whit".

Gray Flycatcher nests in E CAL and E ORE and very locally in Yakima Co., S WASH. It is an uncommon migrant in the deserts and Great Basin of CAL & ORE. A fairly large and pale *Empid*, it is identified by a combination of pale gray upperparts; whitish breast; a long, thin bill with a dark tip to the pale lower mandible; and its unique habit of dipping its tail slowly *downward*. It does not usually flick its wings in migration. The pale plumage does not contrast strongly with the eyering or wingbars, but both features are readily apparent. The tail feathers are edged white, more conspicuously than other *Empids* (except on worn birds in late summer). The call is a strong "whit".

# IDENTIFICATION OF *EMPIDONAX* FLYCATCHERS

Dusky *E. oberholseri*, Hammond's *E. hammondii*, and Least Flycatchers *E. minimus* are the most similar and the most difficult to identify. All are fairly small, show apparent eyerings and wingbars, have rather grayish upperparts and dingy underparts with yellowish bellies (a feature shared by all *Empids* to some degree) and have caused much observer confusion. Not all birds can be identified on plumage characters alone; a combination of plumage, behavior, shape, and vocal characters are often required. Many can be quickly separated, after enough experience, into two groups on the basis of shape: 1) those that look short-tailed and big-headed (most Hammond's and Leasts) and 2) those that look long-tailed and small-headed (most Dusky; Gray Flycatcher also has this shape).

Dusky Flycatcher nests locally in the mountains of B.C. through CAL. It is a fairly common migrant through the interior, much scarser on the coast. It is quite variable in plumage (especially with regards to the amount of darkness on the breast and intensity of yellow on the belly), but most can be identified by a combination of the small-headed, long-tailed shape; grayish throat; long bill, often with an orangeish lower mandible (but can look all-dark in the field); grayish back (without much olive); and call. Dusky Flycatcher does not habitually flick its wings during migration, but is a lazy tail-wagger, flicking upward. The tail feathers (except on worn birds in summer) are edged pale gray, sometimes conspicuously. The call is a mellow "whit".

Hammond's Flycatcher nests locally in higher mountain ranges from C ALASKA through CAL. It is a common migrant through the interior, much more uncommon along the coast. It, too, is somewhat variable in plumage (especially as to the amount of darkness on the breast and sides and the intensity of the yellow on the belly). Most birds can be identified by a combination of small size; short-tailed shape; grayish throat; short, narrow bill with paleness (if any) restricted to the base of the lower mandible; generally olive cast to the back; often dark breastband and sides, giving a "vested" look; and call. The small size, short tail, and short, thin bill are especially good marks in the field. Hammond's Flycatcher is often a nervous wing-and-tail flicker in migration, an habitual character shared only by Western Flycatcher (but this is only a generalization; some birds are rather still). The tail is only narrowly edged with pale gray, usually not conspicuous in the field. The call is a sharp "peek", recalling Pygmy Nuthatch *Sitta pygmaea*, and is unlike any call of other *Empids* in CAL, ORE, and WASH.

# IDENTIFICATION OF *EMPIDONAX* FLYCATCHERS

Least Flycatcher nests in N & E B.C. Vagrants have been recorded in every West Coast state and recently it has been found annually at vagrant "traps" in CAL. It is variable in plumage (especially in regards to the amount of darkness on the breast; some birds overlap the pattern of some Hammond's) and it may be that only the more obvious birds are identified along the West Coast. These birds are identified by a combination of small size (often downright tiny); short-tailed look; whitish throat, often including pale underparts that look as if it is entirely whitish below (but a pale gray breastband and yellowish belly is equally as common a plumage pattern); short, wide bill (almost triangular in shape) with a yellow or orange lower mandible; olive cast to the back; and call. Least Flycatcher does not usually flick its wings during migration, but habitually jerks its tail upward. The tail is only narrowly edged with pale and usually looks evenly-colored in the field. The eyering is often large and conspicuous and the blacker color of the feathers of the wings produce a more striking contrast to the white edgings than is shown by western *Empids* (this feature is true of eastern *Empids* in general). The call is a sharp "wit" or "jip", recalling the note of Yellow-rumped (Audubon's) Warbler *Dendroica coronata,* and is similar to the "whit" notes of Willow, Gray, and Dusky Flycatchers.

## LEAST FLYCATCHER

18 Sep 1974 on SE Farallon I., CAL. *Dave DeSante.*

# YELLOW-BELLIED FLYCATCHER

*Empidonax flaviventris*

Breeds NE North America. Winters C Mexico to Panama.

The Yellow-bellied Flycatcher nests on the West Coast only in NE B.C. It has wandered in summer to E-C ALASKA (and could even breed there). There is only one record on the West Coast south of B.C.: a fall vagrant (but of interest is a record from Tucson, Arizona on 22 Sep 1956†). Its similarity to Western Flycatcher *E. difficilis* makes vagrants especially difficult to identify.

**ALASKA**   One record: 28 Jul 1966 (1†, another seen) at Coal Creek, near the Yukon R. (CFN 83:257).

**CALIFORNIA**   One record: 16 Sep 1976 on SE Farallon I. This bird was trapped, banded, measured, photographed, and released. The record is presently under review by the CAL Records Committee.

# YELLOW-BELLIED FLYCATCHER

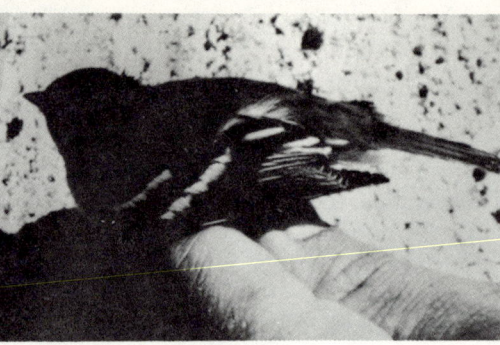

16 Sep 1976 on SE Farallon I., CAL. 1st record. *Ron LeValley*.

I.D. The Yellow-bellied Flycatcher closely resembles Western Flycatcher (see p. 272 for a discussion of Western *Empids*) but is even brighter yellow below and brighter green (not so olive-green) above. It looks shorter-tailed in the field (and does have a shorter tail if measured). The feathers of the wing tend to be blackish (not brownish), producing a more striking contrast to the white edges of the coverts and tertials. The wingbars are white or yellowish (not buffy as on some young Westerns). The eyering is round (not almond-shaped) and if it is broader anywhere it is in front of the eye, not behind it. All these marks are subtle and subjective; their value in the field has yet to be tested.

The Yellow-bellied Flycatcher is said to be rather silent in migration. On the breeding ground it gives an upslurred, whistled "su-wee", rather similar to the call of Western Flycatcher, though more leisurely and less emphatic.

In hand note the sulphur yellow axillaries (not brownish-yellow) and that the 10th primary is longer or equal to the 5th primary. Western Flycatcher has the 5th primary longer than the 10th (except in a few males with wing lengths over 67 mm., in which the 5th and 10th are about equal; most Yellow-bellied Flycatchers have wing lengths less than 67 mm.). For a more thorough discussion of in-hand characters see Phillips, Howe, & Lanyon (1966) and Phillips and Lanyon (1970).

# ACADIAN FLYCATCHER

*Empidonax virescens*

Breeds E North America. Winters Costa Rica to N South America.

The Acadian Flycatcher is mostly restricted to SE U.S. and breeds no closer to the West Coast than the eastern Great Plains. Considering the pattern shown by other eastern vagrants with similar breeding ranges, it is not to be expected often. The difficulty in identifying *Empidonax* flycatchers decreases the likelihood of identifying it as a vagrant; there is only a single specimen taken nearly 50 years ago in B.C. Of interest is another old record from Tucson, Arizona (24 May 1886†).

**BRITISH COLUMBIA**  One record: 9 Jun 1934† at Leonie Lake, near Barriere, Caribou District (C 59:211).

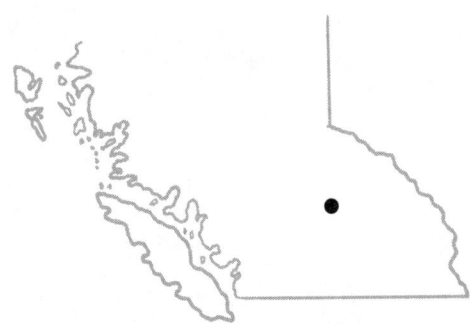

I.D. The Acadian Flycatcher is a fairly large *Empidonax* whose plumage, at least during the spring, does not closely correspond to any western *Empid* (see the *Empid* discussion on p. 272). The upperparts are rather bright green, the throat is white, and the centers of the feathers of the wing coverts and tertials are blackish, contrasting conspicuously with the broad whitish edgings. The bill is long and wide with an orange or yellow lower mandible. Some fall birds become quite yellow below, including the throat, and may be difficult to distinguish from Western *E. difficilis* or Yellow-bellied Flycatchers *E. flaviventris*. See Phillips, Howe & Lanyon (1966) and Phillips & Lanyon (1970) for a discussion of in hand characteristics.

The call of Acadian Flycatcher is a high "peep", recalling the note of Western Flycatcher.

# ALDER FLYCATCHER

*Empidonax alnorum*

Breeds N North America. Winters S Mexico to South America.

The Alder Flycatcher nests in ALASKA and B.C. The only record on the West Coast south of B.C. was a singing bird at a vagrant "trap" in NE ORE.

**OREGON**  One record: 22 Jun 1980 at Enterprise Fish Hatchery, Wal. This bird was singing; details are presently under review by the ORE Records Committee.

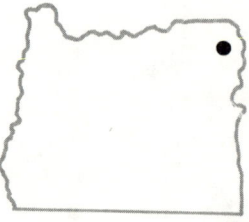

I.D. See the identification essay on *Empidonax* flycatchers beginning on p. 272.

# LEAST FLYCATCHER

*Empidonax minimus*

Breeds E North America. Winters C Mexico to Panama.

The Least Flycatcher nests on the West Coast only in NE B.C. It is a Rarity in every West Coast state. Records in ALASKA and WASH have all been of singing birds in Jun-Jul, but records from CAL and ORE are divided between spring and fall vagrants, with fall records from the coast of CAL predominating. Thanks to increases in coverage and observer expertise, CAL has recently (1975-1979) been averaging nearly 8 Least Flycatchers a year.

**ALASKA** One record: 18 Jun 1969 at Juneau. This species is listed as hypothetical on the state list since, though the bird was singing and well described, it was observed only by a single observer.

**WASHINGTON** Six records, all of singing birds: 21-23 Jun 1958† at Anacortes, Skg. (C 63:181); 1 Jun 1968 at Turnbull NWR, Spk.; 18 Jun-6 Jul 1974 along Umtanum Creek, near Ellensburg, Yak.; Jun-Jul 1975 along Wenas Creek, near Yakima; Jun-Jul 1976 along Oak Creek, near Naches, Yak.; and 28 Jun 1977 at White Mud Lake, near Colville, Stv. The Wenas Creek record has been said to be of a nesting pair, but the details do not support this conclusion. Considering the number of singing males in appropriate habitat, some of which remained for long periods during the summer, it does not seem unlikely that nesting could be proven sometime in the future.

# LEAST FLYCATCHER

**OREGON**  Six records, five from the banding station on Hart Mt., Lake: 1 Jun 1977*, 12 Jun 1977, 8 Oct 1977, 14 Sep 1978, and 15 Sep 1978; and one along the Wenaha R., Wal.: 16 Jun 1977.

**CALIFORNIA**  64 records, graphed below. After the collection of one in Santa Cruz on 29 Jun 1896, none was identified until 1968. Since then it has been found annually spring and fall; half (32) have been recorded at the banding station on SE Farallon I. Mainland birds have been mostly at well-worked desert and coastal vagrant "traps", with fall vagrants predominating. Two wintering individuals have been discovered: 5 Nov 1978-3 Mar 1979 at Filmore, Ven., and 26 Nov 1978-17 Feb 1979 at Brock ranch, Imp. The latest spring record was 8 Jul 1968† on SE Farallon I.

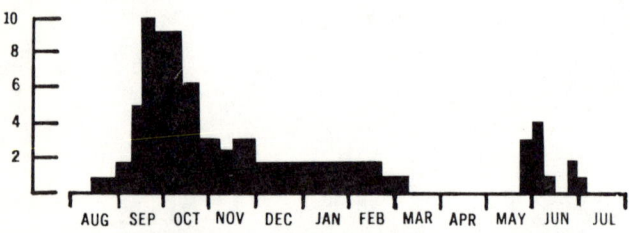

6 Oct 1979 at Pt. Reyes NS, Mrn., CAL. *Peter B. Sands.*

# LEAST FLYCATCHER

I.D. The identification of Least Flycatcher is discussed in the *Empidonax* essay, beginning on p. 272.

# COUE'S FLYCATCHER (GREATER PEWEE)

*Contopus pertinax*

Breeds SE Arizona, SW New Mexico to Nicaragua. Northern populations winter to the south.

The Coue's Flycatcher has been recorded on the West Coast only in S & C CAL. The records to date form a clear pattern of birds arriving in late fall (presumably after "wrong-way" migrations) and remaining to winter locally, often successfully. At least one individual returned for a second winter.

**CALIFORNIA** 16 records, graphed below. At least 9 of the birds were seen locally for over a month and were thought to winter successfully; most of the other birds recorded could have been successful winterers as well. One at Parker Dam, Imp., from 24 Dec 1977-19 Mar 1978* returned (presumably the same individual) for a second winter from 25 Nov 1978-1 Feb 1979. The two early records were both collected: 4 Oct 1952† at the se end, Salton Sea, Imp., and 29 Sep 1965† at Holtville, Imp. The northernmost record was present 6 Dec 1975-18 Feb 1976* at New Brighton SB, S.Cz.

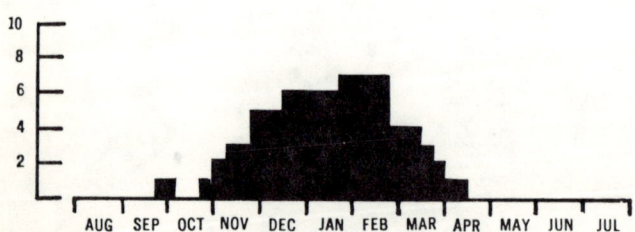

# COUE'S FLYCATCHER

Feb 1978 at Parker Dam, Imp., CAL. *Chris Carpenter.*

29 Dec 1968 at Monterey, CAL. 5th record. *Ronald L. Branson.*

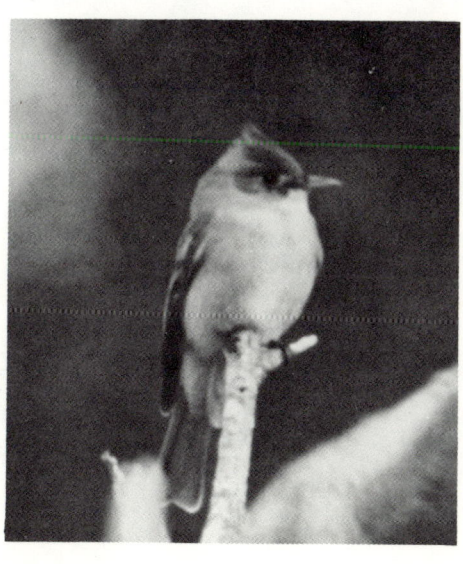

# EASTERN WOOD PEWEE

*Contopus virens*

Breeds E North America. Winters Costa Rica to Peru.

The Eastern Wood Pewee has been recorded on the West Coast only once (possibly twice) in CAL. The species nests north into SE Canada and west to the central Great Plains; there are numbers of West Coast records of other eastern species with similar ranges and one would expect a few more pewee records. The difficulty in separating this bird from Western Wood Pewee *C. sordidulus* may be most responsible for the paucity of reports. Considering what we know of the timing of vagrants, observers should look especially closely at pewees in the late fall (Oct-Nov) and at migrant "traps" in late spring (late May-mid Jun). Of interest to West Coast observers is a record during the fall from Tucson, Arizona (7 Oct 1953†).

**CALIFORNIA**   One undisputed record: 15 Jun 1975* on SE Farallon I. This individual was trapped, banded, measured, photographed, and released. In addition, the CAL Records Committee accepted a record which occurred 18-19 Oct 1974* at Pt. Mugu, Ven., but one of the observers of this bird has expressed misgivings and the record has been resubmitted to the CAL Records Committee for further review. I prefer to consider it a valid record.

# EASTERN WOOD PEWEE

15 Jun 1975 on SE Farallon I., CAL. 1st (or 2nd; see text) record. *Dave DeSante.*

I.D. The Eastern Wood Pewee closely resembles Western Wood Pewee and it may be that only the more clearly marked birds can be identified in the field at our present state of knowledge. In general, Eastern Wood Pewee differs in its tendency to have 1) an all yellow (or nearly all yellow) lower mandible, 2) whiter underparts without the broad gray breastband and sides which produce the "vested" look so common in Western Wood Pewee, and 3) a slightly greener cast to the olive-gray upperparts, especially on the lower back and rump. While any of these differences may be found in samples of Western Wood Pewee, the combination of all three characters appears to be limited to Eastern Wood Pewee. Much observer experience is necessary to correctly gauge the extent of these characters, especially the latter two, which are subjective and subtle. It may be that these species cannot presently be distinguished on plumage characters alone; identification may require a combination of plumage and vocal characters.

The song of Eastern Wood Pewee — a plaintive, whistled "pee-oo-wee" or simply "pee-oo" — is very different from the descending, burry song of Western Wood Pewee. While many Western Wood Pewee sing on migration (especially in the spring), Eastern Wood Pewee (unfortunately) does so less often. Eastern Wood Pewee does often call on migration: a sharply descending, whistled "pee-ur", without burriness. But Western Wood Pewee can also give a clear descending whistle and it seems that only very experienced ears can detect the clearer, more sharply descending quality of the Eastern Wood Pewee call.

# COMMON SKYLARK

*Alauda arvensis*

Breeds Eurasia, N Africa. Northern populations winter from Africa to China and Korea. Has been introduced locally around the world, including Hawaii and S Vancouver I., B.C.

The Common Skylark is a regular spring migrant in small numbers on the outer Aleutians, ALASKA. It has rarely been recorded north or east of the Aleutians, but it was suspected of nesting on St. Paul I., Pribilofs, in 1970. Specimens taken in ALASKA have proved to be the northeasternmost race from Asia: *A. a. pekinensis*. A bird identified as belonging to one of the NE Asia races appeared in CAL during the winter of 1978-79. It apparently wintered successfully here, as it returned briefly during the late fall of 1979.

The European race of Common Skylark *A. a. arvensis* was introduced on southern Vancouver I., B.C., in about 1902. A small population became resident there and eventually spread to the adjacent San Juan I., WASH. The introduced population is now thought to be declining.

**ALASKA** Rare spring migrant on the outermost Aleutian Is. (30 Apr-5 Jun), in flocks of up to 8, and casual there as a fall migrant. Most records away from the outer Aleutians are from the Pribilof Is.: 20 May 1967 on St. George I. and a flock of at least 12 from 1-9 Jul 1970 which included a singing male suspected of breeding. The only other record was on 29 May 1978 at Gambell, St. Lawrence I.

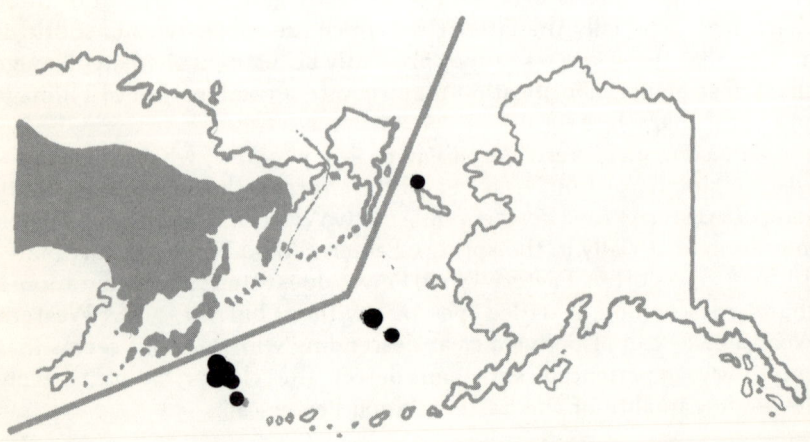

# COMMON SKYLARK

**CALIFORNIA**  One record: 16 Dec 1978-19 Feb 1979* at Pt. Reyes NS, Mrn. This bird (presumably the same individual) returned briefly the next fall from 28 Oct-1 Nov 1979.

Dec 1978 at Pt. Reyes NS, Mrn., CAL. Two views. 1st record. *Al Ghiorso.*

# COMMON SKYLARK

I.D. The Common Skylark illustrated in the standard guides is the European race *A. a. arvensis* which has been introduced on Vancouver I., B.C. All records from ALASKA and CAL appear to be of birds from populations in NE Asia. These birds differ from the nominate, introduced race in a number of ways: 1) they are more richly colored, often with broad reddish edges to the dark feathers of the upperparts, 2) they are strongly buffy-yellow on the face and breast, and 3) the streaks on the nape are narrow, unlike the broad streaks on European (and B.C.) birds. NE Asian races are variable in size: some (e.g. *pekinensis*) are quite large, with a pronounced size difference between sexes, while others (e.g. *kiborti*) are small, averaging smaller than Horned Lark *Eremophila alpestris*. Some races (*pekinensis*) are very reddish, others are more buffy-yellow (*kiborti*), and others tend to be very dark, even blackish (e.g. *intermedia*). None of these characteristics are found on nominate *arvensis*. The CAL bird cannot be assigned to any particular race, but was small and very buffy-yellow, with narrow nape streaks and rusty edges to the feathers of the crown and upper back: it was a vagrant from NE Asia.

Common Skylark might be mistaken for a number of ground-dwelling birds, such as winter-plumaged longspurs *Calcarius sp*. It walks, shows white outer tail feathers, and often joins flocks of Horned Larks and longspurs. Common Skylark lacks wingbars and rusty median wing coverts, has a white belly, has white on only the outer tail feathers, and has a thin white trailing edge to the inner wing; the combination of these characters will separate it from any species of longspur. Some of its habits — crouching, raising its crest, and fluttering on broad wings in flight — are also unlike the habits of longspurs.

Singing birds (as early as Feb-Mar) hover high in the air, giving a long, liquid song (an activity known as "skylarking"). Flight calls of the nominate race include an abrupt "chirrup" and a variety of chirpy notes. Calls of NE Asian birds apparently include other notes, as the CAL bird gave brief preliminary song notes and a short "bjjjrt" call.

# COMMON HOUSE MARTIN

*Delichon urbica*  Plate 6

Breeds Eurasia, N Africa. Winters Africa, S Eurasia.

The Common House Martin has occurred only twice on the West Coast: two birds reached W ALASKA within a few days of each other in Jun 1974.

**ALASKA**  Two records: 6-7 Jun 1974 at Nome, and 12 Jun 1974† on St. Paul I., Pribilofs (A 95:429).

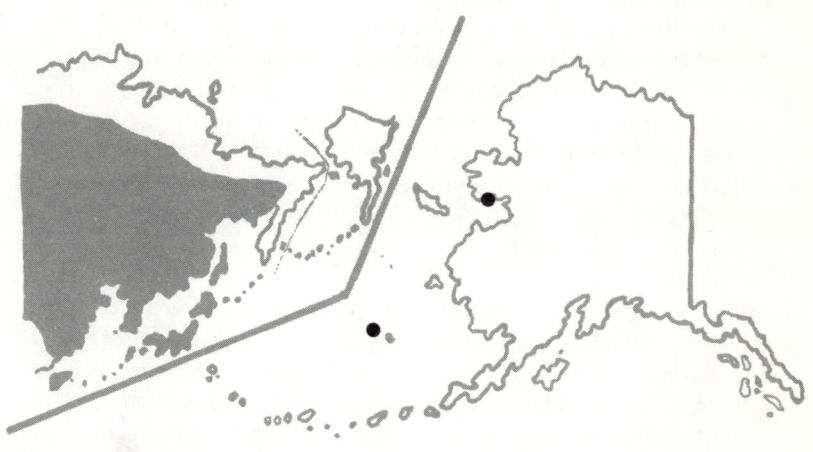

I.D. The Common House Martin resembles Tree Swallow *Iridoprocne bicolor* in size and general appearance, but appears chunkier, with shorter wings and shorter, forked tail. In any plumage the large white rump-patch is distinctive. Adults are steely-blue above and white below. Immatures are slightly duller or more brownish above, and the underparts are faintly washed brown.

# BLUE JAY

*Cyanocitta cristata*

Breeds E North America. Some northern populations winter irregularly to the south.

The Blue Jay seems to be undergoing a range expansion in the northwest portion of its breeding range. It breeds west to E Wyoming and W Alberta and until recently was a Rarity anywhere on the West Coast. But during the 1970s it has become regular in small numbers during the fall and winter in SE B.C. and E WASH (especially around Spokane), with a few birds straying to S WASH, the Puget Sound area, and S Vancouver I. (see M 57:64 and M 59:72 for a discussion of WASH records through 1977). Some birds have lingered throughout the summer and breeding might be expected in the future. Invasions during the fall and winter of 1976-77 and 1977-78 sent birds farther south, especially down the Willamette Valley of ORE, to N CAL, where a diurnal migrant was recorded as far south as San Francisco Bay. Three previous records from CAL occurred far inland and even farther south; these records do not appear to be correlated with invasions elsewhere. A pair nested in E ORE in 1977.

**OREGON**  At least 16 records, all since 1976, except for a bird from late Dec 1973-4 May 1974 at Halfway, Bak., and one in fall 1975 at Malheur NWR, Har. The others first appeared during the invasions of fall & winter 1976-77 (7) and 1977-78 (7). Exact dates have been difficult to trace, but most arrived from Oct-Dec and several remained to winter locally. All were inland except for one at North Bend, Coos (Nov 1976-Apr 1977*). A pair has been present around Union, Uni., since Aug 1976 to at least winter 1979-80. This pair bred during the summer of 1977: an adult and 3 fledglings were seen on 11 Jul and 4 birds were present through 1 Oct 1977 (M 59:70).

**CALIFORNIA**  Eight records: 24 Apr 1950† at Chico, But., 30 Oct 1963-20 Apr 1964 at Iglos, S.Bn. (CB 1:81), 24 Oct 1973* at Panamint City, Inyo, 21 Oct 1977* at Pt. Diablo, Mrn., 30-31 Oct 1977 (2)* at Pt. St. George, D.N., 31 Dec 1977-8 Jan 1978 at Willow Creek, Hmb., mid-Jan-9 Mar 1978* at Fieldbrook, Hmb., and 7 Oct 1978 at the north spit, Humboldt Bay, Hmb.

# BLUE JAY

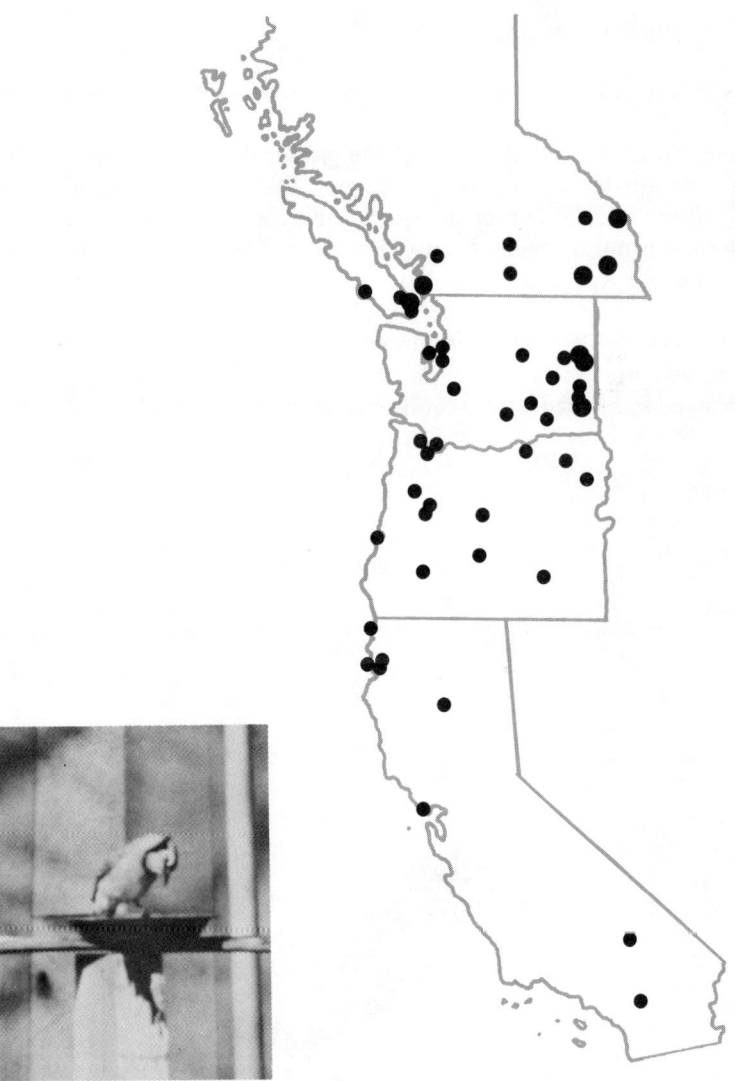

26 Feb 1978 at Fieldbrook, Hmb.,
CAL. 7th record. *Don Roberson.*

# PINYON JAY

*Gymnorhinus cyanocephalus*

Breeds W U.S. to Baja, Mexico. Mostly resident; some irregular wanderings.

The Pinyon Jay is mostly a bird of the pinyon-juniper belt in the Great Basin and high desert areas of E CAL and E ORE. It occasionally wanders afield, often in flocks, in response to variable food supplies. This irregular wandering brought several small flocks into S WASH, where it is a Rarity, during Apr 1967.

**WASHINGTON** One definite record: mid Apr 1967 when several small flocks were present near Goldendale, Klk. (2† taken on 22 Apr). There were two previous undocumented sight records of single birds: Oct 1947 and 17 or 18 Jun 1941, both in Yakima Co. (see WB 7:16).

22 Apr 1967 at Goldendale, Klk., CAL. 1st confirmed record. Specimen in Thompson/Louckhart collection. *Phil Mattocks.*

# GRAY CATBIRD

*Dumetella carolinensis*

Breeds C & E North America. Winters SE U.S. to the West Indies and Mexico to Panama.

The Gray Catbird breeds on the West Coast in S B.C., E WASH, and NE ORE. It is a Rarity in CAL, where nearly all records are from desert oases or coastal vagrant "traps" during the peak of spring and fall vagrant season. This pattern suggests that many of the records may refer to misoriented birds from the east rather than slightly misdirected migrants from nearby western populations. One bird wintered at a C CAL feeder.

**CALIFORNIA** 26 records, graphed below. While fall records are spread among four months, note the narrow 3-week period of spring records. Most birds were at well-worked vagrant "traps": 5 from Deep Springs & Oasis, 4 from Death Valley, 3 from around San Diego and 3 from the Monterey Pen., and 2 each from Santa Barbara and SE Farallon I. An individual wintered from 28 Dec 1973-20 Feb 1974 at Pebble Beach, Mnt. One found dead on 25 Mar 1973 at Los Banos, Mer., could also have been attempting to winter. The first CAL record was 4 Sep 1884 on SE Farallon I.; it was not recorded again in the state until 1964 (C 69:310). It has recently (1974-1979) been averaging about 3 birds a year.

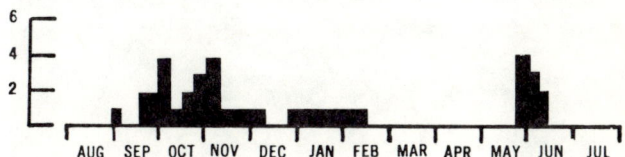

# GRAY CATBIRD

Dec 1973 at Pebble Beach, Mnt., CAL. 8th record. *Ronald L. Branson.*

6 Oct 1979 at Pt. Reyes NS, Mrn., CAL. *Peter B. Sands.*

# BROWN THRASHER

*Toxostoma rufum*

Breeds E North America. Winters SE U.S.

The Brown Thrasher is scarce anywhere on the West Coast, but is technically a Rarity only north of CAL. It has averaged only about 6 records a year in CAL and is so close to our definition of "Rarity" that it is discussed for that state as well. While most records are of spring and fall vagrants, over 15% of the West Coast records are during the winter and a number have been known to winter successfully, returning locally for a second winter (one bird in CAL returned for 4 successive winters).

**CALIFORNIA** 84 records, graphed below. In the case of this species, the graph is misleading. Most records are during the spring and fall; only 15% are during the winter. But winter birds tend to remain locally for long periods (as early as 17 Oct; as late as 17 Apr) and these long stays, graphed by weeks of presence, pile up to form the misleading winter "peak" shown. The graph does show the expected peak in late May-early Jun for eastern vagrants; the interesting peak in late Apr-early May could be of birds moving in normal migration from successful wintering in W Mexico or even CAL (the numbers involved, however, are very small and the statement above is highly speculative). Spring and fall vagrants are most often found at well-worked desert and coastal vagrant "traps": 16 from the Death Valley-Oasis-Deep Springs loop, 8 from the Santa Barbara area, and 7 from SE Farallon I. are examples. Wintering birds prefer residential areas near the coast (or at least this is where they are found, often at feeders); the San Diego, Los Angeles, and Santa Barbara areas have several records each, and one bird returned for 4 successive winters (1971-72 to 1975-76) at Fairfax, Mrn.

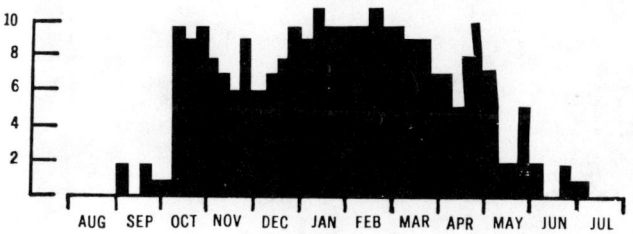

# BROWN THRASHER

**OREGON** Six records: 20 Aug 1940 at Upper Klammath Lake, Klm. (A 58:99), 7 Mar 1954† at Malheur NWR, Har. (C 61:55), Dec 1974-Mar 1975 at Malheur NWR, 25 May 1977 at Shady Cove, Jck., 8 Jul 1978* at Brookings, Cur., and 22 Jun 1979* at Hart Mt., Lake.

**WASHINGTON** Two records: 19-20 May 1963 at Pasco, Frk., and 14 Oct 1972 at the Skagit Game Range, Skg. (M 54:24).

**BRITISH COLUMBIA** Three records: 21-22 Sep 1970 at Penticton (CFN 86:295), 23 Feb-16 Apr 1972 at West Vancouver, and 17-21 Nov 1973 at Long Beach, V.I. (CFN 88:235).

**ALASKA** One record: 27 Sep 1974† at Pt. Barrow.

22 Sep 1970 at Penticton, B.C. 1st record. *Steve R. Cannings.*

1 Apr 1972 at West Vancouver, B.C. 2nd record. *R. W. Phillips.*

# BROWN THRASHER

# CURVE-BILLED THRASHER

*Toxostoma curvirostre*

Breeds SW U.S. to S Mexico. Mostly resident.

The Curve-billed Thrasher has occurred on the West Coast only in S CAL. Winter records along the Colorado R. and near the Salton Sea make up the bulk of the sightings, but twice birds have been reported along the coast during the fall.

**CALIFORNIA**   18 records, graphed below. 13 of the records fall between Nov-Mar and were probably wintering birds; all are from along the Colorado R. (7 records, 6 from the Bard-Laguna Dam area, Imp.) or in the Imperial Valley near the Salton Sea, Imp. (6 records). 3 additional records are from SE CAL: 29 Oct 1924† at Bard, 24 Jun 1973 at Brock ranch, Imp., and 14 Apr 1974* at Brock ranch. Coastal records have been controversial, but there are apparently two good reports (as yet not reviewed by the CAL Records Committee): 6-19 Sep 1965 at Imperial Beach, S.D., and 5 Oct 1979 at the Santa Clara R. mouth, Ven.

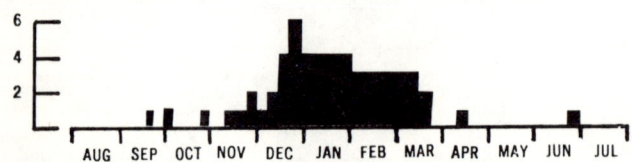

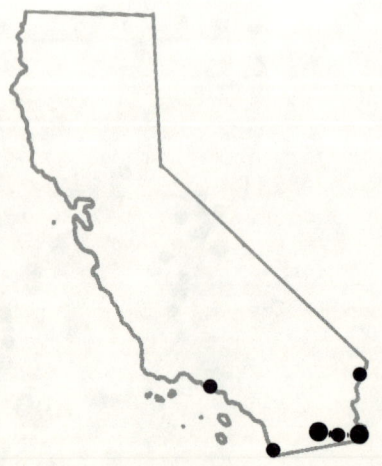

# CURVE-BILLED THRASHER

Feb 1976 at Finney Lake, Imp., CAL. *Dave Harlow*.

I.D. The Curve-billed Thrasher is a lanky grayish thrasher most likely confused with Bendire's Thrasher *T. bendirei*. It can be very difficult to separate from Bendire's and the field guides are misleading in this respect. Eye color is variable and both species may have yellowish eyes. The best mark is the longer, more decurved bill of Curve-billed. Bendire's bill is shorter and straighter, with a diagnostic pale base to the lower mandible (hard to see). Curve-billed is a larger bird (nearly the size of California Thrasher *T. redivivum*) and grayer in color; Bendire's is more compact and rather tannish-brown, with a buffy wash to the breast. Curve-billed tends to have a more distinct whitish throat and the breast spots are larger and blotchy; Bendire's has smaller triangular spots forming a pattern of thin streaks (a pattern more pronounced in fresh fall plumage).

The call of Curve-billed Thrasher is a loud, upslurred "whit-wheet", like a whistle to get someone's attention; it is easily imitated (by humans *Homo sapiens* and Starlings *Sturnus vulgaris*) and often given in winter. The call of Bendire's Thrasher is a blackbird-like "chuck", which is not often heard in winter or migration. For more information see Dunn (1976a).

# CALIFORNIA THRASHER

*Toxostoma redivivum*

Breeds N California to N Baja, Mexico. Mostly resident.

The California Thrasher is a resident of the Coast Ranges of CAL, breeding north to S Humboldt Co. There is only very local fall and winter wandering. A disjunct population exists in Shasta Valley, Sis.; the single record north of CAL is suspected of wandering from this isolated population.

**OREGON** One undisputed record: 20 Jul 1967-4 Feb 1968 at Medford, Jck. This individual visited a feeder irregularly during its stay. There are a few other undocumented reports from this area of S ORE which could well be good; there is potential thrasher habitat here and few observers.

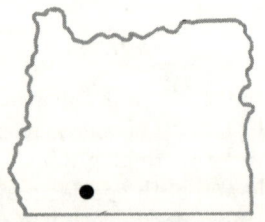

# FIELDFARE
Plate 7

*Turdus pilaris*

Breeds N Eurasia. Winters Europe to India.

The Fieldfare has occurred only once on the West Coast: a bird (presumably a spring overshoot) reached Pt. Barrow, ALASKA.

**ALASKA** One record: 15 Jun 1968† at Pt. Barrow (C 72:480). The specimen was found dead.

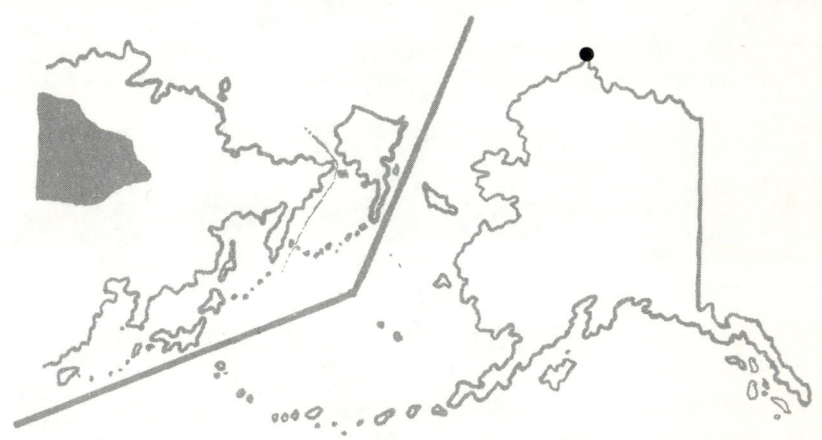

I.D. The Fieldfare is a large, long-tailed thrush slightly larger, but slimmer, than American Robin *T. migratorius*. It is distinguished by a gray head and rump, chestnut back and wings, black tail, and a finely spotted breast washed with a rich buff. The underwing coverts flash white in flight.

The typical flight call is a harsh, chattering, "tchack-tchack-tchack".

# RUFOUS-BACKED ROBIN

Plate 7

*Turdus rufopalliatus*

Breeds W & S Mexico. Wanders irregularly in fall and winter.

The Rufous-backed Robin, an arboreal frugivore, has become a rare, but nearly annual, winter visitor in S Arizona. Birds have twice strayed to SE CAL; one remained to winter locally.

**CALIFORNIA** Two records: 17 Dec 1973-6 Apr 1974* at Imperial Dam, Imp., and 19 Nov 1974 at Saratoga Springs, Death Valley, Inyo.

I.D. The Rufous-backed Robin is similar to American Robin *T. migratorius* but is generally paler, has a rufous wash to the crown and a rufous back, and lacks a white eyering. The breast tends to be more orange-red than that of the American Robin, and the white of the belly extends up into the lower breast as an inverted "V". It is often very secretive, acting more like Varied Thrush *Ixoreus naevius* than American Robin.

# DUSKY THRUSH

Plate 7

*Turdus naumanni*

Breeds NE Asia. Winters SE Asia.

The Dusky Thrush has occurred on the West Coast only on the Aleutians, St. Lawrence I., and Pt. Barrow, ALASKA. All have been recorded during the spring, presumably as a result of spring overshooting. All have been the NE Asian race *T. n. eunomus*.

**ALASKA** 12 records (through May 1980), graphed below. 8 are from the outer Aleutian Is. (Attu-4, Shemya-4); 3 from Gambell, St. Lawrence I.; and one from Pt. Barrow (1-3 Jun 1967). Except for the Barrow record, all birds have been found in the last six years (1975-1980), coinciding with more thorough coverage on Attu I. and at Gambell.

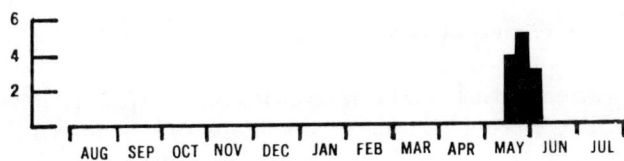

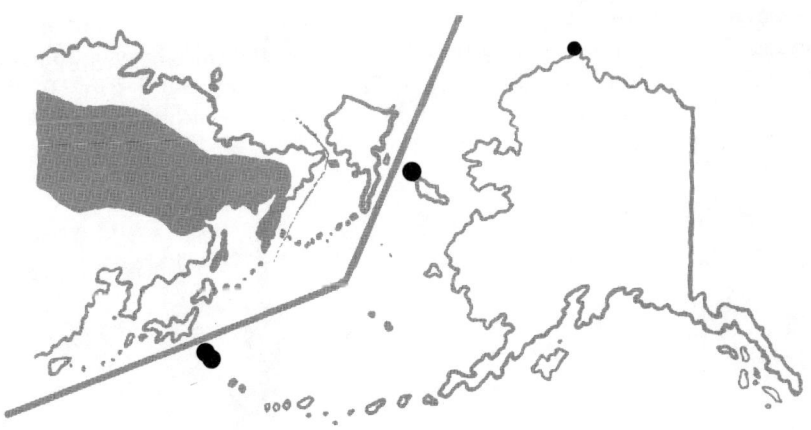

# DUSKY THRUSH

**I.D.** The Dusky Thrush is about the size of American Robin *T. migratorius*. Distinctive are the broad white supercilium; much rusty on the wing and rump; double blackish breastbands, the lower one often broken (there is considerable variation in the extent and pattern of the breast markings); and crescentric flank markings extending to the undertail coverts. The underwing coverts are rufescent. The bill is heavy in proportion to the size of the bird; it is usually dark with a pale base to the lower mandible, but the bill may look yellow with a dark tip in the field. For more detailed description and in-hand photos see BB 53:275.

Calls include a soft clucking note and a wheezy note, rather like that of Common Starling *Sturnus vulgaris*.

# EYE-BROWED THRUSH                       Plate 7

*Turdus obscurus*

Breeds NE Asia. Winters SE Asia, Philippines.

The Eye-browed Thrush has been recorded on the West Coast only in W & N ALASKA. Spring records predominate and recent work on the Aleutians suggest it may be regular there (a couple annually). There are only two fall records.

**ALASKA** 40 records (through spring 1980), graphed below. Nearly all were found during the spring on the westernmost Aleutians (Attu-8, Alaid-6, Nizki-3, Shemya-7, Buldir-4, and Amchitka-5). 19 of these birds occurred during the spring of 1976. Additional spring records come from St. Paul I., Pribilofs (8-9 Jun 1978), Wales, Seward Pen. (3 on 13 Jun 1975), and far north at Barrow (16 Jun 1971). There are only two fall records: 19 Oct 1957† on Amchitka I., and 6 Oct 1962† on St. Paul I.

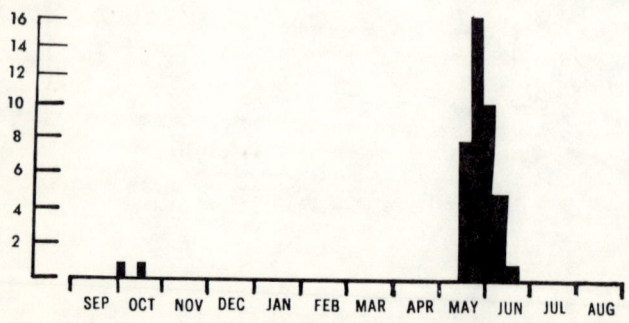

# EYE-BROWED THRUSH

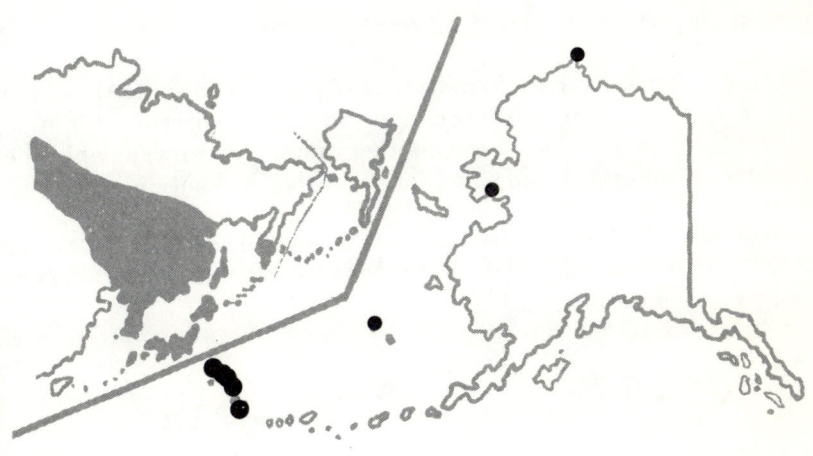

I.D. The Eye-browed Thrush is only slightly smaller than American Robin T. *migratorius* and appears remarkably like that species at a distance in the field. The white supercilium can be seen at close range but it is short (narrowing considerably behind the eye) and inconspicuous and hard to see at a distance. Better characters are its paler appearance, especially paler buffy-orange breast and sides, and the fact that the white of the belly extends upward onto the lower breast as an inverted "V", dividing the orange sides (the reddish breast of American Robin extends down to the white belly and is squarely demarcated from it). Males have a dark gray head, throat, and breast (darker than shown on Plate 7), a white chin, and fairly bright orange sides. Females and immatures often lack any gray on the breast, have white throats, and show only buffy sides. Some birds, of either sex, have gray heads which contrast with the olive-brown back; others are more uniformly colored from crown to back. Immatures may show faint buffy wingbars. The dark tail has whitish corners, similar to those on American Robin.

Calls of Eye-browed Thrush include a very American Robin-like "chuck", a harsh "seee", and a thin "zip-zip". For more information see Parslow (1968).

# WOOD THRUSH

*Hylocichla mustelina*

Breeds E North America. Winters S Texas to Panama.

The Wood Thrush has been found on the West Coast only in CAL, where the four records occurred during either spring or fall migration. Of these four birds, one was collected and another caught and banded, while the other two were caught and eaten (presumably) by domestic cats.

**CALIFORNIA**   Four records: 18 Nov 1967† at Imperial Beach, S.D., 1-11 Aug 1968 at Glendale, L.A. (CB 2:135), 18-19 Jun 1977* near Bolinas, Mrn., and 25-26 Oct 1978 at Imperial Beach, S.D.

18 Nov 1967 at Imperial Beach, S.D., CAL. 1st record. *Alan M. Craig.*

# WOOD THRUSH

18 Jun 1977 at Palomarin, Pt. Reyes NS, Mrn. 3rd record. *Bruce Sorrie.*

# IDENTIFICATION OF *CATHARUS* THRUSHES

Before one attempts to identify a vagrant species of *Catharus* thrush, the observer should be thoroughly acquainted with the two commonest species on the West Coast: Hermit Thrush *C. guttatus* and Swainson's Thrush *C. ustulatus*. *Catharus* thrushes can be very difficult to separate. Identification often depends on a combination of plumage characters and a knowledge of distribution and vocalizations. The discussion below centers on the identification of migrants; habitat and song are very useful during the summer and discussed by the standard guides and such books as Godfrey (1966).

Hermit Thrush is a common nesting species in proper habitat from C ALASKA through S CAL. In the southern part of its West Coast range (such as CAL) it breeds in the higher mountains and moves to the lowlands during the winter (Oct-Apr). It is the only *Catharus* thrush to winter anywhere on the West Coast. It is a small *Catharus* and identified by the combination of 1) rusty-red tail contrasting with gray rump and upperparts, 2) bold spotting on the breast, 3) a thin whitish eyering, 4) grayish flanks, and 5) its habit of frequently flicking its wings. The rusty-red tail can be difficult to see in poor light; too often observers attempt to call a Hermit Thrush some other species because they cannot see the tail color well. The boldly spotted breast, thin white eyering, and wing flicking are also excellent marks. The call is a low "chup" or "chup-chup", very unlike the call of other thrushes.

Swainson's Thrush is a nesting species from C ALASKA through S CAL, preferring riparian areas and deciduous woodlands in the southern part of its West Coast range. It is a common spring migrant through the CAL deserts, but fall migration occurs almost entirely along the coast. There is only *one* acceptable winter record of Swainson's Thrush (an injured bird); all other winter reports (notably on Christmas Counts) are suspected of being in error. Swainson's Thrush is a bit larger than Hermit Thrush and is identified by a combination of 1) richer rufous-brown upperparts, 2) bold buffy eyering, 3) buffy cheeks, 4) a moderately spotted breast washed with buffy (especially on the throat), and 5) buffy-brown flanks. This description is of the typical western race; eastern and Great Basin races, often known as "Olive-backed Thrush", are less easily identified.

# IDENTIFICATION OF *CATHARUS* THRUSHES

They lack the warm rufous-brown tones to the upperparts, having olive-brown upperparts. They can be separated from other species by the buffy eyering, cheek, and throat; and by brownish flanks. On the West Coast there are only a couple sight records of birds fitting "Olive-backed Thrush" (all from vagrant "traps" in CAL). The call note of Swainson's Thrush is a soft "wink", easily distinguished from the calls of other thrushes. For more information on Hermit and Swainson's Thrush identification see Dunn (1977d).

Gray-cheeked Thrush *C. minimus* nests across much of ALASKA and in NW B.C. It is a Rarity south of B.C. on the West Coast. Gray-cheeked Thrush is a large *Catharus* about the size of Swainson's Thrush; it most resembles "olive-backed" races of that species but is easily separated from western Swainson's Thrush. It is identified by the combination of 1) evenly-colored gray-brown upperparts (looks "cold", Swainson's looks "warm". Hermit Thrush can look either way, depending on whether the tail is seen well), 2) gray cheek unicolored with the crown, 3) the lack of an eyering or, at best, a very thin white eyering, 4) boldly spotted breast, washed with pale yellowish-olive on immatures in the fall, and 5) dull slaty-gray flanks. It is separated from Hermit Thrush by its larger size, lack of rusty-red tail, much less distinct eyering, and call. The call of Gray-cheeked Thrush is a downslurred "wheer", similar to the call of Veery (though higher pitched), but easily distinguished from the calls of Hermit and Swainson's Thrush. For more information see Dunn (1977b).

Veery nests locally on the West Coast in deciduous woodlands in S B.C., E WASH, and NE ORE. It is a Rarity in CAL. Veery is about the size of Hermit Thrush but is most often confused with Swainson's Thrush because the standard guides emphasize the rustiness of the upperparts of Veery and fail to emphasize the warm rusty-brown color of the upperparts of western Swainson's Thrush. It is true that eastern races of Veery are even more rusty above than any Swainson's Thrush, but western races are duller and back color is similar to that of some Swainson's Thrush. Veery is recognized by the combination of 1) rusty-red upperparts, 2) very lightly spotted breast (looks almost unspotted at first glance), 3) gray flanks, 4) very thin white eyering, and 5) either a pale gray cheek or a cheek concolor with the nape (but not buffy). The call of Veery is a downslurred "veer", easily separated from the calls of Hermit or Swainson's Thrush. For more information see Dunn (1977f).

# GRAY-CHEEKED THRUSH

*Catharus minimus*

Breeds NE Asia, N North America. Winters West Indes, Central America to C South America.

The Gray-cheeked Thrush has the longest migration route of any American thrush. The migration route is entirely east of the Rockies: it is a Rarity on the West Coast south of its ALASKA and NW B.C. breeding range. All records to date have been during peak vagrant periods on SE Farallon I. and outer Pt. Reyes Pen., CAL.

**CALIFORNIA** Ten records. Eight are from SE Farallon I. (most were banded): 3 Oct 1970 (2†), 28 May-8 Jun 1971, 24 Sep 1974, 11 Jun 1975, 12-14 Sep 1975, 18 Sep 1975, and 10 Oct 1979. The two additional records are from Pt. Reyes NS, Mrn.: 15 Oct 1974 and 31 Oct 1978.

25 Sep 1974 on SE Farallon I., CAL. 3rd record. *Dave DeSante, courtesy Point Reyes Bird Observatory.*

I.D. See the *Catharus* thrush identification essay beginning on p. 310.

# VEERY

*Catharus fuscescens*

Breeds W-C, C, & E North America. Winters Central America to N South America.

The Veery is a local nesting species on the West Coast in S B.C., E WASH, and NE ORE. The migration routes are well east of the West Coast: it is a Rarity in CAL, where the three records are all from late fall at well-worked vagrant "traps".

**CALIFORNIA** Three records: 20 Oct 1973* on SE Farallon I., 12-16 Oct 1974* at Pt. Mugu, Ven., and 5 Nov 1978 at Kelso, S.Bn. All these birds appeared to resemble bright eastern races of Veery, rather than the duller western race.

14 Oct 1974 at Big Sycamore Canyon, Pt. Mugu, Ven., CAL. 2nd record. *Henry M. Brodkin.*

I.D. See the *Catharus* thrush identification essay beginning on p. 310.

# NORTHERN WHEATEAR

*Oenanthe oenanthe*

Breeds N Eurasia, W Alaska, NE Canada. Winters C Africa, India, C China, Philippines.

The Northern Wheatear is a fairly common local breeding bird in W & C ALASKA. Its migration route takes it to the Old World, via W ALASKA and St. Lawrence I.; it is only rarely found as a migrant in the Pribilof or Aleutian Is. The few records from S and SE ALASKA are all from the fall: 21 Oct 1896 at Juneau, "fall" 1966 at Haines, 2 Sep 1967 (5) at Haines, 7 Oct 1967 at Juneau, and 27 Oct 1976 at Hawkins I., Prince William Sound. Fall vagrants have reached the West Coast south of ALASKA. There are also two spring records from the West Coast south of ALASKA; these birds are suspected of being spring migrants returning from wintering somewhere in the New World.

**BRITISH COLUMBIA**   One record: 10-12 Oct 1970 at the Victoria airport on the Saanich Pen., V.I. (CFN 85:258).

**OREGON**   One record: 22 Jun 1977* at Malheur NWR, Har.

**CALIFORNIA**   Two records: 11 Jun 1971† on SE Farallon I. (A 89:895), and 15 Sep 1977 at Shelter Cove, Hmb.

22 Jun 1977 at Malheur NWR, Har., ORE. 1st record. *Bob Ringler.*

# NORTHERN WHEATEAR

12 Oct 1970 at Victoria airport, V.I., B.C. 1st record. *Cy Morehen*.

# NORTHERN WHEATEAR

15 Sep 1977 at Shelter Cove, Hmb., CAL. 2nd record. *George Clarke.*

I.D. The Northern Wheatear male in breeding plumage is illustrated in the standard guides, but female and immature plumages are not pictured. These birds, especially fall immatures (the most likely to occur as vagrants), are very buffy. The upperparts are mostly brownish and the facial mask is reduced to a dusky smudge, while the underparts can be bright buff, especially across the breast. There are broad rusty-buff edgings to the wing coverts and tertials. Shape, the upright stance, and the white rump and tail (the latter with a broad inverted black "T") are the best field marks.

A number of Eurasian wheatears are migratory, but most seem very unlikely candidates for turning up on the West Coast. Perhaps the only species with any reasonable potential for occurring here is Isabelline Wheatear *O. isabellina*. It is similar to female and immature Northern Wheatear but is slightly larger, somewhat larger-headed and larger-billed, and generally paler. More useful is the tail pattern: on Northern Wheatear the crossbar of the inverted "T" occupies about the terminal third of the tail; on Isabelline the crossbar of the inverted "T" occupies the terminal half of the tail. Also helpful is the color of the underwing coverts: gray or black-barred on Northern (appearing as dark as the underside of the flight feathers); clear white or buff on Isabelline (distinctly paler than the underside of the flight feathers). For more information see Kitson (1979a).

# SIBERIAN RUBYTHROAT

Plate 7

*Erithacus calliope*

Breeds NE Asia. Winters SE Asia.

The Siberian Rubythroat has been found annually on the westernmost Aleutian Is., ALASKA, during the last five years (the only years with consistent coverage) during spring and fall migration. It is probably a rare, but regular, migrant on these outer Aleutians, where the records fall into narrow periods during the last week of May-first couple weeks of Jun in spring and late Sept-early Oct in fall. There are only four records away from the outer Aleutians, all in the spring.

**ALASKA**   45 records (through spring 1980), graphed below. Nearly all are from the westernmost Aleutian Is.: Attu (19 records), Nizki (1), Shemya (10), Buldir (4), Kiska (4 — all in Jun 1911), and Amchitka (3). 25 of these records were during the spring; 16 from the fall (10 of the latter occurred during late Sep 1979 on Attu I.). There are four spring records away from the Aleutians: 5 Jun 1977 on St. Paul I., Pribilofs, 6-8 Jun 1978 at Gambell, St. Lawrence I., 13 Jun 1979 at Gambell, and 15 Jun 1979 on St. Paul I.

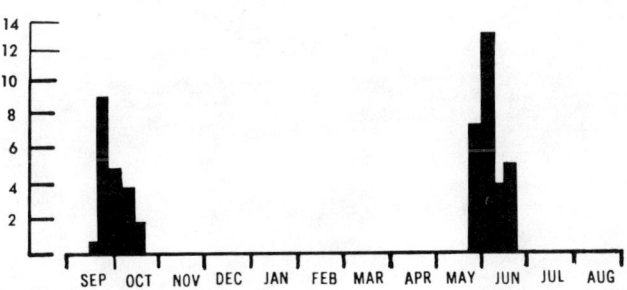

# SIBERIAN RUBYTHROAT

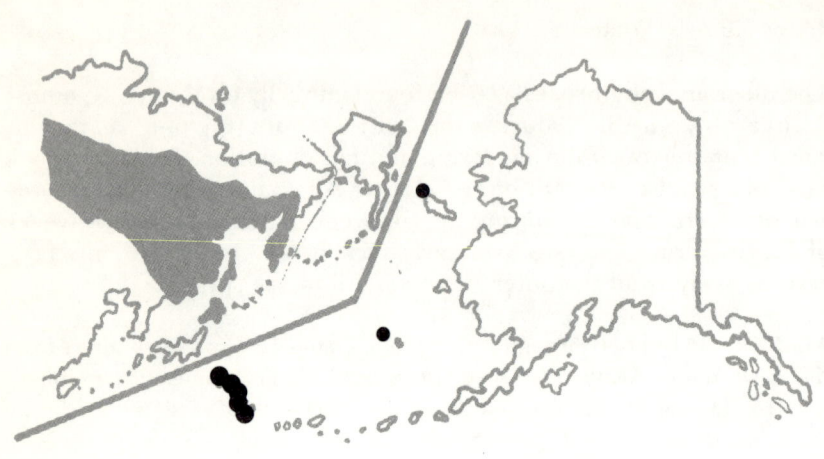

29 May 1979 at Casco Cove, Attu I., ALASKA. *John G. Keenleyside.*

# SIBERIAN RUBYTHROAT

3 Jun 1977 at East Cape, Buldir I., ALASKA. *Robert P. Schulmeister.*

I.D. The Siberian Rubythroat is a chunky, long-legged, short-tailed thrush, distinctly smaller than Hermit Thrush *Catharus guttatus*. Adults are brownish above, dingy whitish-gray below. Males have a bright ruby-red throat bordered by a white malar stripe; females have whitish throats. Adults show a white supercilium contrasting with dark lores; often the most conspicuous mark at a distance. Immatures tend to be buffy-throated and have a shorter whitish or buffy supercilium and a broken eyering, again contrasting with dark lores. The flanks and undertail coverts are washed with buffy; immatures also tend to have buffy breasts. The Siberian Rubythroat is a skulker and often difficult to see for any length of time, preferring short dashes to the next available cover when pressed. It often holds its wings drooped and flicks its tail up to a cocked position.

Calls include a repeated, plaintive, double-noted "chee-wee" and a harsh "churr". Singing birds have been observed during the spring; the song has been likened to that of Gray Catbird *Dumetella carolinensis*. For more detailed information see Lowe (1979).

# WOOD WARBLER

Plate 8

*Phylloscopus sibilatrix*

Breeds Europe. Winters C Africa.

On geographic grounds the Wood Warbler seems to be the most incredible passerine vagrant ever to occur on the West Coast. Breeding on the opposite side of the globe and wintering directly to the south, there was little to suggest this bird would ever occur here. The most likely explanation for its appearance would seem to be that a bird migrated the exact opposite direction as expected and may have flown over the Pole to Alaska. This "wrong-way" (or 180°) misorientation is known for numerous species on occasion (usually immatures in the fall) but the occurrence of Wood Warbler would seem to be among the most spectacular examples. If Wood Warbler can occur, then it would seem that *any* migratory Eurasian bird could occur on the West Coast.

**ALASKA** One record: 9 Oct 1978† on Shemya I. Details of this record are in preparation; look for publication in the near future.

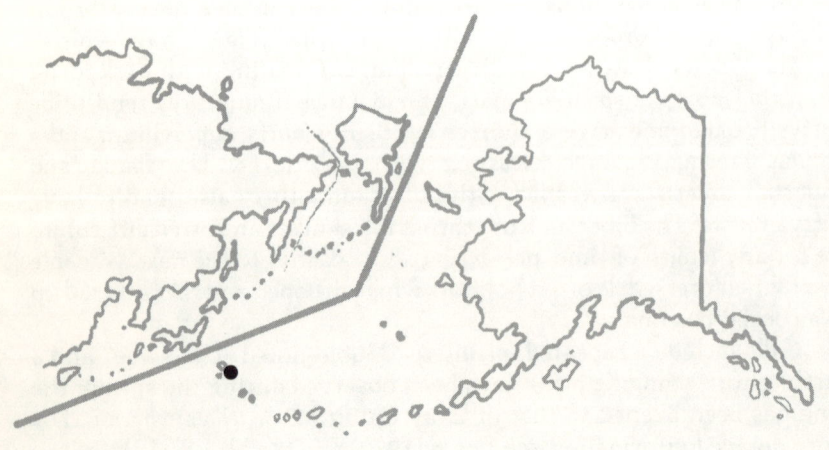

# WOOD WARBLER

**I.D.** The Wood Warbler is one of the more distinctive *Phylloscopus*. It is about the size of Blackpoll Warbler *Dendroica striata*. Its most important features (which in combination distinguish it from all others in its genus) are the bright greenish upperparts (similar to those of a fall Tennessee Warbler *Vermivora peregrina*); clear lemon-yellow throat and upper breast contrasting with the otherwise silky-white underparts; prominent lemon-yellow supercilium accentuated by a thin dusky eye-stripe; fine yellow-green edgings to the flight feathers; and (for a *Phylloscopus*) strikingly long wings which reach half-way down the tail when perched. The legs are orangey-flesh; the bill is somewhat heavier and longer than most other *Phylloscopus*. The underwing coverts and axillaries are lemon-yellow. American warblers with yellow throats, greenish backs, and white bellies also possess conspicuous wingbars, which should eliminate any risk of confusion.

The call is a plaintive, piping "peue", sometimes repeated as a series.

# DUSKY WARBLER          Plate 8

*Phylloscopus fuscatus*

Breeds N Asia. Winters India to SE Asia.

The Dusky Warbler has been found on the West Coast in ALASKA, where there are records of spring and fall vagrants, and in CAL, where a fall vagrant reached SE Farallon I. and provided the first West Coast record of a *Phylloscopus* south of ALASKA.

**ALASKA** Three records: 6 Jun 1977 at Gambell, St. Lawrence I. (AB 32:158), and two birds in early Oct 1978 on Shemya I. Details of the latter records are in preparation; look for their publication in the future.

**CALIFORNIA** One record: 27 Sep 1980† on SE Farallon I. This record occurred just as this book goes to press and identification is best considered tentative at this time, though all preliminary examination points to this species. Details of this extraordinary record will be published elsewhere (*fide* Point Reyes Bird Observatory).

# DUSKY WARBLER

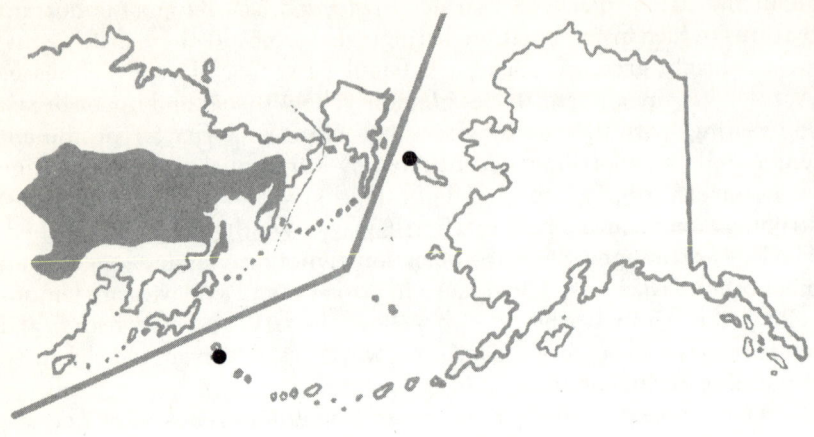

I.D. The Dusky Warbler is a small, nondescript *Phylloscopus* which typically sticks to cover close to the ground; it is skulking and difficult to observe and its call is often the first clue to its presence. It is one of the drabbest of its genus with dark dusky brown upperparts and dull whitish underparts, the latter washed buff on the flanks and undertail coverts. It has a long buffy supercilium (with any whitish restricted to the area before the eye); a short, fine bill; and brownish legs. Unlike other *Phylloscopus*, the rather short tail is slightly rounded at the tip. It is best identified by a combination of the complete lack of greenish or yellowish tones, the fine bill, buffy supercilium, rounded tail-tip, and distinctive harsh call notes. The most similar *Phylloscopus* is Radde's Warbler *P. schwarzi* (a remote possibility as a vagrant): it is separated by its combination of yellowish underparts, whitish supercilium, olive-brown upperparts, strikingly pale legs, and a stout short bill. Radde's Warbler, like Dusky Warbler, has harsh call notes.

The Dusky Warbler has a distinctive harsh "tsack" call which is usually uttered frequently, sometimes in a rapid series of two or three notes. It often calls in flight from one perch to another. It is a frequent wing-flicker.

For more information see Williamson (1976b), Johns and Wallace (1972), and King, Finch, Stallcup & Russell (1978).

# MIDDENDORFF'S GRASSHOPPER WARBLER

Plate 8

*Locustella ochotensis*

Breeds NE Asia. Winters Philippines to Indonesia.

The Middendorff's Grasshopper Warbler has occurred on the West Coast only in ALASKA. Until 1978 there was only a single record (fall bird on Nunivak I.). But one was seen on Shemya I. in fall 1978 and at least six were found on Attu I. in fall 1979. A spring vagrant reached St. Lawrence I. in spring 1979. This recent number of birds suggests the species is more regular in ALASKA than had been suspected, especially on the westernmost Aleutian Is. during the fall.

**ALASKA**  9 records: 15 Sep 1927† at Cape Etolin, Nunivak I., late Sep 1978 on Shemya I., mid-Jun 1979† on St. Lawrence I., and at least six (perhaps 8-1†) from 18-25 Sep 1979 on Attu I. Details of the Shemya I. and St. Lawrence I. records have not yet been published.

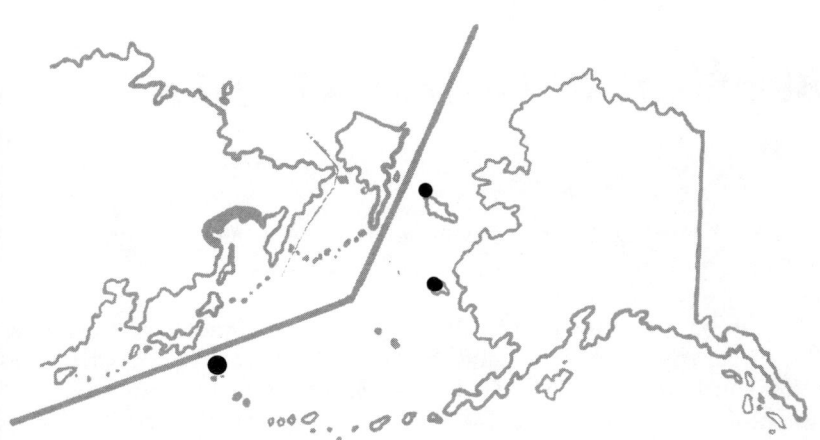

# MIDDENDORFF'S GRASSHOPPER WARBLER

I.D. The Middendorff's Grasshopper Warbler is a large, olive-brown, obscurely streaked *Locustella* with a white-tipped tail, about the size of Yellow-breasted Chat *Icteria virens* or Cactus Wren *Campylorhynchus brunneicapillus*. The upperparts are a dark olive-brown, obscurely streaked on the back, becoming a plain tawny-olive on the rump. All except the central pair of tail feathers are tipped with white. Underparts of adults are a dingy-white, with an olivaceous wash on the sides of the breast to the flanks, and with buffy undertail coverts. The underparts of fall immatures are washed with yellow and show streaks across the lower throat and breast. The similar Pallas' Grasshopper Warbler *L. certhiola*, a possible vagrant, differs in having a paler, warmer cast to the upperparts and more prominent streaking on the back, a rufous (not tawny) rump, and in hand or at close range shows dark subterminal spots on the central tail feathers.

The Middendorff's Grasshopper Warbler is a very skulking bird, keeping close to ground cover and flushing only on close approach.

# BLUE-GRAY GNATCATCHER

*Polioptila caerulea*

Breeds S North America to Guatamala. Northern populations winter to the south.

The Blue-gray Gnatcatcher is a bird of temperate clines, breeding on the West Coast north to N CAL and locally in S ORE. N CAL and ORE birds move south in winter. At least twice vagrants in the fall have wandered north of ORE, where it is a Rarity.

**WASHINGTON**   One acceptable record: 10-16 Nov 1978 at Whidbey I., Isl.

**BRITISH COLUMBIA**   One record: 10-11 Nov 1963 at Victoria, V.I.

# BLUE-GRAY GNATCATCHER

11 Nov 1978 on Whidbey I., Isl., WASH. 1st record. *Dennis Paulson.*

10 Nov 1963 at Victoria, V.I., B.C. 1st record. *G. Allen Poynter.*

# RED-BREASTED FLYCATCHER

Plate 7

*Ficedula parva*

Breeds N Eurasia. Winters N Africa to SE Asia, Indonesia.

The Red-breasted Flycatcher has occurred twice on the West Coast: both were spring vagrants (presumably overshoots) in ALASKA. The specimen taken proved to be the NE Asia race *F. p. albicilla*.

**ALASKA**  Two records: 1 Jun 1977† on Shemya I. (A 95:428), and 5 Jun 1977 at Gambell, St. Lawrence I. (AB 32:158).

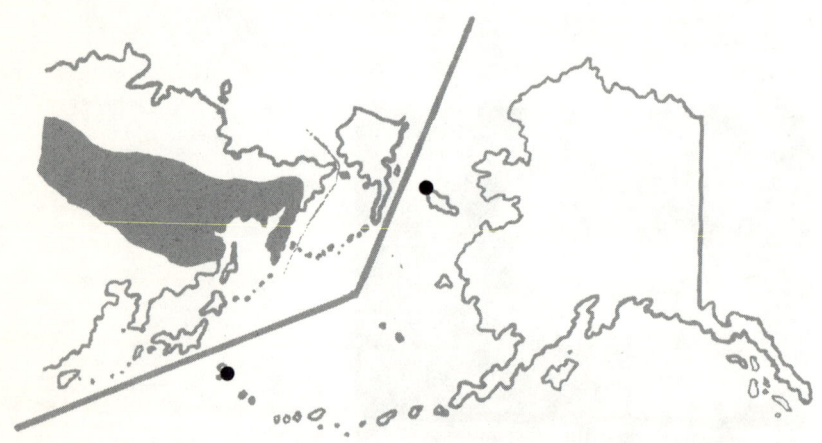

I.D. The Red-breasted Flycatcher is a small, distinctive Old World flycatcher slightly larger than an American Redstart *Setophaga ruticilla;* its general proportions and tail-cocking habits recall that species. Adult males have a reddish-orange throat patch and grayish head; the NE Asia race has a grayish breastband enclosing the reddish throat (the race pictured in European field guides is red-breasted). Females and first-winter birds have plain brown upperparts, a thin buffy eyering, and creamy underparts with a warm buff wash on the throat and breast. First-winter individuals can be aged by the faint wing bar of buff tips on the greater wing coverts. At any time, the species' best field marks are the black tail with large white ovals at each side of the base, which are striking when the tail is flicked upwards or in flight, and the extensive white undertail coverts.

# RED-BREASTED FLYCATCHER

The Red-breasted Flycatcher usually has a less upright stance when perched than other flycatchers. It only occasionally flycatches from an exposed perch. Its call note is often the first sign of its presence and often the best means of following its progress through cover: a dry soft churr or rattle "trrrrr", and a sharp "spic".

# SOOTY FLYCATCHER

Plate 7

*Muscicapa sibirica*

Breeds E Asia. Winters S China, SE Asia to the Philippines.

The Sooty Flycatcher has occurred only once on the West Coast; a fall vagrant which reached the western Aleutian Is., ALASKA.

**ALASKA**   One record: 13 Sep 1977† on Shemya I.

I.D. The Sooty Flycatcher is a small *Empidonax*-sized Old World flycatcher. Adults have dark brown upperparts and a faint wingbar. The throat is white and extends onto the neck as a half-collar. The underparts are broadly smudged with dark on the sides of the breast, sides, and flanks, with a whitish stripe extending from the throat to belly. There is a thin white eyering, but not pale lores. Immatures in the fall appear quite different, with boldly spotted wings (caused by buffy tips to the feathers) and streaking mixed into the dingy underparts.

## SOOTY FLYCATCHER

The Gray-spotted Flycatcher *M. griseisticta* is paler gray-brown above, has whitish underparts with well-defined streaks (without dark sides to the breast), and has a distinct pale loral spot. The Brown Flycatcher *M. latirostris*, a possible vagrant, is similar to Sooty Flycatcher, but is a much paler brown bird above and is cleaner white below, with only light gray sides to the breast, sides, and flanks. These dark areas on the underparts are much reduced in Brown Flycatcher. Adults do not have a wingbar (adult Sooty has a faint buffy wingbar), but fall immature Brown Flycatcher has two buffy wingbars and may be spotted with buff on the upperparts. In any plumage the Brown Flycatcher is a paler bird than Sooty Flycatcher, especially on the underparts. In addition, the wing of Sooty Flycatcher is longer, extending to the half-way point of the tail or beyond at rest; the wingtip of Brown Flycatcher reaches to less than the half-way point of the tail at rest.

Old World flycatchers, like American flycatchers, characteristically sit upright and often sally forth after insects.

# GRAY-SPOTTED FLYCATCHER

*Muscicapa griseisticta*

Plate 7

Breeds NE Asia. Winters S China to New Guinea.

The Gray-spotted Flycatcher has been found on the West Coast only on the outermost Aleutian Is., ALASKA, where all records apparently refer to spring overshoots. All records to date fall within a 10-day period (except for one late bird) in late May-early Jun. More consistent coverage in the western Aleutians in early Jun may prove it to be more regular there than originally suspected.

**ALASKA** 16 records, graphed below. All occurred in just four years: 1956 (1), 1972 (3), 1976 (2), and 1977 (10). Of the 10 in 1977, five were found on Shemya I. from 30 May-5 Jun.

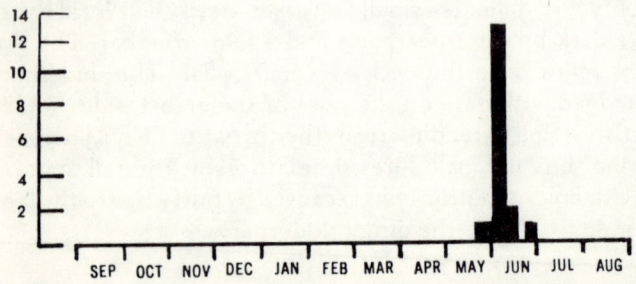

# GRAY-SPOTTED FLYCATCHER

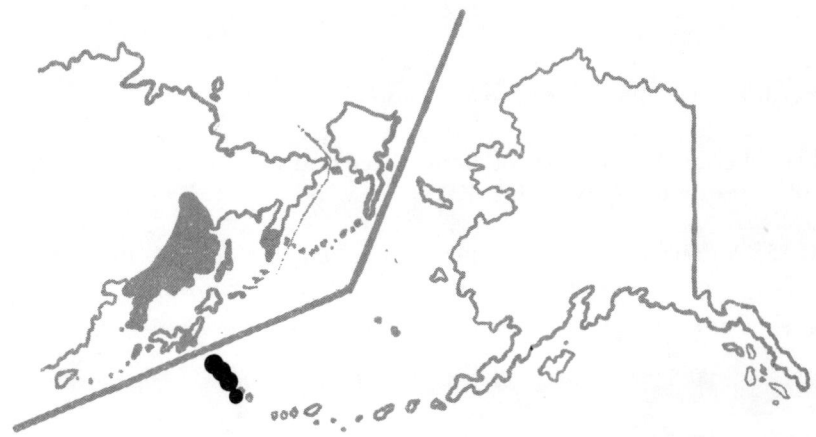

24 Jun 1977 on Buldir I., ALASKA. *Robert P. Schulmeister.*

I.D. The Gray-spotted Flycatcher is a small *Empidonax*-sized Old World flycatcher. It is uniform grayish-brown above with a single indistinct wingbar. The underparts are white with dark gray spots forming streaks across the breast and down the sides to the flanks. The head is rather pale gray and unmarked except for a whitish eyering and a distinct pale loral spot (at close range seen to be a light band connecting over the bill). No other brownish-gray flycatcher combines such distinctly streaked underparts with whitish "spectacles". See Sooty Flycatcher *M. sibirica*.

# SIBERIAN ACCENTOR

Plate 8

*Prunella montanella*

Breeds NE Asia. Winters N China to Japan.

The Siberian Accentor has occurred three times on the West Coast, all as fall vagrants to W & N ALASKA.

**ALASKA**  Three records: 3 Oct 1927† at Cape Etolin, Nunivak I., 13 Oct 1936† at Camp Collier, St. Lawrence I., and "fall" 1951 at Pt. Barrow.

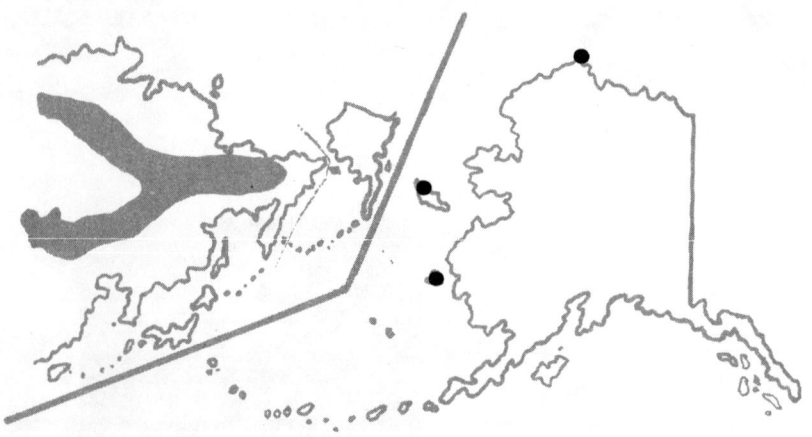

I.D. The Siberian Accentor is a ground-feeding bird slightly larger than a House Sparrow *Passer domesticus*. The bill is thin and sharp-pointed. In any plumage it combines a dark cap and eye-stripe with a broad ochreous supercilium and buffy underparts, a pattern unlike any other similarly-sized bird (see plate). The intensity of the color of the underparts and supercilium varies according to sex and age: fall immatures being the brightest and spring females the dullest.

The habits are rather like ground-feeding pipits, but the wings and tail are often flicked and jerked, rather than the deliberate tail-wagging typical of many pipits.

# IDENTIFICATION OF PIPITS

Before attempting to identify a vagrant pipit, the observer should be familiar with the common Water Pipit *Anthus spinoletta* and its possible variations. For a point of reference we will call the Water Pipit a medium-sized pipit with an average tail length. In general, Water Pipit is drab grayish-brown above and dull white to tawny below, with streaking across the breast. The background color of the breast merges into the color of the belly without sharp demarcation. The back is only indistinctly streaked. Fall birds in fresh plumage are brighter and more heavily streaked on the underparts than adults in winter and spring; by summer all pipits become very worn and bedraggled. While we may, for convenience, consider the common West Coast race of Water Pipit *A. s. pacificus* as the "average" pipit, observers should be aware that other races of Water Pipit occur and may appear different in the field. *A. s. rubescens*, the eastern North America race, is more grayish-brown, less buffy, than *pacificus*; *A. s. alticola*, breeding in the Rockies, is larger and is more richly-colored below with fewer breast streaks; and *A. s. japonicus*, which breeds in NE Asia and has occurred in W ALASKA, is grayer with more distinct back streaking and much heavier streaking on the underparts. In ALASKA, the latter bird has often been misidentified as one or another of the vagrant pipits.

The leg color of Water Pipit is quite variable, from slaty to dingy horn-color. The outer tail feathers are white. Outside of the breeding season it tends to be gregarious, feeding on the ground in flocks. While walking it typically wags its tail. It is not particularly shy and does not prefer dense cover. When flushed, Water Pipit drops back into the habitat with a characteristic bouncing drop, like "bouncing down stairs". Call notes, given in flight, include a soft but clear "pip-pit" or "pip", and a thin "tseep".

For a more thorough discussion of Water Pipit and its races and of all West Coast vagrants see Dunn & Tobish (1981).

# OLIVE-BACKED PIPIT                    Plate 8

*Anthus hodgsoni*

Breeds N & C Asia, Japan. Winters India, SE Asia, Japan, Philippines.

The Olive-backed Pipit has been found on the West Coast during spring and fall migration on the outer Aleutians and on St. Lawrence I., ALASKA. Although considered very rare, recent work on the westernmost Aleutian Is. has recorded it in 4 of the last 5 years (especially on Attu I.) and it may be a rare, but regular, spring migrant there.

Of special interest to West Coast birders is the record of one collected on 16 May 1967 just south of Reno, Nevada (A 85:323). The date strongly suggests that this bird wintered successfully somewhere in the New World.

**ALASKA**   15 records (through spring 1980), graphed below. Except for a bird on 1 Jun 1962† at Gambell, St. Lawrence I., all birds were recorded during the last 5 years (1976-1980). Nearly all these birds were on the outer Aleutians, most in the spring: Attu (9 records), Shemya (1), and Buldir (1). An additional spring record was 6-9 Jun 1977 at Gambell. The only fall records were 24-25 Sep 1979 (2) on Attu I.

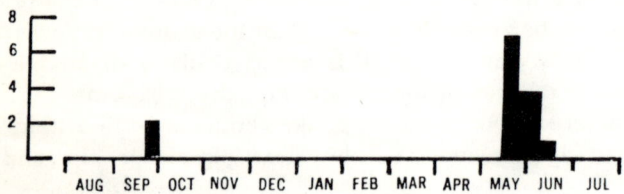

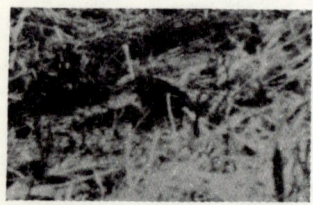

31 May 1980 at Murder Pt., Attu I., ALASKA. *Don Roberson.*

# OLIVE-BACKED PIPIT

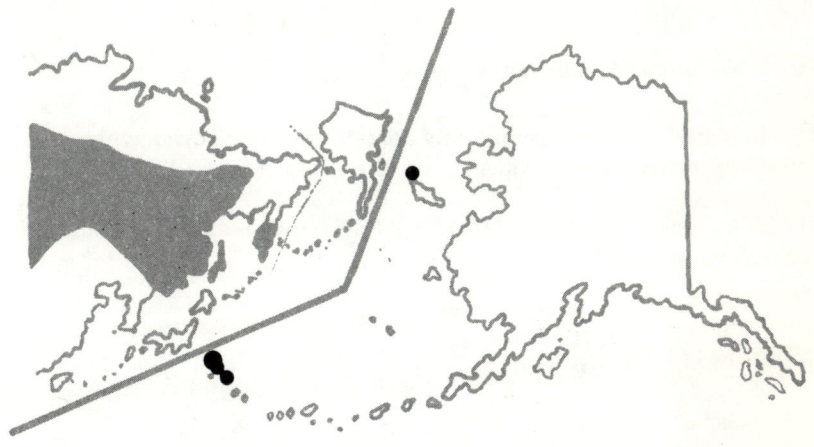

I.D. The Olive-backed Pipit is a most distinctive pipit, about the size of Water Pipit: the combination of olive-green back (only faintly streaked), bright buffy or pumpkin-colored breast with bold thrush-like spots or streaks, and a face pattern including a broad buffy supercilium (brightest before the eye, sometimes paling to white behind the eye) and a pale spot on the ear-coverts behind and below the supercilium, is unlike any other pipit. This pattern is misrepresented in numerous guides but is portrayed on Plate 8. Wear affects the intensity of the olive-green color on the back; fall birds are the brightest, adults in summer may be worn to a dingy olive-gray. The breast is buffy on adults but bright pumpkin-colored on fall immatures; in the latter plumage it is clearly demarcated from the white belly. A NE Asia breeding race of Water Pipit — *A. s. japonicus,* — has been mistaken for Olive-backed Pipit. *Japonicus* lacks the olive-green back, buffy breast, and distinct facial pattern of Olive-backed Pipit.

Olive-backed Pipit feeds on the ground, often with a slinking walk with the tail pumped with each step. When flushed it typically dives back into cover. Only the outer tail feathers are white. The call — a loud "tsee" or "tseet" — is rather like Red-throated Pipit *A. cervinus,* but is louder and more strident. For more information see Kitson (1979b), Dennis (1967), Conder (1979), and Dunn & Tobish (1981).

# TREE PIPIT

Plate 8

*Anthus trivialis*

Breeds N Eurasia. Winters Africa, India.

The Tree Pipit has been found only once on the West Coast, when a male defending territory was collected on the Seward Pen., ALASKA.

**ALASKA** One record: Jun 1972† at Cape Prince of Wales. Details of this record have not yet been published.

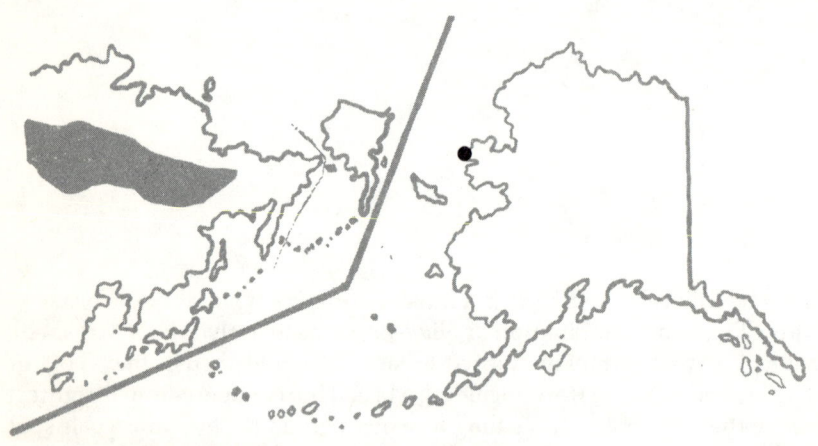

I.D. The Tree Pipit is about the size of Water Pipit (see p. 331 for a discussion of Water Pipit *A. spinoletta* and read also the discussion of Red-throated Pipit *A. cervinus*). The upperparts of Tree Pipit are olive-brown, narrowly but distinctly streaked (except the rump, which is unstreaked). The underparts are creamy-buff with well-defined black streaks across the breast and on the flanks; there is little demarcation between the creamy-buff breast and the off-white belly, and at a distance the appearance is of uniform buffy underparts. The nape streaks are obscure. Only the outer tail feathers are white. The legs are bright pink and the hind claw is short.

# TREE PIPIT

The combination of dingy, narrowly-streaked upperparts, an unstreaked rump, and creamy-buff underparts with well-defined streaks should help to separate this bird from other vagrant pipits. It also differs in not being a ground-dwelling pipit, preferring to perch on vegetation above ground when available. The flight call is different from other pipits: a hoarse buzzing "tee-zee" or "teeze".

For a more thorough discussion see Dunn & Tobish (1981).

# PECHORA PIPIT  Plate 8

*Anthus gustavi*

Breeds NE Asia. Winters Korea, Japan to Borneo.

The Pechora Pipit has occurred four times on the West Coast; all records refer to apparent spring overshoots on St. Lawrence I. and the westernmost Aleutian Is., ALASKA.

**ALASKA**  Four records: May 1937† at Gambell, St. Lawrence I. (C 40:88), 16 Jun 1975 at Gambell, 22 May 1979 on Attu I., and 6 Jun 1979 at Gambell (latter three records discussed in AB 34:317).

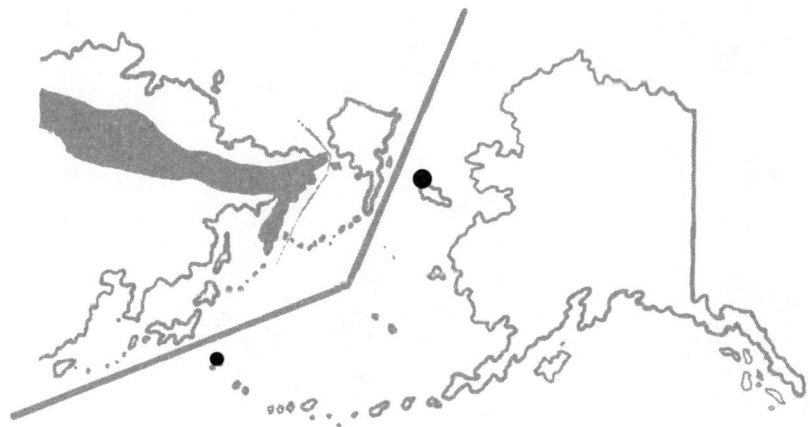

# PECHORA PIPIT

I.D. The Pechora Pipit is about the size of Water Pipit but is slightly longer-tailed (see p. 331 for a discussion of Water Pipit *A. spinoletta* and read the discussion of Red-throated Pipit *A. cervinus*). Pechora Pipit is a dark, heavily streaked bird. The back is blacker than other pipits in spring, having thin rusty edgings to the feathers of the crown and back, giving a striking appearance to the upperparts not shared by other pipits. The underparts are streaked, more heavily in fall than in spring, but the streaks are thinner than those of Red-throated Pipit. A pair of pale lines on the mantle (white in spring, buffy in fall) form "braces", but are less useful than some guides suggest, as they may be indistinct in spring, and fall Red-throated Pipit may show a similar pattern. In any plumage the streaking of the nape is as bold and distinct as that of the crown and back, in contrast to the obscured nape streaks of Red-throated Pipit or Tree Pipit *A. trivialis*. Another useful characteristic is the sharp demarcation between the yellowish-buff background color of the breast and the white belly. The streaking of the breast is squarely cut-off from the unmarked throat.

The bill is heavier than on other pipits discussed here. The legs are pink. Only the outer tail feathers are white (buffy-white in immatures). Pechora Pipit is an extremely skulking bird; when flushed it dives back into the nearest cover. The call is a loud, hard "pwit", often uttered several times in rapid succession: the pitch is low and lacks any sweetness or richness of tone (BB 46:210).

For a more thorough discussion see Dunn & Tobish (1981) and King (1980).

# RED-THROATED PIPIT    Plate 8

*Anthus cervinus*

Breeds NW Alaska, N Eurasia. Winters N Africa, Middle East to Indonesia.

The Red-throated Pipit breeds in the Bering Strait area of W ALASKA. Most birds winter in the Old World; migration brings a few through the western Aleutian Is., especially in the spring (high count of 55+ on 20 May 1979 on Attu I.). Recently it has been found with some regularity along the CAL coast between late Sep-early Nov and other fall migrants have been found in WASH and as far south as Baja, Mexico. About half of the records have involved more than one individual and small flocks of up to 15 have been encountered. The wintering area of these birds is unknown and returning spring migrants have not yet been found. When found on the West Coast south of ALASKA, it is often consorting with flocks of Water Pipit *A. spinoletta*.

**WASHINGTON**   Two records, both at American Camp, San Juan I., S.J.: 14 Sep 1979 and 16 Sep 1979 (different bird).

**CALIFORNIA**   20 records, involving at least 66 individuals, graphed below. Usually encountered singly or in small groups of up to four, but Imperial Beach, S.D., had up to 15 in 1964, up to 10 in 1966 and again in 1967, and 6 in 1974. Multiple records come from Pt. Reyes NS, Mrn. (2 records, 5 birds); Goleta, S.Bb. (3 records, 4 birds); the Oxnard plain, Ven. (3 records, 6 or more birds); Imperial Beach, S.D. (7 records, at least 46 birds, 2†); and San Nicolas I. (2 records, 3 birds). Absent some years, it has been recorded in 1964, 1966, 1967, 1968, 1970, 1974, 1977, 1978, & 1979.

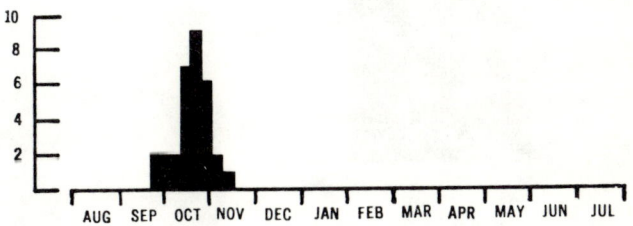

# RED-THROATED PIPIT

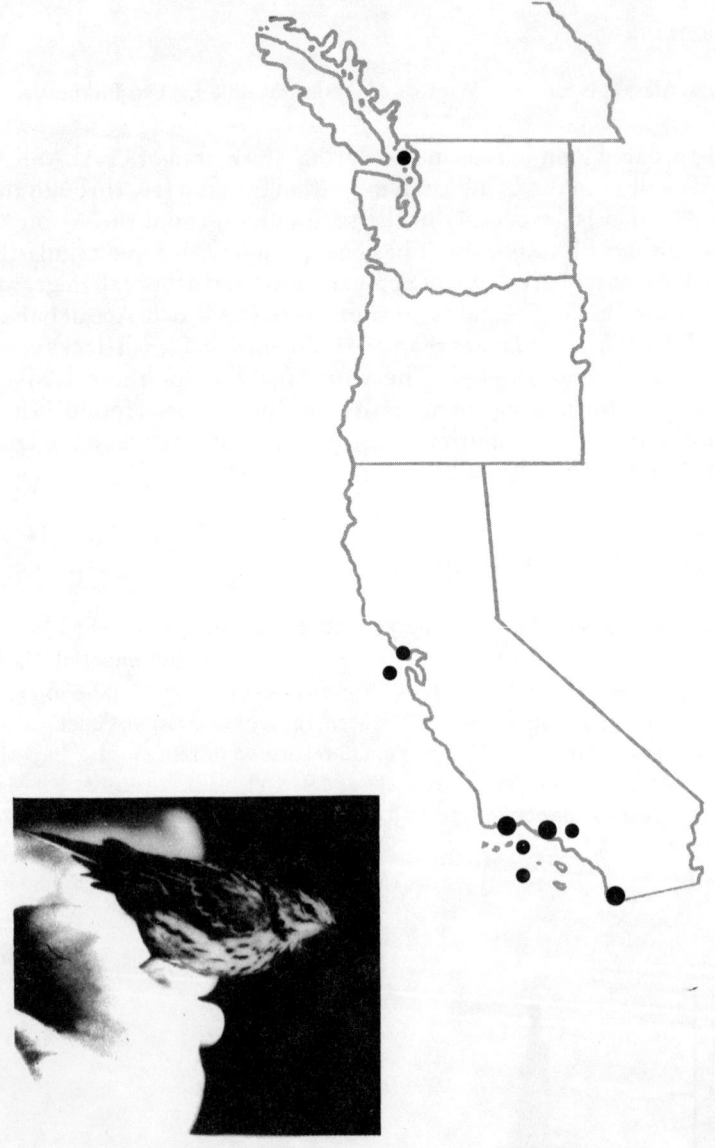

3 Nov 1968 on SE Farallon I., CAL. 4th record. *Henry Robert, courtesy Point Reyes Bird Observatory.*

# RED-THROATED PIPIT

I.D. The Red-throated Pipit is slightly smaller and shorter-tailed than Water Pipit (see p. 331 for a discussion of Water Pipit *A. spinoletta*). Adults in spring and summer have the diagnostic red-brown or pinkish-red throat patch, which is variable in size, often extending onto the upper breast, ear-coverts, and supercilium (on average, males have more red than females). On adults with extensive red, the heavy streaking on the underparts is often restricted to only the lower breast and flanks. At all ages the remainder of the plumage is similar, having a generally dull appearance, lacking any prominent yellowish or olive tones. The crown, back, and rump are heavily streaked with blackish, and there are two whitish stripes on each side of the mantle (although the outer stripe is usually short and indistinct). The underparts of non-breeding birds are heavily streaked with blackish over the breast and flanks, leaving a clear buffy throat and undertail and a whitish belly. There is little contrast between the background color of the breast and belly. The streaking on the breast extends up to the broad dark malar stripe, forming a "U"-shaped pattern around the throat. The wings have two noticeable whitish wing bars and the tail is blackish with white outer tail feathers. The legs are pink.

Red-throated Pipit in fall could be confused with a number of other pipits. It is separated from the *japonicus* race of Water Pipit by the heavily streaked back and by call; from Pechora Pipit *A. gustavi* by a combination of obscurely streaked nape (rather than strongly streaked), the lack of contrast between the background color of breast and belly, the lack of yellowish or creamy background tones to breast, and by call; and from Tree Pipit *A. trivialis* by the lack of olive tones on the upperparts, lack of creamy background color on the underparts, heavily streaked upperparts with whitish "braces", streaked (not plain) rump, long hind claw, and by call.

The flight call is very unlike any other pipit (except Olive-backed Pipit *A. hodgsoni*): a penetrating, wirey, thin "speew" or "psssss", which lasts a full half-second, starting explosively and trailing off to an almost ultrasonic ending. This call is sometimes replaced by, or interspersed with, a less distinctive "chip" note.

For a more thorough discussion see Dunn & Tobish (1981).

# SPRAGUE'S PIPIT

Plate 8

*Anthus spragueii*

Breeds N Great Plains of North America. Winters S-C U.S. to S-C Mexico.

The Sprague's Pipit was first detected on the West Coast in 1974, but has been found nearly annually from Oct-mid Dec in CAL since then. It regularly winters in S Arizona, even as far west as the Arizona side of the Colorado River, and winter records might be expected from the CAL side in the future.

**CALIFORNIA**   9 records: 19-27 Oct 1974 (2-3 birds, 1†) at Imperial Beach, S.D. (WB 6:29), 23 Oct 1975 at Carson, L.A., 22 Nov 1975* at Imperial Beach, 19 Dec 1975 (2 birds) at San Diego, 21-24 Oct 1976* at Carson, 22 Nov 1977 at Imperial Beach, 1-2 Oct 1979 on SE Farallon I., 2 Oct 1979 at Furnace Creek, Inyo, and 23 Oct 1979 at Furnace Creek.

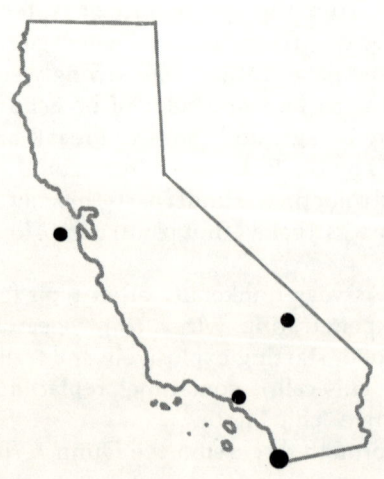

# SPRAGUE'S PIPIT

19 Oct 1974 at Imperial Beach, S.D., CAL. 1st record. *John Luther.*

I.D. The Sprague's Pipit is larger and shorter-tailed than Water Pipit *A. spinoletta* and appears chunkier in the field (see p. 331 for a discussion of Water Pipit). Field guide paintings of Sprague's Pipit tend to be poor; the one in Robbins' guide (1966) does not remotely resemble Sprague's Pipit. Among the best marks of Sprague's Pipit is its buffy, unmarked face, with a large dark eye standing out prominently. This plain-faced look is apparent at a good distance. Sprague's Pipit has dark centers to the feathers of the back and looks heavily streaked in the field; the pale buffy edgings of immatures in the fall include the tip of each feather and can produce a scaly effect to the back. Adults are very pale below and show almost no streaking on the underparts; fall immatures are very buffy below with faint streaking on the breast. The legs are pink. The two outermost tail feathers are white on Sprague's Pipit and show more conspicuously in flight than those of Water Pipit.

Sprague's Pipit is more solitary than Water Pipit and rarely flocks. It does not wag its tail. When flushed it tends to tower high and drop straight back to cover. The call — a loud "pips-QUEET" — is different from other pipits.

For more information see Dunn & Tobish (1981).

# YELLOW WAGTAIL

*Motacilla flava*

Breeds N Alaska, NW Canada, Eurasia, N Africa. Winters S Eurasia, Africa to Australia.

The Yellow Wagtail is a locally common breeding bird in N ALASKA and a common migrant through W ALASKA. It is a regular migrant in small numbers in the western Aleutian Is. It is only rarely recorded in C ALASKA and has only twice wandered to S ALASKA, both times during the fall: 18 Aug 1976 near Cordova, and 28 Sep 1979 in the Copper R. delta. Both records south of ALASKA on the West Coast were fall vagrants (in Sep) which made only brief appearances.

**CALIFORNIA** Two records: 17 Sep 1978 at Pt. Reyes NS, Mrn., and 16 Sep 1979 at Bodega Bay, Son. Both birds were calling and remained only briefly; neither record has yet been reviewed by the CAL Records Committee.

I.D. Covered by the standard guides, but see also the discussion under Gray Wagtail *M. cinerea*.

# GRAY WAGTAIL                                          Plate 8

*Motacilla cinerea*

Breeds Eurasia, N Africa. Winters S Eurasia, Africa to New Guinea.

The Gray Wagtail is a very rare vagrant in ALASKA, where there are several spring records from the Aleutian Is. and St. Lawrence I. (presumably overshoots) and a single fall record from the Pribilof Is. Specimens have proved to be the eastern race *M. c. robusta*.

**ALASKA**  Seven records, six during the spring: 4 Jun 1961† on Amchitka I. (A 92:811), 29 May 1976 on Shemya I., 8 Jun & 11 Jun 1976 on Buldir I., 11 Jun 1976 on Agattu I., and 6-8 Jun 1977 at Gambell, St. Lawrence I. The single fall record was 13 Oct 1962† on St. Paul I., Pribilofs (A 83:134).

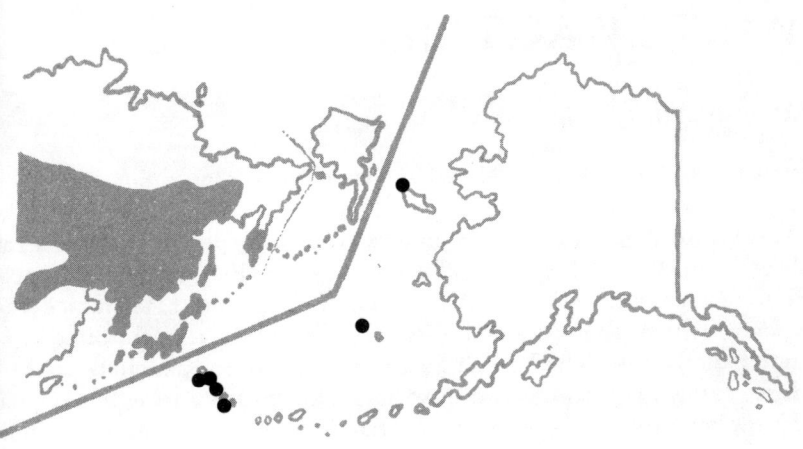

I.D. The Gray Wagtail resembles Yellow Wagtail *M. flava* in general characteristics but appears slimmer and has a noticeably longer tail. Adults have grayish upperparts (lacking any greenish tones as on Yellow Wagtail), blackish wings with white fringes to the tertials, yellow rump, long black tail with white outer tail feathers, and black bill and legs. Adult males have bright yellow underparts and (in breeding plumage) a black chin and throat below a white malar stripe; adult females have whitish underparts except for a yellowish-buff wash across the breast and striking yellow undertail coverts. Immatures in autumn resemble adult

# GRAY WAGTAIL

females. The best distinctions from Yellow Wagtail are the extra-long tail, the lack of obvious whitish wingbars, the gray upperparts, and the bright yellow rump and undertail coverts. A useful additional feature in flight (in any plumage) is the white bases to the secondaries and inner primaries, which form a thin bar across the center of the wing, especially noticeable when viewed from below.

The flight call of Gray Wagtail is a sharp metallic "stit", usually repeated in a rapid two or three note series "stit-it" or "stit-stit-it" higher pitched and sharper than the hard "chizzick" call of White Wagtail *M. alba* and quite different from the wheezy "tsweep" of Yellow Wagtail

# WHITE WAGTAIL

*Motacilla alba*

Breeds NW Alaska, Eurasia, N Africa, Philippines. Winters S Eurasia, Africa.

The White Wagtail is a widespread Old World species which is a rare breeder in W ALASKA, especially on the Seward Pen. and St. Lawrence The race nesting in ALASKA is the northeasternmost Asian race *M. ocularis*, which is gray-backed in spring. This bird has been found as far north as Barrow. The breeding race from Japan to Kamchatka is *M. lugens*, which is black-backed in spring. This bird is a rare, but regular spring migrant on the western Aleutian Is. and one was found far to the east at Glacier Bay (2 Jul 1969). There are a few records of fall migrants in the Pribilof and Aleutian Is., but fall birds are difficult to identify to race and the subspecific designation of most fall migrants is unknown. A fall bird was found far to the southeast at Juneau on 26 Sep 1977.

The White Wagtail is a Rarity on the West Coast south of ALASKA Records are about evenly split between fall vagrants and spring migrants, presumably returning from wintering somewhere in the New World. One spring record (from CAL) was clearly an adult male *lugens* the other spring birds have yet to be identified to race. The fall vagrant which returned to Watsonville, CAL, for two consecutive years has been identified as *lugens*. It was an adult bird which lingered to molt for several weeks each year.

# WHITE WAGTAIL

*Lugens* is a coastal bird and may account for other West Coast Rarity records; *ocularis* is primarily a bird of the interior. Look for a discussion of this entire question, including identification material, in the near future (J. Morlan, *per. com.*; perhaps to be published in *Continental Birdlife*). Recent Russian authorities have separated *lugens* from *ocularis* and other White Wagtails. It is possible that the AOU will consider them separate species in the future.

BRITISH COLUMBIA   One record: 2-21 Mar 1973 at the Coquitlan R. mouth, near Vancouver (CFN 89:318).

OREGON   One record: 3 Feb-26 Mar 1974* at Eugene, Lane.

CALIFORNIA   Five records: 18-29 Oct 1972* at the Santa Clara R. mouth, Ven.; 10 Oct 1974* on SE Farallon I.; 9-11 Oct 1978 at Goleta, S.Bb.; 7 Aug-22 Sep 1979 at the Watsonville sewer ponds, S.Cz., and Pajaro R., Mnt. (*lugens*), this individual returned the next year from 20 Jul to at least 19 Sep 1980; and 22 May 1980 at Tiburon, Mrn. (*lugens*).

22 May 1980 at Tiburon, Mrn., CAL. 5th record. *Leonard Compagno.*

# WHITE WAGTAIL

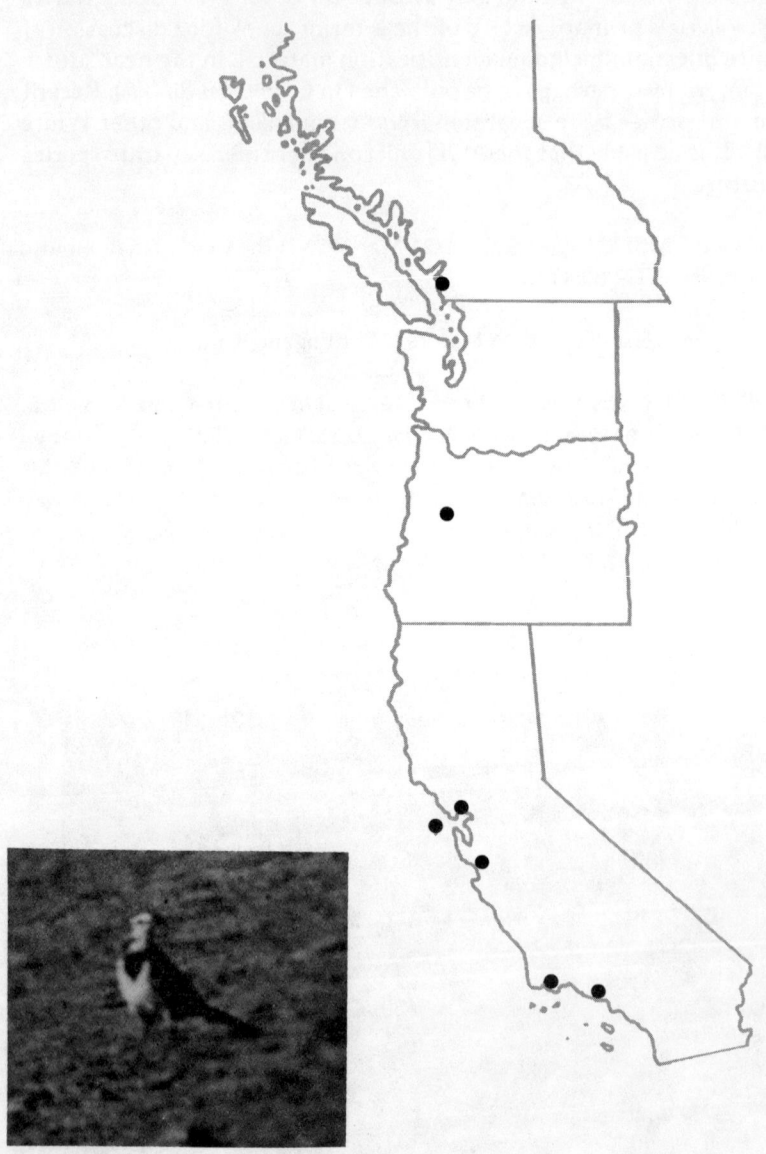

11 Oct 1978 at Goleta, S. Bb.,
CAL. 3rd record. *Paul Lehman*.

# WHITE WAGTAIL

24 Aug 1979 at Watsonville, S.Cz., CAL. 4th record. *Al Ghiorso.*

# PHAINOPEPLA

*Phainopepla nitens*

Breeds SW U.S. to C Mexico. Mostly resident, but some birds move south in winter.

The Phainopepla nests in CAL throughout the southern deserts and north along the eastern edge of the Coast Range to about the San Francisco Bay area and around the edges of the Central Valley. Many of these northern birds withdraw in winter; returning spring birds have been vagrants north to Siskiyou Co., CAL, and twice to S ORE, where it is a Rarity.

**OREGON**  Two records: 17-18 May 1957† at Frenchglen, Har. (C 61:55), and 15 Mar 1961 at Medford, Jck. (M 44:76).

# BROWN SHRIKE

Plate 7

*Lanius cristatus*

Breeds E Asia. Winters SE Asia to New Guinea.

The Brown Shrike has appeared twice in ALASKA: an apparent spring overshoot on St. Lawrence I. and a fall vagrant in the westernmost Aleutian Is.

**ALASKA** Two records: 4-6 Jun 1977 at Gambell, St. Lawrence I. (AB 32:158), and early Oct 1978† on Shemya I. Details of the Gambell bird suggest the northeasternmost breeding race *L. c. cristatus* but the Shemya I. specimen (details of which have yet to be published) is apparently the Korean breeding race *L. c. lucionensis*.

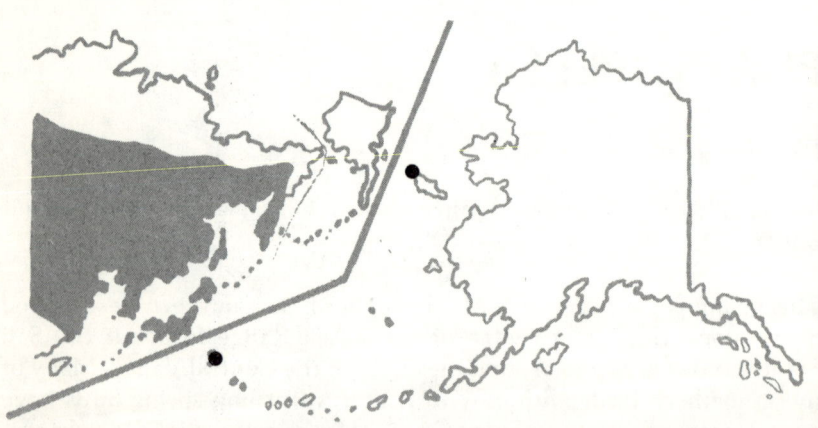

I.D. The Brown Shrike is similar in size and shape to Loggerhead Shrike *L. ludovicianus*, though it is somewhat longer-tailed. Adults are a warm brown above, more rusty on the crown, rump, and tail. The underparts are mostly whitish, with buffy flanks and a buffy wash across the breast. The black mask through the eye is separated from the crown by a narrow white line, apparent in the Korean race collected on the Aleutians, but not apparent in the field on the NE Asia race, presumably the race involved with the St. Lawrence I. sighting.

Immatures are similar to adults, except that the uppperparts and sides of the underparts are narrowly barred with dark. For more information see King, Finch, Stallcup & Russell (1978) and Voous (1979 — brief comparison with selected Asian shrikes).

# WHITE-EYED VIREO

*Vireo griseus*

Breeds E U.S. Winters SE U.S., Cuba to Central America.

The White-eyed Vireo has been found four times on the West Coast. All records were during the 2½ week period between 18 May-8 Jun in CAL.

**CALIFORNIA**  Four records: 4-5 Jun 1969 on SE Farallon I. (CB 2:94), 7-8 Jun 1977* at Pt. Reyes NS, Mrn., 18-21 May 1978 at Pt. Reyes NS, and 31 May-2 Jun 1979 at Oasis, Mono.

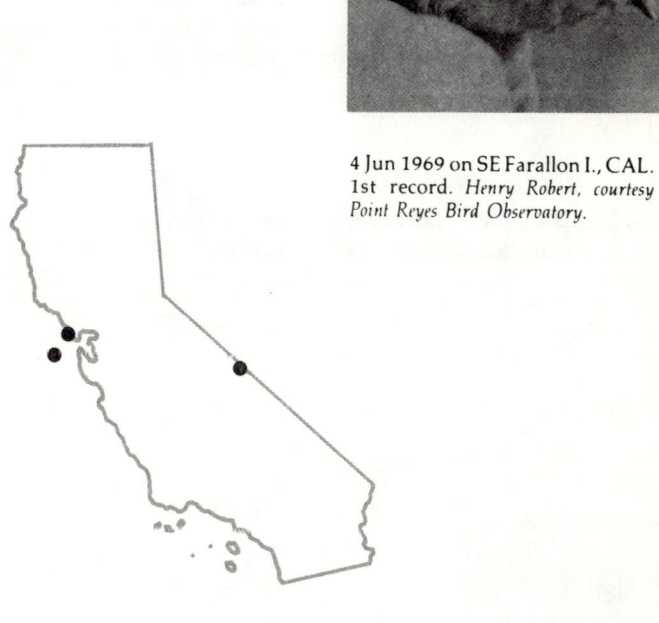

4 Jun 1969 on SE Farallon I., CAL. 1st record. *Henry Robert, courtesy Point Reyes Bird Observatory.*

# YELLOW-THROATED VIREO

*Vireo flavifrons*

Breeds E North America. Winters S Mexico to NW South America.

The Yellow-throated Vireo has occurred on the West Coast only in CAL, where most records are of misoriented spring migrants, but records of fall vagrants and a single wintering individual exist. Most records come from well-worked vagrant "traps" during peak periods for the occurrence of eastern vagrants, but there are three early May records in interior S CAL, about 3-4 weeks earlier than most records of eastern vagrants.

**CALIFORNIA**   14 records, graphed below. 11 are from the spring: 7 May 1963† at Wildrose, Inyo (C 70:186), 24 May 1966 at Cambria, S.L.O., 12-13 Jun 1969 on SE Farallon I., 5-9 May 1976* at Morongo Valley, S.Bn., 23-26 May 1976* at Deep Springs, Inyo, 30 Apr-1 May 1977 at Morongo Valley, 13 Jun 1977 at Morongo Valley, 28-30 May 1978 at Oasis, Mono, 28 May 1978 at Ft. Piute, S.Bn., 3 Jun 1978 at Pt. Reyes NS, Mrn., and 30 May 1979 at Ft. Piute. There are two fall records — 27 Oct 1974 on Santa Catalina I., and 11-18 Sep 1977 at Olema, Mrn. — and a single winter record: 5 Dec 1969-19 Mar 1970 at Riverside.

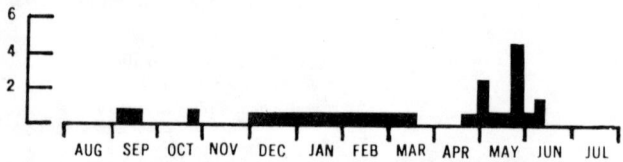

28 May 1978 at Oasis, Mono, CAL. 11th record. *Don Roberson.*

# YELLOW-GREEN VIREO

*Vireo flavoviridis*

Breeds N Mexico to C South America. Northern populations winter to the south.

The Yellow-green Vireo formerly bred in S Texas (and may still occasionally do so) but recently the more consistent area to search for this bird in the ABA area has been S CAL, where one has been found during Sep-Oct in 5 of the last 6 years (1974-1979). Most of the 11 CAL records appear to be of immatures, but there are two records of adults.

Many authorities consider this bird conspecific with Red-eyed Vireo *V. olivaceous*.

**CALIFORNIA** 11 records, graphed below. A specimen taken 1 Oct 1887† at Riverside is the only interior record (A 5:210). The remaining 10 records were along the coast: 22-27 Sep 1964† at Dana Pt., Orn., 23 Sep 1967 at Imperial Beach, S.D., 3 Oct 1967 at Costa Mesa, Orn., 7 Oct 1967† at San Diego, 19-20 Sep 1974 at Imperial Beach, 25 Oct 1976* at Imperial Beach, 15-19 Oct 1977 at Pt. Loma, S.D., 13 Sep 1978 at Pt. Loma, S.D., 22-25 Oct 1978 at Lake Merced, San Francisco, and 8 Sep 1979 at Gaviota, S.Bb.

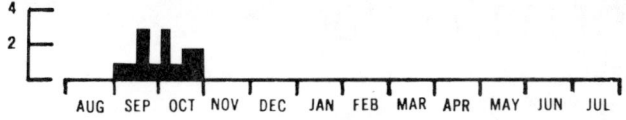

24 Oct 1978 at Lake Merced, San Francisco, CAL. 10th record. *Don Roberson.*

# YELLOW-GREEN VIREO

I.D. The Yellow-green Vireo closely resembles immature Red-eyed Vireo, which have a yellowish wash to the sides, flanks, and undertail coverts. Immature Yellow-green Vireo (which accounts for most West Coast records) is identified by the combination of 1) more yellowish upperparts, producing a distinctive yellow-green cast to the nape, back, rump, and wing and tail edgings, 2) more extensive yellow underparts, often leaving white only on the throat and center of the breast and belly, 3) a duller gray crown (not blue-gray) with less contrasting supercilium bordered by only faint brown, giving the eye a more prominent look on a plain face, and 4) a slightly heavier bill, often fleshy-colored on the lower mandible. In all, it is a large, plain-faced vireo that is much brighter yellow than any immature Red-eyed Vireo. The adult Yellow-green Vireo is less bright, with less extensive yellow on the underparts, but may still be identified by the combination of characteristics noted above. Though the underparts are less yellow than on the immature, they are still broadly washed with yellow-green, not the pure lemon-yellow wash to the sides and flanks of Red-eyed Vireo. For more information see Dunn (1978d).

# PHILADELPHIA VIREO

*Vireo philadelphicus*

Breeds S Canada & NE U.S. Winters Central America to NW South America.

The Philadelphia Vireo nests in NE B.C. It is a Rarity on the West Coast except in that province. Recently it has been found annually in CAL as a very rare fall vagrant and even scarser spring vagrant. Most records fall within the prime periods for eastern vagrants and most were found at well-worked vagrant "traps". In addition, there is one winter record.

**CALIFORNIA**  44 records, graphed below. It has averaged just over 6 birds a year during the most recent five-year period (1975-1979). 4 of the 5 spring records were at eastern desert oases (24-25 May 1976* at Oasis, Mono, 26-27 May 1976* at Scotty's Castle, Inyo, 27-30 May 1976 at Furnace Creek, Inyo, and 14 May 1978 at Scotty's Castle); the lone spring coastal record was on 12 Jun 1975 on SE Farallon I. In contrast, 85% of the fall birds were at coastal sites, including multiples at Pt. Reyes NS, Mrn. (4), SE Farallon I. (4), Carmel R. mouth, Mnt. (3), and the San Diego area (11 — Pt. Loma to Imperial Beach). There is a single winter record: 30 Dec 1978-12 Jan 1979 at Harbor Lake, Palos Verdes Pen., L.A.

# PHILADELPHIA VIREO

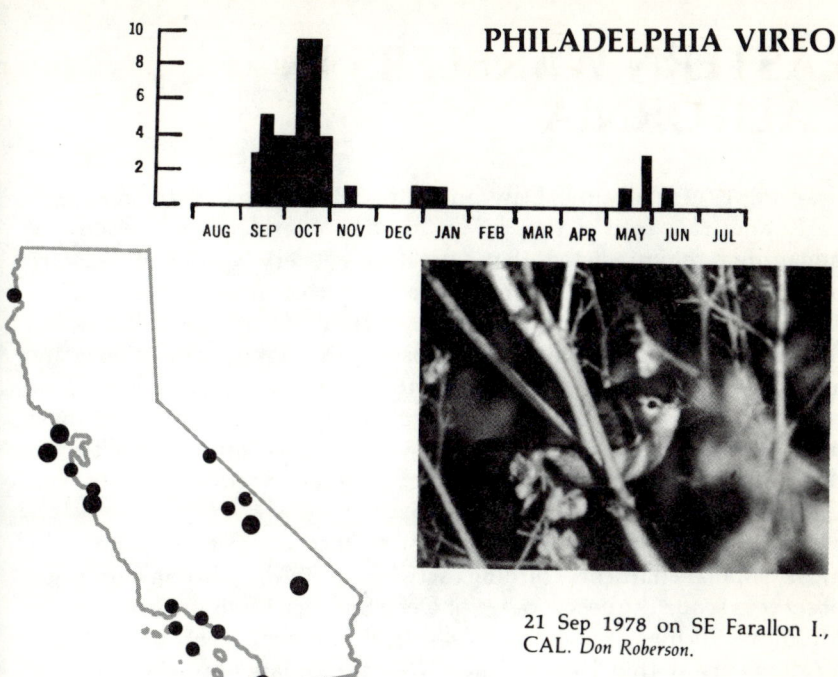

21 Sep 1978 on SE Farallon I., CAL. *Don Roberson*.

I.D. The Philadelphia Vireo is similar in size and shape to Warbling Vireo *V. gilvus*, with which it is often confused, typically being only slightly plumper, shorter-tailed, and more round-headed. Philadelphia Vireo is identified by the combination of 1) more extensively yellow underparts, the yellow covering the entire throat and breast, paling only on the belly and vent; Warbling Vireo is always whitish on the center of the breast and has a whitish throat, but may show very extensive yellow to the sides of the breast, sides, flanks, and undertail coverts (especially immatures in the fall, which are often misidentified as Philadelphia Vireos), 2) a more blue-gray cap and greener back than Warbling, showing some cap-back contrast (Warbling is more evenly grayish colored on the cap and back with little, if any, cap-back contrast), 3) a black eyeline extending forward through the lores to the bill (obscured on some fall immatures); Warbling lacks any black line through the lores, and 4) a straighter supercilium, not arched as in Warbling; the long arched supercilium of Warbling produces a "quizzical" look unique to that species. Fall immatures are brighter yellow below and greener above than adults and often have a single faint yellowish-green wingbar. In any plumage, attention should be drawn to the center of the breast and throat. On Philadelphia Vireo, this is the brightest part of the yellow underparts (matched only by the undertail coverts); on Warbling Vireo, this area is the dullest part of the underparts do not be misled by the bright yellow sides, flanks, and undertail coverts). For more information see Dunn (1978e).

# EASTERN WARBLERS IN CALIFORNIA

In spring 1911, William L. Dawson visited SE Farallon I. off the coast of C CAL and ran into a "wave" of eastern warblers. Surprised but undaunted, he predicted that "practically every species of eastern [*Parulidae*] should report sooner or later at this inhospitable rock" (C 13:171). Not only has this prophecy been fulfilled for the Farallones, but for numerous recently discovered "oases" throughout the deserts and along the coastline of CAL. Some 46 species of warblers have been recorded; 29 of these are thought of as "eastern" warblers. 19 of these birds average more than 4 birds a year in CAL and do not fit our definition of Rarity; most of these, however, are Rarities in other West Coast states.

The search of vagrant "traps" for eastern warblers is perhaps the most popular hardcore birding activity in CAL. Throngs of eager observers scour the desert oases of Deep Springs, Oasis, Scotty's Castle, Mesquite Springs, Stovepipe Wells, and Furnace Creek (the latter 4 locations are within Death Valley NM) during late May-early Jun and again in Oct-Nov; parking has become a major problem at the better patches of cypress trees at Pt. Reyes NS during Sep-Oct; and such S CAL vagrant hot-spots as the Goleta-Santa Barbara area, Pt. Mugu, Pt. Loma, and Imperial Beach are visited daily in early Jun and again in Sep-early Nov. Other outstanding areas — Fairhaven, Hmb. in the NW or the Monterey Peninsula — receive heavy, but erratic, coverage. Very recently "discovered" areas like Ft. Piute, S.Bn., in the desert or Gaviota, S.Bb., on the coast, have only begun to yield their treasures. And, of course, the nets and traps on SE Farallon I. are checked hourly during prime vagrant seasons.

As eastern warblers are so attractive and popular, I have included summaries of their CAL occurrence in the species accounts to follow, even when they do not remotely come within the Rarity definition. If the warbler is covered because it is a Rarity somewhere on the West Coast, it is covered for CAL as well. However, since hundreds of records can be involved, maps and graphs of all records are not included for the more common species. When there are over 100 records for a warbler, its status is described by using tables of per-year averages and by graphing records in a recent "typical" year. Warblers with less than 100 records are discussed as are Rarities, with the use of a map and a graph of all records. There are three additional eastern warblers which do not meet the Rarity definition for any West Coast state or province and which do not have an individual species account. They are briefly discussed below and are included on the table to follow:

# EASTERN WARBLERS IN CALIFORNIA

Palm Warbler *Dendroica palmarum* — Nests in NE B.C. There is but one record for ALASKA (listed in Appendix A), but it has recently averaged nearly 7 birds a year in both WASH & ORE, most records occurring along the coast in late Sep-Nov, with a few birds lingering to winter locally. In CAL, Palm Warbler averages over 170 birds a year and over 150 of these are during the fall, where it is the most common eastern warbler along the coast in Oct-Nov. Nearly 15 birds a year winter along the CAL coast. It is very rare in spring (only about 3 a year) and quite scarce away from the immediate coast.

Northern Waterthrush *Seiurus noveboracensis* — Nests across C ALASKA and N B.C. and locally in NE WASH and C ORE (Crescent Creek, Des., and Little Deschutes R., Klm.). It appears to be a rare, but regular, migrant through E WASH, E ORE, and E CAL. In CAL, it averages over 40 birds a year (about 25 a fall and about 15 during the spring), and is decidedly rarer along the coast than it is in the interior. A very few winter each year in CAL and there are winter records as far north as W WASH. A thorough discussion of the CAL status is in Binford (1971b).

American Redstart *Setophaga ruticilla* — Nests uncommonly in SE ALASKA and breeds across much of the interior of B.C. and locally in E WASH; an isolated small population nests along Crescent Creek, Des., ORE and there is a breeding record from NW CAL (CB 3:87). It apparently migrates regularly in small numbers through E CAL and is one of the most common vagrants along the coast. Over 2000 have been tallied in CAL, where it is the most common "eastern" warbler; it averages some 185 birds a year (about two-thirds of these during the fall). About 8 birds are found wintering in CAL during an average year. A thorough discussion of the CAL status is in McCaskie (1970a).


When discussing eastern warblers in CAL, it is often preferable to group them into various levels of rarity by their recent per-year averages. This gives the observer a feeling for the relative abundance of any warbler encountered. The warblers below (including four rare stragglers from SW U.S.) are ranked by their recent per-year averages (except when there are less than 20 records, when they are ranked by total records) and are broken into six levels of relative abundance:

# EASTERN WARBLERS IN CALIFORNIA

|  | Recent (1975-1979) per-year average (rounded to nearest whole number) | Total CAL records |
|---|---|---|
| American Redstart | 185 | 2150 |
| Palm Warbler | 171 | 1536 |
| Blackpoll Warbler | 118 | 1405 |
| Tennessee Warbler | 94 | 895 |
| Black-and-white Warbler | 79 | 764 |
| Northern Waterthrush | 42 | 537 |
| Chestnut-sided Warbler | 36 | 312 |
| Ovenbird | 33 | 320 |
| Magnolia Warbler | 30 | 325 |
| Northern Parula | 24 | 204 |
| Black-throated Blue Warbler | 21 | 264 |
| Blackburnian Warbler | 18 | 167 |
| Bay-breasted Warbler | 16 | 127 |
| Cape May Warbler | 16 | 121 |
| Black-throated Green Warbler | 15 | 130 |
| Canada Warbler | 10 | 78 |
| Prairie Warbler | 9 | 104 |
| Hooded Warbler | 9 | 70 |
| Painted Redstart | 5 | 54 |
| Prothonotary Warbler | 4 | 33 |
| Yellow-throated Warbler | 4 | 28 |
| Worm-eating Warbler | 3 | 27 |
| Golden-winged Warbler | 2 | 19 |
| Mourning Warbler | 2 | 15 |
| Kentucky Warbler | 1 | 13 |
| Grace's Warbler | 1 | 10 |
| Connecticut Warbler | 1 | 24 |
| Pine Warbler | < 1 | 10 |
| Cerulean Warbler | < 1 | 9 |
| Red-faced Warbler | < 1 | 7 |
| Blue-winged Warbler | < 1 | 7 |
| Louisiana Waterthrush | 0 | 1 |
| Golden-cheeked Warbler | 0 | 1 |

# EASTERN WARBLERS IN CALIFORNIA

The averages and ranking above consider warblers in terms of the year as a whole, but there are some species whose abundance varies greatly by season. Warblers, in general, are more common as vagrants during the fall than during the spring. They are ranked below by season:

| Fall averages (1975-1979) | | Spring averages (1975-1979) | |
|---|---|---|---|
| Palm Warbler | 154 | American Redstart | 51 |
| American Redstart | 124 | Tennessee Warbler | 28 |
| Blackpoll Warbler | 110 | Black-and-white Warbler | 26 |
| Tennessee Warbler | 66 | Ovenbird | 17 |
| Black-and-white Warbler | 42 | Northern Waterthrush | 13 |
| | | Northern Parula | 13 |
| Chestnut-sided Warbler | 29 | Magnolia Warbler | 11 |
| Northern Waterthrush | 26 | | |
| Black-throated Blue Warbler | 21 | Blackpoll Warbler | 8 |
| Magnolia Warbler | 19 | Chestnut-sided Warbler | 7 |
| | | Bay-breasted Warbler | 7 |
| Blackburnian Warbler | 16 | Cape May Warbler | 6 |
| Ovenbird | 15 | Hooded Warbler | 5 |
| Black-throated Green Warbler | 13 | | |
| Northern Parula | 10 | Palm Warbler | 3 |
| Bay-breasted Warbler | 9 | Painted Redstart | 3 |
| Cape May Warbler | 9 | Black-throated Green Warbler | 2 |
| Canada Warbler | 9 | Blackburnian Warbler | 2 |
| Prairie Warbler | 9 | Yellow-throated Warbler | 2 |
| | | Prothonotary Warbler | 1 |
| Hooded Warbler | 3 | Grace's Warbler | 1 |
| Painted Redstart | 2 | Red-faced Warbler | 1 |
| Prothonotary Warbler | 2 | Canada Warbler | 1 |
| Worm-eating Warbler | 2 | Worm-eating Warbler | 1 |
| Yellow-throated Warbler | 1 | Golden-winged Warbler | < 1 |
| Mourning Warbler | 1 | Connecticut Warbler | < 1 |
| Grace's Warbler | 1 | Kentucky Warbler | < 1 |
| Cerulean Warbler | 1 | Mourning Warbler | < 1 |
| Golden-winged Warbler | < 1 | Cerulean Warbler | < 1 |
| Connecticut Warbler | < 1 | Blue-winged Warbler | < 1 |
| Kentucky Warbler | < 1 | Prairie Warbler | < 1 |
| Pine Warbler | < 1 | Black-throated Blue Warbler | < 1 |
| Red-faced Warbler | < 1 | | |
| Blue-winged Warbler | 0 | | |
| Louisiana Waterthrush | 0 | | |
| Golden-cheeked Warbler | 0 | | |

# BLACK-AND-WHITE WARBLER

*Mniotilta varia*

Breeds N-C & E North America. Winters N-C Mexico, S Texas, C Florida to West Indes & NW South America.

The Black-and-white Warbler nests on the West Coast only in NE B.C. It has straggled to ALASKA once. South of B.C. it is considered a Rarity in WASH & ORE, where fall and spring (especially) birds make up the bulk of records. In CAL there has recently been an average of about 80 birds a year. About 2/3 of these are fall vagrants, most along the coast, but the preponderance of spring records are at desert oases in E CAL; Black-and-white Warbler is probably a regular spring migrant there. An average of nearly 10 birds a year winter in CAL, most often in coastal areas. There have also been summering individuals in CAL during most recent years.

**ALASKA** One record: 10-12 Oct 1977 on the Colville R. delta. It was found dead a week later.

**WASHINGTON** 19 records, graphed below. Most have been spring birds in E WASH (where it may be a regular migrant in small numbers). There are three winter records: 10 Dec 1965-27 Mar 1966 at Seattle, King, 28 Dec 1969 at Pt. Roberts, Wha., and 21 Mar 1975 at Tokeland, Pac.

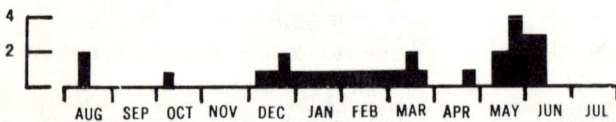

**OREGON** 26 records, graphed below. Most have been spring birds in E ORE (where it may be a regular migrant in small numbers); there are 9 spring records from Malheur NWR, Har, and 3 from the banding station at Hart Mt., Lake. Malheur NWR also dominates the fall records: 5 of the state's 9 fall sightings come from there. The single winter record was 17 Dec 1977-22 Jan 1978* at North Bend, Til.

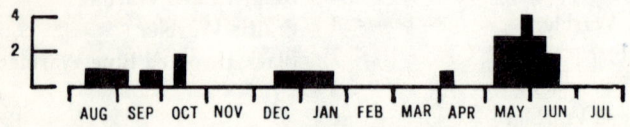

# BLACK-AND-WHITE WARBLER

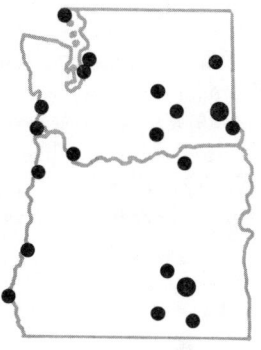

15 Jun 1974 at Kimball SP, Klm., ORE. 8th record. *Gerald B. Smith.*

**CALIFORNIA** 764 records, recently averaging nearly 80 birds a year. 316 records were in N CAL and 448 were in S CAL. 528 occurred during the fall & winter (246 in N CAL; 281 in S CAL). 236 occurred during the spring & summer (70 in N CAL; 167 in S CAL). The table below lists recent (1975-1979) per-year averages:

| CAL | | N CAL | | S CAL | |
|---|---|---|---|---|---|
| fall    = | 42.4 | fall    = | 21.8 | fall    = | 20.4 |
| winter  = | 9.4  | winter  = | 4.6  | winter  = | 4.8  |
| spring  = | 26.4 | spring  = | 7.4  | spring  = | 19.2 |
| summer = | 1.2  | summer = | 1.0  | summer = | .2   |
| TOTAL = | 79.4 | TOTAL = | 34.8 | TOTAL = | 44.6 |

While most of the N CAL records and the majority of fall S CAL records are from coastal areas, the bulk of spring records in S CAL are from desert oases in E CAL (especially the Deep Springs-Oasis-Death Valley loop). Thus it is possible that while many CAL records, especially during the fall, are misoriented vagrants, a small number may regularly migrate through E CAL (and E ORE & E WASH) and may not be misoriented at all. Summer records are mostly along the coast and concentrated in C CAL (Tilden Park, C.C., has a number of records). Winter birds prefer wooded areas near the coast; areas with multiple records include Olema marsh, Mrn., Berkeley-Oakland hills area, C.C. & Ala., the Santa Barbara area,

# BLACK-AND-WHITE WARBLER

and the San Diego area. While there are numerous records of migrants at vagrant "traps", a comparatively high number have been found at coastal residential and wooded areas not on the immediate coastline; there are correspondingly few records for offshore islands. This unusual distribution pattern, the E CAL regular migration route, and the high numbers (comparatively) of winterers all contribute to a status for this bird different from "typical" eastern warblers.

The graph below illustrates the records of Black-and-white Warblers in CAL in 1977. This year has been chosen as illustrating a "typical" pattern of records distribution, though the 88 records in 1977 were somewhat higher than the 79 birds per-year average.

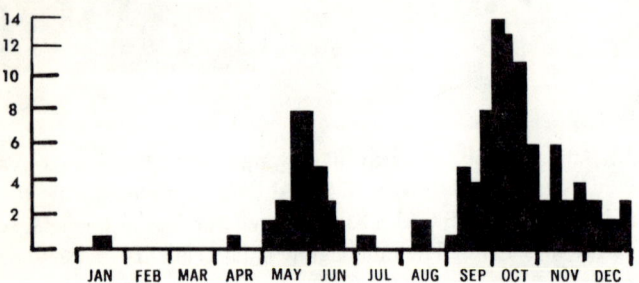

# PROTHONOTARY WARBLER

*Protonotaria citrea*

Breeds E U.S. Winters S Mexico to NW South America.

The Prothonotary Warbler is a very rare vagrant on the West Coast. Over 2/3 of the records were during the fall (including one as far north as SE WASH); all are presumably misoriented immatures. Spring vagrants fall within the pattern of late May-early Jun records shown by numerous eastern vagrants. There is a single winter record from S CAL.

**CALIFORNIA** 33 records, graphed below. Most (22) records are from the fall; 15 of these come from along the coast. A female present 3-7 Dec 1967 at Willow Creek, Mnt., was probably a very late fall vagrant, but a bird wintered from 30 Dec 1978-10 Mar 1979 at Santa Barbara. Areas with multiple records are Deep Springs-Oasis (2 spring, 2 fall); Death Valley NM (1 spring, 4 fall); and the San Diego area (Pt. Loma to Imperial Beach — 4 spring, 3 fall). The northernmost records were 3 Oct 1975* at Pt. Reyes NS, Mrn., and 29 Sep 1978† at McKinleyville, Hmb.

# PROTHONOTARY WARBLER

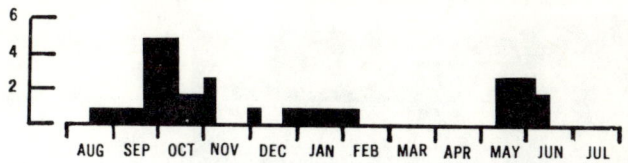

**OREGON**   One record: 19 Aug 1976* at Hart Mt., Lake (WB 8:63).

**WASHINGTON**   One record: 5 Sep 1970 and present for "several weeks" at Richland, Ben.

26 May 1974 at Furnace Creek, Death Valley NM, Inyo, CAL. *Mike Wihler.*

29 Oct 1977 at Stovepipe Wells, Death Valley NM, Inyo, CAL. *Dave Rudholm.*

# PROTHONOTARY WARBLER

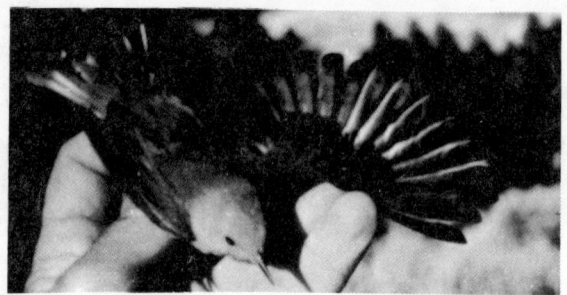

19 Aug 1976 at Hart Mt., Lake, ORE. 2nd record. *L. Richard Mewaldt*.

7 Dec 1967 at Willow Creek, Mnt., CAL. 6th record. *Ronald L. Branson*.

# WORM-EATING WARBLER

*Helmitheros vermivorus*

Breeds E U.S. Winters E-C Mexico, West Indes to Panama.

The Worm-eating Warbler has been found on the West Coast only in CAL, where nearly all records are of spring and fall vagrants, but apparent summering birds have been recorded and an individual wintered in NW CAL.

**CALIFORNIA** 27 records, graphed below. Most (17) are from the fall; 14 of these come from along the coast, including a bird as far north as the Mad R. mouth, Hmb. (14-15 Sep 1975). Most unusual was an individual that wintered far north from 2 Dec 1977-10 Mar 1978* at Sunnybrae, Hmb. Areas with multiple fall records are the Monterey Pen. (3) and the San Diego area (7). 6 of the 9 spring records are from the coast, including 4 records from SE Farallon I. and another from San Nicolas I. A number of spring records are very late (mid-Jun-Jul) and

# WORM-EATING WARBLER

include birds which may have attempted to summer locally: 23 Jun-10 Jul 1977 at Ft. Piute, S.Bn., and 11-21 Jul 1978 at Tilden Park, C.C. Both of these were away from the coast. Other interior records are: 11-13 Oct 1975* at Saline Valley, Inyo, 30 Oct-6 Nov 1975 at Riverside, 27 Nov 1975* at Tapia Park, L.A., 14-16 May 1977 at Yucca Valley, S.Bn., and a most unusual Central Valley record — 31 Oct 1978 at Merced NWR, Mer.

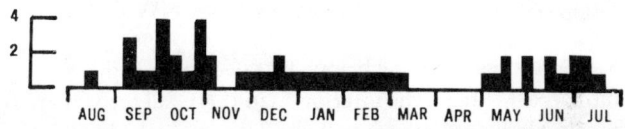

6 Oct 1978 at Pt. Reyes NS, Mrn., CAL. *Al Ghiorso.*

# GOLDEN-WINGED WARBLER

*Vermivora chrysoptera*

Breeds E North America. Winters S Mexico to NW South America.

The Golden-winged Warbler is a very rare vagrant to the West Coast; all the records are from CAL and are about equally split between spring and fall and between the coast and the deserts.

Most unusual is a record of a Golden-winged X Blue-winged Warbler *V. pinus* hybrid ("Brewster's" type) from NW CAL.

**CALIFORNIA**   19 records, graphed below. Just over half of these were during the fall (6 from the coast, 4 from the interior). 3 of these fall records are from far north at Fairhaven, Hmb., as is the lone hybrid record listed later. Three birds were found very late in the fall: 8 Dec 1962 at San Bernardino, 20 Dec 1972 at Claremont, L.A., and 30 Nov 1974 at Big Tujunga Canyon, L.A. Spring records fall within the late May-early Jun pattern shown by many eastern vagrants; the only exception was one on SE Farallon I. (5 Jul 1972). Six spring records come from the Deep Springs-Oasis-Scotty's Castle loop in Inyo & Mono Cos., E CAL; the additional 3 spring records are from offshore islands.

In addition to the Golden-winged Warbler records listed above, an unusual plumaged "Brewster's" type hybrid was found 1 Oct 1973 at Fairhaven, Hmb. (WB 5:58).

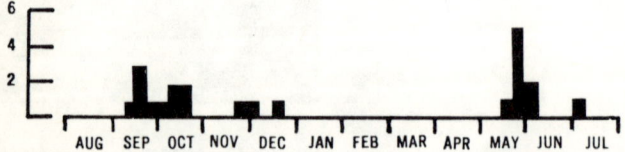

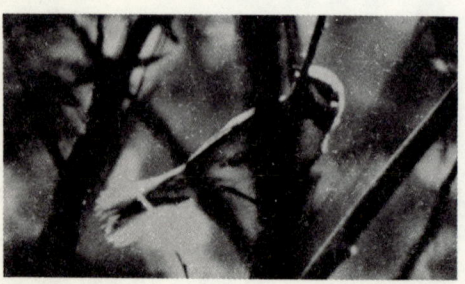

24 May 1979 at Scotty's Castle, Death Valley NM, Inyo, CAL. *Don Roberson.*

# GOLDEN-WINGED WARBLER

21 Sep 1975 at Fairhaven, Hmb., CAL. *Dave Rudholm.*

# BLUE-WINGED WARBLER

*Vermivora pinus*

Breeds E U.S. Winters S Mexico to Panama.

The Blue-winged Warbler has been found on the West Coast only in CAL, where the handful of records are about evenly split between spring and fall vagrants.

**CALIFORNIA**  Seven records: 16 Jun 1954† at Wyman Canyon, Inyo (C 58:75), 13 Sep 1963 at San Francisco, 19 Sep 1964 at Pt. Loma, S.D., 25 Sep 1964 at Imperial Beach, S.D., 19 Sep 1965 at Imperial Beach, 27 May 1975 at Deep Springs, Inyo, and 28 May 1977 at Ft. Piute, S.Bn.

# TENNESSEE WARBLER

*Vermivora peregrina*

Breeds N-C and E North America. Winters S Mexico to NW South America.

The Tennessee Warbler nests on the West Coast across N B.C. and locally in SE ALASKA. It is considered a Rarity in WASH & ORE, where records are split between spring and fall vagrants. It has recently averaged over 90 birds a year in CAL, about 2/3 of which are fall vagrants. Spring records are mostly from desert oases, where the species may be a rare but regular spring migrant. A few winter in CAL irregularly, sometimes in small numbers.

**WASHINGTON** Four records: 30 Aug 1970 at Spokane, 25 Sep 1973 at Seattle, King, 20 May 1974 at Ruby Beach, Jef., and 5 Jun 1977 at Kamiak Butte, Whi.

**OREGON** 13 records, graphed below. Over half of the records fall within the late May-early Jun pattern shown by eastern vagrants in CAL. Nearly all of the records are in E ORE: 8 from the Malheur NWR area, Har. (4 spring, 4 fall) and 2 spring birds at the banding station on Hart Mt., Lake. The summer record is from C ORE: 29 Jul 1976* at Indian Ford Campground, Des. The only coastal record is from the fall: 24 Aug 1977 at the south jetty, Columbia R., Clt.

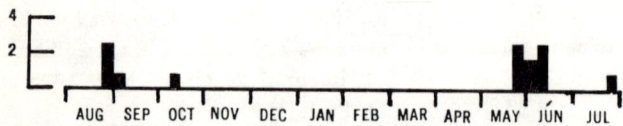

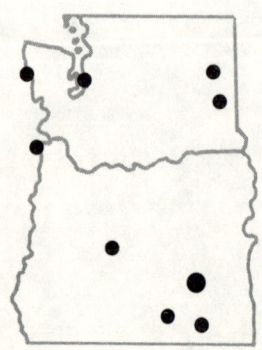

# TENNESSEE WARBLER

9 Jun 1977 at Hart Mt., Lake, ORE. 9th record. L. Richard Mewaldt.

**CALIFORNIA** 895 records, recently averaging nearly 95 birds a year. 413 records were in N CAL and 482 were in S CAL. 684 occurred during the fall & winter (319 in N CAL; 365 in S CAL). 211 occurred during the spring (94 in N CAL; 117 in S CAL). The table below lists recent (1975-1979) per-year averages:

| CAL | | | N CAL | | | S CAL | | |
|---|---|---|---|---|---|---|---|---|
| fall | = | 61.8 | fall | = | 33.4 | fall | = | 28.4 |
| winter | = | 4.6 | winter | = | 2.2 | winter | = | 2.4 |
| spring | = | 27.8 | spring | = | 10.0 | spring | = | 17.8 |
| summer | = | 0.0 | summer | = | 0.0 | summer | = | 0.0 |
| TOTAL | = | 94.2 | TOTAL | = | 45.6 | TOTAL | = | 48.6 |

# TENNESSEE WARBLER

The vast majority of fall records and of N CAL spring records are from the immediate coast (including offshore islands: SE Farallon I., for example, has had 136 records). But nearly half of the S CAL spring records are from desert oases in the interior (especially the Deep Springs-Oasis-Death Valley loop in Inyo & Mono counties), suggesting that Tennessee Warbler may be a regular migrant in small numbers through E CAL (and probably E ORE & E WASH). While coastal birds are probably misoriented, these spring records from E CAL may be of birds on regular migration routes. There are no known records of birds which summered. But wintering individuals are found annually, especially around the San Francisco Bay area (and nearby Marin Co.) and the Santa Barbara area. In the winter of 1977-78, at least 12 birds were found between Dec-Mar; most were thought to winter locally. Several times an individual bird is thought to have returned for a second winter.

The graph below illustrates the records of Tennessee Warbler in 1977. There were 124 records in 1977, somewhat higher than the 95-a-year average, and there was an especially high number of winter birds (peak in late Dec on the graph). But the graph does illustrate the "typical" peaks of occurrence: late May-early Jun and mid-Sep-early Oct.

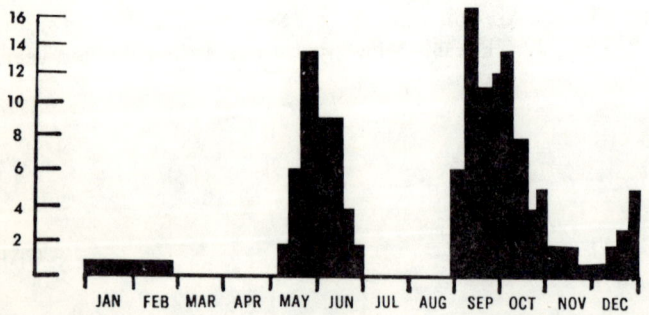

368

# VIRGINIA'S WARBLER

*Vermivora virginiae*

Breeds SW U.S. to N-C Mexico. Winters S Mexico.

The Virginia's Warbler breeds very locally on the West Coast: only in the White Mtns., San Bernardino Mtns., and on Clark Mt., all in SE CAL (see WB 5:49), and perhaps very locally on the east side of the Sierra. It is a vagrant along the coast of CAL, becoming progressively scarser as one moves north, with only a handful of records from N CAL (including one winter record). It is a Rarity north of CAL: there are two records (one spring, one fall) from ORE.

**OREGON**  Two records: 29 May 1977* at Hart Mt., Lake (caught & banded) and 8 Nov 1979* at Eugene, Lane.

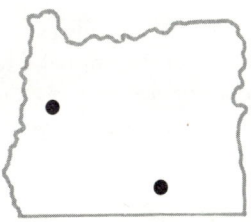

29 May 1977 at Hart Mt., Lake, ORE. 1st record. *L. Richard Mewaldt.*

# NORTHERN PARULA

*Parula americana*

Breeds E North America. Winters W & NE Mexico to the West Indes & Central America.

The Northern Parula is confined as a breeding species to eastern North America and only rarely reaches the West Coast. There are but a handful of records from ORE & WASH, but it is found annually in CAL, recently averaging nearly 25 birds a year. Most records are of spring and fall vagrants (surprisingly, there are more spring records than fall). Several wintering birds have been found (including one in WASH). It has twice been found nesting in coastal C CAL. It seems that if a singing spring vagrant, presumably misoriented, is able to attract a female and find suitable habitat nearby, a pair can successfully nest in areas which are spectacularly distant from the nearest regular breeding areas (central Texas in this case).

**CALIFORNIA**  204 records, recently averaging about 24 birds a year. 80 records were in N CAL and 124 were in S CAL. 85 occurred during the fall & winter (36 in N CAL; 49 in S CAL). 119 occurred during the spring & summer (44 in N CAL; 75 in S CAL). The table below lists recent (1975-1979) per-year averages:

| CAL | | | N CAL | | | S CAL | | |
|---|---|---|---|---|---|---|---|---|
| fall | = | 9.6 | fall | = | 4.4 | fall | = | 5.2 |
| winter | = | 0.8 | winter | = | 0.0 | winter | = | 0.8 |
| spring | = | 12.6 | spring | = | 3.4 | spring | = | 9.2 |
| summer | = | 0.6 | summer | = | 0.6 | summer | = | 0.0 |
| TOTAL | = | 23.6 | TOTAL | = | 8.4 | TOTAL | = | 15.2 |

Unlike most eastern warblers, for which fall records predominate, nearly 60% of the Northern Parulas recorded in CAL occurred during the spring. In S CAL, nearly all these spring birds are from desert oases (especially the Deep Springs-Oasis-Death Valley loop in Inyo & Mono counties), but nearly all the spring records from N CAL are along the coast (including 10 from SE Farallon I.). Most of the fall records anywhere in CAL are from along the coast, though over a third of the S CAL fall records were found at desert oases. There are 10 winter records from CAL, nine of which were in S CAL. Most of these were in the interior (including birds along the Colorado R. and at the south end, Salton Sea); there is only one N CAL winter record: 31 Dec 1973-2 Mar 1974 at Gray Lodge refuge, But.

# NORTHERN PARULA

Several birds have been found summering in coastal N CAL. Twice birds have nested: a male and two females from 18 May-16 Jul 1952 raised three young from two nests at Pt. Lobos, Mnt. (C 60:345) and two males and a female were present 2 Jun-15 Jul 1977 near Olema, Pt. Reyes NS, Mrn. and fledged two young (AB 31:1187).

The graph below illustrates all CAL records during 1977-1979. There were 80 records during these three years (an average of 26+ a year) and the pattern shown is rather typical of the occurrence of this bird:

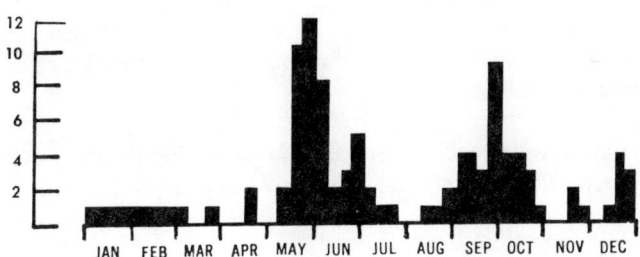

**OREGON** Four records: 22 Jun-3 Jul 1957 at Coos Head, Coos, 19 May 1970 at Malheur NWR, Har., 18 Oct-3 Dec 1972 at Baker, and 30 May 1976* at Malheur NWR.

**WASHINGTON** Three records: 10 Jan-3 Feb 1975 at West Richland, Ben. (M 56(1):12), 13 Jul 1979 at Ocean Shores, G.H., and another 13 Jul 1979 at Neah Bay, Clm.

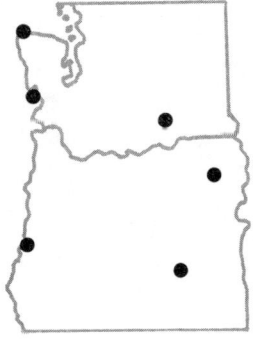

30 May 1976 at Malheur NWR, Har., ORE. 4th record. *Priscilla R. Summers.*

# MAGNOLIA WARBLER

*Dendroica magnolia*

Breeds N North America. Winters S Mexico to West Indes, Central America.

The Magnolia Warbler nests on the West Coast in NE B.C. It is a rare spring and fall vagrant south of B.C., with fall birds predominating. CAL has recently averaged about 30 birds a year. A couple of birds have wintered in CAL.

**ALASKA**   Five records: 1 Oct 1913† about a mile off Humphrey Pt. (on the ice; C 45:49), 10 Jun 1973† along the Chickamin R., SE ALASKA, first week Aug 1976 (2) at Juneau, and 13 Sep 1976† aboard a ship in the Bering Sea at 63°30'N, 166°28'W.

**WASHINGTON**   Two records: 17 Sep 1974 at Leadbetter Pt., Pac., and 21 Oct 1978 at Leadbetter Pt. This species is considered hypothetical on the state list since, though well described, each bird was seen by only a single observer.

**OREGON**   Six records: 18 Sep 1971† at Euchre Creek, Cur., 13 Nov 1974 at Baker, 3 Jun 1978 at Cape Blanco, Cur., 5-6 May 1979* at Salem, Mar., 27 May 1979* at Malheur NWR, Har., and 28 Sep 1979 at Malheur NWR.

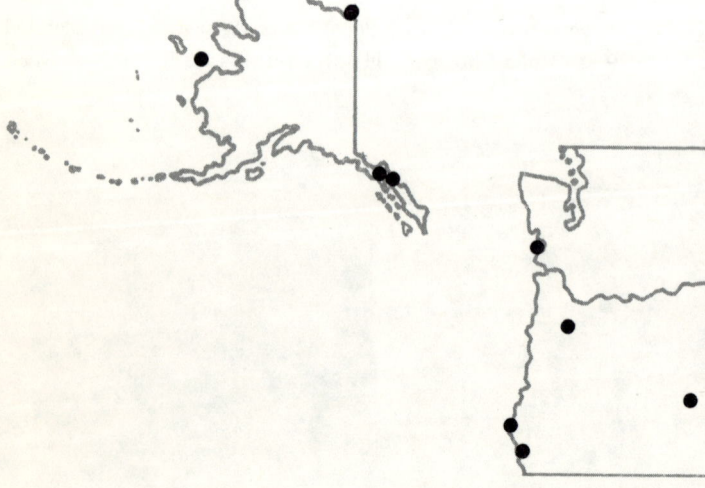

# MAGNOLIA WARBLER

**CALIFORNIA**   325 records, recently averaging nearly 25 birds a year. 209 records were in N CAL and 116 were in S CAL. 218 occurred during the fall and winter (129 in N CAL; 89 in S CAL). 107 occurred during the spring (80 in N CAL; 27 in S CAL). The table below lists recent (1975-1979) per-year averages:

| CAL | | N CAL | | S CAL | |
|---|---|---|---|---|---|
| fall    | = 18.6 | fall    | = 12.6 | fall    | = 6.0 |
| winter  | =  0.4 | winter  | =  0.2 | winter  | = 0.2 |
| spring  | = 10.6 | spring  =  8.2 | | spring  | = 2.4 |
| summer  | =  0.0 | summer  | =  0.0 | summer  | = 0.0 |
| TOTAL   | = 29.6 | TOTAL   | = 21.0 | TOTAL   | = 8.6 |

By far the majority of fall records are along the coast (including 51 from SE Farallon I., which helps to account for the high N CAL count), but about a third of the S CAL fall records are from the interior. As the table indicates, CAL averages about 20 birds a fall but a very high count of 46 fall vagrants was recorded in fall 1974. 64 of the 80 spring records from N CAL occurred on SE Farallon I.; the rest were along the immediate mainland coast. The situation is different in S CAL: well over half of the spring records are from desert oases. There are no known summering birds, but one on 18 Jul 1965 on SE Farallon I. was at a very late date. The records of wintering birds are: 26-27 Mar 1978 at Earp, S.Bn., 2 Jan-27 Apr 1978 at Watsonville, Mnt., and 17 Nov 1978-26 Feb 1979 at Riverside.

The graph below illustrates records from 1977-1979. There were 78 records during these three years (an average of 26 a year) and the patterns formed by the records are typical of the seasonal distribution of this species:

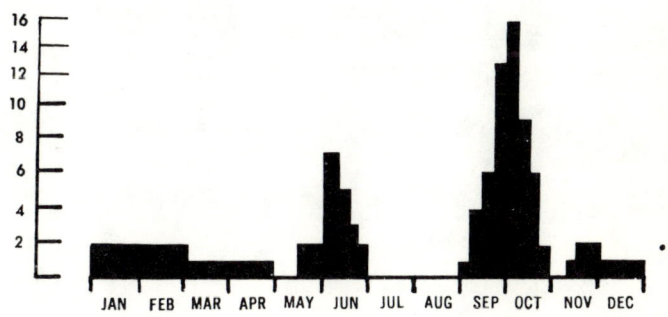

# CAPE MAY WARBLER

*Dendroica tigrina*

Breeds N North America. Winters Caribbean & Yucatan Pen., Mexico.

The Cape May Warbler nests on the West Coast only in NE B.C. It is a Rarity in ALASKA, WASH, and ORE, where there are a handful of spring and fall records. It has recently been averaging about 15 birds a year in CAL, two-thirds of which are fall vagrants. Normally less than 5 spring vagrants a year occur in CAL, but in 1977 a total of 15 were found in early Jun. There are three winter records from CAL. Population levels of Cape May Warbler may fluctuate dramatically (perhaps tied to outbreaks of spruce bud worm) and these fluctuations apparently affect the number of individuals present in any given year along the West Coast. Over half of the West Coast records away from the nesting area occurred during the four-year period between 1974-1977, when populations were said to be high in Canada.

**ALASKA** Three records: 1 Sep 1961† at Haines, SE ALASKA, one found 31 Mar 1970† at Fairbanks which probably died in fall 1969, and 6 Jun 1976† at Pt. Barrow. The latter bird provides a spectacular example of spring overshooting.

**WASHINGTON** One record: 21 Sep 1974 at Bellingham, Wha.

**OREGON** Two records, both at Malheur NWR, Har.: 9 Jun 1967 and 3 Jun 1978*.

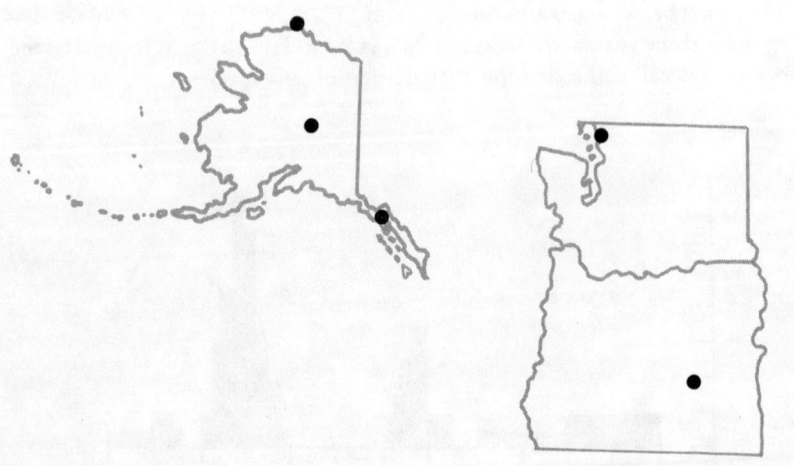

# CAPE MAY WARBLER

**CALIFORNIA**   121 records, recently averaging about 15 birds a year. 73 records were in N CAL and 48 were in S CAL. 81 were found during the fall and winter (42 in N CAL; 39 in S CAL). 40 were found during the spring (31 in N CAL; 9 in S CAL). The table below lists recent (1975-1979) per-year averages:

| CAL | | N CAL | | S CAL | |
|---|---|---|---|---|---|
| fall = 8.8 | | fall = 5.0 | | fall = 3.8 | |
| winter = 0.6 | | winter = 0.2 | | winter = 0.4 | |
| spring = 6.2 | | spring = 4.8 | | spring = 1.4 | |
| summer = 0.0 | | summer = 0.0 | | summer = 0.0 | |
| TOTAL = 15.6 | | TOTAL = 10.0 | | TOTAL = 5.6 | |

23 Feb 1980 at Goleta, S.Bb., CAL. *James M. Greaves.*

# CAPE MAY WARBLER

Most fall records are from vagrant "traps" along the immediate coast (including 14 on SE Farallon I.), though in S CAL coastal fall reports (22) are not too far ahead of fall records from the interior (15). Spring vagrants are mostly along the coast, but over half are from SE Farallon I. (22 records, including 8 in Jun 1977); outer Pt. Reyes Pen., Mrn., accounts for 6 additional spring records. Spring birds in S CAL are split between desert oases (5), the Channel Is. (2), and Pt. Loma, S.D. (2). Looking at annual totals from CAL, it is apparent that the numbers of vagrants increased substantially in 1974-1977, an increase not completely attributable to better coverage by more birders. Until 1974 there were only 24 records from CAL (a five-year average of only 3½ birds a year). In 1974 there were 19 records, in 1975 an additional 19, in 1976 a total of 13, and in 1977 a grand total of 24. While these years were years of rapid increases in coverage and expertise, an examination of SE Farallon I. data (which has had consistent coverage since 1968) reveals these high totals were related to more Cape May Warblers, not just more birders (some 63% of all Farallon records were in these 4 years). Only 8 Cape May Warblers were found in CAL in 1978 (and only 1 on SE Farallon I.), a substantial drop-off from previous years. It can be hypothesized that the high 1974-1977 totals were reflective of high breeding populations (perhaps tied to outbreaks of spruce bud worm) and that we can expect numbers of vagrants on the West Coast to fluctuate (perhaps cyclically) in years to come. There are four winter records: 1 Feb-18 Apr 1976 at Santa Cruz, 5-20 Mar 1978 at Finney Lake, Imp., 29 Dec 1979-Mar 1980 at Goleta, S.Bb., and 31 Jan 1980 at Pacific Grove, Mnt.

The graph below illustrates records from 1977-1979. These 3 years include one of high numbers (24 in 1977), one of low numbers (8 in 1978), and one of average proportions (14 in 1979). The patterns formed by the records are rather typical of the timing of records, though the sharp peak in early Jun is more reflective of spring 1977 than a "typical" pattern of occurrence:

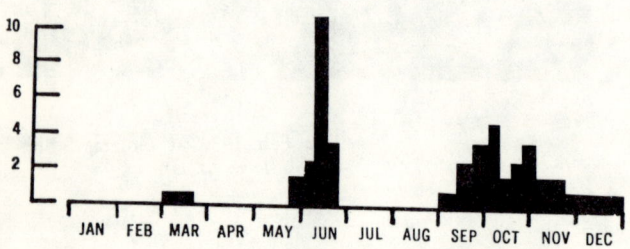

# BLACK-THROATED BLUE WARBLER

*Dendroica caerulescens*

Breeds E North America. Winters Caribbean to Central America.

The Black-throated Blue Warbler is a Rarity anywhere on the West Coast; it has been found only in CAL and ORE. In CAL it averages just over 20 birds a year, nearly all in the last week of Sep through Oct. There are 3 winter records from CAL and only 2 spring records. All of ORE's records are during Sep-Oct except for a single spring vagrant and a summering individual. Most CAL records are coastal, but all of ORE's records are from the interior.

CALIFORNIA   264 records, recently averaging about 21 a year. 120 records were in N CAL and 144 were in S CAL. 259 occurred during the fall (118 in N CAL; 141 in S CAL). The table below lists recent (1975-1979) per-year averages:

| CAL | | N CAL | | S CAL | |
|---|---|---|---|---|---|
| fall = | 20.6 | fall = | 10.6 | fall = | 10.0 |
| winter = | 0.2 | winter = | 0.2 | winter = | 0.0 |
| spring = | 0.4 | spring = | 0.0 | spring = | 0.4 |
| summer = | 0.0 | summer = | 0.0 | summer = | 0.0 |
| TOTAL = | 21.2 | TOTAL = | 10.8 | TOTAL = | 10.4 |

Jan 1975 at San Diego, S.D., CAL.
John Butler.

# BLACK-THROATED BLUE WARBLER

Nearly all of CAL's Black-throated Blue Warblers occur during the fall between 24 Sep-8 Nov. Annual totals were well over average in 1974 (55 records) and 1979 (42 records). The vast majority of birds in N CAL are along the immediate coast (including 34 on SE Farallon I. and 33 on outer Pt. Reyes Pen., Mrn.), but over a third of S CAL records are from the interior (especially desert oases in Mono, Inyo, and S.Bn. counties). A bird on 16-20 Dec 1974 at Morro Bay, S.L.O., might be considered a very late fall vagrant, but three records in CAL may be thought of as wintering birds: 25 Dec 1974-5 Jan 1975 at San Diego, 1 Jan-3 Mar 1975 at Portola Valley, S.M., and 12 Dec 1978-15 May 1979 at Auburn, Sac. For a bird with so many records in CAL, it is somewhat surprising that there are only two spring vagrants: 15-17 Jun 1976 on San Nicolas I., and 26 May 1979 at Scotty's Castle, Inyo.

The graph below illustrates records from 1977-1979. There were 77 records in these three years (an average of about 25 a year) and the pattern formed by the reports is rather typical of the distribution of CAL's Black-throated Blue Warblers:

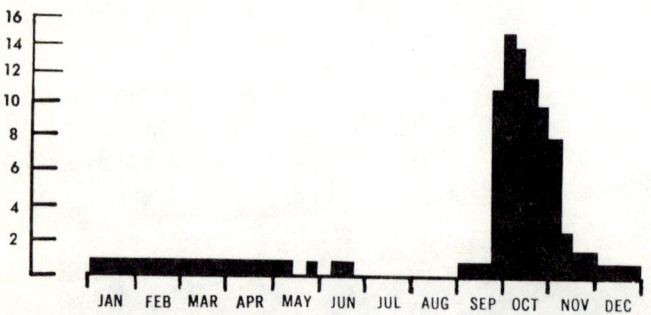

**OREGON** Nine records, seven during the fall and six of these at Malheur NWR, Har.: 9 Oct 1957† (C 61:55), 27 Sep 1960† (C 64:162), 24-26 Oct 1961 (A 82:497), 8 Oct 1969 (CB 2:93), 11 Oct 1970, and 7 Oct 1978*. The additional fall record was 12 Sep 1975 at Hart Mt., Lake. The single spring record was 2-4 May 1963 at Malheur NWR (A 82:497). A bird from 23 Jun-15 Jul 1979* at Still Creek Campground, Mt. Hood, Clk. was probably summering locally.

# BLACK-THROATED BLUE WARBLER

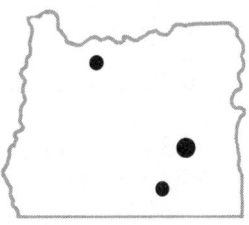

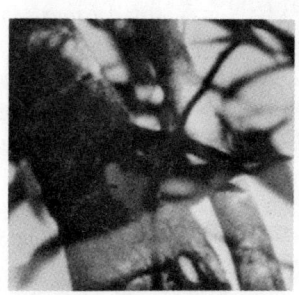

7 Oct 1978 at Malheur NWR, Har., ORE. 8th record. *Priscilla R. Summers.*

9 Oct 1979 at Gaviota, S.Bb., CAL. *James M. Greaves.*

# BLACK-THROATED GREEN WARBLER

*Dendroica virens*

Breeds C-N & E North America. Winters S Mexico to Panama & West Indes.

The Black-throated Green Warbler is very rare anywhere on the West Coast, but singing birds in summer in NE B.C. suggest it may nest there. Most records on the West Coast are fall vagrants in CAL, occurring later than many eastern warblers (most during Oct-early Nov). CAL has recently averaged about 15 birds a year; only 2 a year occur in spring but all of the 4 ORE records were of spring vagrants. There are two winter records from CAL.

**ALASKA** One record: 18 Jul 1941† at Idaho Inlet, Chichagof I., SE ALASKA (A 85:320).

**BRITISH COLUMBIA** One record: 25 Jun 1965† at Chetwynd, NE B.C. (CFN 80:115). This male was collected but several other males were heard singing in the area. This strongly suggests that Black-throated Green Warbler nests in NE B.C., perhaps regularly.

**OREGON** Four records: 13-14 Jun 1974 at the south jetty, Columbia R., Clt., another there 14 Jun 1974, 18 May 1975 at Malheur NWR, Har., and 10 May 1978 at Eugene, Lane (OB 4(2):39).

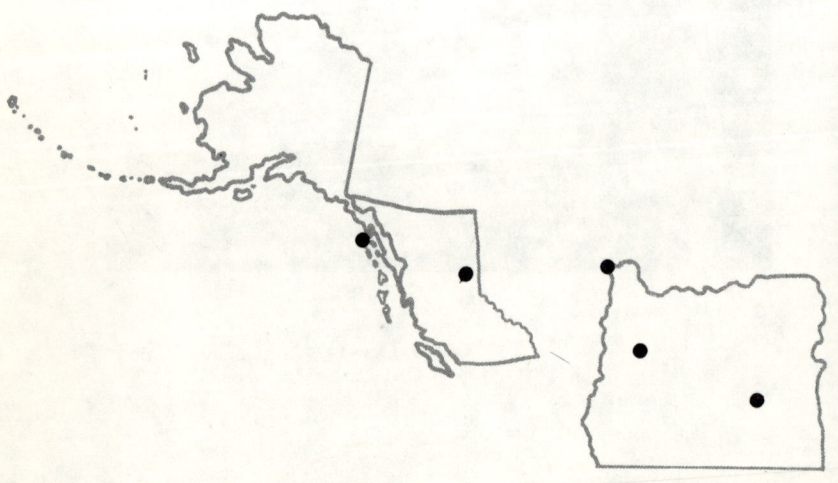

# BLACK-THROATED GREEN WARBLER

**CALIFORNIA**   130 records, recently averaging about 15 birds a year. 34 records were in N CAL and 96 in S CAL. 110 were during the fall (19 in N CAL; 91 in S CAL). Only 18 occurred during the spring (15 in N CAL; 3 in S CAL). The table below lists recent (1975-1979) per-year averages:

| CAL | | N CAL | | S CAL | |
|---|---|---|---|---|---|
| fall   = 12.8 | | fall   = 2.4 | | fall   = 10.4 | |
| winter = 0.4  | | winter = 0.0 | | winter = 0.4  | |
| spring = 2.0  | | spring = 1.4 | | spring = 0.6  | |
| summer = 0.0  | | summer = 0.0 | | summer = 0.0  | |
| TOTAL  = 15.2 | | TOTAL  = 3.6 | | TOTAL  = 11.6 | |

Nearly all of the N CAL fall records and about 70% of the S CAL fall records are from coastal locations (including offshore islands; there are 7 fall records from SE Farallon I.). But 30% of the S CAL fall records are from the interior (especially desert oases in Mono-Inyo-S.Bn. counties); the only N CAL interior record was 5 Nov 1977 at Red Bluff, Teh. Spring records are scarse: 13 of 15 from N CAL were recorded on SE Farallon I. (two in May-Jun 1911 were the first CAL records); the three spring records from S CAL are from the interior (22 May 1976 at Oasis, Mono, and 29 May 1977 at Deep Springs, Inyo) and the Channel Is. (26 May 1975 on Santa Barbara I.). A bird on 23 Dec 1976 at the north end, Salton Sea, Riv., is best considered a late fall migrant, but two records are best viewed as winter records: 16 Dec 1978-6 Jan 1979 at Imperial Beach, S.D., and 22 Dec 1978-24 Feb 1979 at Goleta, S.Bb.

The graph below illustrates records in 1977-1979. There were 44 records during these three years (an average of about 15 a year) and the pattern of distribution is about typical for this species: it is a late fall vagrant, occurring mostly in Oct-early Nov (a pattern later than that for most eastern warblers). Both winter records occurred during these years; winter records in CAL are extraordinary and not to be expected annually:

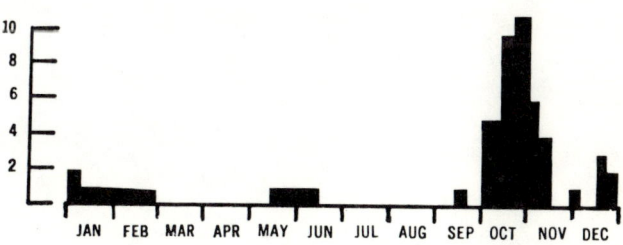

# BLACK-THROATED GREEN WARBLER

I.D. The Black-throated Green Warbler is illustrated in the standard American guides. Observers along the West Coast need to separate it from the similar Townsend's Warbler *D. townsendi;* this can be a confusing proposition during the fall. The back of both birds is green (somewhat brighter on Black-throated Green) but even the dullest immature female Townsend's Warbler will show a more prominent ear-patch and have a yellow wash across the throat and upper breast. Immature female Black-throated Green is dingy below with a yellow throat but a buffy (not yellow) wash across upper breast; the immature male has a blotchy black breastband and does not have yellow on the breast below the breastband. An excellent characteristic to note is the yellow vent (between the legs) of Black-throated Green Warbler (lacking in Townsend's). Several Townsend's X Hermit Warbler *D. occidentalis* hybrids are encountered each year in CAL and can be easily confused with Black-throated Green Warbler. These hybrids usually have bright green backs and mostly unmarked yellow faces (with only a small darkish ear-patch, even less conspicuous than many Black-throated Greens). The hybrid is separated from Black-throated Green Warbler by the yellow on the face extending onto the forehead and by the lack of a yellow vent.

# GOLDEN-CHEEKED WARBLER

*Dendroica chrysoparia*

Breeds Edwards Plateau of S-C Texas. Winters S Mexico to Nicaragua.

The Golden-cheeked Warbler has a very small population restricted to a local breeding area in Texas. The single West Coast record — a fall vagrant on SE Farallon I., CAL — is one of only two North American records away from Texas (the other was found in Florida). The Golden-cheeked Warbler is one of the most spectacularly rare and unexpected species ever to be found on the West Coast.

**CALIFORNIA** One record: 9 Sep 1971† on SE Farallon I. (A 91:411).

I.D. The Golden-cheeked Warbler can be difficult to separate from Black-throated Green Warbler *D. virens* during the fall. Both species have a green back and crown, a yellow face with an indistinct ear-patch, and dingy underparts (males with blotchy black breastband). Golden-cheeked tends to have the green back streaked with black (somewhat like the pattern on the back of fall Blackpoll Warbler *D. striata*) and often shows extensive black on the forehead. It also lacks the yellow vent of Black-throated Green Warbler.

# CERULEAN WARBLER

*Dendroica cerulea*

Breeds SE U.S. Winters W South America.

The Cerulean Warbler has been found on the West Coast only in CAL, where there are 7 records of fall vagrants and 2 of spring vagrants.

**CALIFORNIA** Nine records, seven during the fall: 1 Oct 1947† at the south end, Salton Sea, Imp. (C 49:245), 26 Oct 1967 at Pt. Loma, S.D., 2-5 Sep 1976* at Fairhaven, Hmb., 15-17 Oct 1978 at Pt. Reyes NS, Mrn., 22 Oct 1978 at Pt. Loma, 27 Oct 1978 at the Carmel R. mouth, Mnt., and 25 Oct 1979 at the Carmel R. mouth. The two spring records are: 27 May 1974* at Oasis, Mono, and 26-27 May 1979 at Pt. Loma.

I.D. The Cerulean Warbler can be a confusing species to encounter during the fall and several CAL records were originally misidentified as other eastern species. Cerulean Warbler is a small, short-tailed warbler, usually very active and often preferring the uppermost branches. Immatures of either sex are distinctive and unlike other warblers. The immature male has two bold white wingbars, a conspicuous white supercilium, and thin dark flank streaks on otherwise white underparts (sometimes washed with yellow across the vent). From below the effect is not unlike a female Black-and-white Warbler acting very strangely, but a brief view of the upperparts will dispel this impression. The upperparts

## CERULEAN WARBLER

are grayish-blue (some birds are brighter blue) and narrowly streaked with black on the lower back and rump. Many young males will show a black bar extending from the shoulder to the sides of the breast, looking like a partial breast collar at some angles. The immature female is very different, though the white wingbars and a supercilium are still very conspicous marks. The supercilium and all of the underparts (extending up to the lower face and behind the dingy ear-patch) are yellow (can be bright in some specimens). There are fine indistinct streaks on the flanks. The upperparts are rather bright green, with a blue-green crown and a bluish rump and tail.

15 Oct 1978 at Pt. Reyes NS, Mrn., CAL. 5th record. *Steve Wilson (left); Jeri Langham (right).*

# BLACKBURNIAN WARBLER

*Dendroica fusca*

Breeds C-N & E North America. Winters Central America to W South America.

The Blackburnian Warbler is very rare anywhere on the West Coast. It is most often recorded as a fall vagrant in coastal CAL, where the recent average was about 16 birds a fall. There are only a few spring records in CAL and one which could have summered. Three spring-summer birds in B.C. were probably non-breeders wandering west of the nearest breeding areas (local population in C Alberta).

**BRITISH COLUMBIA** Three records: 9 Jul 1930† at Thorson's Landing, Peace R. district, NE B.C., 25 Aug 1960 at Fleetwood, and 12-14 May 1974 at Kerrisdale.

**WASHINGTON** One record: 10 Sep 1979 at Ocean Shores, G.H. This species is considered hypothetical on the state list because, though the bird was very well described, it was seen by only a single observer.

10 Oct 1978 at Pt. Reyes NS, Mrn., CAL. *Al Ghiorso.*

# BLACKBURNIAN WARBLER

**CALIFORNIA**  166 records, recently averaging about 18 birds a year. 90 records were in N CAL and 84 in S CAL. 153 (some 92%) were found during the fall (83 in N CAL; 79 in S CAL). There are only 12 spring records (7 in N CAL; 5 in S CAL). There are no winter records. The table below lists recent (1975-1979) per-year averages:

| CAL | | | N CAL | | | S CAL | | |
|---|---|---|---|---|---|---|---|---|
| fall | = | 16.4 | fall | = | 10.0 | fall | = | 6.4 |
| winter | = | 0.0 | winter | = | 0.0 | winter | = | 0.0 |
| spring | = | 1.8 | spring | = | 0.8 | spring | = | 1.0 |
| summer | = | 0.0 | summer | = | 0.0 | summer | = | 0.0 |
| TOTAL | = | 18.2 | TOTAL | = | 10.8 | TOTAL | = | 7.4 |

The vast majority of CAL records are of fall vagrants and nearly all of these are from vagrant "traps" along the immediate coast (including 29 records from SE Farallon I.). Even S CAL, which has numerous vagrant "traps" in the eastern desert regions, has less than 20% (14 records) from the interior. Autumns with high totals of Blackburnian Warblers were 1974 (24 records) and 1979 (23 records). There are very few spring records. In N CAL, 5 of the 7 spring records are from SE Farallon I. (the two exceptions were at Pt. Reyes NS, Mrn.: 6 May 1974 and 12 Jun 1976). The five S CAL spring records were on the Channel Is. (26-27 May 1975 and another 29 May 1979 on Santa Barbara I. and 17 Jun 1976 on San Nicolas I.) and in E CAL (26 May 1976 at Oasis, Mono, and 31 May 1976 at Deep Springs, Inyo). A male seen 6 Aug 1972 at Buck's Lake, Plu., was in the mountains and at a very early date for a fall migrant; it could well have summered locally and is best considered a summer record.

The graph below illustrates records from 1977-1979. The 54 records during these three years were just about the average number (18 a year) and the pattern formed by the timing of the records is rather typical of the distribution of Blackburnian Warblers, which peak in early Oct:

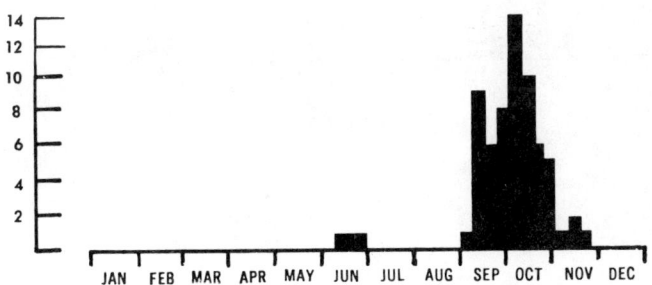

# YELLOW-THROATED WARBLER

*Dendroica dominica*

Breeds SE U.S. Winters extreme SE U.S., S Mexico to Central America & West Indes.

The Yellow-throated Warbler has been found on the West Coast only in CAL, where there are a handful of records of spring and fall vagrants. Most of those identified to race have been the white-lored western race *D. d. albilora*, but there is a fall records of the yellow-lored eastern race *D. d. dominica*.

**CALIFORNIA** 30 records (through spring 1980) graphed below. Records are fairly evenly split between spring (17) and fall (13). Areas with multiple records are the San Diego area (7, including 4 on Pt. Loma), coastal Santa Barbara Co. (3), the Carmel R. mouth, Mnt. (2), SE Farallon I. (3), Pt. Reyes NS, Mrn. (2), and the Deep Springs-Oasis-Death Valley loop in Inyo-Mono counties (7). The only inland record away from the latter area was on 2 Sep 1978 at Dog I., Teh, in the Central Valley, N CAL. The spring distribution of records is interesting since it is very different from most eastern warblers. Most eastern warblers occur in late May-mid-Jun (and 10 Yellow-throated Warblers occurred then) but there 4 early spring records — 23-25 Apr 1974* at San Diego, 18 Apr 1979 at Pt. Loma, 29 Apr 1979 at Encinitas, S.D., and 12 May 1979 at Santa Monica, L.A. — and two fairly late spring records — 8 Jul 1969 on SE Farallon I. and 23 Jun-3 Jul 1979 at Pt. Reyes NS.

About 20 birds have been identified in hand or in the field as the western race *D. d. albilora*. A bird banded and photographed which was present from 15 Oct-5 Nov 1969 on Pt. Loma was identified as the eastern race *D. d. dominica* (CB 3:17).

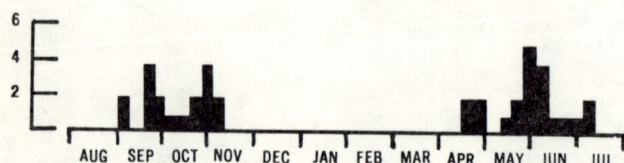

# YELLOW-THROATED WARBLER

5 Sep 1976 at Pt. Reyes NS, Mrn., CAL. *Al Ghiorso.*

25 Oct 1979 at Gaviota, S.Bb., CAL. *James M. Greaves.*

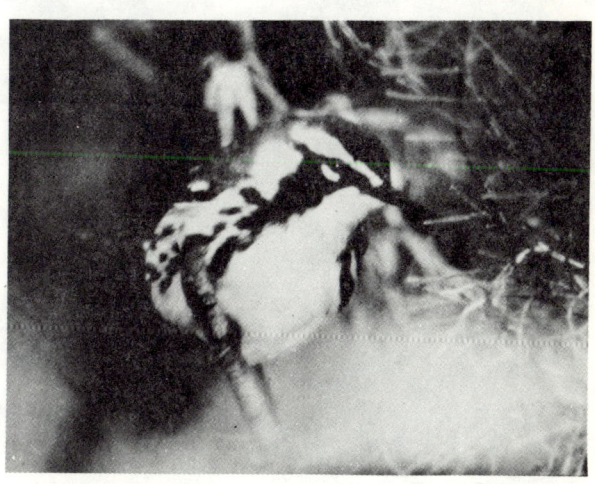

# GRACE'S WARBLER

*Dendroica graciae*

Breeds SW U.S. to Nicaragua. U.S. populations winter from N Mexico to Central America.

The Grace's Warbler in the United States is thought of as a summer bird of the mountains of S Utah, SW Colorado, E Arizona, and W New Mexico, but a small number breed on Charleston Mt., Nevada, just across the border from CAL. Ten Grace's Warblers have reached CAL. The spring birds have been singing males in S CAL mountains, probably spring overshoots which found apparently suitable habitat and were defending territory. It could possibly nest in the future if a female can be attracted. The fall records are of vagrants along the coast and there are two records of wintering birds in coastal Santa Barbara Co.

**CALIFORNIA** Ten records, three of which were singing males during the spring-summer in what could be suitable breeding habitat: 30 May 1974 on Clark Mt., S.Bn. (WB 5:50), 15 Jun-3 Jul 1975* at Arrastre Creek, S.Bn., and 21 May 1977* on Clark Mt. 5 records are of fall vagrants: 29 Oct 1966 at San Diego, 8 Sep 1968 at San Diego (both CB 1:77), 20-22 Sep 1977* at Imperial Beach, S.D., 24-25 Sep 1977 at Imperial Beach, and 30 Sep 1979 near Malibu, L.A. The two winter records were in coastal Santa Barbara Co.: 6 Jan-2 Apr 1980 at Santa Barbara and 24 Feb-11 Apr 1980 at Carpinteria.

8 Sep 1968 at Pt. Loma, S.D., CAL. 2nd record. *Alan M. Craig.*

# CHESTNUT-SIDED WARBLER

*Dendroica pensylvanica*

Breeds C-N & E North America. Winters Central America.

The Chestnut-sided Warbler is a rare bird anywhere on the West Coast. Singing birds in summer have been found in the interior of B.C. and it was thought to have nested there in the past; the westernmost regular breeding area is central Alberta and this species may occasionally wander west in summer and even nest irregularly in B.C. Chestnut-sided Warbler is considered a Rarity in WASH and ORE, but it has recently averaged over 35 birds a year in CAL. Most birds in CAL are fall vagrants, but a small number of spring vagrants are found annually and there are both winter and summer reports.

**BRITISH COLUMBIA**   Said to have nested at Tupper Creek in NE B.C. in 1944 (CEN 86:390) but hard evidence is lacking. 5 recent records, two of which were singing males in the interior: 22 Jun 1971 at Red Pass, Mt. Robson PP, and 21 Jun 1972 at Prince George. The 3 additional records were vagrants along the coast: 27 Jul 1966 at Pt. Grey, Vancouver, 29 Sep 1974 at Reifel refuge, Vancouver, and 19-21 Jun 1979 at Vancouver.

**WASHINGTON**   Three records, all spring vagrants: 18 Jun 1960† at Columbia NWR, near Othello, Grn. (C 72:246), 19 Jun 1975 at Leavenworth, Che., and 11 Jun 1977 at Palouse Falls SP, Frk. (M 59:102).

**OREGON**   11 records, graphed below. 6 birds were spring vagrants: 3 at Malheur NWR, Har., 2 at the banding station on Hart Mt., Lake, and 2 from the coast (12-17 Jun 1974* at Coos Head, Coos, and 31 May 1979* at Florence, Lane). All three fall vagrant records are from Malheur NWR. Two additional records are hard to label: 7 Jul 1979⁴ at Ochoco Creek Campground, Crk., and 19 Aug 1979 at Roseburg, Dgl. They could be of a very late spring vagrant and a very early fall vagrant, but both birds were in forested areas in the interior and at dates which could easily be those of birds which were summering locally.

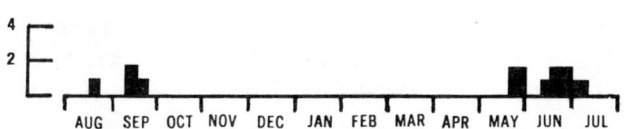

# CHESTNUT-SIDED WARBLER

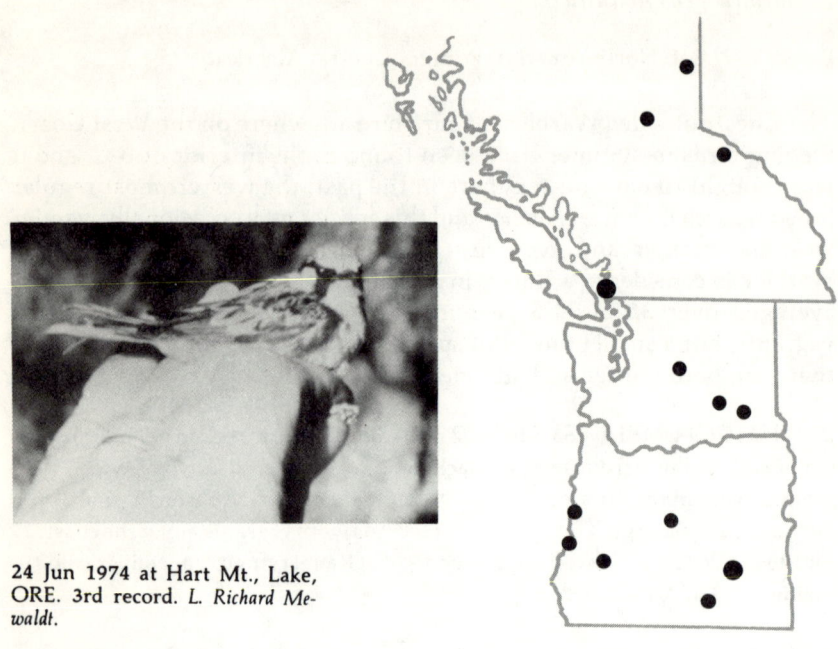

24 Jun 1974 at Hart Mt., Lake, ORE. 3rd record. *L. Richard Mewaldt.*

**CALIFORNIA** 312 records, recently averaging about 36 birds a year. 206 records were in N CAL and 106 were in S CAL. 251 were during the fall (170 in N CAL; 81 in S CAL). 58 were during the spring (33 in N CAL; 25 in S CAL). The table below lists recent (1975-1979) per-year averages:

| CAL | | N CAL | | S CAL | |
|---|---|---|---|---|---|
| fall = | 28.8 | fall = | 20.6 | fall = | 8.2 |
| winter = | 0.2 | winter = | 0.2 | winter = | 0.0 |
| spring = | 7.0 | spring = | 3.8 | spring = | 3.2 |
| summer = | 0.4 | summer = | 0.4 | summer = | 0.0 |
| TOTAL = | 36.2 | TOTAL = | 25.0 | TOTAL = | 11.4 |

# CHESTNUT-SIDED WARBLER

As the table indicates, fall vagrants make up the bulk of CAL records. Most fall birds are found at vagrant "traps" along the coast (including offshore islands; there are 64 fall records from SE Farallon I.), but about 35% of fall birds in S CAL are from interior locations, especially desert oases in E CAL. In 1974, 55 Chestnut-sided Warblers were found during the fall — well over the less-than-30 a fall average. 1974 has been the only fall which brought exceptional numbers of this species to CAL. The distribution of spring records is sharply divided: in N CAL all spring vagrants have been along the immediate coast (including 19 from SE Farallon I.), but in S CAL some 80% (20 of 25 records) of the birds have been found at desert oases in E CAL (especially the Deep Springs-Oasis-Death Valley loop in Mono-Inyo counties). There are a few records of very late fall migrants in CAL (an example is 18 Dec 1979 at the south end, Salton Sea, Imp.), but a bird from 25 Nov 1976-3 Jan 1977 at the Carmel R. mouth, Mnt. is best considered a winter record. 3 records from the interior of N CAL are difficult to label: 25 Jun 1976 at Convict Lake, Mono, 7 Jul 1976 at Silver King Creek, Alp., and 19 Aug 1979 at Lundy Canyon, Mono. All were along the east edge of the Sierra and could refer to late spring and early fall vagrants. I have chosen to consider the first bird as a spring vagrant, but the latter two birds, present in Jul-Aug in forested locations in the mountains, could well have summered locally and are listed as summer records in the tables above.

The graph below illustrates records from 1977-1979. There were 105 records during these three years (an average of 35 a year) and the pattern of occurrence shown in these years is rather typical of the timing of Chestnut-sided Warblers in CAL, except that the winter record noted above occurred during these years and winter birds are extraordinary in CAL:

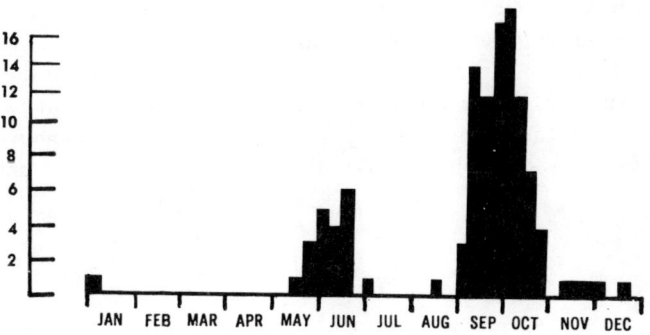

# BAY-BREASTED WARBLER

*Dendroica castanea*

Breeds N North America. Winters NW South America.

The Bay-breasted Warbler nests in NE B.C. It is very rare anywhere on the West Coast away from B.C. It has recently averaged just over 15 birds a year in CAL and the pattern of records in that state has changed during the last decade. Until 1975, most CAL records were of fall vagrants and spring birds were extremely scarce. But from 1975-1979 there have been nearly as many spring birds (37) as those during the fall (44). Concurrent with this development was a substantial increase in numbers in 1974-1977 (averaging over 20 birds a year in those four years), followed by a reduction to more normal figures in 1978-79. Indeed, if those productive years are not included, the most recent 5-year average of Bay-breasted Warbler in CAL would be about 6 birds a year. Cape May Warbler *D. tigrina* also showed increases in 1974-1977 not related to a simple increase in birdwatchers; it may well be that the numbers of vagrants fluctuate periodically in response to population levels on the breeding ground. It has been hypothesized that factors such as a spruce bud worm outbreak in Canada will greatly increase numbers of certain warblers and these population peaks can be noted at distant points by comparing annual totals of vagrants.

**ALASKA** One record: 23 May 1951 at College, near Fairbanks.

**OREGON** Four records: 6 Jul 1963† at upper Klammath Lake, Klm. (C 66:76), 7 Jun 1976 at Malheur NWR, Har., 27 Jun 1976* at Howard Prairie Res., Jck., and 13-22 Aug 1976 at Crescent Creek Campground, Klm. Three of these records occurred in late Jun-mid-Aug; they could refer to late spring or early fall vagrants, but were recorded at locations in the interior during times which could indicate summering individuals. Where do spring vagrants on the West Coast eventually stop? They are hopelessly misoriented and well behind the normal migration schedule. It may well be that some simply stop at what passes for appropriate habitat and summer locally. There now seems to be enough summer reports of eastern warblers in the West to suggest this does happen from time to time.

# BAY-BREASTED WARBLER

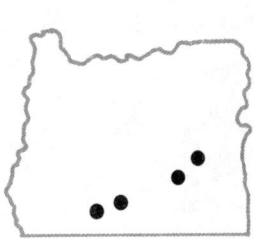

**CALIFORNIA**  127 records, recently averaging about 16 birds a year. 74 records were in N CAL and 53 in S CAL. 75 occurred during the fall (38 in N CAL; 37 in S CAL). 52 occurred during the spring (36 in N CAL; 16 in S CAL). The table below lists recent (1975-1979) per-year averages:

| CAL | | N CAL | | S CAL | |
|---|---|---|---|---|---|
| fall | = 8.8 | fall | = 5.0 | fall | = 3.8 |
| winter | = 0.0 | winter | = 0.0 | winter | = 0.0 |
| spring | = 7.4 | spring | = 5.2 | spring | = 2.2 |
| summer | = 0.0 | summer | = 0.0 | summer | = 0.0 |
| TOTAL | = 16.2 | TOTAL | = 10.2 | TOTAL | = 6.0 |

Most fall records are from vagrant "traps" along the immediate coast. In N CAL all fall records are coastal (including 14 from SE Farallon I.), except for one found dead on 31 Oct 1977 at Sacramento. About 30% of S CAL fall records are from desert oases or other interior locations. The general discussion above focuses on the shift in patterns in CAL, with spring records nearly equalling fall records during very recent times, and the sharp peak in numbers during the mid-1970s. As suggested, population levels of Bay-breasted Warbler may be cyclical. Thus the West Coast receives high numbers of vagrants during some years and few birds during other periods. There are no winter records in CAL; late birds (such as 12 Dec 1976 at the Carmel R. mouth, Mnt.) are best treated as late fall vagrants. The pattern of spring records sharply differs between north and south: in N CAL nearly all spring vagrants are coastal (including 20 records, some 55%, from SE Farallon I.), with the only exception being a bird at Grenada, Sis., in Jun 1978; in S CAL nine of the 16 spring records are from interior points, especially the Deep Springs-Oasis-Death Valley loop in Inyo-Mono counties.

# BAY-BREASTED WARBLER

The graph below illustrates records from 1977-1979. There were 46 Bay-breasted Warblers during these three years (an average of about 15 a year) and the pattern shown by the timing of these reports is rather typical of the distribution of this species in CAL:

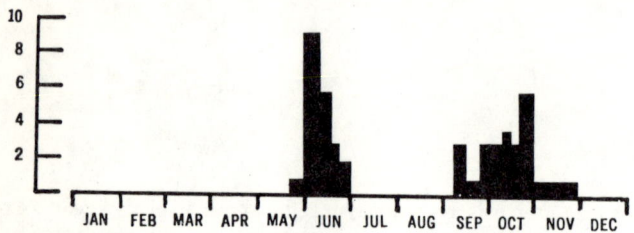

17 Jun 1977 at Pt. Reyes NS, Mrn., CAL. *Al Ghiorso.*

I.D. The fall Bay-breasted Warbler can be difficult to separate from Blackpoll Warbler *D. striata* (see the discussion under that species). It differs in having 1) paler buffier-yellow throat and breast, without faint breast streaking, 2) a pinkish-buff (or even chestnut) wash to the flanks, sometimes extending onto the undertail coverts but often contrasting with white undertail coverts, 3) warmer yellow-green upperparts, and 4) less contrasting face pattern. Most (but not all) have black legs.

# BLACKPOLL WARBLER

*Dendroica striata*

Breeds N North America. Winters N & W South America.

The Blackpoll Warbler nests across much of ALASKA and N B.C., but the regular migration routes are entirely east of the Rockies; indeed, most move during the fall to NE North America and fly across the Atlantic to South America (see *Bird-Banding* 34:107). The first record of the Blackpoll Warbler south of B.C. on the West Coast was not recorded until 1961, but since that time observers working vagrant "traps" along the immediate coast of CAL have found it in numbers during the fall; CAL has recently averaged 110 birds a fall. Spring birds make up less than 5% of CAL records (most from offshore islands or desert oases). It is still very rare in ORE and WASH (in contrast to the numbers in CAL), with records split between spring and fall. McCaskie (1970) discussed the 238 records on the West Coast south of B.C. through 1969. He suggested several hypotheses which could account for the numbers of fall vagrants; "mirror image" misorientation of immatures and a large population size were advanced as the most credible. The 1176 records during the 1970s show very much the same pattern of occurrence as those in the 1960s and McCaskie's discussion remains the best explanation of the status of Blackpoll Warbler in CAL. Numbers of Blackpoll Warblers fluctuate annually along the West Coast; exceptionally high numbers occurred in 1974 (by far the highest numbers), 1975, and 1979.

**WASHINGTON** One record: 20 Sep 1976 at Ocean Shores, G.H. This species is considered hypothetical on the state list because, though the bird was well-described, it was seen by only a single observer.

**OREGON** Seven records, four from the fall: 7 Sep 1967† at Malheur NWR, Har., 16 Sep 1974 at Cape Blanco, Cur., 12 Sep 1975 at Malheur NWR, and 6-8 Sep 1979 at Fields, Har. There are two records of spring vagrants — 29 May 1974* at Malheur NWR, and 1 Jun 1977* at Hart Mt., Lake — and a bird inland on 28-29 Jun 1977 at Summit Spring, Jef., which could have been either a late spring vagrant or attempting to summer locally.

# BLACKPOLL WARBLER

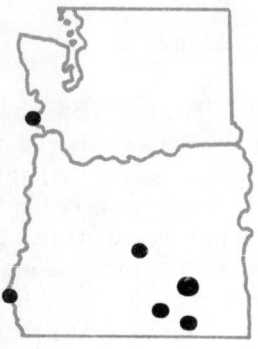

29 May 1974 at Malheur NWR, Har., ORE. 2nd record. *C. F. Zeillemaker.*

**CALIFORNIA** Approximately 1405 records, recently averaging about 120 birds a year. 879 records were in N CAL and 526 were in S CAL. 1333 were recorded during the fall (833 in N CAL; 500 in S CAL). 72 were found during the spring (46 in N CAL; 26 in S CAL). The table below lists recent (1975-1979) per-year averages:

| CAL | | N CAL | | S CAL | |
|---|---|---|---|---|---|
| fall = | 110.0 | fall = | 68.2 | fall = | 41.8 |
| winter = | 0.0 | winter = | 0.0 | winter = | 0.0 |
| spring = | 7.8 | spring = | 4.2 | spring = | 3.6 |
| summer = | 0.0 | summer = | 0.0 | summer = | 0.0 |
| TOTAL = | 117.8 | TOTAL = | 72.4 | TOTAL = | 45.4 |

As the table suggests, about 95% of the CAL records occurred during the fall. The vast majority of these are from the immediate coast (including offshore islands — SE Farallon has 293 records, about 35% of the N CAL total). Only in S CAL are there any considerable numbers from the interior — about 9% of fall reports — and these are mostly from desert oases in Mono-Inyo-S.Bn. counties. N CAL interior records are very scarce and there is only one from the mountains (17 Sep 1977 at Christmas Valley, S Lake Tahoe, E.D.) and but three from the Great Basin, all at Honey Lake, Las.: 23 Sep 1961 (only days after the first CAL record — 15 Sep 1961† at Mahogany Flats, Inyo), 12 Sep 1975, and 10 Sep 1976. Numbers

# BLACKPOLL WARBLER

of fall vagrants fluctuate widely and there only a few years which have recorded the "average" number. Very high counts were in 1974 (249), 1975 (163), and 1979 (155); in contrast only 51 were reported in the fall of 1978. There are an average of 8 spring birds a year: those in N CAL tend to be recorded on SE Farallon I. (32 records, some 78% of the N CAL total), while those in S CAL are most often found at desert oases in the Deep Springs-Oasis-Death Valley area (about 57% of the S CAL spring total). Two SE Farallon I. records are difficult to label: 1-16 Aug 1969 and 8-12 Aug 1973. Both were spring-plumaged females that were banded and both may have been extremely late spring vagrants. There are no known summering or winter records; the latest fall record is 22 Nov 1979 at Pt. Loma, S.D. Nearly all banded birds or specimens which have been aged are of immatures during the fall.

The graph below illustrates records in 1977. There were 117 records during 1977 and it is chosen as a "typical" year. It is interesting to compare this graph with that published by McCaskie (1970): there is very little difference in the timing of records. 50% of the 1961-1969 records occurred during the two weeks between 24 Sep-8 Oct. In 1977, about 45% of the records were found during these same two weeks. The only anomaly about 1977 was the spring peak; it typically occurs in early Jun, not late Jun:

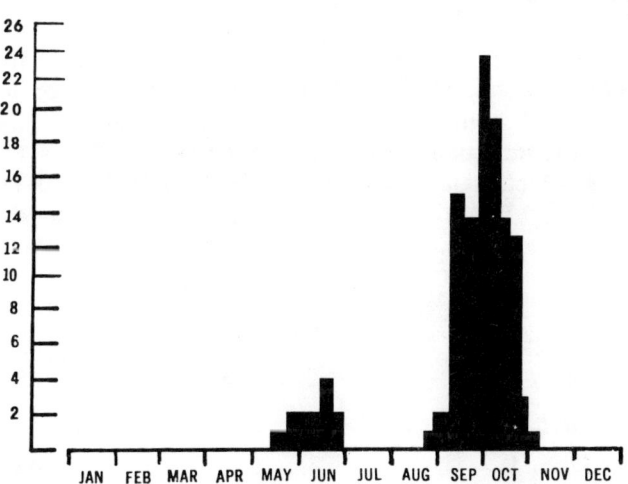

# BLACKPOLL WARBLER

25 Sep 1977 at Pt. Reyes NS, Mrn., CAL. *Al Ghiorso.*

I.D. The Blackpoll Warbler is in drab plumage during the fall, but it is *the* vagrant warbler to learn and serves as a point of comparison for other species (it is the commonest coastal fall vagrant in Sep). It is olivaceous-green above with two bold white wingbars and fine, but distinct, back streaks. The throat and breast are washed yellow, sometimes bright, sometimes dull. Almost always there are fine breast streaks. The belly and undertail coverts are gleaming white and the tail shows conspicuous white spots from below and in flight. A dark line extends from the bill through the eye and onto the ear-coverts, setting off a well-marked supercilium. This face pattern is characteristic of the species and helps to distinguish it from Bay-breasted *D. castanea* and Pine Warbler *D. pinus* (see the discussions under those species for additional separating characteristics). Leg color is not reliable; they are most often a pale pink or flesh, but can be quite dark brown and may look blackish in the field. Blackpoll Warbler lacks any trace of a buffy wash to the breast or flanks. For more information see McCaskie, DeBenedictis, Erickson, & Morlan (1979, p. 66).

# PINE WARBLER

*Dendroica pinus*

Breeds E North America, N West Indes. Winters SE U.S., West Indes, Central America.

The Pine Warbler has been found on the West Coast only in CAL, where there are a handful of fall vagrant records and a single record of a wintering individual. All fall birds were at vagrant "traps" along the coast (including SE Farallon I.), but the wintering bird was at an obscure desert location.

**CALIFORNIA** Ten records, nine from the fall: 22 Oct 1966† at Imperial Beach, S.D., 28 Oct 1967 at Pt. Loma, S.D., 5 Oct 1970 at Pt. Reyes NS, Mrn., 18 Sep 1971 at Imperial Beach, 21 Sep 1973* on SE Farallon I., 19 Oct 1974 on SE Farallon I., 13-16 Oct 1976* at Pt. Loma, 15 Oct 1979 at Gaviota, S.Bb., and 16 Oct 1979 on SE Farallon I. Note that six of the records occurred during the two weeks between 13-28 Oct. The sole winter record was 4-26 Feb 1978 at Regina, Imp.

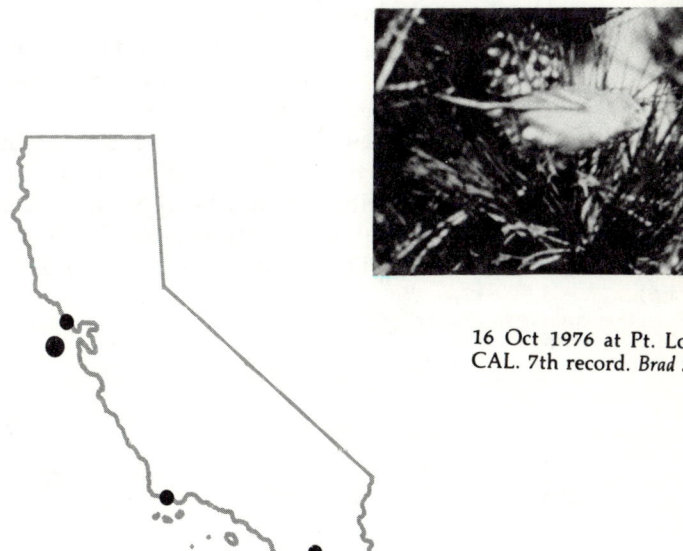

16 Oct 1976 at Pt. Loma, S.D., CAL. 7th record. *Brad Schram*.

# PINE WARBLER

I.D. The Pine Warbler is often confused during the fall with Blackpoll Warbler *D. striata* and a number of CAL reports of Pine Warbler have proved to be Blackpoll Warblers with dark legs and only faint back streaks. Fall Pine Warblers differ considerably between the sexes, yet neither the immature male nor immature female closely resembles Blackpoll Warbler, despite the standard field guides' suggestions to the contrary. The immature male is a bright, deep yellow on the throat and breast. The greenish upperparts, especially the back, are washed with brown. Fall Blackpoll are lemon-yellow on the throat and breast and the upperparts are olivaceous green. The streaks on the breast of Pine Warbler are coarser and become small spots on the sides, unlike the fine gray breast streaks of Blackpoll, but the gleaming white belly, undertail coverts, and tail spots are similar in both birds (lack of buffy-pink wash to flanks helps separate Pine from Bay-breasted Warbler *D. castanea* in the fall). Finally, Pine Warbler does not have the dark eyeline look of Blackpoll Warbler; instead there is a yellowish supercilium and eyering, which combine with pale lores and a pale half-collar extending up behind the darker ear-coverts to produce a face pattern very unlike Blackpoll Warbler. The immature female is even more distinctive, lacking most of the yellow color of the male. It is a dingy brown above and a paler buffy brown below, often blotchy on the breast. Any yellow color is reduced to a pale wash on the breast. The face pattern is as described for the male, showing a pale buffy spot on the lores, a buffy supercilium and indistinct eyering, and a pale half-collar (reminiscent of Prairie Warbler *D. discolor*). The legs of both sexes are black. In sum, the fall Pine Warbler is a large, stocky, short-tailed warbler with two conspicuous wingbars and a characteristic face pattern and is either olive-brown above and deep yellow on the breast or dingy brown above, paler buffy-brown below. For more information see McCaskie, DeBenedictis, Erickson & Morlan (1979, p. 66).

# PRAIRIE WARBLER

*Dendroica discolor*

Breeds E U.S. Winters West Indes, E Central America.

The Prairie Warbler has been found on the West Coast only in CAL. There it is a very rare fall vagrant, averaging about 9 birds a fall. Nearly all of the fall records are from the immediate coast. Spring birds are almost unknown and there is but one summer record.

**CALIFORNIA** 104 records, recently averaging 9 birds a year. 59 records are from N CAL and 45 from S CAL. 101 records (some 97%) were during the fall (58 in N CAL; 43 in S CAL). There are only two spring records and an additional bird which was thought to summer locally. The table below lists recent (1975-1979) per-year averages:

| CAL | | N CAL | | S CAL | |
|---|---|---|---|---|---|
| fall    | = 8.6 | fall    | = 6.0 | fall    | = 2.6 |
| winter  | = 0.0 | winter  | = 0.0 | winter  | = 0.0 |
| spring  | = 0.2 | spring  | = 0.0 | spring  | = 0.2 |
| summer  | = 0.2 | summer  | = 0.0 | summer  | = 0.2 |
| TOTAL   | = 9.0 | TOTAL   | = 6.0 | TOTAL   | = 3.0 |

Nearly all of the fall records are from the immediate coast (including offshore islands; there are 13 records from SE Farallon I.); the only exceptions were birds inland on 11-28 Nov 1976 at Scotty's Castle, Inyo, 15-16 Oct 1977 at Oasis, Mono, 24 Oct-2 Nov 1977 at the south end, Salton Sea, Imp., and 26 Nov-11 Dec 1977 at Corcoran, Kng. Autumns with higher than average numbers of Prairie Warblers were 1974 (12), 1977 (11), and 1979 (17). There is only one record of a clear spring vagrant — 29 May 1976 at Furnace Creek, Inyo — but a bird on 19 Jul 1973 at Pacific Grove, Mnt., is best treated as a very late spring vagrant. A male present 2 Jun to at least 1 Jul 1978 at Tollhouse Springs, Inyo, in the White Mtns., was apparently attempting to summer; the story of this bird is very unusual. Presumably setting up territory but attracting no female Prairie Warbler, it was observed singing, skirmishing violently with a female Black-throated Gray Warbler *D. nigrescens* (attempted copulation or simply agression? Whichever, the female Black-throated Gray was left dazed and bloody), and on 1 Jul was found carrying food and feeding, of all things, two fledgling Lesser Goldfinch *Carduelis psaltria* (*Western Tanager* 46 (7):5).

# PRAIRIE WARBLER

The graph below illustrates records of Prairie Warbler in 1976-1979. There were 43 records during these four years (an average of about 11 a year); four years (instead of the usual three) are included on the graph since the timing of vagrants has varied erratically during some recent years and the longer period of records better illustrates the timing of this species in CAL. One spring and one summer record occurred in these years; such records are extraordinary:

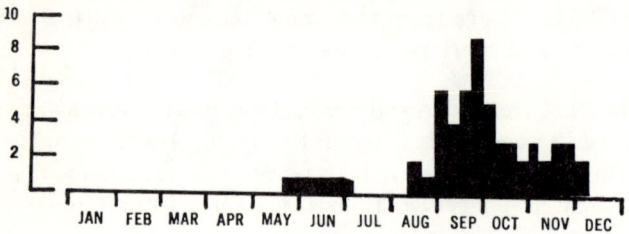

26 Nov 1977 at Corcoran, Kng., CAL. *John Luther*.

I.D. The Prairie Warbler in the fall is obscurely marked and can be confusing. It is olive green above and mostly yellow below, with two white wingbars, white undertail coverts, and white tail spots. Fine dark streaks are restricted to the sides and flanks. Immature males show "shadowy" dark face markings where breeding-plumaged males have the distinctive black pattern, but immature females have these face markings reduced to only obscure patterns. Pale lores and a whitish broken eyering characterize the immature female face. Excellent field marks include a yellowish "half-collar" extending up from the shoulder to behind the olive ear-coverts and the fact that the whitish wingbars do not contrast conspicuously against dark wing feathers (contrasting wingbars against dark wings is characteristic of Blackpoll *D. striata*, Bay-breasted *D. castanea*, Magnolia *D. magnolia* and several other eastern warblers with yellow on the underparts). A good discussion is in *Continental Birdlife* 1:119.

# OVENBIRD

*Seiurus aurocapillus*

Breeds N & E North America. Winters SE U.S., NE Mexico to West Indes, NW South America.

The Ovenbird nests on the West Coast in NE B.C. A specimen was said to have been taken in ALASKA in the 1800s; south of B.C. it is a very rare spring and fall vagrant. CAL has recently averaged about 33 birds a year; the records are fairly evenly split between spring and fall and there are two records of wintering individuals.

**ALASKA** One possible record: 30 May 1867† above Nulato, on the Yukon R., but this specimen was destroyed during the Chicago fire and the species has been relegated to the state's hypothetical list. Others were said to have been seen at Ft. Yukon in summer 1867 and nesting was suspected. There is no recent data to support this conclusion.

**WASHINGTON** Five records: 15 Nov 1956† at Spokane (M 38:7), 5 Jun 1972† at Richland, Ben., 16 Jun 1973 at Sullivan Lake, P.O., 12 May 1977 at Pullman, Whi., and 12 Nov 1979 at Ephrata, Grn.

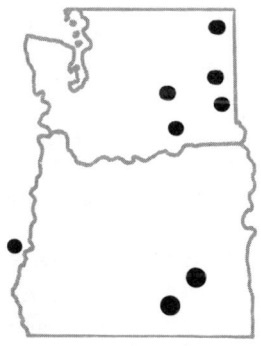

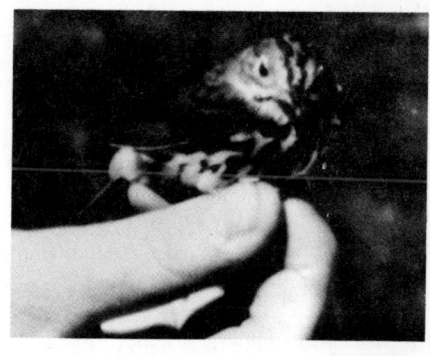

5 Jun 1972 at Richland, Ben., WASH. 2nd record. *Robert E. Woodley.*

# OVENBIRD

**OREGON** Ten records, graphed below. These few records fit very well into the pattern shown by much higher numbers in CAL (see WB 6:114, which lists several of the records). All but one were in E ORE: 5 from Malheur NWR, Har. (4 spring, 1 fall) and 4 from Hart Mt., Lake (3 spring, 1 fall). The single coastal record came aboard a boat offshore Coos Bay on 6 Jun 1970.

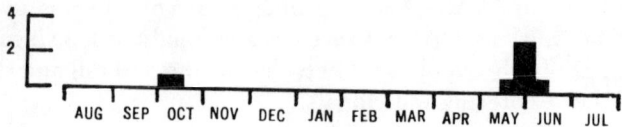

**CALIFORNIA** 320 records, recently averaging about 33 birds a year. 198 records were in N CAL and 122 in S CAL. 145 were recorded during the fall (84 in N CAL; 61 in S CAL). 173 were found during the spring (114 in N CAL; 59 in S CAL). The table below lists recent (1975-1979) per-year averages:

| CAL | | N CAL | | S CAL | |
|---|---|---|---|---|---|
| fall | = 15.4 | fall | = 9.8 | fall | = 5.6 |
| winter | = 0.4 | winter | = 0.0 | winter | = 0.4 |
| spring | = 17.4 | spring | = 11.8 | spring | = 5.6 |
| summer | = 0.0 | summer | = 0.0 | summer | = 0.0 |
| TOTAL | = 33.2 | TOTAL | = 21.6 | TOTAL | = 11.6 |

Records from N CAL are nearly all from the coast, including SE Farallon I. (the island has 65% of the fall records and 78% of the spring records — probably the retiring habits of this bird make it difficult to find when cover is available; cover is extremely limited on SE Farallon I.). There are six spring records from the N CAL interior and a single interior fall record from N CAL (2 Oct 1979 at Chico, But.). Interior birds make up a high percentage of S CAL records (36% during the fall and 55% during the spring). Most were at desert oases in Inyo-Mono-S.Bn. counties. Ovenbird is one of the few eastern warblers which is as common in spring as in fall. There are two winter records from S CAL: 12 Feb-9 Apr 1977 at Riverside, and 28 Dec 1977-4 Jan 1978 at San Francisquito Canyon, L.A.

# OVENBIRD

The graph below illustrates records from 1977-1979. There were 94 birds during these three years (an average of 31 a year) and the pattern formed by the reports is rather typical of the timing of this bird in CAL (except for the two unusual winter records during these years):

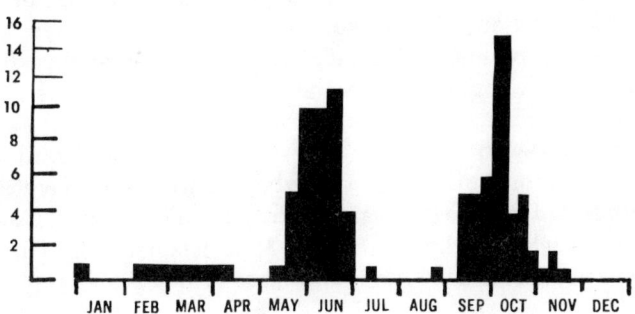

# LOUISIANA WATERTHRUSH

*Seiurus motacilla*

Breeds E U.S. Winters N-C Mexico to West Indes, NW South America.

The Louisiana Waterthrush has been found only once on the West Coast: a fall vagrant in CAL over 60 years ago. Considering that the bird winters in W Mexico, the paucity of records is surprising. Louisiana Waterthrush arrives on its breeding grounds very early in the spring and leaves very early in the fall; it has been suggested that since most vagrant birding at prime locations is done in late May-early Jun and Sep-Oct, birders may miss a few of these birds in Apr or early May and in Aug. A record from Baja, Mexico on 27 Apr 1964 tends to support this suggestion.

**CALIFORNIA** One record: 17 Aug 1908† at Mecca, Riv. (C 10:236).

# LOUISIANA WATERTHRUSH

I.D. The Louisiana Waterthrush is similar to Northern Waterthrush *S. noveboracensis* and the discussion by the standard guides tends to emphasize the unspotted throat of Louisiana and its whitish supercilium. Most Louisiana Waterthrush have white throats, but some have large spots on the throat, and a few Northern Waterthrush have white throats. The entire supercilium of Louisiana Waterthrush is not white, but only that portion of the supercilium *behind* the eye. Better characteristics to separate Louisiana from Northern Waterthrush are 1) a supercilium which widens behind the eye and is immaculate white in that area (Northern has a supercilium which narrows behind the eye and it is buffy or yellowish, except in a few worn birds which may look whitish), 2) cinnamon-buff flank patch which contrasts with white belly and white undertail coverts (the flanks and undertail coverts of Northern are typically washed yellowish), and 3) a heavier bill. For more information see Binford (1971a) and Wallace (1976b).

# KENTUCKY WARBLER

*Oporornis formosus*

Breeds E U.S. Winters E-C Mexico to NW South America.

The Kentucky Warbler has been found on the West Coast only in CAL, where there are a handful of spring records and a couple of fall records. Over half of the birds were found on offshore islands where cover is very reduced; the retiring nature of this species makes it especially difficult to locate on the mainland.

**CALIFORNIA** 13 records, graphed below. 11 were recorded during the spring and 7 of these were on offshore islands: 6 on SE Farallon I. (2 Jun 1969, 3 Jul 1972†, 1-3 Jun 1974*, 16 Jun 1975, 18 Jun 1976, and 11-12 May 1979) and another on Santa Barbara I. (1 Jun 1973*). The additional spring records are: 4 Jun 1968 at Pt. Loma, S.D. (CB 1:37), 27 May 1977* at Ft. Piute, S.Bn., 8 Jun 1977 at Oasis, Mono (singing male), and 30 Apr 1979 at Little Lake, Inyo. The two fall records are: 21-23 Nov 1972 at Eureka, Hmb., and 24 Oct 1979 at Imperial Beach, S.D.

# KENTUCKY WARBLER

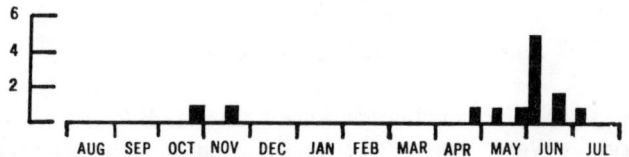

4 Jun 1968 at Pt. Loma, S.D., CAL. 1st record. *Alan M. Craig.*

# CONNECTICUT WARBLER

*Oporornis agilis*

Breeds C-N North America. Winters N South America.

The Connecticut Warbler breeds locally in NE B.C. It is a Rarity anywhere on the West Coast away from B.C. and the only records to date are from CAL, where the few records are split between spring and fall vagrants. Over half of the CAL records are from offshore islands where there is little cover; the retiring habits of this species make it difficult to locate on the mainland.

**CALIFORNIA** 24 records, graphed below. 16 of these were recorded on offshore islands: 14 on SE Farallon I. (8 fall, 6 spring), 1 on Santa Barbara I. (31 May 1974), and 1 on San Nicolas I. (29-30 Sep 1974). Most of the remaining records are coastal: Imperial Beach, S.D. (27 Sep 1963, 29 Sep 1974), Pt. Loma, S.D. (4 Jun 1968), Pebble Beach, Mnt. (27 Sep 1964), Santa Cruz (22 Oct 1978), and Pt. Reyes NS, Mrn. (26 Sep 1974*, 29 Sep 1974*). The only interior record was 22 Sep 1974* at Stovepipe Wells, Death Valley NM, Inyo.

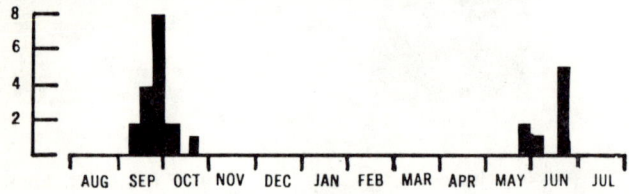

19 Jun 1976 on SE Farallon I., CAL. *Bruce Sorrie.*

# MOURNING WARBLER    CONNECTICUT WARBLER

Mourning Warbler (left) and Connecticut Warbler (right). 25 Sep 1974 on SE Farallon I., CAL. 4th record (Mourning) and 15th record (Connecticut). Dave DeSante.

# MOURNING WARBLER

*Oporornis philadelphia*

Breeds N North America. Winters Central America to NW South America.

The Mourning Warbler nests locally in NE B.C. and might even interbreed with MacGillivray's Warbler *O. tolmiei* in this area (M 57:68; some authorities consider the two birds conspecific). It has been recorded on the West Coast away from B.C. only in CAL, where a handful of fall vagrants outnumber the few spring vagrants. About half of the records are from SE Farallon I., where there is almost no available cover; the retiring habits of this bird make it difficult to locate on the mainland, as does its similarity to the common MacGillivray's Warbler.

**CALIFORNIA**   15 records, graphed below. 12 of these were during the fall and 7 of the birds were located on SE Farallon I. The additional fall records are coastal — 3 Oct 1968 (C 72:373), 19 Sep 1975 at Pt. Reyes NS, Mrn., 2 Sep 1979 at Pt. Mugu, Ven., and 27-30 Sep 1979 at Pt. Reyes NS — except for one on 10 Nov 1979† at Baker, S.Bn., which was not only from the interior but very late. There are three spring records: 12 Jun 1968† at Deep Springs, Inyo, 29 May 1976* at Furnace Creek, Inyo, and 4 Jun 1977 at Mesquite Springs, Inyo.

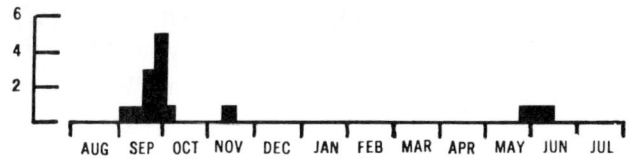

# MOURNING WARBLER

28 Sep 1979 at Pt. Reyes NS, Mrn., CAL. *Al Ghiorso*.

I.D. The Mourning Warbler is very similar to MacGillivray's Warbler *O. tolmiei*. Some authorities consider them conspecific, though Hall (1979) found very few specimens of hybrids and Salt (1973) found they did not respond to the playback of each other's song in the suggested overlap zone in Alberta. Whatever their eventual taxonomic status, all but breeding-plumaged males can be difficult to separate in the field.

In spring, adult male Mourning is distinguished by the absence of prominent eye-arcs (the incomplete eye-ring) always found on MacGillivray's. The contrasting black "apron" at the base of the gray throat is a fairly good characteristic, though an occasional MacGillivray's will show this pattern. Most Mourning Warblers have gray lores (MacGillivray's lores are black), but some populations of Mourning Warbler are predominantly black-lored. Spring female MacGillivray's also has the characteristic eye-arcs, but spring female Mourning are more variable: some show incomplete eyerings and some even have complete eyerings. Females of both species have complete grayish hoods but show a paler area on the throat, which is usually whitish. A female Mourning Warbler in the spring with an eyering can be difficult to identify; it might be distinguished by shape and eyering characteristics discussed for birds in the fall.

# MOURNING WARBLER

In the fall both sexes of Mourning Warbler immatures have incomplete eyerings and must be very carefully distinguished from MacGillivray's. Female Mourning may be easier to identify. It shows very little suggestion of a hood (both sexes of fall MacGillivray's look distinctly hooded) and the throat is yellow, merging into the yellow breast. Thus the entire underparts are deep yellow; the head and neck are grayish, the back olive, and there is an incomplete eyering. Both Common Yellowthroat *Geothlypis trichas* and Nashville Warbler *Vermivora ruficapilla* can be confused with immature female Mourning Warbler, but both of these birds have a paler belly (whitish or brownish) than the yellow breast and undertail coverts. Immature male Mourning Warbler is more similar to MacGillivray's, especially to female MacGillivray's which tend to have a paler throat (less of a hood) than males. Many young male Mourning Warblers have a yellowish wash to the throat similar to immature females and can be separated on that characteristic (immature female MacGillivray's, if it shows any yellow on the throat at all, has it restricted to an obscure wash about the chin). Immature female MacGillivray's usually has a whitish or grayish throat, but some immature male Mourning can have a whitish throat. These birds are most similar. They can be very carefully separated by 1) the shape of the eyering — always bold eye-arcs in MacGillivray's, but thinner and more complete (only slightly broken before and behind the eye) in Mourning, 2) by the shorter tail of Mourning Warbler, which is often apparent in the field on any age or plumage of Mourning Warbler, and 3) by the lower throat pattern (where the pale throat meets the yellow breast) — the grayish color of the neck extends down into this area on MacGillivray's, tending to separate the yellow breast from pale throat by a darker area (looking more hooded); on Mourning the whitish or yellowish throat meets the yellow breast squarely and the grayish color is restricted to the sides of the neck.

Both species can be very secretive but, in general, Mourning is more apt to forage above ground away from dense cover than is MacGillivray's (there are, though, plenty of exceptions). Some observers detect a different quality to the chip notes of the two species.

In hand, nearly all birds can be separated by a formula based on a wing (W) minus tail (T) measurement. 98% of MacGillivray's males have $W - T = 11$ mm. or less and 98% of MacGillivray's females have $W - T = 10$ mm. or less; 98% of Mourning Warblers (of either sex) have $W - T = 10$ mm. or more. For more information on in-hand characteristics see Lanyon & Bull (1967) and Hall (1979).

# RED-FACED WARBLER

*Cardellina rubrifrons*

Breeds SW U.S. to NW Mexico. Winters C Mexico to Guatamala.

The Red-faced Warbler nests in the U.S. in the mountains of C Arizona to SW New Mexico. It has very rarely strayed to S CAL, but three of the records are of males possibly defending territory in the mountains during May-Jul. Should a singing male attract a vagrant female, nesting could occur in the future.

**CALIFORNIA** Seven records, six during the spring and three of these were males in forested mountain habitat: 14 Jun 1973* at Buckhorn Campground, San Gabriel Mtns., L.A., 17 May-22 Jun 1975* on Clark Mt., S.Bn., and 17 Jun-2 Jul 1978 (1 or 2 birds) at Charlton Flats, San Gabriel Mtns., L.A. The additional spring records are: 30 May 1970† at Brock ranch, Imp. (CB 1:145), 21-24 May 1977 at Pt. Loma, S.D., and 4 Jun 1977 at Morongo Valley, S.Bn. The lone fall record is 26 Aug 1974 at Mission Gorge, S.D.

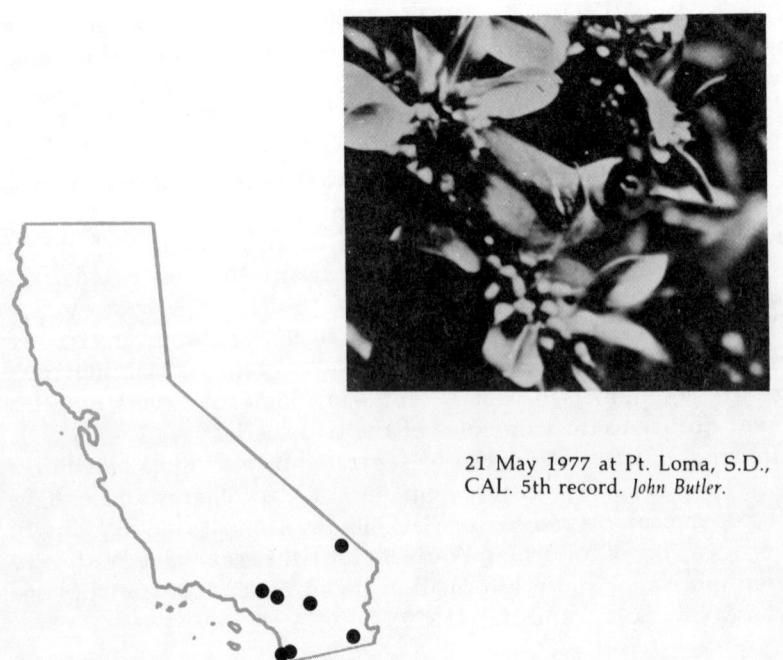

21 May 1977 at Pt. Loma, S.D., CAL. 5th record. *John Butler.*

# HOODED WARBLER

*Wilsonia citrina*

Breeds E U.S. Winters E-C & S Mexico to Central America.

The Hooded Warbler is very rare anywhere on the West Coast; it nests no nearer than E Texas (although there were two apparent pairs in Arizona in summer 1979). It has been an extremely rare vagrant in CAL, but was found more often in the late 1970s and a recent average there is almost nine birds a year. West Coast records are about evenly split between spring and fall vagrants, but a summering bird has been found in CAL and there is a winter record from CAL and another far north in WASH.

**CALIFORNIA** 71 records (through summer 1980), graphed below. 34 records were in N CAL and 36 were in S CAL. 30 were recorded during the fall (16 in N CAL; 14 in S CAL). 39 were found during the spring (18 in N CAL; 21 in S CAL). The table below lists recent (1975-1979) per-year averages:

| CAL | | N CAL | | S CAL | |
|---|---|---|---|---|---|
| fall | = 3.4 | fall | = 2.0 | fall | = 1.4 |
| winter | = 0.2 | winter | = 0.0 | winter | = 0.2 |
| spring | = 5.2 | spring | = 2.4 | spring | = 2.8 |
| summer | = 0.0 | summer | = 0.0 | summer | = 0.0 |
| TOTAL | = 8.8 | TOTAL | = 4.4 | TOTAL | = 4.4 |

Most fall records are from along the coast (only 2 on SE Farallon I.), but there are a few from areas in the Coast Range in N CAL and about half of S CAL fall records are from desert oases in the interior. Most spring records in N CAL are coastal (8 from SE Farallon I.), but 15 of the 21 spring records in S CAL are from interior locations. The only winter record was 17 Dec 1977-27 Jan 1978 at San Diego. A bird summered in N CAL during Jul-Aug 1980 at Tilden Park, C.C. Areas with more than two records are SE Farallon I. (10), San Diego area (4), Kelso, S.Bn. (4), Death Valley NM, Inyo (4), Deep Springs, Inyo (4), Oasis, Mono (4), Ft. Piute, S.Bn. (3), San Francisco (3), and Pt. Reyes NS, Mrn. (3). The northernmost record was 2 Oct 1971* at Fairhaven, Hmb.

# HOODED WARBLER

The graph below illustrates all CAL records:

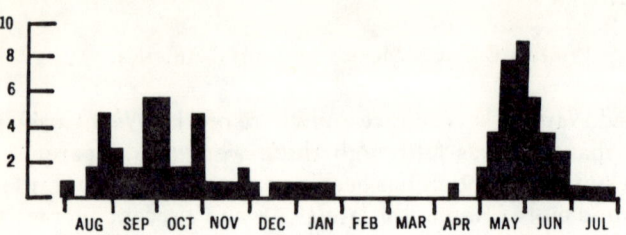

**OREGON** Three records: 20 Jul 1974* at Washburn SP, Lane, 20 May 1977* at Malheur NWR, Har., and 10 Jul 1979 at Washburn SP.

**WASHINGTON** One record: 31 Dec 1975-4 Apr 1976 at Seattle, King.

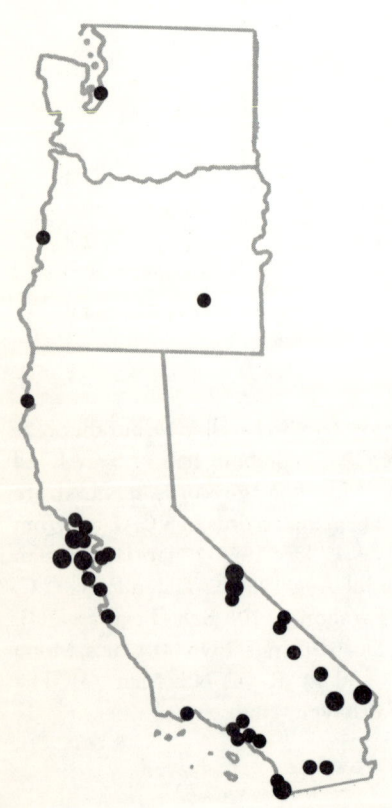

15 Apr 1977 at Kelso, S.Bn., CAL.
*Steve Cardiff.*

31 Oct 1975 at Mesquite Spring, Death Valley NM, Inyo, CAL.
*John Luther.*

# CANADA WARBLER

*Wilsonia canadensis*

Breeds N & E North America. Winters N & W South America.

The Canada Warbler is a rare nesting species in NE B.C. It is rarely found on the West Coast away from that province; the only records are a bird found dead in ALASKA and a number of fall vagrants (and a handful of spring records) in CAL, where it has recently been averaging nearly 10 birds a year.

**ALASKA**  One record: an individual found dead on 25 Jul 1965† at Barrow.

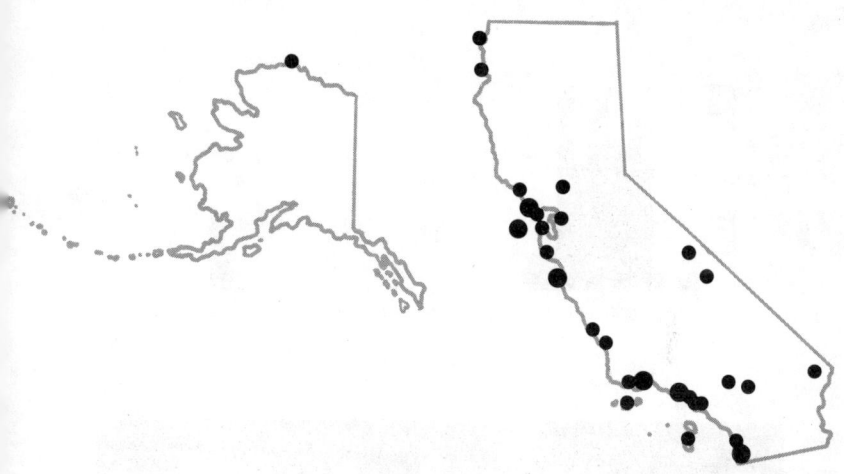

**CALIFORNIA**  78 records, graphed below. 37 records were in N CAL and 41 in S CAL. 71 (about 90%) were recorded during the fall (33 in N CAL; 38 in S CAL). Only 7 have been found during the spring. The table below lists recent (1975-1979) per-year averages:

| CAL | | N CAL | | S CAL | |
|---|---|---|---|---|---|
| fall | = 8.8 | fall | = 4.6 | fall | = 4.2 |
| winter | = 0.0 | winter | = 0.0 | winter | = 0.0 |
| spring | = 1.0 | spring | = 0.6 | spring | = 0.4 |
| summer | = 0.0 | summer | = 0.0 | summer | = 0.0 |
| TOTAL | = 9.8 | TOTAL | = 5.2 | TOTAL | = 4.6 |

# CANADA WARBLER

Nearly all of the fall records are from the coast (including 14 from SE Farallon I.); the only exceptions were on 5-6 Oct 1968 (2) at Barton Flats, S.Bn., 28 Sep 1976 at Morongo Valley, S.Bn., and 14-17 Sep 1977 at Davis, Yolo. Areas with multiple fall records include the San Diego area (15), the Monterey Pen. (6), Pt. Reyes NS, Mrn. (6), coastal Santa Barbara Co. (5), and Pt. Mugu, Ven. (3). The northernmost record was 10 Sep 1978 at Pt. St. George, D.N. A female in heavy molt on 8 Aug 1973 on SE Farallon I. was on a very early date for a fall vagrant. 4 of the 7 spring records are from SE Farallon I.; the others were in the interior of S CAL: 13 Jun 1967 in the Panamint Mtns., Inyo (C 72:373), 21 May 1969 at Deep Springs, Inyo, and 3 Jun 1978 in the Sacramento Mtns., S.Bn.

The graph below illustrates all CAL records:

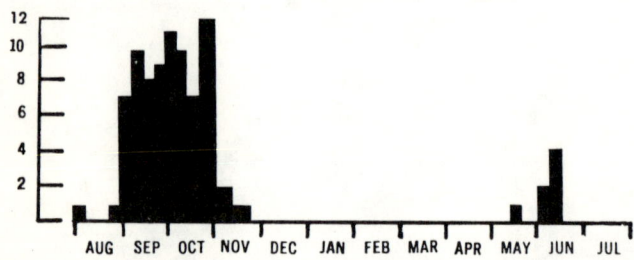

13 Oct 1979 at Gaviota, S.Bb., CAL. *James M. Greaves.*

# PAINTED REDSTART

*Myioborus picta*

Breeds SW U.S. to Central America. Northern populations winter from N Mexico south.

The Painted Redstart is a nesting bird in the mountains of E Arizona and SW New Mexico. It strays to CAL annually. There are 10 records of birds in summer in potential breeding habitat; four times pairs have been present and a nesting attempt (unsuccessful) was documented in summer 1974. There are also numerous records of spring and fall vagrants and 7 winter records from CAL; some birds have returned for consecutive winters. The one record north of CAL was a late fall vagrant far to the north in coastal B.C.

**CALIFORNIA** 54 records, graphed below, recently averaging 5 birds a year. As the graph suggests, records are well scattered throughout the seasons. 10 summer records are of birds in forested mountain habitat which could have been potential breeding habitat. There are four instances of pairs in such habitat: 23 May-29 Jul 1974 at Agua Dulce Campground, Laguna Mtns., S.D., 28 May-15 Jul 1974 at South Fork Campground, San Bernardino Mtns., S.Bn., 30 May-2 Jul 1975 at South Fork Campground, and 20-28 Jun 1977 in the New York Mtns., S.Bn. The nest and 4 young of the first pair listed were found on 6 Jul 1974, but the nest was deserted by 13 Jul, perhaps due to disturbance by cattle (Unitt, 1974; all records to this date are also listed here). 5 birds have been found during May-Jun on Clark Mt., S.Bn.; there is also potential breeding habitat here. One bird was found in what is termed N CAL on 4 Jul 1969 near Springville, Tul., in the southern Sierra Nevada. There are 7 winter records, two of which were of birds which returned for three consecutive years: 14 Jan-Mar 1942, Sep 1942-Feb 1943, and 26 Sep 1943-23 Mar 1944 at Altadena, L.A.; and 14 Dec 1952, 23 Dec 1953-30 Mar 1954, and 27 Sep 1954-Mar 1955 at Mill Creek Canyon, San Bernardino Mtns., S.Bn.

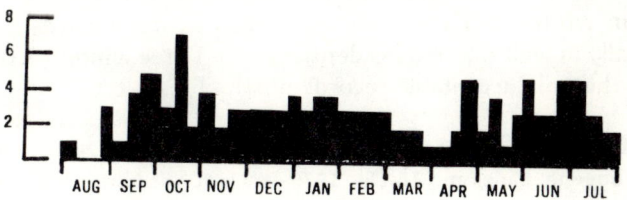

# PAINTED REDSTART

**BRITISH COLUMBIA**  One record: 4-5 Nov 1973 at Vancouver (WB 6:67).

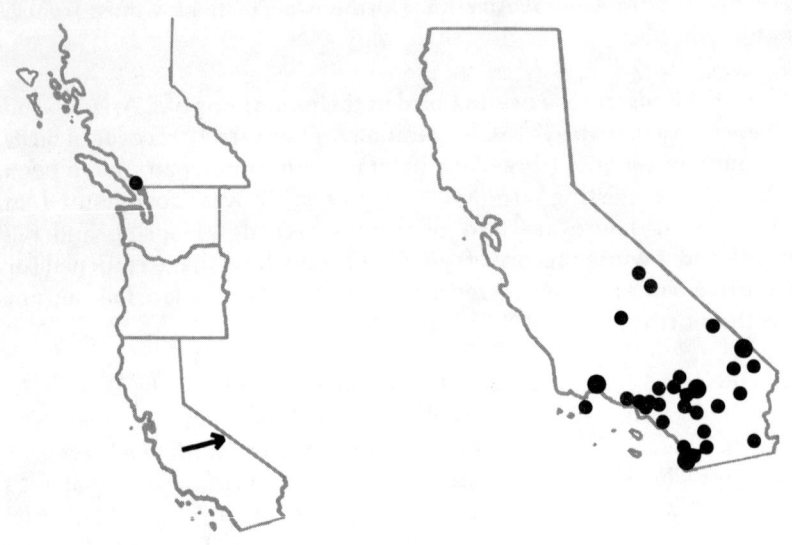

# HOODED ORIOLE

*Icterus cucullatus*

Breeds SW U.S. to S Mexico. U.S. populations winter in Mexico.

The Hooded Oriole nests on the West Coast throughout much of CAL, where its range has expanded northward in recent decades following the planting of Washington Fan Palms, a preferred nesting tree, and now is found locally as far north as Humboldt Co. Much of the population withdraws in winter, but there are numerous winter records from S CAL, especially in well-planted residential areas. Three winter records in W ORE are the only acceptable records north of CAL.

**OREGON**  Three records: 9-29 Dec 1976* at Depoe Bay, Lnc., 24 Dec 1978-28 Feb 1979* at Eugene, Lane, and 16 Dec 1979-Jan 1980* at North Bend, Coos.

# HOODED ORIOLE

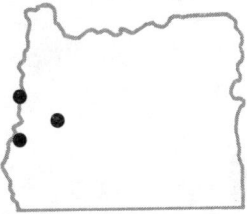

Jan 1979 at Eugene, Lane, ORE. 2nd record. *Tom Lund.*

29 Dec 1976 at Depoe Bay, Lnc., ORE. 1st record. *Tom Crabtree.*

I.D. Female and immature Hooded Orioles can be difficult to separate from other female and immature orioles. Size, bill shape, color of underparts, and call are important characteristics. The Hooded Oriole is slightly smaller than Northern Oriole *I. galbula* and looks slimmer and longer-tailed in the field. The bill is more decurved than other American orioles (the bill of Northern Oriole is rather straight). The entire underparts are yellowish-green. Both races of Northern Oriole have paler bellies than the breast — yellowish-green breast and whitish belly on "Bullock's" Oriole, the nesting race from S B.C. through CAL; orangish breast and buff to pale gray belly on "Baltimore" Oriole, the nesting race in N.E. B.C. and a rare spring and fall vagrant from WASH to CAL (a few winter each year in CAL, where it is nearly as common in winter as "Bullock's"). The call of Hooded Oriole is a whistled "wheet", very unlike the call of any other North American oriole; it does have a chatter similar to Northern Oriole.

Orchard Oriole *I. spurius*, which is a rare vagrant in CAL (averaging about 13 birds a year, mostly spring and fall vagrants, but a few winter annually), must be carefully distinguished. Orchard Oriole is distinctly smaller than Hooded Oriole, being not much larger than House Finch *Carpodacus mexicanus*. The bill is shorter and appears less sharply decurved. The underparts are entirely clear yellow, lacking the greenish tones of Hooded. The tail of Orchard looks shorter in the field and is often jerked from side to side. The call is a sharp "chuck", very unlike the call of other orioles. For more information see Dunn (1975).

# STREAK-BACKED (SCARLET-HEADED) ORIOLE

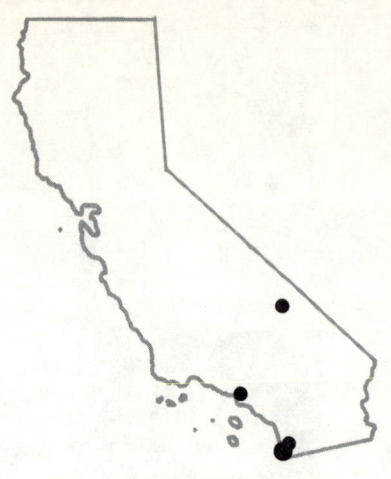

*Icterus pustulatus*

Breeds W Mexico to Costa Rica. Some northern populations wander during the non-breeding season.

The Streak-backed Oriole is primarily a Mexican species which occasionally wanders north to Arizona, where most records occur between Dec-Mar (but there is a mid-summer record — 31 Jul 1952). 5 birds have straggled to CAL during fall-winter and another was recorded during the spring some fifty years ago.

**CALIFORNIA** Six records: 1 May 1931† at Lake Murray, La Mesa, S.D. (A 48:606), 22 Sep 1962 and another 13 Oct 1962 at Imperial Beach, S.D. (A 81:358), 8 Oct 1963 at Imperial Beach, 2-5 Jan 1966 at Rancho Park, L.A., and 6 Nov-11 Dec 1977* at Furnace Creek, Inyo.

**I.D.** The Streak-backed Oriole is a large, bright oriole combining a black throat and a distinctly streaked back in most plumages. Adult males can become very red-orange about the head; females and young males are more orange-headed. The back is olive (or yellow in adult male) with rows of oval black spots forming streaks. The wing coverts are broadly edged with white, reduced in young birds, but usually looking more white-winged than most other American orioles. The combination of a black throat, orange or red-orange head, and streaked back will separate Streak-backed Oriole from the nesting species in North America. Very young females (Jul-Aug) lack black throats and streaked backs; their bulk and fairly straight, heavy bills will recall Scott's Oriole *I. parisorum*. They are distinguished by their brighter yellow-olive coloration, much white on the wing, and black lores. By Sep, the black on the throat and back becomes apparent.

# SCOTT'S ORIOLE

*Icterus parisorum*

Breeds SW U.S. to C Mexico. Winters NW Mexico to S Mexico.

The Scott's Oriole nests in S CAL. It is extremely rare in N CAL, where the six records include apparent spring overshoots, fall vagrants, and one wintering individual. The single record north of CAL was a male at a feeder in winter.

**WASHINGTON**   One record: 11 Feb-Mar 1980 at Chehalis, Lew.

I.D. The adult male Scott's Oriole is easily identified by the marks described in the standard guides. Females and immatures can be more difficult. Scott's Oriole is a large, heavy oriole with a long, stout, only slightly decurved bill. The plumage is reminiscent of Hooded Oriole *I. cucullatus,* but is a darker grayish-green color, lacking any yellow tones. The belly may be a dull grayish-green (but not distinctly paler or whitish as in Northern Oriole *I. galbula*). The back is narrowly streaked with dusky, unlike other North American orioles. Most female and many immature Scott's Orioles show black flecking on the throat. Some young males remain in this same dull plumage into the spring, picking up only more black on the throat; others will have a plumage intermediate between immature and adult male by spring. For more information see Dunn (1975b).

# RUSTY BLACKBIRD

*Euphagus carolinus*

Breeds N North America. Winters E North America.

The Rusty Blackbird nests across C ALASKA and N B.C. It is a Rarity in WASH and ORE, with the few records falling between Sep-Mar. It is a rare bird in CAL, but it is averaging nearly 12 birds a year and does not fit our definition of a Rarity there. There are 92 records in CAL; most appeared during Nov, when there is a sharp peak, especially at locations east of the Sierra. Nearly all records fall between mid-Oct and Mar; fall migrants (as noted) are in the majority but there are a number of records of wintering individuals along the coast. There are only two records of spring migrants. The status of this bird in CAL is thoroughly discussed in McCaskie (1971).

**WASHINGTON** Ten records, graphed below. Seven were in E WASH, where more thorough coverage may prove it to be regular in late fall (similar to the situation in CAL). The three coastal records were 10-19 Dec 1972 at Lumni Flats, Wha., 31 Dec 1978 at Bellingham, Wha., and 20-25 Oct 1979 at Ocean Shores, G.H.

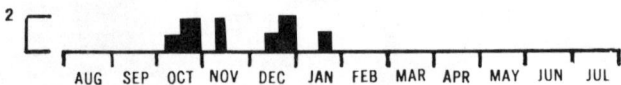

**OREGON** Two records: 20 Mar 1959† at Tillamook (C 62:140), and 13-14 Nov 1977* at Baskett Slough NWR, Polk.

7 Nov 1978 at Pt. Reyes NS, Mrn., CAL. *Al Ghiorso.*

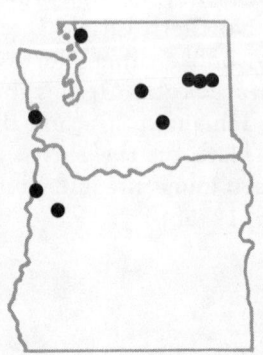

# GREAT-TAILED GRACKLE

*Quiscalus mexicanus*

Breeds SW U.S. to W South America. Some northern populations winter to the south.

The Great-tailed Grackle is undergoing a rapid and spectacular range expansion in western North America. It was only first recorded on the West Coast at Imperial Dam, on the Colorado River in extreme SE CAL, in Jun 1964; by the early 1970s numbers were nesting along the CAL side of the Colorado R. and a few birds appeared to be colonizing areas around the south end of the Salton Sea. The first grackle reached the S CAL coast in Feb 1977. In May 1977 a few appeared farther north in the interior at Furnace Creek, Death Valley NM.; they now appear to be established there. In the late 1970s numbers begin to appear elsewhere along the coast and in the interior of S CAL. A bird reached San Francisco in Jun 1978 for the first N CAL record. By the summer of 1980 a pair had nested in San Francisco and birds had been found in the N Central Valley. The first records north of CAL also occurred in spring 1980, when 3 individuals where found in E ORE. It seems likely that this species will continue to consolidate its numbers at scattered CAL localities and will probably continue to expand it range. It could even be nesting in ORE and WASH by the end of the next decade.

**OREGON** Three records: 18-24 May 1980 at Malheur NWR, Har., 1st week of Jun 1980 at John Day, Grn., and 5-6 Jun 1980 at Island City, Uni.

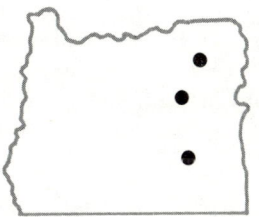

# COMMON GRACKLE

*Quiscalus quiscula*

Breeds N-C & E North America. Northern populations are migratory.

The Common Grackle is an uncommon local breeder in NE B.C.; it is a Rarity on the West Coast away from that province. Most Rarity records occurred as spring and fall vagrants, but there are summer reports from ALASKA and winter records from W WASH and S CAL. The Common Grackle has seemed to be expanding its range westward in recent years and it might be expected with more frequency on the West Coast. All records to date appear to be of the western "bronzy" race *Q. q. versicolor*.

**ALASKA** Six records: 17 Jun 1943† at Wainwright, 20-21 Jul 1959† at Ogotoruk Creek, W ALASKA, 28-29 Aug 1966 at Yakutat, 12 May 1971 at Fairbanks, 10 Aug 1974 at Juneau, and 17 Jul 1976 at Tazlina Glacier, C ALASKA.

**WASHINGTON** Three records: 22 Oct 1950† at Paradise Creek, Whi. (only 130 yards west of the Idaho state line), 26-27 Jun 1965 at Seattle, King (M 47:19), and 4 Dec 1974-18 Jan 1975 at Olympia, Thr.

**OREGON** One record: 28 May 1977* at Malheur NWR, Har. (WB 8:156).

**CALIFORNIA** 13 records (through spring 1980), graphed below. 12 of these occurred during the last five years. Seven come from the interior during the spring: 21-26 May 1975* at Furnace Creek, Inyo, 30 Apr 1976* at Morongo Valley, S.Bn., 28 May 1977* at Scotty's Castle, Inyo, 30 May-8 Jun 1977* at Deep Springs, Inyo, 22 May 1979 at Scotty's Castle, 9 Jun 1979 near Blythe, Riv., and 24-25 May 1980 at Furnace Creek. Another spring record — 22 May 1979 at West Pittsburg, C.C. — comes from the San Francisco Bay delta. Most of the fall records are from near the coast: 20 Nov 1969† at El Cajon, S.D., 11 Oct 1975 at Arcata, Hmb., and 13 Oct 1977 at Hayward, Ala.; an additional fall record was in E CAL: 7 Oct 1979 at Furnace Creek. The single winter record is from the S CAL coast: 9 Feb-26 Mar 1977* at Carlsbad, S.D.

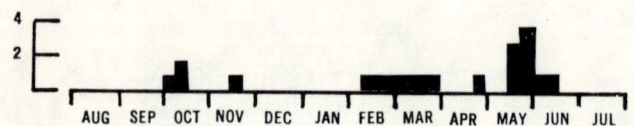

# COMMON GRACKLE

28 May 1977 at Scotty's Castle, Death Valley NM, Inyo, CAL. 6th record. *Linda S. Terrill.*

5 Mar 1977 at Carlsbad, S.D., CAL. 5th record. *Paul Lehman.*

24 May 1975 at Furnace Creek, Death Valley NM, Inyo, CAL. 2nd record. *Dave Rudholm.*

# SCARLET TANAGER

*Piranga olivacea*

Breeds E North America. Winters N South America.

The Scarlet Tanager is a Rarity anywhere on the West Coast. Fall vagrants are most often recorded (peak in late Oct-Nov), but there are a number of spring vagrant records during late May-Jun. A spring overshoot reached Pt. Barrow, ALASKA, far to the north.

**ALASKA** Two records: 25 Jun 1934† at Barrow, and 7 May 1977 at Cordova.

**BRITISH COLUMBIA** One record: 14 Nov 1926† at Comox, V.I.

**OREGON** Two records: 31 May 1979 at Malheur NWR, Har., and 13 Jun 1979* at Hart Mt., Lake. Both records were of adult males; the latter bird was netted and banded.

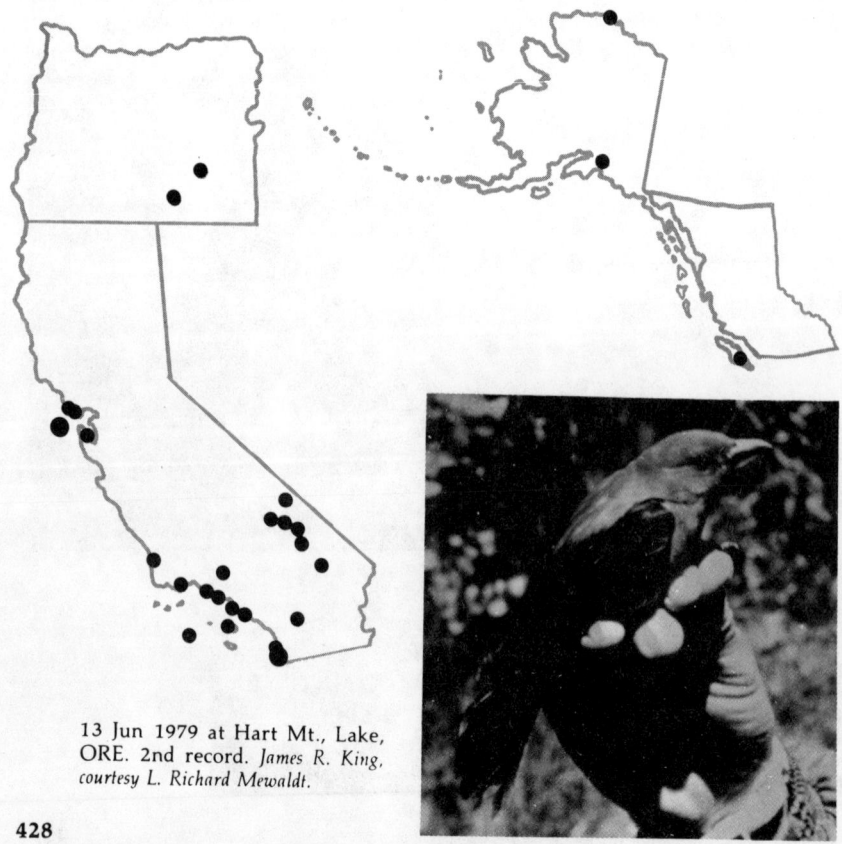

13 Jun 1979 at Hart Mt., Lake, ORE. 2nd record. *James R. King, courtesy L. Richard Mewaldt.*

# SCARLET TANAGER

**CALIFORNIA** 33 records, graphed below. Most records were along the coast, but there are a number from the desert oases in E CAL. Areas with multiple records include Death Valley NM, Inyo (6), the San Diego area (7 — Pt. Loma to Imperial Beach), and SE Farallon I. (3).

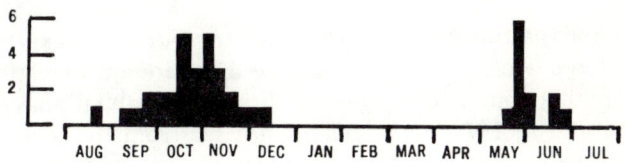

# SUMMER TANAGER

*Piranga rubra*

Breeds S U.S. to N Mexico. Winters S Baja, N Mexico to N & W South America.

The Summer Tanager nests on the West Coast along the CAL side of the Colorado R. and very locally elsewhere in SE CAL. Fall and spring vagrants have reached N CAL, mostly along the coast, and there are winter and mid-summer records. The single record north of CAL was a spring vagrant. Many out-of-range records of Summer Tanager in CAL are suspected of referring to the nominate eastern race *P. r. rubra* and specimen records tend to support this hypothesis; the ORE record could also be of a vagrant from the east.

**OREGON** One record: 14 Jun 1979* at Hart Mt., Lake. This male was netted and banded.

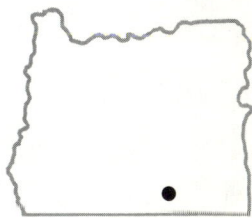

14 Jun 1979 at Hart Mt., Lake, ORE. 1st record. *James R. King, courtesy L. Richard Mewaldt.*

# PYRRHULOXIA

*Cardinalis sinuatus*

Breeds SW U.S. to C Mexico. Mostly resident.

The Pyrrhuloxia is normally a resident of the Sonoran desert; it has rarely wandered west to CAL. Most records are during spring or summer; singing birds in potential breeding habitat have been encountered and in 1977 a pair nested not far from the Colorado R. There are three records of birds in winter; one returned to the same location for three consecutive winters.

**CALIFORNIA** Eight records, two during the spring — 28 Apr 1974 at the south end, Salton Sea, Imp., and 23 May 1974* at Brock ranch, Imp. — and three during the summer: 14 Jul 1974 at Palos Verde, Imp., 18 Jul 1974* at Westmorland, Imp., and 6 Jun-Jul 1977* (pair) at Chemuhuevi Wash, north of Vidal Junction, S.Bn. This pair built a nest and incubated eggs, but the eventual success of this attempt is unknown. There are three winter records: 24 Feb-6 Mar 1971 at Heise Springs, Imp. (CB 2:99) — the same bird returning 31 Dec 1971-27 Mar 1972 and 28 Jan-23 Mar 1973; 17 Dec 1972-19 Feb 1973 at Calipatria, Imp.; and 23 Dec 1977 at Brock ranch, Imp.

23 Jul 1977 at Chemuhuevi Wash, north of Vidal Juction, S.Bn., CAL. 8th record. *Kent Van Vuren.*

# ROSE-BREASTED GROSBEAK

*Pheucticus ludovicianus*

Breeds N-C and E North America. Winters S Mexico to NW South America.

The Rose-breasted Grosbeak nests in NE B.C. It is one of the commoner "eastern" species to be encountered on the West Coast south of B.C. (except WASH, where it is unaccountably scarse). It seems to be a regular migrant, in small numbers, east of the Sierra in CAL, especially during the spring. It now averages nearly 95 birds a year in CAL: about 62% in spring, 30% in fall, 7% winter locally, and 1% summer locally (but there is no evidence of nesting). Desert oases concentrate birds, as do coastal vagrant "traps", and account for the bulk of the records during migration. Winter birds are most often at feeders in residential areas, especially in coastal S CAL, and this species seems equally likely to winter in the state as its western counterpart, the Black-headed Grosbeak *P. melanocephalus*.

The Rose-breasted Grosbeak remains a Rarity in ORE & WASH, perhaps due to few observers in the eastern areas of these states and the paucity of concentrating points. Most Rarity records are during spring migration, but a number of summer records exist. Occasional nesting might be expected in the future (there is a nesting record as close as S B.C. — summer 1977 near Kamloops).

**WASHINGTON** Three records: 2 May 1956† at Sprague, Lnc. (M 57:57), 22 Jun 1979 at Tacoma, Prc., and 29 Jun 1979 (2) at Wenas Creek, Yak.

**OREGON** 14 records, graphed below. Migration patterns parallel those in CAL and eastern sites (especially Malheur NWR, Har.) have produced most records. The only records from W ORE are: 25-30 Dec 1972* at Lake Oswego, Clk., 25 Jun 1973 at Eugene, Lane, 27 Sep 1977† at Mt. Angel, Mar., and 16-17 May 1978 at Portland, Mul. A pair of grosbeaks present 21 Jun-3 Jul 1976* at Cold Springs Campground, Des., built a nest but apparently no eggs were laid and the identity of the female has been questioned (possibly Black-headed Grosbeak).

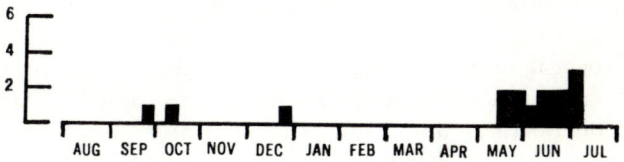

# ROSE-BREASTED GROSBEAK

Jun 1976 at Indian Ford Campground, west of Sisters, Des., ORE. 5th record. *Steve Gordon.*

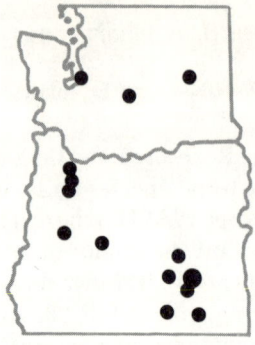

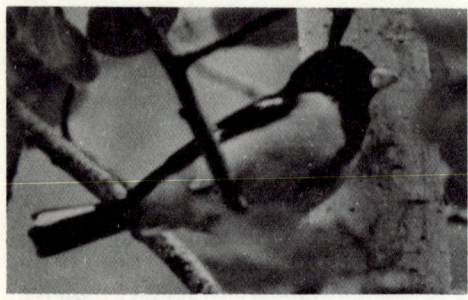

I.D. The adult male Rose-breasted Grosbeak is easily identified by the standard guides. Female and immature birds are more difficult to separate from similarly-plumaged Black-headed Grosbeaks *P. melanocephalus*. Immature males tend to have a rosy or dark buff breast and bright rosy underwings. Females are best distinguished by a whitish (sometimes buffy) breast crossed by heavy dark streaks and by whitish head stripes; female Black-headed tends to have a buffy or orangey-brown breast crossed with fine streaks and usually has buffy head stripes. Black-headed Grosbeaks in spring and summer can become worn and look white-breasted in the field; these ambiguous individuals can prove difficult to identify. With experience, the call note is useful. Rose-breasted Grosbeak has a high, squeaky "eek" call, separatable with practice from the lower, sharper "ik" call of Black-headed Grosbeak. For more information see Dunn (1977a).

# BLUE GROSBEAK

*Guiraca caerulea*

Breeds S U.S. to Costa Rica. Winters S Baja, N-C Mexico, and Cuba to Panama.

The Blue Grosbeak nests in S CAL and north locally through the Central Valley in N CAL. It is very rare in winter, but the only N CAL winter record was far north at the head of the Central Valley (3 Jan 1976 at Redding, Sha.). The only West Coast record north of CAL was also in winter: a female-plumaged bird which visited a feeder in ORE.

# BLUE GROSBEAK

**OREGON**  One record: 4-17 Jan 1975* at Corvallis, Ben. (M 57:44).

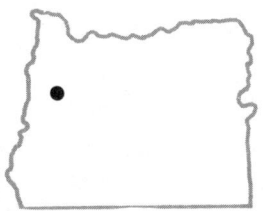

# INDIGO BUNTING

Jan 1975 at Corvallis, Ben., ORE. 1st record. M. S. Eltzroth.

*Passerina cyanea*

Breeds E U.S. Winters S Mexico, West Indes to Panama.

The Indigo Bunting breeds west to New Mexico and has nested in Arizona. There are numerous records from the West Coast, but it remains a Rarity in every state and province except CAL. Cal has recently averaged about 55 Indigo Buntings a year and it is one of the commoner "eastern" species to be found in that state. About 65% of the records are of spring vagrants and it appears to be regular in small numbers in E CAL during spring migration. About 30% of the records are of fall vagrants; these tend to appear along the coast. But 5% of the recent CAL records are of birds which remained to summer locally. Numerous records have involved singing males on territory, but as yet no pure pair has been found nesting (though this possibility is expected to occur in the near future). At least 5 male Indigo Buntings have been paired with female Lazuli Buntings *P. amoena*; in N CAL these have included a male feeding young in Jul 1979 at Ukiah, Men., and an apparent hybrid, probably from a pair which included a singing male present at Olema, Mrn., for the last 4 summers (1976-1979). Winter records are very scarce (only 3 from N CAL), but they (along with a few ORE records) suggest that Indigo Bunting is more likely to be found in winter on the West Coast than its western counterpart Lazuli Bunting.

There are spring records north of CAL, but the bulk of Rarity records are of males during the summer, sometimes defending territory (pioneers for a rapidly expanding population?). There are also a few fall records (north as far as S ALASKA) and a handful of winter records (surprisingly half of ORE records occurred from Nov-Jan).

# INDIGO BUNTING

14 Jul 1973 at Pend O'reille SP, P.O., WASH. 2nd record. *James F. Acton.*

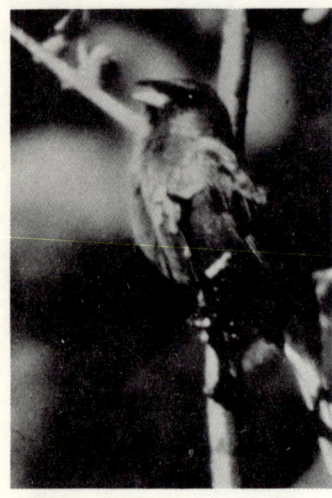

**OREGON** Eight records, four during the spring and summer: 14-21 Apr 1972 at Medford, Jck., 7 Jun 1975 at Eugene, Lane, 20 Jul 1976 at Little Alvord Creek Canyon, Steens Mt., Har., and another that summer at nearby Pike Creek (both males defending territory). The four additional records were during the late fall and winter: 1 Dec 1974-early Jan 1975 at Leaburg, Lane, 29 Nov-4 Dec 1975 at Eugene, Lane, 9 Nov 1977 at Eugene, and 2-7 Nov 1979* at Corvallis, Ben.

**WASHINGTON** Three records, all singing males in summer: 23 Jun-13 Jul 1958 at Forks, Jef. (M 47:45), 7-14 Jul 1973 at Pend Oreille SP, P.O., and 25 Jun 1977 at Chewelah, Stv.

**BRITISH COLUMBIA** Ten records, graphed below. Nine have been during the spring and summer and all of these were from the interior except for one present 1-2 Jun 1973 at Lions Bay, West Vancouver (CFN 88:232). The lone fall record was 1 Sep 1977 at Golden.

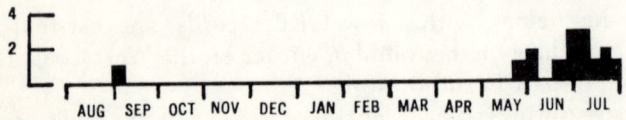

**ALASKA** One record: 3 Sep 1973 at Anchorage. This species is considered hypothetical on the state list because, though the bird was well described, it was seen by only a single observer.

# VARIED BUNTING

*Passerina versicolor*

Breeds SW U.S. to Guatamala. Northern populations winter to the south.

The Varied Bunting is an extremely rare straggler to the West Coast: both records come from SE CAL. An old record of a winter flock on the Colorado River, from which specimens were taken, is very unusual as winter records from Arizona are unknown (some have questioned the origin of the specimens, suggesting they were taken in Mexico, but there is no evidence to support this suggestion). The recent Death Valley record, occurring during the late fall when other Arizona-Mexico species tend to appear, was on a much more expected date.

**CALIFORNIA** Two records: 8 Feb 1914† (2 taken from flock of 15-20) at Blythe, Riv. (C 16:18), and 18-21 Nov 1977* at Mesquite Spring, Death Valley NM, Inyo.

18 Nov 1977 at Mesquite Spring, Death Valley NM, Inyo, CAL. 2nd record *Don Roberson.*

# PAINTED BUNTING

*Passerina ciris*

Breeds SE U.S. to N Mexico. Winters N Mexico, U.S. Gulf Coast to Panama & Cuba.

The Painted Bunting has occurred on the West Coast as a misoriented migrant. Most acceptable records are of fall vagrants at traditional vagrant spots in CAL. Two spring records at expected dates (late May-Jun) are also acceptable (including the lone record from ORE). Through the years, reports of adult males near population centers or during the winter at feeders have been rejected as probable escapes from captivity. It was a popular cage bird in the past, but it has been illegal to hold this species since the early 1970s and adult males that now appear during established patterns of occurrence are best considered wild birds, unless special circumstances suggest a particular individual is suspect.

**CALIFORNIA**  17 acceptable records, graphed below. Due to the number of questionable reports, those acceptable are listed. Most have been birds in non-adult male plumage at coastal vagrant "traps" (probably immatures): six at Imperial Beach, S.D. (14-15 Sep 1962† — A 81:358, 11 Oct 1962, 10 Nov 1962, 28 Sep 1963, 21-24 Sep 1974, & 12 Oct 1974); two at Pt. Loma, S.D. (22 Sep 1963, 11 Sep 1975*), and two on SE Farallon I. (10 Sep 1975, 28 Sep 1979 — both banded). Fall records of females or immatures in the interior are: 31 Aug 1971 at Deep Springs, Inyo, 27-28 Nov 1976* at Scotty's Castle, Inyo, and 13 Nov 1978 near Blythe, Riv. Acceptable records of adult-plumaged males are all during the fall in the interior of S CAL: 21 Oct 1972 at Kelso, S.Bn., 4 Nov 1972 at Furnace Creek, Inyo, and 4 Oct 1977 at Vallecitos, S.D. The only spring record was a singing non-adult-male-plumaged bird on 24 Jun 1966† at Santa Rosa, Son., in the Coast Range of N CAL (Bolander & Parmeter, 1978).

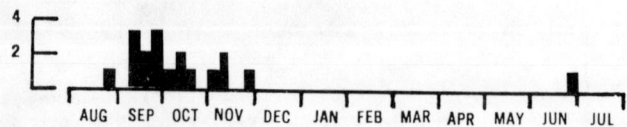

**OREGON**  One record: an adult male on 2 Jun 1963† at Malheur NWR, Har. (A 82:497). The specimen proved to be the western race *P. c. pallidior*.

# PAINTED BUNTING

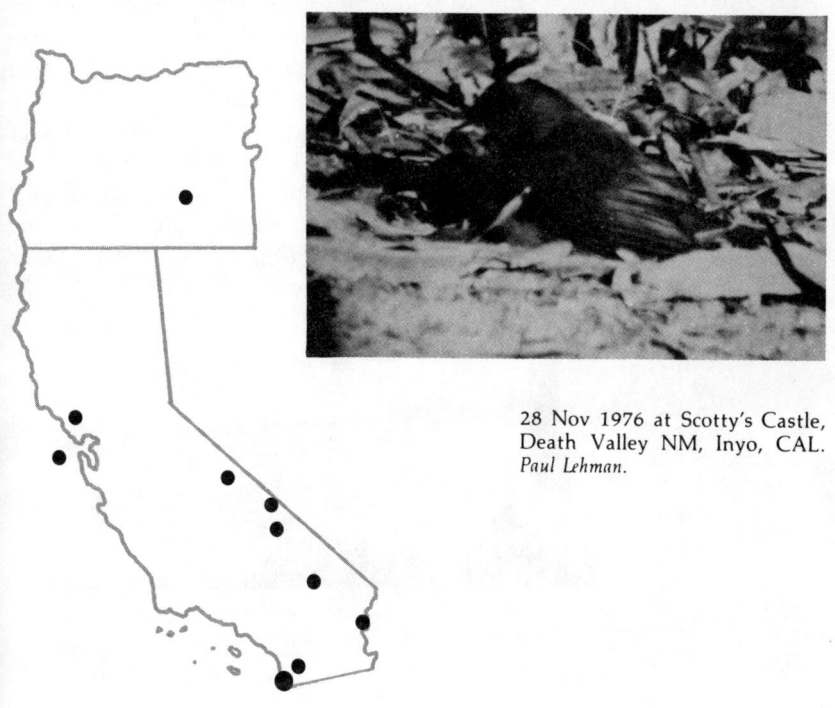

28 Nov 1976 at Scotty's Castle, Death Valley NM, Inyo, CAL. *Paul Lehman.*

# DICKCISSEL

*Spiza americana*

Breeds E North America. Winters C Mexico to N South America.

The Dickcissel is a rare vagrant to the West Coast. Most records are of misoriented fall vagrants; there are only a handful of spring records and but four of winter birds (one far north in B.C.). In CAL, Dickcissel has been averaging about 7 birds a year and does not fit into our definition of Rarity; the definition has been stretched in this case to include a discussion of CAL records, as the bird is strictly a vagrant there and the pattern formed by the records illustrate its distribution on the West Coast.

# DICKCISSEL

**CALIFORNIA** 83 records, graphed below. 70% of the fall records were along the coast (including offshore islands: SE Farallon has 4 fall records, as does San Nicolas I.). Areas with multiple fall records include Imperial Beach, S.D. (24 records, 13 of which were during Sep-Oct 1963), Goleta, S.Bb. (8), Pt. Reyes NS, Mrn. (6), and Death Valley NM, Inyo (10). The 11 spring records are split between the coast (SE Farallon I. — 5, Santa Barbara I. — 1, Pt. Reyes NS — 1) and the deserts of E CAL (Death Valley NM — 3, Deep Springs, Inyo — 1). A bird on 7 Dec 1976 at Santa Cruz was a very late fall vagrant; there are only three records of wintering birds: 2 Dec 1963-16 Mar 1964 at San Diego, Dec 1967-9 Apr 1968 at Pacific Grove, Mnt., and 26 Jan-27 Mar 1977 at Los Osos, S.L.O.

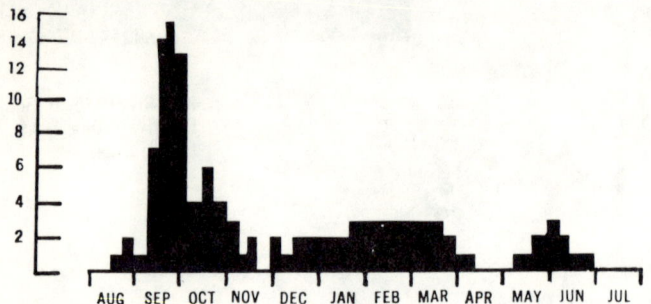

**OREGON** One record: 30 Nov-6 Dec 1979* at Lakeside, Coos.

**BRITISH COLUMBIA** Three records: 12 Jun 1922† at Vaseaux Lake, 14 Nov 1960-14 Jan 1961 at Victoria, V.I., and 3 Jun 1976 at Tofino, V.I. The wintering bird was netted and banded.

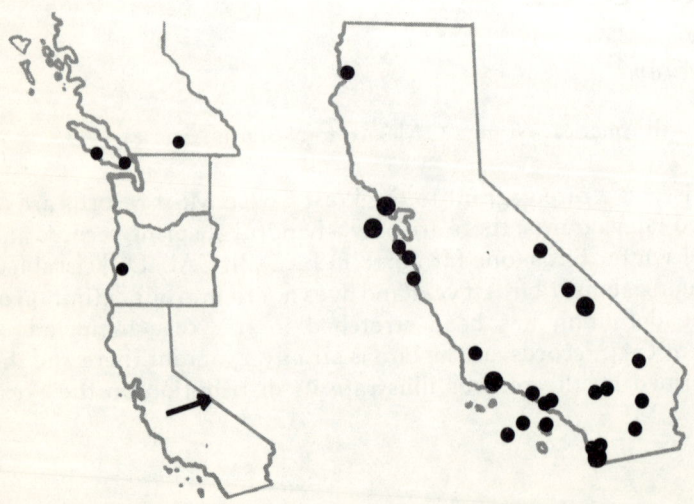

# DICKCISSEL

2 Dec 1979 at Lakeside, Coos, ORE. 1st record. *Owen Schmidt*.

# BRAMBLING

Plate 9

*Fringilla montifringilla*

Breeds N Eurasia. Winters S Eurasia.

The Brambling is a regular migrant on the westernmost Aleutian Is. and can even be fairly common there at times: over 200 were present during the last two weeks of May 1980 on Attu I. Fall birds have been recorded widely in ALASKA away from the Aleutians. Five birds have wintered along the West Coast from SE ALASKA to ORE. The large numbers in ALASKA, its apparent tendency to wander toward the south-east in the fall, and its ability to utilize feeders during the winter are all reasons we can expect more records of this bird along the West Coast south of ALASKA in the future.

Of interest to West Coast observers are records from Nevada (31 Oct-1 Nov 1978 at Sutcliffe), Montana (19 Nov-3 Dec 1978 at Swan Lake), and South Dakota (15 Dec 1979-Mar 1980 at Bismarck).

# BRAMBLING

**ALASKA** Rare regular migrant on the western Aleutians during the spring (9 May-22 Jun) and fall (17 Sep-17 Oct). In most years there are only a few birds, in flocks up to ten, but a flock of 50 was seen on Shemya I. in fall 1978 and well over 200 (perhaps up to 500) were on Attu I. from 15-30 May 1980. A minimum of 150 were seen on 18 & 20 May, in flocks up to 100, but numbers decreased dramatically after 22 May. Spring birds have reached the Pribilof Is., St. Lawrence I., Hooper Bay, and Pt. Barrow; fall birds have strayed to the Pribilof Is. and Pt. Barrow. There are four records from S & SE ALASKA, three of which wintered: 23 Dec 1969-15 Apr 1970† at Juneau, 6 Nov 1977-Apr 1978 at Cordova, 6-16 Nov 1978 at the Buskin R. mouth, Kodiak I., and late Nov 1978-Feb 1979 at Bird Creek near Anchorage.

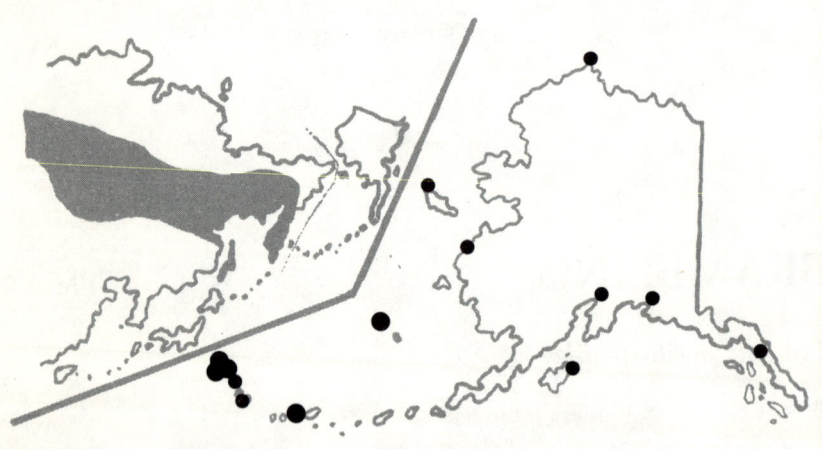

**BRITISH COLUMBIA** Two records: 7 Feb-early Mar 1971 at Tlell, Graham I., Q.C.I., presumably the same bird returning 5 Feb 1972; and another present 7-9 Nov 1971 at Reifel refuge, Vancouver (both discussed in CFN 88:486).

**OREGON** One record: 22 Nov 1967-31 Mar 1968* at Portland, Mul.

# BRAMBLING

Mar 1968 at Portland, Mul., ORE. 1st record. *Christy Brindle.*

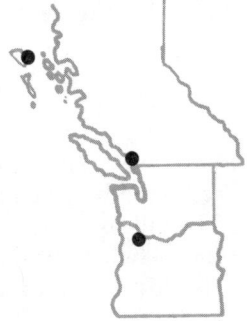

25 Feb 1971 at Tlell, Graham I., Q.C.I., B.C. 1st record. *Jennifer Davies.*

I.D. The Brambling is a small finch, slightly longer, but slimmer, than a House Sparrow *Passer domesticus*. Males in breeding plumage are distinctive, with black head and back, and orange breast and shoulder (see Plate 9). Females and immatures are less conspicuously marked, but the combination of a white rump band, broad orangeish wingbars, pale orange breast, and unmarked face are not found on any American finch. The crown and nape are mottled dark brown.

The white rump is especially prominent in flight. The flight call is a distinctive, nasal "zneer", interspersed with various chirpy notes.

# HAWFINCH

Plate 9

*Coccothraustes coccothraustes*

Breeds Eurasia. Winters S Eurasia.

The Hawfinch has been recorded on the West Coast only as a spring and fall vagrant in ALASKA, where the records are scattered between the Aleutian Is., the Pribilof Is., and St. Lawrence I. The fall specimen was judged to be the Japanese breeding race *C. c. japponicus* (which has also been taken in the spring on the Commander Is. just west of the Aleutians), but the spring specimen was thought to be intermediate between *japponicus* and the nominate race and may have originated on mainland NE Asia.

**ALASKA** 12 records (through spring 1980), graphed below. 11 were found during the spring and ten of these were on the outer Aleutians: 6 on Attu I. (3 on 26 May 1976, singles on 23 May 1978, 18 May 1980, & 23 May 1980), and 4 on Adak I. (31 May 1971 — 2, 1†; 5 Jun 1971; & 28 Jun 1971). The additional spring record was on 6-7 Jun 1978 at Gambell, St. Lawrence I. The only fall record was 1 Nov 1911† on St. Paul I., Pribilofs.

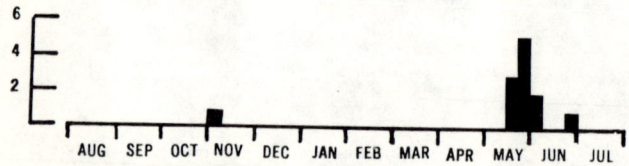

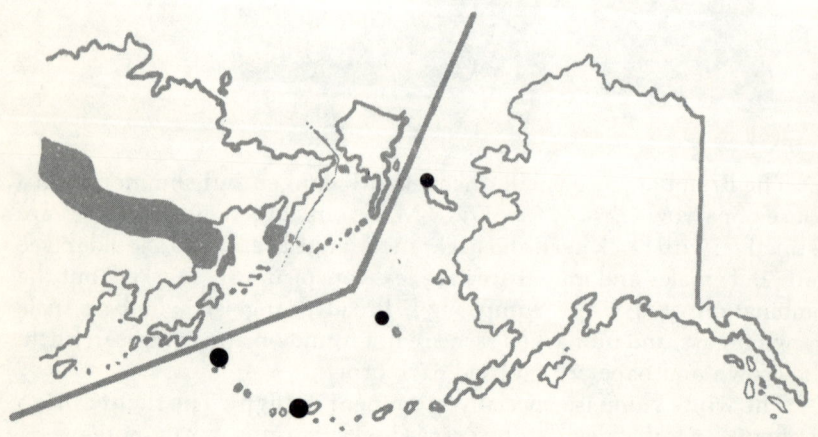

# HAWFINCH

9 Jun 1971 on Adak I., ALASKA.
4th record. *Daniel D. Gibson.*

I.D. The Hawfinch is a large distinctive finch about the size of Evening Grosbeak *Hesperiphona vespertina*. All ages and sexes have a huge bill, thick neck, tawny upperparts, white wing patch (very conspicuous in flight as a broad wingbar), and very short white-tipped tail, a combination of features not found on any American finch. The heavy bill is mettalic blue in spring, becoming a dull gray or horn-color by winter. Also unique are the spatulate-tipped inner primaries and secondaries, although these are rarely discernible in the field.

The flight is undulating. In flight the broad wingbar, combined with white bases to the primaries, form a long white bar down the center of the wing which is very conspicuous from above and below. This white bar in the wing on the largely grayish, big-headed, short-tailed finch helps identify it in flight at a distance.

The call is a sharp, distinctive, metallic "tzik", uttered when perched and in flight.

# EURASIAN BULLFINCH  Plate 9

*Pyrrhula pyrrhula*

Breeds N & C Eurasia. Some populations are resident, others are migratory to S Eurasia, and others stage irregular movements south.

The Eurasian Bullfinch wanders to ALASKA irregularly. Although there are records of apparent spring overshoots, more typically it seems to be a fall straggler, sometimes moving inland where it has been recorded during the winter. This tendency to wander east in winter might produce records on the West Coast south of ALASKA in the future.

**ALASKA** Ten records, three apparent spring overshoots: May 1936† at Gambell, St. Lawrence I., Jun 1959 at Gambell, and 18-21 May 1978 on Attu I., western Aleutians. Three records, involving 6 birds, during the fall: 12 Oct-4 Nov 1927 (4 birds, 1†) on Nunivak I., 27 Sep 1977 on Shemya I., western Aleutians, and 1st week of Nov 1977 at Anchorage. Three birds have appeared during the winter: 10 Jan 1867† at Nulato, W ALASKA, 10-11 Mar 1962 at Petersburg, and 9 Feb 1978 at Anchorage (see AB 32:389). The Nulato specimen proved to be the type specimen of *P. p. cassinnii*, which was later found to be the Kamchatka breeding race.

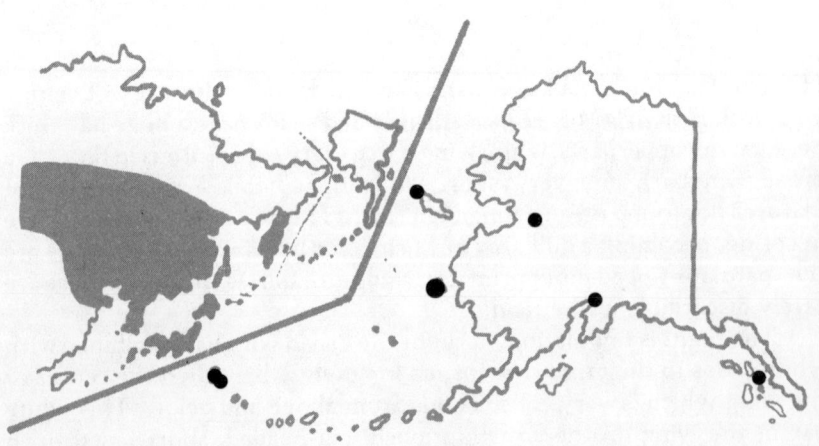

# EURASIAN BULLFINCH

I.D. The Eurasian Bullfinch is a distinctive small finch combining the features of a chunky body, stubby bill, black face and cap, gray back, white rump, and black tail — a pattern not found on any American finch. Males have a rosy-red face, neck, throat and breast (see Plate 9); females and immatures are warm pinkish-brown or pinkish-gray in these areas. Immatures are washed with dark tawny on the upperparts. The greater wing coverts are white, forming a conspicuous wingbar both on the ground and in flight. The white rump on the small chunky bird is an excellent characteristic to note in flight.

The discussion above and the painting on Plate 9 illustrate the breeding races in NE Asia and the Kamchatka Pen.; males from the breeding races on the Kurile Is. and in Japan (which could occur in ALASKA) are easily distinguishable in the field. The rosy-red color is restricted to the face and throat; the breast is grayish (or if rosy at all, it is distinctly paler than the face). The back is brownish, tinged rusty (not mostly gray), and the white in the wing is reduced.

The call is a very plaintive, piping, soft "hew".

# COMMON ROSEFINCH       Plate 9

*Carpodacus erythrinus*

Breeds Eurasia. Winters S Eurasia.

The Common Rosefinch has occurred on the West Coast only in W ALASKA, where all but one of the records are of spring vagrants. It has been found during five of the last nine springs; in 1977 numbers appeared at Gambell, St. Lawrence I., where the high count reached 18 birds.

**ALASKA** Nine records, eight during the spring: 4 Jun 1972† at Old Kashunuk Village in the Yukon-Kuskokwim R. delta (A 91:185), 9 Jun 1973 at Gambell, St. Lawrence I., 3 Jun 1975 on Buldir I., western Aleutians, 14-18 Jun 1975 at Gambell, 22 May 1976 (2) on Attu I., western Aleutians, 21 Jun 1976 (2) on Buldir I., 1-9 Jun 1977 at Gambell (this record involves 18 birds — 6 males, 12 females — and should probably be considered more than one record, since only a few birds were present early in this period and numbers gradually increased to the high count on 6 Jun), and 11 Jun 1977 on St. Paul I., Pribilofs. The only fall record was on 31 Aug 1977 on Shemya I., western Aleutians.

# COMMON ROSEFINCH

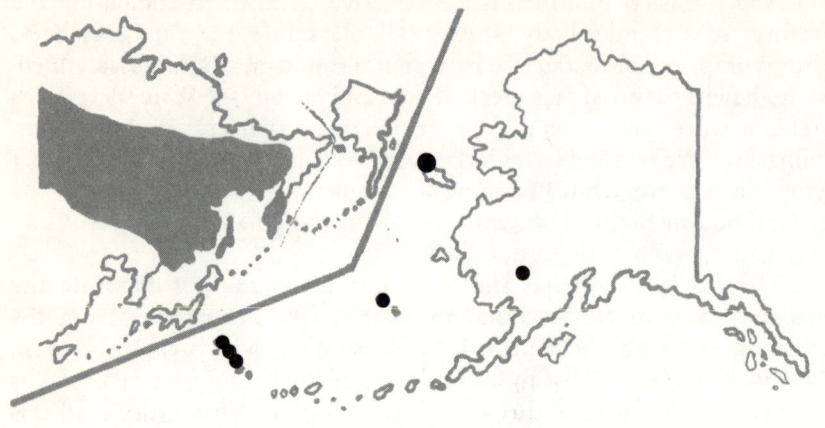

Jun 1975 at Gambell, St. Lawrence I., ALASKA. *John G. Keenleyside.*

I.D. The Common Rosefinch generally resembles American finches of the genus *Carpodacus*. The adult male has a purer red crown, throat and breast than the purple-red color on Purple Finch *C. purpureus* and the often more orange-red color on House Finch *C. mexicanus*. Like Purple Finch, Common Rosefinch has an unstreaked belly, flanks, and undertail coverts. Females and immatures are very plain-faced, with the beady black eye the most prominent feature. The upperparts of females and immatures are plain, with two whitish wingbars, and the underparts are obscurely streaked across the breast, enclosing the white throat.

## COMMON ROSEFINCH

A number of Asian species of *Carpodacus* exist, but all are more extensively colored than Common Rosefinch: males have a more distinct facial pattern and females are more heavily streaked below.

The call of Common Rosefinch is a plaintive "whooeep", utterred in flight and when perched. The song is a monotonous repetition of the same simple whistled phrase "teetu-ti-teu".

# BLACK ROSY FINCH

*Leucosticte atrata*

Breeds N Great Basin mtns. of U.S. Winters in Great Basin lowlands.

The Black Rosy Finch breeds on Steens Mt., Har., and perhaps elsewhere in E ORE. Intergrade populations with Gray-crowned Rosy Finch *L. tephrocotis* might also be present, as they are in nearby Idaho mnts. It is a Rarity away from ORE along the West Coast; the only records are of winter birds in E CAL among large flocks of Gray-crowned Rosy Finch.

Most authorities consider this bird conspecific with Gray-crowned Rosy Finch; it would not be a surprise to find it "lumped" within the very near future.

**CALIFORNIA**   Five records: 15 Jan 1904† at Bodie, Mono (C 30:191), 19 Nov 1949 (2†) at Westgard Pass, Inyo (C 71:733), 11-20 Nov 1972 (2-3) at Westgard & Gilbert Passes, White Mtns., Inyo, 28 Nov 1975 at Westgard Pass, and 31 Mar 1980 at Conway Summit, near Bridgeport, Mono.

An additional record of two specimens taken on 30 Mar 1941 at Hallelujah Junction, Las., is not from CAL. The birds were collected in Nevada a few hundred yards away from the CAL border (G. McCaskie, *per. com.*).

# ORIENTAL GREENFINCH             Plate 9

*Carduelis sinica*

Breeds NE Asia. Winters China, Taiwan.

The Oriental Greenfinch has been found on the West Coast only as a spring or fall vagrant on the westernmost Aleutian Is., ALASKA. Small flocks were recorded in spring 1976 and fall 1977.

**ALASKA** Nine records (through spring 1980), five during the spring: four records on Buldir I. — 22 May 1976 (flock of six), 8 Jun 1976, 14 Jun 1976 (flock of five), 4 Jun 1977†, and one record on Attu I. — 17-18 May 1980. There are four fall records: three on Shemya I. — 5 Sep 1977 (flock of four, 1†), 11 Sep 1977, 18 Sep 1977 (two, 1†), and another on Buldir I.: 19 Aug 1976.

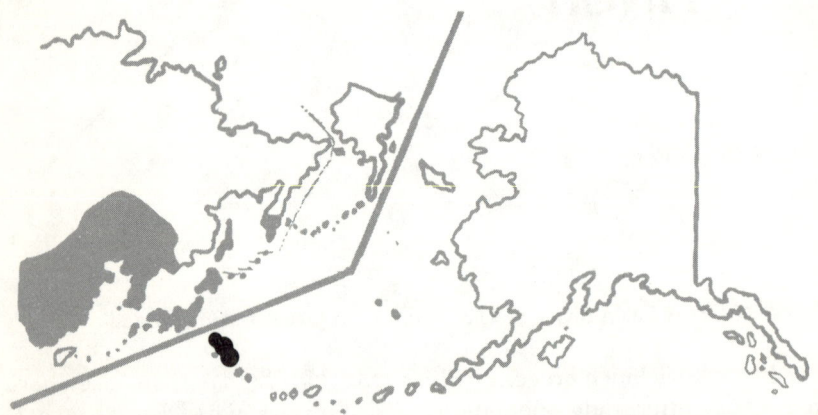

I.D. The Oriental Greenfinch is a small finch a bit larger and chunkier than Common Redpoll *C.flammea*. The extensive yellow patch in the wing of all ages and sexes, formed by yellow bases to the primaries, and the yellow patches at the sides of the base of the tail will recall Pine Siskin *C. pinus,* but these yellow patches stand out even more prominently on the dark-plumaged Oriental Greenfinch. Males have a grayish head, tawny-green back and wings, greenish breast and rump, and yellow undertail coverts and underwing linings. Females are a sandy-brown, with somewhat grayer face, and are most easily identified by the yellow patches in the wing and tail. Immatures resemble females, but the centers of the upperpart feathers are darker and the bird looks obscurely streaked. The large pinkish bill, contrasting with the plain dark head, is an additional field mark at any age or of either sex.

## ORIENTAL GREENFINCH

In flight, males look all dark tawny-green with prominent yellow wing stripe and yellow base to the tail; these features can be noted during brief views or at a distance. The call is said to be a "thin, rather high-pitched metallic tinkle" (King & Dickinson, 1975).

# COMMON REDPOLL

*Carduelis flammea*

Breeds N North America, N Eurasia. Winters erratically and irregularly south to N U.S., C Eurasia.

The Common Redpoll nests in ALASKA and N B.C. It is a winter visitor (numbers varying widely during irregular invasions) on the West Coast south to NE ORE with some regularity. Some years it reaches SE ORE and apparently there was a major southern invasion in 1899, as a flock reached NE CAL. There is only one record in CAL during this century.

Some authorities consider this bird conspecific with Hoary Redpoll *C. hornemanni*, a very similar species which nests in ALASKA and is a scarce winter visitor to N B.C. The generally rarer Hoary is often found in winter with flocks of Common Redpoll. Specimens have been taken throughout the interior of B.C., as far south as Okanagan and Grindrod in SE B.C. Observers in E WASH and E ORE might look for it during invasion winters, but any sighting needs to be well documented (there are undocumented reports from WASH, where it is listed as hypothetical).

**CALIFORNIA** Three records: 30 Nov-23 Dec 1899 (flock from which 3† were taken) near Eagle Lake, Las. (C 4:45), 23 Dec 1899† in Plumas Co., and 22 May 1969† at Manilla, Hmb. The latter bird is the only recent record and was taken on an exceptionally late date for this species to be this far south.

# COMMON REDPOLL

I.D. The Common Redpoll is very similar to Hoary Redpoll *C. hornemanni*. Standard field guides emphasize the larger size, paler color, and unstreaked pale rump of Hoary Redpoll. Size and paleness are quite variable in Common Redpoll and are not of much value in separating out the Hoary, but these features can be useful to first draw one's attention to a possibly interesting bird. Hoary Redpoll can be identified by the combination of 1) an unstreaked pale rump, well seen, and 2) pure white and unstreaked undertail coverts. In addition, Hoary Redpolls have shorter, more conical bills which give the face a "pushed-in" look, but some Common Redpolls can also appear this way. The presence of "pantaloons" — the long shaggy tarsal feathers — is apparently of little value as the two birds overlap widely in this characteristic.

# LESSER GOLDFINCH

*Carduelis psaltria*

Breeds W U.S. to NW South America. Mostly resident, though some birds withdraw from colder areas in winter.

The Lesser Goldfinch nests widely in CAL and ORE and very locally in S WASH (especially around Lyle, Klk.). There is only one record north of WASH, a probable spring overshoot just across the international border in SW B.C.

**BRITISH COLUMBIA** One record: 17 May 1958† at Huntingdon (M 39:25, C 44:33).

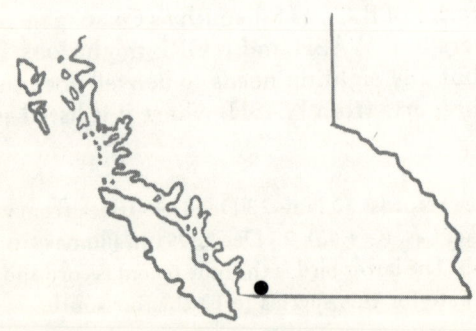

# WHITE-WINGED CROSSBILL

*Loxia leucoptera*

Breeds N North America, N Eurasia. Wanders widely and erratically.

The White-winged Crossbill is an eruptive species, wandering widely in fall and winter and sometimes staging invasions which bring nesting birds to areas in which they do not breed regularly. It nests regularly in C ALASKA and N B.C. It is a rare breeding bird in the Cascade Mtns. of WASH and winter records are scattered widely in that state. In ORE, it has been taken in summer in the Wallowa Mtns. (1938) and migrant and winter records are scattered about the state and birds have reached the coast in late fall. A major eruptive movement of White-winged Crossbills occurred during the winter of 1977-78. A flock of 40 reached the coast of SW WASH and scattered birds were found along the ORE coast and in the Cascades of both states. During this eruption a flock was found in N CAL, the only record for that state. The invasion of 1977-78 continued into the summer; birds were found summering in several counties of NE ORE and the first ORE nesting record occurred in Grant Co. Though its occurrence in ORE is erratic and irregular, it does not seem to be a Rarity there and can only claim that status in CAL.

**CALIFORNIA** One record: 1 Sep 1978* (flock of 12) at Mosquito Lake, Trn.

# LARK BUNTING

*Calamospiza melanocorys*

Breeds C North America. Winters SW U.S. to C Mexico.

The Lark Bunting is an irregular migrant and winter visitor to the West Coast in CAL. Over 160 records exist for CAL, including flocks of 20-40 birds; most occurred during the fall and winter, but spring vagrants are found annually as well. Records through 1970 are discussed in Wilbur,

# LARK BUNTING

Carrier & McCaskie (1971). Lark Bunting has recently (1975-1979) been averaging about 12 records a year, some of which pertain to small flocks. In 1978, following draught-ending rains, a nest was found in the Lanfair Valley, S.Bn., CAL, which fledged young — a brief but substantial expansion of the breeding range (nearest known regular breeding areas are in NW New Mexico and E Colorado).

Lark Bunting is a Rarity north of CAL on the West Coast. Records are well scattered throughout the year and include every season.

**OREGON** Four records: 2-3 Jan 1967† at Corvallis, Ben., 6 Aug 1969 (2) at Yaquina Head, Lnc., early Jan-4 May 1972 at Portland, Mul., and 15 Sep 1979* (2) at Cape Blanco, Cur.

**WASHINGTON** Two records: 16 Jun 1967 at Marietta, Wha., and 2 Sep 1973 at Cape Flattery, Clm.

**BRITISH COLUMBIA** Five records, four from the interior during the spring and summer: 1 Aug 1906† at Chilliwack (A 32:107), 8 Jun 1914† at Okanagan Landing, 28 May 1939† at Wistaria, and 26 May 1953† along Dollyvarden Creek, Kootenay NP. The single coastal record is of a fall vagrant: 5 Oct 1975 at Vancouver.

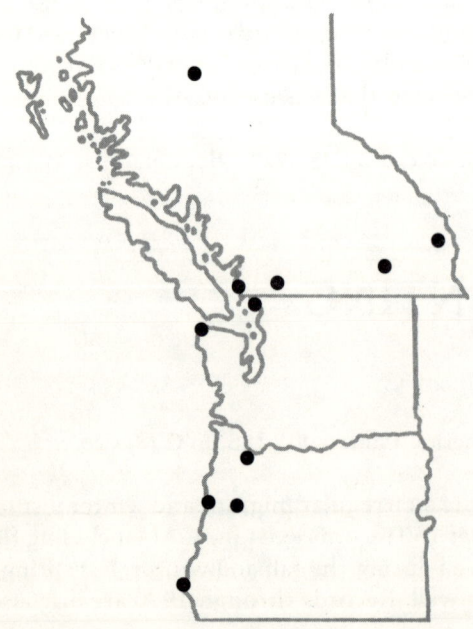

# BAIRD'S SPARROW

*Ammodramus bairdii*

Breeds C North America. Winters SW U.S. to N-C Mexico.

The Baird's Sparrow is a prairie bird which winters in the SW U.S. west to SE Arizona. The only record for the West Coast is of a fall vagrant on the Farallon Is., CAL. It might be looked for in winter along the CAL side of the Colorado R. in open grass habitat, but searches to date in these areas have yielded no signs of this secretive sparrow.

**CALIFORNIA**   One record: 28 Sep 1969† on SE Farallon I.

# LE CONTE'S SPARROW

*Ammospiza leconteii*

Breeds N-C North America. Winters S-C U.S.

The Le Conte's Sparrow has been recorded on the West Coast only as an extremely rare spring and fall vagrant. All records fall with narrow periods: mid-Oct–mid-Nov in the fall and late May in the spring.

**WASHINGTON**   One record: 29 May 1964† at Kennewick, Ben. This bird was killed when it struck a window.

**CALIFORNIA**   Seven records, six during the fall: 13 Oct 1970† on SE Farallon I.; 19 Oct 1974 at Pacific Grove, Mnt.; 27 Oct-1 Nov 1974 at Furnace Creek, Inyo, and a second bird present there on 28 Oct 1974; 16 Nov 1974* at Wildcat Canyon, Richmond, C.C.; and 23-24 Oct 1976 at Little Lake, Inyo. The only spring record was 21-24 May 1977* at Furnace Creek.

# LE CONTE'S SPARROW

19 Oct 1974 at Pt. Pinos, Pacific Grove, Mnt., CAL. 2nd record. *Ronald L. Branson.*

I.D. The Le Conte's Sparrow is a distinctive bird, but the standard guides tend to tone down its bright colors and contrasts and this has caused it to be confused with immature Grasshopper Sparrow *A. savannarum*. Both species show a white median stripe on the crown and magenta stripes on a gray nape. The Le Conte's Sparrow is distinguished by 1) its bright orange (not just buffy) breast and supercilium, 2) a sharp contrast between the orange breast and white belly, 3) distinct black streaks on the sides and flanks, 4) a blackish back streaked with buff, 5) gray cheeks, and 6) a powder blue (not white) eyering. For a more thorough discussion see Dunn (1976b).

# SHARP-TAILED SPARROW

*Ammospiza caudacuta*

Breeds N-C & NE North America. Winters E & SE U.S.

The Sharp-tailed Sparrow nests locally in NE B.C. (Peace R. district). Migration takes it well east of the West Coast, but apparently a few birds regularly winter in coastal salt marshes in CAL: an average of five birds a year have been found recently in these marshes in winter. Much of the habitat is unaccessible and there may be other undetected birds wintering each year as well. In habitat that is checked regularly, a few birds are found nearly every year at the same locations. Away from the apparent regular wintering spots, Sharp-tailed Sparrow is extremely rare. There are only 3 fall records at non-wintering areas and two records of spring migrants in the interior.

**CALIFORNIA** Very rare wintering bird in extensive salt water coastal marshes. Several were taken in 1891 & 1896 at Milpitas, S.Cl., and two wintered at Venice, L.A., in 1944; these marshes are now gone. Areas were it may winter annually include marshes at the east end of Dumbarton Bridge, S.Cl. (recorded in winters of 1962-63, 1963-64, 1970-71*, 1972-73, 1973-74, and 1978-79), Palo Alto, S.Cl. (winters of 1977-78, 1978-79), Bolinas Lagoon, Mrn. (winters of 1976-77, 1977-78, 1978-79 — up to 4 birds present), Morro Bay, S.L.O. (winters of 1952-53 and 1970-71 — 5 birds present in 1953), and Newport Bay, Orn. (recorded annually since winter 1970-71 — up to 3 birds present). Dates of wintering birds stretch from 17 Oct-6 May; a bird was singing at Palo Alto on 23 Apr 1979 (presumably just before departing). Fall records away from the wintering areas are: 2 Nov 1963 at Imperial Beach, S.D., 12 Oct 1975 at Pacific Grove, Mnt., and 4 Oct 1977* at Neary's Lagoon, Santa Cruz. An interesting inland sighting in late winter was on 29 Mar 1975 at Imperial Dam, Imp., on the Colorado R. There are two records of apparent spring migrants (or spring vagrants) in E CAL: 26 May 1976* at Oasis, Mono, and 27-29 May 1976* at Furnace Creek, Inyo.

8 Feb 1978 at Palo Alto, S.Cl., CAL. *Al Ghiorso.*

# SHARP-TAILED SPARROW

I.D. All records of Sharp-tailed Sparrow in CAL are suspected of pertaining to the bright prairie-nesting race *A. c. nelsoni*. This race is pictured in the standard field guides but the bright colors are muted and other species of sparrows are sometimes misidentified as Sharp-tailed Sparrow. The face and breast of Sharp-tailed Sparrow are bright ochre-orange, much more orange than any regularly occurring West Coast sparrow and approaching the brightness of Le Conte's Sparrow *A. leconteii*. These bright colors, combined with the features of gray cheeks, dark gray cap, unstreaked gray nape, white stripes on a dark back, and smudgy streaks to the sides of the breast and to the sides and flanks, will identify this bird. For a more thorough discussion see Dunn (1976b).

# CASSIN'S SPARROW

*Aimophila cassinii*

Breeds SW U.S., N Mexico. Northern populations move south in winter.

The Cassin's Sparrow has been recorded on the West Coast only in CAL, where the few records fall into two distinct subdivisions: 1) misoriented spring and fall vagrants, all records of which are from SE Farallon I., and 2) spring and summer nomads in potential breeding habitat in the interior of S CAL, probably in response to an environmentally shifting breeding range (see Hubbard, 1977). Most of the latter birds have been singing males defending territory for a brief time and then disappearing.

# CASSIN'S SPARROW

**CALIFORNIA** Perhaps 25 records, but over 15 of these occurred during the spring & summer of 1978 in potential breeding habitat in SE CAL, following heavy drought-ending rains which produced lush vegetation. Up to 15 singing males were in the Lanfair Valley, S.Bn., from 21 May-7 Jun, and another singing bird was s. of Barstow, S.Bn., from 8-16 May 1978. A non-singing bird away from breeding habitat occurred that same spring: 2 May 1978 at the north end, Salton Sea, Riv. A site at El Cajon, S.D., has held a singing bird three times: 15-30 May 1970, 8-11 May 1976*, and 10-12 Jun 1978. Records of spring and fall vagrants are from SE Farallon I.: 25 Sep 1967, 11-12 Jul 1969, 22-23 Sep 1969†, 2-4 Jun 1970†, and 12 Jun 1975.

11 Jul 1969 on SE Farallon I., CAL. 2nd record. *Malcolm Coulter, courtesy Point Reyes Bird Observatory.*

I.D. The Cassin's Sparrow is a mid-sized, generally grayish and nondescript sparrow with a flat-crowned, long-billed, and long-tailed shape. Singing males are easily recognized by their distinctive song and "skylarking" habits. The standard field guides are generally adequate, but fail to note the white tips to the outer tail feathers, best seen in flight, which help distinguish it from the similar Botteri's Sparrow *A. botterii*, a possible vagrant to the West Coast. A good painting of Cassin's Sparrow is in Hubbard (1977) and an article dealing with the Cassin's vs. Botteri's problem is expected in *Continental Birdlife* in 1981.

# BLACK-THROATED SPARROW

*Amphispiza bilineata*

Breeds Great Basin & SW U.S. to N-C Mexico. Northern populations winter to the south.

The Black-throated Sparrow nests on the West Coast in the desert of SE CAL and the Great Basin of NE CAL and SE ORE. It is a Rarity on the West Coast north of ORE, where all records appear to be of spring overshoots in May-Jun. Hunn (1978) has suggested that drought conditions within the breeding range contribute to vagrancy in this species and summarizes all records of western vagrants.

**WASHINGTON** Five records: 31 May 1908 near Brooks Lake, Dgl. (pair, including singing male), 23-24 May 1959 at Ohanapecosh Ranger Station, Mt. Ranier NP, Prc., 28 May 1970 at Horsehaven Hills, near Mabton, Yak., 16 May 1976 at Pt. Grenville, G.H., and 10 May 1977 at Walla Walla. See Hunn (1978) for more details.

**BRITISH COLUMBIA** One record: 8 Jun 1959† at Murtle Lake, Wells Gray PP (CFN 75:162).

# SAGE SPARROW

*Amphispiza belli*

Breeds Great Basin & coastal C CAL to Baja, Mexico. N Great Basin populations winter in SW U.S.

# SAGE SPARROW

The Sage Sparrow nests on the West Coast in CAL, E ORE, and E WASH. There is a single record north of WASH: a fall vagrant which proved to be of the migratory N Great Basin race *E. b. nevadensis*.

**BRITISH COLUMBIA**   One record: 2 Oct 1930† at Lulu I., Vancouver (M 13:1).

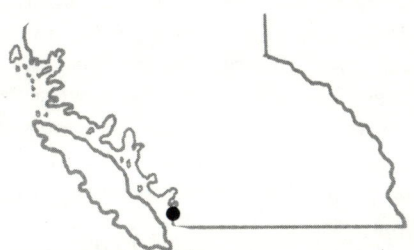

# GRAY-HEADED JUNCO

*Junco caniceps*

Breeds on mtns. in the Great Basin of U.S. Winters at lower elevations from SW U.S. to NW Mexico.

The Gray-headed Junco nests in the White Mtns. and on Clark Mt. in E CAL. It is a Rarity north of CAL, where the single acceptable record is of a bird at a feeder in the fall.
   Some authorities consider this bird conspecific with Dark-eyed Junco *J. hyemalis*.

**BRITISH COLUMBIA**   One record: 8-10 Nov 1975 at Qualicum Beach, V.I. (M 57:51).

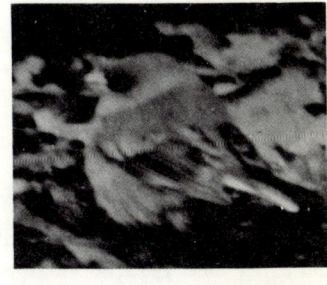

8 Nov 1975 at Qualicum Beach, V.I., B.C. 1st record. *Neil K. Dawe.*

# CLAY-COLORED SPARROW

*Spizella pallida*

Breeds N-C North America. Winters S Texas to S Mexico.

The Clay-colored Sparrow nests on the West Coast in NE B.C. It had been thought to be very rare on the West Coast south of B.C., but CAL has recently (1975-1979) averaged over 35 birds a year. Nearly 90% of the CAL records occurred during the fall and most appear to be misoriented immatures. The coast receives most of these birds, but a substantial number have occurred in the interior, especially at desert oases. Spring vagrants in CAL mostly fall into the late May-early Jun pattern shown by many eastern vagrants. A few have wintered in coastal C & S CAL.

The Clay-colored Sparrow is considered a Rarity in ORE and WASH. ORE records are of wintering birds and there is an additional winter record from WASH. This species may be attempting to breed near Spokane, WASH; most of the state's records come from that area and several have been found there throughout the summer, though evidence of nesting is lacking.

**WASHINGTON**   12 records, graphed below. 8 records are from near Spokane (4 spring, 2 summer, 2 fall), where the species may be attempting to nest. 3 singing males and female were present in Spokane Valley from 26 Jun-8 Jul 1979, but no evidence of nesting was obtained. Such evidence might be obtained in this area in the future. There is a late fall record from the Skagit flats, Skg., — 8 Nov 1976 — and a wintering individual was present there from Dec 1974-20 Apr 1975. The two additional state records were during the spring and summer: 2-9 Jul 1977 at Valley, Stv., and 21 Apr 1979 at St. Andrews, Dgl.

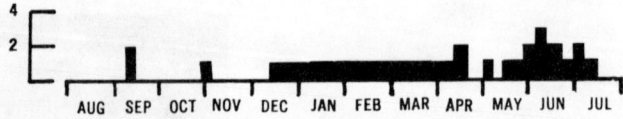

**OREGON**   Three records, all during the winter: 2 Feb-8 Mar 1974* at Eugene, Lane, 14 Dec 1975 at Tillamook, and late Dec 1979-Mar 1980* at Nehalem Meadows, near Mohler, Til.

# CLAY-COLORED SPARROW

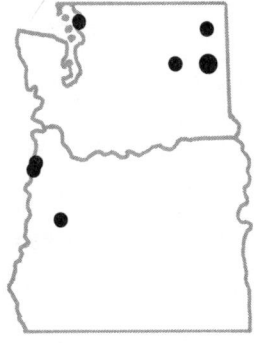

Nov 1975 at Furnace Creek, Death Valley NM, Inyo, CAL. *Herbert Clarke.*

I.D. The standard field guides are generally adequate to distinguish adult Clay-colored Sparrow, but more information is needed to separate immature Clay-colored Sparrow (which account for most CAL records) from immature Chipping Sparrow *S. passerina* and Brewer's Sparrow *S. breweri*. Chipping Sparrow is the darkest of the three, with a diagnostic dark gray rump (best viewed in flight — Clay-colored and Brewer's have a paler brown-gray rump), and mostly dusky-gray underparts. Early in the fall, immature Chipping is heavily streaked on the breast (Aug-Sep), a feature not shared by either Clay-colored or Brewer's. Both immature Chipping and immature Clay-colored have a whitish median stripe on the crown, a whitish supercilium, and a dark cheek patch. Brewer's Sparrow is separated from these birds by its pale sandy-brown color, the lack of a whitish median stripe (the crown is finely streaked with black), and by a thin white eyering. By Oct, when immature Chipping Sparrow has lost its breast streaks, the best points separating it from Clay-colored Sparrow are 1) the brighter buffy breast of Clay-colored Sparrow, 2) the contrast between a gray nape and the rest of the head and breast of Clay-colored Sparrow, looking like a gray collar at a distance (Chipping may have a gray nape, but it does not contrast much from the head and breast), 3) often a brighter pink bill on Clay-colored Sparrow, 4) a dark line through the lores on Chipping Sparrow (lacking on Clay-colored), and 5) a crisper face pattern and noticeable whitish malar stripe of Clay-colored Sparrow. For more information see Simon (1977) and Dunn (1975a).

The soft "tsip" call note of Clay-colored Sparrow is similar to the call of Brewer's Sparrow, but is distinguishable with practice from the sweeter "tseet" note of Chipping Sparrow.

# FIELD SPARROW

*Spizella pusilla*

Breeds E North America. Winters E U.S. to NE Mexico.

The Field Sparrow has occurred only once on the West Coast: a spring vagrant reached SE Farallon I., CAL. Though a rather common species in the East, its relatively short migration routes and the mostly north-south migration direction may lessen the chances of "mirror-image" misoriented birds from reaching the West Coast.

**CALIFORNIA**   One record: 17 Jun-9 Jul 1969 on SE Farallon I. (CB 2:27).

17 Jun 1969 on SE Farallon I., CAL. 1st record. *Henry Robert, courtesy Point Reyes Bird Observatory.*

# BLACK-CHINNED SPARROW

*Spizella atrogularis*

Breeds SW U.S. to S-C Mexico. Northern populations winter to the south.

The Black-chinned Sparrow nests on the West Coast in CAL, regularly north in the foothills around the Central Valley to Lake and Mariposa Cos., and occasionally eruptive movements will bring nesting birds north to Tehama Co. These irregular eruptions have sent Black-chinned Sparrows north of CAL in 1970, 1971, 1977, and 1979. During these springs it was found near Medford, in S ORE, and pairs there in summer 1970 and 1977 may have nested, though evidence is lacking.

# BLACK-CHINNED SPARROW

**OREGON**   6 records, all near Medford, Jck. Four were at Roxy Ann Butte: 7 Jun-2 Jul 1970 (pair), 15 May 1971, late May-29 Jul 1977* (pair), and Jun 1979. An additional two singing males were present 10 miles ne. of Medford on 23 May 1979 and one was still present on 11 Jun 1979. Nesting was suspected in 1970 and 1977, but no evidence was obtained.

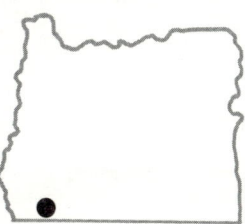

14 Jun 1977 at Roxy Ann Butte, near Medford, Jck., ORE. 3rd record. *Otis Swisher.*

# SWAMP SPARROW

*Melospiza georgiana*

Breeds N North America. Winters E U.S.

The Swamp Sparrow nests on the West Coast in NE B.C. More than 20 a year have been found recently in CAL, nearly all during the late fall and winter, and it might be thought of as regular in winter there in small numbers. It is still considered a Rarity in ORE and WASH. All records in those states are during the late fall and winter and it might be regular there in small numbers as well, but its secretive habits and the comparatively few observers in those states may contribute to the few records. A very high percentage of all records on the West Coast south of B.C. are along the coast; some areas — such as Olema marsh, Mrn., CAL — concentrate birds during the winter (there were 22 there in winter 1974-75). Fall birds are found annually at patches of cover in the deserts and Great Basin areas of E CAL, but records during spring migration are very scarce.

# SWAMP SPARROW

**WASHINGTON**   Six records: 24 Feb-8 Apr 1973 at Lake Sammamish SP, King (WB 4:31), 20 Oct 1974 at Sun Lakes Campground, Grn., 22 Dec 1974 at Anacortes, Skg., late Dec 1974 at Lummi flats, Skg., 28 Dec 1974 at Wiser Lake, Wha., and 23 Nov 1979 at Ocean City SP, G.H.

**OREGON**   12 records, graphed below. The peak in late Dec probably reflects the more thorough coverage during Christmas Counts rather than a true peak; most of the birds probably wintered locally. All records are from W ORE; 6 were at Fern Ridge Res., near Eugene, Lane.

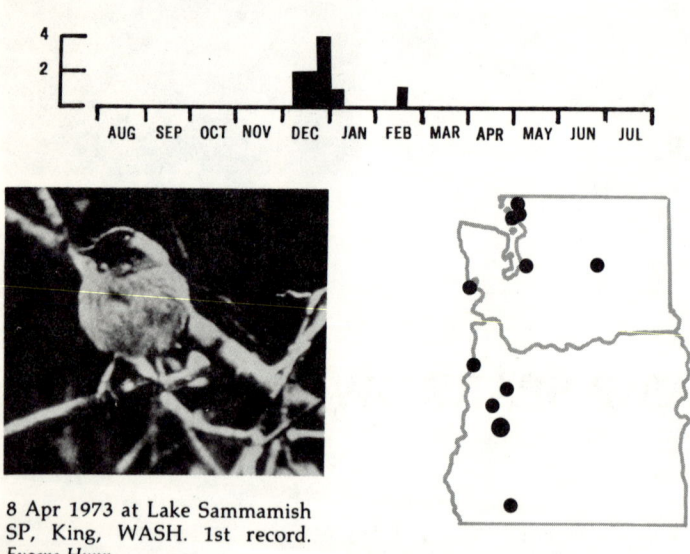

8 Apr 1973 at Lake Sammamish SP, King, WASH. 1st record.
*Eugene Hunn.*

# McCOWN'S LONGSPUR

*Calcarius mccownii*

Breeds N Great Plains of North America. Winters SW U.S. to N-C Mexico.

The McCown's Longspur is considered a Rarity anywhere on the West Coast. Although it is not on the list of birds to be reviewed by the CAL Records Committee (perhaps because there are areas where it may be looked for with success during most years), it has recently averaged less than 4 birds a year (1975-1979) and meets our definition. The records on

# McCOWN'S LONGSPUR

the West Coast are easily separated into two patterns: 1) apparent spring overshoots west of the Alberta breeding range in the interior of B.C., and 2) late fall and winter records from CAL, often with flocks of Horned Lark *Eremophila alpestris* and other longspurs.

**BRITISH COLUMBIA** Three records, all spring records in the interior: 1 Jun 1887† at Chilliwack, 20 Jun 1890† at Chilliwack, and 29 May 1930† at Newgate.

**CALIFORNIA** 34 records, involving at least 84 birds, graphed below. There are several fall records from Imperial Beach, S.D. (5 records) and from open fields in eastern L.A. Co. (4); other fall records are scattered through E CAL. The only coastal record from N CAL was 16 Oct-7 Nov 1978 (2) at Pt. Reyes NS, Mrn. All the winter records are from Great Basin areas in NE CAL, especially Honey Lake, Las. (3 records, up to 3 birds on 31 Dec 1974), or open areas of SE CAL, especially the Imperial Valley, Imp. (9 records, sometimes small flocks, up to 20 birds in winter 1966-67).

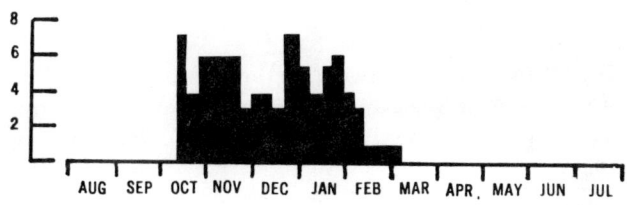

# CHESTNUT-COLLARED LONGSPUR

*Calcarius ornatus*

Breeds N Great Plains of North America. Winters SW U.S. to C Mexico.

The Chestnut-collared Longspur does not nest on the West Coast, but numbers of fall migrants and wintering birds, sometimes in flocks, appear annually in CAL. Numbers fluctuate from year to year. Fall birds are most often found in the Great Basin of NE CAL, the deserts of E & SE CAL, and in open fields along the coast. Small numbers, sometimes involving flocks, winter in the Great Basin (especially Honey Lake, Las.; a flock of 180 wintered there in 1974-75), the Imperial Valley, and occasionally SW CAL.

Chestnut-collared Longspur is a Rarity north of CAL. Interior records during the spring in B.C. and the coastal fall record in ORE might be expected, but the spring and summer reports along the coast are surely exceptional.

**BRITISH COLUMBIA** 4 records, two from the interior: 8 Jul 1921† at Kispiox Valley, and 29 May 1930† at Newgate. Two spring records are from the coast: 18 Jun 1972 at Faber Inlets, Barkley Sound (CFN 87:66), and 1-3 May 1977 at Victoria, V.I.

**WASHINGTON** Two records: 7 Jul 1974 at Tokeland, Pac., and 24-26 Jun 1975 at Pt. Grenville, G.H. (both discussed in M 60:108).

**OREGON** Two records, one during the fall: 9 Oct 1974 (3) at Bayocean spit, Tillamook Bay, and one from the spring: 1 May 1976* at Fern Ridge Res., near Eugene, Lane.

18 Jun 1972 at Faber Islets, Barkley Sound, B.C. 3rd record. *David F. Hatler.*

# CHESTNUT-COLLARED LONGSPUR

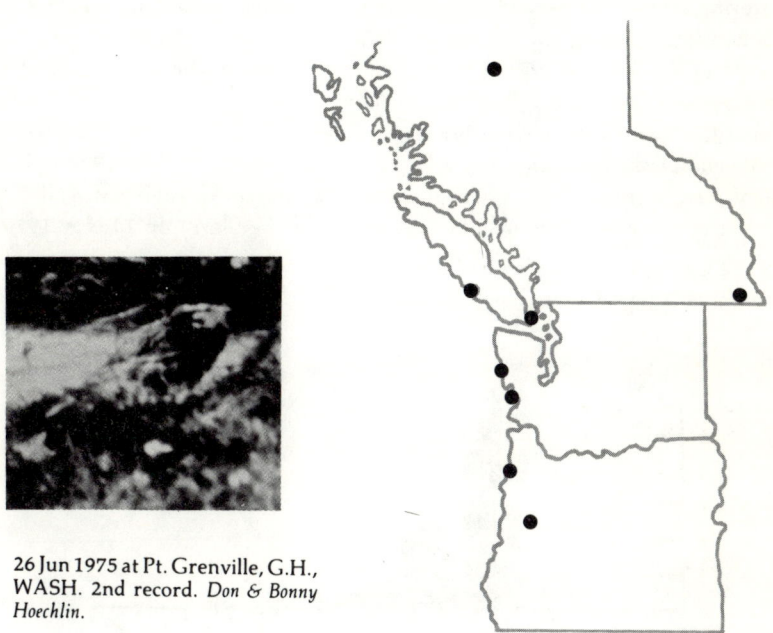

26 Jun 1975 at Pt. Grenville, G.H., WASH. 2nd record. *Don & Bonny Hoechlin.*

# SNOW BUNTING

*Plectrophenax nivalis*

Breeds N North America, N Eurasia. Winters south to N U.S., C Europe.

The Snow Bunting nests in N & W ALASKA. It is a regular wintering bird on the West Coast from C ALASKA to ORE, numbers decreasing as one moves farther south. It is more common along the coasts of WASH & ORE than it is in the interior, and only small numbers reach the interior of those states. It is a Rarity in CAL, where most records are in the late fall. There are also a number of winter records.

# SNOW BUNTING

**CALIFORNIA** 54 records, graphed below. Most records, and nearly all the wintering birds, have been in coastal NW CAL. High counts include 4 birds near Arcata, Hmb., during the winter of 1972-73, and up to 9 present near Lake Talawa, D.N., during winter of 1974-75. Along the coast, the southernmost bird was present 2 Dec 1972-11 Jan 1973 at Alameda, Ala. Interesting records inland west of the Sierra were 4 Nov 1961 at Sacramento NWR, Gln., 19-30 Nov 1977 at Monticello Dam, Yolo, and one very far south from 23-27 Dec 1978 at Kelso Valley, near Mohave, Kern. There are 5 records from the Great Basin of NE CAL; another bird was exceptionally far south east of the Sierra on 14 Nov 1970 at Scotty's Castle, Death Valley NM, Inyo. The single spring record was of an adult male on 11 May 1978 at Cape Mendocino, Hmb.

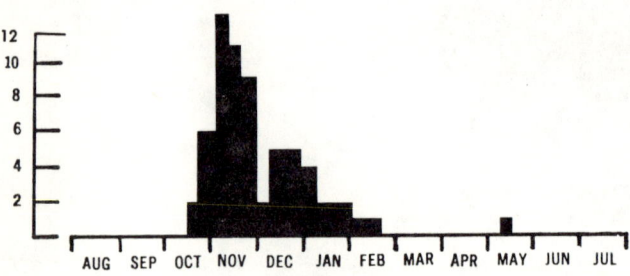

27 Nov 1977 at Monticello Dam, Yolo, CAL. *Herbert Clarke.*

# McKAY'S BUNTING

*Plectrophenax hyperboreus*

Breeds islands in Bering Sea. Winters Bering Sea coast of Alaska.

The McKay's Bunting is a common breeder on Hall and St. Matthew Is., a rare breeder on St. Lawrence I., and a very rare nesting bird on the Pribilof Is. Wintering birds are usually restricted to the Bering Sea coast of W ALASKA and Nunivak I., but during the winter of 1978-79 birds were seen far to the east and south, appearing at Women's Bay, Kodiak I., ALASKA (2 to 4 birds) and two birds were found much farther south in W WASH. Another was even farther south, on the ORE coast, in winter 1980.

**WASHINGTON** Two records, both at Ocean Shores, G.H.: a bird in nearly clean breeding plumage was present 16-18 Dec 1978 and one in winter plumage was present 16 Dec 1978-3 Mar 1979.

**OREGON** One record: 23 Feb-2 Mar 1980 at the south jetty, Columbia R., Clt.

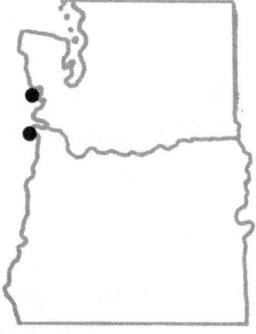

23 Dec 1978 at Ocean Shores, G.H., WASH. 2nd record. *Robert M. Evans.*

# LITTLE BUNTING

Plate 9

*Emberiza pusilla*

Breeds N Eurasia. Winters India, S Asia to Philippines.

The Little Bunting as been found only twice in ALASKA; both records are of fall vagrant immatures.

**ALASKA** Two records: 6 Sep 1970† aboard a ship in the Chukchi Sea nearly 200 miles north-west of Icy Cape (A 91:417), and 8 Sep 1977† on Shemya I., western Aleutians.

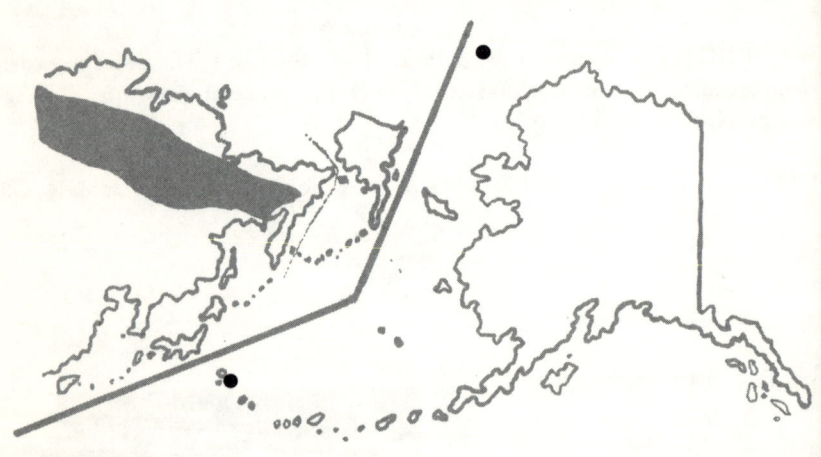

I.D. The Little Bunting is a small, compact, rather short-tailed bunting; in size and "nervous" behavior it recalls Lincoln's Sparrow *Melospiza lincolnii*. Males in breeding plumage have a diagnostic head pattern of rufous or chestnut median stripe on the crown, blackish lateral crown stripes, and rufous supercilium and cheeks (the latter outlined in black); otherwise the plumage resembles that of females and immatures. Useful features at all ages are the small, sharply triangular bill; the shuffling "close-to-the-ground" gait; the habit of raising its crown feathers when alert; and the rather straight-sided tail which is not flirted or flicked so frequently as with other buntings, thus the white outer tail feathers are often not apparent.

# LITTLE BUNTING

As well as the small size and structural features, other characteristics which help identify females and immatures are 1) brownish (not rusty) lesser wing coverts (although these feathers are usually covered when perched), 2) two fairly prominent, thin, white wingbars, 3) rusty or warm-brown median crown stripe bordered by blackish lateral crown stripes, 4) a thin, pale eyering, 5) rusty "face" and front end of supercilium, 6) whitish underparts with fairly profuse, fine, black streaking across the breast and down the flanks, and 7) a call note which is a hard, sharp, clicking "tic", sometimes repeated in a series.

Female and immature Common Reed Bunting *E. schoeniclus* resemble Little Bunting. The Common Reed Bunting is best distinguished by 1) a larger size (about that of a small, slim House Sparrow *Passer domesticus*), 2) a stouter bill with slightly rounded culmen, 3) a dull buff median crown stripe with chestnut lateral crown stripes, 4) buffy supercilium, 5) coarser streaking on the underparts, 6) rusty lesser wing coverts, 7) "fuller" tail which is frequently flicked open to reveal the white outer tail feathers, and 8) a call note which is typically a clear "syew" or "tsew", quite different from Little Bunting's "tick". Immature Pallas' Reed Bunting *E. pallasi* is of similar size to Little Bunting, but has the proportions and behavior of Common Reed Bunting, has much less well-defined streaking and facial pattern, and has a pale rump. Immature Rustic Bunting *E. rustica* resembles Common Reed Bunting in size but has whiter underparts with rusty streaks across the breast (forming a more or less well defined breast band) and which extend down the flanks, a whitish supercilium, a pale patch on the nape, and a habit of raising its crown feathers when alert. Its call — a hard "pit" or "jit" — is somewhat similar to the ticking note of Little Bunting, though is perhaps less sharp. For a more thorough discussion of the field characteristics of Little Bunting see Wallace (1976a).

# RUSTIC BUNTING

Plate 9

*Emberiza rustica*

Breeds N Eurasia. Winters S Europe, S-C Asia.

The Rustic Bunting appears to be a regular spring migrant in small numbers on the westernmost Aleutian Is., ALASKA and there are a few records there from the fall as well. It is very rare away from the Aleutians; there are spring records on St. Lawrence I. and a couple possible sightings much farther south on the West Coast (B.C. and CAL, see Appendix C).

**ALASKA**  Over 60 records, all but three of which are from the western Aleutian Is. About 85% of the records were found during the spring; minimum numbers of spring records (through 1980) from individual islands are: Attu (30), Nizki (1), Alaid (1), Shemya (6), Buldir (7), Kiska (4), and Amchitka (1). Dates stretch from 11 May-19 Jun, with a sharp peak during the last two weeks of May. Fall records date from 15 Sep-27 Oct and come from Shemya I. (1), Amchitka I. (2), and Adak I. (5 — C 58:235). The three spring records away from the western Aleutians were at Gambell, St. Lawrence I.: 10-11 Jun 1973 (2) and 4-9 Jun 1976.

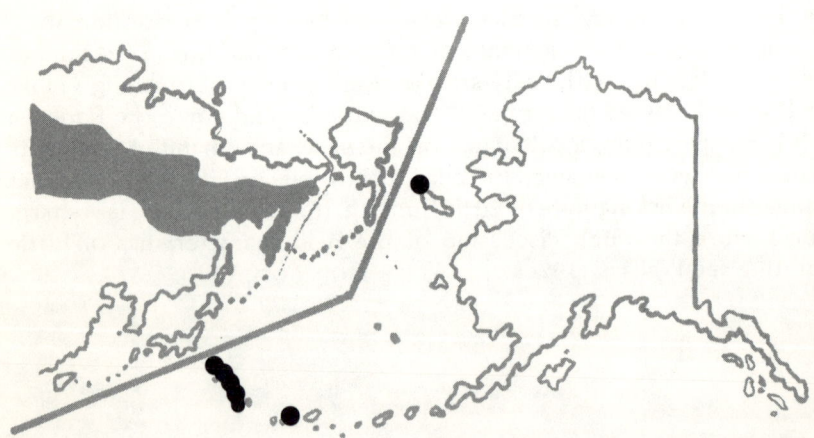

**I.D.** The Rustic Bunting is about the size of Lapland Longspur *Calcarius lapponicus*, but looks slimmer and longer-tailed in the field. Males in breeding plumage are easily recognized by the black head with a white post-ocular stripe, the habit of raising the crown feathers when alert, rusty back, and a rusty breastband. Females and immatures lack the black on the head and rusty back, but show a trace of the male's head pattern,

# RUSTIC BUNTING

usually show a pale spot towards the rear of the ear-patch, have erectile crown feathers, and have some rusty streaking across the breast and on the flanks. The breast streaking usually forms an irregular breastband setting off the white throat. The outer tail feathers are white, conspicuous when the tail is fanned or flitted. Some Rustic Buntings may have rather chestnut cheeks and have been confused with Little Bunting *E. pusilla* (see that discussion), but note the larger size, heavier bill, lack of an eyering, rusty streaking on the breast and flanks (not fine black streaks), and rusty lesser wing coverts.

The call note of Rustic Bunting is a hard "jit" or "pit", recalling the note of Dark-eyed Junco *Junco hyemalis*.

# GRAY BUNTING  Plate 9

*Emberiza variabilis*

Breeds NE Asia. Winters S Japan, E Asia.

The Gray Bunting has been found on the West Coast only on the westernmost Aleutian Is., ALASKA, where both records could refer to spring overshoots.

**ALASKA**  Two records: 18 May 1977† on Shemya I. (A 95:428), and 29 May 1980 on Attu I. The specimen is of an adult male; the sight record appears to be of an immature male.

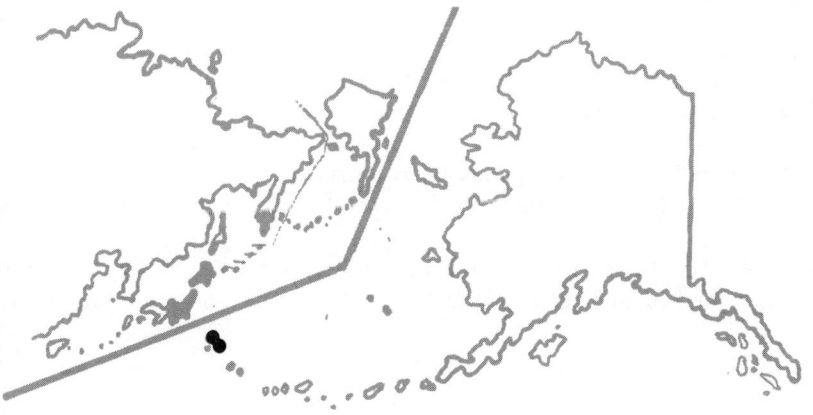

# GRAY BUNTING

I.D. The Gray Bunting is a large, heavy-billed bunting about the size of Lapland Longspur *Calcarius lapponicus*. Males in breeding plumage are essentially all slate gray, including the rump and wing coverts, except for olive-brown edgings to the scapulars and tertials and dark streaking on the back. The gray underparts become paler on the belly. Females are dingy in appearance, with a streaked back and olive and rusty edgings to the scapulars; smudgy gray-brown streaks on dingy underparts; a rather plain brownish face with a paler tan median stripe on the crown and an off-white malar stripe; and chestnut edgings to the rump. This chestnut rump (best viewed in flight) is an excellent field mark. Females in winter may also show rusty streaks on the back, nape, and crown. Immature males resemble females, but the entire rump and uppertail coverts are chestnut (a conspicuous mark in flight). There are rusty edgings to the wing coverts and scapulars, and the underparts are mostly clouded with gray, paling only towards the belly. All ages and sexes have heavy, long bills which are distinctly two-tone — dark culmen and tip and a pale base to the lower mandible. This bill pattern recalls that of Fox Sparrow *Passerella iliaca*.

# PALLAS' REED BUNTING          Plate 9

*Emberiza pallasi*

Breeds NE Asia. Winters E Asia.

The Pallas' Reed Bunting has been found on the West Coast only in ALASKA, where the two records were of apparent spring overshoots.

**ALASKA**  Two records: 11 Jun 1968† at Barrow (Pitelka, 1974), and 28 May 1973 at Gambell, St. Lawrence I. (C 76:108). The two records are of adult males.

# PALLAS' REED BUNTING

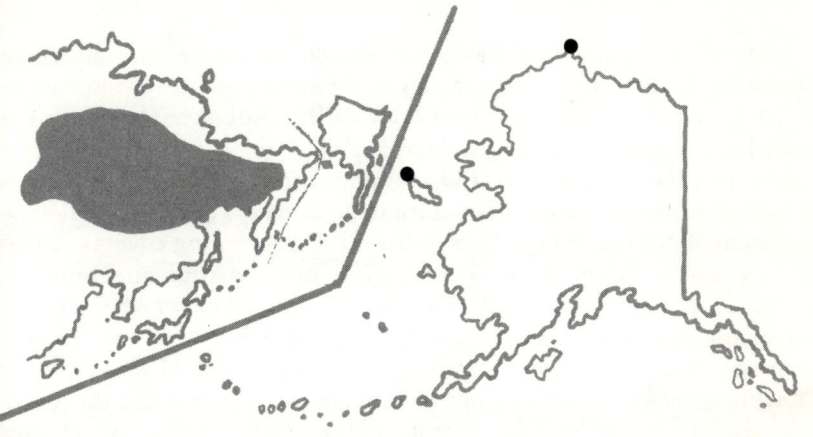

11 Jun 1968 at Pt. Barrow, ALASKA. 1st record. Museum of Vertebrate Zoology, U.C. Berkeley #163423. *Don Roberson.*

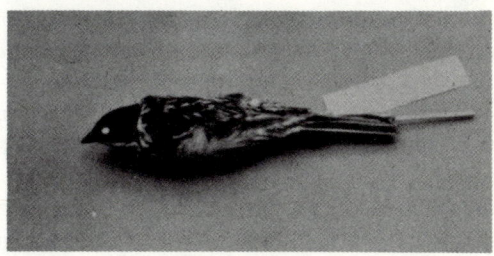

I.D. The Pallas' Reed Bunting is best compared to Common Reed Bunting *E. schoeniclus* (see that account). It is similar in its plumage patterns and might be thought of as a small version of that species. The male in breeding plumage is separated from Common Reed Bunting by black streaking on a pearly-gray (not rusty brown) back, a conspicuous whitish rump, and often a yellow-orange wash to the white collar. Males in winter or in transition show variable amounts of black on the crown, ear-coverts, and throat, often with a pale supercilium, but continue to lack the Common's very rusty edgings to the wings and back and continue to show a distinct pale rump.

# PALLAS' REED BUNTING

Female and immature Pallas' are similar to female and immature Common, but are generally smaller and buffier. Identification can be difficult and little work has been done on this subject. That which is published (Kitson, 1978b) compares Pallas' only to the nominate European race of Common and contains some errors (the article is presently under revision). Separation of female Pallas' from female Common of NE Asian races is possible if the lesser wing coverts can be seen. These are dull brownish on Pallas', but chestnut on Common. Lesser wing coverts are usually covered by other feathers when at rest, but might be noted in flight. Females of the northeasternmost race of Common — *E. s. pyrrhulina* — are larger and rustier than Pallas', usually showing extensive rusty edgings to all wing coverts (not just the lesser wing coverts) and to the back. Females of the race *E. s. minor* — which may breed on the Kamchatka Pen. — may be much more similar to female Pallas'. They appear to be as small as Pallas', often as buffy, and can look pale-rumped. Tentative feature which may separate Pallas' from these birds are 1) lack of rusty lesser wing coverts (diagnostic if seen), 2) lack of outlining to the entire cheek patch, showing only a dark corner to the lower rear edge of cheek patch (see Plate 9), and 3) the presence of pale wingbars on Pallas' females. Both NE Asia races of Common may have the heavy malar stripe clearly demarcated from the finer breast streaks and this is not an important difference between the two buntings (contrary to the suggestion on Plate 9). A more thorough discussion of this entire problem is in preparation; look for its publication elsewhere (C. Wilds, *per. com.*).

Some Pallas' have slightly rusty cheeks and might be confused with the similarly-sized Little Bunting *E. pusilla*, but note the lack of an eye-ring, the indistinct breast streaks, the pale rump, a stouter bill, and habits. Pallas' often flicks its tail (as does Common Reed Bunting), displaying the white outer tail feathers; Little Bunting does not typically indulge in this habit.

The calls — a trisyllabic "pee-see-oo" and a "ch-reep", recalling House Sparrow *Passer domesticus* — are unlike those of Common Reed or Little Bunting (Kitson 1979b).

# COMMON REED BUNTING    Plate 9

*Emberiza schoeniclus*

Breeds N Eurasia. Winters S Eurasia, N Africa.

The Common Reed Bunting has been recorded on the West Coast only on the westernmost Aleutian Is., ALASKA, where the four records are of apparent spring overshoots.

**ALASKA**   Four records: 29 May 1975† on Buldir I. (C. 80:314), 26 May 1977 on Attu I., 4 Jun 1977† on Shemya I., and 24-31 May 1980 on Attu I. Specimens have been identified as the race *E. s. pyrrhulina*, which breeds in Japan and the Kurile Is., but the 1980 sight record may have been of the smaller NE Asia race *E. s. minor*.

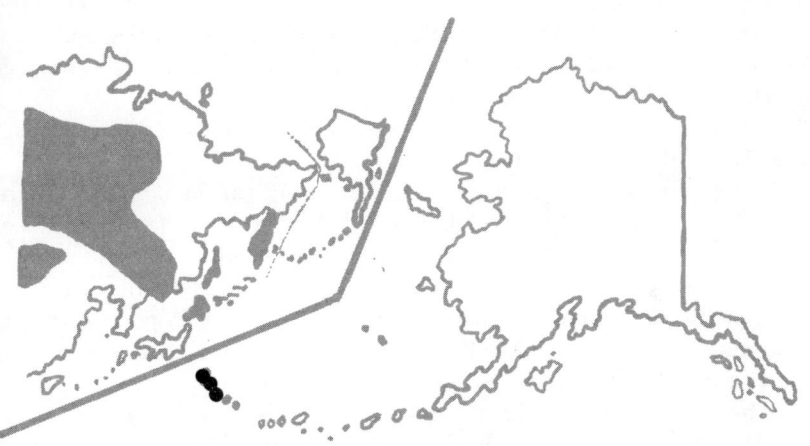

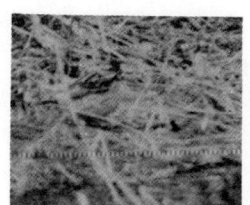

25 May 1980 at Massacre Valley, Attu I., ALASKA. 4th record. *Don Roberson.*

# COMMON REED BUNTING

I.D. The Common Reed Bunting is a widespread Palearctic bunting about the size of Lapland Longspur *Calcarius lapponicus*. Males in breeding plumage are characterized by a black head and throat, divided by a white malar stripe; a bright white collar; black and buffy streaked back; and rusty-edged tertials and wing coverts. In non-breeding plumage males may retain blotches of black on the head and throat, but much of the head and nape is washed with brown and there is often a pale supercilium.

Females and immatures lack the black on the head, showing instead a buffy supercilium on a warm brown head and broad dark malar stripe. On some birds, this malar stripe merges into broad streaks on the underparts; on other birds the malar stripe is clearly separated from finer breast streaks. Birds of the race *E. s. pyrrhulina* usually have rusty flank streaks and considerable rusty to all wing coverts and to the back. The little known race *E. s. minor* is smaller, lacks rusty flank streaks, and may lack rusty to the back. It does have the diagnostic chestnut lesser wing coverts of all Common Reed Buntings.

The tail is frequently flicked, showing the extensive white on the outer two tail feathers.

Some plumages of Common Reed Bunting can be confused with Little Bunting *E. pusilla* and Pallas' Reed Bunting *E. pallasi* (see those accounts), but note the heavy bill, lack of an eyering, and diagnostic chestnut lesser wing coverts. Wallace (1976a) discusses the Little v. Common Reed Bunting problem with reference to European races of Common. A discussion of the Pallas' v. Common Reed Bunting problem is in preparation (C. Wilds, *per. com.*).

The typical call is a clear, plaintive "tsew". There is a variety of other calls, but they do not approach the sharp "tic" note of Little Bunting, the hard "pit" of Rustic Bunting *E. rustica*, or the calls of Pallas' Reed Bunting.

# APPENDIX A — ADDITIONAL ALASKA RARITIES

The following species have recently averaged less than four birds a year in ALASKA and meet our definition of Rarity there, but are not considered Rarities in any other West Coast state or province. As explained in the introduction, these species are listed here rather than having main text accounts. More information on most of these records is in Kessel & Gibson (1978).

**Flesh-footed Shearwater** *Puffinus carneipes* — 7 records, all between Jul-Sep, in the Gulf of Alaska and west to the central Aleutians.

**Black-crowned Night-Heron** *Nycticorax nycticorax* — Two records, both by single observers and thus considered hypothetical on the state list, though details are good. Both are from W ALASKA — Apr 1975 on Atka I., central Aleutians, and 3 Apr 1979 on St. Paul I., Pribilofs — and it is suspected that the nominate Eurasian race, which breeds in Japan and has been recorded on the Commander Is., is responsible for the records. Black-crowned Night-Heron is nearly a Rarity in B.C.: there is only a tiny locally-breeding population near Vancouver.

**Wood Duck** *Aix sponsa* — Two records in SE ALASKA: 11-12 May 1969 at Juneau, and 10 Jul 1976 at Hot Springs Slough, Stikine R.

**Turkey Vulture** *Cathartes aura* — One record: early May 1979 at Delta Juction, C ALASKA. This is the northernmost record in North America.

**Wilson's Phalarope** *Stegnopus tricolor* — 9 records, all between early May-late Jun. Records scattered in SE and E Central ALASKA, but two records north to N ALASKA, including one at Pt. Barrow (9 Jun 1962†).

**South Polar Skua** *Catharacta maccormicki* — 15 records, all between late Jul-early Nov. Nearly all were in the Gulf of Alaska, but one was extremely far north about 60 miles off Icy Cape, N ALASKA (29 Sep 1970). South Polar Skua is found in small numbers off the West Coast from Jun-Nov, with numbers peaking in Aug-Oct. Skuas have recently been split into three species; excellent discussions of their taxonomy and identification are in Devillers (1977) and Devillers (1978).

**Western Gull** *Larus occidentalis* — One record: 8 Jun 1975† about 50 miles offshore in Bristol Bay. The bird had been banded on SE Farallon I., CAL, on 22 Jun 1973.

**Ring-billed Gull** *Larus delawarensis* — At least 17 records: records are scattered throughout the seasons. Most are from the coast of SE and S ALASKA, but has been recorded north in the interior to Fairbanks (3-4 May 1978, 30 Apr 1978).

**Franklin's Gull** *Larus pipixcan* — Three records: 14-18 May 1971 at Tuxedni NWR, Cook Inlet, 16 Jun 1976 at Chiniak Bay, Kodiak I., and 20-22 Jun 1976 on St. Paul I., Pribilofs.

**Northern Pygmy Owl** *Glaucidium gnoma* — 21 records, all between late Aug–mid-May in SE ALASKA, west to Yakutat. It may be a regular winter visitor.

**Whip-poor-will** *Caprimulgus vociferus* — One record: 22 Nov 1972† at West Petersburg, Kupreanof I., SE ALASKA. Whip-poor-will is recorded annually on the West Coast only in S CAL, where a small population presumably breeds very locally in the San Bernardino Mtns., San Jacinto Mtns., Laguna Mtns., and on Clark Mt. (see CB 2:33 *et al*). A vagrant of the nominate eastern race has also been found in S CAL: 14 Nov 1970 at Pt. Loma, San Diego (CB 2:37).

**Anna's Hummingbird** *Calypte anna* — 25 records, scattered througout the seasons, all at sugar-water feeders in SE ALASKA except for one nw. to Cordova, S ALASKA (13 Nov-19 Dec 1971). Apparently becoming more common and may not remain within Rarity status for long.

**Eastern Kingbird** *Tyrannus tyrannus* — 26 records, all between Jun-Sep. Most records are from SE ALASKA, but birds have appeared as far north as Pt. Barrow and as far west as St. Paul I., Pribilofs.

# APPENDIX A

**Western Kingbird** *Tyrannus verticalis* — Three records: 28 Jun 1964† near Susitna R. bridge, Denali Hwy., C ALASKA, 16 Aug 1973 at the Copper R. delta, S ALASKA, and 9 Jun 1978 at Skagway, SE ALASKA.

**Dusky Flycatcher** *Empidonax oberholseri* — One record: 19 Jul 1976† at Icy Cape, NW ALASKA.

**Purple Martin** *Progne subis* — 18 records, all late May-late Jul. Records are scattered widely: as far north as Wainwright, as far west as Wales, Seward Pen.

**Mountain Chickadee** *Parus gambeli* — 8 records, 6 of which were during the winter on the SE ALASKA mainland. One taken on 6 Aug 1974 in Warm Pass Valley, north of Skagway, SE ALASKA, could indicate local breeding.

**Clark's Nutcracker** *Nucifraga columbiana* — 5 records, all in winter in SE ALASKA.

**Bobolink** *Dolichonyx oryzivorus* — One record: 23 Jun 1976† at Pt. Barrow.

**Western Meadowlark** *Sturnella neglecta* — 5 records, all between late Sep-early Jan. Most were in SE ALASKA, but one was taken in late Sep 1959 in the Brooks Range in NW ALASKA.

**Yellow-headed Blackbird** *Xanthocephalus xanthocephalus* — 8 records, between Jun-Oct. Records are widely scattered: as far north as Pt. Barrow, as far west as Pt. Hope.

**Evening Grosbeak** *Hesperiphona vespertina* — 6 records, sometimes involving flocks, all in SE ALASKA.

**Purple Finch** *Carpodacus purpureus* — Two records, both in SE ALASKA: 11 Apr 1974 at Auke Bay (flock of 20-25 birds), and 8 Nov 1975 at Juneau.

**White-throated Sparrow** *Zonotrichia albicollis* — 10 records, most in C and SE ALASKA. Records span the seasons. One was far north at the Colville R. delta (5 Jun 1973).

# APPENDIX B — POSSIBLE VAGRANTS FROM EURASIA

There are numerous species of birds in the world which might occur as vagrants on the West Coast. Some of these have been illustrated on Plate 10, whose facing page also briefly discusses a few identifying characteristics. It is not the purpose of this book to attempt to discuss in any detail the status or identification of possible vagrants, but a few of the more likely have been pictured and others are listed below. Active observers in Alaska will want to have available European and Asian guides; those in California should peruse Mexican field guides. Possible vagrants from NE Asia, to be looked for especially in Alaska, are discussed in this Appendix. The listings are not meant to be comprehensive; indeed such a list would contain most of the migratory birds of the world. Wood Warbler *Phylloscopus sibilatrix* would not have made this list, yet it has been recorded in Alaska. Taking into consideration the breeding range and the migratory pattern, those listed would seem to be among the most likely to occur in the future. Identification material is kept to a minimum or omitted (and information from Plate 10 is not repeated), but I have attempted to note particularly valuable material published elsewhere when appropriate. Single observer records, while not sufficient to place a species on the North American list, are also indicated when the details of the record suggest the identification was correct (*fide* Daniel D. Gibson).

**Lesser White-fronted Goose** *Anser erythropus*. Smaller and darker than Greater White-fronted Goose *A. albifrons*. Distinguishing marks include a shorter bill with a steep, higher forehead, a yellow eye-ring, and the fact that the wings extend beyond the tail.

**Hobby** *Falco subbuteo.* Plate 10. Single observer record: 19 Sep 1977 at Cordova. This sighting was very brief and, at best, is considered "possibly correct".

**Common Water Rail** *Rallus aquaticus.* Size and shape like Virginia's Rail *R. limicola,* but face, neck, and breast gray.

**Northern Lapwing** *Vanellus vanellus.* Large plover with black crest, black face and breast, and striking black and white underwing pattern.

**Eurasian Curlew** *Numenius arquata.* Briefly discussed under Far Eastern Curlew *N. madagascariensis,* p. 133.

**Little Curlew** *Numenius minutus.* Very similar to nearly extinct Eskimo Culew *N. borealis,* but white underwing coverts, more finely marked underparts, and more extensively pale base to lower mandible (see Farrand, 1977).

**Common Redshank** *Tringa totanus.* Fairly large, stocky *Tringa* with white secondaries, white rump extending up back in a wedge, red legs, red base to straight, relatively heavy bill.

**Nordmann's Greenshank** *Tringa guttifer.* Discussed under Common Greenshank *T. nebularia,* p. 141.

**Eurasian Woodcock** *Scolopax rusticola.* Much larger than American Woodcock *Philohela minor,* with barred underparts, darker upperparts.

**Pintail Snipe** *Gallinago stenura.* Plate 10. Similar to Common Snipe *Capella* (=*Gallinago*) *gallinago,* but buff mottling to upperwing coverts. Differs from NE Asia race (*G.g. gallinago*) by barred underwings and lack of prominent trailing edge to secondaries; from American race (*G.g. delicata*) by browner upperparts, feathers edged in buff (not narrowly in white). For more see Kitson (1978) and Gibson (1978).

**Solitary Snipe** *Gallinago solitaria.* A very large snipe, mostly ginger brown, with only a whitish crown stripe and pair of creamy lines on back.

**Common Kingfisher** *Alcedo atthis.* Tiny, stocky kingfisher with green crown and wings, blue back, rump, and tail, and orange-red underparts.

**Eurasian Nutcracker** *Nucifraga caryocatactes.* Shaped like Clark's Nutcracker *N. columbiana,* but plumage mostly brown, speckled with white.

**Siberian Thrush** *Turdus sibirica.* Plate 10.

**Redwing** *Turdus iliacus.* Plate 10.

**Mistle Thrush** *Turdus viscivorus.* Very large thrush; evenly gray-brown upperparts, boldly spotted underparts.

**Isabelline Wheatear** *Oenanthe isabellina.* Discussed under Northern Wheatear *O. oenanthe,* p. 316.

**Stonechat** *Saxicola torquata.* Plate 10; for a much fuller discussion of NE Asia races see Robertson (1977). Single observer record: 6 Jun 1978 at Gambell, St. Lawrence I.

**Rufous-tailed Robin** *Erithacus sibilans.* Size of Bluethroat *Luscinia svecica;* olive-brown upperparts with dark rufous tail and rump, olive-brown scaling on whitish throat, breast, and flanks.

**Siberian Blue Robin** *Erithacus cyane.* Plate 10.

**Red-flanked Bluetail** *Tarsiger cyanurus.* Plate 10. See also BB 66:3.

**Daurian Redstart** *Phoenicurus auroreus.* Similar to European Redstart *P. phoenicurus* (see a European guide) but white patch in wing; female with buffy eyering.

**Willow Warbler** *Pylloscopus trochilus.* Plate 8. This species has previously been listed (e.g. ABA Checklist) as having occurred on the West Coast on the basis of a specimen found dead on 11 Jun 1968 at Pt. Barrow, ALASKA (Pitelka, 1974). During the course of the research for this book, the author examined the specimen and, though struck with the lead gray color of the bird, noted the presence of wingbars. Subsequent examination against a wing-formula

# APPENDIX B

key strongly suggested the specimen was of an Arctic Warbler *P. borealis*, not of a Willow Warbler. This situation was brought to the attention of Dr. Frank Pitelka, who sent the specimen to the National Museum of Natural History in Washington, D.C. It is their preliminary conclusion that the bird is indeed an Arctic Warbler (G. Watson, *fide* F. Pitelka, *per. com.*). Willow Warbler should not be listed as having occurred on the West Coast (or anywhere in North America) at this time. These examinations, incidentally, took place after the commission of the color plates for this book. Willow Warbler is illustrated on Plate 8, rather than Plate 10, where it belongs. The illustration on Plate 8 is of the NE Asia race — *P. t. yakutensis* — which is much grayer than European races and lacks much (if any) yellow on the underparts.

**Radde's Warbler** *Phylloscopus scharzi* — Briefly discussed under Dusky Warbler *P. fuscatus*, p. 322. For a thorough discussion see Johns & Wallace (1972).

**Chiffchaff** *Phylloscopus collybita*. Very similar to Willow Warbler *P. trochilus* (discussed above and illustrated on Plate 8), but is generally dingier above and below, and has black legs and feet (Willow may have dark brown legs, but usually shows pale feet). NE Asia race — *P. c. tristis* — is grayish-brown above, buffy white below. It differs from European birds by lacking much (if any) yellow on the underparts. Browner coloration and buffy supercilium may be useful in separating Chiffchaff from gray NE Asia race of Willow Warbler. See Williamson (1976b).

**Yellow-browed Warbler** *Phylloscopus inornatus*. Plate 10. The painting on Plate 10 does not illustrate this species well. It is a small, active, short-tailed *Phylloscopus* with a dumpy shape recalling Golden-crowned Kinglet *Regulus satrapa*. The lower wingbar is more prominent than the upper, and both are bordered on their rear edge by a dark bar. There is a faint crown stripe, dark-tipped lower mandible, and pale legs. The call — a loud whistled "weest" — is often given during migration and is a useful field characteristic. See BB 62:89 and an excellent photo and discussion in BB 73:158.

**Pallas' Warbler** *Phylloscopus proregulus*. Nearly as small and active as Golden-crowned Kinglet *Regulus satrapa*, with prominent yellow supercilium and wingbars, a crown stripe, and pale yellow rump patch. See BB 57:508.

**Greenish Warbler** *Phylloscopus trochiloides*. Very similar to NE Asia race of Chiffchaff *P. colybita*, but short single clear wingbar (faint wingbar suggested on some Chiffchaff). Call — a House Sparrow-like "chee-wee" — is unlike Chiffchaff. See BB 48:499 and Kitson (1979a).

**Gray's Grasshopper Warbler** *Locustella fasciolata*. Larger than Middendorff's Grasshopper Warbler *L. ochotensis*, with olive-brown upperparts and a white throat contrasting with grayish breast. No white tips to tail. See Williamson (1976a).

**Lanceolated Warbler** *Locustella lanceolata*. Plate 10. Tiny, drab-colored *Locustella* with gorget of fine breast streaks. Creeps on ground like a mouse. See BB 51:243.

**Pallas' Grasshopper Warbler** *Locustella certhiola*. Briefly discussed under Middendorff's Grasshopper Warbler *L. ochotensis*, p. 324.

**Richard's Pipit** *Anthus novaeseelandiae*. Large, bulky, long-legged pipit with tawny upperparts and heavily streaked, buffy underparts. Call — an explosive, rasping "schreep" — is unlike other pipits. See BB 56:285, 292; 65:287.

**Eurasian Siskin** *Carduelis spinus*. Similar to Pine Siskin *C. pinus*, but male has greenish-yellow back, yellow rump, and black cap and chin; female more similar, but has yellow rump, heavier bill. Single observer record: 4 Jun 1978 on Attu I.

**Pine Bunting** *Emberiza leucocephala*. Plate 10. See *Scottish Birds* 5:225.

**Yellow-breasted Bunting** *Emberiza aureola*. Plate 10. See BB 52:161; 53:229. Single observer record: 26-27 Jun 1978 at Gambell, St. Lawrence I. (*Birding* 11:154).

# APPENDIX C — SELECTED REPORTS NOT USED

Numerous reports of rare birds on the West Coast have been published that lack convincing details or substantiation. These questionable reports have not been used as records in this book. The process through which some of these reports were screened, especially those taken from the pages of *American Birds*, is discussed in the Introduction on page xiv. Major reference works on the states and provinces usually include a "hypothetical" list of reports discarded by the authors (it is unfortunate that some states use "hypothetical" to describe adequately documented sight records without a photograph). The published reports of the Records Committees in California and Oregon also include a listing of rejected records. It is not the purpose of this brief Appendix to repeat the information found in those publications. The listing below is only a selected list of certain published records which are not used in this book, but which have either been accepted by a local Records Committee or have otherwise been widely publicized. The reasons for the choice not to use the report is also given. It is the author's judgement that these records are not adequately documented or are suspected of being incorrectly identified, but it is very possible that some good reports, for one reason or another, are either listed here or were rejected in the general compilation process described previously. A few other records that were not included are discussed in the main text under the appropriate species account.

**Yellow-billed Loon** *Gavia adamsii*
- CAL   8-26 Dec 1977 at Grant Lake, Mono. Details are sketchy and it appears this report will not pass the CAL Records Committee. There are still no acceptable inland records from CAL.

**Least Grebe** *Podiceps dominicus*
- CAL   There are several additional published reports (e.g. C 49:125 and C 62:223), but none contain substantiating details and all but the single good record are widely discarded.

**Short-tailed Albatross** *Diomedea albatrus*
- WASH  3 May 1970 off Westport, G.H. Published in CB 1:113.
- ORE   30 Sep 1979 off Newport, Lnc. Accepted by ORE Records Committee.
- CAL   20 Apr 1978 off Santa Cruz. Published in WB 11:47 and accepted by CAL Records Committee. All of these three reports are documented by photographs. It is now thought by several West Coast observers (and the author concurs) that the photos are of old or aberrant Black-footed Albatross *D. nigripes* or hybrids or just unidentifiable, but certainly not Short-tailed. See page 8 for more details.

**Manx Shearwater** *Puffinus puffinus*
- ORE   12 Sep 1979 at Gearhart, Clt. Accepted by ORE Records Committee. This report, like a number of others recently from ORE and WASH, is very sketchy, does not distinguish the race involved, and appears inadequate as a first state record. The date is early when compared to the typical pattern in CAL. But a number of reports of small black-and-white shearwaters off ORE and WASH recently suggest that it will be adequately documented for those states in the future.

**Bar-tailed Godwit** *Limosa lapponica*
- WASH  2 Jul 1974 at Neah Bay, Clm. Published in Mattocks, Hunn, and Wahl (1976) and elsewhere, but examination of the photograph suggested the bird was a worn Marbled Godwit *L. fedoa*. The report would be of the earliest fall vagrant on the West Coast.

**White-rumped Sandpiper** *Calidris fuscicollis*
- B.C.  20 Apr 1977 at Victoria, V.I. A month earlier than any other West Coast record and the details are poor. Published in *American Birds* (this is a good example of *American Birds* published reports which are thought to be inadequately documented; many others are not included in the Appendix).

# APPENDIX C

**Long-toed Stint** *Calidris subminuta.*
    ORE    3 Sep 1979 at Tillamook Bay. Accepted by ORE Records Committee. Photographs of this bird have been widely circulated to West Coast observers. All except those in ORE agree (and the author concurs) that the photos are of a Least Sandpiper *C. minutilla,* or, at best, fail to distinguish the bird from that species. Interestingly, this bird was identified in the field as a Temminck's Stint *C. temminckii* and was not relabelled for several months.

**Least Tern** *Sterna albifrons*
    ORE    19 Aug 1973 (4) at the Suislaw R. mouth, Til., and 30 Sep 1978 off Newport, Lnc. Both accepted by ORE Records Committee. Both sight records are sketchy and fail to distinguish from, among other birds, Common Tern *S. hirundo.* A group of 4 this far north would be extraordinary and the Sep report would be extremely late.

**Golden-winged** *Vermivora chrysoptera* **X Blue-winged Warbler** *V. pinus*
    ORE    14 Jun 1977 at Indian Ford campground, Des. Accepted by ORE Records Committee. The details are very brief and do not distinguish this bird from, among other possibilities, a Yellow-rumped Warbler *Dendroica coronata.*

**Rusty Blackbird** *Euphagus carolinus*
    ORE    15 Sep 1979 at Malheur NWR, Har. Accepted by ORE Records Committee. Details do not exclude the possibility of juvenile Brewer's Blackbird *E. cyanocephalus.* The report would be of the earliest fall record on the West Coast.

**McCown's Longspur** *Calcarius mccownii*
    ORE    8 Aug 1976 in Harney Co. Accepted by ORE Records Committee. Details are very brief and inadequate to document what would be an extraordinary mid-summer record of this species.

**Rustic Bunting** *Emberiza rustica*
    B.C.    26 Oct 1971 (2) at Queen Charlotte City, Q.C.I. Published in *American Birds.* This is a single observer report with fairly good details and might be considered borderline. It is included here as a reference if a pattern of records should develop in the future. There is also a single observer sight record from the fall in S CAL which has not been submitted to the CAL Records Committee. It may also be of this species and observers on the West Coast south of ALASKA should be alert to the possibility of finding this bird.

# APPENDIX D — SELECTED ADDITIONAL RECORDS (1980)

The short list below is of a selected few records from 1980 which add substantially to our knowledge of the occurrence of each species. Most birds were discovered shortly before this book went to press and are included here at the last possible date. A few additional records from fall 1979, inadvertently omitted from the main text, are also noted to complete the picture for those species through 1979.

**Mongolian Plover** *Charadrius mongolus*
    CAL    13 Sep-3 Oct 1980 at Moss Landing, Mnt. First CAL record.

**Bar-tailed Godwit** *Limosa lapponica*
    ORE    16 Sep 1979 at Coos Bay and 17 Sep 1979 at Bandon, Coos. There were thus 7 records for ORE through 1979.

**White-rumped Sandpiper** *Calidris fuscicollis*
    CAL    8-15 Aug 1980 at Edwards marsh, Antelope Valley, L.A. Fifth record for CAL and the first fall record for the West Coast south of ALASKA.

**Ruff** *Philomachus pugnax*
    B.C.    9-10 Sep 1979 and 24-25 Sep 1979 at Victoria, V.I. Thus there were 11 records for B.C. through 1979.
    ORE    18 Jan 1980 at Coquille, Coos. Second record for ORE and the first winter record on the West Coast north of CAL.

**Black-billed Cuckoo** *Coccyzus erythropthalmus*
    CAL    8-15 Sep 1980 at Pt. Reyes NS, Mrn. Fourth CAL record.

**Common Skylark** *Alauda arvensis*
    CAL    25 Oct 1980 and subsequently at Pt. Reyes NS, Mrn. Presumably this is the same individual returning for an unprecedented third winter in CAL.

# LITERATURE CITED

Key to standardized journal abbreviations is on page xv.

Abbott, Dennis J. III and Davis W. Finch. 1978. First Variegated Flycatcher record for the United States. AB 32:161.

Ainley, David G. 1976. The occurrence of seabirds in the coastal region of California. WB 7:33.

American Birding Association. 1975. *ABA Checklist: Birds of Continental United States and Canada.* Austin, Texas: ABA. With annual supplements.

American Ornithologists' Union. 1957. *Check-list of North American Birds.* 5th ed. Baltimore: AOU.

———. 1973. 32nd supplement to the A.O.U. Check-list of North American Birds. A 90:411.

———. 1976. 33rd supplement to the A.O.U. Check-list of North American Birds. A 93:875.

Balch, Lawrence G. 1980. A brief guide to the identification and status of Asian species in Alaska. *Birding* 12:12.

Binford, Laurence C. 1971a. Identification of Northern and Louisiana Waterthrushes. CB 2:1.

———. 1971b. Northern and Louisiana Waterthrush in California. CB 2:77.

———. 1978. Lesser Black-backed Gull in California, with notes on field identification. WB 9:141.

———. 1979. Fall migration of diurnal raptors at Pt. Diablo, California. WB 10:1.

Binford, Laurence C. and J. V. Remsen, Jr. 1974. Identification of the Yellow-billed Loon. WB 5:111.

———. 1975. Status of the Yellow-billed Loon in the Western United States and Mexico. WB 6:7.

Bolander, Gordon L. and Benjamin D. Parmeter. 1978. *Birds of Sonoma County, California.* Napa, California: Parmeter.

Byrd, G.V., D.D. Gibson, and D.L. Johnson. 1974. The birds of Adak Island, Alaska. C 76:288.

Byrd, G.V., J.L. Trapp, and D.D. Gibson. 1978. New information on Asiatic birds in the Aleutian Islands, Alaska. C 80:308.

Campbell, R. Wayne and Patrick T. Gregory. 1976. The Buff-breasted Sandpiper in British Columbia, with notes on its migration in North America. *Syesis* 9:123.

Campbell, R. Wayne and Wayne C. Weber. 1976. Occurrence and status of the Tufted Duck in British Columbia. *Syesis* 9:25.

Conder, Peter. 1979. Britain's first Olive-backed Pipit. BB 72:2.

Contreras, Alan. 1978. The status of vagrant warblers in Oregon. OB 4 (3):2.

Cramp, Stanley and K.E.L. Simmons, eds. 1977. *The Birds of the Western Palearctic.* Vol. 1. Oxford: Oxford Univ. Press.

Dawson, William L. 1924. *Birds of California.* 4 vols. San Diego: South Moulton Co.

DeBenedictis, Paul. 1971. Wood Warblers and Vireos in California: The nature of the accidental. CB 2:109.

Dement'ev, G.P. and N.A. Gladkov, eds. 1951-1954. *The Birds of the Soviet Union.* 6 vols. Transl. 1968 by Israel Program for scientific translations, Jerusalem. Clearinghouse for Federal Scientific and Tech. Inf., Springfield, Va.

Dennis, Roy H. 1967. Olive-backed Pipits on Fair Isle; a species new to Britain and Ireland. BB 60:161.

DeSante, David F. 1973. An analysis of the fall occurrences and nocturnal orientations of vagrant wood warblers in California. Unpubl. PhD. Diss., Stanford Univ., Palo Alto.

DeSante, David F. and David G. Ainley. 1980. *The Avifauna of the South Farallon Islands, California.* Studies in Avian Biology, No. 4. Cooper Ornithological Society.

Devillers, Pierre. 1970. Identification and distribution in California of the *Sphyrapicus varius* group of sapsuckers. CB 1:47.

———. 1972. The juvenal plumage of Kittlitz's Murrelet. WB 3:33.

———. 1977. The Skuas of the North American Pacific Coast. A 94:417.

———. 1978. Distribution and relationships of South American Skuas. *Le Gerfaut* 68:374.

Dunn, Jon. 1975a. Field Notes — Clay-colored Sparrow. *Western Tanager* 41 (9):4.

———. 1975b. Field Notes — Immature orioles. *Western Tanager* 41 (10):7.

———. 1976a. Field Notes — Bendire's and Curve-billed Thrashers. *Western Tanager* 42 (10):4.

———. 1976b. Field Notes — Grasshopper, LeConte's, and Sharp-tailed Sparrows. *Western Tanager* 42 (8):4.

———. 1976c. Field Notes — The identification of pipits. *Western Tanager* 43 (3):5.

———. 1977a. Field Notes — Female grosbeaks. *Western Tanager* 43 (6):5.

———. 1977b. Field Notes — Gray-cheeked and Wood Thrushes. *Western Tanager* 44 (3):5.

———. 1977c. Field Notes — Hammond's and Dusky Flycatchers. *Western Tanager* 43 (8):5.

———. 1977d. Field Notes — Hermit and Swainson's Thrushes. *Western Tanager* 44 (1):5.

———. 1977e. Field Notes — Least Flycatcher. *Western Tanager* 43 (9):4.

———. 1977f. Field Notes — Veery. *Western Tanager* 44 (2):5.

———. 1977g. Field Notes — Western Flycatcher. *Western Tanager* 43 (7):5.

———. 1977h. Field Notes — Willow Flycatcher. *Western Tanager* 43 (10):5.

———. 1978a. Field Notes — Ash-throated and Wied's Crested Flycatchers. *Western Tanager* 45 (3):4.

———. 1978b. Field Notes — The *Endomychura* murrelets. *Western Tanager* 44 (8):8.

———. 1978c. Field Notes — Great Crested and Olivaceous Flycatchers. *Western Tanager* 45 (4):5.

———. 1978d. Field Notes — Red-eyed and Yellow-green Vireos. *Western Tanager* 45 (1):9.

———. 1978e. Field Notes — Warbling and Philadelphia Vireos. *Western Tanager* 44 (10):9.

———. 1978f. The Races of Yellow-bellied Sapsucker. *Western Tanager* 44 (7):1.

———. 1979a. Field Notes — Ageing sandpipers. *Western Tanager* 46 (2):6.

———. 1979b. Field Notes — Black, Vaux's, and Chimney Swifts. *Western Tanager* 45 (9):11.

———. 1979c. Field Notes — Immature Red-shouldered and Broad-winged Hawks. *Western Tanager* 45 (8):13.

———. 1979d. Field Notes — Northern and Louisiana Waterthushes. *Western Tanager* 45 (10):7.

———. 1979e. Field Notes — Semipalmated Sandpiper. *Western Tanager* 46 (4):6.

———. 1979f. Field Notes — The *Tyrannus* Flycatchers. *Western Tanager* 45 (5):5.

———. 1979g. Field Notes — Western and Least Sandpipers. *Western Tanager* 46 (3):6.

Dunn, Jon and Kimball Garrett. 1981 (MS at this time). *Birds of Southern California: an annotated checklist*. Los Angeles: Los Angeles Audubon Society.

Dunn, Jon and Thede Tobish. 1981. Identification and status of pipits in North America. *Continental Birdlife* (MS at this date).

Dwight, Jonathan. 1925. The Gulls of the World. *Bull. of Am. Museum of Nat. History* 52:63-401. New York.

Eisenmann, Eugene. 1955. *The Species of Middle American Birds*. New York: Linnaean Society of New York. Transactions, Vol. 7.

Elkins, Norman. 1979. Neararctic landbirds in Britain and Ireland: a meteorological analysis. BB 72:417.

Farrand, John Jr. 1977. What to look for: Eskimo and Little Curlews compared. AB 31:137.

Finch, Davis W., William C. Russell, and Edward V. Thompson. 1978. Pelagic Birds in the Gulf of Maine, Part 1. AB 32:140.

Fisher, Allan C. 1979. Mysteries of bird migration. *National Geographic* 156:154.

Fix, David M. 1979. Occurrence and identification of the Stilt Sandpiper in Oregon. OB 5 (2):6.

Flint, V.E., R.L. Bohme, Yu V. Kostin, and A.A. Kuznetsov. 1968. *Birds of the U.S.S.R.* In Russian. Moscow.

Foxall, Roger A. 1979. Presumed hybrids of the Herring Gull and the Great Black-backed Gull. AB 33:838.

Gabrielson, Ira N. and Stanley G. Jewett. 1940. *Birds of Oregon*. Oregon State Univ.

Gabrielson, Ira N. and F. C. Lincoln. 1959. *The Birds of Alaska*. Stackpole Co. and Wildl. Mgnt. Inst.

Gibson, Daniel D. 1978. Separation of Tattlers and Snipe. *'Elepaio* 39 (1):8. Published by the Hawaii Audubon Society.

Godfrey, W. Earl. 1966. *The Birds of Canada*. Nat. Mus. Canada Bull., No. 203. Paintings by John A. Crosby.

Gould, Patrick S., Warren B. King, and Gerald Sanger. 1974. "Red-tailed Tropicbird" in King, Warren B., ed., *Studies of Seabirds in the Central and Eastern Pacific Ocean*, pp. 206-231.

Grant, Peter B. 1978. Field identification of West Palearctic gulls. Part 1. BB 71:145. Covers Black-headed, Slender-billed, Bonaparte's and Gray-headed Gulls.

———. 1979. Field identification of West Palearctic gulls. Part 2. BB 72:142. Covers Common (Mew), Mediterranean, Laughing, Franklin's, and Ring-billed Gulls.

———. 1980. Field identification of West Palearctic gulls. Part 3. BB 73:113. Covers Audouin's, Herring, Lesser Black-backed, Great Black-backed, and Great Black-headed Gulls.

Grinnell, Joseph and Alden H. Miller. 1944. *The Distribution of the Birds of California*. Pacific Coast Avifaua No. 27. Berkeley: Cooper Ornithological Society.

Hall, George A. 1979. Hybridization between Mourning and MacGillivray's Warblers. *Bird-banding* 50:101.

Harper, Peter C. and F. C. Kinsky. 1979. *Southern Albatross and Petrels: An Identification Guide*. Wellington, N.Z.: Price Milburn.

Harrison, Craig. 1979. Short-tailed Albatross. *Oceans* 12 (5):24.

Hoffman, W., W. P. Elliott and J. M. Scott. 1975. The occurrence and status of the Horned Puffin in the western United States. WB 6:87.

Hubbard, John P. 1977. Status of Cassin's Sparrow in New Mexico and adjacent states. AB 31:933.

Hunn, Eugene S. 1978. Black-throated Sparrow vagrants in the Pacific Northwest. WB 9:85.

Isleib, M. E. "Pete" and Brina Kessel. 1973. Birds of the North Gulf Coast — Prince William Sound Region, Alaska. *Biological Papers of the Univ. of Alaska*, No. 14.

Jehl, Joseph R., Jr. 1968. Relationships in the Charadrii (shorebirds): a taxonomic study based on color patterns of the downy young. *Memoir* 3. San Diego: San Diego Soc. of Nat. History.

———. 1974. Middle American Near-shore Avifauna. A 91:689.

Jehl, Joseph R. and Suzanne Bond. 1975. Morphological variation and species limits in murrelets of the genus *Endomychura*. *Trans. San Diego Soc. Nat. History* 18:9.

Jewett, Stanley G., W.P. Taylor, W. T. Shaw and J. W. Aldrich. 1953. *Birds of Washington State*. Univ. Washington Press, Seattle.

Johns, R. J. and D. I. M. Wallace. 1972. Field identification of Dusky and Radde's Warblers. BB 65:497.

Johnsgard, Paul A. 1968. *Waterfowl: their biology and natural history*. Lincoln: Univ. of Nebraska Press.

Johnson, Ned K. and Kimball L. Garrett. 1974. Interior bird species expanding breeding range into Southern California. WB 5:45.

Keeton, William T. 1979. Avain orientation and navigation: a brief overview. BB 72:451.

Kenyon, K. W. 1961. Birds of Amchitka Island, Alaska. A 78:305.

Kenyon, K. W. and R. E. Phillips. 1965. Birds from the Pribilof Islands and vicinity. A 82:624.

Kessel, Brina and Daniel D. Gibson. 1978. *Status and distribution of Alaska birds*. Studies in Avian Biology No. 1. Cooper Ornithological Society.

King, Ben F. 1980. The second through fourth records for North America of the Pechora Pipit. AB 34:317.

King, Ben F. and Edward Dickinson. 1975. *A Field Guide to the Birds of South-East Asia*. Boston: Houghton Mifflin.

King, Ben F., Davis Finch, Richard Stallcup and Will Russell. 1978. First North American sightings of Brown Shrike and Dusky Warbler and second record of Red-throated (Red-breasted) Flycatcher. AB 32:158.

King, Warren B. 1967. *Seabirds of the Tropical Pacific Ocean*. Preliminary Smithsonian Identification Manuel. Washington, D.C.: Smithsonian Institute.

———. ed. 1974. *Pelagic Studies of Seabirds in the Central and Eastern Pacific Ocean*. Washington, D.C.: Smithsonian Institute.

Kitson, Alan R. 1978. Identification of Long-toed Stint, Pintail Snipe and Asiatic Dowitcher. BB 71:558.

———. 1979a. Identification of Isabelline Wheatear, Desert Warbler and three *Phylloscopus* warblers. BB 72:5.

———. 1979b. Identification of Olive-backed Pipit, Blyth's Pipit, and Pallas' Reed Bunting. BB 72:94.

Lanyon, Wesley E. and John Bull. 1967. Identification of Connecticut, Mourning, and MacGillivray's Warblers. *Bird-banding* 39:187.

Larrison, E. J. and K. G. Sonnenberg. 1968. *Washington birds: their location and identification*. Seattle: Seattle Audubon Society.

Loomis, L. M. 1918. Review of the *Procellariiformes*. Proc. Cal. Acad. Sci., 4th ser., vol 2, pt. 2:93.

Lowe, A. R. 1979. Siberian Rubythroat: new to Britain and Ireland. BB 72:89.

Luther, John S., Guy McCaskie and Jon Dunn. 1979. Third report of the California Bird Records Committee. WB 10:169.

Mattocks, Philip W., Eugene S. Hunn and Terence R. Wahl. 1976. A Checklist of the birds of Washington State, with recent changes annotated. WB 7:1.

McCaskie, Guy. 1970. The occurrence of four species of *Pelecaniformes* in the Southwestern United States. CB 1:117.

———. 1970a. The American Redstart in California. CB 1:41.

———. 1970b. The Blackpoll Warbler in California. CB 1:85.

———. 1971. Rusty Blackbirds in California and Western North America. CB 2:55.

———. 1973. A second look at the exotic waterfowl. *Birding* 5:45.

McCaskie, Guy, Paul DeBenedictis, Richard Erickson and Joseph Morlan. 1979. *Birds of Northern California: an annotated field list*. Berkeley: Golden Gate Audubon Society.

Miliotis, Paul S. and P. A. Buckley. 1975. Ross' Gull in Massachusetts. AB 29:643.

Munro, J. A. and I. McT. Cowan. 1947. *A Review of the Bird Fauna of British Columbia*. British Columbia Prov. Museum, Spec. Pub. 2.

Murphy, Robert Cushman. 1952. The Manx Shearwater: a species of worldwide distribution. Am. Mus. Novit. #1586.

Nisbet, I. C. I. 1963. American passerines in western Europe, 1951-1962. BB 56:204.

Oregon Bird Records Committee. 1980a. Historic Actions Report. OB 6:82.

———. 1980b. Review list of the Oregon Bird Records Committee. OB 6:78.

Palmer, Ralph S., ed. 1962. *Handbook of North American Birds*. Vol 1: Loons through flamingos. New Haven: Yale Univ. Press.

———. 1976. *Handbook of North American Birds*. Vols. 2 & 3: Waterfowl. New Haven: Yale Univ. Press.

Parslow, J. L. F. 1968. Eye-browed Thrushes in Northamptonshire, Hebrides, and Scilly: a species new to Britain and Ireland. BB 61:218.

Payne, R. B. and C. J. Risley. 1976. Systematics and evolutionary relationships among the herons. Museum of Zoology Misc. Pub. No. 150. Ann Arbor: Univ. of Michigan.

Peterson, Roger Tory. 1947, 1980. *A Field Guide to the Birds*. Boston: Houghton Mifflin.

———. 1961. *A Field Guide to Western Birds*. Boston: Houghton Mifflin.

———. 1963. *A Field Guide to the Birds of Texas and Adjacent States*. Boston: Houghton Mifflin.

Peters, James L. 1979. *Check-List of Birds of the World*. Vol. 1, 2nd ed. Ernst Mayr and G. William Cottrell, eds. Cambridge, Mass.: Museum of Comparative Zoology.

Phillips, Allan R. 1975. The migrations of Allen's and other hummingbirds. C 77:196.

Phillips, Allan R., Marshall A. Howe and Wesley E. Lanyon. 1966. Identification of the flycatchers of Eastern North America, with special emphasis on the genus *Empidonax*. Bird-banding 37:153.

Phillips, Allan R. and Wesley E. Lanyon. 1970. Additional notes on the flycatchers of Eastern North America. Bird-banding 41:190.

Pitelka, Frank A. 1974. An avifaunal review for the Barrow region and North Slope of arctic Alaska. *Arctic and Alpine Research* 6:161.

Porter, R. F., Ian Willis, Steen Christensen and Bent Por Nielsen. 1976. *Flight identification of European raptors*. 2nd ed. London: T. & A.D. Poyser, Ltd.

Pough, Richard H. 1957. *Audubon Western Bird Guide*. New York: Doubleday and Co., Inc. Illustrated by Don Eckelberry.

Prater, A. J., J. H. Marchant and J. Vuorinen. 1977. *Guide to the Identification and Ageing of Holarctic Waders*. British Trust for Ornithology.

Pratt, H. Douglas. 1976. Field identification of White-faced and Glossy Ibises. *Birding* 8:1.

Remsen, J. V., Jr. 1977. The species of special concern list: an annotated list of declining or vulnerable birds in California. California Fish & Game.

Richardson, W. J. 1972. Autumn migration and weather in eastern Canada — a radar study. AB 26:10.

———. 1974. Spring migration over Puerto Rico and the western Atlantic — a radar study. Ibis 116:172.

———. 1976. Autumn migration over Puerto Rico and the western Atlantic — a radar study. Ibis 118:309.

Robertson, Iain S. 1977. Identification and European status of eastern Stonechat. BB 70:237.

Robbins, Chandler S., Bertel Bruun and Herbert S. Zim. 1966. *Birds of North America: A Guide to Field Identification*. New York: Golden Press. Illustrated by Arthur Singer.

Rogers, Dennis. 1979. Status of Red-shouldered Hawk in Oregon. OB 5(1):4.

Ryan, Richard H. 1972. A guide to North American waterfowl escapes. *Birding* 4:159.

———. 1976. Escapes, exotics, and accidentals. *Birding* 8:223.

Salt, W. R. 1973. *Alberta vireos and wood warblers*. Publ. No. 3, Prov. Mus. and Archives of Alberta.

Sanger, Gerald. 1974. "Laysan Albatross" in *Pelagic Studies of Seabirds in the Central and Eastern Pacific Ocean*, Warren B. King, ed, Smithsonian Institute, pp. 129-153.

Sauppe, Barry, Bruce A MacDonald, and David M. Mark. 1978. First Canadian and third North American record of the Spoonbill Sandpiper. AB 32:1062.

Sealy, S. G., J. Bedard, M.D.F. Udvardy and F. H. Fay. 1971. New records and zoogeographical notes on the birds of St. Lawrence Island, Bering Sea. C 73:322.
Schreiber, R. W. and R. L. DeLong. 1969. Brown Pelican status in California. AFN 23:57.
Short, Lester, Jr. 1969. Taxonomic aspects of avian hybridization. A 86:84.
Simon, David. 1977. Identification of Clay-colored, Brewer's, and Chipping Sparrows in fall plumage. *Birding* 9:189.
Sladen, W. J. L. 1966. Additions to the avifauna of the Pribilof Islands, Alaska. A 83:130.
Slater, Peter. 1970. *A Field Guide to Australian Birds, Non-Passerines.* Adelaide: Rugby, Ltd.
Small, Arnold. 1974. *The Birds of California.* New York: Winchester Press.
Stiles, F. Gary. 1971. On the field identification of California hummingbirds. CB 2:41.
———. 1972. Age and sex determination in Rufous and Allen's Hummingbirds. C 74:25.
Wallace, D. I. M. 1970. Identification of Spotted Sandpiper out of breeding plumage. BB 63:168.
———. 1974. Field identification of small species of the genus *Calidris.* BB 67:1.
———. 1976a. Distinguishing Little and Reed Buntings. BB 69:465.
———. 1976b. A review of waterthrush identification. BB 69:27.
———. 1979. Review of British records of Semipalmated Sandpiper and claimed Red-necked Stints. BB 72:264.
Wallace, D. I. M. and M. A. Ogilvie. 1977. Distinguishing Blue-winged and Cinnamon Teals. BB 70:290.
Warham, John, W. R. P. Bourne and H. F. I. Elliott. 1974. Albatross identification in the North Atlantic. AB 28:585.
Weber, Wayne C. and R. Wayne Campbell. 1976. Occurrence of the Smew in British Columbia, with comments on other North American records. AB 32:1059.
Wilbur, Sanford R. 1973. The Red-shouldered Hawk in the Western United States. WB 4:15.
———. 1974. The literature of the California Least Tern. U.S. Dept. of the Interior, Bureau of Sport Fisheries and Wildlife, Special Scientific Report — Wildlife No. 175. Washington, D.C.
Wilbur, Sanford R., W. Dean Carrier, and Guy McCaskie. 1971. The Lark Bunting in California. CB 2:73.
Williams, T.C., P. Berkeley and V. Harris. 1977. Autumnal bird migration over Miami studied by radar: a possible test of the wind drift hypothesis. *Bird-banding* 48:1.
Williams, T.C., J.M. Williams, L.C. Ireland and J. M. Teal. 1977. Autumnal bird migration over the western North Atlantic Ocean. AB 31:251.
Williamson, Kenneth. 1960. Juvenile and winter plumages of the marsh terns. BB 53:243.
———. 1976a. The genera *Cettia, Locustella,* and *Acrocephalus:* Identification for ringers. B.T.O. ident. guide No. 1.
———. 1976b. The genus *Phylloscopus:* Identification for ringers. B.T.O. ident. guide No. 2.
Wahl, Terence R. 1975. Seabirds in Washington's offshore zone. WB 6:117.
———. 1979. Seabirds in the northwestern Pacific Ocean and south central Bering Sea in June 1975. WB 9:45.
Winter, Jon. 1973. The California Field Ornithologists Records Committee report 1970-1972. WB 4:101.
Winter, Jon and Guy McCaskie. 1975. 1973 report of the California Field Ornithologists Records Committee. WB 6:135.
Unitt, Philip. 1974. Painted Redstarts attempt to breed in California. WB 5:94.
———. 1977. The Little Blue Heron in California. WB 8:151.
Vaurie, Charles. 1959, 1965. *The Birds of the Palearctic Fauna.* 2 vols. London: Witherby.
Voous, K. H. 1973. List of recent holarctic bird species, Non-Passerines. *Ibis* 115:612.
———. 1977a. List of recent holarctic bird species, Passerines (Part 1). *Ibis* 119:223.
———. 1977b. List of recent holarctic bird species, Passerines (Part 2). *Ibis* 119:376.
———. 1979. Capricious taxonomic history of Isabelline Shrike. BB 72:573.
Zimmerman, Dale. 1975. The changing seasons. AB 29:23.

# INDEX TO PHOTOGRAPHERS

The listings followed by a dagger (†) are photographs of specimens.

Acton, James F. (Jim) 167, 434
Ash, Dewayne 84
Baldridge, Frank 243
Branson, Ronald L. 3, 91, 171, 193, 268, 285, 296, 362, 454
Brindle, Christy 441
Brodkin, Henry M. 313
Buckley, Paul 3
Butler, John 11, 53, 160, 261, 377, 414
Campbell, R. Wayne 16, 128, 197
Cannings, Steve R. 298
Cardiff, Steve 248, 416
Carl, G. Clifford 7
Carpenter, Chris 285
Clarke, George 316
Clarke, Herbert 32, 41, 120, 131, 210, 244, 461, 468
Compagno, Leonard 345
Copper, Robert 61, 201, 229, 245
Coulter, Malcolm 457
Crabtree, Tom 129, 421
Craig, Alan M. 308, 390, 409
Davies, Jennifer 441
Davis, Tom 30
Dawe, Neil K. 51, 459
Day, Robert H. 185, Plate 11
Delaney, Linda (see also Terrill, Linda S.) 49, 63, 156, 157, 183
DeSante, Dave 126, 276, 287, 312, 411
Drent, Rodulf H. 137
Eltzroth, M S 433
Evans, Robert M. 469
Fryer, Ralph 206
Garrett, Kimball 245
Gibson, Daniel D. 443; courtesy of: 84
Gilligan, Jeff 123, 124, Plate 11
Ghiorso, Al 88, 251, 289, 347, 363, 386, 389, 396, 400, 412, 424, 455
Gnagey, Joe 197
Goodwill, J. E. V. 190
Gordon, Steve 432
Greaves, James M. 160, 172, 375, 379, 389, 418
Greyell, Bob 261
Harlow, Dave 301
Hatler, David F. 464

Heinemann, Dennis 213
Henningsen, Lillian 227
Hetrick, Wes 35
Hoechlin, Don 57, 82, 467 (with Bonny)
Holtzclaw, Truman 184
Hunn, Eugene 464
Johnston, Stuart 255
Keenleyside, John G. 123, 318, 446
King, James R. 428, 429
Kirchner, Lothar 86
Knapton, Richard 144
Kornet, Chris 226
Langham, Jeri 18, 39, 72, 114, 135, 187, 198, 385
Lehman, Paul 346, 427, 437
Lemon, Enid 55
LeValley, Ron 11, 278
Lewis, Jim 43
Lineham, Charles 240
Lucas, Robert 202
Lund, Tom 131, 182, 421
Luther, John 175, 220, 341, 404, 416
MacDonald, Bruce A. 83
Maisel, Gerald Plate 11
Marshall, David R. 88
Mattocks, Phil 294 (†)
McCaskie, Guy; courtesy of 35
McLean, Louis 5
McQueen, Larry B. 50, 102
Mewaldt, L Richard 362, 367, 369, 392; courtesy of: 226, 428, 429
Meyer, Darlene 175
Morehen, Cy 315
Myers, J. P. Plate 11
Nehls, Harry B. 123, 132, 155, 171, 180, 208, 217 (†)
O'Brien, Robert E. 2, 188
Oldfield, Michael 58
Paulson, Dennis 9, 125, 202, 325
Pearcy, William 215
Phillips, R. W. 298
Point Reyes Bird Observatory; courtesy of: 43, 227, 264, 312, 338, 349, 457, 462
Poynter, G Allen 91, 115, 266, 325
Remsen, Van 87, 91, 97, 159, 175, 211, 233
Ringler, Bob 314
Roberson, Don 11, 18, 22, 38, 75, 89 (†), 103, 107 (†), 109 (†), 141, 146, 149, 151 (†), 166, 201, 216, 332, 350, 351, 353, 364, 435, 475 (†), 477

**491**

Robert, Henry 338, 349, 462
Robertson, Ian 86
Rudholm, Dave 103, 113, 157, 232, 258, 361, 365, 427
Sands, Peter B. 282, 296
Sansone, Lawrence 105, Plate 11
Schmidt, Owen 188, 439
Schram, Brad 67, 119, 120, 263, 401
Schulmeister, Robert P. 83, 319, 329
Sian, Ervio 94, 95, 177
Smith, Gerald B. 359
Smith, Jan 220
Sorrie, Bruce 16, 309, 410
Steeves, John B. 196
Summers, Priscilla R. 371, 379
Swisher, Otis 463
Tait, Ian 264
Terrill, Linda S. (see also Delaney, Linda) 427
Wahl, Terence R. 52, 130
Wihler, Mike 7, 361
Williams, J. E. 93
Wilson, Steve 3, 168, 385
Witzeman, Robert 41
Woodley, Robert E. 405
Van Vuren, Kent 430
Verbruggue, William 92
Zamzow, Gary 201
Zeillemaker, C. F. 398

# INDEX TO COMMON NAMES

Main text accounts and color illustrations are **boldfaced**.

Accentor, Siberian **330**, **Plate 8**
Albatross, Black-browed 12
　　Black-footed 7-9
　　Gray-headed 12
　　Laysan 8, **10-12**
　　Shy (see White-capped)
　　Short-tailed 5, **6-9**, 11, **Plate 1**
　　Royal 5, 13
　　Wandering **4-5**, 8, 13, **Plate 1**
　　White-capped **12-13**, **Plate 1**
Anhinga **45**
Ani, Groove-billed **228-229**

Auklet, Crested **218**
　　Parakeet **216-217**
　　Rhinoceros 217
Bittern, Least **57-58**
Blackbird, Rusty **424**
　　Yellow-headed 480
Bluetail, Red-flanked 481, Plate 10
Bobolink 480
Booby, Blue-faced (see Masked)
　　Blue-footed **38-40**, 42
　　Brown **40-42**, 43
　　Masked **37**, 43
　　Red-footed **42-43**, **Plate 1**
Brambling **439-441**, **Plate 9**
Bullfinch, Eurasian **444-445**, **Plate 9**
Bunting, Common Reed 471, 476, **477-478**, **Plate 9**
　　Gray **473-474**, **Plate 9**
　　Indigo **433-434**
　　Lark **451-452**
　　Lazuli 433
　　Little **470-471**, 473, 476, 478, **Plate 9**
　　McKay's **469**
　　Painted **436-437**
　　Pallas' Reed 471, **474-476**, **Plate 9**
　　Pine 482, **Plate 10**
　　Rustic 471, **472-473**, **Plate 9**
　　Snow **467-468**
　　Varied **435**
　　Yellow-breasted 482, **Plate 10**
Canvasback 85
Catbird, Gray **295-296**
Chickadee, Mountain 480
Chiffchaff 482
Coot, American 112, **Plate 5**
　　Eurasian 112, **Plate 5**
Cormorant, Double-crested **44-45**
　　Neotropic **44-45**
　　Olivaceous (see Neotropic)
Crane, Common **108**, **Plate 1**
　　Sandhill 108
Crossbill, White-winged **451**
Cuckoo, Black-billed **227-228**, 484
　　Common 222, **223-224**, **Plate 6**
　　Oriental **222**, 223, **224**, **Plate 6**
　　Yellow-billed **225-226**
Curlew, Bristle-thighed **134**
　　Eskimo 481
　　Eurasian **133**, 481
　　Far Eastern **133**, **Plate 5**
　　Little 481
　　Long-billed 133

Dickcissel **437-439**
Dotterel **125-126**, **Plate 3**
Dove, White-winged 221
Duck, American Black **78-79**
    Ring-necked 88
    Spotbill **80**, **Plate 2**
    Tufted **85-88**
    Wood 479
Dunlin 174
Eagle, Bald 98-99
    Steller's Sea **99-100**, **Plate 2**
    White-tailed **98-99**, **Plate 2**
Egret, Cattle **51-52**
    Chinese **55-56**, **Plate 1**
    Great **47-48**
    Little 54, 56
    Reddish **48-49**
    Snowy 52, **54-55**, 56
Eider, Common 89
    King **90-91**
    Steller's **92-93**
Falcon, Peregrine 107
    Prairie 107
Fieldfare **303**, **Plate 7**
Finch, House 446
    Purple 446, 480
Flycatcher, Acadian **279**
    Alder 273, 274, **280**
    Ash-throated 265, **266-267**, 269
    Brown 328
    Coue's **284-285**
    Dusky 272, 275, 276, 480
    Gray 274, 276
    Gray-spotted **328-329**, **Plate 7**
    Gray-streaked (see Gray-spotted)
    Great Crested **264-265**
    Hammond's 272, 275, 276
    Identification of *Empidonax* 272-276
    Least 275, 276, **281-283**
    Olivaceous **268-269**
    Red-breasted **326-327**, **Plate 7**
    Red-throated (see Red-breasted)
    Scissor-tailed **260-261**
    Siberian (see Sooty)
    Sooty **327**, **Plate 7**
    Streaked 263
    Sulphur-bellied **260-261**
    Variegated 263
    Western 273, 275, 277, 278, 279
    Wied's Crested 267
    Willow 273, 274
    Yellow-bellied **277-278**

Frigatebird, Magnificent **46-47**
Fulmar, Northern 14
Gadwall 75
Gallinule, American Purple 111
    Common **111**
Garganey 77, **81-83**, **Plate 2**
Gnatcatcher, Blue-gray **324-325**
Godwit, Bar-tailed **130-132**
    Black-tailed **126-127**, 129, **Plate 5**
    Hudsonian 127, **128-129**
    Marbled 132
Goldfinch, Lesser **450**
Goose, Bean **68-69**, **Plate 2**
    Emperor **71-73**
    Greater White-fronted 69, 480
    Lesser White-fronted 480
    Ross' **70**
Grackle, Common **426-427**
    Great-tailed **425**
Grebe, Least **4**
Greenfinch, Oriental **448-449**, **Plate 9**
Greenshank, Common **140-141**, **Plate 5**
    Nordmann's 141, 481
Grosbeak, Black-headed **431-432**
    Blue **432-433**
    Evening 480
    Rose-breasted **431-432**
Gull, Black-headed **196-198**
    Black-tailed **194-195**
    Bonaparte's 196, 198, 200, 203
    Franklin's 199, 479
    Great Black-backed **189**, 193, 196
    Herring 192
    Ivory **204**
    Laughing **199-200**
    Lesser Black-backed **192-193**, 196, **Plate 5**
    Little 196, **200-203**, 207
    Ring-billed 479
    Ross' **205-207**
    Sabine's 205
    Slaty-backed **189-192**, 195
    "Yellow-footed" 191
Gyrfalcon **106-107**
Hawfinch **442-443**
Heron, Little Blue **52-52**
    Louisiana (see Tricolored)
    Tricolored **50**
Hobby 480, **Plate 10**
Hoopoe **246**, **Plate 6**
Jacksnipe, Eurasian **150-151**, **Plate 3**

Jay, Blue **292-293**
    Pinyon **294**
Junco, Gray-headed **459**
    Dark-eyed 459
Kestrel, American 106
    Eurasian **105-106, Plate 10**
Kingbird, Cassin's **257**
    Couch's 255, 256
    Eastern 480
    Gray **254**
    Thick-billed **258-259**
    Tropical **254-256**, 259
    Western 256, 257, 480
Kingfisher, Common 481
Kite, Mississippi **96-97**
    White-tailed **96**
Kittiwake, Black-legged 207
    Red-legged **204-205**
Knot, Great **152, Plate 3**
    Red 152
Longspur, Chestnut-collared **466-467**
    McCown's **464-465**
Loon, Common 2
    Yellow-billed **1-3**
Mallard 78, 80
Mallard X American Black Duck 78-79
Martin, Common House **291, Plate 6**
    Purple 480
Meadowlark, Western 480
Murre, Common 212
    Thick-billed **210-212**
Murrelet, Craveri's 215, **216**
    Kittlitz's **212-213**
    Marbled 213
    Xantus' **214-215**
Night Heron, Black-crowned 57, 479
    Yellow-crowned **56-57**
Nightjar, Jungle **234-235, Plate 6**
Nutcracker, Clark's 480
    Eurasian 481
Oriole, "Baltimore" 421
    Hooded **420-421**
    Northern 421
    Orchard 421
    Scarlet-headed (see Streaked-backed)
    Scott's **432**
    Streak-backed **422, Plate 6**
Ovenbird 356, 357, **405-407**
Owl, Boreal 234
    Common Scops **229-230, Plate 6**
    Hawk **233**
    Northern Pygmy 470
    Snowy **231-233**

Oystercatcher, American **113-114**
    Black 113
Parula, Northern 235, 357, **370-371**
Peeps (see Stints)
Pelican, Brown **36**
Petrel, Black-winged 17
    Bonin 17
    Cape **13-14, Plate 1**
    Cook's 17, **18-20**
    Gould's 17
    Mottled **14-17**, 18
    Pycroft's (see Stejneger's)
    Scaled (see Mottled)
    Stejneger's **20-21**
    White-winged (see Gould's)
Phainopepla **347**
Phalarope, Wilson's 139, 174, 479
Plover, Common Ringed **116-118**
    Little Ringed **115-116, Plate 3**
    Mongolian **122-124, Plate 3**
    Mountain **124**
    Piping **119-121**
    Semipalmated 116, 117, 122
    Snowy **121**
Pipit, Identification of 331
    Indian Tree (see Olive-backed)
    Olive-backed **332-333, Plate 8**
    Pechora **335-336**, 339, **Plate 8**
    Red-throated 333, 336, **337-338, Plate 8**
    Richard's 482
    Sprague's **340-341, Plate 8**
    Tree **334-335**, 336, 339, **Plate 8**
    Water 331, 333, 339, 341
Pochard, Common **84-85, Plate 2**
Puffin, Horned 216, **218-221**
    Tufted 219
Pyrrhuloxia **430**
Rail, Common Water 480
    Yellow **109-110**
Redhead 85, **Plate 2**
Redpoll, Common **449-480**
    Hoary 449-450
Redshank, Common 481
    Spotted **136-138, Plate 5**
Redstart, American 355, 356, 357
    Daurian 481
    Painted **419-420**
Redwing 481, **Plate 10**
Robin, American 304, 307
    Rufous-backed **304, Plate 7**
    Rufous-tailed 481
    Siberian Blue 481, **Plate 10**

Rosefinch, Common **445-446**, **Plate 9**
Rosy Finch, Black **447**
    Gray-crowned **447**
Rubythroat, Siberian **317-319**, **Plate 7**
Ruff 172, 174, **184-188**, **Plate 11**
Sandpiper, Baird's 153, 158, 169, 174, 183, 188
    Broad-billed 151, **178-179**, **Plate 3**, **Plate 11**
    Buff-breasted 172, 174, **181-184**
    Common **146-147**, **Plate 3**
    Curlew **173-175**
    Green 139, **141-142**, 143, **Plate 5**
    Least 154, 162, 165, 166, **Plate 4**
    Marsh **138-139**, **Plate 5**
    Rufous-necked (see Stint, Rufous-necked)
    Semipalmated **155-158**, 161, 163, **Plate 4**
    Sharp-tailed 166, **169-172**, **Plate 3**
    Solitary 142, 143
    Spoonbill **176-177**, **Plate 4**
    Spotted 146, 147, **Plate 3**
    Stilt 139, 174, **179-180**
    Terek **145-146**, **Plate 3**
    Upland **135**
    Western 154, 155, 157, 161, 163, 177, **Plate 4**
    White-rumped **167-169**
    Wood 139, **142-143**, **Plate 5**, **Plate 11**
Sapsucker, Yellow-bellied **250-252**
Scaup, Greater 88
    Lesser 88
Sea Eagle, Steller's (see Eagle, Steller's Sea)
Shearwater, "Black-vented" Manx **25-27**
    Flesh-footed 479
    Greater **23**
    Manx **24-27**
    "Newell's" 25
    Pink-footed 22, 26
    Sooty 14
    Streaked **22-23**, **Plate 1**
    "Townsend's" 25
    "White-vented" Manx **24-27**
Shrike, Brown **348**
Siskin, Eurasian 482
Skua, South Polar 479
Skylark, Common **288-290**
Smew **93-95**, **Plate 2**

Snipe, Common 151, 481
    Pintail 481
    Solitary 481
Sora 110
Sparrow, Baird's **453**
    Black-chinned **462-463**
    Black-throated **458**
    Botteri's 457
    Brewer's 461
    Cassin's **456-457**
    Chipping 461
    Clay-colored **460-461**
    Field **462**
    Grasshopper 454
    LeConte's **453-454**, 456
    Sage **458-459**
    Sharp-tailed **455-456**
    Swamp **463-464**
    White-throated 480
Spoonbill, Roseate **60-61**
Stilt, Black-necked **114-115**
Stint, Identification of 153-154
    Little 158, 161, **162-163**, **Plate 4**
    Long-toed **165-167**, **Plate 4**
    Rufous-necked 158, **159-161**, 163, 177, **Plate 4**
    Temminck's **164-165**, **Plate 4**
Stonechat 481, Plate 10
Stork, Wood **58**
Storm-Petrel, Band-rumped **30-31**
    Galapagos (see Wedge-rumped)
    Harcourt's (see Band-rumped)
    Leach's 28, 31
    Least 30
    Wedge-rumped **29-30**
    Wilson's **27-29**, 30, 31
Swallow, Tree 291
Swan, "Bewick's" **64-65**
    Tundra 64-65, 67-68
    Trumpeter 64, **65-68**
    Whistling (see Tundra)
    Whooper **64-65**
Tanager, Scarlet **428-429**
    Summer **429**
Tattler, Gray-tailed **148-149**, **Plate 3**
    Polynesian (see Gray-tailed)
    Wandering 149
Teal, Baikal **75-77**, 83, **Plate 2**
    Blue-winged 83
    Cinnamon 83
    Falcated **73-75**, **Plate 2**
    Green-winged 77, 83

Tern, Common Black 209
　　Least **207-208**
　　Sandwich **208**
　　White-winged Black **209-210, Plate 5**
Thrasher, Brown **297-299**
　　California **302**
　　Curve-billed **300-301**
Thrush, Dusky **305-306, Plate 7**
　　Eye-browed **306-307, Plate 7**
　　Gray-cheeked 311, **312**
　　Hermit 310
　　Identification of *Catharus* 310-311
　　Mistle 481
　　Siberian 481, **Plate 10**
　　Swainson's 310
　　Wood **308-309**
Tree Duck (see Whistling Duck)
Tropicbird, Red-billed **32-33**, 34
　　Red-tailed **33-34**, 35, **Plate 1**
　　White-tailed 33, **34-35**
Veery 311, **313**
Vireo, Philadelphia **352-353**
　　Red-eyed 352
　　Warbling 353
　　White-eyed **349**
　　Yellow-green **351-352**
　　Yellow-throated **350**
Vulture, American Black **95**
　　Turkey 479
Wagtail, Gray **343-344, Plate 8**
　　White **344-347**
　　Yellow **342**, 343-344
Warbler, Bay-breasted 356, 357, **394-396**, 400, 402, 404
　　Black-and-white 365, 357, **358-360**
　　Blackpoll 356, 357, **397-400**, 402, 404
　　Black-throated Blue 356, 357, **377-379**
　　Black-throated Green 356, 357, **380-382**, 383
　　Blue-winged 356, 357, 364, **365**
　　Canada 356, 357, **417-418**
　　Cape May 356, 357, **374-376**
　　Cerulean 356, 357, **384-385**
　　Chestnut-sided 356, 357, **391-393**
　　Connecticut 356, 357, **410-411**
　　Dusky **321-322, Plate 8**
　　Golden-cheeked 356, 357, **383**
　　Golden-winged 356, 357, **364-365**
　　Golden-winged X Blue-winged **364**
　　Grace's 356, 357, **390**
　　Gray's Grasshopper 482
　　Greenish 482
　　Hooded 356, 357, **415-416**
　　Kentucky 356, 357, **408-409**
　　Lanceolated 482, **Plate 10**
　　MacGillivray's 411, 412-413
　　Magnolia 356, 357, **372-373**, 404
　　Middendorff's Grasshopper **323-324, Plate 8**
　　Mourning 356, 357, **411-413**
　　Nashville 413
　　Pallas' 482
　　Pallas' Grasshopper 324, 482
　　Palm 355, 356, 357
　　Parula (see Parula, Northern)
　　Pine 356, 357, 400, **401-402**
　　Prairie 356, 357, **403-404**
　　Prothonotary 356, 357, **360-362**
　　Radde's 322, 482
　　Red-faced 356, 357, **414**
　　Tennessee 356, 357, **366-368**
　　Townsend's 382
　　Townsend's X Hermit 382
　　Virginia **369**
　　Willow 481, **Plate 8**
　　Wood **320-321, Plate 8**
　　Worm-eating 356, 357, **362-363**
　　Yellow-browed 482
　　Yellow-throated 356, 357, **388-389**
Waterthrush, Louisiana 356, 357, **407-408**
　　Northern 355, 356, 357, 408
Wheatear, Isabelline 316, 481
　　Northern **314-316**
Whip-poor-will 479
Whistling Duck, Black-bellied **63**
　　Fulvous **62**
Wigeon, Eurasian 75
Willet **144**
Woodcock, Eurasian 481
Woodpecker, Acorn **249**
　　Northern Three-toed **253**
　　Nuttall's **249**
　　Red-headed **248**
Wood Pewee, Eastern **286-287**
　　Greater (see Flycatcher, Coue's)
　　Western 286, 287
Wryneck, Eurasian **247, Plate 9**
Yellowlegs, Greater 138, 141
　　Lesser 138, 139, 143, 188
Yellowthroat, Common 413